THE UNANIMITY RULE IN THE REVISION OF TREATIES: A RE-EXAMINATION

EDWIN C. HOYT

★

THE UNANIMITY RULE IN THE REVISION OF TREATIES A RE-EXAMINATION

WITH A FOREWORD BY

PHILIP C. JESSUP

Hamilton Fish Professor of International Law and Diplomacy, Columbia University, New York

MARTINUS NIJHOFF / THE HAGUE / 1959

Copyright 1959 by Martinus Nijhoff, The Hague, Netherlands
All rights reserved, including the right to translate or to
reproduce this book or parts thereof in any form

PRINTED IN THE NETHERLANDS

FOREWORD

In international law the authority of the writers has been great and the Statute of the International Court of Justice still takes cognizance of them as subsidiary sources. Yet it has been widely recognized that on many points writers, even of the most respectable authority, have merely repeated the statements of their predecessors, sometimes with the result that error or some individual dogma or predilection has been perpetuated. The three-mile limit of territorial waters, for example, was long identified with the range of cannon and with the famous dictum of Galiani until modern historical research revealed more accurately its historical origin in the practice of states. The very definition of international law as a law of which only states were subjects impelled to somewhat far-fetched inclusions of certain political entities as "states," and has had at last to yield at least to the concept that an international organization may also be a subject of international law. The long repetition of the essential attributes of states – sovereignty, independence, equality – has not altered the realities of the very great differences between states in respect of each of these attributes. As Cardozo said of definitions, if our preconceived notions of international law do not accord with the facts of international life, so much the worse for those old notions; they must be revised to be brought into line with reality.

Each new scholarly investigation or reappraisal of the practice of states, of the actualities of international life, is therefore to be welcomed for the light which it throws on some one of our traditional precepts of international law. My former colleague at Columbia University, Professor Edwin C. Hoyt, has rendered this service in his re-examination of the unanimity rule in the revision of treaties.

It should be borne in mind that Professor Hoyt is concerned with the problem of the *revision* of treaties and therefore does not deal with all aspects of the unanimity rule, although much of his

material does have a broader impact, as for example on the question of unanimity as a rule of conference procedure which he expressly omits from his own focus of study. The author naturally reminds us in his introduction of the famous Declaration of London of 1871, but his illuminating analysis of that text and the surrounding facts brings ready agreement to his conclusion that at most the Declaration "was a denial of a right of unilateral denunciation, rather than an affirmation of a requirement of unanimity" in the revision of multilateral treaties. He continues to show on what a frail foundation rests the traditional acceptance of this aspect of the unanimity rule. He shows also that while insistence on the unanimity rule may be traced in large part to a fear that its abandonment would weaken the fundamental rule, *pacta sunt servanda*, this conclusion does not follow. Nor will any state seeking to justify repudiation of a bilateral treaty obligation find any comfort between the covers of this book.

This study emphasizes the point that as treaties began to attain a quasi-legislative function, principles drawn from the private law of contracts were seen to have less applicability and to be in need of readaptation or even of abandonment. A starting point was furnished when international law acknowledged that a peace treaty concluded at the end of a war was valid even though imposed upon the unwilling vanquished state; the familiar element of contractual consent was not necessary. Notions of effectiveness and of substantial interest came to dominate as territorial and political regimes were modified by or under the leadership of the Great Powers composing the Concert of Europe. But, the author notes, concessions were made to time-honored contractual principles. Thus it was still acknowledged that no state would be bound by the new obligations of a revised treaty to which it refused its consent – *ex consensu advenit vinculum*. Likewise it was conceded that "no treaty among other parties deprives a state of any substantive acquired rights (*res inter alios acta*)." And as already noted, the principle *pacta sunt servanda* still made illegal the unilateral abrogation of a treaty of permanent character.

Procedurally, Professor Hoyt brings out that there may be "conference unanimity without unanimous consent of the parties, or unanimity of the parties without conference unanimity, and there is no necessary connection between the two." Partic-

ularly he shows from the sample cases of treaties defining special regimes of a territorial character which he analyzes, that "there is no support in practice for the theory that a treaty which purports to revise an earlier agreement, without the consent of all the parties, is void *ab initio.*" Practice does not indicate that all the parties to an earlier treaty have any general right to take part in negotiations respecting revision, although they cannot be bound by some new treaty concluded without their participation or consent.

He also inclines to the view, which is of special interest in this era of international organization, that in some instances the right of withdrawal is substituted for the supposed right to deny the validity of a modification of an administrative regime without the consent of all the parties.

It is not the purpose of this Foreword to present a digest of Professor Hoyt's conclusions. The points which have been mentioned are designed to indicate the scope of this re-examination of one application of the traditional unanimity rule. In the present writer's opinion, the conclusions reached are sound. They have an impact upon basic norms of international law and require careful consideration by all international lawyers.

PHILIP C. JESSUP

*Hamilton Fish Professor of
International Law and Diplomacy
Columbia University, New York*

ACKNOWLEDGEMENTS

This book had its origin in a study that I made as a participant in a seminar in international law held at Columbia University in 1954–55. Other members of this group, Hans N. Blix, Paul I. Eeckman, Omar Z. Ghobashy, Gordon G. Henderson, Jirina M. Hrazdilova, I. Joel Larus and Guenther Weissberg made available to me the results of their research on individual treaty regimes. Their contributions were of great value. They are of course not responsible for my conclusions.

May, 1958   EDWIN C. HOYT

TABLE OF CONTENTS

Foreword   v

Abbreviations   XII

Introduction   1
    1. A Statement of the Problem   1
    2. Opinions of Writers   3
    3. The Declaration of London   6
    4. Some Related Problems   9

Part I. GENERAL TREATIES

I. NONPOLITICAL CONVENTIONS   17
    1. Their Terminable Character   17
    2. The Authority of Periodic Revisory Conferences   20
    3. The Method of *inter se* Agreements   28
    4. The Method of Denunciation   39
    5. Outright Departures from the Unanimity Principle   41
    6. Law-making Treaties   46
    7. Summary   49

II. TREATIES OF A CONSTITUTIONAL CHARACTER   52
    1. The Covenant of the League of Nations   52
    2. The Statute of the Permanent Court of International Justice   55
    3. The Charter of the United Nations   62
    4. The Constitution of the International Labor Organization   66
    5. The Constitution of the World Health Organization   68
    6. Replacement of the League of Nations by the United Nations   72
    7. Summary   78

III. MULTIPARTITE PEACE SETTLEMENTS   82
    1. The Treaty of Vienna, 1815   82
    2. The Treaties of Paris, 1856, and Berlin, 1878   87
    3. The Treaty of Versailles   93
        a) Subsequent revision of parts of the settlement   93
        b) Its effect on the status of Belgium   97
        c) Its effect on the rights of Switzerland   99

TABLE OF CONTENTS

4. The Italian Peace Treaty, 1947	102
a) The Naval, Military and Air Clauses	102
b) The Free Territory of Trieste	108
5. Agreements concerning Germany	112
6. Summary	112

PART II. SPECIFIC TERRITORIAL REGIMES

IV. THE REGIMES OF INTERNATIONAL RIVERS: THE RHINE AND THE DANUBE   117

1. The Period 1815 to 1918	117
a) The Central Commission of the Rhine	117
b) The European Commission of the Danube	121
2. Revisions after World War I	128
a) The Rhine	128
b) The Danube	133
3. The Later History of the Danube Regime	142
a) The breakdown of the international system	142
b) The Belgrade Convention	147
4. Summary	152

V. THE REGIME OF THE TURKISH STRAITS   156

1. 1840 to 1914: the Principle of Unanimity of the Great Powers	156
2. Wartime Diplomacy	159
3. The Lausanne Conference, 1922–1923	162
4. The Montreux Conference of 1936	169
5. The Negotiations of 1945–1946	174
6. Summary	176

VI. INTERNATIONAL REGIMES IN COLONIAL AFRICA   179

1. The treaties of Madrid, Berlin and Brussels	179
2. The Algeciras Conference	184
3. The French Protectorate in Morocco	187
4. Revision of the Acts of Berlin and Brussels by the Peace Conference of 1919	191
5. The Tangier Convention of 1923	196
6. The Revision of the Tangier Statute in 1928	204
7. Tangier since 1945	206
8. Summary	210

VII. TREATY REGIMES REINFORCED BY CUSTOM   214

1. The Aaland Islands	214
a) The Convention of 1856	214
b) The Opinion of the League of Nations Commission of Jurists	219
c) Later Treaties	222

2. The Suez Canal		227
a) The Convention of 1888		227
b) The British reservation		229
c) Discussions of revision in 1956		234
3. Summary		241
VIII. CONCLUSIONS		245
Selected Bibliography		253
Index		261

ABBREVIATIONS

A.J.I.L.	American Journal of International Law.
B.F.S.P.	British and Foreign State Papers.
BRIT. DOCS.	British Documents on the Origins of the War, 1898–1914. 11 vols. Gooch and Temperley edition 1927–1938.
B.Y.I.L.	British Year Book of International Law.
DANUBE CONFERENCE (1921)	Conférence Internationale pour l'Etablissement du Statut Définitif du Danube. Paris, 1921.
DANUBE CONFERENCE (1948)	Conférence Danubienne, Béograd, 1948. Recueil des Documents.
DEGRAS	Soviet Documents on Foreign Policy. 3 vols. Jane Degras edition, 1953.
DOCUMENTS ON INTERNATIONAL AFFAIRS	Documents on International Affairs. Annual volumes, 1928–1954. Issued under the auspices of the Royal Institute of International Affairs, London.
GROSSE POLITIK	Germany, Auswärtiges Amt. Die Grosse Politik der Europäischen Kabinette 1871–1914. 40 vols. 1924–1927.
HARVARD DRAFT CONVENTION	Research in International Law, Harvard Law School, Convention on the Law of Treaties, James W. Garner, Reporter. Supplement to the American Journal of International Law, vol. 29, 1935.
L.N.T.S.	League of Nations Treaty Series.
MALLOY	Treaties, Conventions, International Acts, Protocols and Agreements between the United States of America and Other Powers (1776–1909) 2 vols. Compiled by William M. Malloy, 1910.
MILLER DIARY	David Hunter Miller, My Diary at the Paris Peace Conference. 21 vols. 1924.
NOUV. REC. GÉN.	Nouveau Recueil Général de Traités. Continuation of the "Recueil des Principaux Traités" compiled by Georg Friedrich von Martens.
SURVEY OF INTERNATIONAL AFFAIRS	Survey of International Affairs. Annual volumes by Arnold J. Toynbee and others (1920–1946) and Peter Calvocoressi (1947–1953). Issued under the auspices of the Royal Institute of International Affairs, London.
T.I.A.S.	United States Treaties and Other International Acts Series.
U.N.T.S.	United Nations Treaty Series.

INTRODUCTION

1. A STATEMENT OF THE PROBLEM

The often-asserted rule of customary international law that a treaty may not be terminated or revised without the consent of all of the parties is one that has been taken for granted without serious analysis. The appropriateness of the rule as applied to multipartite treaties is open to serious question. Such treaties, intended to regulate matters of common concern, can serve their purpose effectively only if they are open to all of the states affected by the subject matter. If they are to retain their usefulness in the face of changing conditions, they must also be capable of frequent revision. Yet the larger the number of participating states, the more difficult it becomes to comply with the traditional requirement of unanimous consent.

It is apparent that in its modern multipartite form the treaty has been pressed into a role quite different from its original one of recording simple bilateral bargains. It has now emerged as the essential legal instrument of a new effort to bring multipartite organization into the world of sovereign states. In the light of this important development a reexamination of the content and status of the unanimity rule is long overdue.

The principle of unanimity was stated by the Harvard Research in International Law, in 1935, as follows:

A later treaty may supersede an earlier one, only when the parties to the later treaty include all the parties to the earlier one.[1]

A treaty may be denounced by a party only when such denunciation is provided for in the treaty or consented to by all other parties.[2]

The rule can be traced to the basic principle, *pacta sunt servanda*. In former days it had to be read with the qualification that consent could legitimately be compelled – by the victor in a war, or often by a demand backed by the threat of war. With this qualification the rule caused no concern when treaties were mainly

[1] HARVARD DRAFT CONVENTION 1013.
[2] *Id*. at 1173.

bipartite, or concluded between a few states only. When changes became necessary the parties discussed the matter, in its political context, and either came to a new agreement or went to war about it. This study attempts no answer to the broad problem of peaceful change – what legal means replaces force as an instrument for securing consent. It must be noted, however, that the rule of unanimity becomes a much more sweeping generalization when it is read without the qualification that consent may be compelled. To require consent of every party is to make revision more difficult than original agreement, for even signature of all parties is not consent, unless the treaty is one which takes effect on signature, and formal consent to the new treaty is not given until each state by ratification agrees to be bound by it. One may also contrast the asserted weakness of the international legislative process that is implicit in the unanimity requirement with the position of customary international law, which is continually subject to questioning and re-examination in the light of changing conditions. It would seem that the rules governing treaty revision must also in some way meet the requirements of effectiveness.

Various alternatives to the unanimity requirement are logically possible. The parties to a treaty are ordinarily the states most interested in the subject matter at the time the treaty is drawn up. But this situation may change. Suppose a treaty made between states A, B, C and D, all bordering on an international river, on the subject of river navigation. When revision of the treaty becomes in order, D is no longer a riparian and citizens of State E have important river shipping interests. It would be reasonable to invite E to participate and to omit D. E's participation would contribute to the effectiveness of the new regime, while D, whose interest is now negligible, might insist on a *quid pro quo* for its consent. Such a situation might seem better served by a rule of consent of the states having a substantial interest in the subject matter, than by a rule of unanimity of previous parties. If a rule of substantial interest were applied, D would still be protected by the principle that the new treaty would not bind her, being *res inter alios acta*, and the other parties would not be hampered in their freedom to contract among themselves.

Other questions are: Is the practice of unanimity a rule of consent of the parties to previous treaties, or is it a principle of

conference procedure? Is there a basis for a more liberal interpretation of the requirement of consent which would recognize some earlier stage of participation in the revision process as consent to the opening of revision, so as to eliminate a right of veto thereafter? Under what circumstances are some of the parties entitled to vary their treaty obligations *inter se?* If they do so, are they later entitled to question the validity of their new agreement in a dispute among themselves? Is failure to assert the right to participate the equivalent of consent? Are different rules applicable to different kinds of treaties? Are there circumstances in which the consent of other states, not parties to the earlier treaty, may be required for its revision? Has the unanimity principle been replaced in practice by a principle of majority approval?

2. OPINIONS OF WRITERS

Only a few writers have directed their attention to the rule of unanimity as applied to revision. Their views may be cited as hypotheses to be tested against practice.

The editors of the Harvard Draft, while affirming the rule of unanimity as stated above, acknowledged one qualification. This was the permissibility of *inter se* agreements, as to which they stated:

> Two or more of the States parties to a treaty to which other States are parties may make a later treaty which will supersede the earlier treaty in their relations *inter se*, only if ... the later treaty is not so inconsistent with the general purpose of the earlier treaty as to be likely to frustrate that purpose.[1]

As to an *inter se* agreement inconsistent with the purpose of an earlier, more general agreement, they did not go so far as to say it would be void, but only stated that the obligation of the earlier treaty would take priority if parties to the earlier treaty insisted upon it.[2]

Sørensen, who wrote on the subject in 1938, assumed the existence of the principle of unanimous consent. He saw the problem in all instances as one of interpreting the intent of the original agreement as to the permissibility of variations by *inter se*

---
[1] HARVARD DRAFT CONVENTION 1016.
[2] *Id.* at 1024–1026.

agreement. He thought that a treaty could be revised without unanimity, as between the states wishing to do so, only if the parties to the treaty did not intend to exclude such action, and if the new agreement was left open to accession by all the original parties.[1] In some cases, he thought, this intent would be obvious, as with a convention to demilitarize a certain territory, or to limit armaments, or to create an international organ. In other cases the intent might be to provide a minimum amount of protection but not to prevent other agreements giving greater protection, or (as with agreements for pacific settlement) to establish a principle but not to attach the same importance to use of the body named in the agreement. However, "in all cases where there is a general undertaking it is always open to any party to object to the other parties departing from the terms of the collective treaty in their mutual relations." [2] The question then "can only be decided by interpreting the particular collective treaty involved." [3]

Scelle has taken a different view.[4] Regarding revision as essentially a legislative task, he believes the unanimity rule to be incompatible with social necessities, and thinks that a halting evolution towards the majority principle is discernible. The question of revision amounts, in his view, to a dispute between the proponents of revision and its opponents:

To the obligation of the signatories to respect the treaty while it is in force corresponds equally the obligation of the other signatories to consent to modifications or to the abrogation of the stipulations which have ceased to correspond to social necessity. Who shall oblige the interested parties to discuss revision, to consent to it and to effectuate it, such is the problem.[5]

Scelle suggested that in any dispute on these matters the prin-

---

[1] Sørensen, *The Modification of Collective Treaties without the Consent of all the Contracting Parties*, 9 NORDISK TIDSSKRIFT FOR INTERNATIONAL RET 150 (1938).

[2] *Id.* at 172.

[3] *Id.* at 173. Sørensen raised, but did not answer, the question whether, if a revising agreement was illegal by this test, the consequence would be that the new agreement was invalid, or that the other parties were entitled to withdraw from the collective treaty, or that the matter involved "the usual consequences of a state's illegal acts." *Ibid.*

[4] Georges Scelle, *La Revision dans les Conventions Générales*, 42 ANNUAIRE DE L'INSTITUT DE DROIT INTERNATIONALE (1948), 1; see also SCELLE, THÉORIE JURIDIQUE DE LA REVISION DES TRAITÉS (Publications of the Graduate Institute of International Studies, Geneva, No. 16, 1936).

[5] 42 ANNUAIRE at 6–7. (Translated.)

ciple of unanimity should fall before the principle that no one can be a judge in his own cause.[1]

Tobin, who studied diplomatic practice in the matter of termination of treaties, concluded as to revision that, "failure of one or more signatories of a treaty to participate in a revision need not render that revision invalid," and that, "failure to assert the right to participate when the revision is public knowledge appears to be equivalent to an implied acceptance of the new settlement ..."[2] He also concluded that there was a distinction between the rights of great powers and those of other parties in the matter of revision.[3] His study, however, tended to mingle legal principles with political ones.

Lauterpacht discussed the problem in his reports on the law of treaties for the International Law Commission.[4] He took the view that later inconsistent agreements were void if they did not receive the consent of all parties and if they contradicted an essential purpose of an earlier agreement, but he suggested that this rule should not apply to multilateral conventions and that as to these a "substantial majority" would suffice for revision.[5]

Fitzmaurice, Lauterpacht's successor as rapporteur on this subject, sees no such exception, and believes that unanimity is required for the termination of any treaty by a new agreement.[6] He states, however, that the parties may agree, "either by actual participation in the new treaty, or, without such participation, by assenting to the termination when the new treaty comes into force."[7] He also asserts the validity of majority action as a revision purely *inter se*, "leaving the regime of the existing treaty to continue as between [the parties to the new treaty] and the par-

---

[1] *Id.* at 49–50 (citing the advisory opinion of the Permanent Court of International Justice in the case concerning Interpretation of Article 3, para. 2, of the Treaty of Lausanne, P.C.I.J., Ser. B, No. 12 [1925]). *Cf.* the suggestion by Sir Arnold McNair that in regard to political treaties there exists an obligation to accede to a request to confer if revision is asserted to be necessary to meet new conditions. MCNAIR, THE LAW OF TREATIES 370 (1938).

[2] TOBIN, THE TERMINATION OF MULTIPARTITE TREATIES 225 (1933).

[3] *Id.* at 217–219.

[4] Lauterpacht, *First Report on the Law of Treaties*, U.N. Doc. No. A/CN.4/63 (1953) 198–208; *Second Report on the Law of Treaties*, U.N. Doc. No. A/CN. 4/87 (1954) 35–53.

[5] Lauterpacht, *Second Report on the Law of Treaties* 35, 51 ff. *Cf.* Lauterpacht's comments on the unanimity rule in the matter of consent to reservations. *Infra* at p. 11.

[6] Fitzmaurice, *Second Report on the Law of Treaties*, U.N. Doc. No. A/CN. 4/107 (1957), 37–38.

[7] *Id.* at 38.

ties not subscribing to [it], as also between the latter parties themselves." ¹

3. THE DECLARATION OF LONDON

The classic statement of the requirement of unanimity, and the precedent generally referred to on later occasions on which the rule has been invoked, is the Declaration of London of January 17, 1871. It stated:

> The plenipotentiaries of North Germany, Austria-Hungary, Great Britain, Italy, Russia and Turkey, assembled today in Conference, recognize that it is an essential principle of the Law of Nations that no Power can liberate itself from the engagements of a Treaty, nor modify the stipulations thereof, unless with the consent of the Contracting Powers by means of an amicable arrangement.²

An examination of the circumstances surrounding this declaration is enlightening. Its signatories were the parties to the Treaty of Paris of 1856, which imposed on Russia, after the Crimean War, the provisions concerning demilitarization of the Black Sea. ³ Russia had seized upon the diversion presented by the Franco-Prussian War to denounce that part of the treaty. In a circular note announcing this action she asserted that it was justified by previous violations of other clauses of the treaty by other parties. Russia also suggested that she was ready to come to a new understanding with the other parties to the treaty.⁴ The British government in reply denied the right of Russia to free herself from the treaty, and stated: "That right belongs only to the Governments who have been parties to the original instrument." ⁵ Although Russia had made sure of Prussian consent, and the other powers, preoccupied with the situation in Western Europe, were in no position to prevent her action, the matter was brought before a conference of the powers held at London as the proper formal mode of procedure. In view of the political realities the conference could only confirm Russia's action with the sanction of all the parties to the previous treaty, and this was done in the Treaty of London.⁶ The Declaration of London was

---

¹ *Id.* at 38–39.
² 3 HERTSLET, THE MAP OF EUROPE BY TREATY 1904.
³ 46 BRITISH AND FOREIGN STATE PAPERS [hereafter cited: B.F.S.P.] 8.
⁴ 3 HERTSLET, THE MAP OF EUROPE BY TREATY 1892.
⁵ 3 *id.* 1898.
⁶ 3 *id.* 1919.

the first act of the conference, signed on the day it opened – January 17, 1871. The new treaty was signed on March 13. France, for reasons of the war and disorder at home, had no representative at the proceedings until the meeting of March 13 and did not participate in the drafting of the declaration or of the treaty. On taking his seat in the conference the French representative merely announced his acceptance of the provisions already drawn up and declared that he welcomed the occasion to support "the salutary rule of the European society – that is, *not to bring about any essential change in international relations without the examination and consent of all the Great Powers.*" [1] (Emphasis added.)

In this history the following points are noteworthy:

1. The conference was essentially a face-saving device, called to give legal form to what was already a *fait accompli*. As Hall stated, "The force of its assertion may have been impaired by the fact that Russia, as the reward of submission to law, was given what she had affected to take." [2]

2. On its facts the London Declaration was a denial of a right of unilateral denunciation, rather than an affirmation of a requirement of unanimity. The word "all" has been read into the declaration by later commentators to make the phrase "consent of all the Contracting Powers." This is probably correct as a matter of interpretation of the intent of the conferees, but, if so, that part of their declaration was, in the circumstances of the case, "dictum" rather than "holding." [3]

3. The French plenipotentiary's version of the declaration, expressed in terms of the European balance of power, suggests that some of the parties had in mind the preservation of political rather than legal principles.

It has been suggested by Verdross and Ross that the declaration cannot be taken literally because the parties must not have intended to do away with every ground of one-sided release from treaties, including such widely-relied-on grounds of release as breach by another party or material change of circumstances.

---

[1] 61 B.F.S.P. 1220.
[2] HALL, A TREATISE ON INTERNATIONAL LAW 412 (8th ed. 1924).
[3] The repetition of the words of the London Declaration in the Resolution of the Council of the League of Nations, of April 17, 1935, with reference to German repudiation of provisions of the Treaty of Versailles, was similarly a protest against unilateral denunciation. LEAGUE OF NATIONS, OFF. J., 16th year 551 (1935).

These writers therefore believe that the correct meaning of the declaration is only that a state should not declare a treaty terminated without first having notified the other parties and sought to reach agreement with them.[1] Verdross adds that if there is a disagreement whether circumstances have changed in such a way as to require revision, this disagreement, like every other international dispute, must be decided "by the normal means of pacific settlement." [2] If thus watered down, there is little left of the London Declaration.

Article 10 of the Convention on Treaties, adopted at Havana in 1928 by the Sixth Conference of American States,[3] is also cited as an official reassertion of the unanimity principle, although it also omitted the word "all" and therefore did not in terms require unanimity as opposed to some form of majority consent. It repeated the language of the London Declaration almost word for word:

> No State can relieve itself of the obligations of a treaty or modify its stipulations except by the agreement, secured through peaceful means, of the other contracting parties.

The meaning of Article 10 of the Havana Convention is limited, however, by Article 17, which provides:

> Treaties whose denunciation may have been agreed upon [4] and those establishing rules of international law, can be denounced only in the manner provided thereby.
>
> In the absence of such a stipulation, a treaty may be denounced by any contracting State, which State shall notify the others of this decision, provided it has complied with all the obligations therein.
>
> In this event the treaty shall become ineffective, as far as the denouncing State is concerned, one year after the last notification, and will continue in force for any other signatory States, if any.

Article 17 of the Havana Convention has been severely criticized. Hudson believed it could "hardly be said to state existing law." [5]

---

[1] VERDROSS, VÖLKERRECHT 157 (3d ed. 1955); ROSS, TEXTBOOK OF INTERNATIONAL LAW 221 (1947).

[2] VERDROSS, op. cit. supra at 157.

[3] 4 HUDSON, INTERNATIONAL LEGISLATION 2378. This Convention entered into force with respect to only seven of the twenty-one American Republics, not including the United States.

[4] Comparison with the original text of this Article, as drafted by the Commission of American Jurists at Rio de Janeiro in the preceding year, makes it clear that this was a reference to provisions inserted in the original treaty. 2 COMISION INTERNACIONAL DE JURISCONSULTOS AMERICANOS, ACTAS, REUNION DE 1927, 216.

[5] 1 HUDSON, INTERNATIONAL LEGISLATION lvii n.

Urrutia believed it referred only to treaties of limited effect or having in view successive obligations. He wrote: "Its application would not be possible in the case of a treaty of permanent effect; it would otherwise be contrary to principle." [1] Unfortunately, Articles 10 and 17 were both approved, by the Commission of American Jurists and by the Havana Conference, without substantial discussion, so that it is not possible to say just how they were reconciled in the minds of the participants.

4. SOME RELATED PROBLEMS

A similar question of the degree of consent required arises with respect to treaty reservations.[2] In this field also a rule of unanimity was formerly thought to apply. The Harvard Draft Convention stated that:

a State may make a reservation when ratifying only with the consent of all other States which are signatories and of all the States which have acceded to the treaty prior to the ratification by that State.[3]

It now appears, however, that the trend in this field is clearly away from the requirement of unanimity.[4] The International Court of Justice, which was asked in 1951 to give an advisory opinion on the effect of reservations to the Genocide Convention, held in effect that a state which had made a reservation to which some of the parties to the convention had objected might nevertheless be regarded as a party to the convention by such parties as were willing to accept the reservation.[5] The court stressed as

---

[1] Urrutia, *La Codification du Droit International en Amérique*, 22 RECUEIL DES COURS 201 (1928). (Translated).

[2] The connection between the principles governing reservations and those applicable to revision was stated in a memorandum submitted to the International Court of Justice by the International Labor Office, in the Case Concerning Reservations to the Convention on Genocide: "[International conventions] are subject to modification at any time if the consent of all the States concerned can be obtained. Where this principle is applicable it is natural to regard a reservation which is in effect a modification of the provisions of the treaty in its application to one or more parties, as being admissible if it receives the assent of the other parties." RESERVATIONS TO THE CONVENTION ON GENOCIDE – PLEADINGS, ORAL ARGUMENTS, AND DOCUMENTS 235 (I.C.J. 1951).

[3] HARVARD DRAFT CONVENTION 889.

[4] The Pan-American Union has followed a different practice at least since 1938. For summary of this practice, see the Statement of the Organization of American States to the International Court of Justice in the Genocide Case, PLEADINGS, ORAL ARGUMENTS, AND DOCUMENTS 15.

[5] Reservations to the Convention on the Prevention and Punishment of the Crime

central the two principles – of consent and of the intention of the parties:

> It is well established that in its treaty relations a State cannot be bound without its consent, and that consequently no reservation can be effective against any State without its agreement thereto. It is also a generally recognized principle that a multilateral convention is the result of an agreement freely concluded upon its clauses and that consequently none of the contracting parties is entitled to frustrate or impair by means of unilateral decisions or particular agreements, the purpose and *raison d'être* of the convention.[1]

It found no intent in this instance to exclude all reservations, since the integrity of the convention as adopted was less important in the view of the drafters than universality in its acceptance. A test of compatibility was still to be applied to each reservation by each of the other parties to the convention. The conclusions of the Court on this point were as follows:

> (a) that if a party to the Convention objects to a reservation which it considers to be incompatible with the object and purpose of the Convention, it can in fact consider that the reserving State is not a party to the Convention;
>
> (b) that if, on the other hand, a party accepts the reservation as being compatible with the object and purpose of the Convention, it can in fact consider that the reserving State is a party to the Convention.[2]

Subsequently, in a Resolution of January 12, 1952, the United Nations General Assembly rejected a report of the International Law Commission which favored the requirement of unanimous consent, and directed the Secretary-General, as to future conventions of which he was depository, not to pass on the effect of reservations, but to leave the legal conclusions to be drawn by each other party for itself.[3] In 1954, when it was necessary to decide how to deal with reservations to the proposed Covenant of

---

of Genocide [1951] I.C.J. Rep. 14. Four judges disagreed and believed there was an existing general rule of law "that, without the consent of all the parties, a reservation ... cannot become effective and the reserving State cannot become a party." *Id*. at 41.

[1] *Id*. at 21. The United States in its statement to the Court had emphasized the same principles as the essential elements in all determinations regarding treaties. It opposed a unanimity requirement and urged that to allow the largest possible number of states to become parties would accord with the purpose of the Genocide Convention. PLEADINGS, ORAL ARGUMENTS, AND DOCUMENTS 23 ff. It also stated that "in almost all cases, consent should reasonably be implied from a failure to object within a reasonable period of time." *Id*. at 45.

[2] *Id*. at 29–30.

[3] U.N. GENERAL ASSEMBLY RESOLUTION No. 598 (VI) (1952).

Human Rights, the United Kingdom, which had strongly supported the unanimity principle before the International Court of Justice in 1951, urged instead that reservations should be deemed to be accepted only if two-thirds of the parties accepted them or raised no objection.[1] Professor Lauterpacht, as rapporteur on the law of treaties for the International Law Commission in 1953-54, also advocated the abandonment of the unanimity principle in the matter of reservations. He stated:

[While] it is proper to apply the fundamental notions of the general principles of the law of contract, that analogy must stop short of a reasoning which in effect transforms the requirement of consensual agreement into a negation thereof. That point is reached when the will of one party frustrates the will of all the others by rendering ineffective their consent to reservations appended by a State. ... In the chain of relationships brought about by reservations to a multilateral treaty *the element of consent ... can be secured only by way of giving an opportunity to withdraw from the treaty to the State or the small minority of States who find it necessary to oppose the general desire of other contracting parties.*[2] (Emphasis added).

It should be noted before leaving this topic that, while the unanimity principle as to reservations was similar to the one stated for revision, no question of revising an already binding agreement was involved. If the contract analogy is applied, the question is rather as to the form the original agreement will take, the reserving state being in the position of making a new offer which the other parties may accept or reject. The variation of the contract after it becomes legally effective is a further step. However, the effect of reservations not accepted by all is to splinter the agreement into a series of bilateral obligations similar to those which result if some of the parties are permitted to make a revision of a treaty, to be effective only amongst themselves.

The question of whether unanimity should be the voting rule of international conferences is also a matter distinct from the rule of unanimity in treaty revision. The problem of voting exists at every conference, whether revisory or initial. A conference may take its decisions by majority vote but still require

---

[1] Lauterpacht, *Second Report on the Law of Treaties*, U.N. Doc. No. A/CN.4/87 (1954) 31–33; see also *Reservations to Multilateral Conventions*, by G. G. Fitzmaurice, Second Legal Adviser to the British Foreign Office, 2 INT'L AND COMP. L.Q. 1, 23–24 (1953), where this procedure is suggested as a general residual rule; RESERVATIONS TO THE CONVENTION ON GENOCIDE — PLEADINGS, ORAL ARGUMENTS, AND DOCUMENTS 417 ff. (I.C.J. 1951).

[2] *First Report on the Law of Treaties*, U.N. Doc. No. A/CN. 4/63 (1953) 114–115.

unanimous ratification before its work takes effect, or it may adhere to unanimity in voting but not fulfill the requirement of unanimous consent of all parties to a treaty which is being revised. Unanimity as a rule of conference procedure is outside the scope of this study, but the practice in regard to it will be noted where it is encountered, both in an effort to distinguish rules of conference procedure from the requirements of revision (the two are often confused), and because the practice in regard to the one principle has had its influence on the other.[1]

A third problem which has a bearing on the requirement of revision is the question whether consent of the parties to a previous treaty may be tacit or implied. The question of implied consent is a general problem of international law which is not limited to treaty matters, and it is not treated exhaustively here. It is assumed here that the principle is correctly stated in the Harvard Draft: "It is conceivable that the consent of a State might be tacit or result from implication, if it is clear that the giving of its consent was intended." [2]

In the matter of revision we might expect, as Scelle suggested, a gradual evolution in the direction of some form of majority principle similar to that in regard to acceptance of reservations. We have seen as well that some doubt remains whether the customary rule of consent of the parties was ever in fact as rigid a requirement as it is sometimes said to be. There is now a body of state practice in the matter that extends back more than one hundred years, during which time multipartite treaties have been assuming constantly increasing importance in ordering the world's affairs. From a re-examination of this practice it should be possible to discern the character of the customary rule and its present status and substance. It is hoped that this study may serve to point out areas of agreement as to principle, to focus attention on areas of disagreement or uncertainty where efforts to reconcile opposing points of view are needed, and to show trends of development of the law. Such a study seems especially perti-

---

[1] On unanimity as a rule of conference procedure, see DUNN, THE PRACTICE AND PROCEDURE OF INTERNATIONAL CONFERENCES (1929); Jenks, *Some Constitutional problems of International Organizations*, 22 B.Y.I.L. 11 at 34–42 (1945); RICHES, MAJORITY RULE IN INTERNATIONAL ORGANIZATION, A STUDY OF THE TREND FROM UNANIMITY TO MAJORITY DECISION (1940); cf Lande, *Revindication of the principle of Legal Equality of States*, 62 POL. SCI. Q. 258, 398 (1947).

[2] HARVARD DRAFT CONVENTION 1163.

nent in view of the presently pending efforts of the International Law Commission to codify the law of treaties.

The treaties to be considered fall into four general categories:

1. Conventions which provide for co-operation on economic and social matters or lay down new rules of international conduct. These treaties, having the least political content, might be expected to show the farthest progress away from the restrictions of strict unanimity. However, the requirements of revision will be less strict wherever the original intent was to create obligations binding only so long as they served the convenience of the parties.

2. The constitutions of international organizations. Here the problem is mainly one of constitutional interpretation, but the practice is nevertheless instructive with regard to the basic assumptions of the parties, their willingness to give up the requirement of unanimity by provision of a different rule in advance, and the connection between the rules of revision and the right of withdrawal.

3. Multipartite peace settlements. Several special factors distinguish these treaties and tend to diminish the general significance of instances of their revision. Among such factors are strong political content, the principle of separability of parts of such settlements, and the fact that the revision of boundaries does not ordinarily imply revision of the treaties which created them.

4. Treaties establishing specific territorial regimes. These are frequently established to avert political disputes. They combine political importance, intended permanence and frequent revision and thus provide the best test of the requirements of revision.

PART I

GENERAL TREATIES

CHAPTER I

NONPOLITICAL CONVENTIONS

1. THEIR TERMINABLE CHARACTER

The treaties which enlist the widest participation are those which establish international administrative unions or provide for co-operation on economic and social matters. Such treaties do not affect the balance of power, or any state's "vital interests," but they have a high value of mutual convenience. We will hereafter refer to them as "nonpolitical conventions." [1]

The very purpose of nonpolitical conventions requires them to be participated in by many states. They are therefore usually open to accession by any state willing to accept the obligations they contain. [2] On the other hand, they are generally open to denunciation by any party. On the next page there is given a representative list of such treaties concluded between 1850 and 1914, which indicates the extent to which provisions on these subjects were included.

It is evident that a right of denunciation of a multipartite treaty, if such exists, has a close connection with the requirements of revision. The Convention of 1886 on the Sealing of Railway Cars Subject to Customs Inspection expressed it in a provision that each of the interested states reserved the right to propose revisions and that in default of agreement on the subject the state which proposed the changes would have the right to consider itself no longer bound. [3] Conversely, if parties X, Y and Z refuse their consent to a revision desired by all the other parties, the latter can as a last resort terminate their obligations by denouncing the treaty, and then proceed to conclude a new treaty among themselves. The fact that this possibility exists is likely to influence dissenting parties to adapt themselves to the views of a group

---

[1] The term is used by DE VISSCHER: THEORY AND REALITY IN PUBLIC INTERNATIONAL LAW 322 (Corbett trans. 1957).
[2] In the absence of a provision of the treaty on the subject there is no legal basis for making a distinction as to the right to participate in revision between original parties and states which have become parties by accepting an invitation to accede.
[3] 22 NOUV. REC. GÉN. (2 sér.) 42.

Provisions of Nonpolitical Conventions

Subject	Year	Open to accessions	Denunciation permitted	Limited to a term of years	Reference to the possibility of revision
Sanitary	1851	X	X	X	
,, (draft)	1859	X	X	X	
,,	1893		X	X	X
,,	1894	X	X	X	X
Red Cross	1864	X			
,,	1906	X	X		
Sugar	1864	X		X	X
,,	1902	X	X	X	
Telegraph	1865	X			X
,,	1868	X			X
,,	1872	X			X
,,	1875	X	X		X
Postal	1874	X	X	X	X
,,	1878	X	X		X
Weights & Measures	1875	X	X		
Submarine Cables	1884	X	X	X	
Phylloxera	1878	X	X		X
,,	1881	X			X
Industrial Property	1883	X	X		X
Patents (Pan Am.)	1889	X	X		X
Trade Marks (Pan Am.)	1889	X	X		X
Copyright	1886	X	X		X
Sealing of railway cars	1886		X		X
Publication of tariffs	1890	X	X		X
Rail transport rules	1890		X	X	X
Measurement of vessels	1898		X		
Inst. of Agriculture	1905	X			
Off. of Public Health	1907	X	X	X	X
Opium	1912	X	X		
White Slave Traffic	1904	X	X		
Obscene publications	1910	X	X		
Motor Traffic	1909	X	X		
Fur Seals	1911		X	X	X

of states which includes those most powerful and important in the particular treaty system.

The practice of inserting a provision specifically permitting denunciation became standard very soon after this type of convention came into use. The Geneva Convention of 1864 for the

Amelioration of the Condition of the Wounded in Armies in the Field[1] did not speak of denunciation, nor did the International Telegraph Conventions[2] of 1865, 1868 and 1872, but in the next revision of the Telegraph Convention in 1875 there was inserted an article permitting denunciation.[3] Even before this there was an implicit acknowledgment that the right to withdraw existed.[4] The Conventions for Protection against Cholera, drafted at Paris in 1851[5] and 1859,[6] contained denunciation provisions, as did the Treaty of 1874 which instituted the Postal Union[7] and the 1875 Convention on Weights and Measures.[8] The Convention of 1864 to limit controls on the production and export of sugar omitted a denunciation clause but instead limited the convention to a term of ten years.[9] When the usual denunciation clause was omitted from the Sanitary Convention of 1912, which revised one of 1903, the British delegate stated at the time of signature that it was understood by his government that the right of denunciation continued as in the previous conventions.[10] In some other instances the reference to denunciation was framed in a way that shows that the parties assumed the right and were most concerned with limiting the manner of its exercise. Thus the Conventions of 1904 [11] and 1910,[12] for Suppression of the White Slave traffic and Obscene Publications, and the one of 1912, Regulating the Trade in Opium and other drugs,[13] state only that if one of the parties denounces the convention, such action shall not terminate the convention for the other parties. It therefore seems justified to conclude, in respect to nonpolitical conventions generally, that they are ordinarily intended to be terminable at will, or on notice,

---

[1] 55 B.F.S.P. 43.
[2] See pp. 20–23, *infra*.
[3] 66 B.F.S.P. 19.
[4] See statement made by the Austrian representative in 1872, quoted at pp. 21-22, *infra*.
[5] DE CLERCQ, RECUEIL DES TRAITÉS DE LA FRANCE 141.
[6] FRANCE, MINISTÈRE DES AFFAIRES ETRANGÈRES, PROTOCOLES DE LA CONFÉRENCE SANITAIRE INTERNATIONALE, Annex to Protocol No. 37 (1859).
[7] 65 B.F.S.P. 13.
[8] 2 MALLOY, TREATIES, CONVENTIONS, ETC. BETWEEN THE UNITED STATES OF AMERICA AND OTHER POWERS [hereafter cited: MALLOY] 1924.
[9] 54 B.F.S.P. 29.
[10] 108 B.F.S.P. 279.
[11] 97 B.F.S.P. 95.
[12] 103 B.F.S.P. 244, 251.
[13] 105 B.F.S.P. 490.

2. THE AUTHORITY OF PERIODIC REVISORY CONFERENCES

and that in the absence of special indications of a contrary intention the right of denunciation, if not specifically included, is to be implied.

Nonpolitical conventions usually make some reference to the possibility of revision.[1] A recent practice is to specify in terms the number of parties whose agreement will be required before changes will be effective. Such provisions show that there is nothing inevitable about the unanimity requirement, but they do not answer the question as to what is the residual rule in the absence of agreement on the subject in advance. A provision found in the sugar convention of 1864 and some other early nonpolitical conventions reserved to the 'High Contracting Parties,' as distinguished from other states which might take advantage of the opportunity of acceding, the power to introduce, 'by common accord,' such modifications as might prove necessary.[2] This provision appears to have been intended to avoid undue difficulty in meeting the assumed requirement of unanimous consent.[3] However, most common among the earlier provisions for revision was a clause which simply committed the parties to consider revision periodically, without specifying whose consent would be necessary to make the revision effective. The original Telegraph Convention of 1865, for example, stated (Article 56) that it was to be subjected to "periodic revisions, at which all the Powers which have taken part in it shall be represented." [4] This seemed to create an obligation to attend which would justify a conference in ignoring any absentees.[5]

---

[1] Sometimes revision is not mentioned, but the convention is concluded for a term of years, making reconsideration necessary at the expiration of the set period. See table, p. 18, *supra*.

[2] 54 B.F.S.P. 29; see also the Convention Respecting the Creation of an International Office of Weights and Measures of 1875, 2 MALLOY 1924, the Convention for the Publication of Customs Tariffs, of 1890, 82 B.F.S.P. 340, and the Agreement of 1907 Respecting the Creation of an International Office of Public Health, 100 B.F.S.P. 466.

[3] See the discussion with regard to the adoption of the similar clause in the General Act of Berlin, of February 26, 1885, p. 182, *infra*.

[4] In the French, "seront représentées." FRANCE, MINISTÈRE DES AFFAIRES ETRANGÈRES, DOCUMENTS DIPLOMATIQUES DE LA CONFÉRENCE TÉLÉGRAPHIQUE INTERNATIONALE DE PARIS 1 (1865). Similar provisions appear in the Postal, Rail Transport, Industrial Property, Copyright and Phylloxera Conventions.

[5] The Telegraph Convention of 1875 made this more explicit, providing (Art. 15)

The suggestion that the failure of some parties to attend a conference would not prevent revision was borne out in early revisions of the Telegraph Convention. Luxembourg was not represented at the conference of 1872. Great Britain sent only technical representatives to the conference held at St. Petersburg in 1875, which completely rewrote the convention, and therefore did not sign the revised convention.[1] She acceded to it only after the date on which it had gone into effect in accordance with its terms.[2] Luxembourg, which took no part in the conference, also acceded after the convention had gone into effect.[3] When the initial treaty of the Postal Union was revised in 1878, one member of the Union, Persia, took no part, and it was provided in a final protocol that she should be "admitted nevertheless to sign the Convention later, provided she affirms her adhesion by a diplomatic act with the Swiss Government before April 1, 1879."[4] The same procedure, allowing later accession as a privilege rather than a right, was followed as to absent members in later revisions.[5] There was no attempt in any of these instances to preserve the rights of non-consenting parties under the old agreements.

A provision to allow the making of interim decisions between conferences without unanimity was inserted in the Telegraph Convention in 1868, but it was eliminated in 1872, apparently for reasons as much practical as legal. This provision allowed questions of interpretation of the convention to be referred to a special commission, in which any contracting state which thought it necessary to do so could take part. The decisions of the commission were to have, for states not represented, "the same validity as if they had taken part."[6] The elimination of this provision in 1872 was made on the motion of the Austrian representative, who stated:

The Convention is based on the agreement of all the contracting States and, if one wishes to preserve their unanimity, it is of importance that

---

that all member states were "entitled" to be represented ("pourront se faire représenter") at future conferences. 66 B.F.S.P. 19.

[1] 66 B.F.S.P. 19.
[2] 67 B.F.S.P. 47.
[3] 69 B.F.S.P. 623–624.
[4] DOCUMENTS DU CONGRÈS POSTAL DE PARIS 641 (1878). Persia did accede on June 1, 1878, 69 B.F.S.P. 276.
[5] 76 B.F.S.P. 27 (1885); 83 B.F.S.P. 513 (1891); 89 B.F.S.P. 65 (1897).
[6] 59 B.F.S.P. 322.

no one of them find in its dispositions obstacles which might lead it to refuse to continue its participation.[1]

Revision was therefore reserved to the regular conferences of the union.

As the time of the first treaties of the Telegraph and Postal Unions the principle of consent of the parties to previous treaties was not distinguished from the principle of unanimity as a rule of international conferences, whether revisory or not. However, the acceptance of the authority of the Conference to revise the convention made conference procedure all-important, and here the Telegraph and Postal Unions showed an early trend away from the requirement of unanimity. [2] The Telegraph Conference of 1871–72 adopted the following rules to govern its meetings:

No amendment is adopted unless it receives the absolute majority of the number of States represented.

In case of equality, it is considered as rejected.

* * *

Each of the contracting States may oppose the adoption of a new conventional disposition by declaring its formal refusal to adhere to it.

This veto may be absolute or conditional and under reservation of new instructions which the delegate would elicit from his Government. It may apply to a vote already taken and in which the opposing delegate was unable to take part.[3]

The next conference, held at St. Petersburg in 1875, also adopted this rule, in identical language, but it was agreed that the word "veto" had really been improperly used to describe this right, and that what was meant was only that any delegate was entitled to warn his colleagues that the adoption of a certain amendment would make it impossible for him to sign or for his government to ratify the new acts.[4] The 1872 convention made no provision for

---

[1] DOCUMENTS DE LA CONFÉRENCE TÉLÉGRAPHIQUE INTERNATIONALE DE ROME 479–480 (1872).

[2] Some of the great powers in effect received weighted representation through separate representation for the administrations of dependent territories. See CHAMBERLAIN, JESSUP, LANDE, LISSITZYN, INTERNATIONAL ORGANIZATION 35–38 (1955).

[3] DOCUMENTS (1872) at 236.

[4] This incident of the St. Petersburg conference is referred to in DOCUMENTS DE LA CONFÉRENCE TÉLÉGRAPHIQUE INTERNATIONALE DE BRUXELLES 56–57 (1928). At the 1928 conference an attempt was made to eliminate this provision from the conference rules, the Belgian delegate stating that in fact it had no significance, but it was decided to let it remain, while calling attention to the interpretation adopted in 1875 at St. Petersburg. *Id.* at 52–53, 56–57.

ratification, but it stated that it was concluded "under reserve of approval" of the contracting governments, and it was agreed that this meant that "if one of the Governments used its right of refusing its approval of the tariffs drawn up by the Conference, these would have no validity for any of the States and it would be necessary to proceed to establish them anew." [1] This requirement was satisfied in practice by tacit acquiescence. [2] No state ever attempted to prevent the application of decisions adopted by the Conference. The provision that each delegation should be entitled to oppose the adoption of any proposal tending to modify the previous convention, as modified by the interpretation placed on it at St. Petersburg, continued to appear in the rules of procedure of successive conferences. It did not appear in the rules of procedure for the revisory conference on Radiotelegraphy of 1912, [3] but it was included by some accident in the initial draft of the rules of procedure to govern the Radiotelegraph Conference of 1927. It was then stricken out by general approval after the British delegate had observed that its meaning was unclear and that it served no purpose.[4] The rules of procedure for the Madrid Conference of 1932, which abrogated the previous Telegraph and Radiotelegraph Conventions and replaced them with a single Telecommunications Convention, made it clear that the principle of consent was preserved only in the right to withdraw. They stated:

In general, delegations which cannot make their opinion prevail on a new conventional or regulatory provision must endeavor to adopt the opinion of the majority.

In any case, if a proposed measure appears to a delegation to be of such a nature as to prevent its government from ratifying the new acts, it may express a formal refusal (definitive or provisional) to adhere to the vote of the majority.[5]

[1] DOCUMENTS (1872) 1, 672.
[2] The revised convention of 1875, which put all of the detailed regulations into a Règlement which was to be revised periodically by conferences of representatives of telegraphic administrations, provided also that these revisions were not to become executory until they received the approval "of all the Governments of the Contracting States." 66 B.F.S.P. 19. Article 80, para. 9, of the Règlement however, provided that if modifications were proposed a failure to reply would be interpreted as consent.
[3] DOCUMENTS DE LA CONFÉRENCE RADIOTÉLÉGRAPHIQUE DE LONDRES 3 (1912).
[4] 2 DOCUMENTS DE LA CONFÉRENCE RADIOTÉLÉGRAPHIQUE INTERNATIONALE DE WASHINGTON 76 (1927).
[5] 2 DOCUMENTS DE LA CONFÉRENCE TÉLÉGRAPHIQUE INTERNATIONALE DE MADRID XLIII (1932). Another provision (Art. 21), giving votes at the conference to certain colonies, protectorates, etc., was the subject of considerable debate.

The initial treaty of the Postal Union, of 1874, provided for periodic congresses, at which, it was specified, each country would have one vote.[1] The first congress was held at Paris in 1878. One of the rules of procedure which it adopted to regulate its sessions seemingly limited the majority principle. It stated:

> The definitive adoption of acts having a diplomatic character is dependent upon the approbation of the contracting Governments and upon ratifications which shall be exchanged in the ordinary forms.[2]

However, the final protocol which was signed along with the new convention showed that this meant no more than that a state would not be bound without its consent. It said: "In case one or another of the contracting parties should not ratify the Convention, this Convention shall be nonetheless valid for the parties."[3] The same provision was adopted in the 1912 revision of the Convention of 1906 which made applicable to radiotelegraphy some of the provisions of the Telegraph Convention.[4] The majority principle of the Postal Union was made still more explicit in 1939, when the eleventh Postal Congress adopted the following procedural rule to govern its sessions: "Questions which cannot be decided by common accord are settled by voting. The absolute majority decides."[5] Practical reasons prevented any dissenting government from carrying its opposition to a new provision to the point of withdrawal from the Union.

In two instances the Telegraph Union purposely excluded members from a revisory conference. The exclusion of the U.S.S.R. from the Radiotelegraph Conference held at Washington in 1927 was occasioned by the fact that its government was not recognized by the United States, which issued the invitations. A Soviet protest to the director of the Union's International

---

[1] 65 B.F.S.P. 13.

[2] DOCUMENTS DU CONGRÈS POSTAL DE PARIS 371 (1878).

[3] DOCUMENTS DU CONGRÈS POSTAL DE PARIS 641 (1878). The Postal Convention of 1878 provided in Article 20 that between congresses proposals for changes might be circulated by the Bureau of the Union on the request of any member. Changes in certain articles of the convention would take effect only if approved by all members, but changes in other articles would take effect if two-thirds voted in their favor, and if the proposals concerned only interpretation of existing provisions they could be adopted by a simple majority. 69 B.F.S.P. 210.

[4] 105 B.F.S.P. 219. Of the parties to the 1906 agreement, Brazil and Turkey in fact did not ratify the 1912 convention, and Bulgaria ratified it only after it had gone into effect. *Id.* at 224. Mexico was absent from the 1912 conference, but acceded later. *Id.* at 260.

[5] 1 DOCUMENTS DU CONGRÈS POSTAL DE BUENOS AIRES 607 (1939).

Bureau was unavailing.¹ In 1947 the invitation to the Atlantic City Telecommunications Conference which the Bureau of the Union had sent to Spain as a member country was withdrawn at the request of the United States after the United Nations had adopted its resolution of December 12, 1946, recommending that the Franco Government of Spain be debarred from membership in international agencies that were to be brought into relationship with the U.N.² Spain was allowed to accede, however, in 1951.

While in practice these unions did not allow themselves to be fettered by lack of unanimity, they did adhere strictly to their own internal administrative law. In 1927, an important question having arisen in the Telegraph Union over regulations dealing with telegrams in code language, it was proposed to deal with it in the course of the radiotelegraph conference being held that year in Washington, instead of waiting until the next scheduled telegraph conference. Invitations to attend were therefore sent by the United States Government to those members of the Telegraph Union which were not members of the radiotelegraph conference, and a plenary session of the telegraph conference was convened. However, this action was reconsidered and the matter postponed to the next regular telegraph conference after several delegations had objected to the irregularity of the procedure being followed and had called attention to the controversial nature of the question to be considered.³ It was pointed out that although the great majority of the members of the Telegraph Union were represented, some were not and of these Luxembourg had explicitly reserved its rights.⁴ The primary objection, however, was the fact that the Règlement, while allowing the date of a conference to be advanced, did not authorize any change of the place fixed for the next meeting (in this instance, Brussels).

[1] 2 DOCUMENTS DE LA CONFÉRENCE RADIOTÉLÉGRAPHIQUE DE WASHINGTON 731 (1927). The Soviet letter stated: "The Union of Soviet Socialist Republics participating in the Convention of international radiotelegraphy, its right to be represented at all the Conferences convoked by virtue of this convention is incontestable."

[2] U.S. DEP'T OF STAPE PUB. NO. 3177, REPORT OF THE UNITED STATES DELEGATION TO THE INTERNATIONAL TELECOMMUNICATION CONFERENCE AT ATLANTIC CITY 2–3 (1947).

[3] 2 DOCUMENTS DE LA CONFÉRENCE RADIOTÉLÉGRAPHIQUE INTERNATIONALE DE WASHINGTON 366–370, 373–379 (1927).

[4] *Id.* at 374.

It was thus a question of internal administrative law of the Union The matter was settled eventually at the Brussels Conference of 1928, where a compromise solution was adopted by a vote of 47 to 4, with three abstentions and six members not represented.[1]

The Convention of 1924 of the European Rail Transport Union also provided for periodic revisory conferences.[2] Portugal, a party to the 1924 Convention, did not take part in the conference held in 1933, but the conference nevertheless produced a new, revised convention.[3] The new convention provided in Article 60(2):

> The entry into force of the new convention resulting from a Conference of revision produces the abrogation of the previous convention even with regard to those of the contracting parties which may not have ratified the new Convention.[4]

Article 63 provided for the eventuality of non-ratification by some member states by permitting the Swiss Government, after it should have received the ratifications of fifteen states, to contact the "interested Governments" and "examine with them the possibility of putting the Convention in force." Pursuant to this provision the Swiss Government invited the contracting parties to a meeting on November 17, 1937, to determine the date of entry into force of the revised convention. Nineteen governments had by then ratified it, and Portugal had acceded.[5] Bulgaria and Finland did not attend the meeting, but all of the other signatories to the 1933 convention met and signed a protocol which brought the convention into operation.[6]

---

[1] DOCUMENTS DE LA CONFÉRENCE TÉLÉGRAPHIQUE INTERNATIONALE DE BRUXELLES 82–83, 89 (1928). The absent members were Argentina, Austria, Egypt, Ireland, Poland and Uruguay.

[2] 2 HUDSON, INTERNATIONAL LEGISLATION 1393. This was a revision of the original Convention of 1890 (82 B.F.S.P. 771) with the participation of all of its parties except Russia.

[3] 6 HUDSON, INTERNATIONAL LEGISLATION 527.

[4] In a discussion of this provision during the later revisory conference held in 1952 it was supported on the ground that it was important to guarantee the unification of the law of railway transport and undesirable to allow of a situation where states which had not ratified the new convention might demand of those which had ratified it that in traffic with them the old convention remain in force. 1 ACTES DE LA CONFÉRENCE INTERNATIONALE SUR LE TRANSPORT PAR CHEMINS DE FER, BERNE 485–486 (1952).

[5] The Portuguese accession was effective June 14, 1938. 192 L.N.T.S. 391.

[6] 192 L.N.T.S. 627. Spain, Greece and Turkey, although they had not ratified, signed this protocol. Bulgaria ratified the convention on August 23, 1938. 192 L.N.T.S 391.

Following World War II the Western European countries felt that there was an urgent need to revise the provisions of the convention which dealt with carriage of "containers." They therefore requested an extraordinary revision conference, to deal with this subject only.[1] Article 60 of the 1933 Convention provided that such a conference might be held on the request of one-third of the contracting states, and twelve governments concurred in the request for the extraordinary conference in this instance, which was enough to satisfy the requirement.[2] The conference was held at Berne on May 8–13, 1950.[3] Bulgaria, Finland, Poland, Portugal and Rumania were not represented. Sixteen states eventually signed the Additional Convention on May 13, 1950, and Portugal adhered to it.[4] This was the first occasion on which a majority of the member states made changes over the active protest of a minority. Hungary and Czechoslovakia had walked out of the conference, asserting that the 1933 convention had been violated.[5] However, the conference had been properly called, the precedent of 1933 had shown that a new convention could be adopted without the participation of one party, and Articles 60 and 63[6] of the 1933 convention established that failure of a minority to ratify should not prevent effective revision. The disregard of the active protests of Hungary and Czechoslovakia was but a small additional step.

No one hesitated to take that step. The additional convention provided that it should come into force "among the States which have ratified it" after notice from the Swiss Government "affirming the practical possibility of putting it in force." The Swiss Government gave such notice on February 28, 1951, when, out of the sixteen signers, France, Finland, Austria, Sweden, Denmark and Switzerland had ratified; Italy, Belgium, the Netherlands and Norway had indicated that they would ratify soon; and Portugal had adhered.[7]

Since the agreement of 1950 was not called a revision, but an additional convention, the Eastern European states which did

[1] 58 BULLETIN DES TRANSPORTS PAR CHEMINS DE FER 1 (1950).
[2] *Id.* at 81.
[3] *Id.* at 177–178.
[4] *Id.* at 178, 225, 341, 417.
[5] N. Y. Times, May 18, 1950.
[6] *Supra*, p. 26.
[7] 59 BULLETIN DES TRANSPORTS PAR CHEMINS DE FER 69 (1951).

not ratify were considered as remaining parties to the Union.[1] In 1952 they returned to the fold to participate in the next revisory conference, and they signed the new convention adopted at Bern on October 25, 1952.[2]

When it came to adoption of the rules of the 1952 conference, Article 11 of which provided that proposals were adopted by majority vote, a Polish delegate remarked that if the rule of unanimity were followed it would avoid complications as to acceptance of the conventions. No one supported his view.[3]

3. THE METHOD OF *INTER SE* AGREEMENTS

The Convention of 1883 which established the Union for the Protection of Industrial Property[4] provided that revisory conferences should be held periodically. It also specifically reserved to the parties the right to make separately, as between themselves, special agreements on the same subject "in so far as such agreements do not contravene the stipulations of the present Convention." Industrial property rights were not mere administrative conveniences, but matters touching important financial interests. For this reason, and because of the interest in preserving the degree of uniformity which had been achieved, in the subsequent history of this union, and of the similar union established in 1886 on the subject of copyrights, the method of *inter se* agreements which had been envisaged in the initial convention was used wherever unanimity was found unattainable.

When the first revisory conference of the Industrial Property Union was held in 1886, it produced sharp differences of opinion.[5] At the outset there was a debate over whether revision should be attempted at all. A statement by the delegate of Great Britain reflected some confusion of legal and practical considerations:

---

[1] 2 ACTES DE LA CONFÉRENCE INTERNATIONALE SUR LE TRANSPORT PAR CHEMINS DE FER, BERNE 244 (1952).

[2] CMD. No. 9065 (1954).

[3] 2 ACTES DE LA CONFÉRENCE INTERNATIONALE SUR LE TRANSPORT PAR CHEMINS DE FER, BERNE 226, 230 (1952).

[4] 74 B.F.S.P. 44.

[5] The rules adopted by the 1886 conference provided that each member state should have one vote. 14 NOUV. REC. GÉN. (2 sér.) 596–597. The previous conference had not adopted any formal rules of procedure. See FRANCE, MINISTÈRE DES AFFAIRES ETRANGÈRES, CONFÉRENCE INTERNATIONALE POUR LA PROTECTION DE LA PROPRIÉTÉ INDUSTRIELLE (1883).

If the result of this Conference was the modification of the text of the Convention, and if the Governments were not in agreement to accept unanimously the modifications proposed, would the rejection by a minority produce the withdrawal of all the States composing that minority? Or rather must one consider the present Convention as the charter of the Union, which cannot be modified without the unanimous consent of all the contracting States? [1]

Without specifically answering this question, the conference decided by a vote of five to four, with three abstentions, that it would not attempt to revise the convention. [2] Instead, it produced a protocol containing additional articles, which were to be effective only for the states which ratified them. [3] The next conference, held in 1890, produced two special agreements, and also two protocols, one concerning the expenses of the International Bureau and the other concerning the interpretation and application of the convention.[4] Norway, Sweden and Belgium, apparently fearing that the protocols also might be put in effect without the consent of all parties, ratified them only with the condition that they should be approved by all the other members of the union.[5] This condition was evidently accepted by the other signatories, for the protocol concerning the expenses of the Bureau was brought into effect only on January 1, 1898, after the adherences of Serbia and the Dominican Republic, the last two members to announce their acceptance,[6] and the protocol of interpretation and application never took effect.[7] The conference of 1900 adopted an act which revised certain articles of the convention.[8] It was hoped that this agreement would be accepted by all of the parties, but the conference agreed that if at the end of the time specified for ratification all the states of the Union were not prepared to deposit their ratifications, it would be up to the governments which had ratified to decide whether this act

[1] 14 NOUV. REC. GÉN. (2 sér.) 604.
[2] *Id.* at 605.
[3] *Id.* at 665, 659.
[4] *Id.* at 187–219.
[5] *Id.* at 224.
[6] 89 B.F.S.P. 30.
[7] The Swiss Government announced in 1896 that it would not take effect since entry into force "was dependent upon unanimous ratification ... by the several contracting States and certain of them having refused to ratify it." 98 B.F.S.P. 447.
[8] UNION INTERNATIONAL POUR LA PROTECTION DE LA PROPRIÉTÉ INDUSTRIELLE, ACTES DE LA CONFÉRENCE DE BRUXELLES, PREMIÈRE ET DEUXIÈME SESSIONS, 1897 et 1900, 407 (1901).

should be put in effect among themselves.[1] This eventuality did in fact materialize, and in 1902 the parties which had ratified it decided to apply it among themselves without waiting for further ratifications.[2]

In 1911 the procedure of *inter se* agreement, formerly limited to clearly supplementary provisions, was extended to a complete revision of the convention. The Convention of 1911 provided:

> This Act, ... shall, as regards the relations between the countries which ratify it, replace [all the previous Acts.] However, the aforementioned Acts shall remain in force as regards relations with the countries which shall not have ratified the present Act.[3]

The result of this sort of provision, repeated in subsequent revisions of 1925 and 1934, was that, while thirty-eight countries were listed as members of the union in 1947, the 1934 text was in effect among only fourteen of them, while for seventeen the 1925 text was applicable and for seven, the text of 1911.[4]

The Convention of 1886 which instituted the International Copyright Union[5] contained an explicit requirement of unanimity:

> It is understood that no change in the present Convention shall be binding on the Union (valable pour l'Union), except by the unanimous consent of the countries composing it.

The fact that such a clause was thought necessary suggests the implication that without it the convention might have been effectively revised without the consent of all. It was added to the text on the proposal of the British delegate, who suggested that some countries might hesitate to modify their internal legislation to adapt it to the international convention if they feared that it might soon be revised.[6] There was, however, a provision (Art. 15), similar to the one in the industrial property convention, which

---

[1] *Id.* at 398.

[2] 92 B.F.S.P. 807 (footnote). All of the states not having ratified in 1902 did eventually ratify or accede.

[3] 104 B.F.S.P. 116.

[4] See UNION INTERNATIONALE POUR LA PROTECTION DE LA PROPRIÉTÉ INDUSTRIELLE, ACTES DE LA CONFÉRENCE RÉUNIE À NEUCHÂTEL 11 (1947).

[5] 77 B.F.S.P. 22. The formal title of the union was "International Union for the Protection of Literary and Artistic Works."

[6] ACTES DE LA DEUXIÈME CONFÉRENCE INTERNATIONALE POUR LA PROTECTION DES OEUVRES LITTÉRAIRES ET ARTISTIQUES RÉUNIE À BERNE 52–53 (1885). The clause thus inserted was maintained in all later revisions of the convention.

allowed member governments to adopt in the form of special agreements among themselves improvements in the convention which all members were not ready to sign. As with the industrial property convention, all subsequent changes were introduced by *inter se* agreements.[1]

Separate treaties on these subjects were in force among the American states.[2] Treaties on patents and trade-marks concluded at Buenos Aires in 1910 provided that they were to supersede previous treaties on the same subjects "as far as the relations between the signatory States are concerned."[3] However, in 1923 eighteen states, this number not including Peru although it had ratified the trade-mark convention of 1910, concluded a new trade-mark convention which provided that it should become effective when ratified by one-third of the signatory states, "and from that moment the Convention signed on August 20, 1910, shall cease to exist."[4] It was added that this was to be without prejudice to private rights previously acquired.

The method of *inter se* agreements has become the one most commonly applied in the revision of nonpolitical conventions. It was used in 1906 in the revision of the 1864 Geneva Convention for the Amelioration of the Condition of the Wounded in Armies in the Field, although that convention had made no provision at all for revision, and although the 1906 convention contained, in Article 24, an important departure from the provisions of the earlier convention.[5] (This was a new provision which stated that

[1] For the results in terms of the provisions binding on the various parties, see UNION INTERNATIONAL POUR LA PROTECTION DES OEUVRES LITTÉRAIRES ET ARTISTIQUES, ACTES DE LA CONFÉRENCE DE ROME 9–13, 62–63 (1928).

[2] The Pan-American treaties on copyrights show no departures from the practice of unanimity in the matter of signature of revising agreements, but ratification by all parties to a previous agreement was never treated as a prerequisite of effective revision as between the parties which did ratify. For the history of the Inter-American convention, see 2 LADAS, THE INTERNATIONAL PROTECTION OF LITERARY AND ARTISTIC PROPERTY 635 ff. (1938); texts, *id.*, 1175–1191.

[3] 3 MALLOY 2930, 2935.

[4] 2 HUDSON, INTERNATIONAL LEGISLATION 992.

[5] 99 B.F.S.P. 968; *cf.* 55 B.F.S.P. 43. The new convention was to come into force for each ratifying power six months after the deposit of its ratification. It provided:

> The present Convention, when duly ratified, shall supersede the Convention of August 22, 1864, in the relations between the contracting States.
>
> The Convention of 1864 remains in force in the relations between the parties who signed it but who may not also ratify the present Convention.

Six parties to the original convention did not participate in the revision, and three others did not sign the new convention. ACTES DE LA CONFÉRENCE DE GENÈVE 13–15, 23 ff. (1906).

the convention should "cease to be obligatory if one of the belligerent Powers should not be signatory to the Convention.")

The method of *inter se* agreements was used also in the transfer to United Nations organs of functions which were exercised by organs of the League of Nations under the terms of a number of nonpolitical conventions.

As to functions assigned to the Permanent Court of International Justice this transfer was made in Articles 36 and 37 of the Statute of the new International Court of Justice. Article 36 provided that declarations accepting the compulsory jurisdiction of the Permanent Court should, "as between the parties to the present Statute," be deemed to be acceptances of the compulsory jurisdiction of the International Court of Justice, and Article 37 provided:

> Whenever a treaty or convention in force provides for reference of a matter to a tribunal to have been instituted by the League of Nations, or to the Permanent Court of International Justice, the matter shall, *as between the parties to the present Statute*, be referred to the International Court of Justice. (Emphasis added).

It was necessary also to transfer the functions exercised by the Secretary-General of the League of Nations as depository of treaties. Such functions under the narcotics conventions, for example, included receiving notices of ratifications and denunciations, solicitation of additional signatures, informing the parties of such occurrences, and in certain circumstances calling a new conference. A resolution of the United Nations General Assembly of February 12, 1946, recorded the assent of the members of the United Nations to the assumption of these functions by the U.N. Secretariat.[1] In addition such a transfer was approved by all of the members of the League of Nations in one of the resolutions adopted by the Assembly on April 18, 1946, when the League itself was terminated.[2] Nevertheless, and despite the purely formal nature of the change, the United Nations Secretariat proposed to the Economic and Social Council in September, 1946, as to the narcotics conventions, that specific amendments be introduced in the texts of the various conventions by a protocol to be signed by the parties thereto.[3] In the form

---

[1] U.N. GENERAL ASSEMBLY RESOLUTION No. 24 (I) (1946).
[2] LEAGUE OF NATIONS OFF. J., Spec. Supp. No. 194, at 278 (1946).
[3] U.N. Doc. No. E/116 (1946).

adopted by the Economic and Social Council the parties to the protocol would undertake to apply the amendments "as between themselves" and they would come into force in respect of each convention "when a majority of the Parties thereto have become Parties to the present Protocol." [1] Another paragraph was inserted in the resolution to direct the Economic and Social Council and the Secretary-General to suspend all action under the protocol and the narcotics conventions with respect to the Franco Government in Spain, for as long as that government remained in power, and this even though Spain was a party to the conventions of 1912, 1925 and 1931. Some opposition to this amendment was expressed in the drafting committee and in the Council, but the opposition was based, not on legal grounds, but on fear of weakening the international control system.[2]

After approval by the Economic and Social Council the draft protocol was examined by the Sixth (Legal) Committee of the General Assembly, and found to be in proper form.[3] The Committee asked and answered several questions, among them the following:

> (iii) What will be the legal position of those parties to the original instruments which do not become parties to the protocol?
>
> * * *
>
> With regard to question (iii) above, it is clearly competent to any number of the parties to the original instruments to make amendments in them which are binding *as between themselves*. This is exactly what article 1 of the protocol does.[4]

The Committee went on to state that those parties to the original instruments which did not become parties to the protocol would still remain bound, by virtue of the original instruments, *vis-a-vis* the parties which did sign the protocol, although the original machinery of control would be altogether dissolved. The resolu-

---

[1] U.N. ECONOMIC AND SOCIAL COUNCIL OFF. REC. 3d Sess., Supp. No. 4, at 45 ff. (1946).

[2] U.N. Docs. Nos. E/AC./12/4, E/AC./12/5; see also U.N. ECONOMIC AND SOCIAL COUNCIL OFF. REC. 3d Sess., Plenary 57–61 (1946). On Aug. 3, 1955, the Economic and Social Council finally decided to invite Spain to become a party to this protocol. 10 INTERNATIONAL ORGANIZATION 164 (1956).

[3] U.N. GENERAL ASSEMBLY OFF. REC. 1st Sess., 2d pt., Sixth Committee, 206 ff. (1946).

[4] U.N. GENERAL ASSEMBLY OFF. REC., 1st Sess., 2d pt. Sixth Committee, 208 (1946).

tion and draft protocol were approved by the General Assembly on November 19, 1946.[1]

On October 20, 1947, the General Assembly approved a resolution and protocols in similar form transferring functions under the Conventions of 1921 and 1933 on Traffic in Women and Children and under the Convention of 1923 on Traffic in Obscene Publications.[2] The amendments in this case included one change of substance, the elimination from the conventions in question of the so-called colonial application clause.[3] The elimination of the clause was proposed by the U.S.S.R. and approved over the vigorous opposition of the United Kingdom.[4] In spite of this important change it was again provided that the amendments should come into force in respect of each convention when a majority of their parties had become parties to the protocol.[5] However, in the following year a similar proposal to eliminate a colonial application clause in connection with transfer of League of Nations functions under the 1928 Convention on Economic Statistics was rejected in the Legal Committee of the Assembly (by seventeen votes to thirteen, with fourteen abstentions) after it had been stated by the Assistant Secretary-General in charge of the Legal Department that a revision of substance, as distinguished from purely formal modifications to adapt the text to the new situation resulting from the dissolution of the League of Nations, would require the consent of all the signatories of the convention, including certain states not members of the United Nations.[6]

Also in 1948, revisions of the same nature were made in three previous conventions, of 1904 and 1910, dealing with suppression of the white slave traffic and obscene publications.[7] These amend-

---

[1] U.N. GENERAL ASSEMBLY OFF. REC., 1st Sess., 2d pt., Plenary, 986 ff. (1946); U.N. GENERAL ASSEMBLY RESOLUTION No. 24 (1), at 81 (1946); The amendments were in force with respect to all the previous conventions, having been accepted by a majority of the parties in each case, by February 3, 1948. See STATUS OF MULTILATERAL CONVENTIONS OF WHICH THE SECRETARY-GENERAL ACTS AS DEPOSITARY, U.N. Doc. No. ST/LEG/3, at p. VI-4 (1955).

[2] U.N. GENERAL ASSEMBLY RESOLUTION No. 126 (II) (1947).

[3] See Art. 14 of the Convention of 1921 on Traffic in Women and Children. 1 HUDSON, INTERNATIONAL LEGISLATION 726.

[4] U.N. GENERAL ASSEMBLY, OFF. REC., 2d Sess., Plenary, 340–355 (1947).

[5] Art. 5 of the draft protocol, U.N. GENERAL ASSEMBLY RESOLUTION No. 126 (II) (1947).

[6] U.N. GENERAL ASSEMBLY OFF. REC., 3d Sess., 1st pt., Sixth Committee, 292–296 (1948). *Cf.* position taken by the Secretariat in 1951, *infra*, p. 36.

[7] U.N. GENERAL ASSEMBLY RESOLUTION No. 256 (III) (1948).

ments concerned depository functions entrusted by the conventions to the French Government and which France had asked to transfer to the United Nations. It was recognized that France, unlike the extinct League of Nations, "might continue to possess certain obligations until acceptance of the transfer by all the parties." [1] Nevertheless the revision protocol agreed on by the General Assembly provided that the amendments should take effect when approved by a definite number (less than all) of the parties to the conventions.[2] Although Spain was a party to all three conventions, she was not invited to sign the amending protocols.

The Economic and Social Council had decided in 1947 that it would be desirable to have one convention uniting all of the agreements concerning the traffic in women and children.[3] This project resulted in the preparation of a draft convention which was approved by the General Assembly on December 2, 1949, and opened for signature by U.N. members and by "each non-member State which the appropriate organ of the United Nations may invite to do so" (a formula excluding Spain) on March 21, 1950.[4] This convention was intended to consolidate all of the previous conventions and also to introduce desirable alterations. It provided that it should come into force on the deposit of two ratifications. Article 28 stated:

> The provisions of the present Convention shall supersede in the relations between the Parties thereto the provisions of the international instruments referred to ..., each of which shall be deemed to be terminated when all the Parties thereto shall have become Parties to the present Convention.

A draft of a single convention to unify all of the international agreements relating to narcotic drugs was prepared by the Secretariat in 1951 at the request of the Economic and Social Council.[5] The Legal Department of the Secretariat now seemed to reverse the position it had taken in 1948 with respect to amendment of

---

[1] Statement on behalf of the Secretariat, U.N. GENERAL ASSEMBLY OFF. REC., 3d Sess., 1st pt., Sixth Committee, 511 (1948).
[2] Twenty in the case of the White Slavery Conventions, and thirteen in the case of the Obscene Publications Convention, U.N. GENERAL ASSEMBLY RESOLUTION No. 256 (III) (1948).
[3] U.N. ECONOMIC AND SOCIAL COUNCIL RESOLUTION No. 83 (V) (1947).
[4] U.N. GENERAL ASSEMBLY RESOLUTION No. 317 (IV) (1949).
[5] U.N. Doc. No. E/CN.7/AC.3/3 (1951).

the convention on economic statistics.[1] In a commentary to accompany the draft single convention [2] it stated:

> Over the years, ideas have changed concerning the conditions which have to be fulfilled before international treaties can be amended. Whereas in the past the opinion used to be that multilateral conventions could not be amended except with the unanimous consent of all the original Contracting Parties, the point has now been reached where the possibility of amending multilateral agreements with the concurrence of a more or less large number of the original Parties is admitted. Thus, in the case of the Protocols approved by the United Nations General Assembly, transferring to the United Nations functions previously exercised either by the League of Nations or by a particular government, States which had not taken part in the conference of plenipotentiaries that drew up the original Convention, participated in the revision of the Convention. ... It may therefore be concluded that in this respect the evolution has been sufficient to allow a conference of plenipotentiaries to amend a convention when not all the original Parties to it are represented at the conference.

In respect to the coming into force of the amendments the comment noted a development of practice parallel to that of the possibility of revision:

> In the past, ... the entry into force of the amendments depended upon unanimous concurrence on the part of the old Parties. This rule has changed in the course of time and the modern view is that, even if the possibility of amendments coming into force as the result of a decision by a certain majority of the original Contracting Parties was not contemplated in the initial Convention – and that was the case of the present international instruments on narcotic drugs – that fact did not prevent these amendments from coming into force. But in this instance one firm principle has emerged, which is, that States which remain Parties to earlier instruments are bound by the texts of these instruments, without *ipso facto* being bound by the amendments.

At its ninth session, 1954, the Commission on Narcotic Drugs decided that entry into force of the convention should depend on acceptance by at least twenty-five states, but to ensure the effectiveness of the new convention it provided that this number must include three of the principal drug manufacturing countries and three of the principal opium producing countries.[3]

In 1953 the now-familiar procedure was applied again to effect the transfer to U.N. organs of functions assigned to the

---

[1] *Supra*, p. 34.

[2] U.N. Doc. No. E/CN.7/AC.3/4/Rev. 1, at 41 (1951).

[3] U.N. ECONOMIC AND SOCIAL COUNCIL OFF. REC., 18th Sess., Supp. No. 8, at 11 (1954). The manufacturing countries were defined as follows: Belgium, France, Federal Republic of Germany, Italy, Japan, Netherlands, Switzerland, United Kingdom, United States. The producing countries were: Bulgaria, Greece, India, Iran, Turkey, U.S.S.R., Yugoslavia.

League of Nations in the Slavery Convention of 1926. This time there was a brief discussion in the Legal Committee as to whether the procedure of adopting an amending protocol was really necessary.[1] The representative of the United Kingdom supported the adoption of the protocol but observed that it was "a pure formality" and "not to be regarded as throwing any doubt whatever on the Secretary-General's depository functions under the General Assembly's resolution 24 (I) of 12 February 1946."[2] A representative of the Secretariat stated:

[The Secretary-General] had carried out the administrative functions assigned to him under resolution 24 (I) with regard to conventions to which there had been no protocols, and no State had ever raised any objection. Since there were precedents for either course of action, the Secretary-General felt that whether or not there should be a protocol in the present case was a matter of policy to be decided by the General Assembly.[3]

In respect to the undertaking in the Slavery Convention to communicate to the Secretary-General of the League of Nations laws and regulations which the parties enacted in applying the convention, the Legal Department of the Secretariat called attention to the Advisory Opinion of the International Court of Justice in *the Case of the International Status of South-West Africa*,[4] in which the Court found an obligation to render to the United Nations annual reports previously submitted to the League under the Mandate.[5] Despite this debate, however, the procedure of an amending protocol open for signature by the parties to the previous convention was again chosen.[6]

Considerations of practical effectiveness were controlling in the revision, by a conference held at the Hague in 1955, of the Warsaw Convention concerning private law rules for international carriage by air.[7] All of the parties to the Warsaw Convention did not participate in the Hague Conference.[8]

[1] U.N. GENERAL ASSEMBLY OFF. REC., 8th Sess., Sixth Committee, 48–53 (1953).
[2] *Id.* at 48.
[3] U.N. GENERAL ASSEMBLY OFF. REC., 8th Sess., Sixth Committee, 52 (1953).
[4] [1950] I.C.J. Rep. 128, discussed *infra*, pp. 76–78.
[5] U.N. Doc. No. E/AC.7/L. at 142 (1953).
[6] U.N. GENERAL ASSEMBLY RESOLUTION No. 794 (VIII) (1953). The amendments were to come into effect when twenty-three parties to the previous convention (of the possible total of forty-four) should have become parties to the protocol.
[7] 5 HUDSON, INTERNATIONAL LEGISLATION 100. On the subject of revision the Warsaw Convention provided only that any contracting party might call for a revisory conference (Art. 41).
[8] See 2 INTERNATIONAL CIVIL AVIATION ORGANIZATION. INTERNATIONAL CONFERENCE ON PRIVATE AIR LAW, THE HAGUE 70 (1955).

No state represented at the Hague suggested that unanimity of the parties to the Warsaw Convention would be required for revision, but most of those which expressed themselves upon the point agreed that the consent of a substantial proportion of the parties to the Warsaw Convention should be required.[1] Typical was the comment of the German Federal Republic:

> The essential importance of the Warsaw Convention of the 12th of October, 1929, lies in the fact that, throughout the world, it has created a uniform legal basis for international air traffic. ... Everything should, therefore, be avoided that might endanger the present uniformity in air traffic law. A revision of this Convention or the conclusion of an additional Protocol can, therefore, be advocated only if it may be assumed with certainty that the great majority of the signatory States to the Warsaw Convention will also ratify the Additional Protocol.[2]

The United States, in its reply, reserved opinion on the number of ratifications which should be required, stating that it depended, in part at least,

> upon the decision of the conference concerning whether states who become parties to the protocol would thereby consider themselves no longer bound by the existing provisions of the Warsaw Convention with respect to states not yet parties to the protocol or whether they would consider that two contractual relations existed.[3]

The United Kingdom urged the "practical difficulties of having two inconsistent sets of obligations," and suggested that it would be better to have an entirely new convention, with a requirement that the states ratifying it denounce the Warsaw Convention.[4]

---

[1] 2 *id.* at 145 ff. Sweden suggested that ratification by two-thirds of the parties to the Warsaw Convention should be required before the protocol came into force, Venezuela suggested three-fourths and Australia thirty-five (there were forty-two in all). The United Kingdom considered that ratification by twenty parties would be sufficient.

[2] 2 INTERNATIONAL CONFERENCE ON PRIVATE AIR LAW, THE HAGUE 157 (1955).

[3] 2 *id.* at 188.

[4] 2 INTERNATIONAL CONFERENCE ON PRIVATE AIR LAW, THE HAGUE 183 (1955). The British view was adopted by a subcommittee on methods of revision, which gave the following example of conflicting obligations which might arise if the Warsaw Convention were not denounced [2 *id.* at 102]; "States A, B and C are bound by the Warsaw Convention, but only States A and B are bound by the Protocol. In litigation in the Courts of State A involving nationals of States B and C, State A will be obliged *towards State B* (which has accepted the Protocol) to give effect to the amended Convention and *towards State C* (which has not accepted the Protocol) to give effect to the existing Convention. If, therefore, the carrier is a national of State C, that State will be entitled to complain of a breach of an international obligation if its national carrier is not given the benefit of the limit of liability under the Warsaw Convention; but if, at the same time, the passenger or consignor or consignee is a national of State B, that State will be entitled to complain if its national passenger

The conference rejected this proposal because of fears of destroying the uniformity already prevailing. The delegates were all agreed that it was possible to have two co-existing systems of relationships. No one referred to the interest of the Warsaw parties in uniformity under their convention which would be destroyed if a majority made a new agreement *inter se*. The Hague Protocol, adopted on September 28, 1955, provided that as between the parties ratifying it the convention and the protocol should be one single instrument known as "the Warsaw Convention as amended at the Hague, 1955." It was to apply only to transport both originating and terminating in territories of parties to the protocol. It was left to each party to make its own decision as to whether to denounce the original Warsaw Convention.[1] The protocol provided that it would come into effect among the ratifying states as soon as thirty ratifications were deposited.[2] There was no distinction in this regard between the ratifications of parties to the Warsaw Convention and those of other participants in the conference.

4. THE METHOD OF DENUNCIATION

In 1881 Austria-Hungary, France, Germany, Switzerland and Portugal wished to revise the Convention of September 17, 1878, on Measures to be taken against Phylloxera. Italy and Spain had been signatories of the 1878 convention but had not ratified it. The parties first named stated in Article 1 of their convention of 1881 that they were leaving the International Convention of 17 September, 1878, "pour en conclure une nouvelle." [3] Since that time the method of revision by denunciation of a previous convention has been resorted to on a number of occasions.

The terms of the Paris Convention on Aerial Navigation, of 1919,[4] assumed a basic requirement of unanimity for revision. It established a permanent International Commission for Air Navigation (CINA), and gave it the power to amend, by three-fourths majority, certain regulations contained in Annexes A to

or consignor or consignee is not given the benefit of the higher limit of liability under the Protocol. State A would, therefore, be subject to conflicting obligations towards States B and C."
[1] 1 INTERNATIONAL CONFERENCE ON PRIVATE AIR LAW, THE HAGUE 319–321 (1955).
[2] Art. 22, 2 *id*. at 10.
[3] 73 B.F.S.P. 323.
[4] 11 L.N.T.S. 174.

G. However, it excepted from this procedure Annex H, dealing with customs, which the convention called "matière dans laquelle les gouvernements n'avaient pas voulu abandonner *leur droit de veto aux décisions d'une majorité.*" [1] (Emphasis added.) As to revision of the convention itself, it was provided that amendments, which could be proposed by two-thirds of the states represented on the Commission, "must be formally adopted by the contracting States before they become effective." [2] This provision was taken to mean that *all* contracting States must consent, and such was the procedure followed with respect to all amendments made in the convention until 1944.[3]

On September 11, 1944, however, when the United States issued invitations to an International Civil Aviation Conference to be held in Chicago for the purpose of reaching agreement on world air routes and a new aviation convention, interest rather than participation in the prewar agreements seemed to be the criterion for inclusion. The invitations were sent to nations associated with the United Nations in the war and to "the European and Asiatic neutral nations, in view of their close relationship to the expansion of air transport which may be expected along with the liberation of Europe." [4] Under this formula Argentina, a party to the Paris Convention, was not invited.[5]

The Chicago Convention on International Civil Aviation [6] was intended to replace the Paris Convention and also the Pan-American Convention on Commercial Aviation which had been adopted at Havana in 1928.[7] It accomplished this by providing, in Article 80:

---

[1] See Art. 34 of the convention.
[2] *Ibid.*
[3] Amendments were in the form of protocols containing a clause similar to the following, taken from the protocol of an amendment opened for signature Oct. 27, 1922:
"It shall come into force so soon as the States at present contracting parties to the Convention shall have deposited their ratifications.
"States which shall become contracting parties to the Convention may adhere to this Protocol". 1 HUDSON, INTERNATIONAL LEGISLATION 379.
[4] 1 U.S. DEPT. OF STATE PUB. NO. 2820, PROCEEDINGS OF THE INTERNATIONAL CIVIL AVIATION CONFERENCE 11 (1948).
[5] In fact, however, Argentina was the first state to take advantage of Article 92 of the Chicago Convention, which permitted adherence by States which remained neutral during the war. 2 *id.* at 1401.
[6] T.I.A.S. No. 1591.
[7] 4 HUDSON, INTERNATIONAL LEGISLATION 2354. A Spanish-American Convention

Each contracting State undertakes, immediately upon the coming into force of this Convention, to give notice of denunciation of the Convention relating to the Regulation of Aerial Navigation signed at Paris on October 13, 1919 or the Convention on Commercial Aviation signed at Habana on February 20, 1928, if it is a party to either. As between contracting States, this Convention supersedes the Conventions of Paris and Habana previously referred to.

The method of denunciation was also employed in the Convention of 1926 on Motor Traffic, which provided that each contracting party should denounce the convention of 1909, [1] and in the protocol of 1946 establishing the World Health Organization which provided that the parties should denounce the 1907 Agreement respecting the Creation of an International Office of Public Health.[2]

5. OUTRIGHT DEPARTURES FROM THE UNANIMITY PRINCIPLE

There are also a number of instances in which less than all of the parties to a nonpolitical convention, in adopting a revised agreement, have terminated the old one entirely without going through the formality of exercising the right to denounce it.[3] The revision of the Convention of June 7, 1905, which instituted the International Institute of Agriculture[4] is a particularly interesting example because it contained no denunciation clause. It

---

on Aerial Navigation of Nov. 1, 1926, was also signed by the Latin-American states, Spain and Portugal. 3 HUDSON, INTERNATIONAL LEGISLATION 2019. Several of the contracting states were parties to the Paris Convention. However, it was not intended as a revision of the Paris Convention, which it closely paralleled, and it provided in Art. 42 that it was not intended to cancel other air agreements previously concluded. So few states ratified that the "Ibero-American Aerial Navigation Commission" which it envisaged never came into existence, and Lissitzyn concluded in 1942 that it retained "only historical significance." LISSITZYN, INTERNATIONAL AIR TRANSPORT AND NATIONAL POLICY 372n. (1942). The parties to the Chicago convention of 1944 did not bother to denounce it. It has been pointed out that the Paris and Havana conventions were inconsistent and that several states signed both of them, and Panama actually became a party to both. HARVARD DRAFT CONVENTION 1028; Warner, *The International Convention for Air Navigation and the Pan American Convention for Air Navigation: A Comparative and Critical Analysis*, 3 AIR LAW REVIEW 225 (1932). The Havana Convention, however, envisaged such a case, according priority to earlier inconsistent treaties (Art 30).

[1] 3 HUDSON, INTERNATIONAL LEGISLATION 1859.
[2] 9 U.N.T.S. 66. See also Article 25 of the Pan-American Postal Convention of November 9, 1926. 3 HUDSON, INTERNATIONAL LEGISLATION 2043.
[3] One such instance is the replacement in 1923 of the Latin-American Trade-mark Convention of 1910, p. 31, *supra*.
[4] 2 MALLOY 2140.

was revised in 1926 by an amending protocol which raised the permissible maximum of financial assessments against member states.[1] Only thirty-eight among the fifty-four parties to the convention in 1926 signed the amending protocol. The United States was among the parties to the convention which did not sign it. The United States finally adhered to the protocol as of August 25, 1934, explaining when it did so that it had been voluntarily paying contributions in accordance with the terms of the protocol since July 1, 1933, but that it recognized no obligation to do so except from the date of its adherence.[2] The note acknowledged, however, that the protocol had become effective for the powers which signed it.

After the establishment of the Food and Agriculture Organization of the United Nations the International Institute of Agriculture was terminated and its assets transferred to FAO. This was accomplished as follows: on July 16, 1945 the United Nations Interim Commission on Food and Agriculture recommended to the governments of the United Nations that the Institute should be merged with FAO "in due course after FAO has been formally established and the necessary authority given both by FAO and by parties to the International Institute of Agriculture." [3] Subsequently a protocol to terminate the Convention of 1905 was drawn up, dated March 30, 1946, for signature by the parties to the Convention.[4] It provided that it should come into force upon its acceptance by thirty-five members of the Institute. There were some fifty parties to the 1905 Convention at the time, and besides the defeated states, at least Costa Rica, Mexico, Ethiopia and New Zealand, all parties to the Convention, did not sign the protocol. Though the protocol provided that it should come into force "as between the parties" to it, it also stated that the Institute should "be brought to an end" by the Permanent Committee of the Institute after it should have collected all the assets of the Institute and turned them over to FAO. The protocol came into force with thirty-five final acceptances on January

---

[1] 3 HUDSON, INTERNATIONAL LEGISLATION 1857.

[2] 5 HACKWORTH, DIGEST OF INTERNATIONAL LAW 82–83. The instrument of adherence, effective as of August 25, 1934, was not deposited until January 15, 1936.

[3] UNITED NATIONS INTERIM COMMISSION ON FOOD AND AGRICULTURE, SECOND REPORT TO THE GOVERNMENTS OF THE UNITED NATIONS (1945).

[4] T.I.A.S. No. 1719.

28, 1948. On February 27, 1948, the Permanent Committee of the International Institute of Agriculture adopted a Final Act announcing the dissolution of the Institute.[1] The Permanent Committee was an executive body on which all members of the Institute were represented. Its ordinary authority, under the terms of the 1905 Convention, was limited to the collection of information, and its normal business was conducted by majority rule. The published text of the Final Act does not indicate by what vote it was adopted.

The protocol of 1946, besides providing for the termination of the Institute, also stated that thereafter the powers, rights or duties attributed to the Institute by a series of international conventions[2] should devolve upon FAO instead. There was no provision for approval of such action by the parties to the conventions.

There do not appear to have been any objections to these procedures.

In the revision of the international agreements to regulate whaling so as to prevent the extermination of whales, unanimity was sought, but was dispensed with when it proved unattainable. The 1937 London Agreement on this subject was signed and ratified by the United Kingdom, the United States, Germany, Norway, New Zealand and Ireland.[3] Canada, Denmark and Mexico acceded to it.[4] After World War II two whaling agreements were concluded which, referring to the interruption of whaling by the war and an emergency need for whale oil, introduced *less* restrictive regulations by temporary amendments to the 1937 Agreement. The first of these was an amending protocol, signed at London on February 7, 1944, to apply to the first season in which whaling operations were resumed after the war.[5] Ireland and Mexico were not signatories, but the protocol provided that it was not to come into force until all of the parties to the

---

[1] 18 DEP'T OF STATE BULL. 828 (1948).

[2] These conventions dealt with locust control, plant protection, marking of eggs, and standardization of methods of cheese and wine analysis and the keeping of herdbooks.

[3] 7 HUDSON, INTERNATIONAL LEGISLATION 754. Additional restrictions were added by an amending agreement of 1938. 7 *id.* 762.

[4] Argentina, Australia, South Africa, the Netherlands, Chile, France, Sweden and the U.S.S.R. also became parties to the 1937 agreement after World War II.

[5] 9 HUDSON, INTERNATIONAL LEGISLATION 111.

1937 Agreement except enemy Germany and occupied Denmark had ratified it or acceded to it.[1] However, when Ireland did not in fact accede to the protocol, the other parties signed a supplementary agreement to bring the 1944 protocol into force "without awaiting the accession of the Government of Eire." [2]

A similar amendment to the 1937 Agreement, continuing the relaxed restrictions through the 1946–47 whaling season, was opened for signature at London on November 26, 1945.[3] This time Ireland was omitted from the list of states whose ratification or accession was stated to be required before the amendment to the 1937 Agreement would come into force. Nevertheless, it was again impossible to secure formal consent of all the parties, and again a supplementary protocol was signed, this one to bring the amendment into force "without awaiting ratification by the Governments of Mexico and the Netherlands." [4] However, there was evidence of acquiescence by those two governments, though not of Ireland.[5]

On December 2, 1946, by another supplementary protocol, the protocol of November 26, 1945, was extended to apply to the

[1] The Final Act of the London Whaling Conference of 1944 stated: "that, as this Protocol makes certain temporary amendments to the Agreement of 1937, Governments who are parties to that instrument (other than Governments with whom diplomatic relations are suspended by reason of hostilities) should be invited either to sign the present Protocol or to accede thereto ...." CMD. No. 6510 (1944).

[2] 145 B.F.S.P. 908. This agreement, which the United States signed subject to ratification, was sent to the Senate accompanied by a report of Secretary of State Byrnes which merely stated: "As provided in ... the aforementioned protocol of February 7, 1944, that protocol could not come into force until instruments of ratification thereof or accession thereto had been deposited on behalf of the Governments of the United Kingdom of Great Britain and Northern Ireland, the United States of America, Canada, Eire, Mexico, New Zealand and Norway. Such instruments have been deposited for each of those Governments with the exception of the Government of Eire. The supplementary protocol of October 5, 1945, has therefore been signed with a view to bringing into force the protocol of February 7, 1944 at the earliest practicable date in order that it will be effective during the 1945–1946 whaling season." 13 DEP'T STATE BULL. 872 (1945). Still unratified by the United States and by then obsolete, the supplementary protocol was withdrawn from the Senate on Apr. 8, 1947. 16 DEP'T STATE BULL. 727 (1947). It had been in force, however, among the other parties.

[3] 9 HUDSON, INTERNATIONAL LEGISLATION 114.

[4] 148 B.F.S.P. 511.

[5] A report of Acting Secretary of State Acheson which was sent with the supplementary protocol to the Senate stated: "The Governments of Mexico and the Netherlands, according to information received officially by the Department, have given assurances that the procedure provided for by the supplementary protocol for the purpose of bringing the protocol of 1945 into force in its entirety meets with their approval." 16 DEP'T STATE BULL. 1005–1006 (1947). This supplementary protocol was ratified by the United States.

1947-48 season.[1] This supplementary protocol provided that it should come into force when notifications of acceptance had been given "by all the Governments parties to the said Protocol of November 26, 1945." This meant that Mexico and Ireland, as well as Sweden – newly a party to the 1937 Agreement which this agreement further amended for the season of 1947-48 – were again ignored.[2]

On March 15, 1946, meanwhile, another supplementary protocol had been signed by ten of the parties to the 1937 Agreement, again ignoring Ireland.[3] This agreement further relaxed the 1937 provisions so as to allow any factory ship not reaching the Antarctic whaling grounds before Nov. 24, 1945, to continue operations for two months longer than the 1937 Agreement allowed.

Finally, at the Washington International Whaling Conference of November-December, 1946, fifteen states, including all of the principal producers except Japan, signed a new Whaling Convention.[4] Ireland and Sweden had been invited to the conference, but sent only observer delegations and did not sign the convention.[5] Mexico was not represented. The parties to the new Convention agreed to establish an International Whaling Commission, which would take decisions by majority vote (Art. 3). The Commission was empowered to amend the regulations, but it was provided that any government should have the right to present an objection to any amendment of the schedule and in such a case the amendment should not be binding on the objecting state.[6] Article 10 (4) of the convention provided that it should come into force for the ratifying governments as soon as it should have been ratified by at least six of the signatories, including the Netherlands, Norway, the U.S.S.R., the United Kingdom (principal whaling states), and the United States. These were the states whose support was necessary to make the new agreement

---

[1] T.I.A.S. No. 1708.
[2] The Netherlands had signed this supplementary protocol.
[3] 146 B.F.S.P. 498.
[4] 9 HUDSON, INTERNATIONAL LEGISLATION 117.
[5] 15 DEP'T STATE BULL. 1101 (1946).
[6] Art. 5 (3) of the convention. The first amendments to the schedule were made at the meeting of the International Whaling Commission at London May 30 to June 7, 1949. France objected to one amendment, which therefore came into force for the other parties but not for France. T.I.A.S. No. 2092.

6. LAW-MAKING TREATIES

It may be asked whether conventions of the 'law-making' type — those which are intended to establish or affirm rules of international law — have different characteristics from the nonpolitical conventions we have been considering. The 1928 Havana Convention on Treaties seemed to reflect an opinion that law-making treaties were not denouncable in the absence of specific provisions authorizing denunciation, although the article on this subject was confusingly expressed.[1] However, many law-making treaties, following the pattern we have already outlined, include denunciation clauses. The texts of the conventions on the law of nationality which were adopted by the 1930 Hague Conference for the Codification of International Law all contained such provisions.[2] There is also a denunciation clause in the Genocide Convention of December 9, 1948.[3] The Draft Covenants on Human Rights omit it but suggest instead a procedure for amendment by two-thirds of the parties.[4] The Hague Conventions of 1899 and 1907, in part declaratory of existing law and in part establishing new law, all had denunciation provisions. The Convention of 1899 on the Law and Customs of War on Land[5] provided in Article 5:

> In the event of one of the High Contracting Parties denouncing the present Convention, such denunciation would not take effect until one year after the written notification made to the Netherland Government. ...

The rapporteur of the committee which drafted this provision explained it to the conference as follows:

> Article 5 concerns denunciation. It is evident that the Convention should not be a perpetual engagement. What, then, should the procedure be if one of the contracting Parties desires to withdraw?

---

[1] See p. 8, *supra*.

[2] League of Nations Pub. No. C. 351. M. 1930. V., at 89, 99, 119. The drafting committee also conceded that nothing would prevent the conclusion of *inter se* agreements, even if not entirely in accordance with the principles contained in the conventions. *Id*. at 68.

[3] GENERAL ASSEMBLY RESOLUTION No. 260 (III) (1948).

[4] U.N. ECONOMIC AND SOCIAL COUNCIL OFF. REC. 18th Sess., Supp. No. 7, at 62 (1954).

[5] 2 MALLOY 2042.

Although, in principle, this last hypothesis should not be provided for, it nevertheless seemed more prudent to consider it. A case might arise where a state, on the eve of war, might suddenly announce its intention to denounce the Convention. In order to avoid abuses of this kind, it was decided to specify the method of procedure in the matter of denunciation in a clause tending rather to restrict its effect than to encourage its exercise. Moreover, states will adhere more readily to a contractual engagement, if they know in advance that, according to the letter of the law, they may free themselves at a given time, without making their denunciation appear almost violent, as it would in the absence of a special clause.[1]

This statement was ambiguous enough so that there could be found in it arguments either for or against an implicit right of denunciation. However, once the conference decided that the convention "should not be a perpetual engagement," the right of denunciation was inescapable.

The Treaty for the Renunciation of War (Kellogg-Briand Pact), an attempt to create new law, was clearly intended to be a permanent undertaking, as appears from its wording and from the preceding negotiations.[2] An exception to the usual rule, it contains no denunciation clause. However, the permanence of the new consensus that aggressive war is inadmissible depends on factors unrelated to procedural rules of treaty revision.

Doubts have been expressed whether it would be permissible for some of the parties to a law-making treaty to vary its rules by an *inter se* agreement.[3] However, even the customary principles of international law are not regarded as immutable, and there would seem to be no good reason why conventionally-established principles should be more so. In fact international practice, as indicated above, affords several instances in which the right to revise a law-making convention by *inter se* agreement was recognized. A further instance was provided by the Hague Conference of 1907, when it revised, as between some of the parties, the Convention of 1899 on the Laws and Customs of War on Land. The new Convention of 1907 provided that the earlier convention should still remain in force "as between the Powers which signed it and which do not also ratify the present Conven-

[1] 1 PROCEEDINGS OF THE HAGUE PEACE CONFERENCE (James Brown Scott ed. 1920) 209; *cf. id.* 154–155.

[2] U.S. TREATY SERIES No. 796; DEP'T OF STATE PUB. NO. 468, TREATY FOR THE RENUNCIATION OF WAR 9, 11 (1933).

[3] Hudson wrote in 1930 that to do so would be "contrary to the spirit of codification." Hudson, *The First Conference for the Codification of International Law*, 24 A.J.I.L. 461 (1930).

tion."[1] Spain, China, Honduras and Nicaragua, parties to the 1899 convention, did not participate in the 1907 conference. Hudson noted that this produced anomalous conditions, so that the United States and France, which were bound *inter se* by the convention of 1907, remained bound to Great Britain and Italy by the convention of 1899.[2] However, the legal validity of the revision was not disputed at the Second Hague Conference.

The delegates to the Second Hague Conference were concerned instead with unanimity as a principle of conference procedure.[3] In all preliminary votes unanimity was not insisted on, but unanimity (counting abstentions as consent) does seem to have been required in the ultimate decision on the inclusion of a convention in the Final Act. In the one instance where a dissident minority pressed a formal objection to such adoption the convention was regarded as rejected. This was the case of the Compulsory Arbitration Convention. It was not a revision of a former agreement. Furthermore, not even the states signing it would have been bound by it if they had chosen later not to ratify. Nevertheless, although thirty-two states, a majority of the conference, voted for the inclusion of this convention in the Final Act, the opposition of nine states, led by Germany, was enough to defeat it.[4] Schücking reports that the advocates of the Compulsory Arbitration Convention subsequently held two meetings at a hotel to consider whether they should not conclude the convention between themselves. He adds:

> The plan did not succeed, and it must be said, indeed that it would perhaps have been in violation of good faith. For so long as the principle of unanimity ... holds good at international conferences, the majority lays itself open, in my opinion, to the just reproach of disloyal and therefore, indeed, of illegal conduct, if in the room of an hotel it adopts as a resolution a plan which was defeated in the hall of the conference. ...[5]

There was a later debate among scholars as to whether the opposition of one or a few states would similarly be a legal obstacle to conference action. Huber believed that it would be, while

---

[1] 2 MALLOY 2269 (Art. IV).
[2] 1 HUDSON, INTERNATIONAL LEGISLATION lvi.
[3] SCHÜCKING, THE INTERNATIONAL UNION OF THE HAGUE CONFERENCES 209–223 (Fenwick transl. 1918).
[4] *Id.* at 212.
[5] *Id.* at 219.

Zorn and Schücking thought that an undefined "quasi-unanimity" would suffice.[1] Schücking states:

> It is inconceivable that when the huge body of diplomatic representatives of the entire civilized world has been brought together, and when after proceedings of months in length they have come to an agreement, that the opposition of a single Balkan state, such as Montenegro, or perhaps of another state which has just been adopted into the family of nations from the group of half-civilized states, should obstruct a work of the civilized states as a body. And yet that was the situation that was accepted as law before the Hague Conferences.[2]

Schücking proposed that a three-fourths majority should be made the rule of the next conference. He noted that for practical realization of their project the lesser states, even if in the majority, would be inclined to make very far-reaching concessions to obtain the co-operation of the powerful states.[3]

This debate turned entirely on conference procedure rather than on the requirements of revision. It shows a drift away from the unanimity principle, although the president of the Second Hague Conference still called it "the first principle of every conference."[4] Where there was unanimity of those attending the conference there was no hesitation about revising the conventions of the previous conference, even though some of the parties were not present.

7. SUMMARY

The history of nonpolitical conventions affords many indications that the participants assumed the existence of a rule of unanimous consent for revision. However, in actual practice the lack of unanimity has never operated to block changes which practical considerations required. It has usually been relatively easy to find ways of circumventing it.

The terminable character of nonpolitical conventions makes it always possible to denounce the old convention and then conclude a new one. In most instances, however, denunciation is too drastic a remedy because the parties do not want to risk the degree of co-operation already achieved. Other methods of prac-

---

[1] *Id.* at 210–212.
[2] *Id.* at 215–216.
[3] *Id.* at 221.
[4] 2 DEUXIÈME CONFÉRENCE INTERNATIONALE DE LA PAIX (1907), ACTES ET DOCUMENTS 171 (1909).

tically effective revision have therefore been developed. One of these is acceptance of the authority of a periodic revisory conference. Agreement on this step transforms the question into one of conference procedure. Unanimity was originally the accepted principle governing conference voting, and departures from that principle were the subject of serious discussion in the early nonpolitical conferences. Before 1914, however, unanimity in conference voting at nonpolitical conferences had been generally abandoned. In the international unions which accepted the principle of periodic conference revision the basic principle that no state could be bound without its consent was preserved only in the option to withdraw from international co-operation in the field involved.

A commoner method for the revision of nonpolitical conventions has been the *inter se* agreement, which leaves the previous agreement also still valid except in the relations between parties to the new agreement. The particular advantage of this method is that it is considered to leave the obligations of other parties under the original convention still binding on them. This was expressly stated in the Geneva Convention of 1906 concerning the Condition of the Wounded in Armies in the Field, and it was stated in regard to the Narcotics Conventions by the Sixth Committee of the General Assembly in 1946. It was the reason for following the *inter se* method in the revision of the Warsaw Convention concerning international carriage by air.

The International Court of Justice has held in another context that none of the contracting parties to a multipartite convention is entitled to frustrate or impair by means of a particular agreement the essential purpose of the convention,[1] and the same principle was affirmed by the editors of the Harvard Draft Convention on the Law of Treaties.[2] However, no instance has been found of any protest against a projected *inter se* agreement on this ground, and law-making conventions as well as other nonpolitical conventions have been revised in this manner. Instances such as the revision of the Warsaw Convention on private air law show that the interest of the parties to the original agreement in

---

[1] Case concerning Reservations to the Convention on Genocide [1951] I.C.J. Rep. 14 at 21, discussed at pp. 9–10, *supra*.
[2] See p. 3 *supra*.

uniformity thereunder is not considered enough to make *inter se* revision improper. The parties, however, ordinarily make their own decision as to the appropriateness of *inter se* revision, and compatibility with the purpose of the original convention is no doubt taken into account.

Where there is no provision in advance for periodic revisory conferences, and where *inter se* revision is impractical, the parties to nonpolitical conventions do not hesitate to revise them outright despite a lack of unanimity. When the Convention Instituting the International Institute of Agriculture was revised in this manner in 1926, the United States (not a party to the revision) refused to recognize that any new obligation was binding on it, but conceded that the revision was effective for the powers which were parties to it. When Ireland withheld her consent to the temporary relaxation of the 1937 Whaling Agreement after World War II, the other parties put it in effect nevertheless, and they converted this temporary departure from unanimity into a permanent one by excluding Ireland from later revisions. They apparently considered her failure to consent as an indication of lack of interest..

Where unanimity is not required it is replaced by some form of majority approval of the revised acts. In the case of the unions with periodic revisory conferences the essential requirements may be in the conference voting rules. Where revision, as distinguished from purely supplemental provisions, is accomplished by *inter se* agreement, it is ordinarily provided that the agreement will become effective on ratification by a stated majority. This frequently provides (as with the Narcotics and Whaling Conventions) that the majority must include a number of the states most important in the particular activity under regulation.

CHAPTER II

TREATIES OF A CONSTITUTIONAL CHARACTER

Treaties creating international organizations such as the League of Nations, the United Nations or the World Court are distinguishable from the international unions considered in the last chapter not merely in degree but also in kind. They are gropings toward international government which awaken fears of restrictions of national sovereignty.

Such treaties ordinarily provide an explicit procedure for amendment, and where such provisions are included they usually allow amendment by something less than unanimous consent. Because future revision is usually dealt with explicitly, there is only a very limited body of practice on revision in the absence of a prescribed amendment procedure. Our inquiry concerns the residual rules which apply in the absence of such provisions. Nevertheless, the inclusion of such provisions is informative insofar as it shows a belief that the requirement of unanimity in revision should be abandoned. The practice in relation to the adoption of amendment and withdrawal provisions is also interesting for what it shows concerning the use of the right of withdrawal as an alternative means of preserving the principle of consent.

1. THE COVENANT OF THE LEAGUE OF NATIONS

In the course of drafting the Covenant of the League of Nations Wilson stated his opinion, in private discussion, that a state had the power to denounce any treaty. He thought a majority of the delegates to the Paris Peace Conference would agree with him that a state had the right to withdraw from the League under the Covenant as originally drafted – without any specific provision on the subject.[1] However, the view of Wilson's advisers and of Lord Robert Cecil was to the contrary, and Wilson, knowing that the Senate would insist on this right, concluded

[1] 1 MILLER, THE DRAFTING OF THE COVENANT 293 (1928).

that explicit authorization for withdrawal was essential. His proposal that withdrawal should be permitted at the end of ten years was opposed by the representative of France, not from opposition to the right to withdraw, but because it might contain a suggestion that the League was experimental rather than permanent,[1] and it was provided instead (Art. 1, para. 3):

> Any Member of the League may, after two years' notice of its intention so to do, withdraw from the League, provided that all its international obligations and all its obligations under this Covenant shall have been fulfilled at the time of its withdrawal.

Authorization of withdrawal had also become essential in the view of the small states when it was decided to allow amendment of the Covenant by less than unanimous vote, reserving a veto only to the states represented in the Council.[2] Representatives of the Netherlands and Switzerland stated that this amendment provision would constitute a limitation of the sovereignty of the small states.[3] To meet their objection the following paragraph was added to Article 26:

> No such amendment shall bind any Member of the League which signifies its dissent therefrom, but in that case it shall cease to be a Member of the League.

The veto in the matter of revision was therefore given up by all except the States represented in the Council, and the principle of consent was preserved instead by the right to withdraw. The Covenant appears to have been the first important multipartite treaty in which the authorization of revision by a special majority vote was made explicit. The precedent thus set has been followed subsequently in numerous other multipartite treaties, particularly those of the organizational type.

While unanimity was thus expressly abandoned in this instance as a requirement of revision, it was still preserved as a rule of conference procedure. The Commission on the League of Nations, the committee of the Paris Peace Conference which drafted the Covenant, operated under the unanimity rule. This was the result of a ruling made by President Wilson, as its chair-

---

[1] 1 *id.* at 343; *cf.* 2 *id.* at 535.
[2] Article 26, para. 1: "Amendments to this Covenant will take effect when ratified by the Members of the League whose Representatives compose the Council and by a majority of the Members of the League whose Representatives compose the Assembly."
[3] 2 MILLER, THE DRAFTING OF THE COVENANT 632 (1928).

man. A majority of the Commission had voted in favor of a Japanese amendment which would have inserted a reference to the equality of nations, but the representative of Great Britain announced his objection and President Wilson ruled that "any objection insisted upon was an obstacle to the adoption." [1] Early drafts of the Covenant avoided specifying unanimity for decisions of the Council and Assembly. The Smuts plan of December, 1918, had suggested that unanimity be replaced with a three-power veto. It stated:

> The league is therefore in this dilemma, that if its votes have to be unanimous, the league will be unworkable; and if they are decided by a majority, the Great Powers will not enter it; and yet if they keep out of it they wreck the whole scheme. Clearly neither unanimity nor mere majority will do.[2]

Smuts suggested that the Council, which would have a majority of great-power permanent members, should have the rule that no resolution would be valid if three or more members voted against it. He felt that this limit, while preventing the Council from passing a resolution against which there was a strong feeling, would not substantially impair its working efficiency.[3] The three-power veto was included in the drafts of the Covenant prepared by President Wilson, but it was dropped from the combined Hurst-Miller draft which was the basis of the Commission's work.[4] Finally the Commission, without discussion, adopted an explicit unanimity requirement.[5] Miller, who was present, commented:

> [It] seems clear that it was agreed that the ordinary international rule is generally as applicable to the Council and to the Assembly as to other international Conferences.[6]

The result was Art. 5 of the Covenant, which provided that decisions at any meeting of the Assembly or of the Council should require "the agreement of all the Members of the League represented *at the meeting*." (Emphasis added.) It should be noted that this version of unanimity as a matter of conference procedure gave no veto to absent states.

---

[1] 1 MILLER, THE DRAFTING OF THE COVENANT 465 (1928); see also 2 *id.* at 392.
[2] 2 *id.* at 39.
[3] 2 *id.* at 42.
[4] *Ibid.*
[5] 2 *id.* at 339.
[6] 1 *id.* at 316.

It may be noted here that when it came to drafting the Charter of the United Nations, twenty-six years later, the participants were ready to modify this "ordinary international rule" of conference procedure. The San Francisco Conference took its decisions on substantive questions by two-thirds vote of those present and voting.[1] In the realm of conference procedure it has been said that "the battle to substitute majority decision for the requirement of unanimity has now been largely won." [2]

2. THE STATUTE OF THE PERMANENT COURT OF INTERNATIONAL JUSTICE

The Statute of the Permanent Court of International Justice contained no provision for withdrawal.[3] In the mood of the United States Senate this became an important issue when American accession to the Court was proposed. Senator Lenroot inquired of the Department of State as to whether withdrawal was possible, and on Dec, 30, 1925, he was advised by Assistant Secretary Olds:

> While there can be no question that the United States would have the power to withdraw from the Permanent Court at any time, still distinction between the power to take such action and the propriety thereof can be clearly drawn. I feel therefore that to avoid the possibility of future misunderstanding, and particularly to strengthen the regard which should be had for international agreements, an appropriate reservation should be incorporated in the resolution by which the United States adheres to the statute of the Permanent Court recognizing and reserving the right of the United States to withdraw from the Court.[4]

The Senate appended a reservation, specifying that it must be accepted by all the signatory powers, "That the United States may at any time withdraw its adherence to the said Protocol. . . ." [5] As Mr. Hackworth, then Legal Adviser of the Department of State, said when he was questioned in 1945 about the

---

[1] GOODRICH AND HAMBRO, CHARTER OF THE UNITED NATIONS 16–17 (2d ed. 1949) The authors note that the great powers nevertheless had "an effective veto" because the Conference was unwilling to chance the possibility that one of the Sponsoring Governments would refrain from joining the organization.
[2] Jenks, *Some Constitutional Problems of International Organizations*, 22 B.Y.I.L. 34 (1945).
[3] 6 L.N.T.S. 379.
[4] 5 HACKWORTH, DIGEST OF INTERNATIONAL LAW 299 (1943).
[5] S. Doc. No. 45, 69th Cong., 1st Sess., (1926).

above reservation, "That was the safe thing to do."[1] It should be noted, however, that the fact that states commonly insist on provisions or reservations explicitly recognizing a right of withdrawal does not establish that in the absence of such provision a right to withdraw would not exist.

When the question of acceptance of the United States reservations was discussed at the first Conference of Signatories of the Protocol of Signature of the Statute of the Permanent Court, there was a division of opinion as to whether the reservation of the right to withdraw would give the United States any greater right than it would have had if the reservation were not expressed.[2] Some speakers believed that the right to withdraw was implicit. M. Osusky (Czechoslovakia) stated that "every international convention of the same type as the Statute of the Court implied the right of denunciation, even if no formal provision were made for it," and M. Denichert (Switzerland):

It would appear that the Statute was an international Convention of the collective type and could be denounced. As long as there were no provisions to the contrary, a State might withdraw at will, after having given reasonable notice of its intention.[3]

M. Buero (Uruguay) connected the matter of withdrawal with that of amendment, and asked: "Had Members of the League the right to prevent the alteration of the Statute by their own single vote, or was their only alternative to withdraw . . . ?"

A number of other speakers disagreed with the view that a right to withdraw was implicit, but some of them were concerned with the fact the Court was an essential part of the machinery of the League of Nations, so that the whole League structure would be affected if states which were members of the League, while retaining such membership, sought to withdraw from the Court. Thus M. Rolin (Belgium) thought that the conference could grant the right of denunciation to a state not a Member of the League without its being necessary to give an opinion on "the infinitely more serious question whether a State might remain a Member of the League and yet denounce the Protocol [of Signature]." He

[1] *Hearings before the Senate Committee on Foreign Relations on the Charter of the United Nations,* 79th Cong., 1st Sess., 348 (1945).
[2] MINUTES OF THE CONFERENCE OF STATES SIGNATORIES OF THE PROTOCOL OF SIGNATURE (1926) at 12–19 (League of Nations Pub. No. V. LEGAL 1926. V. 26).
[3] MINUTES OF THE CONFERENCE OF STATES SIGNATORIES OF THE PROTOCOL OF SIGNATURE (1926) at 12–13, 15.

was ready to recognize that the United States was at liberty to withdraw its adherence.¹

Others, however, denied on principle the existence of any general right to withdraw. M. Castberg (Norway) stated that.

> He could not agree with the opinion expressed by several delegates, according to which a convention which contained no provisions relating to denunciation might, as a general rule, be denounced by one of the signatories at any given time without previous notice or with such previous notice as it might care to give. That was a dangerous theory, which would tend to make the privileges conferred by conventions of this nature practically valueless.²

And M. van Eysinga (Netherlands) reminded the conference of the Declaration of London of 1871.³ In the last analysis, however, all were ready to grant the privilege of withdrawal to the United States.

The desire to bring in the United States also had its effect on the conclusions of the parties to the Court's Statute with regard to the requirements of revision.

The Statute, as prepared by the Council and approved by the Assembly of the League of Nations, contained no procedure for future amendment.⁴ The question of what procedure would apply in these circumstances was first raised when the United States Senate attached to its resolution of January 27, 1926, concerning United States accession to the Court a reservation which provided: ". . . that the Statute for the Permanent Court of International Justice adjoined to the Protocol shall not be amended without the consent of the United States."⁵ At the first Conference of Signatories of the Court's Statute, held in September, 1926, several delegates inquired what the amendment procedure would be, the United States' reservation aside.⁶ M. de Vasconcellos (Portugal) suggested the possible alternative that the matter should be treated as governed by the amendment procedure provided in Article 26 of the League Covenant (ratification by all of the Members represented in the Council and by a

---

¹ *Id.* at 13. To the same effect, see the remarks of M. Pilotti (Italy), *id.* at 15–16.
² *Id.* at 17.
³ *Id.* at 15.
⁴ Judge Hudson called this omission "an amazing lack of foresight." HUDSON, THE PERMANENT COURT OF INTERNATIONAL JUSTICE 130–131 (1943).
⁵ SEN. DOC. NO. 45, 69th Cong. 1st Sess. (1926).
⁶ MINUTES OF THE CONFERENCE OF STATES SIGNATORIES OF THE PROTOCOL OF SIGNATURE (1926) at 14 ff.

majority of the entire League membership). This was the course later to be adopted by the ILO in the matter of withdrawals.[1] However, what seemed to be the prevailing view was expressed by M. Rolin (Belgium), in whose opinion, since the Statute had been brought into effect by a separate diplomatic instrument, it could only be revised "with the formal consent and ratification of all the Members signatories" of that instrument.[2] It is impossible to tell how much this opinion may have been influenced by desire to facilitate accession by the United States.

By 1928 there was a consensus that some amendments were necessary, and the League Assembly recommended to the Council that the Statute should be examined with this purpose in view.[3] Amendments to eighteen articles of the Statute, and four new articles, were drafted by a Committee of Jurists which met in March, 1929.[4] The Council then called a conference of the states parties to the Statute, which met in Geneva, September 4–12, 1929, examined the amendments and drafted a protocol to put them in force.[5] The amendments were not far-reaching. Judge Hudson notes that perhaps their most striking feature was "that they failed to deal with the chief *lacuna* in the Statute ..., its lack of provision for a method of amendment." [6] This failure is explained by the fact that the Committee of Jurists and the Conference of Signatories of 1929 were also concerned with drafting a protocol for the accession of the United States, which, as we have seen, had insisted that the Statute should not be amended without its consent.[7] The revision protocol was approved and

---

[1] *Infra*, p. 66.

[2] MINUTES OF THE CONFERENCE OF STATES SIGNATORIES OF THE PROTOCOL OF SIGNATURE (1926) at 18.

[3] For a detailed account of the proceedings to amend the Statute, continuing from 1928 to 1935, see HUDSON, THE PERMANENT COURT OF INTERNATIONAL JUSTICE 130–141 (1943).

[4] League of Nations Doc. No. C. 166. M. 66. 1929. V.

[5] MINUTES OF THE CONFERENCE REGARDING THE REVISION OF THE STATUTE OF THE PERMANENT COURT OF INTERNATIONAL JUSTICE AND THE ACCESSION OF THE UNITED STATES OF AMERICA TO THE PROTOCOL OF SIGNATURE (League of Nations Doc. No. C. 514. M. 173. 1929. V.).

[6] HUDSON, THE PERMANENT COURT OF INTERNATIONAL JUSTICE 137 (1943).

[7] The Protocol relating to United States Accession provided, "No amendment of the Statute of the Court may be made without the consent of all the Contracting States." MINUTES OF THE 1929 CONFERENCE OF SIGNATORIES, 83. As acceptance of the United States' reservations necessitated changes in the Court's procedure, especially as to advisory opinions, this protocol also provided that it should come into orce only after ratification by all states which had ratified the original protocol of

opened for signature by the Assembly of the League of Nations on September 14, 1929.[1] It was hoped that the amendments might become effective before September 1, 1930, the date for new elections of judges, and for this reason the revision protocol contained the following provision:

> 4. The present Protocol shall enter into force on September 1st, 1930, provided that the Council of the League of Nations has satisfied itself that those [parties to the Statute] whose ratification of the present Protocol has not been received by that date, have no objection to the coming into force of the amendments to the Statute of the Court which are annexed to the present Protocol.[2]

In spite of this provision and all exhortations to haste, by September 9, 1930, only thirty-two out of forty-five parties to the Statute had ratified the revision protocol. Eight others had stated they would raise no objection to the coming into force of the amendments, but Brazil and Uruguay had stated they could not agree without parliamentary authorization, Cuba had expressed opposition, and Abyssinia and France had expressed no opinion. The Council therefore had to conclude that the conditions laid down in paragraph 4 of the protocol had not been fulfilled.[3] The First Committee of the League Assembly noted the Council's decision and concluded "that the Protocol of September 14th, 1929, could not now come into force until it has been ratified by all the States which ratified the former Protocol of December 16th, 1920." [4]

The importance of early ratification of the Protocol of Revision was again urged before the First Committee of the Assembly in 1932 in a report of M. Pilotti on the coming into force of the protocol. He stated:

> May I be permitted, in this connection, to direct your attention to the following consideration: The Statute of the Court is a multilateral instrument setting up an international collective body. Accordingly, it is not possible for successive editions of that instrument to remain simultaneously in force, one such edition binding certain States *vis-a-vis* a first group of other States, another binding those same States *vis-a-vis* a second group: It is impossible – to take only one example – for judges

signature. All but the Latin-American members ultimately did ratify it, and Hudson notes that the real obstacle to its entry into force was the failure of ratification by the United States. HUDSON, *op. cit. supra* at 236.

[1] *Id.* at 135–136.
[2] LEAGUE OF NATIONS OFF. J., 10th year 1843 (1929).
[3] LEAGUE OF NATIONS OFF. J., 11th year 1313 (1930).
[4] LEAGUE OF NATIONS OFF. J., Spec. Supp. No. 84 at 131 (1930).

to find themselves at the same time under two different systems. Hence, by not ratifying, a small minority of the States concerned may prevent a reform which is deemed desirable by the large majority. This is an unsatisfactory situation and one open to such drawbacks that it need perhaps only be indicated for the remedy to be found.[1]

By 1935 all of the States which had ratified the Protocol of Signature of the Statute had also ratified the Revision Protocol, except for Brazil, Panama and Peru. These three states had each taken steps to obtain the necessary approval by their Legislatures, and Panama and Peru had stated that they had no objection to having the amendments enter into force. Therefore, the Secretary-General, at the direction of the League Council, announced that the Protocol would enter in force on February 1, 1936, unless specific objections were received before then. None were received and the protocol came into force on that date.[2]

Hudson concluded that the requirement of unanimity was satisfied by this procedure, and stated:

Action by the parties to the Protocol of Signature with a view to amendment of the Statute is governed by a general principle of international law that in the absence of specific provisions to the contrary the stipulations of an international instrument can be modified only with the consent of all parties. . . . It is to be noted, however, that the general principle of international law does not require that such consent be manifested in any particular way; it may even be informal.[3]

Revision was next considered after World War II. The work of preparing the draft statute for a new International Court of Justice was entrusted to a Committee of Jurists which met at Washington from April 9th to 20th, 1945, in advance of the United Nations Conference at San Francisco. At this meeting Mr. Read (Canada), later Judge of the Court, referred briefly to "the difficulty that the present Statute was regarded as incapable of amendment without the consent of all the signatories."[4] How-

---

[1] NINTH ANNUAL REPORT OF THE PERMANENT COURT OF INTERNATIONAL JUSTICE, P.C.I.J., Ser. E, No. 9 at 57 (1933). Max Huber (Switzerland) made a similar statement. *Id.* at 60–61.

[2] HUDSON, THE PERMANENT COURT OF INTERNATIONAL JUSTICE 140 (1943).

[3] *Id.* at 132.

[4] 14 U.N. CONF. INT'L ORG. DOCS. 57 (1945); see also 14 *id.* 185. For a list of the states parties to the Statute of the Permanent Court as of December 31, 1942, see HUDSON, PERMANENT COURT OF INTERNATIONAL JUSTICE 666 (1943). The list includes a number of states which had withdrawn from the League of Nations, since such withdrawal was not construed as effecting denunciation of the Protocol of Signature of the Statute of the Court. *Id.* at 129, 217–218, 255–256.

ever, the Chairman, Mr. Hackworth (United States) stated that the only task of the Committee was consideration of the Statute and that other questions such as the continuance of the Permanent Court of International Justice were "political questions" which "were not of concern to this technical group." [1] Mr. Fitzmaurice (United Kingdom) remarked that if a new court were created it did not matter what became of the old one. It would die a natural death because its League of Nations election machinery would no longer exist.[2]

The Committee decided to leave the question whether to establish a new court or reform the old one to be decided by the San Francisco Conference.[3] Its report emphasized, however, the importance of acting in accordance with strict legality. It stated:

> The Committee has not disregarded the fact that among the United Nations there are many which are parties to the Statute of the Court drawn up in 1920 and revised in 1929, and that on that account they are bound not only to one another, but also with respect to States which do not appear among The United Nations. Hence the obligation for the former of adjusting the situation arising between them and those States for that reason. That adjustment was not within the province of the Committee: it did not undertake to prejudge it. It should be also borne in mind that in building up an institution of international justice the regular channels must be followed with special strictness.[4]

The San Francisco Conference decided in favor of the creation of a new court. An important factor in this decision was the circumstance that a number of parties to the 1920 Statute were not represented at San Francisco and, in the words of a subcommittee report,

> the negotiations with the parties not thus represented which would be required for effecting modifications in the 1920 Statute would encounter difficulties and might be very protracted.[5]

This report further noted that, since the existence of two World Courts was "not to be contemplated." steps would undoubtedly be taken by the parties to the Statute of the old Court to bring it to an end.[6]

The Conference also adopted the recommendation of the Com-

[1] 14 *id.* 58.
[2] 14 *id.* 187.
[3] 14 *id.* 822–823.
[4] 14 *id.* 853.
[5] 14 *id.* 383.
[6] 13 *id.* 385.

mittee of Jurists that an explicit amendment procedure, allowing amendment of the Statute by less than unanimous consent should be provided so as to fill "a regrettable lacuna in the Statute." [1] The Court's Statute was made "an integral part" of the U.N. Charter (Article 92 of the Charter), and it was provided in Article 69 of the Statute that amendments to it should be by the same procedure as was provided for amendments to the Charter.[2] Since all Members of the United Nations were *ipso facto* parties to the Statute of the Court (Article 93 of the Charter), they could withdraw from the Court only by withdrawing from the U.N.[3]

After the San Francisco Conference it remained only to terminate the existence of the old court. All of the judges resigned on January 31, 1946, and with the dissolution of the League of Nations there was no method of replacing them. All of the parties to the Court's statute except Albania, Siam, Spain and the defeated enemy states also went through the form of recording their assent to the court's dissolution.[4]

3. THE CHARTER OF THE UNITED NATIONS

The Dumbarton Oaks Proposals [5] provided that amendments to the Charter of the prospective United Nations Organization should come into force "for all members of the Organization" when adopted by two-thirds vote of the Assembly and ratified by

---

[1] 14 *id.* 852.
[2] *Infra*, pp. 62–63.
[3] Later, pursuant to Article 93, paragraph 2, Switzerland and several other states which were not Members of the U.N. became parties to the Statute. The conditions under which such states were admitted as parties to the Statute contained no reference to the possibility of withdrawal. See [1947–48] I.C.J. YEARBOOK 30–31. It seems, however, that they must be on an equal footing with other parties in this respect and that the right of withdrawal is therefore to be implied. *Cf.* the practice with respect to withdrawal from the I.L.O., *infra*, p. 66.
[4] LEAGUE OF NATIONS OFF. J., Spec. Supp. No. 194 at 225, 277–278 (1946). Siam soon became a party to the Statute of the new court, and Albania and Spain were in default of their obligations to contribute to the court's support. See LEAGUE OF NATIONS, BOARD OF LIQUIDATION, FINAL REPORT 37–38, 40 (League of Nations Doc. No. C. 5. M. 5. 1947). Spain was also under edict of ostracism by the General Assembly Resolution of February 9, 1946, U.N. GENERAL ASSEMBLY RESOLUTION NO. 32 (I) (1946); see also 6 U.N. CONF. INT'L ORG. DOCS. 232. The Members of the United Nations had declared their intention "to require, under the terms of the peace treaties or in some other appropriate form," the assent of the defeated enemy states. See LEAGUE OF NATIONS OFF. J., Spec. Supp. No. 194 at 225 (1946).
[5] 11 DEP'T STATE BULL. 368 (1944).

all of the permanent members of the Security Council and a simple majority of the other members. By thus reserving a veto only to the most important powers, the proposals followed the League of Nations precedent. They were entirely silent, however, on the subject of a right of withdrawal. This was open to two interpretations, one of which was chosen by Great Britain, the other by the United States. The official British commentary stated: "States would have no right of withdrawing voluntarily; the intention is that membership of the Organisation shall be permanent." [1] The United States view was that since the organization was one of sovereign states, as contrasted with a federal union, "all members would possess the faculty of withdrawal." [2] The attitude of the Soviet Union was closer to that of the United States than to the British view. At the 9th Plenary Session of the San Francisco Conference Mr. Gromyko, stressing the voluntary nature of the Organization, referred to the right of withdrawal as "an expression of state sovereignty" and said that in the opinion of the Soviet Delegation it would be wrong to condemn beforehand the grounds on which any state might find it neces-

---

[1] CMD. NO. 6571 (para. 22) (1944).

[2] 7 U.N. CONF. INT'L ORG. DOCS. 265. When hearings on the Charter were held before the Senate Foreign Relations Committee, the matter of withdrawal was a subject of assiduous questioning and it was made clear that the United States saw no limitation on the right of withdrawal other than the possible penalty of an adverse world opinion. *Hearings before the Senate Committee on Foreign Relations on the Charter of the United Nations.* 79th Cong., 1st Sess., 232–237, 346–348, 646–649 (1945). The following testimony, at pp. 234–235, is particularly instructive:

> Senator TUNNELL. Doctor, in the absence of a surrender of the right of withdrawal, would not a sovereign state retain that right?
> Mr. PASVOLSKY. That is right.
> The CHAIRMAN [Senator Connally]. That was the theory we proceeded upon, was it not?
> Mr. PASVOLSKY. That is right.
> The CHAIRMAN. We proceeded upon that theory in drafting this report of the committee.
> Mr. PASVOLSKY. That is right.
> The CHAIRMAN. I sat in with the committee when that report was prepared.
> Senator GEORGE. Then, Docter, is it your answer that the Member state has an absolute right to withdraw?
> Mr. PASVOLSKY. Yes, Senator.
> Senator GEORGE. Absolute?
> Mr. PASVOLSKY. Yes.
> Senator GEORGE. Unqualified?
> Mr. PASVOLSKY. Yes. But it is on notice that it will have to justify it.
> Senator GEORGE. You mean that it might incur the displeasure of the peace-minded people of the earth?
> Mr. PASVOLSKY. Yes, Senator.

sary to exercise its right of withdrawal from the Organization.[1]

In the view of the small states represented at the San Francisco Conference the right to withdraw was closely connected with the requirements of revision. The small states all favored a procedure whereby unanimity would not be required for revision or amendment. They were united in opposition to the granting of the veto over amendments to the great powers. The alternative of ratification of amendments by some sort of qualified majority was proposed by Australia, Brazil, Costa Rica, Ecuador, Mexico and Venezuela.[2] In addition to these, the representatives of Canada, Uruguay, Colombia, New Zealand and the Netherlands all spoke out against the concession of any veto over amendment.[3] The representative of Belgium, while ready to eliminate the veto, conceded that it was "politically impractical" to do so.[4] Australia and a few other states suggested that the voting procedure of a future special conference to consider revision, and the procedure for ratification of amendments proposed by such a conference, "should be left up to the good sense and wisdom of the members of that Conference." The Australian representative added that if the veto were applied to the process of ratification it would be necessary "to examine the possibilities of the right of withdrawal from the Organization." [5]

The farthest concession that the great powers were prepared to make was to allow, in addition to specific amendments proposed by the General Assembly (and subject to the veto), an alternative method of revision by a General Conference.[6] Such revision was still to be subject to the veto. Article 109 of the Charter provided:

1. A General Conference of the Members of the United Nations for the purpose of reviewing the present Charter may be held at a date and place to be fixed by a two-thirds vote of the members of the General Assembly and by a vote of any seven members of the Security Council. . . .

2. Any alteration of the present Charter recommended by a two-thirds vote of the conference shall take effect when ratified . . . by two-thirds

[1] 1 U.N. CONF. INT'L ORG. DOCS. 619.
[2] 7 *id*. 138–140.
[3] 7 *id*. 144–252, *passim*.
[4] 7 *id*. 231.
[5] 7 *id*. 229–230. A similar position was taken by Mexico, Uruguay, India, Canada and New Zealand. 7 *id*. 229, 236–237, 242–243.
[6] 7 *id*. 566; *cf*. 7 *id*. 145.

of the Members of the United Nations including all of the permanent members of the Security Council.[1]

The small states reluctantly accepted this formula.[2]

It was this decision to preserve a veto over amendments for the permanent members of the Security Council which made the right to withdraw indispensable in the view of the small states.[3] Even Belgium and the Netherlands, which had opposed recognition of the right to withdraw, now conceded its necessity.[4] The Belgian delegate stated his belief that such a right, in the event of the blocking of an amendment by the veto, would be based on the principle, *rebus sic stantibus*.[5] The delegate of the Ukraine, on the other hand, supported the right of withdrawal for the opposite reason that, since unanimity in revision was not required, "the right of withdrawal was necessary to protect the sovereignty of the states." [6] Even the United Kingdom delegation now conceded "that the power to withdraw was implicit in the Charter as it stood." [7]

The Conference refrained from stating the right of withdrawal in the Charter itself, for fear of representing withdrawal "as something normal or probable," and the following interpretive statement, approved in plenary session, was adopted instead:

> The Committee adopts the view that the Charter should not make express provision either to permit or to prohibit withdrawal from the Organization. The Committee deems that the highest duty of the nations which will become Members is to continue their cooperation within the Organization for the preservation of international peace and security. If, however, a Member because of exceptional circumstances feels constrained to withdraw, ... it is not the purpose of the Organization to compel that Member to continue its cooperation in the Organization.[8]

The statement added in particular that withdrawal would be per-

---

[1] The Article added that if such a conference should not be held before the tenth annual session of the General Assembly the proposal to call such a conference should be put on the agenda of that session. For consideration of the question by the Assembly in 1955, see 10 INTERNATIONAL ORGANIZATION 137–138 (1956). See also WILCOX AND MARCY, PROPOSALS FOR CHANGES IN THE UNITED NATIONS (1955).

[2] 7 *id.* 243–244. The delegate of Mexico had observed: "To pretend that an amendment may come into force, notwithstanding the non-ratification by one or more of the permanent members of the Security Council, would probably amount to forcing said members to withdraw from the Organization." *Id.* at 237.

[3] 7 U.N. CONF. INT'L ORG. DOCS. 576, 243–244, 262.

[4] *Id.* at 244, 263.

[5] *Id.* at 263.

[6] *Id.* at 262–264.

[7] 4 *id.* 123.

[8] 7 U.N. CONF. INT'L ORG. DOCS. 328–329; 1 *id.* 620.

missible if a Member's rights and obligations were changed by a Charter amendment in which it had not concurred and which it found itself unable to accept, or if an amendment accepted by the necessary majority in the Assembly or in a General Conference failed to secure the ratification needed to bring it into effect.

4. THE CONSTITUTION OF THE INTERNATIONAL LABOR ORGANIZATION

The Constitution of ILO was incorporated in the Treaty of Versailles (Part XIII) and in the other peace treaties of 1919-1920. It was specified in Article 422 that amendments to this part of the treaty might be adopted by a majority of two-thirds of the delegates to the Conference of the Organization, but would take effect only when ratified by the states represented on the Council of the League of Nations and by three-fourths of the members of the League. Questions of interpretation of the Constitution were to be referred to the Permanent Court of International Justice. Article 403 stated: "Except as otherwise provided in this Part of the present Treaty, all matters shall be decided by a simple majority of the votes cast by the Delegates present."

There was no separate provision for withdrawal from the Organization, but since membership in the League of Nations automatically carried with it membership in ILO, it was logical to apply the rules concerning withdrawal which were contained in the League Covenant. When the United States, not a member of the League, accepted membership in ILO nothing was said about the possibility of withdrawal.[1] However, when Japan, which announced her withdrawal from the League in 1933, purported in 1938 to withdraw from ILO without giving notice, the organization took the position that the period of notice prescribed by the Covenant should be regarded as applying also, by analogy, to ILO. Japan ignored this ruling, but the United States and Brazil (the latter had withdrawn from the League while remaining a member of ILO) both stated that they accepted the obligation to give two years notice in the event of withdrawal.[2]

---

[1] The United States became a member on August 20, 1934, fixing the sole condition that it assumed no obligations under the Covenant of the League of Nations. 30 A.J.I.L. Supp. 67 (1936).

[2] INTERNATIONAL LABOUR CONFERENCE, 27th Sess., Report IV (1) at 86 (1945). In

The Instrument of Amendment of the ILO Constitution which was adopted by the 27th Session of the Labor Conference at Paris in 1945 restated this existing practice of the organization. The amended text now explicitly provides that no member may withdraw without giving two years notice and having paid up all of its obligations to the organization.[1] A Committee on Constitutional Questions appointed by the Governing Body, reporting in advance of the Paris session, had commented on the practice of the organization concerning withdrawals, as follows:

> The Constitution itself makes no provision for withdrawal and it would have been a tenable view that its provisions, being designed, as they explicitly state, to create a "permanent" organisation, were intended to be binding in perpetuity. Largely as the result of the political situation in the 30's, this view has not prevailed, but the existence of the right of withdrawal rests on a customary basis and the only procedure of withdrawal sanctioned by custom involves the giving of the two years' notice provided for in the Covenant. While, therefore, even though nothing were done to define the position further by the adoption of any text on the subject, the requirement of notice would, in the view of the International

---

1945 the following states which were not members of the League were members of ILO: Brazil, Chile, Haiti, Hungary, Peru, Rumania, Spain, the United States and Venezuela. The matter of the admission of new states to the International Labor Organization involved a question of interpretation of Article 387 of the Treaty of Versailles, which stated, "... Membership of the League of Nations shall carry with it membership of the said organization." The issue arose whether this meant that membership of ILO must remain identical with membership in the League of Nations. Although Article 423 provided that "any question or dispute relating to the interpretation of this Part of the present Treaty" should be referred for decision to the Permanent Court of International Justice, the Conference of ILO chose not to ask the Court's help. Germany and Austria were admitted to membership, with only one dissenting vote, when the Supreme Council of the Allies recommended such action to the Conference, during the peace negotiations with those states. INTERNATIONAL LABOUR CONFERENCE, 1st Sess., Record of Proceedings, 26 (1919). However, when the question arose whether Finland also should be admitted to membership, the Conference sidestepped the question of principle and decided instead to let Finnish delegates participate in the work of the Conference in a non-member capacity. See THOMAS, THE INTERNATIONAL LABOUR ORGANISATION 38–39 (1931). The Conference had before it an opinion of its legal adviser, Manley O. Hudson, to the effect that Article 387 envisaged "a complete parity between the League of Nations and the Labor Organization, so far as the membership is concerned." He distinguished the case of Germany and Austria as "an exception made to induce the signature of [the treaties of peace]." 2 SHOTWELL, THE ORIGINS OF THE INTERNATIONAL LABOR ORGANIZATION 496 (1934). In 1934, however, in connection with the admission of the United States, the Conference had to face the issue squarely. The unanimous vote to invite the United States to become a member was a clear decision that ILO membership was a separate matter from League of Nations membership. INTERNATIONAL LABOUR CONFERENCE, 18th Sess., Record of Proceedings, 463–466 (1934). See also Jenks, *The Relation between Membership of the League of Nations and Membership of the International Labour Organization*, 16 B.Y.I.L. 79 (1935).

[1] INTERNATIONAL LABOUR CONFERENCE, 27th Sess., Record of Proceedings, 470 (1945).

Labour Office, continue to be applicable, it would clearly be preferable that there should be some authoritative text defining the position.[1]

C. W. Jenks, Legal Adviser to the ILO, has given his view that, while it is "undesirable" in a function of permanent importance to permit the unilateral withdrawal of individual states, the proceedings of the San Francisco Conference have made it clear

> that at the present stage in the development of world organisation, the elimination of all withdrawal provisions from the constitutional instruments of specialized international organisations, so far from eliminating the danger of withdrawal from such organisations would merely result in confusion in cases in which States purported to withdraw despite the absence of any provisions defining the procedure for such withdrawal.[2]

5. THE CONSTITUTION OF THE WORLD HEALTH ORGANIZATION

While the World Health Organization is clearly of a non-political character, it is interesting to consider it here because of the different attitude taken in that organization with respect to withdrawal.

The drafters of the Constitution of WHO placed greater emphasis on the principle of universality than had the San Francisco Conference. The Technical Preparatory Committee, which met before the World Health Conference of 1946 and prepared preliminary drafts, emphasized the world-wide character of the struggle against disease and deliberately omitted any mention of the possibility of withdrawal.[3] However, after the Health Conference had decided that amendments might come into force when accepted by two-thirds of the members, it was pointed out by the delegate of Norway that this "would open the possibility of certain members of the Organization being bound by decisions of other States against their will." [4] The conference agreed that this was unacceptable, and there was read into the record without objection a "declaratory Statement," that:

> A member is not bound to remain in the Organization if its rights and

---

[1] INTERNATIONAL LABOUR CONFERENCE, 27th Sess., Report IV (1) at 87 (1945).

[2] Jenks, *Some Constitutional Problems of International Organisations*, 22 B.Y.I.L. 11, 23 (1945).

[3] Minutes of the Technical Preparatory Committee for the International Health Conference, WHO, OFFICIAL RECORDS, No. 1 at 26 (1946).

[4] WHO OFFICIAL RECORDS, No. 2 at 74 (1946).

obligations as such were changed by an amendment of the Constitution in which it has not concurred and which it finds itself unable to accept.[1]

There was no veto in the matter of amendments and no reference to withdrawal under any other conditions.

When acceptance of the Constitution of WHO was being considered in the United States Congress, the Senate Foreign Relations Committee apparently overlooked the declaratory statement of the Health Conference, for it stated that "it would be possible for the obligations of the United States vis-à-vis the Organization to be drastically changed without the consent of our Government." [2] Congress therefore added to its joint resolution authorizing acceptance an interpretative paragraph which stated:

> [Sec. 4.] In adopting this joint resolution the Congress does so with the understanding that, in the absence of any provision in the World Health Organization Constitution for withdrawal from the Organization, the United States reserves its right to withdraw from the Organization on a one-year notice: *Provided, however,* That the financial obligations of the United States to the Organization shall be met in full for the Organization's current fiscal year.[3]

This faced the Secretary-General of the United Nations with a problem. Article 82 of the WHO Constitution placed upon him the duty of informing states parties to the Constitution of the dates when other states had become parties. If the "understanding" concerning withdrawal were to be treated as a reservation, it would be his duty to inquire of each of the other parties whether they consented to the reservation, and the delay would be such that no action could be taken before the first World Health Assembly, scheduled for June 24, 1948. The Secretary-General chose simply to refer the acceptance of the United States to the Executive Secretary of WHO, stating:

> I regret that in view of the provision in Section 4 of the joint resolution to which the acceptance of the United States is subject, I am not in a position to determine whether the United States has become a party to the Constitution. However, I am prepared to be guided by the action of the Health Assembly in regard to this matter, since under Article 75 of the Constitution it is a competent body to settle any question concerning the interpretation or application of the Constitution.[4]

---

[1] *Ibid.*
[2] S. REP. NO. 421, 80th Cong., 1st Sess., 7 (1947).
[3] T.I.A.S. No. 1808 at 127.
[4] WHO OFFICIAL RECORDS, No. 13 at 382 (1948); *cf.* Schachter, *The Developmen*

After a brief discussion in the Health Assembly on July 2, 1948, in which no objections were raised, the Assembly President announced that "the United States ratification of our Constitution is unanimously accepted by this Assembly." [1] A speech by the Indian delegate had urged that no "mere lawyer's argument" should control. He urged that the Assembly should "lay down as a principle of general application that any Member State may determine its membership on a year's notice." [2] No specific action was taken on this proposal. The Secretary-General of the United Nations subsequently notified the United States that it was considered a party to the WHO Constitution as from June 21, the date of deposit of its instrument of acceptance with the Secretary-General.[3]

Subsequent practice demonstrated, however, that the general right to withdraw was conceded only to the United States and that other members might legally withdraw only if the Constitution should be amended without their consent. This issue was tested by the decision of the U.S.S.R., Byelorussia and the Ukraine in 1949 to cease their participation in WHO. Their action was announced in telegrams from Deputy Ministers of Health in those countries to the Director-General of WHO. The telegrams stated that those countries no longer considered themselves members of the organization.[4] The Director-General promptly replied, stating:

Because Constitution of WHO makes no such provision I cannot accept your communication as a withdrawal from the Organization. Your communication will be submitted to third session of Executive Board. ...[5]

of *International Law Through the Legal Opinions of the United Nations Secretariat*, 25 B.Y.I.L. 122–127 (1948). Mr. Schachter, Senior Legal Counsellor of the United Nations Legal Department, believed that it could not be inferred from the Constitution of the WHO that unilateral withdrawal would be permitted, and that the United States' "understanding" was, strictly speaking, a reservation of a right beyond that allowed by the Constitution. He concedes, however, that the Secretariat's communication "assumed that the World Health Assembly was competent to decide, by interpretation of the Constitution, that the apparent reservation of the United States need not be considered inconsistent with the provisions of the Constitution." *Id.* at 125.

[1] WHO OFFICIAL RECORDS, NO. 13 at 80 (1948).
[2] *Id.* at 78.
[3] T.I.A.S. No. 1808 at 128. Schachter takes this to be "further confirmation of the view of the Secretary-General that the Resolution of the World Health Assembly was to be considered not as signifying consent to the reservation by the parties but rather as an interpretation by the competent organ that the ratification was not inconsistent with the terms of the Constitution." Schachter. *op. cit. supra* 125.
[4] WHO OFFICIAL RECORDS, No. 17 at 52 (1949).
[5] *Ibid.*

TREATIES OF A CONSTITUTIONAL CHARACTER 71

The Executive Board approved the Director-General's action and referred the matter to the second Health Assembly.[1] The Assembly, however, did not press the assertion that there was no general right of withdrawal. It was evident that opinion was divided on the point.[2] A new question was raised as to whether communications received from Deputy Ministers of Health, instead of from Ministers of Foreign Affairs, should be accepted as notices of withdrawal.[3] The Director-General suggested that they should not.[4] The Assembly chose not to commit itself to any legal views but to concentrate on an appeal to the three states to reconsider their action.[5] In the meantime, in an effort to keep the matter open, these three states and Albania, Bulgaria, Czechoslovakia, Hungary, Poland and Rumania, which took similar action, were carried on WHO's books as "inactive members." The arrears of contributions of the U.S.S.R. alone at the end of 1955 amounted to $ 3, 606,681.[6]

In July, 1955, the U.S.S.R. returned to the fold with an announcement in the Economic and Social Council that, "In order to extend its share of international cooperation in the medical field the Soviet Union was joining WHO." [7] The language assumes that the Soviet Union had not been a member. However, the Assistant Director-General of WHO replied that "he was very pleased to hear that the Union of Soviet Socialist Republics wished to *resume* its participation in WHO." [8] (Emphasis added.) The Organization continued to maintain that the absent members had not withdrawn, and the latter ultimately conceded this principle by agreeing to pay token contributions (5% of the amount assessed each year) for the years in which they did not actively participate.[9] In the course of discussion of the conditions of readmission of the absent members, the Norwegian re-

---

[1] *Id*. at 19.
[2] WHO OFFICIAL RECORDS, No. 21 at 114–115, 303–308 (1949).
[3] *Id*. at 139, 303–304, 306.
[4] *Id*. at 139.
[5] See the statements by the delegates of India, Australia and Switzerland, *id*. at 304–306, and Assembly resolution, *id*. at 353. The Swiss delegate commented, however, that "his delegation was of the opinion that any Member of the Organization had the right to withdraw from it." *Id*. at 306. The United States, having already secured its right to withdraw, took no part in the discussion.
[6] WHO OFFICIAL RECORDS, No. 70 at 17 (1956).
[7] U.N. ECONOMIC AND SOCIAL COUNCIL OFF. REC., 20th Sess., 31 (1955).
[8] *Id*. at 34.
[9] WHO OFFICIAL RECORDS, No. 71 at 19, 153–164 (1956).

presentative commented on "the fact that WHO was the only international organization in existence which had no provision for withdrawal from membership." He added:

The original decision to that effect in 1946 had been based on the feeling then prevalent that the world had reached a stage where such a provision was unnecessary. Time had proved that thinking to be premature and he accordingly considered that once the present situation had been settled the Health Assembly should take steps to amend the Constitution.[1]

No other delegates took up the last suggestion.[2]

6. REPLACEMENT OF THE LEAGUE OF NATIONS BY THE UNITED NATIONS

There was a departure from the principle of unanimous consent when the United Nations Charter was put into effect on October 24, 1945,[3] while it was not arranged to terminate the League of Nations until April 18, 1946. This was not, strictly speaking, a revision of the Covenant, but the adoption of a new obligation inconsistent with the former one. By Article 103 of the Charter the members of the League which signed it agreed that their obligations under the Charter should prevail over obligations imposed by the League Covenant, although under Article 20 of the Covenant League members had undertaken to enter into no engagements inconsistent with its terms.

The League of Nations had forty-one members in 1945, without counting Austria, which was dropped from the list of member states as of March 18, 1938,[4] or Estonia, Latvia and Lithuania, which had been incorporated into the U.S.S.R. in 1940. Not all of these League member states were included when the United States, the United Kingdom, the U.S.S.R. and China issued invitations to the United Nations Conference at San Francisco. The criterion for inclusion was whether a state had declared war on Germany or Japan by March 1, 1945.[5] Later, this test was relaxed

---

[1] *Id.* at 155.

[2] For the amendment and withdrawal provisions of other specialized agencies, see U.N. Secretariat, *Handbook of Final Clauses* 120–125, 183–194 (Doc. No. ST/LEG/1) (1951). See also Jenks, *Some Constitutional Problems of International Organizations*, 22 B.Y.I.L.11 at 65–68 (1945).

[3] On ratification by the five permanent members of the Security Council and a majority of the other signatories (Art. 110).

[4] See LEAGUE OF NATIONS, BOARD OF LIQUIDATION, FINAL REPORT 31, 40–41 (League of Nations Doc. No. C. 5. M. 5. 1947).

[5] For the invitations, see 12 DEPT. STATE BULL. 394 (1945).

so far as to allow the participation of Argentina, on the insistence of the Latin-American states, and of Denmark, which was thought to have resisted the German occupation to the extent of its power, but membership in the League of Nations was not mentioned as a reason for admitting these two states to the Conference.[1] Thirty-one of the forty-one members of the League were represented at San Francisco and signed the United Nations Charter. Those not represented were:

Afghanistan	Poland
Albania	Portugal
Bulgaria	Siam
Finland	Sweden
Ireland	Switzerland

The absence of Poland was only the result of failure of the inviting powers to agree on which Polish Government should be recognized. This matter was settled and Poland signed the United Nations Charter on October 15, 1945. Albania was hardly to be considered as a League member, having given notice of withdrawal from the League in April, 1939, though the Assembly refused to approve this action because Albania was in arrears in its League contributions.[2] It was also a debatable point whether Albania was still to be considered as an enemy state.[3] Finland and Bulgaria were clearly in this category, and Siam was at war with France. However, there was no good reason for the exclusion of Afghanistan, Ireland, Portugal, Sweden and Switzerland except their failure to declare war on Germany or Japan.

There would have been no insuperable obstacle to terminating the League before bringing the United Nations Charter into operation. In addition to the provision for withdrawal on two years' notice, the Covenant provided that the Assembly might deal with "any matter within the sphere of action of the League" (Art. 3), a provision that could easily authorize termination, though an Assembly decision would require unanimity of the Members represented at the meeting.[4] However, the termination of the League was taken for granted at San Francisco, without

---

[1] 1 U.N. CONF. INT'L ORG. DOCS. 345–359; 5 *id.* 155–156, 376–381, 460.

[2] LEAGUE OF NATIONS, BOARD OF LIQUIDATION, *op. cit. supra*, 37–38.

[3] U.N. SECURITY COUNCIL OFF. REC., Supp. No. 4 at 84, 97–98 (1946).

[4] In addition there was no reason why a wider consent should be required for termination than for amendment (which required only ratification by two-thirds, including all members represented on the Council).

any discussion of the manner in which this formality was to be accomplished.[1]

The Charter was signed at San Francisco on June 26, 1945. It was only three months later that the first steps were taken to terminate the League through its own machinery. On September 20, 1945, the League's Acting Secretary-General called the attention of all League members to the decisions taken at San Francisco and suggested that the League's Supervisory Commission should formulate provisional terms of transfer of League assets to the U.N., subject to final decision of the Assembly at a meeting early in 1946. He concluded as follows:

> In view of urgency of matter would welcome telegraphic acknowledgment of above communication with any observations Members of League may wish to submit. ... Unless therefore I receive replies from Governments before October 5th I shall assume their assent to programme.[2]

No dissent was expressed.

Subsequently the Acting Secretary-General summoned the League Assembly to meet in Geneva on April 8, 1946.[3] Delegations were present from all member states except Albania, Bulgaria, Ethiopia, Haiti, Iraq, Liberia and Siam.[4] On April 18 the members present unanimously resolved that the League of Nations should cease to exist, "except for the sole purpose of the liquidation of its affairs as provided in the present resolution."[5] A Board of Liquidation was set up to represent the League for this purpose. On the completion of its work it was to make a report to the Member Governments and then declare itself dissolved.

The transfer of the League's tangible assets involved the disposal of property owned in common rather than revision of treaty obligations. It was the subject of a common plan worked

---

[1] The Conference authorized the Preparatory Commission, which was to function until a Secretary-General should be elected, to make a study of how far it would be desirable to transfer to the U.N. certain functions, activities and assets of the League. However, neither the Conference nor the Preparatory Commission were concerned with the legal formalities of accomplishing the transfer. 1 U.N. CONF. INT'L ORG. DOCS. 628; REPORT OF THE PREPARATORY COMMISSION OF THE UNITED NATIONS, ch. 11 (1945).

[2] LEAGUE OF NATIONS OFF. J., Spec. Supp. No. 194 at 10 (1946).

[3] *Id.* at 9.

[4] *Id.* at 25, 54. Colombia was represented only by an observer. Austria sent a delegation claiming the right to participate. Such a right was denied, although the Austrian representatives were permitted to remain as observers. *Id.* at 49.

[5] *Id.* at 269–272.

out by the League's Supervisory Commission and the Preparatory Commission of the United Nations,[1] which was also approved in the Assembly Resolution of April 18, 1946.[2] Buildings were valued at cost to the League, less depreciation, an amount considerably less than current value.[3] The plan provided that the shares in these assets of Members of the League which were members of the United Nations were to be credited to them on the books of the United Nations. The shares of members were to be calculated in proportion to the total amounts of their contributions since the League's inception. The shares of Members of the League which were not members of the United Nations on Dec. 31, 1946, were to be disposed of by agreement with the States concerned.

The decision to dissolve the League of Nations and distribute its assets in this manner, unanimously adopted by the members present, met the requirement for ordinary decisions of the Assembly under Art. 5 of the Covenant. Whether termination was a decision within the Assembly's competence would be a question of interpretation of the Covenant rather than of general rules of treaty revision.[4] However, it may be noted also that none of the member states which were absent from the last Assembly expressed any disagreement with the method followed in liquidating the League and disposing of its assets. Sovereignty in Bulgaria was being exercised by a Commission of the Allied Powers, and Bulgaria was ultimately required, by Art. 7 of the Peace Treaty, to accept the arrangements made for the liquidation of the League. Ethiopia, Iraq and Liberia had all been represented at San Francisco and had signed the United Nations Charter. They also proceeded to settle their League accounts in accordance with the scheme of distribution approved by the League Assembly and accepted credits on the books of the U.N. for their shares of the League assets.[5] Siam, which became a member of the United Nations on November 17, 1946, did likewise.[6] Albania was the only other absentee.

[1] *Id.* at 273.
[2] *Id.* at 270.
[3] Report of the Finance Committee, approved by the Assembly on April 18, 1946, *id.* at 267.
[4] See Jenks, *Some Constitutional Problems of International Organizations*, 22 B.Y.I.L. 68–70 (1945).
[5] See LEAGUE OF NATIONS, BOARD OF LIQUIDATION, *op. cit. supra* at 9, 29, 47–48.
[6] *Id.* at 36.

A number of questions concerning the transfer to United Nations organs of functions entrusted to organs of the League of Nations under nonpolitical conventions have been discussed in the previous chapter.[1] One other question that arose in connection with the transition from the League system to that of the United Nations must also be noted. This was the question of the South African Mandate for South-West Africa.[2]

The refusal of South Africa to propose a trusteeship agreement for the territory ultimately resulted in a request by the General Assembly for advice from the International Court of Justice. The Court's opinion, of July 11, 1950, held (1) that South Africa continued to have international obligations under the mandate; (2) that no legal obligation was imposed on South Africa by Chapter 12 of the Charter (the trusteeship system); and (3) that South Africa acting alone had no competence to modify the international status of the territory. Such competence was said to rest with the Union of South Africa acting with the consent of the United Nations.[3]

The Court rejected South Africa's contention that the mandate had lapsed when the League of Nations ceased to exist. It held that the mandate, created in the interest of the inhabitants of the territory and of humanity in general, constituted "an international status for the territory," recognized by all League Members including South Africa. It found in Article 10 of the Charter, which authorized the General Assembly to discuss any questions within the scope of the Charter, a competence of the Assembly to exercise the supervision over the mandated territory previously exercised by the League, and it found South Africa to be obliged to submit to this supervision by the General Assembly and to render annual reports to it.

Two judges dissented from the part of the opinion which held that South Africa was obliged to submit to supervision by the

[1] See pp. 32–37, *supra*.
[2] All of the states holding Mandates except South Africa agreed to replace them with new trusteeship agreements under Chapter 12 of the United Nations Charter. These changes gave rise to no problem of revision. The mandates had originally been assigned by agreement of the Principal Allied and Associated Powers of 1919 and approved by the Council of the League of Nations. Agreement to the new arrangements by the Principal Allied and Associated Powers (the United States, Britain, France, Italy and Japan) created no problem, and the League of Nations had gone out of existence before the first of the trusteeship agreements was approved.
[3] International Status of South-West Africa [1950] I.C.J. Rep. 128.

General Assembly. These were Sir Arnold McNair and Judge Read. Judge Read's opinion contains the follwoing statement in support of the principle of unanimous consent:

> It is a principle of international law that the parties to a multilateral treaty, regardless of their number or importance, cannot prejudice the legal rights of other States. The United Nations, by signing and ratifying the Charter, could and did establish the competence of the Organization to perform functions in relation to the mandated territories. They could not, in law, transfer functions from the League to the Organization, without the consent and authority of the League, or of Members of the League whose legal rights would thus be impaired. Consequently, while the Charter had come into force and the organization of the United Nations had come into being before the dissolution of the League, the legal rights of many States, which were not members of the new Organization, as regards the mandated territories including South-West Africa, remained in full force and vigor.[1]

This statement was dictum, since the only issue was raised by South Africa, which did sign the Charter and was clearly bound by everything in it. The real ground of Read and McNair's dissent was that the Charter did not in terms provide for any supervision by the Assembly before a trusteeship agreement was concluded. In another part of his opinion Judge Read emphasized lack of consent by South Africa to the transfer to the United Nations of the functions, powers and responsibilities of the League in respect of mandates.[2]

The opinion of Sir Arnold McNair concluded that administrative supervision by the League Council had lapsed, but not the substantive obligations owed to former members of the League under the Mandate agreement. However, he believed that South Africa's obligations were not merely contractual, and that the mandate, like a conveyance, created a status "valid *in rem*" which would survive the extinction of all contractual obligations. He explained this concept as follows:

> From time to time it happens that a group of great Powers, or a large number of States both great and small, assume a power to create by a multipartite treaty some new international regime or status, which soon acquires a degree of acceptance and durability extending beyond the limits of the actual contracting parties, and giving it an objective existence. This power is used when some public interest is involved, and its exercise often occurs in the course of the peace settlement at the end of a great war. ...

---

[1] [1950] I.C.J. Rep. at 165.
[2] *Id.* at 172.

After citing the examples of the demilitarization of the Aaland Islands and the dedication of the Kiel Canal as an international waterway by the Versailles Treaty, he continued:

The mandates System seems to me to be an *a fortiori* case. . . . In my opinion the new régime established in pursuance of this "principle" [Art. 22 of the Covenant] has more than a purely contractual basis, and the territories subjected to it are impressed with a special legal status, designed to last until modified in the manner indicated in Article 22.[1]

Article 22 of the Covenant did not itself suggest how a mandate should be terminated, but Article 7 of the South African Mandate provided that the consent of the Council of the League should be required for any modification thereof. McNair did not specify how, in his opinion, a mandate might be terminated, the League Council no longer existing. Under the holding of the majority of the Court this competence would be in the Assembly.

7. SUMMARY

While the founders of international organizations intend them to be permanent and do not want even to suggest the possibility of their demise, states have in the last analysis generally insisted on the right to withdraw, a position which is not at all surprising when it is remembered that the right of secession is often preserved even within federal states. Practice seems to suppport the conclusion that with regard to treaties of the constitutional type the right to withdraw, even if not expressed, is to be implied, in the absence of a clear contrary intent. It is particularly insisted upon by the great powers and is regarded as the means of preserving the principle of national sovereignty. The case of WHO is exceptional. It is the only one where there was a clear intent to create a universal organization and therefore to exclude withdrawal except in the case of adoption of an amendment which the state was unwilling to accept. The parties (except for the United States) were willing to go so far only because of its clearly nonpolitical character. As has been noted in the case of nonpolitical conventions, recognition of the right to withdraw makes it always possible, in the last analysis, to get around the unanimity rule.

Starting with the Covenant of the League of Nations, the parties to treaties of a constitutional character have been willing to adopt express provisions which abandon unanimity as a re-

[1] *Id.* at 153–155.

TREATIES OF A CONSTITUTIONAL CHARACTER 79

quirement of revision. Although in the more far-reaching organizations a veto for some powers is retained, this is a political necessity rather than an application of a legal principle. Where the requirement of unanimity for amendment is abandoned, the right of withdrawal becomes the means of preserving the principle that no state shall be bound by any new obligation without its consent. In the one instance of a modern constitutional treaty which made no provision for amendment without unanimity, the Statute of the World Court, the oversight was remedied in 1945. In the meantime it was assumed that unanimous consent for amendments would be necessary, but it is impossible to tell to what extent this assumption was influenced by the desire to secure the accession of the United States, which had stated that it would be a condition of its participation that no amendment be allowed without its consent. The decision made at San Francisco to create a new court instead of revising the old one also reflected the assumption that in the absence of a special provision the consent of all parties would be required for revision. The practice in regard to revision of the Statute of the Court in the 1930's shows that the requirement of unanimous consent was satisfied by informal consent, short of ratification of the amendments, provided that consent was clearly intended.

It may be noted that the adoption of a special provision authorizing revision by a defined majority is a form of unanimous consent, given in advance instead of *ad hoc*. The consent is to a possible deprivation of treaty rights. There is no consent to be bound by an amendment which the member state may find it impossible to accept.[1] The right to refuse to be bound by such an amendment is preserved by the option to withdraw.

The discussions of the San Francisco Conference on amendment and withdrawal are particularly interesting because they show that in that single instance the small powers were willing to go a step further and allow binding revision without unanimous con-

---

[1] The one instance in which advance consent *to be bound* may be intended, is that in which a defeated state is required in a peace treaty to accept future arrangements to be agreed on by the victors. However, the decision of the Permanent Court of International Justice in the Case concerning Territorial Jurisdiction of the International Commission of the River Oder makes it seem likely that the defeated state still would not be legally bound by the provisions of the later treaty unless it became a party. P.C.I.J., Ser. A, No. 23 (1929). The peace treaty might nevertheless operate as a *renunciation of rights* under previous treaties. See pp. 106–108, *infra*.

sent, while they strenuously opposed the retention of a veto over revision by a few states. It was because of the possibility of a veto which would thwart the desire of a majority to revise the Charter that the small states regarded the right of withdrawal as essential. The United States and the Soviet Union insisted upon it to guard national sovereignty.

In the case of treaties of a constitutional character, the alternative of revision by *inter se* agreement seems inconsistent with the need to preserve a single functioning organization. The statements of Pilotti and Huber, rejecting such a procedure in regard to amendment of the Statute of the Permanent Court of Justice, to which no one disagreed, support this principle.[1]

When less than all of the members of the League of Nations committed themselves to the Charter of the United Nations before they had abrogated the Covenant of the League, the question which resulted was one, not of revision, but of the effect of inconsistent treaty obligations. Revision of the Covenant was not intended. The legality of the procedure followed in terminating the League was a question of interpretation of the provisions of the Covenant. Customary rules were not involved. Nor was any question of treaty revision involved when the assets of the League were transferred to the U.N., but only questions of the rights of the parties in property owned in common.

The history of international organizations shows a trend, similar to that we have noticed in nonpolitical conferences, away from unanimity as a rule of conference procedure.[2] However,

[1] We may note parenthetically that in its statement to the Court in the case concerning *Reservations to the Convention on Genocide* the United States government made a distinction between "organizational" treaties and other treaties, which appears to be equally pertinent with respect to *inter se* agreements. In the statement which the United States furnished to the International Court of Justice it said:

> The "organizational" type of treaty ... establishes an international organization and sets forth the constitution or character of the organization in terms so finely balanced and interrelated that a reservation disturbing that situation would seriously affect the powers, functions and procedures of the organization. In the case of such a treaty there would come a point at which a reservation, accepted by some parties and rejected by others, would foster genuine confusion by creating a special new set of rules among the reserving States and those accepting the reservation, and as a practical matter impair if not prevent attainment of the purpose of the treaty - namely the establishment and functioning of a single efficient organization.

RESERVATIONS TO THE CONVENTION ON GENOCIDE - PLEADINGS, ORAL ARGUMENTS, AND DOCUMENTS 33 (I.C.J. 1951).

[2] On this subject see Jenks, *Some Constitutional Problems of International Organizations*, 22 B.Y.I.L. 34–42 (1945).

whereas in the rules of nonpolitical conferences unanimity had generally been abandoned by 1914, in the Commission on the League of Nations, a political conference, unanimity was still the rule. It was abandoned only at San Francisco in 1945. As has been noted previously, this is a different question from the matter of unanimity of consent of parties to a previous treaty, though the two have been often confused.

CHAPTER III

MULTIPARTITE PEACE SETTLEMENTS

1. THE TREATY OF VIENNA, 1815

Treaties of peace concluding general wars usually deal with a great variety of subjects requiring settlement. Though some of these subjects concern a limited number of parties, other members of the victorious coalition participate in the drafting or at least give their support and approval. For convenience all of the settlements, no matter how diverse, are usually assembled in one general act. Peace treaties sometimes specifically state special means for revision of some of their parts, but even where there is no specific provision on the subject, clauses which have an interest limited to some of the parties are generally modified by those parties acting alone.[1] This practice became established with respect to revisions of the General Act of the Congress of Vienna. There were some initial protests, but they were pressed less seriously with the passage of time.

The important parts of the Vienna settlement were each the subject of separate agreements of the powers most directly interested, and the decision to include all of these separate agreements in a single Act was made late in the proceedings, at a conference of the five principal powers of May 23, 1815.[2] They agreed that to embody all of the results of the Congress in one general and common instrument would be "more solemn and appropriate" than simply to present a collection of individual treaties, and they accepted Metternich's proposal that the more important articles from the separate treaties or protocols should be included in the body of the General Act, while all of them

---

[1] *Cf.* Palieri, *La formation des traités dans la pratique internationale contemporaine*, 74 REC. DES COURS 465–542 (1949). Palieri suggests that the interested states are free to modify parts of a general settlement which are of private application, because of a "general rule by which each State is free to make what it will of its rights and to renounce them or to use them as means of exchange against other advantages." *Id.* at 532 (Translated).

[2] 2 B.F.S.P. 738.

should also be appended in full, as Annexes having the same force and validity as the General Act itself.[1]

The General Act was signed on June 9, 1815, by seven of the eight powers which had signed the French Peace Treaty of 1814.[2] These were: Austria, France, Great Britain, Prussia, Russia, Portugal and Sweden. Spain, insisting on reservations, was not permitted to sign but did accede two years later. All of the other powers represented at the Congress were invited to accede to the General Act, and eventually nearly all of them did so.

Annex XVI concerned arrangements for international rivers. Here the General Act specified that revision would require only unanimous agreement of the riparian states.[3]

Annex XVII was a Règlement on the rank of diplomatic agents, which had been agreed to by the representatives of the eight principal powers on March 19, 1815. This agreement was revised by the five principal powers at the Congress of Aachen, in 1818, without consulting the other three signatories of the original Règlement, not to speak of the other states which had acceded to the General Act.[4]

Annexes I and II were treaties between Russia, Prussia and Austria concerning the division of Poland. Article I of the General Act repeated the provision of these treaties that the Duchy of Warsaw should be reunited to the Russian Empire, as a separate Kingdom irrevocably and perpetually linked to Russia "by its Constitution." In Article I of the General Act it was stated that the Czar reserved the right "to give to this State, enjoying a distinct administration, the interior improvement which he shall judge proper." In 1831 the Czar suppressed the Constitution which he had granted to Russian Poland, taking the precaution of securing in advance the consent of Austria and Prussia. Russia did not consult any of the other signatories of the General Act. Palmerston protested that such action was inconsistent with the Treaty of Vienna.[5] In this case there was a disagreement as

---

[1] Art. 118 of the General Act stated: "[The Annexes] are considered as integral parts of the arrangements of the Congress and shall have everywhere the same force and validity as if they were inserted, word for word, in the General Treaty." *Id.* at 54.
[2] *Id.* at 3.
[3] Revision of the provisions concerning the Rhine is considered in Chapter IV, *infra*.
[4] 5 B.F.S.P. 1090.
[5] 37 B.F.S.P. 1424.

to the correct interpretation of the treaty, Russia taking the position that the grant of the Polish Constitution "was not a necessary consequence of the Treaty of Vienna, but a spontaneous act" of the Czar.[1] However, the Russian note added that this view was shared by Prussia and Austria, which were the other parties "more especially concerned." England maintained that her appeal was to the General Act, "and to that Treaty His Majesty's Government cannot admit that Austria, Prussia, and Russia were Contracting Parties in greater or more special degree than the other Powers who signed it." [2] The protest was without effect.

Annex X consisted of a treaty between Austria, England, Prussia and Russia which provided for the union of Belgium and Holland, and the position of Luxembourg as a Duchy of the German Confederation under the rule of the King of the Netherlands. The important provisions of this treaty were also repeated in the body of the General Act. One of these provisions (Article 67 of the General Act) provided that the commander of the Luxembourg fortress should be named by the King of the Netherlands. When this provision was revised in 1816-17 to provide for the naming of the Luxembourg commander by the King of Prussia, this was approved by a series of treaties between each of the parties to the Annex and the King of the Netherlands, but without the participation of the other parties to the General Act.[3] Again, in the years 1830-39, only the five great powers, Holland and Belgium participated in the conferences on the Belgian question which finally terminated the union of Holland and Belgium, and there was no reference to the other parties to the Act of Vienna. The protocol of the initial conference stated that the participants were meeting "in their capacity as signatories of the Treaties of Paris and of Vienna, which constituted the Kingdom of the Netherlands," a reference evidently to the Annex rather than to the General act. The protocol also refer-

---

[1] *Id.* at 1431.
[2] *Id.* at 1438. Great Britain again claimed a right to intervene with regard to Poland during the Polish revolt of 1863, and proposed the calling of a conference of Great Britain, Austria, France, Prussia, Portugal, Spain and Sweden, as the parties to the Act of Vienna (with no reference to other states which had acceded). Russia maintaining the same position as in 1831, nothing came of the suggestion. 53 *id.* 897–918.
[3] 7 *id.* 3.

red, however, to the responsibility of the great powers for the maintenance of the peace of Europe and stated that the King of the Netherlands was invited to participate pursuant to the terms of the Protocol of Aachen of November 15, 1818.[1] This was a document in which the five great powers had stated their firm resolve to maintain the principle of "intimate union" among themselves for the sake of maintenance of the peace of Europe.[2] They continued by stating that, to better attain this aim, they would invite other states to any future conferences among themselves, if matters of special interest to those states were to be dealt with. The principle put first was that of the unity of the great powers. Participation of lesser states was to be accorded as a privilege.

Again, in 1867, the great powers met to create a new status for Luxembourg, consequent upon the termination of the German Confederation. They decided that the King of the Netherlands should participate "as the territorial sovereign," Belgium as a party to the treaties of 1839, and Italy as a new great power. There was no suggestion that other parties to the Treaty of Vienna had any rights in the matter, and when Spain asked to be invited she based her claim (which was at once rejected), not on the Treaty of Vienna but on the fact that Italy had been admitted.[3]

It may be said that the principle of separability was not really involved in these instances since the pertinent provisions of the Vienna Act were of the nature of "executed conveyances," so that future disposition of the territories in question arose in each case as a new matter, unaffected by past treaties. The view that treaties of territorial settlement have fulfilled their function when the new boundaries have been surveyed and the administrative transfers have been completed seems generally valid.[4] This

[1] 18 B.F.S.P. 728.
[2] 6 *id.* 14.
[3] *Correspondence Respecting the Grand Duchy of Luxemburg*, CMD. No. 3866 (1867).
[4] BRIERLY, THE LAW OF NATIONS 266–267n. (5th ed. 1955); Hyde, *The Revision of Treaties and of Settlements Registered in Treaties*, 2 HUNGARIAN QUARTERLY 203 at 206 (1936); TOBIN, THE TERMINATION OF MULTIPARTITE THEATIES 50–51, 144–146 (1933). McNair has suggested that certain other permanent rights pertaining to territory might likewise exist thereafter independent of the treaty which created them. McNair, *Les effets de la guerre sur les traités*, 59 REC. DES COURS 537–555 (1937); *cf.* Palieri, *La formation des traités dans la pratique international contemporaine*, 74 REC. DES COURS 465 at 532 (1949).

means that it is inaccurate to speak of the revision of such treaties. A later attempt to change the boundaries which the treaty created arises as a new matter, requiring the consent of the state in possession, but not necessarily the consent of the parties to the previous treaty. Under this test, the new dispositions respecting Poland concerned no states except Russia and Poland unless the Treaties of Vienna could be construed as going beyond a territorial transfer and constituting an international undertaking to maintain Poland's autonomous status. The main argument was on that point.

However, other parts of the Treaties of 1815, which clearly sought to create permanent status and a continuing obligation, were also revised separately. One such provision was the constitution of Cracow in perpetuity as a free territory, its neutrality guaranteed by Austria, Prussia and Russia. This had been the subject of a treaty between those three powers which became Annex III to the Vienna Act, and the same provisions were also inserted in the body of the Act. In 1846 Austria, Prussia and Russia agreed to "revoke" the articles of their treaties on this subject and return the territory to the possession of Austria.[1] Palmerston again protested, stating:

> It is demonstrable, ... that with whomsoever may have originated the plan of erecting Cracow and its territory into a free and independent State, that plan was carried into effect by stipulations to which all the Powers were equally parties, and consequently it is not competent for 3 of those Powers by their own separate authority to undo that which was established by the common engagements of the whole. ....[2]

The reply of Prince Metternich was accompanied by a memorandum of law.[3] It argued that the insertion in the Act of Vienna of the various separate treaties which had been concluded between individual powers added nothing to the obligatory force of those treaties nor deprived the contracting parties of the capacity to modify them by agreement among themselves. A series of later agreements among the German states which modified territorial clauses of the Act of Vienna was cited as proof of this capacity. The effect of reciting such provisions in the Vienna Act, it was said, was only to give the parties to that Act

---

[1] 35 B.F.S.P. 1088.
[2] *Id.* at 1085.
[3] *Id.* at 1100.

the right to intervene in the event of a dispute among the parties to the separate treaties. Since the three parties to the treaties concerning Cracow had reached agreement in this instance, there was no occasion for other powers to interfere. The Austrian memorandum added that what had happened in relation to Holland and Belgium served the three powers as a precedent:

> If the three Courts had, in regard to Cracow, followed a different procedure from that which was then observed, and if they had associated in this affair the Courts of Spain, of Portugal, and of Sweden, not to mention other difficulties, they would have cast a shadow of doubt on the acts of public law by which Belgium had been separated from Holland.[1]

The published correspondence does not record what answer, if any, was made to this argument by Great Britain.

When the German Confederation, established by a Treaty among the German States which was incorporated in the Act of Vienna, was dissolved in 1866, none of the the non-German powers claimed a right to be consulted.[2] There had been a diplomatic correspondence, initiated by France, on the possibility of assembling a Conference of the Powers, but the discussion had been in general terms relating to the means of preserving the peace of Europe and the balance of power rather than to rights of parties to the Act of Vienna.[3]

Despite the provision of Article 118 of the Vienna Act that the annexes were to have the same force and effect as if they were inserted, word for word, in the General Treaty, theer is no case in which the proponents of revision of any of the annexes sought the consent of other parties besides the signatories of the annexes in question.[4]

2. THE TREATIES OF PARIS, 1856, AND BERLIN, 1878

The principle of separability was also demonstrated with respect to the Treaty of Paris of 1856.[5] This treaty was concluded between the six great powers of Europe, and Turkey, whose inde-

---

[1] *Id.* at 1104. (Translated).
[2] The protest of the King of Hanover, on the annexation of his kingdom by Prussia, is printed in 3 HERTSLET, THE MAP OF EUROPE BY TREATY 1742.
[3] 57 B.F.S.P. 378–412.
[4] *Cf.* TOBIN, THE TERMINATION OF MULTIPARTITE TREATIES 216–217.
[5] 46 B.F.S.P. 8.

pendence and territorial integrity the powers collectively guaranteed. It had two annexes, a convention on the Straits and a convention on the Aaland Islands. The Straits convention was concluded between the same seven powers as the general treaty.[1] The convention which provided for the demilitarization of the Aaland Islands was concluded between only three of the powers, Britain, France and Russia. Article 33 of the Treaty of Paris stated that it should have "the same force and validity as if it formed a part" of the treaty. It is curious that the powers still clung to this formula after the experience of the separate revision of the arrangements annexed to the Vienna Act. It seems to have been resorted to as a compromise. The minutes of the conferences at Paris show that the demand for demilitarization was first put forward by the representative of France, as a "special condition proposed in the interests of Europe."[2] Russia's delegate announced his acceptance of the stipulation, but asked that it be put 'in a separate act which would be concluded between France, Great Britain, and Russia, since these Powers alone have taken part in the acts of war of which the Baltic has been the theatre." The Austrian representative then suggested that the separate act be, nevertheless, annexed to the general treaty, and this suggestion was adopted.[3] In any event, when revision of the status of the islands came under discussion in 1907–08 none of the parties to the parties to the negotiations ever suggested consulting Austria, Italy, and Turkey, and Sir Arthur Nicolson told the Russian Foreign Minister, "I did not quite see how the Aaland Islands could be a question of interest to Germany who was not a party to the 1856 treaty." Certain German officials referred to Article 33 of the Treaty of Paris in private memoranda, but their official claims were not based on it, but rather on their political interest as a Baltic power.[4]

The Treaty of Paris contained a collective guarantee of the independence and territorial integrity of Turkey. Because of this guarantee, its territorial dispositions were removed from the operation of the usual rule that territorial provisions have fulfilled their function when the necessary transfers have been com-

[1] Discussed *infra*, Ch. V.
[2] 46 B.F.S.P. 67, 71.
[3] *Ibid.*
[4] The Aaland Islands Convention is discussed at greater length in Ch. VII, *infra*.

pleted.[1] In this case they clearly interested all the signatories, which were the six great powers, and Turkey, the object of the guarantee. The right of all of them to participate in the revision of the Near Eastern settlement was emphatically asserted in the Declaration of London of 1871.[2] It was asserted again when Russia, after her military victory over Turkey in 1878, sought to dictate new territorial changes.

In this instance, England had warned Russia beforehand, on January 14, 1878:

> that, in the opinion of Her Majesty's Government, any Treaty concluded between the Government of Russia and the Porte affecting the Treaties of 1856 and 1871 must be an European Treaty, and would not be valid without the assent of the Powers who were parties to those Treaties.[3]

The language was an assertion of the authority of the Concert of the great powers, as well as of the unanimity principle. Russia was forced by British military pressure to submit her separate treaty with Turkey, which would have brought wide changes in the arrangements of 1856,[4] to be revised by a Congress of the powers held at Berlin. All of the signatories of the Treaty of 1856 participated in the Congress and signed the resulting treaty.[5]

At this great-power gathering unanimity was the rule of conference procedure. At the first session Bismarck, in his capacity as President, stated that he considered it "incontestable that the minority in the Congress shall not be bound to acquiesce in a vote of the majority," though he suggested that resolutions of the majority concerning procedural matters should be regarded as decisions of the Congress, provided that no formal protest was entered by the minority.[6] In spite of these rules, however, it was evident that Turkey was "less equal" than the other powers. When all of the latter had agreed that the Turkish provinces of Bosnia and Herzegovina should be "occupied and administered" by Austria-Hungary,[7] and only the Turkish representative objected to this new infringement of Turkish sovereignty, Bismarck

[1] *Supra*, pp. 85-86.
[2] *Supra*, p. 6.
[3] CMD. NO. 1923, Doc. No. 6 (1878).
[4] 69 B.F.S.P. 732.
[5] For text of the treaty, see *id*. at 749.
[6] *Id*. at 982.
[7] This was the subject of previous agreements between Austria and Russia. 2 PRIBRAM, THE SECRET TREATIES OF AUSTRIA-HUNGARY, 1879–1914 188–203· (1921)

sternly warned him, "in the name of the majority of the Congress and especially of the neutral Powers," that the intervention of the Congress had gained for Turkey other provinces and that the resolutions of the Congress formed a whole from which he could not accept the benefits while repudiating the disadvantages.[1] Turkey had no choice but to consent.[2]

The newly independent Balkan states were all excluded from the Congress of Berlin, and the Treaty of Berlin was signed by the same seven powers as had signed the Treaty of Paris. It redrew the map of the Balkans, recognized the independence of Rumania, Serbia and Montenegro, provided an autonomous status for Bulgaria and Eastern Roumelia, and obliged Turkey and the Balkan countries not to discriminate against relgious minorities. It authorized Austrian "occupation and administration," but not annexation, of the Turkish provinces of Bosnia and Herzegovina. With these changes, it renewed the Paris guarantee of the integrity of the Ottoman Empire.

In 1885–86 conferences of the powers were held in Constantinople to deal with a Bulgarian invasion of Eastern Roumelia, and modifications of certain provisions of the Berlin Treaty were unanimously agreed upon.[3] In the course of these conferences there were references to the Declaration of London, and the British representative stated his conception of that principle in the following terms:

> It was a matter at that time of re-establishing the principle that international stipulations cannot be modified by any act of a single Power. ... Clearly no modification of the text of an Article of the Treaty of Berlin can be made except with the unanimous consent of the Powers, and this is precisely the view which the British Government has always taken.[4]

In 1896 there were revolutionary disturbances and massacres of Armenian Christians in Turkey. These developments prompted Lord Salisbury to propose that the six European Powers should agree among themselves what changes in the government and administration of the Turkish Empire were necessary and that any resolution on which the six powers were unanimous should be forcibly imposed on Turkey. His proposal emphasized

---

[1] 69 B.F.S.P. 958.
[2] *Id.* at 1069.
[3] 77 B.F.S.P. 335, 386.
[4] *Id.* at 382. (Translated).

the political principle of the Concert of the great powers as the basis for unanimity:

> It is an object of primary importance that the concert of Europe should be maintained; and as long as any of the Powers, or any one Power, is not satisfied with the expediency of the recommendations that are put forward, no action in respect to them can be taken. But if any recommendations made by the Ambassadors should approve themselves to all the Powers as measures suitable for adoption, it must not be admitted, at the point we have at present reached, that the objections of the Turkish Government can be an obstacle to their being carried into effect.[1]

In fact the powers were unable to agree on such joint action as Lord Salisbury suggested, but this result was occasioned by political rather than legal considerations. Mutual jealousy counselled maintenance of the *status quo*.[2]

In all of these instances it was apparent that Turkey would not be permitted to block a change in the Near Eastern settlement if all of the great powers were able to agree on it. Although the diplomatic correspondence contained frequent references to the need for "consent of all the Powers." what was often meant was "consent of all the great powers." The consent of each of these would have been required because of their collective guarantee of the settlement, even if no rule of unanimous consent of parties to previous treaties had been assumed.

An important change in the territorial settlement of the Treaty of Berlin was made unilaterally on October 5, 1907, when Austria announced her annexation of Bosnia and Herzegovina, the Turkish provinces under her "administration" since 1878. Russia, which had made a preliminary bargain with Austria to trade Russian consent to annexation of the provinces for Austrian support of changes in favor of Russia at the Straits, had not contemplated announcement of the annexation as a *fait acompli* but had envisaged a conference of the powers. She sought to avoid a complete diplomatic defeat by requiring Austria to submit the question to such a conference.[3] Russia's Foreign Minister, Izvolski, made the demand for a conference in a circular despatch in which he referred to the Declaration of London of 1871 and to the complete

---

[1] CMD. NO. 8304 (1897). The Circular is quoted and discussed in LANGER, THE DIPLOMACY OF IMPERIALISM 333 ff. (1951).
[2] LANGER, *op. cit. Supra* at 334–350.
[3] 5 BRIT. DOCS. 383 ff., 807–808; 1 FAY, ORIGINS OF THE WORLD WAR 375–376 (1929); SHOTWELL AND DEÁK, TURKEY AT THE STRAITS 78–80 (1940).

analogy of the new situation to the earlier Russian demand for revision.[1] He stated:

> It seems in fact evident that Austria-Hungary having been invested with the right of occupying Bosnia and Herzegovina ... not by a private arrangement with Turkey, but by the Treaty of Berlin, no modification of these rights can take place without an agreement among all the powers signatory to the said Treaty.

The British, French and Italian Governments also supported the necessity of a conference of the signatory powers.[2] The British Foreign Minister pointed out that the status of the provinces remained Turkish by the Treaty of Berlin. He also cited the Declaration of London and stated, "It was an exceeding bad precedent to attempt to alter a Treaty arbitrarily at the will of one party." [3]

The Bosnian crisis of 1907–08 was finally resolved by the surrender of Russia in the face of a determined stand taken by Austria, supported by Germany. However, as had been the case in 1871, the legal form of unanimous consent of the parties to the previous treaty was resorted to as a face-saving device. Turkish consent was given in exchange for Austria's payment of an indemnity for the loss of property of the Sultan.[4] All of the Powers, by prearrangement according to a formula proposed by Germany, accepted an Austrian invitation to give their formal consent to the Austro-Turkish agreement involving the nullification of Article 25 of the Treaty of Berlin.[5] British, Italian and French consent was made contingent on the modification also of Article 29, to provide concessions to Montenegro.

One must conclude that in the revision of the treaties of 1856 and 1878 the maintenance of the authority of the Concert of the great powers was a constant consideration. It was assumed that they could act in their collective capacity only if they were unanimous. It was apparent, however, that Turkey would not be allowed to block treaty revision on which the great powers might agree. All of the declarations affirming the requirement of unanimous consent for revision were aimed at attempts at *unilateral* revision.

[1] 5 BRIT. DOCS. 533 ff.
[2] 5 *id*. 415–422.
[3] 5 *id*. 420.
[4] 102 B.F.S.P. 180.
[5] 5 BRIT. DOCS. 638 ff., 718–733, 776, 786, 794.

3. THE TREATY OF VERSAILLES

a) *Subsequent revision of parts of the settlement*

The Treaty of Versailles [1] had twenty-seven signatories and 440 articles on a wide variety of subjects, of interest to varying groups of powers. A number of its parts contained special provisions for their own revision which named the parties to be consulted.[2] Even where such provisions were absent, however, parts of the treaty were later separately revised. In no case were all the parties to the treaty consulted in the revision of any part of it.

Article 428 provided that, as a guarantee for the execution of the treaty by Germany, the Rhineland would be occupied by Allied and Associated troops for fifteen years after the coming into force of the treaty. A separate agreement on this subject was also concluded between Belgium, France, Great Britain, the United States (the occupying powers) and Germany.[3] The United States did not ratify this agreement, but American troops participated in the occupation until January, 1923.[4] There were three zones of occupation, which, according to Article 429 of the treaty, were to be relinquished respectively at the end of five, ten and fifteen years. After November 30, 1929, only the French remained in occupation of the third zone, which extended from the Saar to Mainz. Its evacuation was agreed to five years ahead of time by an agreement concluded at the Hague on August 30, 1929, [5] as an incident of the adoption of a new plan for settlement of the reparation question, between Belgium, Great Britain, France and Germany – i.e., the occupying powers which were parties to the separate agreement concerning the occupation. The participants did not solicit the adhesion of any other powers.

The provisions concerning the Rhine have been revised by separate action of the states named to the Central Commission of the Rhine.[6] Revision of the provisions concerning the Danube

---

[1] On the revision of this treaty generally, see STEPHENS, REVISIONS OF THE TREATY OF VERSAILLES (1939). For text of the Treaty, see 13 FOREIGN REL. U.S., THE PARIS PEACE CONFERENCE 1919 (1947).
[2] See Arts. 26, 377, 378, 422, and Part VIII, Annex II, par. 22.
[3] 13 FOREIGN REL. U.S., PARIS PEACE CONFERENCE 1919, 762.
[4] *Id.* at 773.
[5] 104 L.N.T.S. 473.
[6] *Infra*, Ch. IV.

has been treated as a matter concerning only the states named to draw up a navigation statute for the river.[1] The reparation provisions (Part VIII of the treaty) were also treated as of concern to a limited number of parties, and the manner in which these provisions were subsequently revised shows how acceptance of the principle of separability frees the parties from assumptions concerning the unanimity rule and opens the door to revision based frankly on consent of the principally interested states.

Article 233 of the Treaty of Versailles provided that the amount Germany must pay as reparation was to be determined by an Inter-Allied Reparation Commission, whose composition, powers and method of procedure were charted in Annex II to this part of the treaty. It was to be composed ordinarily of delegates of the United States,[2] Great Britain, France, Italy and Belgium, though in certain questions concerning Japanese interests a Japanese delegate was to replace the delegate of Belgium, and in questions relating to Austria, Hungary, or Bulgaria the place of Belgium was to be taken by Yugoslavia.[3] The Commission was given "wide latitude as to its control and handling of the whole reparation problem," and it was authorized to amend the provisions of Annex II by unanimous vote of the governments represented on the Commission.

Early decisions taken by the powers represented on the Commission acting alone are explainable by the wide powers left to the Commission and its authority to interpret this part of the treaty.[4] Later, however, they scrapped the provisions of the treaty and substituted other arrangements. These sweeping changes began when the Dawes Plan was put into effect in 1924.

Article 237 provided that the initial calculation of the proportional reparation shares of the various allies should be made "by the Allied and Associated Governments." In fact, however, it was made by several agreements between the six governments represented on the Commission and Portugal.[5] The only states

---

[1] *Infra*, Ch. IV.

[2] The United States did not ratify the treaty, but was represented on the Commission by an unofficial observer.

[3] The other Allied and Associated Powers were entitled to be represented by Assessors when their claims were under examination, but without the right to vote.

[4] Paragraph 12 of Annex II. See 13 FOREIGN REL. U.S., PARIS PEACE CONFERENCE 1919, 485–486, 881.

[5] *Id*. at 441–442, 849–860.

outside the Commission to which these agreements assigned shares of reparations were Rumania, Portugal and Greece. These governments, with the United States and those represented on the Commission, were invited to the London Conference of 1924 which was to put into operation the Dawes Plan reparations machinery. In addition, Czechoslovakia, Poland, Brazil, Siam, Liberia and Cuba, as "the other powers directly interested in the reparation settlement", were sent notes assuring them that they would be kept informed and given a hearing on matters pertaining to their interests.[1] The Dawes Plan created an Arbitral Tribunal of Interpretation between the Reparation Commission and the German government, and set up other new machinery which substantially superseded the Reparation Commission.[2] It was put into effect by agreements between Germany and the nine governments represented at the London Conference.[3]

Still more far-reaching changes in the reparation provisions were proposed in the "Young Plan" of 1929. It contemplated reduction of the total reparation bill, abolition of the Reparation Commission, and an end to the joint liability of Germany for any Austrian, Bulgarian or Hungarian indebtedness.[4] The plan had been prepared by a Committee of Financial Experts which had been instructed by the governments of Germany, Belgium, France, Great Britain, Italy and Japan to draw up "a complete and final settlement of the question of reparations."[5] When the plan was ready these six governments summoned a conference at the Hague to put it into effect. The matter of invitations to the conference was referred to in its Final Act, of January 20, 1930:

> The [six] Governments..., taking the view that the conclusions of this report concerned also the Governments of Greece, Portugal, Poland, Roumania, Czechoslovakia and Jugoslavia as well as the Governments of Canada, the Commonwealth of Australia, New Zealand, the Union of

---

[1] CMD. NO. 2184 (1924). Haiti, Peru and Bolivia, which had also filed claims, were not mentioned. For list of claims filed, see 13 FOREIGN REL. U.S., PARIS PEACE CONFERENCE 1919, 470 ff.
[2] 13 FOREIGN REL. U.S., PARIS PEACE CONFERENCE 1919, 385–386.
[3] 19 A.J.I.L. Supp. 23–52 (1924). An ambiguous report by a commission of jurists composed of Sir Cecil Hurst and M. Fromageot had stated that to put the Dawes Plan into operation without running counter to the Treaty of Versailles would require an agreement with Germany and also "an understanding on certain points between the Allied Governments." CMD. NO. 2270 at 132–136 (1924).
[4] 13 FOREIGN REL. U.S., PARIS PEACE CONFERENCE 1919, 390–391.
[5] *Id.* at 928.

South Africa and India, invited these Governments to take part in the negotiations and agreements affecting them.[1]

All of these governments signed the agreement which put the new plan into effect.[2] Although Poland and Czechoslovakia, which had made large reparation claims, were included, a number of other states which had filed claims with the Reparation Commission had not been invited to participate in this revision. The new agreement provided, moreover, that it would go into effect when ratified "by four out of the five powers principally concerned, viz. Belgium, Great Britain, France, Italy and Japan." [3] There was thus to be required not even unanimity of the principally interested states.

The United States feared that this agreement would jeopardize the priority of its special claims in respect of army costs. It therefore notified the Agent-General for Reparation Payments, a new Dawes Plan official, that the United States would reserve all of its rights under existing treaties.[4] It did not claim that the new arrangements were invalid. The United States subsequently reached a direct agreement on this subject with Germany.[5]

The Lausanne Agreement of July 9, 1932, which was intended to put an end to the reparation regime entirely, but which did not come into force, was signed by the same governments as had put the Young Plan into effect.[6] It was to be effective on ratification by Germany, Belgium, France, the United Kingdom, Italy and Japan.[7]

The reparation provisions were thus repeatedly revised without regard for any requirement of unanimity. Practical effectiveness was the governing consideration. The other signatories never questioned this assumption of authority by the most interested creditor nations.[8]

---

[1] Text in 24 A.J.I.L. Supp. 259 (1930). The United States had chosen to abstain from official participation in any of the reparation agencies, but it was represented at the Hague by an observer.
[2] *Id.* at 262.
[3] *Id.* at 270.
[4] 13 FOREIGN REL. U.S., PARIS PEACE CONFERENCE 1919, 394.
[5] *Id.* at 942.
[6] *Id.* at 406.
[7] *Ibid.*
[8] STEPHENS, *op. cit. supra*, 258–259.

b) *Its effect on the status of Belgium*

The effects of the Treaty of Versailles on the previous treaties concerning the Rhine and the Danube are considered elsewhere.[1] Its effects on the treaties which established the status of Belgium, Luxembourg and Switzerland must also be considered.

The neutrality of Belgium was established and guaranteed by three treaties of April 19, 1839, a treaty of separation between Holland and Belgium,[2] a treaty between the five great powers and Holland,[3] and one between them and Belgium,[4] the last two guaranteeing the entire settlement and Belgium's independence and perpetual neutrality.

The experience of World War I caused Belgium to decide on the termination of her neutral status. The method of doing this was considered by the Peace Conference. The Commission on Belgian and Danish Affairs, charged by the Supreme Council of the Allies with the study "of the present status, in law and in fact, of the Treaties of 1839," [5] refrained from expressing an opinion on whether the treaties could be said to have been terminated by the fact of their violation, but concluded that, in any event, they should be revised.[6] As to the states which should participate in the revision, the Commission concluded that they were Holland, "those of the guarantor great powers which have fulfilled their obligations," and Italy, Japan and the United States, as great powers represented at the conference and having general interests. This formula left out Russia. An accompanying explanatory note stated:

Of the guarantor powers, three have failed to fulfill their obligations: Prussia and Austria-Hungary by their aggression in 1914; Russia by the Treaty of Brest-Litowsk.[7]

The British Government had previously stated its view that the reason for ignoring Russia was that "for the present [she] is non-existent." [8]

---

[1] *Infra*, ch. IV.
[2] 27 B.F.S.P. 1000.
[3] *Id.* at 990.
[4] *Id.* at 1000.
[5] 10 MILLER DIARY 26.
[6] *Id.* at 176–177.
[7] *Id.* at 179.
[8] 5 *id.* 33.

The Dutch government was in agreement with the composition of the revisory conference as envisaged by the Allies, and agreed to attend.[1] Such a meeting to work out the details of revision was still pending when the Treaty of Versailles was signed.

Article 31 of the Treaty of Versailles dealt with the subject as follows:

> Germany, recognizing that the Treaties of April 19, 1839, which established the status of Belgium before the war no longer conform to the requirements of the situation, consents to the abrogation of the said Treaties and undertakes immediately to recognize and to observe whatever conventions may be entered into by the Principal Allied and Associated Powers, or by any of them, in concert with the Governments of Belgium and of the Netherlands, to replace the said Treaties of 1839. ...

The representatives of the United States, Great Britain, France, Italy, Japan, Belgium and the Netherlands studied the question until March, 1920, and drafted a project for an agreement between Belgium and the Netherlands and a collective treaty, but disagreements between Belgium and the Netherlands concerning replacement of waterways clauses of the Treaties of 1839 (which placed severe restrictions on Belgium's access to the sea and to the Rhine) prevented a settlement.[2] The Netherlands apparently raised no objection to the termination of Belgium's neutralized status.

Negotiations between the Netherlands and Belgium continued, and in 1926 they signed with France and the United Kingdom a treaty recognizing the abrogation of the Treaties of 1839 and the termination of Belgium's neutralization.[3] It was interesting, in view of the attitude taken at the Peace Conference in regard to Russia, that this treaty provided that the U.S.S.R. (as well as Austria, Germany and Hungary) should be invited to adhere to it. The treaty never took effect because the Netherlands Parliament refused its approval. From the terms of this treaty McNair concludes that it was the view of the British government that,

> although for all practical purposes the guarantee clauses of the Treaties of 1839 had been rendered obsolete by the Treaties of Peace of 1919 and 1920 ..., as a matter of strict law it was necessary that that fact should

---

[1] 14 *id.* 80.

[2] 13 FOREIGN REL. U.S., PARIS PEACE CONFERENCE 1919, 136.

[3] BELGIUM, MINISTÈRE DES AFFAIRES ÉTRANGÈRES, DOCUMENTS DIPLOMATIQUES RELATIFS À LA REVISION DES TRAITÉS DE 1839, 24 (1929).

be formally put on record by all the five guaranteeing Powers (or their successors) and Holland.[1]

However, Belgium and France, which had entered into a military understanding in 1920, had shown that they regarded the neutralized status of Belgium as already terminated.[2] Great Britain, Germany, France, Belgium and Italy also stated in the preamble to the 1925 Locarno Treaty of Mutual Guarantee that they were "taking note of the abrogation of the treaties for the neutralisation of Belgium." [3] Assuming that Russia had lost the right to object, the termination of this status involved no real departure from unanimity since the Netherlands raised no objection to this change. The real issue, as has been said, concerned the river clauses of the treaties of 1839 and here the Versailles Treaty purported to make no changes.[4]

c) *Its effect on the rights of Switzerland*

At the conclusion of World War I France wished to terminate the special neutralized zone of Upper Savoy (French territory since 1860). Its special status had resulted from the treaties of 1815 which guaranteed the neutrality of Switzerland, and had been affirmed by a treaty of 1816 between Switzerland and Sardinia.[5] When Savoy was ceded to France by Sardinia in 1860, Switzerland protested to the Sardinian Government on the basis of the Treaty of 1816, and also asked the intervention of the powers signatory of the treaties of 1815, protesting agianst any occupation of the territory by France "until the Powers of Europe shall have pronounced their opinion." [6] The matter was settled by France's concession, expressed in the treaty of cession, that the King of Sardinia could only transfer the territories "on the conditions upon which he himself possesses them." [7] To terminate this status France first secured Switzerland's consent,

---

[1] MCNAIR, THE LAW OF TREATIES 372 (1938).
[2] *Id.* at 370.
[3] 3 HUDSON, INTERNATIONAL LEGISLATION 1693.
[4] On effect of the Versailles Treaty on the status of Luxembourg see McNair, *Les effets de la guerre sur les traités,* 59 REC. DES COURS 575 (1937).
[5] 1 HERTSLET, THE MAP OF EUROPE BY TREATY 421 (Article 7).
[6] 2 *id.* 1415, 1435.
[7] 2 *id.* 1429 (Article 2).

subject to approval by the Swiss Federal Council.[1] It was then provided in Article 435 of the Treaty of Versailles:

... The High Contracting Parties take note of the agreement reached between the French Government and the Swiss Government for the abrogation of the stipulations relating to this zone which are and remain abrogated.

Despite this categorical language, Switzerland's consent was not complete without the approval of the Federal Council, and that was not given until March 16, 1928.[2] Switzerland notified the French government that it could accept the provisions of Article 435 only with the understanding that nothing would be definitively settled until the Federal Council had ratified the agreement.[3] It also asked that the parties to the Treaty of Peace should also seek the accession "of the signatory Powers of the Treaties of 1815 ... which are not signatories of the present Treaty of Peace." [4] Pursuant to this request the adherence of Spain and Sweden was in fact later obtained.[5]

At the same time as she sought the termination of the neutralization of Savoy, France sought also to end the so-called "Free Zones" of Upper Savoy and Gex, where French customs lines had been withdrawn in favor of Switzerland. The free zone of Upper Savoy had been agreed to by Sardinia and Switzerland (fulfilling commitments made to the eight powers at Vienna) in their Treaty of 1816 which confirmed the neutrality of Upper Savoy, and it became one of the conditions accepted by France on the transfer of the territory to her in 1860.[6] The Gex zone was provided for in the Second Peace of Paris of November 20, 1815.[7] That treaty stated that in addition to certain cessions to Switzerland, the line of the French custom-houses should be "placed to the West of the Jura, so that the whole of the Pays de Gex shall be without that line." Switzerland was not a party to the Second Peace of Paris. However, this provision was an amplification of a

[1] 5 FOREIGN REL. U.S., PARIS PEACE CONFERENCE 1919, 487–488 (1944).
[2] 1 GUGGENHEIM, TRAITÉ DE DROIT INTERNATIONAL PUBLIC 116 n. (1953).
[3] See Annex to Article 435 of the Treaty of Versailles.
[4] *Ibid.*
[5] April 8, 1920, and March 22, 1921, respectively. P.C.I.J., Ser. C, No. 17–1, Vol. II, 563 (1929).
[6] *Supra*, p. 99.
[7] 1 HERTSLET, MAP OF EUROPE BY TREATY 342. This was a treaty between the principal four Allies and France, acceded to later by Spain and Portugal. 3 DE CLERQ RECUEIL DES TRAITÉS DE LA FRANCE 100.

provision of the declaration of the eight powers (Art. 79 of the Vienna Act), which Switzerland had formally accepted.

Article 435 of the Treaty of Versailles also declared that the stipulations of the Treaties of 1815 and other supplementary acts concerning the Free Zones were "no longer consistent with present conditions" and stated that it was "for France and Switzerland to come to an agreement" to settle the status of these territories. With the adherence of Spain and Sweden to the stipulations of this Article, the consent of all interested parties, except Switzerland, had been obtained. On August 7, 1921, France and Switzerland signed a customs agreement to replace the Free Zones regime, but Swiss ratification was subject to a plebiscite and failed when the vote went against the convention.[1] In 1923 France established her customs line at the political frontier, but she subsequently agreed with Switzerland to submit the dispute to the Permanent Court of International Justice.

The judgment of the Permanent Court, given June 7, 1932, was in favor of Switzerland.[2] The Court interpreted Article 435 as not intended *per se* to abrogate the earlier treaty provisions, but only as a declaration of disinterestedness, leaving the matter to be settled by France and Switzerland. However, the Court added:

> Even if it were otherwise, it is certain that, in any case, Article 435 of the Treaty of Versailles is not binding upon Switzerland, who is not a Party to that Treaty, except to the extent to which the country accepted it.[3]

As to the former Sardinian zones it was clear that Switzerland had the rights of a party to the previous treaties. As to the Gex zone this was less clear, but the Court found that here also, taking the treaties of 1815 all together as a composite territorial arrangement, Switzerland must be regarded as a party. It followed that none of the treaties could be abrogated without Swiss consent.[4]

The Court went on to state that even if Switzerland were not

[1] 2 HUDSON, WORLD COURT REPORTS 448 (1935).
[2] Case concerning the Free Zones of Upper Savoy and the District of Gex, P.C.I.J., Ser. A/B, No. 46 (1932).
[3] *Id.* at 141.
[4] France had made no argument that an existing treaty relation between France and Switzerland could have been abrogated by the Treaty of Versailles without Swiss consent. She confined herself to arguing that Switzerland was not a party, or that she had given her consent to the abrogation, or that the obligation had lapsed by virtue of a change in circumstances. P.C.I.J., Ser. C, No. 17–1, Vol. II, 530–634 (1929).

to be regarded as a party she might still have a treaty right as a third-party beneficiary. On this subject the Court observed:

> It cannot be lightly presumed that stipulations favourable to a third State have been adopted with the object of creating an actual right in its favour. There is however nothing to prevent the will of sovereign States from having this object and this effect. The question of the existence of a right acquired under an instrument drawn between other States is therefore one to be decided in each particular case: it must be ascertained whether the States which have stipulated in favour of a third State meant to create for that State an actual right which the latter has accepted as such.[1]

In their dissent Judges Altamira and Hurst protested vigorously against the possibility of third-party rights, stating:

> ... we wish to make every reservation in regard to a theory seeking to lay down, as a principle, that rights accorded to third Parties by international conventions, to which the favoured State is not a Party, cannot be amended or abolished, even by the States which accorded them, without the consent of the third State. ...[2]

4. THE ITALIAN PEACE TREATY, 1947

a) *The Naval, Military and Air Clauses*

Part IV of the Italian peace treaty [3] (Naval, Military and Air Clauses) limited the Italian army to 185,000 men and put comparable limitations on Italy's navy and air force. There was a specific provision concerning revision of this part of the treaty. Article 46, entitled "Duration of Application," stated:

> Each of the military, naval and air clauses of the present Treaty shall remain in force until modified in whole or in part by agreement between the Allied and Associated Powers and Italy or, after Italy becomes a member of the United Nations, by agreement between the Security Council and Italy.

This provision evidently assumed that unanimity would be required, in the absence of Security Council action, for any generally effective revision of these clauses, for a proposal by Australia, which would have allowed revision of any part of the treaty by less than unanimity of the signatories, though reserving a veto

---

[1] P.C.I.J., Ser. A/B, No. 46 at 147–148 (1932).
[2] *Id.* at 185. *Cf. infra*, pp. 220, 242.
[3] T.I.A.S. No. 1648.

for the United States, France, Great Britain and the U.S.S.R., was rejected by the Peace Conference.[1]

It was only to be expected that Italy would seek every means to escape from the restrictions which the treaty imposed on her.[2] She had protested from the first that the treaty was an affront to her national conscience and asked for recognition of the principle that the treaty could be revised through bilateral accords with the interested states and through the United Nations. [3] The replies to this request were largely noncommittal. However, the British and American governments expressed qualified approval of the principle of revision via bilateral agreements, except as to provisions affecting the rights and interests of the Allied and Associated Powers as a whole. As to the latter the British government assumed that unanimity would be necessary. Its note of February 8, 1947, to the Italian government pointed out that provision had already been made in Article 46 for the possibility of revising the military, naval and sir clauses, and added:

> It is, of course, plain that those other provisions of the Peace Treaty which affect the rights and interests of the Allied and Associated Powers as a whole cannot be modified except by agreement between all the Governments concerned. It would clearly not be appropriate for His Majesty's Government to express any comment on a matter which concerns the signatories of the Treaty as a whole.
>
> However, in so far as the Treaty confers on any individual Allied Power certain rights affecting only that Power and Italy, there would seem to be nothing to exclude the possibility of the Allied Power concerned, for its part and without prejudice to the rights of other Allied Powers, agreeing with the Italian Government to the modification of those rights in particular cases.[4]

The United States' reply was less specific. It stated:

> As you know, provision is made in Article 46 of the Italian Treaty for possible future modification of the military, naval and air clauses. Also, it is the view of this Government that means exist under the United Nations Charter for eventual peaceful changes in the provisions of treaties by agreement among the States concerned. Further, as regards provisions of the Italian Treaty which confer on any one of the Allied and Associated Powers rights affecting only that power and Italy, there would surely be

---

[1] VEDOVATO, IL TRATTATO DI PACE CON ITALIA, DOCUMENTI E CARTA 194 (1947); cf. id. at 188.

[2] The coming into force of the treaty was not even dependent on Italian ratification. See Article 90 of the Treaty, and letter of the British ambassador to the Italian Minister of Foreign Affairs, Feb. 8, 1947, VEDOVATO, op. cit., supra at 560.

[3] VEDOVATO, op. cit., supra at 554, 565–567.

[4] VEDOVATO, op. cit. supra at 559.

no bar to a future modification which might be agreed upon between Italy and the power concerned.[1]

The last part of this statement was a recognition of the principle of separability.

Even before the treaty was signed, a number of Latin American states sought to place suggestions for its revision on the agenda of the United Nations General Assembly.[2] Representatives of the United States and the United Kingdom welcomed discussion of revision, stating they regarded the treaty as less than ideal.[3] However, the item was ultimately withdrawn by its sponsors.

Revision of the military clauses became urgent for many of the signatories in 1951, when it was desired to increase Italy's contribution to the defense effort of the North Atlantic Community.[4] Italian efforts now met a favorable response in Washington, London and Paris. The problem was to find a legal way of doing it.

On the occasion of a visit by Prime Minister de Gasperi to Washington, on September 26, 1951, a Joint Declaration was issued by the United States, France and the United Kingdom. It noted that Italy was "still prevented by an unjustifiable [Soviet] veto from obtaining membership in the United Nations in spite of the provisions of the treaty," [5] and that the restrictions and disabilities to which Italy was subject under the peace treaty were no longer in accord "with the situation prevailing today." It then stated:

> Each of the three governments, therefore, declares hereby its readiness to give favorable consideration to a request from the Italian Government to remove so far as concerns its individual relations with Italy, and with-

---

[1] *Id.* at 564.
[2] U.N. Doc. No. A/369 (1947).
[3] U.N. GENERAL ASSEMBLY OFF. REC., 2d Sess., General Committee 15–18 (1947).
[4] The United States Senate appended to its approval of the stationing of American troops in Europe a paragraph stating:

> It is the sense of the Senate that the United States should seek to eliminate all provisions of the existing treaty with Italy which impose limitations upon the military strength of Italy and prevent the performance by Italy of her obligations under the North Atlantic Treaty to contribute to the full extent of her capacity to the defense of Western Europe.

S. Res. 99, 82d Cong., 1st Sess., (1951). Text in 24 DEP'T STATE BULL. 637 (1951).

[5] The preamble to the treaty stated that it would "form the basis of friendly relations between them, thereby enabling the Allied and Associated Powers to support Italy's application to become a member of the United Nations and also to adhere to any convention concluded under the auspices of the United Nations; . . .".

out prejudice to the rights of third parties, those permanent restrictions and discriminations now in existence which are wholly overtaken by events or have no justification in present circumstances or affect Italy's capacity for self-defense.[1]

Simultaneously with the issuance of this declaration, Secretary of State Acheson expressed hope that all the governments signatory to the treaty would give it their full concurrence.[2]

The Soviet Union of course protested, as did Poland, Czechoslovakia and Albania (which, though not a signatory, had acceded to the treaty).[3] However, the protest was framed in political rather than legal terms. It charged that the three governments wished to use Italian manpower and resources for aggressive purposes and to turn Italy into a dependent country. It stated that the U.S.S.R. had no objection in principle to revision of restrictions set by the Italian Peace Treaty and admission of Italy to the United Nations, on condition of analogous revision and admissions for Bulgaria, Hungary, Finland and Rumania.

The formula of individual renunciation of rights having been settled upon, events now moved rapidly. On December 8, 1951, Italy submitted a formal request for revision to the twenty-one allied parties [4] to the peace treaty. The Italian request stated that the treaty had been based on the assumption of universal adherence to the principles of the United Nations and an equal status for Italy as a member of that organization. This assumption had not been fulfilled. Therefore Italy asked agreement of the twenty-one states,

that the spirit reflected by the preamble [5] no longer exists, ... and that the military clauses, articles 46–70 and the relevant annexes, which restrict Italy's right and capacity to provide for her own defense, are not consistent with Italy's position as an equal member of the democratic and freedom-loving family of nations.

The reply of the United States concurred in this Italian statement and released Italy "from its obligations to the United States under Articles 46–70 and Annexes relevant thereto." [6] Thirteen

[1] 25 DEP'T STATE BULL. 570 (1951).
[2] *Id.* at 564.
[3] KEESING'S CONTEMPORARY ARCHIVES 11928 (1951). Text of the Soviet note is in 25 DEP'T STATE BULL. 649 (1951).
[4] This number included Pakistan, which had stated that it considered India's ratification to be binding on it also 49 U.N.T.S. 126.
[5] *Supra*, p. 104, n. 5
[6] For the exchange of notes between Italy and the United States, see T.I.A.S. No. 2461.

other signatories to the treaty also agreed to the Italian request, and Mexico and Iraq, which had acceded to the treaty, as authorized in Article 88,[1] did so as well. Czechoslovakia, Poland, the Soviet Union and Yugoslavia rejected the Italian proposal, as did Albania.[2] Ethiopia made no reply.[3] The Soviet answer was a protest against the adhesion of Italy to "the agressive Atlantic bloc." It stated that the Soviet Union would be disposed to adhere to a revision of the treaty and to the elimination of its restrictions only if Italy withdrew from that alliance.[4] The Yugoslav radio indicated that Yugoslav approval was contingent on a settlement of the problem of Trieste.[5]

The score thus finally stood at 16 parties to the peace treaty (including Italy) in favor of the revision, 5 opposed and 1 (Ethiopia) remaining silent. On February 9, 1952, after the U.S.S.R. had vetoed Italian admission to the United Nations for the fifth time, Italy protested to the Soviet Union that this action violated the pledge given in the preamble to the peace treaty to support the Italian application,[6] and stated that in consequence of this violation Italy could not adhere further on its part to the obligations imposed on Italy by the treaty with respect to the U.S.S.R.[7]

Reviewing the facts as to the revision of this part of the peace treaty, it is evident that the western powers, while lending their agreement to Italy's contention that the assumption underlying the treaty, of universal adherence to the principles of the United Nations, had failed of realization, took their legal stand on a right of individual parties to renounce their own treaty rights, leaving it up to Italy to decide whether the rights of non-acceding states could be disregarded. It was not an instance of *inter se*

---

[1] Art. 88 provided: "Any member of the United Nations, not a signatory to the present Treaty, which is at war with Italy, and Albania, may accede to the Treaty and upon accession shall be deemed to be an Associated Power for the purposes of the Treaty."

[2] Byelorussia and the Ukraine apparently never deposited separate ratifications of the treaty. 49 *U.N.T.S.* 126. They therefore had no rights under the treaty, Art. 89 of which provided: "The provisions of the present Treaty shall not confer any rights or benefits on any State named in the Preamble as one of the Allied and Associated Powers or on its nationals until such State becomes a party to the Treaty by deposit of its instrument of ratification."

[3] SURVEY OF INTERNATIONAL AFFAIRS (1951) 45.

[4] 10 ANNALI DI DIRITTO INTERNAZIONALE 94–95 (1952).

[5] SURVEY OF INTERNATIONAL AFFAIRS (1951) 45.

[6] *Supra*, p. 104, n. 5.

[7] Text in N.Y. Times, Feb. 10, 1952.

agreement because it was impossible for Italy to do away with the military restrictions without affecting her treaty relations with the dissenting parties. There is ample precedent, however, for individual renunciation by certain parties to a multipartite treaty of the right to rely on restrictions which the treaty imposed on another party.[1] By Article 141 of the Treaty of Versailles Germany renounced for her part the right to rely on the restrictions on French rule in Morocco flowing from the Act of Algeciras, and by Article 152 of the same treaty she consented for her part to Great Britain's assumption of the powers conferred on Turkey by the Suez Canal Convention. In 1936 the British delegation to the Montreux Conference justified their consent to Turkish fortification of the Straits as an individual renunciation of rights under the Lausanne Convention.[2] In 1938 Greece, Rumania, Yugoslavia, Italy, France and Great Britain waived, in so far as they were concerned ,the application of the military, naval and air clauses of the Treaty of Peace with Bulgaria.[3] In 1953, the United States renounced in favor of Japan the rights given it by Article 3 of the Japanese Peace Treaty of September 8, 1951, to administer the islands of the Amami Oshima group.[4] It did not ask the consent of any of the other parties and there were no protests.

The legitimacy of such action appears to depend upon whether there was any obligation in the matter running between the victorious powers. The bilateral form in which such treaties have been drafted, all of the Allied and Associated Powers being one party, and the defeated state the other party seems to lend some support to the view that the only obligation runs between the defeated state and each of the allied states. There is little authority, however, on this point.[5]

[1] The validity of such renunciation is stated by Fitzmaurice in his Second Report for the International Law Commission on the Law of Treaties. U.N. Doc. No. A/CN.4/107 at 39–40. He adds: "A renunciation or waiver of its rights by one of the beneficiaries cannot of itself (whatever the practical effect) impair the rights of the others as a matter of law, or absolve the party subject to the obligations concerned from continuing to perform them in relation to, or as respects, any non-renouncing party." *Id.* at 96. He also states that renunciation, though legally effective, may entail the payment of damages if injury to the other party results. *Id.* at 96–97.

[2] *Infra*, p. 171. See also Japan's individual renunciation of rights under the Montreux Convention. Article 8(b) of the Japanese Peace Treaty of 1951. T.I.A.S. No. 2490.

[3] 8 HUDSON, INTERNATIONAL LEGISLATION 80.

[4] 29 DEP'T STATE BULL. 208 (1953).

[5] See the U.S. commentary on the Treaty of Versailles. 13 FOREIGN REL. U.S., THE

Whatever the legality of the renunciation by the Allied Powers, the Italian government had to rely on other grounds of release. It rested its case on its claim of violation of the preamble by the Soviet Union and its contention as to change of circumstances, for which it had the affidavit of the three Western powers in their tripartite declaration of September 26, 1951.

b) *The Free Territory of Trieste*

Revision of the treaty provisions concerning Trieste provides further evidence in support of the principle of separability.

Article 21 of the Peace Treaty provided for the creation of the Free Territory of Trieste. Italian sovereignty over the area was terminated. A permanent statute (Annex VI) was to come into force at a time to be fixed by the Security Council of the United Nations. Until that time a provisional regime (Annex VII) should apply. Article 1 of this Annex stated that pending assumption of office by the Governor of the Territory, who was to be appointed by the Security Council, the Free Territory should "continue to be administered by the Allied military commands within their respective zones." [1]

The scheme envisaged in the peace treaty proved impossible of execution. Italy, Yugoslavia and the Security Council were never able to agree on a Governor, and it was alleged by the western powers that Yugoslavia had illegally incorporated her zone into her national territory. Therefore, on March 20, 1948, the United States, United Kingdom and France proposed that the Free Territory should be restored to Italian sovereignty. They suggested that this should be done by an additional protocol to the treaty of peace, to be agreed upon by themselves, the U.S.S.R. and Italy, and then submitted to the Security Council for approval "in view of the special responsibilities assumed by the Council in connection with the Free Territory of Trieste." No explanation was given for the proposed exclusion of Yugoslavia.[2]

PARIS PEACE CONFERENCE 1919 at 59 (1947); ROUSSEAU, DROIT INTERNATIONAL PUBLIC 36 (1953); Fitzmaurice, *The Juridical Clauses of the Peace Treaties*, 73 REC. DES COURS 259 at 261–262 (1948).

[1] The zones of administration of the British-American and Yugoslav military commands ("Zone A" and "Zone B", respectively) which were referred to in Annex VII had been established by a 1945 military agreement between the United States, the United Kingdom and Yugoslavia. U.S. EXEC. AGR. SER. No. 501.

[2] See the press statement issued by United States, United Kingdom and France,

The Soviet reply, dated April 13, 1948, was in part as follows:

> the treaty ... was prepared by the Council of Foreign Ministers and examined in detail at the Paris Conference, with the participation of 21 states. ...
>
> Hence it stands to reason that the proposal to decide the question of the revision of the treaty of peace with Italy in respect to one or another of its parts by means of correspondence or the organization of private conferences is considered unacceptable by the Soviet Government as violating the elementary principles of democracy.[1]

In answer to the Soviet note, the United States and the United Kingdom now hastened to explain that they had never intended to exclude any of the parties to the Treaty from also participating in its revision, and that they had meant the "preliminary meeting" of the five powers to be followed by consultation with all the other signatories.[2]

The Yugoslav government, on the other hand, maintained that the way to proceed was by a bilateral agreement between Italy and Yugoslavia,[3] and the three western powers eventually came around to this view also as the only way to a practical solution. The United States informed the Soviet Union in November, 1951:

> As the Soviet Government knows, the United States has for some time favored a constructive settlement of the Trieste question by the parties directly concerned. This would be in the direct interest of the Italian and Yugoslav peoples.[4]

On October 8, 1953, the United States and the United Kingdom jointly announced their decision to terminate their administration of Zone A and to withdraw their troops. They stated that their administration had never been intended to be permanent and that when it proved impossible to reach agreement with the other signatories of the peace treaty to set up the permanent regime they found themselves "faced with a situation not contemplated in the Treaty." They had employed their good offices in the hope of promoting a settlement between Italy and Yugoslavia, but without success. In these circumstances, the declara-

---

March 20, 1948. 18 DEP'T STATE BULL. 425 (1948); also notes to Italy and to the U.S.S.R., *id.* at 453, 522.

[1] *Id.* at 549.
[2] U.N. SECURITY COUNCIL OFF., REC., 3d year, 350th meeting 5–6, 12 (1948); 18 DEP'T STATE BULL. 549 (1948).
[3] DOCUMENTS ON INTERNATIONAL AFFAIRS (1947–1948) 256.
[4] 25 DEP'T STATE BULL. 912 (1951).

tion said, the two governments had decided "to bring the present unsatisfactory situation to an end" by returning Zone A, in view of its predominantly Italian character, to Italian administration.[1]

Yugoslavia called this a violation of the peace treaty, threatened to regard the arrival of Italian troops in Zone A as an act of aggression, and proposed direct talks between Yugoslavia, the United Kingdom, the United States and Italy.[2] Italy suggested a five-power conference, including France.[3] The Soviet Union repeated its charges of violation of the treaty.[4] In view of the strong Yugoslav reaction it was impossible to implement the decision to withdraw the British and American troops.

On October 12, 1953, the U.S.S.R. brought the matter to the Security Council.[5] The Soviet delegate argued that no country had a right to depart from the decisions made in the treaty without the agreement of all twenty-one signatories.[6] His plea fell on deaf ears. It was apparent that the other members of the Security Council, including three of the smaller parties to the peace treaty (China, Greece and Pakistan), agreed that direct negotiations between the most interested powers offered the only hope of a solution. By a vote of 8 to 1 (Lebanon abstaining) they adjourned the discussion to wait the result of such negotiations.[7] This was not an abdication of interest by the other parties to the treaty, however, The prevalent view was probably expressed by the representative of France when he stated:

> Mr. Vyshinsky has told us that not three or five but twenty-one States are concerned in the Trieste dispute. But I am sure that if, at the conclusion of the negotiations and conversations now being held, a final agreement were reached – as we hope it will be – not only among the three great Powers but also between the two parties fundamentally concerned in the dispute, Yugoslavia and Italy, none of the other signatories to the Treaty of Peace would assume the responsibility of blocking the agreement, the conclusion of which would provide definite assurance that all threats to international peace and security in the area of the territory of Trieste would be averted.[8]

The prediction of the French delegate proved to be correct

---

[1] 29 DEP'T STATE BULL. 529 (1953).
[2] DOCUMENTS ON INTERNATIONAL AFFAIRS (1953) 291–295, 297–298.
[3] *Id.* at 300.
[4] *Id.* at 295.
[5] U.N. Doc. No. S/3105 (1953).
[6] U.N. SECURITY COUNCIL OFF. REC., 8th year, 628th meeting, 14, 23 (1953).
[7] *Id.*, 647th meeting, 10 (1953).
[8] *Id.*, 628th meeting, 18 (1953).

(although France herself was left out of the negotiations). On October 5, 1954, Italy, Yugoslavia, the United States and the United Kingdom signed a Memorandum of Understanding, which divided the Free Territory between Italy and Yugoslavia.[1] It recited the fact that it had proved impossible to put into effect the relevant provisions of the peace treaty, but it bound Italy to maintain the Free Port at Trieste in accordance with Treaty Annex VIII. A statement by Secretary of State Dulles explained that the participation of the United States and the United Kingdom had been only to extend "their good offices."[2] The Soviet Government accepted the agreement in a letter stating:

> ... The agreement concerning the Free Territory of Trieste was reached as a result of an understanding between Yugoslavia and Italy, as the countries immediately interested, and is acceptable to those countries. In view of this circumstance, and also of the fact that the above-mentioned agreement between Yugoslavia and Italy will promote the establishment of normal relations between them and thus contribute towards a relaxation of tension in that part of Europe, the Soviet Government takes note of the above-mentioned agreement.[3]

No one objected to this settlement of the problem by agreement of the two states directly concerned. In contrast to the procedure followed in regard to the military clauses of the Italian Peace Treaty, the approval of other signatories of the treaty was not requested. The agreement was communicated to the Security Council for information only[4] and it would have been put in effect even if Soviet consent had not been given.

This solution accords with the principle of separability. The fact that no objections were raised showed general recognition that the interested states were Italy and Yugoslavia.[5] The result can also be justified on another legal basis. The coming into force of the permanent statute of the territory was dependent on a future agreement by the members of the Security Council. Until that time the treaty provided for a provisional

---

[1] 31 DEP'T STATE BULL, 556 (1954).
[2] *Ibid.*
[3] U.N. Doc. No. S/3305 (1955).
[4] U.N. Docs. Nos. S/3301, S/3351 (1955).
[5] It might have been different if the Free Territory had ever been a going concern. Other states, particularly Austria, might eventually have acquired customary rights through reliance on the international regime. *Cf.* ch. VII *infra*.

regime only. Its provisional character was another justification for its termination by the occupying powers. They were under no duty to maintain it in force indefinitely when the expected agreement in the Security Council proved unattainable.[1]

5. AGREEMENTS CONCERNING GERMANY

The initial post-war agreements between the principal allies concerning settlement of the problem of Germany were also of a temporary or provisional character, looking to subsequent elaboration of permanent peace settlements. The Potsdam Agreement of August 2, 1945, provided that a permanent German settlement should be drawn up by the Council of Foreign Ministers [2] (where the rule of conference unanimity prevailed), and the agreement of June 5, 1945, establishing a quadripartite Control Council for Germany provided:

> 2. The Control Council, whose decisions shall be unanimous, ... will reach agreed decisions on the chief questions affecting Germany as a whole.[3]

These were nothing more than agreements to agree. None of the parties had the intention of denying to themselves the right to take further action in the eventuality (which for political reasons they did not want to mention at the time) that they would be unable to reach the necessary further agreements. Because of the temporary nature of these agreements, no questions of treaty revision were involved when, after the breakdown of attempts to reach agreement in the Control Council and Council of Foreign Ministers, the three western powers concluded separate agreements concerning the parts of Germany under their control.

6. SUMMARY

Several factors tend to distinguish peace settlements from other multipartite treaties in the matter of revision. One of these is the fact that political realities play a major role. Where a

---

[1] *Cf.* Fitzmaurice, *The Juridical Clauses of the Peace Treaties*, 73 REC. DES COURS 259 at 280–281 (1948).
[2] S. DOC. NO. 123, 81st Cong., 1st Sess. 34 (1949).
[3] CMD. NO. 6648 (1945).

disadvantageous settlement has been imposed by force on a defeated state the latter is likely to find some legal pretext for ending the restrictions as soon as it can get the consent of enough states to make it politically possible to do so.

A second factor is the principle that the revision of boundaries, unless protected by some explicit international guarantee, requires only the consent of the state in possession. Treaty provisions which establish new boundaries are "executed" or "transitory." After the transfers are made they have no continuing effect.

A third factor is the principle of separability. Where a peace treaty includes diverse provisions on unrelated matters, of concern to varying numbers of the parties, it is the practice to treat the various sections of the treaty as separable and to revise them by negotiations among the parties directly interested in the subject matter, without the necessary participation of all signatories of the peace treaty. All of the great powers, as well as most of the smaller states, have relied on this principle at one time or another. Germany, Austria and Prussia did so concerning Poland and Cracow, and Great Britain and France in regard to the Aaland Islands. Many parts of the Treaty of Versailles were revised separately, and all of the western powers assumed the separability of the clauses on Trieste. The effect of this characteristic of multipartite peace settlements is to free the parties from prior assumptions concerning the rule of unanimous consent and to open the way to revision frankly based on the agreement of the most interested states – i.e., those whose co-operation will be necessary to make the new arrangements effective.

If a treaty imposes obligations or restrictions on one party (in the case of a peace treaty, the defeated state) in favor of each of the other parties, the latter are entitled to renounce their rights unilaterally, or to consent so far as they are concerned to the termination of the restrictions. Such action would be a legal wrong only if there was an additional obligation running between the group of favored states, to maintain the restrictions. It is a matter of interpretation of the treaty whether it is intended to create such an additional obligation. In the revision of the military clauses of the Treaty of Peace with Italy of 1947, political considerations no doubt dictated the result. However, the western

allies thought that they saw a legal way to release Italy by the method of individual renunciation. This left upon Italy the onus of justifying the termination of the restrictions as against non-consenting powers on grounds of changed circumstances, prior violation, or self-defense.

It is important to note that Italy did not contend that the fact that a substantial majority of the parties were willing to end the restrictions was enough to terminate the rights of the non-consenting states. She relied instead on the other grounds mentioned above.

Revision is a legal problem only with respect to treaty provisions intended to be permanent. Sections of a peace settlement which are of a provisional nature, intended to remain in force only pending elaboration of a permanent agreement, are terminable if the permanent agreement does not follow within the time specified or within a reasonable period. In the elaboration of new arrangements the unanimity principle is not involved, except as a question of conference procudure.

It has sometimes been suggested that the great peace settlements have a law-creating effect beyond the immediate parties.[1] This idea is reminiscent of the nineteenth century concept that the concert of the great powers held a mandate to make decisions which would be legally binding upon the smaller states.[2] It is not borne out by the history of the settlement of 1919. There was no disregard of Dutch rights in the termination of Belgium's neutralized status, nor any intended disregard of Swiss rights in the provisions concerning the neutral zone of Savoy and the Free Zones. The decision of the World Court in the *Free Zones* case supports the proposition that not even a general peace treaty of the authority of the Treaty of Versailles could abolish substantive treaty rights of a non-participating state without that state's consent.[3] A war may produce such a change of circumstances as to make the termination of a previous treaty proper, but this is another matter.

---

[1] McNair, *So-called State Servitudes*, 6 B.Y.I.L. 111 at 122–123, 126 (1925); McNair, *The Functions and Differing Legal Character of Treaties*, 11 B.Y.I.L. 100 at 112 (1930).

[2] See Lande, *Revindication of the Principle of Legal Equality of States, 1871–1914*, 62 POL. SCI. Q. 258, 398 (1947).

[3] Further material on this point is considered at pp. 153, 189–190, *infra*.

PART II

SPECIFIC TERRITORIAL REGIMES

CHAPTER IV

THE REGIMES OF INTERNATIONAL RIVERS THE RHINE AND THE DANUBE

1. THE PERIOD 1815 TO 1918 [1]

a) The Central Commission of the Rhine

The Treaty of Paris of May 30, 1814, between the four Allies and France provided that navigation on the Rhine should be "free," although subject to regular tolls, and that the coming Congress to be held at Vienna should establish principles to regulate such tolls and should consider the application of similar principles to other international rivers.[2] When the Congress assembled it entrusted these tasks to its Commission on Rivers, which was composed of the representatives of France, Prussia, England and Austria. Russia, alone of the great powers, had chosen not to take part in this commission, suggesting that it be limited to the four powers named, as those "more directly interested." [3]

This commission drafted general principles for international rivers – those separating or traversing more than one state, which became Articles 108 to 116 of the General Act of the Congress of Vienna.[4] The principles were not automatically applicable, but were to be applied in each case by a special agreement of the riparian states. They were: freedom of navigation for all "in respect to commerce," [5] limited and uniform tolls, and regulation of navigation by common action of the riparian states. Article 116 of the General Act specified that unanimity of the riparian states should be required for future revisions of such regulations.[6]

The commission, though it included two non-riparian states, also drew up a set of articles specifically concerning the Rhine. When it came to this work it invited Holland, Nassau, Hesse-

---

[1] On this period generally see CHAMBERLAIN, THE REGIME OF THE INTERNATIONAL RIVERS: DANUBE AND RHINE (1923).
[2] 1 B.F.S.P. (pt. 1) 151.
[3] 2 CHODZKO, LE CONGRÈS DE VIENNE 527 (1864).
[4] 2 B.F.S.P. 7.
[5] This ambiguous phrase reflected failure to agree on the exclusion of limitations in favor of the boats of riparian states.
[6] "Once the regulations have been drawn up, they shall not be changed except with the consent of all the Riparian States."

Darmstadt, Baden and Bavaria, as the other Rhine riparians, to participate.[1] All of these, as well as England, Austria, France and Prussia, signed the Rhine articles, which were included in Annex 16 to the General Act.[2] There was to be a single system for the collection of river tolls, to be controlled by a Central Commission of the Rhine made up of representatives of the riparians. The first task of the Central Commission was to be the drafting of more detailed regulations concerning tolls and river navigation, to be approved by "the Governments of the Rhine." Article 17 provided:

> The Central Commission shall take its decisions by an absolute plurality of votes which shall be given in perfect equality. But ... its decisions shall not be obligatory for the Riparian States until their consent shall have been given by their Commissioners.

These articles, as well as Article 16 of the General Act, made it clear that the non-riparian signatories of the Vienna articles should have no voice in future revision. On the basis of Article 17, which was repeated in the navigation acts of 1831 and 1868 the Central Commission followed a system of unanimity in its deliberations on all important matters.[3]

Conflicts of interest between the Netherlands and Prussia, the principal upstream riparian, delayed for some time agreement on the more detailed regulations. The Netherlands was reluctant to allow the tidewater streams within her territory (the Leck and the Waal) to be considered part of the conventional Rhine, and Prussia countered by maintaining the practice of forced transfer of cargo at Cologne which was legal under a Napoleonic regulation of 1804, continued in effect by the Vienna Articles pending entry in force of the new detailed regulations. England, as a non-riparian, had no voice in the Commission's deliberations, but she supported Prussia diplomatically.[4] In 1831, however, the riparians signed a new navigation convention.[5] Its preamble recited their failure to agree as to what waters within the Netherlands were intended to be regulated by the Vienna articles. It outlined the positions taken in this dispute as follows:

[1] Switzerland apparently did not ask to be included.
[2] 2 B.F.S.P. 163.
[3] VAN EYSINGA, LA COMMISSION CENTRALE POUR LA NAVIGATION DU RHIN 113 (1935).
[4] CHAMBERLAIN, *op. cit. supra* at 193–194.
[5] 18 B.F.S.P. 1076.

[a] *Position of the Netherlands*]
that its rights of sovereignty extended without any restriction whatever over the sea which bathes its states, even where it mingles with the waters of the Rhine, and that, according to the conferences preliminary to the Act of the Congress of Vienna, only the Leck should be regarded as the continuation of that river in the Netherlands.

[b] *Position of all the other riparian states*]
that the Act of the Congress of Vienna had placed restrictions on the exercise of these rights, insofar as they might apply to ships passing from the Rhine to the high seas, and vice-versa, and that, under the denomination of the Rhine, the said Act had meant all the course, all the branches and all the mouths of that river in the Netherlands, without any distinction.[1]

Although all of the other riparian states were ranged against the Netherlands on this issue, the preamble to the convention of 1831 stated that the conferees had thought it best to leave these disagreements aside, with each party reserving its own interpretation in respect to them, and to proceed to establish regulations for the navigation of the Rhine itself. The Netherlands, however, stated its consent that both the Leck and the Waal should be considered as parts of the Rhine (Article 2), thus narrowing the dispute to the question of access to the sea. It did not consent to any jurisdiction of the Rhine Commission below Krimpen on the Leck or Gorkum (Gorinchem) on the Waal, these limits excluding the ports of Rotterdam and Dordrecht, respectively.[2] In Article 19 the requirement of riparian unanimity for revision was explicitly stated: "The present Regulation shall have the force of a Convention and shall not be altered except by a common accord." There was no provision for denunciation.

Although the Convention of 1831 declared navigation to be "entirely free ... in respect to commerce," as had the Vienna articles, it was made clear that the river was only open to boatmen with permits from one of the Rhine governments.[3] The position taken by the English representative at Vienna, in favor of opening navigation to ships of all nations, had been supported only by Baden, the furthest upstream riparian.[4] Control thus remained firmly in the hands of the riparian states.

---

[1] *Ibid.* (Translated.)
[2] VAN EYSINGA, *op. cit. supra* at 100–101.
[3] CHAMBERLAIN, *op. cit. supra* at 199.
[4] *Id.* at 179.

In 1868 the 1831 convention was replaced by the new Convention of Mannheim.[1] This convention was signed by all of the parties to the act of 1831 excepting Nassau, which had by this time been annexed by Prussia. The dispute between the Netherlands and the other riparians as to whether the jurisdiction of the Commission legally extended below Gorkum and Krimpen continued unresolved, but the Netherlands made good its position in fact. Van Eysinga states that in 1893 the end of the Waal and the Leck, at Gorkum and Krimpen respectively, were marked by the Commission by erecting beacons at those points.[2]

After the Franco-Prussian War France, no longer a riparian, lost her representation on the Rhine Commission and her right to participate in revisions of the Mannheim Convention.[3] When various articles of the Mannheim Convention were revised thereafter, it was done without French participation.[4] A new representative of Alsace-Lorraine was appointed by the German Emperor. Other small riparians were now absorbed in the German Empire, but as the new German constitution left the control of river navigation to its states they maintained their representation on the Rhine Commission. The Netherlands, protected by the requirement of unanimity for binding decisions of the Commission, did not object to this alteration of its character. In fact the Commission took no decisions of substance without unanimity.[5] On one occasion a German attempt to modify the convention to permit the reintroduction of river tolls failed because the Netherlands refused to give its consent.[6]

---

[1] 59 B.F.S.P. 470. The river tolls were now abolished.

[2] VAN EYSINGA, *op. cit. supra* at 101. These were points at which in previous times the Rhine actually entered the sea, before land reclamations extended the waterway.

[3] She was again treated as a party, however, in 1919. *Infra*, p. 129.

[4] 2 RHEINURKUNDEN 379, 437 (1918). The war with Prussia did not, *per se*, operate to terminate the rights of France, for Art. 18 of the Additional Convention of December 11, 1871, restored to force the previous treaties between France and the German States, and Art. 12 of the Peace Treaty expressly revived "Treaties of Navigation." 62 B.F.S.P. 81, 98. The Convention of Mannheim nowhere explicitly stated that it could be revised without the consent of all of its signatories if some of them ceased to be riparians, but such a condition seemed to be implicit. Its terms were applicable only to "boats belonging to the navigation of the Rhine," defined in Art. 2 as "boats having the right to fly the flag of one of the riparian States."

[5] Memorandum submitted by the Netherlands to the Peace Conference of 1919. 12 MILLER DIARY 6, 18.

[6] VAN EYSINGA, *op. cit. supra* at 117.

b) *The European Commission of the Danube*

It was forty years before circumstances seemed to permit the application to the Danube of the principles of the Act of Vienna. Following the Crimean War, however, the great powers and Turkey agreed by the Treaty of Paris that the Vienna principles should in future be applied.[1] They entrusted the urgent task of clearing a navigable channel at the river's mouth to a "European Commission," composed of one delegate of each signatory power. Only two of these powers (Austria and Turkey) were riparians.[2] The European Commission was expected to be a temporary body, and it was planned that permanent responsibility for the regulation of river navigation would be assumed by a "River Commission," composed of representatives of the riparian states. The latter were given two years in which to elaborate rules of navigation. Thereafter, the Treaty of Paris provided, the signatory powers would meet in a conference and pronounce the dissolution of the European Commission, and the River Commission would thenceforth enjoy the powers that the European Commission had possessed and see to the maintenance of the entrance channel.

In the immediate sequel to the Treaty of Paris, the River Commission, on which were represented Austria, Turkey, Bavaria and Wurtemberg, met and drafted a Navigation Act which was signed at Vienna on November, 7, 1857.[3] It provided for free navigation for sea-going ships, but reserved other river navigation for ships of the riparian states. In 1858 this Navigation Act was submitted for approval to a conference of the signatories of the Treaty of Paris. The British representative opposed it, on the ground that the principle of freedom of navigation required that the river be open to the ships of all nations, and maintained

---

[1] 48 B.F.S.P. 8. Articles 15 to 19 concern the Danube. Improvement of navigation at the Danube entrance had been an object of particular importance to Great Britain, whose imports of Danube grain increased rapidly after the repeal of the corn laws in 1846. The obstacles to shipping in the form of shoaling of the bar at the river mouth, wrecks, inadequate pilots and absence of aids to navigation are described in diplomatic correspondence presented to Parliament in 1853. CMD. NO. 1669 (1853).

[2] Under the Treaty of Paris Russia gave up part of Bessarabia and was thus no longer a riparian. This was the subject of Article 20 which provided that in exchange for the restoration of territories occupied by the Allies in the Crimea, "et pour mieux assurer la liberté de la navigation du Danube," Russia consented to a "rectification" of her frontier in Bessarabia.

[3] 16 NOUV. REC. GÉN. (pt. 2) 75.

that the work of the River Commission could not be put into effect until it had received the approval of all of the signatories of the Treaty of Paris.[1] In contrast to the situation respecting the Rhine, in this instance the other non-riparian powers all backed the British objection, and they outnumbered the riparians by five to two, so that the River Commission was unable to assume jurisdiction at the river mouth. Austria was not opposed to "European" control at the river mouth,[2] but she refused to admit that the lack of agreement on the subject among the signatories of the Treaty of Paris could prevent the riparians from putting their navigation act into effect on the upper river.[3] The Turkish Government, while maintaining also that it was entitled to place the act in execution by virtue of sovereign right, agreed to refrain from doing so pending a solution of the question by the parties to the Treaty of Paris.[4] The Vienna Navigation Act thus went into effect above the "Iron Gates," a natural obstacle to navigation at the Austrian frontier, and it remained the regime of the upper river until 1918, when by the Treaty of Bucharest Germany and Austria forced Rumania to accept its application to the Rumanian river as well.

The failure to agree on the application of the River Commission's regulations to the river mouth still left the powers with the need to keep the entrance in navigable condition and to provide for policing the maritime portion of the river. They were unwilling to entrust these tasks to Turkey, and they therefore kept the European Commission in existence. The first of a series of prolongations of its term was agreed upon at a conference held in 1858.[5] Each was the subject of unanimous agreement by the parties to the Treaty of Paris.

It it important to recognize the character of this regime. The European Commission, which thus took over a function for which it was not at first intended, was not a riparian body but an organ of the Concert of Europe, of which the Treaty of Paris was an instrument. Turkey, the territorial sovereign on that

---

[1] 48 B.F.S.P. 123–131.
[2] See the instructions of the Austrian Emperor to his plenipotentiaries at the Congress of Paris, HAJNAL, THE DANUBE 92 (1920).
[3] 48 B.F.S.P. 131.
[4] *Ibid.*
[5] *Id.* at 132.

part of the river, had been taken under the collective protection of the great powers by the terms of that treaty.[1] The regime of the maritime Danube thus became part of the body of "European" matters for which the great powers considered themselves jointly responsible. This situation prevailed until 1914. Because of it one cannot be sure that insistence on obtaining the consent of all signatories of the Treaty of Paris for any changes in the jurisdiction of the European Commission was due to formal requirements of treaty revision. It is probable that the need to maintain the unity of the Concert of the great powers was a more important consideration in the minds of the statesmen concerned.[2]

The European Commission now proceeded to draw up rules for the navigation and policing of the river mouth. A Public Act on this subject was adopted unanimously at Galatz on November 2, 1865, and approved by a conference of the powers held at Paris in the following year.[3]

Rules of procedure for the European Commission which were drawn up in 1879 show that it took its decisions on administrative questions by majority vote, but that on matters of principle (questions de fond) unanimity was necessary.[4]

Great Britain continued her efforts to extend the right of free navigation, and the authority of the European Commission. At the Paris Conference of 1866 she proposed that the competence of the Commission be extended upstream to Braila, the head of navigation for sea-going ships.[5] The representatives of Italy, France, Austria and Prussia agreed to the proposal.[6] However, under the then-accepted conference rule of unanimity, the matter was dropped when it encountered opposition by Turkey.[7] The same proposition was raised again by Great Britain in 1871.[8] Turkey again declined, and the powers deferred to her wishes,

---

[1] Articles 7 and 8 of the Treaty of Paris. 46 *id.* 12.
[2] *Cf.* TOBIN, THE TERMINATION OF MULTIPARTITE TREATIES 218–221 (1933). *Cf.* pp. 87–92, *Supra.*
[3] 55 B.F.S.P. 93; 56 *id.* 624.
[4] STURDZA, RECUEIL DE DOCUMENTS RELATIFS À LA LIBERTÉ DE NAVIGATION DU DANUBE 130 (1904).
[5] 57 B.F.S.P. 552–553.
[6] *Id.* at 578–579, 595.
[7] *Id.* at 595–596.
[8] 61 *id.* 1214.

the German representative observing that Turkish interests were more directly affected than those of any other power.[1]

By the Treaty of Berlin of 1878 the powers recognized the independence of Rumania, which thus replaced Turkey as the principal riparian of the lower river. Turkey no longer objecting, and Rumania not being represented, Great Britain now succeeded in getting agreement of the powers to extend the jurisdiction of the European Commission upstream as far as Galatz, in Rumanian territory, to be exercised "in complete independence of the territorial authority." [2] Rumania was given a seat on the European Commission.[3] The treaty also recognized the independence of Serbia, while Bulgaria became an autonomous and tributary principality under the suzerainty of Turkey (Article 34 and Article 1, respectively). Russia returned to the river mouth as riparian of the northernmost of the three river mouths, the Kilia arm. Neither Rumania nor Serbia were invited to sign the Treaty of Berlin, but by the treaty their independence was established, and neither state contested its validity. The European Commission, including its Rumanian member, agreed in 1881 to amend its Public Act of 1865 so as to apply its regulations as far as Galatz.[4] The purpose of this Additional Act, as stated in its preamble, was "to place the Public Act of 2 November 1865 in harmony with the stipulations of the Treaty of Berlin."

The Treaty of Berlin had directed the European Commission, together with representatives of Serbia and Bulgaria, to draft regulations for the section of the river from Galatz to the Iron Gates. This effort soon bogged down in the face of Rumania's refusal to agree to participation in the administration of that part of the river by the European Commission. A draft was finally agreed to at Galatz by all except Rumania. It provided for an administration by a Commission to be composed of representatives of Austria, Rumania, Serbia, Bulgaria and one other member (in rotation) of the European Commission. In the face of this

---

[1] *Id.* at 1223. These developments afford an interesting comparison with the Powers' later disregard of Rumanian wishes in the same matter, after Rumania had replaced Turkey as the riparian power. *Infra*, pp. 125–126.

[2] 69 *id.* 749 (Arts. 43, 53).

[3] *Id.*, Art. 53.

[4] Additional Act of May 28, 1881, 72 B.F.S.P. 7.

holdout by Rumania the British government proposed a conference of the powers to meet at London to consider (1) prolongation of the term of the European Commission, (2) extension of its powers to Braila and (3) the draft regulations.[1] As Judge Negulesco later observed, this was an attempt to make good the lack of unanimity on the European Commission by the unanimity of the powers assembled in London.[2]

In advance of the conference the great powers tried to induce Rumania not to resist the proposals on which all the great powers had agreed.[3] These efforts failed. When the conference opened Great Britain nevertheless proposed the admission of Rumania, but this was opposed by the representative of Germany on the ground that a great-power conference of this nature would be governed by the unanimity principle. Hence to admit Rumania would be to give her a veto power. His view was recorded as follows:

Count Munster feels he must oppose the admission of Rumania on the same footing as the Great Powers. The plenipotentiary of Germany readily admits the great interest which Rumania possesses in the happy solution of the questions pending before the Conference. Nevertheless, the German Government would favor conserving the European character of the Conference by abstaining from placing Rumania on an equality with the Great Powers. If while, maintaining the principle of unanimity in the Conference, one gave a voice to Rumania, one would create for her a position which would be not at all desirable – that of being able, at her wish, to impose her veto. Rumania therefore ought to be admitted only as a guest and not as mistress of the house.[4]

This point of view was accepted, and Rumania and Serbia were invited only to send observers.[5] Serbia accepted representation on this unequal basis, but Rumania declined.

Without Rumania, the conference was able to act unanimously. It produced the Treaty of London of 1883, signed by the parties to the treaties of Paris and Berlin (the six great powers and Turkey).[6] It purported to extend the jurisdiction of the European Commission from Galatz to Braila and it "adopted" and "declared applicable" the regulations for the middle river which

[1] CMD. NO. 3525 (1883).
[2] Case concerning Jurisdiction of the European Commission of the Danube, P.C.I.J Ser. B, No. 14 at 92 (1927).
[3] CMD. NO. 3525 at 47 (1883).
[4] Protocol of February 10, 1883, STURDZA, RECUEIL DE DOCUMENTS 421. (Translated.)
[5] *Id.* at 421–422.
[6] 74 B.F.S.P. 20.

Rumania had refused to sign.[1] It also prolonged for a period of twenty-one years the powers of the European Commission, with the proviso that at the expiration of that period its term should be considered to be renewed in successive three-year periods unless one of the contracting parties should notify the others, one year before the expiration of one such period, of its intention to propose modifications of the constitution or powers of the Commission. It also provided that the Commission should cease to exercise jurisdiction over one of the Danube mouths, the Kilia arm, which ran through Russian territory.

In this instance the great powers were unable to make all of their dispositions effective. Rumania immediately protested.[2] Expressly accepting the provision extending the life of the European Commission, she stated that she would regard as not binding the other decisions taken without her participation. She affirmed, as an incontestable principle of international law, "that no State is bound to execute on its territory European decisions which it has not discussed and to which it has not previously consented."[3] In addition Rumania noted that in 1866 and 1871 the powers had not thought they had the right to extend the jurisdiction of the European Commission from Galatz to Braila over the opposition of Turkey. How then could they now extend it to a new part of Rumanian territory by a decision taken without Rumanian participation?[4]

In addition to her rights as a riparian, Rumania claimed that she was entitled to participate by virtue of her position as a member of the European Commission and as a signatory of the 1881 Additional Act of the Commission. The Rumanian note added that the Act of 1881 was a convention validly concluded and ratified, which could not be modified unilaterally. Indeed now-accepted principles of state succession would support Rumania's claim that she should be regarded as a party to the

---

[1] In the view of one commentator, this provision was only the expression of a recommendation ("un voeu"), in the expectation that Rumania would ultimately assent. SAINT CLAIR, LE DANUBE 160–161 (1899).

[2] STURDZA, RECUEIL DES DOCUMENTS 416-a.

[3] *Id*. at 416-e. (Translated.)

[4] The action of the London Conference also seemed at variance with the principles declared by the Congress of Vienna: regulation of navigation by common action of the riparian states, and the principle that "once the regulations have been drawn up, they shall not be changed except with the consent of all the Riparian States." *Supra*, p. 117.

treaty provisions of a localized character entered into by her predecessor, Turkey, with specific application to her territory.[1] The powers in admitting Rumania to a seat on the European Commission and allowing her to sign the act of 1881 would seem to have conceded this point.

King Carol I of Rumania said of the Treaty of London that it was "un traité appelé à demeurer lettre morte." [2] The regulations for the middle river were never placed in effect. The European Commission did in fact extend its functions to the section between Galatz and Braila, but Rumania never ceased to contest the legality of such action. As will be seen, in the changed atmosphere after the First World War she finally succeeded in ending this exercise of international jurisdiction.

The Treaty of London was the last significant treaty concerning the Danube before the First World War.[3] By the Treaty of Bucharest, which the Central Powers imposed on Rumania on May 7, 1918, Articles 24 to 26 of which concerned the Danube,[4] Rumania agreed to conclude with Germany, Austria-Hungary, Bulgaria and Turkey a new navigation act for the entire navigable river. The European Commission was henceforth to be composed only of representatives of states situated on the Danube or on the European shores of the Black Sea.[5] Presumably if the war had been won by the Central Powers, the Allies would have been required to accept a new regime of this character.

---

[1] Jenks, *State Succession in Respect of Law-making Treaties*, 29 B.Y.I.L. 105 at 112–116, 120 (1952). Bismarck on one occasion stated that he "regarded it as in accordance with the law of nations that Bulgaria should remain under the authority of the treaties by which she was bound under the Government of the Porte." *Id.* at 129.

[2] Sofronie, *Le Statut International du Danube Maritime et la Position de la Roumanie* 48 REVUE GÉNÉRALE DE DROIT INTERNATIONAL PUBLIC 65 (1941–1945).

[3] Two Sanitary Conventions, prescribing measures to be taken at Sulina in time of cholera epidemics were concluded in 1893 and 1897. Rumania was not a signatory of the first convention (19 HERTSLET, COMMERCIAL TREATIES 240), but did sign the second, which contained almost identical requirements. STURDZA, RECUEIL DE DOCUMENTS 812.

[4] 10 NOUV. REC. GÉN. (3 sér.) 856. In Article 259 (6) of the Treaty of Versailles, Germany renounced the benefits of the Treaty of Bucharest, and in Article 292 she also recognized its abrogation. There were similar provisions in the Peace Treaties with Austria, Hungary and Bulgaria. Turkish acceptance of similar provisions was envisaged in Articles 259 and 277 of the (unratified) Treaty of Sèvres. 113 B.F.S.P. 652.

[5] Russia is not mentioned in the Treaty, but this provision apparently envisaged the future participation of Russia or the Ukraine.

2. REVISIONS AFTER WORLD WAR I

a) *The Rhine*

At the end of the First World War France and her allies sought to change the character of the Central Commission of the Rhine, converting it from a riparian to an international body, and to change its procedure so that decisions would be taken by majority vote instead of by unanimity. England was to secure her aim of making the Rhine a truly international river, France to secure representation equal to that of Germany, and Belgium to secure for the first time recognition of her status as a Rhine power.[1] It was obvious that these changes would require the consent of the Netherlands.

Article 354 of the Treaty of Versailles stated:

> As from the coming into force of the present Treaty, the Convention of Mannheim of October 17, 1868 ... shall continue to govern navigation on the Rhine, subject to the conditions hereinafter laid down.
>
> * * *
>
> Within a maximum period of six months from the coming into force of the present Treaty, the Central Commission referred to in Article 355 shall meet to draw up a project of revision of the Convention of Mannheim. ...
>
> Further, the modifications set out in the following Articles shall immediately be made in the Convention of Mannheim.
>
> The Allied and Associated Powers reserve to themselves the right to arrive at an understanding in this connection with Holland, and Germany hereby agrees to accede if required to any such understanding.

The principal modifications were in Articles 355 and 356. Exclusive riparian control was to be abandoned and the river was to be opened unreservedly to vessels and crews of nonriparians. Switzerland, as well as Belgium, was to be admitted to the Rhine Commission. France was to have an especially privileged position, and the headquarters of the Central Commission was to be transferred from Mannheim to the French town of Strasbourg. The text of these articles was as follows:

---

[1] Belgium's waterways all connected with the Rhine and her ports handled an important share of Rhine traffic. Her rights had hitherto depended on separate treaties with the riparian states.

Article 355

The Central Commission provided for in the Convention of Mannheim shall consist of nineteen members, viz:

- 2 representatives of the Netherlands;
- 2 representatives of Switzerland;
- 4 representatives of German riparian States;
- 4 representatives of France, which in addition shall appoint the President of the Commission;
- 2 representatives of Great Britain;
- 2 representatives of Italy;
- 2 representatives of Belgium.

Whatever be the number of members present, each Delegation shall have the right to record a number of votes equal to the number of representatives allotted to it.

If certain of these representatives cannot be appointed at the time of the coming into force of the present Treaty, the decisions of the Commission shall nevertheless be valid.

Article 356

Vessels of all nations, and their cargoes, shall have the same rights and privileges as those which are granted to vessels belonging to the Rhine navigation, and to their cargoes.

None of the provisions contained in Articles 15 to 20 and 26 of the above-mentioned Convention of Mannheim ... shall impede the free navigation of vessels and crews of all nations. ...

It seems clear that France was regarded as a state bound by the obligations of the Mannheim Convention at the time the Versailles Treaty was drawn up. The first French draft of the Rhine clauses had this preamble:

> France having, as a consequence of her sovereignty being substituted for that of Germany over the Reichsland [Alsace-Lorraine], recovered all the rights granted to her by the Convention for the navigation on the Rhine ...[1]

With the rights must have gone the duties as well.

Despite the categorical language of the Treaty clauses the French representative did acknowledge from the first that negotiations with the Netherlands would be necessary.[2] However, the Netherlands was not allowed to participate in the drafting of the Rhine clauses. It was only on March 16, 1919. after this work had been completed by the Waterways Commission of the Peace

---

[1] 11 MILLER DIARY 285.
[2] *Id.* at 281.

Conference, that the Netherlands Delegation was allowed to state its case.[1]

The Netherlands submitted a memorandum defending the Convention of Mannheim.[2] It noted that under the previously existing system each riparian state had "a right to one vote, decisions having to be unanimous, which is not inconvenient in practice." It argued that a commission of the type of the European Danube Commission, including delegates of nonriparian states, "would be inadvisable in the Dutch delta." It cautioned the Conference to bear in mind "that the powers of the present Central Commission ... do not extend below Gorkum and/or Krimpen." These arguments produced no changes in the treaty, except that, instead of stating that the Netherlands was "invited to adhere," the noncomital reference to a possible future understanding with the Netherlands was substituted.[3]

When the text of the Rhine articles became known, the Netherlands Government protested against the discrimination between states in the matter of votes in the Central Commission. It noted the intention expressed in Article 354 "to arrive at an understanding with the Netherlands" and warned that "the Act of 1868 ... cannot be denounced and cannot be modified without the co-operation of the Netherlands." [4]

[1] 12 id. 6, 18.
[2] Id. at 18–21.
[3] See Article 354, quoted at p. 128, supra.
[4] Letter to the Secretary General of the Peace Conference, June 23, 1919. 12 MILLER DIARY 251–253. Article 354 of the Versailles Treaty also contained the provision that a contemplated General Convention on waterways having an international character should apply also to the Rhine, and should prevail, in case of conflict, over the provisions of the Mannheim Convention. This provision caused the Netherlands to send another note to the Peace Conference, in which it claimed the right to participate in the preparation of the General Convention. 8 FOREIGN REL. U.S., THE PARIS PEACE CONFERENCE 1919, 492. The General Convention was ultimately drawn up at the Conference on Freedom of Communications and Transit which was held at Barcelona in 1921. 1 HUDSON, INTERNATIONAL LEGISLATION 645. It entered into force October 31, 1922. It was signed and ratified by Great Britain, France and Italy, among others. Germany had agreed in advance to accept it. The Netherlands participated in the Conference, but its representative did not sign the convention because of an unwillingness to accept a definition of "waterways of international concern" which would have extended international control to the waters of the Rhine delta below Gorkum and Krimpen. Switzerland also abstained from signing the Barcelona Convention, and Belgium did not ratify. By Article 13 of the Barcelona Convention the contracting states undertook "not to apply among themselves" any provisions of previous river treaties which might conflict with the rules of the General Convention, but such previous treaties were not to be considered as abrogated. The Barcelona Statute therefore operated only as an *inter se* agreement and did not affect the rights possessed by the Netherlands under the Mannheim Convention. In the

The Treaty of Versailles was signed on June 28, 1919. It came into force, for those parties ratifying, on January 10, 1920. After it had been signed, the Waterways Commission of the Peace Conference, on August 20, 1919, directed the attention of the Supreme Council of the Allies to the necessity of opening negotiations with the Dutch Government.[1] The Supreme Council decided, on October 2, 1919, to invite the Netherlands to negotiate with the other powers represented on the Central Commission,[2] but these negotiations did not begin until after the peace treaty had come into force. The Netherlands did not adhere to the Versailles modifications of the Mannheim Convention until September 8, 1923.[3] By an agreement of January 21, 1921, however, she had agreed to adhere, subject to certain changes, "as soon as possible." [4]

Even before the 1921 agreement the Central Commission, composed as required by the Versailles Treaty but without Netherlands participation, held its first meeting on June 21, 1920, at its new Strasbourg headquarters and commenced its work.[5] The Netherlands gave its consent to the transfer of the Commission's archives from Mannheim to Strasbourg.[6] After the agreement of January 21, 1921, the Netherlands sent delegates to participate on the Commission, without waiting for formal adherence to the Treaty clauses.[7] In 1921 the Netherlands permitted the Commission to undertake a voyage of inspection in Netherlands' waters.[8] In spite of this administrative cooperation, however, the Netherlands did not concede that the Treaty had created any new rights or obligations in Dutch waters, and in the 1921 agreement and an additional protocol of March 29, 1923, the other powers represented on the Commission met the Netherlands'

---

case concerning the Territorial Jurisdiction of the International Commission of the River Oder, P.C.I.J., Ser. A, No. 23 (1929) it was held that it was not the intention of the Treaty of Versailles to apply the General Convention so as to affect the rights of a state which had not ratified it. *A fortiori* it could not affect the rights of the Netherlands, which was not a signatory.

[1] 8 FOREIGN REL. U.S., THE PARIS PEACE CONFERENCE 1919, 493.
[2] *Id.* at 483–485.
[3] 117 B.F.S.P. 540–543.
[4] 20 L.N.T.S. 111.
[5] VAN EYSINGA, *op. cit. supra* at 114.
[6] *Ibid.*
[7] *id.* at 115.
[8] *Id.* at 119.

conditions in this respect.[1] It was provided that the Netherlands should have a third representative on the Commission and that the Commission's jurisdiction should not be extended to any new waterways in Netherlands territory without her consent. In a return to the original provision on this subject drafted at Vienna in 1815, it was agreed that resolutions of the Central Commission, while they might be adopted by majority vote, should not be obligatory for any state which refused to approve them.[2] Although these agreements with the Netherlands constituted a revision of the Versailles Treaty in respect to its Rhine clauses, the Supreme Council did not think it necessary to obtain the agreement of any of the signatories of that treaty other than those represented on the Rhine Commission.

The work of further revising the Mannheim Convention was only begun in 1924. After prolonged negotiations all of the states members of the Central Commission except the Netherlands signed on May 4, 1936, a *modus vivendi* whereby certain parts of a new draft regulation would go into effect on January 1, 1937[3]. France would have abandoned her permanent chairmanship and each government would have had thenceforth only one vote in the Central Commission. It was anticipated that signature by the Netherlands would be obtained by the effective date, but this was not referred to in the agreement.

In fact the Netherlands gave its adherence to this agreement on November 14, 1936. It never went into effect, however, because it was denounced on the same date by Germany, which at the same time denounced all of the river clauses of the Treaty of Versailles.[4] This was only the last step in the sweeping unilateral repudiation by Germany of the terms of the Treaty of Versailles.[5]

[1] 20 L.N.T.S. 111–117.
[2] *Supra*, p. 118.
[3] 36 NOUV. REC. GÉN. (3 sér.) 769. Switzerland was included as a party to this agreement.
[4] DOCUMENTS ON INTERNATIONAL AFFAIRS (1936) 283–285; 36 NOUV. REC. GÉN. (3 sér.) 800. The *modus vivendi* had specified that it might be denounced by any party up to November 15, 1936. France and Belgium also denounced it following the German action. CHIESA, LE RÉGIME INTERNATIONAL DU RHIN ET LA PARTICIPATION DE LA SUISSE 137 (1952).
[5] *Supra*, p. 7, n. 3. Foreign Secretary Eden, speaking in the House of Commons on November 16, 1936, said that protracted negotiations had been in progress with a view to reconciling Germany's desiderata concerning her rivers with the interests of

In 1937 Italy also withdrew her representative from the Rhine Commission.[1] This was regarded as a renunciation of Italy's rights, so that when the functions of the Central Commission were resumed on a provisional basis in 1945 by agreement between the United Kingdom, France, Belgium, the Netherlands and the United States (as a power occupying riparian territory), Italy was not included.[2] Switzerland, which was still not a party to the treaties on the subject, indicated her approval of the 1945 agreement in a letter to the British Foreign Office, and retained her seat on the Commission. Again, no other parties to the treaty of Versailles were asked to consent to this revision of Article 354. In April of 1950 the Central Commission reported that the Federal Republic of Germany had been admitted to a place on the Commission with rights and obligations equal to those of the other governments there represented.[3] Despite the return of Germany, the United States also continued to be represented.[4]

b) *The Danube*

The end of World War I brought still greater political changes to the Danube. Three of the parties to the previous treaties, Austria-Hungary, Germany and Turkey, were defeated, so that it seemed possible to compel their consent to new arrengements, and there was no government of Russia recognized by the victorious powers. There was a whole group of new riparian states. In this situation the victorious powers were able to internationalize the entire river under a regime that included representation of non-riparian states.

Guiding principles of the new regime were set out in the peace treaties.[5] They provided that the nationals, property and flags of all states should be treated with perfect equality. The powers of the European Commission on the maritime section of the river

the other powers concerned, and expressed regret that the German government should "once again have abandoned procedure by negotiation in favour of unilateral action." DOCUMENTS ON INTERNATIONAL AFFAIRS (1936) 285.

[1] [1955] 1 ANNUAIRE FRANÇAIS DE DROIT INTERNATIONAL 508 n. 2.

[2] T.I.A.S. No. 1571. This agreement provided that each government represented in the Commission should have one vote.

[3] 22 LA NAVIGATION DU RHIN 246 (1950).

[4] [1955] 1 ANNUAIRE FRANÇAIS DE DROIT INTERNATIONAL 508.

[5] See Articles 331–332, 346–349 of the Treaty of Versailles. The same provisions appeared in the treaties with Austria, Hungary and Bulgaria.

were left unchanged, but "as a provisional measure" only Great Britain, France, Italy and Rumania were to be represented on that commission. "From the point where the competence of the European Commission ceases" the river was to be administered by a new International Commission, composed of representatives of the riparian states and one representative of each non-riparian state represented on the European Commission. The language concerning the extent of the competence of the European Commission was left intentionally ambiguous because of the unresolved dispute with Rumania over the sector between Galatz and Braila.

The peace treaties provided that a definitive statute should be laid down "by a Conference of the Powers nominated by the Allied and Associated Powers," which was to meet within one year. The defeated riparian states were to be present in a consultative capacity, but they agreed in advance to accept the statute which the conference produced.[1] The Allied and Associated Powers nominated Belgium, France, Great Britain, Greece, Italy, Rumania, the Serb-Croat-Slovene State (Yugoslavia) and Czechoslovakia to draft the definitive statute.[2] The Convention instituting this statute was signed by these states and by Germany, Austria, Bulgaria and Hungary at Paris on July 23, 1921.[3]

At the conference of 1921 there was an interesting discussion of the requirements for future revision of this convention. The original French draft which served as the basis of discussion provided, as to both the European Commission and the International Commission:

> The powers of [each Commission] shall only be modified or come to an end as the result of an international agreement in which all of the States signatory to the present Convention shall have been invited to participate.[4]

This language seemed to mean that a state could not prevent revision by refusing to attend a revision conference. It did not answer the question whether unanimity of the states which did attend the conference would be required.

---

[1] See Articles 348–349 of the Treaty of Versailles.

[2] In addition to the riparian states and the European Commission powers, Greece was included because of the size of her fleet in maritime Danube traffic and Belgium because of her commercial interest in the importation of Danube grain (said to be 34% of all Rumanian exports in 1911).

[3] 26 L.N.T.S. 173.

[4] DANUBE CONFERENCE (1921) 85, 89.

The Rumanian delegate asked amendment of the clause in so far as the European Commission was concerned so as to substitute "States represented on the Commission" for "States signatory to the present Convention." The Greek and Belgian delegations then objected to allowing *modification* of the powers of the European Commission without the accord of all the states which took part in elaborating the Statute. Accordingly the words, "be modified or" were eliminated.[1] The final text of Article 7 stated:

> The powers of the European Commission can only come to an end as the result of an international agreement concluded by all the States represented on the Commission.

Only the Yugoslav and German representatives raised the objection that the European and International Commissions had been provided for in the peace treaties and could be abolished only by agreement of all 44 signatories of those treaties.[2] There was an answer to this insofar as concerned the European Commission, since the peace treaties provided that that commission "reassumed" the powers it possessed before the war, and the prewar treaties permitted termination of the Commission by agreement of the member states. This justification, however, would not extend to termination of the International Commission, a pure creation of the peace conference. The representatives of France, Great Britain, Italy and Rumania were not deterred by the German-Yugoslav argument, but they ultimately accepted the desire of the smaller states to insert a clause permitting general revision of the convention in place of the one dealing with modification or termination of the powers of the International Commission.[3] The strict view of the powers of the 1921 conference which had been taken by Germany and Yugoslavia was also expressed by two of the judges of the Permanent Court of International Justice in the *Case concerning Jurisdiction of the European Commission of the Danube between Galatz and Braila.*[4] Judge Nyholm, in his separate opinion, observed that the 1921 Statute was, in relation to the treaty of Versailles, "as a regulation compared with a law." It might amplify the provisions of the

[1] *Id.* at 135–136, 547–548.
[2] *Id.* at 975–976.
[3] *Id.* at 975–979.
[4] P.C.I.J., Series B, No. 14 (1927), discussed *infra* pp. 140–142.

treaty, but "any decision taken by it in contradiction of the Treaty would be null, and might so be regarded by each of the Powers signatory of the Treaty of Versailles." [1] Judge Negulesco, dissenting, said:

> The Statute of theDanube could not modify the provisions of the Treaty of Versailles; for 26 Powers had taken part in that Treaty, whereas at the Convention on the Danube only twelve Powers were represented. ... [2]

The majority of the Court, however, relied on the fact that all of the parties to the dispute before it were parties to the Statute, and refused to question its validity.

The discussion at the 1921 conference of the form revision should take showed assumption by most of those present that unanimity of some sort would be required. It remained unclear whether this should be unanimity of the parties to the 1921 convention or unanimity of those present at a revision conference.[3] The preponderant view perhaps favored the latter assumption, and the British and Greek delegates stated in particular that the ill-will of one state should not be permitted to prevent revision.[4] For this reason the conference rejected a proposal that a revisory conference should occur only if the members of the European Commission unanimously agreed to it.[5] Only the British delegate suggested that a future conference should be allowed to set its own rules, and that a simple majority might be enough in all cases.[6] This view evoked alarm from the other delegates, particularly Rumania's, who could not admit that the territorial power might be outvoted. The Belgian delegate seemed to express the sense of the conference when he stated,

> that the conditions in which revision would operate should remove the fears which have been expressed. A conference which would meet to undertake revision on the basis of a program outlined in advance must not necessarily succeed in realizing the entire program. If this embraced ten articles, unanimous agreement might be reached on a certain number of them, eight for example, and not on the other two; these last would consequently escape revision.[7]

---

[1] *Id.* at 73.
[2] *Id.* at 129.
[3] DANUBE CONFERENCE (1921) 976, 1070, 1097–1099, 1160–1165.
[4] *Id.* at 1098, 1165.
[5] *Id.* at 1165.
[6] *Id.* at 1163–1164. The delegate was J. G. Baldwin, British representative on the European Commission of the Danube.
[7] *Id.* at 1164. (Translated.)

The British delegate then declared,

> that the opinion which he expressed previously must be considered as a purely personal opinion: he had thought that it was impossible to bind the future Conference in advance. However, since according to the statement of the Plenipotentiary of Belgium there exists a well-established international jurisprudence on this point, he declares that it is not at all in his intention to contradict it.[1]

The French delegate, whose original formula, as has been indicated, was ambiguous on the point, did not participate in this discussion. The final text of the article concerning general revision (Article 42) was as follows:

> At the expiration of five years from the date of its coming into force, the present statute may be revised if two-thirds of the signatory States so request and specify the stipulations which appear to them to require revision. This request shall be addressed to the Government of the French Republic, which will summon, within six months, a Conference in which all the States signatory of the present Convention shall be invited to take part.

The effect of the 1921 regime on the rights of Russia remains to be considered. Russia was no longer a riparian after World War I, but this factor was not determinative. As we have seen, the European Commission was not a riparian body.

The post-war composition of the European Commission was dealt with in the Treaty of Versailles by Article 346. It provided:

> The European Commission of the Danube reassumes the powers it possessed before the war. Nevertheless, as a provisional measure, only representatives of Great Britain, France, Italy and Rumania shall constitute this Commission.

This was the only provision of the treaty which detracted from Russia's pre-war rights. Its wording was chosen by the Commission on the International Regime of Ports, Waterways and Railways of the Peace Conference in preference to a British draft which would have simply excluded the enemy states. The change was suggested by the representative of France, at a meeting on March 25, 1919, in the following terms:

> Mr. Claveille supported the British text subject to an amendment specifying the States which should continue to be represented on the Commission, which was preferable to stating those which should in future be excluded. Russia, for instance, was formerly represented, and it was difficult to say how her case should be dealt with.[2]

[1] *Ibid.* (Translated).
[2] 11 MILLER DIARY 417–418.

The civil war in Russia was then being fought, and its outcome remained in doubt when the treaties were signed. Viewed as a provisional measure, Article 346 was therefore not unreasonable.

However, the terms of the 1921 convention implied a further denial of Russia's rights. Article 4 made it discretionary with the other members of the Commission whether Russia should ever be readmitted, and placed her in the same position as states which had never been parties to the prewar treaties. It stated:

> The European Commission is composed provisionally of representatives of France, Great Britain, Italy and Rumania. . . .
>
> Nevertheless, any European State which, in future, is able to prove its possession of sufficient maritime, commercial and European interests at the mouths of the Danube may, at its request, be accorded representation on the Commission *by a unanimous decision of the Governments already represented*. (Emphasis added.)

The discussions of this provision in the drafting conference did not consider the position of Russia. They were all concerned with the claims of other states represented at the conference that they, too, should be included on the European Commission.[1] The conference ultimately took the view that it had no power to deliberate on the composition of the European Commission as established by Article 346 of the Treaty of Versailles.[2]

In respect to the maritime Danube the 1921 Convention merely confirmed the European Commission in the powers it exercised under the previous treaties, which were expressly maintained in force except as modified in the new act. This fact would seem to preclude explanation of the disregard of Russia's preexisting rights as an application of the principle *rebus sic stantibus*.

The Soviet government did not in fact protest against the substantive provisions of the new regime.[3] However, it soon

---

[1] DANUBE CONFERENCE (1921) 124–132, 519–525.

[2] *Id.* at 536–537. The German representative, however, emphasized that the composition of the European Commission fixed by Article 346 was provisional and said he interpreted this to mean that it was not intended to exclude permanently the states formerly represented. *Id.* at 524–525.

[3] An exposition of Russian views concerning other river provisions of the Treaty of Versailles was given in a note addressed in August, 1922, to the government of Latvia respecting the river Niemen. This note reserved opinion as to whether that river should be administered by an international commission as envisaged in the applicable section (Art. 342) of the Versailles Treaty, and insisted that the question in all its aspects must be decided with the participation of Russia and Byelorussia, in a conference of all riparians, including riparians of tributaries flowing into the Niemen below Grodno, the point from which it was proposed to declare the river

sought the readmission of Russia to the European Commission.[1] A request to this effect made in 1925 was denied, ostensibly on the ground that the amount of Russian shipping on the Danube was insufficient.[2] It was thus apparently treated as a new application under Article 4. The Soviet government again sought admission to the European Commission in 1934, offering at that time to adhere to the 1921 Convention. According to M. Vyshinsky, who mentioned this fact at the 1948 Belgrade Conference, Great Britain "wrote only a formal note and gave no substantial answer," and France made no reply.[3]

Assuming that the lack of a recognized Russian Government was original justification for the enactment of a provisional regime, it is nevertheless hard to reconcile with the traditional principle of unanimity this permanent denial of Russia's pre-war rights. At the Belgrade Conference in 1948 the British spokesman stated that the U.S.S.R. had excluded itself from recognition of rights flowing from the treaties concluded by the Tsarist government.[4] The Soviet government, however, had not conceded this much. Its general attitude in regard to such treaties was stated in 1924, in response to an inquiry from the Director of the International Intermediary Institute, as follows:

A general abrogation of all the treaties concluded by Russia under the former regime and under the Provisional Government never took place. However, it hardly follows that all these treaties are susceptible of being reconfirmed. It will be in place to examine this question from the point of view of the clause *"rebus sic stantibus"* for each State and each treaty separately.[5]

Perhaps the British spokesman meant that Russia could not pick and choose as to which treaties to continue in effect. The French

international. It also drew attention to the fact that the international character of the Niemen had been established by the Acts of the Congress of Vienna, of which Russia was a signatory, and continued, "The Russian government has always firmly insisted that no international acts to which Russia was a signatory can be altered without like participation of the Russian government." 3 KLIUCHNIKOV AND SABANIN, MEZHDUNARODNAIA POLITIKA NOVEISHOGO VREMENI V. DOGOVORAKH, NOTAKH I DEKLARATZIIAKH (pt. 1) 200–201 (1928).

[1] MANCE, INTERNATIONAL RIVER AND CANAL TRANSPORT 67 (1945).
[2] *Ibid.*
[3] CONFÉRENCE DANUBIENNE, BEOGRAD 1948, RECUEIL DES DOCUMENTS [hereafter cited: DANUBE CONFERENCE (1948)] 109. In 1936 the Soviet Minister in Rumania sought to get the support of that government for the Russian candidacy. DUVERNOY, LE RÉGIME INTERNATIONAL DU DANUBE 139 (1941).
[4] DANUBE CONFERENCE (1948) 103.
[5] HARVARD DRAFT CONVENTION 1118–1119.

note which informed the Soviet government of French recognition of that government *de jure* on October 28, 1924, and proposed opening negotiations for a general treaty, stated that pending such negotiations the treaties, conventions and arrangements having existed between France and Russia would have no effect. The Soviet government, acknowledging receipt of this communication on October 29, 1924, stated its willingness to open negotiations on these terms.[1] As to France, therefore, it appears that there was agreement to regard the Danube treaties as at an end so far as Russia was concerned. With respect to other states the question of what pre-war Russian treaty relations survived had remained obscure. Jenks, writing in 1936, concluded that the abnormality of the relations between Russia and the other parties to the pre-war treaties justified revising them without her in 1919-21.[2]

Turkey also was excluded from the 1921 conference. This reflected the view that she had forfeited her rights as a consequence of the war. The Treaty of Sèvres of 1920, which provided explicit Turkish acceptance of the new regime resulting from the other peace treaties,[3] never took effect in consequence of the revolution that took place in Turkey. However, by Article 25 of the Treaty of Lausanne of July 24, 1923, Turkey undertook "to recognize the full force and effect of the Treaties of Peace and additional Conventions concluded by the other Contracting Powers with the Powers who fought on the side of Turkey." [4]

The dispute between Rumania and the other powers concerning the competence of the European Commission on the Rumanian part of the river between Galatz (upstream limit until 1883) and Braila (upstream limit by the Treaty of London) was referred to the Permanent Court of International Justice in 1927, for an advisory opinion.[5] The Court was asked to decide whether, "under the law at present in force, the European Commission

---

[1] 53 JOURNAL DU DROIT INTERNATIONAL 673 (1926).

[2] Jenks, *The Montreux Conference and the Law of Peaceful Change*, 2 NEW COMMONWEALTH QUARTERLY (1936–37), 242–251.

[3] 113 B.F.S.P. 751 (Art. 348).

[4] GREAT BRITAIN, TREATY SERIES No. 16 (1923) 25. For a view that the exclusion of Russia and Turkey was justified by cessation of their role as great European Powers and of their interest in the navigation of the river mouths, see HAJNAL, LE DROIT DU DANUBE INTERNATIONAL 228 (1929).

[5] Case concerning Jurisdiction of the European Commission of the Danube between Galatz and Braila, P.C.I.J., Series B, No. 14 (1927).

had the same powers on the sector from Galatz to Braila as on the sector below Galatz."

The postwar treaty provisions, intentionally vague on this issue, were as follows:

Treaty of Versailles

[Art. 346] The European Commission of the Danube reassumes the powers it possessed before the war.

[Art. 347] From the point where the competence of the European Commission ceases, the Danube shall be placed under the administration of an International Commission. ...

The 1921 Statute

[Art. 5] The European Commission retains the powers which it possessed before the war.

[Art. 6] The authority of the European Commission extends, under the same conditions as before, and without any modification of its existing limits, ... from the mouths of the river to the point where the authority of the International Commission commences.

[Art. 9] The authority of the International Commission extends over the Danube between Ulm and Braila.

In a nine to one decision the Court held that the European Commission did have the same powers between Galatz and Braila as on the sector below Galatz. The majority, taking in conjunction Articles 6 and 9 of the 1921 Statute, found a "plain meaning" that the territorial competence of the European Commission should extend to Braila.[1] They refused to consider whether there was any inconsistency between the Statute and the Treaty of Versailles, holding on this point that,

as all the Governments concerned in the present dispute have signed and ratified both the Treaty of Versailles and the Definitive Statute, they cannot, as between themselves, contend that some of its provisions are void as being outside the mandate given to the Danube Conference under Afticle 349 of the Treaty of Versailles.[2]

Judge Moore, who wrote a concurring opinion, was even more emphatic. He said:

That the law at present in force is first of all the Definitive Statute of July 23rd, 1921, a treaty signed and ratified by all the Parties to the present controversy, is undisputed;

* *
*

---

[1] *Id.* at 22–37.
[2] *Id.* at 23.

The question whether this extension [from Galatz to Braila] was based on "tolerance" or on the Treaty of London of 1883, is now immaterial. No matter what the pre-war basis of the extension may have been, the Statute has supplied a basis of legal permanence.[1]

None of the members of the Court relied on the Treaty of London of 1883. The majority opinion noted the finding of a League of Nations' committee of inquiry that the clause of the Treaty of London extending the authority of the Commission to Braila, because of Rumania's refusal to consent, "was not amongst those in force before 1914." [2] Judge Nyholm believed that the war, in which all of the parties to the previous Danube treaties had participated, had "abolished" the prior treaties, so that they could recover importance only insofar as they were incorporated by reference in the Versailles Treaty.[3]

3. THE LATER HISTORY OF THE DANUBE REGIME

a) *The breakdown of the international system*

Despite the advisory opinion of the Permanent Court of International Justice, Rumania continued her efforts to limit the jurisdiction exercised by the European Commission on her territory. Negotiations conducted with the assistance of the League of Nations Advisory and Technical Committee for Communications and Transit resulted, on December 20, 1929, in agreement by England, France, Italy and Rumania on the text of a Convention to settle the matter.[4] In this first effort at revision of the

---

[1] *Id.* at 80–81. Judge Nyholm disagreed with these views although he concurred in the result on the basis of the situation of fact existing before the war. His opinion stated: "The mandate given by the Allied and Associated Powers, to a limited number of Powers, assembled in conference at Paris, does not contain an authorization to depart from the principles and rules contained in the Treaty. Although the Conference had the power to amplify these rules, any decision taken by it in contradiction of the Treaty would be null, and might be so regarded by each of the Powers signatory of the Treaty of Versailles." *Id.* at 73.

[2] *Id.* at 17. The Committee did find a "usage having juridical force."

[3] P.C.I.J., Series B, No. 14, 72 (1927).

[4] LEAGUE OF NATIONS OFF. J., 11th year, 189–192 (1930). The draft agreement affirmed the applicability of the regulations of the European Commission as far as Braila but provided that trials of infractions, formerly conducted by officials of the Commission, should go before new "navigation tribunals" to be instituted by the Rumanian government, with appeals to a new three-judge "Navigation Court" at Galatz, composed of the President of the Court of Appeal of Galatz (President) and two judges chosen by majority of the European Commission, one to be a national of a state represented on the European Commission and one a national of a state not so represented.

1921 Convention the principle of unanimous consent was adhered to. By letter of the chairman of the Committee for Communications and Transit to the Secretary-General of the League, the text of the new agreement was sent to the League Council with the request that assent of the parties to the 1921 convention be invited.[1] This letter stated:

> In the opinion of the special Committee and of the delegates to the European Commission of the Danube, the text, which these delegates consider might be embodied in a Convention between the Powers represented on the European Commission of the Danube, ... involves the modification of certain provisions of the international treaties, instruments or arrangements maintained in force by Articles 5 and 6 of the Convention instituting the definitive Statute of the Danube and, previously, by Article 346 of the Treaty of Versailles. ...
>
> If the Council agrees with the Advisory and Technical Committee and decides to support its recommendations, I have the honour to request it ... to ask the Secretary-General to communicate the attached draft Convention (Appendix I) – which the Powers represented on the European Commission of the Danube propose to conclude – to the other Powers parties to the Convention instituting the Definitive Statute of the Danube, and further to request him to invite the representatives of all the Powers parties to the said Convention to sign a protocol in which, by a joint declaration, they would signify their assent to the modifications proposed in the legal regime of the maritime portion of the Danube.

On December 5, 1930, all of the signatories to the 1921 Convention, which had thus received notice of the provisions of the proposed convention, by a joint declaration, did give their assent to the proposed Convention.[2] In fact the draft convention was not put into effect, and the European Commission powers agreed instead on a *modus vivendi* whereby the Commission would refrain from exercising jurisdiction between Galatz and Braila.[3] However, the attention to securing the consent of all signatories in this instance may be contrasted with the procedure followed in the more sweeping revision which followed in 1938–39.[4]

Germany withdrew from the International Commission of the Danube on November 15, 1936, when she denounced all the provisions of the Versailles Treaty respecting German rivers.[5] The annexation of Austria on March 13, 1938, withdrew still another

---

[1] *Id.* at 188.
[2] LEAGUE OF NATIONS, OFF. J., 12th year, 735–745 (1931).
[3] 6 HUDSON, INTERNATIONAL LEGISLATION 364–367.
[4] *Infra*, pp. 144–145.
[5] 36 NOUV. REC. GÉN. (3 sér.) 800.

section of the river from international administration. Germany nevertheless renewed her efforts to secure admission to the European Commission, supported now by her Axis partner, Italy. Wishing to appease both Germany and Rumania in the face of the new political situation, the other European Commission powers were now ready to accept changes in the Commission's composition and powers, and on August 18, 1938, the United Kingdom, France and Rumania signed at Sinaia an agreement which restored to Rumania most of the powers which the European Commission had exercised.[1] New navigation and police regulations for the maritime Danube were to be drawn up by the European Commission "on the basis of proposals presented by the Rumanian Government" (Article 3). The jurisdiction to try offenses against the regulations passed to Rumania. Responsibility for river works passed to a Rumanian "Maritime Danube Board." The European Commission was to remain in existence, shorn of effective power, as a supervisory and consultative body to which reports were to be made. It was provided in Article 23 that the agreement should enter into force only upon ratification or accession by all the states represented on the European Commission. By a separate convention signed at Bucharest March 1, 1939, Italy acceded to the Sinaia agreement, and Germany was admitted to the European Commission.[2] The two acts came into force simultaneously on May 13, 1939.

On March 2, 1939, the texts of the two agreements had been transmitted by France, the United Kingdom and Rumania to the governments of the states signatory to the 1921 convention. Yugoslavia alone replied reserving her rights and questioning the legality of these acts adopted without the consent of all the signatories to the 1921 Convention. She asked whether the agreements were to be regarded as a modification of the mandate of the European Commission as defined in the 1921 Convention, or as a new international act.[3]

[1] 1 U.S. DEP'T OF STATE, DOCUMENTS AND STATE PAPERS 269 (1948).
[2] *Id.* at 273.
[3] The Yugoslav note of April 12, 1939, is referred to in Marcantonatos, *L'évolution du Statut International du Danube Maritime de 1938 à 1948*, 1 REVUE HELLÉNIQUE DE DROIT INTERNATIONAL 142–143 (1948). The author states that serious international events which followed soon after prevented further discussion of the questions Yugoslavia raised. Greece did not protest, but asked that she also be admitted to the European Commission. *Id.* at 145–148.

The legal position taken by the British and French governments in this regard appeared at the 1948 Belgrade Conference, where the validity of the 1938–39 agreements was challenged. Their representatives then stated that the effect of the Sinaia Agreement was to diminish the powers of the European Commission in favor of the territorial sovereignty of Rumania, and that Article 7 of the 1921 Convention, providing that the powers of the European Commission might come to an end through agreement by all of the States represented on that Commission, by necessary implication authorized diminution of those powers by similar agreement. They argued that this was not a revision of the 1921 Statute for which, under Article 42, a new conference of all the signatories would have been required.[1] However, the minutes of the 1921 Conference show clearly that Article 7 was not intended to authorize modification of the powers of the European Commission and that for that purpose a revisory conference would be required.[2] The British and French argument is further weakened by the fact that in 1929 the same governments had thought it necessary to obtain the consent of all signatories for the much less extensive modifications of the power of the European Commission which they then envisaged.[3]

In September, 1940, Germany convened a conference of the Danubian states at Vienna for the purpose of terminating the International Commission. This had been a fixed object of German policy since 1936. It was proposed to substitute for the International Commission a "Council of the Fluvial Danube." which would exclude the United Kingdom and France.[4] Although the object was riparian control, the treaty rights of Italy, Germany's Axis partner, were respected, but non-riparian Greece, a signatory of the 1921 Convention which was still at peace with Germany and Italy, was excluded.

Russia at once claimed the right to participate. She was now again a riparian, having forced Rumania to return Bessarabia

[1] DANUBE CONFERENCE (1948), 101–103, 149.
[2] *Supra*, pp. 134–135.
[3] The author of a recent German work concludes that the procedure followed in 1938 was an example of "a tendency in international law practice to alter parts of multilateral treaties through unilateral agreements among the parties most interested relying on the tacit or later-expressed consent of the other parties." WEGENER, DIE INTERNATIONALE DONAU 28 (1951).
[4] MARCANTONATOS, *op. cit. supra* at 150 .

two months previously, and her claim was based on this fact. Previous treaties were not mentioned when on September 10, 1940, she informed Germany "that the Soviet Union, as a Danubian State, cannot remain indifferent to the navigation regime of the Danube and cannot but take part in the decision of questions relating to the Danube."[1] Germany had not wanted to liquidate the European Commission.[2] She informed Russia that the purpose of the Vienna Conference was only to abolish the International Commission, of which Russia had never been a member, and that Germany recognized Russia's right to a seat on the European Commission.[3] However, Russia insisted that one new commission should be created for the whole river, and on October 26, 1940, Russia, Germany and Italy announced their decision to disssolve both the International and European Commissions and replace them with a "United Danube Commission" composed of representatives of Russia, Germany, Italy, Rumania, Bulgaria, Hungary, Slovakia and Yugoslavia. It was announced that representatives of Russia, Germany, Rumania and Italy would meet in Bucharest on October 28, 1940, to establish a provisional regime for the maritime Danube.[4]

Rejecting a British protest against Russian participation in the Bucharest conference as a violation of neutrality, the Soviet government stated on November 2, 1940, that the formation of a new Danube commission with the participation of the U.S.S.R. was the correction of an injustice committed by the Treaty of Versailles and other treaties on the strength of which Russia was kept out of the river commissions.[5] The statement added:

> The Danube Commission must naturally be composed of representatives of States situated on or closely connected with the Danube and using the Danube as a trade channel (for instance, Italy).
>
> It is clear that Great Britain, being thousands of kilometres distant from the Danube, cannot be classed as such a State.

Except for the reference to Italy, included in deference to German insistence, this statement clearly foreshadowed the position taken by the Soviet government in 1948 at Belgrade.

---

[1] 3 DEGRAS, SOVIET DOCUMENTS ON FOREIGN POLICY 470 (1953).
[2] GAFENCU, PRELUDE TO THE RUSSIAN CAMPAIGN 68–76 (1946).
[3] The Times (London) July 5, 1946.
[4] 3 DEGRAS, *op. cit. supra*, 475.
[5] *Id.* at 476.

The negotiations at Bucharest failed to produce agreement, however, and they were adjourned *sine die* on December 21, 1940.[1]

b) *The Belgrade Convention*

After the war, when the Paris Peace Conference in the fall of 1946 considered the question of the Danube in connection with peace terms for Bulgaria, Rumania and Hungary, Russia opposed any mention of the Danube in the treaties, maintaining that its regulation was a matter that concerned only the riparian states.[2] The United States and Great Britain proposed including in the peace treaties clauses affirming the traditional principle of free navigation, and the British proposed in addition the calling of "a conference of all interested states" to establish the new permanent international regime for the Danube.[3] Later, the United States, Great Britain and France joined in proposing a provision for calling a conference in which Rumania, Bulgaria and Hungary were to take part, "together with France, the U.S.S.R., the United Kingdom, the United States and the Danubian States."[4] When this proposal was adopted by the Economic Committee, Belgium and Greece submitted statements to the Conference reserving their rights as signatories of the 1921 Convention.[5] In the Council of Foreign Ministers on November 27, 1946, Molotov suggested the inclusion of the Ukraine, and Bevin then proposed that Greece also be invited.[6] However, in the face of Russian (not to speak of Yugoslav and Czech) opposition to the calling of any conference at all, Great Britain and France never urged the inclusion of all of the signatories to the 1921 Convention. Great Britain did maintain, however, that the 1921 Convention would remain in force until a new instrument should be drawn up.[7]

In a declaration adopted by the Council of Foreign Ministers on December 6, 1946, it was finally agreed to hold a conference

---

[1] GAFENCU, *op. cit. supra*, 80–84.
[2] BYRNES, SPEAKING FRANKLY 131, 149 (1947).
[3] D.S. DEP'T STATE PUB. NO. 2868, PARIS CONFERENCE TO CONSIDER THE DRAFT TREATIES OF PEACE 1946, SELECTED DOCUMENTS 675–676 (1947).
[4] *Id.* at 754.
[5] *Id.* at 966–967.
[6] The Times (London), November 29, 1946.
[7] The Times (London), October 1, 1946.

to draw up a new conventional regime of navigation on the Danube, "to be composed of representatives of the Danubian States: the U.S.S.R., the Ukrainian S.S.R., Bulgaria, Rumania, Yugoslavia, Czechoslovakia, and Hungary, and representatives of the following States, members of the Council of Foreign Ministers; the United States, the United Kingdom and France."[1] The declaration provided that Austria should take part in the conference "after the question of a Treaty with Austria has been settled."

The Danube Conference opened in Belgrade on July 30, 1948, The United States offered a draft convention providing for one river commission to be composed of the riparians (including the U.S.S.R., the Ukraine and Austria) and France, Great Britain and the United States.[2] Early in the conference the French delegate declared his insistence on the need to respect the "acquired rights" of the parties to the previous treaties.[3] The British representative made the same point, citing the writings of Sir Arnold McNair.[4] He pointed out that Belgium, Greece and Italy, even though not at the conference, all had rights which must be observed. The French and British delegates both also argued that the unanimity rule must be observed.[5] The United States supported the claim of Austria to be represented in the conference, on the ground of her interest as a riparian. This proposal was defeated, seven to two, despite the presence of the other former enemy states.

The western powers were regularly outvoted at Belgrade. The Soviet bloc presented a solid front, determined to return the river to riparian control and caring nothing for the principle of unanimity.[6] The delegations of Yugoslavia, Czechoslovakia, Bul-

[1] 18 DEP'T STATE BULL. 736 (1948).
[2] 1 U.S. DEP'T OF STATE, DOCUMENTS AND STATE PAPERS, 494 (1948).
[3] DANUBE CONFERENCE (1948) 55.
[4] *Id.* at 61. The reference to McNair appeared to be to that author's opinion that certain types of permanent rights (public or private) originally created or recognized by treaty, take on an objective existence independent of the future existence of the treaty itself. McNair placed rights to navigate a river in this category, as well as fishing rights and rights of nationals to acquire property within another treaty state. McNair, *Les Effets de la Guerre sur les Traités*, 59 REC. DES COURS 523 at 537–555 (1937).
[5] The French delegate stated, "No majority ... can abrogate the existing Statute without the previous consent of all the interested parties," and the British delegate, "without the assent of all the signatories, treaties cannot be abrogated." DANUBE CONFERENCE (1948) 55, 61.
[6] The communist *coup d'état* in Czechoslovakia had taken place in February 1948. The rift between Yugoslavia and the Soviet Union had already become public, but it had no effect on this conference.

garia, Rumania and Hungary, all signatories to the 1921 Convention, took the position that because of changed political and economic conditions the 1921 Convention was no longer in effect and the conference therefore had *carte blanche* to establish a new regime.

The principal attacks on the 1921 regime were delivered by Vyshinsky, representing the Soviet Union. He insisted that the administration of the river should be by the riparians alone. He argued strongly that the 1921 Convention could not be considered as being in force.[1] His argument on this point was as follows: (1) since it was concluded without the participation of the U.S.S.R. and excluded her from the European Commission, the 1921 Convention was itself a violation of the treaties of 1856, 1878 and 1883; (2) it was in any case rendered a nullity when in 1938-39 it was modified without the participation of several signatories; and (3) Great Britain, France and the United States themselves recognized its inapplicability when they did not suggest inviting Italy, Belgium and Greece to the Belgrade Conference, which would have been the required procedure under Article 42 of the 1921 Convention.[2] From the events of 1921 and 1938-39 Vyshinsky drew the conclusion that the principle of the inviolability of acquired rights was a fiction and that there existed a practice of modifying international conventions without regard for the wishes of certain individual signatory states.[3]

A British suggestion that the question of the validity of the 1921 Convention be submitted to the International Court was rejected by seven votes to three.[4]

The Convention, as signed by the U.S.S.R., the Ukraine, Bulgaria, Czechoslovakia. Hungary, Rumania and Yugoslavia on August 18, 1948, stated in Article 1, in the same terms as the peace

[1] DANUBE CONFERENCE (1948) 63–71.
[2] Thereafter Great Britain and France belatedly suggested that Italy, Belgium and Greece should be invited. *Id.* at 101, 151. Greece addressed a communication to the Conference in which she demanded the right to participate and reserved her rights. Belgium and Italy reserved their rights under the 1921 Convention but did not ask to participate. *Id.* at 233.
[3] "Il faut tenir compte des faits historiques, car ils existent, et si la pratique existait déjà de modifier les conventions internationales indépendamment de la volonté de tel ou tel participant aux Conventions précédentes, alors á quoi bon se réclamer de certains 'droits acquis' lorsque sont en jeu les intérêts des signataires influents de ces conventions." *Id.* at 69.
[4] *Id.* at 177–178, 227.

treaties with Rumania, Bulgaria and Hungary: "Navigation on the Danube shall be free and open to the nationals, vessels of commerce and goods of all States on a footing of equality. ..."[1] It provided for a new Danube Commission, composed of one representative for each riparian state, which would be responsible for seeing to the execution of the Convention, carrying out river improvements and establishing navigation regulations. Its decisions were to be taken by majority vote, except that no river works should be undertaken without the approval of a state on whose territory the work would be effected. A conference for revision might be called by a majority of the signatory states, and revisions would enter into force upon ratification by six signatories. The new regime was declared to apply from the Black Sea to Ulm, in Germany, even though neither Germany or Austria was a signatory. An additional Protocol by the same signatories declared the 1921 Convention to be no longer in effect.[2]

Great Britain, France, the United States, Belgium, Greece and Italy all protested against the action of the conference, denying its validity and stating that they would consider the 1921 Statute to be still in effect.[3] The United States' note, delivered November 15, 1949, when the new convention was put into effect by the signatories, stated:

> [This convention] signed over the objections of the Governments of France, the United States, Austria, and the United Kingdom, and in contravention of the well-established rights of Belgium, Greece and Italy, violates the concept of international waterways which has been recognized in Europe for more than 130 years. ... It seeks to deprive the United Kingdom, France, Italy, Belgium, and Greece, without their consent, of treaty rights established by international agreement in 1921 and disregards the legitimate interests of nonriparian states.[4]

It is noteworthy that this protest did not speak of unanimity, but emphasized customary river law and the invalidity of any attempt to deprive non-consenting states of their pre-existing treaty rights.

The Soviet reply to the notes of the United States, Great Britain and France called attention to the fact that the 1921 Convention had been concluded without the participation of the

---
[1] *Id.* at 373.
[2] *Id.* at 395.
[3] DANUBE CONFERENCE (1948) 243–249; 21 DEP'T STATE BULL. 832 (1949).
[4] 21 DEP'T STATE BULL. 832 (1949).

Soviet Union and had admitted non-riparian countries to the river commissions, which, it asserted, was contrary to "the generally recognized principle that the right to regulate navigation on international rivers belongs only to the riparian governments and is to be effectuated by common agreement among them." [1] It stated that the 1948 Convention, "unanimously adopted by the governments of the Danube, participating in the Conference," re-established legality in these respects. The Soviet Government added that it would not consider the protests of Belgium, Italy and Greece, since by the decision of the Council of Foreign Ministers of December 12, 1946, they were not included in the conference.

The French, Italian and British delegates, to indicate their non-recognition of the action of the Belgrade Conference, held an extraordinary session of the European Danube Commission at Rome on March 9, 1953, at which they announced that the Commission would continue in existence until it should be dissolved with the agreement of all its members, and that it would sit provisionally at Rome.[2]

Yugoslavia soon accused the Soviet Union of attempting to dominate the new Danube Commission and denying Yugoslavia's right to participate.[3] On June 2, 1951, the Yugoslav Government announced that its delegation had walked out of the fourth session of the Commission "after fruitless attempts to prevent the adoption of new rules of navigation that would have given the Soviet Government complete control of the river." [4] Yugoslavia refused to recognize the validity of the navigation rules adopted by the Commission in her absence and stated that she would establish her own regulations on the Yugoslav section of the river.[5] In 1953, however, the Commission compromised with Yugoslavia, accepting her demands for a share in the administrative posts as the price of renewed Yugoslav co-operation.[6]

[1] FANDIKOV, MEZHDUNARODNO-PRAVOVOI REZHIM DUNAIA 252–253 (1955).(Translated). *Cf.* the principles stated in the Act of Vienna, *supra*, p. 117.
[2] COMMISSION EUROPÉENNE DU DANUBE, TEXTES DU REGLEMENT DE LA COMMISSION EUROPÉENNE DU DANUBE ET DES ACCORDS CONCERNANT LE DANUBE MARITIME 16, 18 (1954).
[3] 4 INTERNATIONAL ORGANIZATION 542 (1950).
[4] 5 *id.* 845 (1951).
[5] *Ibid.*
[6] 8 *id.* 416–417 (1954).

An annex to the Belgrade Convention provided that an Austrian representative should be admitted to the new Danube Commission after the conclusion of a treaty with Austria, and it was reported in 1958 that beginning with the previous year Austrian and West German experts were now participating in the Commission's activities.[1] There was an indication that the new Danube Commission was attaining somewhat wider practical recognition, for it was also reported that the Commission had established "active cooperation ... with the Economic Commission for Europe and the International Navigation Congress of Brussels."[2]

4. SUMMARY

The history of the conventional regulation of the Rhine and the Danube is a history of contention between the proponents of riparian control and the proponents of a broader internationalization. In both cases the essential consent for changes in the régime proved to be that of the riparians.

The two regimes were quite different in their inception. On the Rhine, control was in the hands of the riparians from the start, and unanimity of the riparian states was a practical necessity if uniform regulations were to be applied to the entire river. The veto exercised by each riparian state was more than a legal principle. It was backed up by a practical veto *power*. The European Commission of the Danube, on the other hand, was an organ of the Concert of the great powers. The riparian power, Turkey, had been taken under their collective protection, and its successor, Rumania, was treated also as if under the tutelage of the great powers. In the nineteenth century, therefore, the guiding principle was that of the Concert of Europe. Unanimity was applied as a rule of great-power conference procedure. Because of this rule of conference procedure the great powers were unwilling to admit Rumania to their Conference of 1883, despite her clear interest as a riparian in the subject of river regulation. On the basis of recognized principles, Rumania as the successor to Tur-

---

[1] 9 REVUE OF INT. AFFAIRS (YUGOSLAV), No. 189 at 10 (Feb. 16, 1958). The Austrian State Treaty of May 15, 1955 had provided in the same terms as the 1947 peace treaties that navigation on the Danube should be open to all. T.I.A.S. No. 3298 (Art. 31).

[2] 9 REVIEW OF INT. AFFAIRS (YUGOSLAV), No. 189 at 10 (Feb. 16, 1958).

key should have been regarded as a party to the treaty provisions concerning the Danube. The fact that she was not so regarded again demonstrates the view of the great powers that they held a special legal mandate in this "European" matter. The ultimate failure of great power dictation in the face of Rumania's continued insistence on her sovereign rights was a revindication of the principle of the equality of states.[1] However, the rights Rumania insisted upon, with ultimate success, were her customary rights as territorial sovereign rather than procedural rights of treaty revision.

On the Rhine the idea of a special legislative mandate of the Paris Peace Conference of 1919 was rebutted, and the principle of the riparian veto again affirmed, by the Netherlands' successful insistence on the ineffectiveness of the Treaty of Versailles to make changes on her part of the river so long as she withheld her consent. This was an instance of some of the parties negotiating a new instrument without according to every party to the previous treaties the right to participate in the negotiations. They relied on their ability to get the Netherlands' subsequent consent. While by the terms of the treaty it was made applicable without awaiting the Netherlands' approval, the parties did not contend that it could have any effect on the river in Netherlands territory until such approval was obtained. The Netherlands, for its part, did not assert the total invalidity of this treaty provision but only its ineffectiveness on Netherlands territory. The attempts of the Allies in the Treaty of Versailles to replace riparian control with broader internationalization, and to exert supranational control by replacing unanimity with majority voting in the Rhine Commission, were largely abandoned in the face of the Netherlands' refusal to consent, and the agreements of 1921, 1923 and 1926 restored the riparian veto, except as to changes made only *inter se*.

On the Danube, after World War I, a true international regime was attempted. The majority of delegates to the 1921 conference still took for granted the unanimity principle, as a rule of conference procedure. They seemed also agreed, however, that a state which did not attend a revisory conference would lose its

---

[1] See Lande, *op. cit. supra*.

veto. Once present, they thought, any state would find it hard to maintain a unilateral opposition in the face of the united opinion of the other interested states. The exclusion of Russia was an abnormal case, but it also indicated that non-participation by a single state, whatever the reason, would not prevent action by a revisory conference. On matters on which the delegates present were united the 1921 conference was not concerned about possible inconsistencies between its work and previous treaties. The opinion of the Permanent Court of International Justice in the *Danube* case laid down the corollary principle that parties to a later agreement will not be heard to contend, in a dispute between themselves, that their agreement was void for inconsistency with a previous treaty (even though the previous treaty was the Treaty of Versailles).

In 1929 the powers represented on the European Commission recognized that in the absence of a revisory conference changes would require the unanimous consent of all the parties to the convention. This was called for by explicit terms of the 1921 Convention as much as by customary principles. Later, however, in a period of increasing international tension, the European Commission powers did not seek the consent of the other signatories when they modified the regime.

The return to riparian control on the Danube was begun at the insistence of Rumania and Germany in 1938–40, and completed by Russia and her satellites in 1948.

At the Belgrade Conference of 1948, Russia and her satellites replaced the 1921 convention without the consent of the non-riparian signatories. It should be noted, however, that the Soviet bloc did not assert a right to ignore the treaty rights of the minority as much as it challenged the existence of those rights by asserting the invalidity of the 1921 Convention (on grounds of prior violation, changed circumstances and its character as an imposed settlement). The Belgrade Conference abandoned unanimity as a principle of conference procedure, replacing it by majority voting. The Western powers did not fail to protest against this procedure, but the protests of Great Britain and France were weakened by the fact that in the preceding negotiations they had themselves agreed to exclude from the conference the smaller non-riparian signatories of the 1921 Convention, although it was

apparently the expectation that their consent to the revision would be secured at some later stage.

Subsequent protests of the Western powers were based on the illegality of interference with their pre-existing rights and on customary principles of river law. The Soviet Government took its official position on the Vienna principle that the control of navigation on international rivers is a matter to be settled by common agreement of the riparians only.

CHAPTER V

THE REGIME OF THE TURKISH STRAITS

1. 1840 TO 1914: THE PRINCIPLE OF UNANIMITY OF THE GREAT POWERS

In the nineteenth century the great powers in effect exercised a collective protectorate over Turkey. The regime of the Straits was a matter of pre-eminent strategic importance to at least two of the great powers, and its importance to them made it a bargaining counter for the others. Under these circumstances political considerations were paramount. Approval of these powers for any change in the regime would have been required even if no prior treaties had been involved.

The first convention on the subject was signed in 1840 by Great Britain, Austria, Prussia, Russia and Turkey.[1] It resulted from the war against Turkey by Mehemet Ali, the rebellious Pasha of Egypt, who was favored by France, and the unwillingness of England to allow the Straits to be protected by Russia alone. It provided that the four European powers should cooperate to defend the Straits against any attack by Mehemet Ali but should thereafter simultaneously withdraw their forces when deemed no longer necessary by the Sultan. The powers also agreed to respect "the ancient rule of the Ottoman Empire, in virtue of which it has at all times been prohibited for Ships of War of Foreign Powers to enter the Straits of the Dardanelles and the Bosphorus." In the following year the principle of closure to ships of war was made the subject of a new convention in which France joined.[2]

As appears from the preambles to both conventions, the basic idea was a joint undertaking by the European great powers to protect the Sultan in his sovereign rights as a security for the preservation of the peace of Europe, and an undertaking by the Sultan on his part to maintain the closure principle in the future. In Article 3 of the second convention it was stated that the Sultan reserved the right to communicate the convention "to all the

---

[1] 2 HERTSLET, THE MAP OF EUROPE BY TREATY 1008.
[2] 29 B.F.S.P. 703.

Powers with whom the Sublime Porte is in relations of friendship, inviting them to accede thereto," but this provision was never made use of.

A convention annexed to the Treaty of Paris of 1856 maintained the rule respecting the Straits essentially without change.[1] Prussia was not an original participant in the Congress of Paris. However, when it came to consideration of the Straits Convention, of which she was a signatory, the Congress unanimously agreed that she should be invited to participate in the deliberations.[2] The invitation stated that the Congress considered it "of European interest that Prussia, signatory of the Convention concluded at London July 18, 1841, participate in the new arrangements to be undertaken."[3] Prussia's representatives accordingly joined the Congress on March 18, 1856, at its 11th Session, and Prussia signed the Peace Treaty as well as the new Straits Convention. In these treaties, Sardinia (later Italy), in right of her participation as an ally in the Crimean War, joined the great power signatories of the earlier conventions.

The Treaty of London of 1871 again affirmed the principle of the closure of the Straits.[4] However, the following important exception was added, without opposition on the part of Russia:

with power to His Imperial Majesty the Sultan to open the said Straits in time of peace to the vessels of war of friendly and allied Powers, in case the Sublime Porte should judge it necessary in order to secure the execution of the stipulations of the Treaty of Paris of March 30, 1856.

At the Congress of Berlin in 1878 Lord Salisbury argued that this provision should be interpreted to mean that the powers were bound to respect the Sultan's independent determination in the matter of admitting foreign warships, while Russia supported the principle of mandatory closure of the Straits to the warships of all powers.[5] In 1881 Russia secured German and Austrian recognition of her interpretation of the treaty provisions.[6]

During the Russo-Japanese war, however, the Russians found themselves for the first time seriously hampered by their inabil-

[1] 46 B.F.S.P. 18.
[2] *Id.* at 70.
[3] *Id.* at 84.
[4] 3 HERTSLET, THE MAP OF EUROPE BY TREATY 1919.
[5] 69 B.F.S.P. 1070, 1075; see also 4 BRIT. DOCS. 58.
[6] 1 PRIBRAM, THE SECRET TREATIES OF AUSTRIA-HUNGARY 37.

ity to make use of their Black Sea fleet, and after the war it became an important aim of Russian policy to secure a change which would permit passage of the Straits by Russian warships while maintaining closure as to other powers. Her method of going about the matter showed that Russia recognized that consent of all the great powers would be required for any peaceful modification of the regime.

The subject was taken up with England during the negotiations leading up to the Anglo-Russian agreement of 1907. The British were willing to bargain. In a memorandum of November 16, 1906, Sir Charles Hardinge, Permanent Under-Secretary for Foreign Affairs, wrote:

> It is probable that the Russian Government will now desire a modification of the *status quo*, and if it is thought desirable to make some concession to Russia in return for other advantages to be obtained during the pending negotiations, and if this is a concession upon which they set store, it would be possible to promise to the Russian Government our support in obtaining the consent of the Powers to a modification of Article II of the Treaty of London in the sense of the declaration made by Lord Salisbury at the 18th sitting of the Berlin Congress. ...
> By a change in this sense the Russian fleet would, *with the consent of the Sultan*, be able to freely navigate the Straits without hindrance; ...[1]

The memorandum also discussed the possibility that the Russian Government might demand an exclusive right of passage for their warships while the Straits remained closed to all others, and concluded, on strategic grounds, that even this might be conceded.[2] In the negotiations that followed, however, the British Government, fearing "a storm in public opinion," declined to go this far in a formal agreement. The Russian Ambassador acknowledged that the consent of the other powers would be necessary for a change in the existing regime.[3] Though no formal commitment was obtained from England, the Russian Foreign Minister expressed his pleasure at the sympathetic attitude shown by the British, and stated his anticipation that a favorable moment would soon arrive for revision of the Straits regime.[4]

Russia also sought the consent of the other great powers for the modification of the Straits regime in her favor. On September

---

[1] 4 BRIT. DOCS. 58, 59.
[2] *Id.* at 59–60.
[3] *Id.* at 279–281.
[4] *Id.* at 295–296.

16, 1908, Izvolski, Russian Foreign Minister, entered into the so-called "Buchlau Bargain" with the Foreign Minister of Austria, connecting the matter of the Straits with Austria's desire to annex the Turkish provinces of Bosnia and Herzegovina, but apparently assuming that both projects, involving modification of the Treaty of Berlin, would have to be confirmed by a conference of the powers.[1] In the sequel, Izvolski failed to secure the consent of the powers for his part of the bargain. France was noncommital and England remained opposed to a one-sided opening of the Straits. Still pursuing the same goal, Russia concluded a secret agreement with Italy on October 24, 1909, whereby, in return for Russian recognition of Italian interests in Tripoli and Cyrenaica, Italy promised to consider favorably Russia's interests in the question of the Straits.[2] After the outbreak of war between Italy and Turkey in 1911 Russia made further tentative overtures for a conference to open the Straits, but withdrew them upon meeting a negative response.[3]

2. WARTIME DIPLOMACY

With Turkish participation in World War I, and especially with the opening of the Allied attack on the Dardanelles on February 19, 1915, matters entered a new phase. In a memorandum to the British and French governments, dated March 4, 1915, Russia asked her allies to recognize that Constantinople, both sides of the Bosporus, and the West shore of the Dardanelles and the Sea of Marmora should be included in the Russian Empire.[4] The British agreed to this request on March 12, and the French on April 10, 1915.[5] None of the three allies so much as referred to the rights of the then still neutral Italy, even though negotiations had begun as early as February with a view to bringing Italy into the war on their side.

The negotiations with Italy culminated, after the accord with

---

[1] *Supra*, p. 91.
[2] 1 UN LIVRE NOIR, DIPLOMATIE D'AVANT-GUERRE D'APRÈS LES DOCUMENTS DES ARCHIVES RUSSES 357 (1922).
[3] SHOTWELL AND DEÁK, TURKEY AT THE STRAITS 87–88 (1940); 9 BRIT. DOCS. 320ff., 346–350.
[4] 1 KONSTANTINOPOL I PROLIVY PO SEKRETNYM DOKUMENTAM B. MINISTERSTVO INOSTRANNYKH DEL 252 (Adamov ed. 1925); see also 6 TEMPERLEY, A HISTORY OF THE PEACE CONFERENCE OF PARIS 5 ff. (1924).
[5] 1 KONSTANTINOPOL I PROLIVY 275–277, 295.

Russia, in the secret London agreement of April 26, 1915, between England, France, Russia and Italy.[1] Italy was promised extensive territorial rewards for joining the war, mostly at the expense of Austria. Article 9 provided that, in the event of a partition of Asiatic Turkey, Italy should receive a just share of the Mediterranean region adjacent to the province of Adalia. Nothing was said about the Straits. On April 26 also, Italy acceded to the Anglo-French-Russian Declaration of September 5, 1914, in which each of the allies agreed not to conclude a separate peace. This declaration stated:

> The four Governments agree that, whenever there may be occasion to discuss the terms of peace, none of the Allied Powers shall lay down any conditions of peace without previous agreement with each of the other Allies.[2]

Italy declared war on Austria-Hungary on May 23, 1915, and on Turkey August 21, 1915.[3]

Before signing the agreement with Italy of April 26, 1915, Russia was at pains to be sure that it would not be construed to affect the previous agreement on Constantinople and the Straits. On this point she requested specific assurances from England and France.[4] The British replied with a memorandum stating that there was no need to request Italy to join in the Straits accord, "which naturally remains in full force," and that, in the opinion of Sir Edward Grey, it would be wiser not to raise the question. Grey suggested that it would be preferable, after Italy had adhered to the agreement to conclude no separate peace, "to let her know that the matter of Constantinople and the Straits must be accepted by her, as a question already decided, since her own demands had been met."[5] There was also a formal exchange of notes between Russia, France and Great Britain, in which they agreed that the prior allied agreements on the future

---

[1] Text printed in 5 TEMPERLEY, *op. cit. supra* 384.

[2] *Id.* at 392.

[3] There was no formal declaration of war against Germany until July 28, 1916.

[4] 1 KONSTANTINOPOL I PROLIVY 326–327.

[5] *Id.* at 327–328. The wording given above is a retranslation from the Russian. The original memorandum was in English. See also *id.* at 325 for opinion of Sir Arthur Nicolson, reported by the Russian Ambassador in London, that the agreements of the allies prior to the adhesion of Italy, including the one on Constantinople and the Straits, "do not concern her and in any case remain unshakable. At the moment of peace objections of Italy, if any are made, need not be feared." (Translated).

peace remained in force and were not susceptible to any revision as a consequence of the alliance with Italy.[1]

Italy nevertheless heard rumours. Early in April, 1916, Grey informed the Russian ambassador that he had been questioned on the matter by the Italian ambassador, but that, considering that Italy had no right to demand that she be informed of facts which preceded her entry into the alliance and concerning which she had raised no question at that moment, he had avoided the ambassador's questions.[2]

After the belated Italian declaration of war on Germany,[3] Italy was finally informed, on October 5, 1916, of the Straits agreement. Under the circumstances, the Italian government did not waste time in protests. In a note to the Russians of November 19, 1916, it stated:

> [The Italian Government], rightfully inspired with a feeling of confidence and friendship in respect to its allies, whose reciprocal sympathies it does not doubt, will not linger over the circumstance that these agreements were concluded without its knowledge and contrary to all its expectations. The royal government will confine itself to defining, from the present moment, the principal points to which it would like to direct the attention of the allied governments, so as to attain a wording of the treaties in question based on full equality with the other contracting governments, which the royal government considers a matter of great importance.[4]

The note went on to state that the question of Constantinople and the Straits had always been a particular object of attention for Italian policy in the Mediterranean and that the attainment of Russia's aims would create a new situation of great importance.[5] On December 2, 1916, by an exchange of notes with her allies, Italy adhered to the Straits agreement, "on condition that the war be prosecuted to a victorious conclusion, that Italy realize her aspirations in the East and elsewhere, ... and that she enjoy all advantages secured to France and Great Britain."[6]

It thus appears that England, France and Russia reached a firm agreement to alter the regime at the Straits without

---

[1] *Id.* at 334 (and see also 332).
[2] *Id.* at 412–413.
[3] July 28, 1916.
[4] 1 KONSTANTINOPOL I PROLIVY 347–348. (Translated).
[5] Italy also spelt out in this note in more detail than previously, her own claims on Turkish territory, and insisted upon the right of free passage of the Straits and a free port at Constantinople.
[6] 1 KONSTANTINOPOL I PROLIVY 354–355. (Translated).

consulting Italy, a neutral party to the previous treaties. However, the agreement was preliminary only. They counted on securing Italy's consent at the peace conference.[1]

3. THE LAUSANNE CONFERENCE, 1922–1923

After World War I, the Allies, Turkey and Russia all treated the previous agreements concerning the Straits as at an end and approached the question as one calling for new regulation.[2]

Nevertheless, Russia's right to participate eventually in the new arrangements concerning the Straits was generally conceded. The first attempt to deal with the question was made in the draft treaty of Sèvres, which the Allies sought unsuccessfully to impose on Turkey immediately following the war.[3] By it the Straits, neutralized and opened to the warships as well as the merchant ships of all nations, would have been placed under the control of an International Straits Commission which would act "in complete independence of the local authority." Article 40 provided for the composition of the Commission:

> The Commission shall be composed of representatives appointed respectively by the United States of America (if and when that Government is willing to participate), the British Empire, France, Italy, Japan, Russia (if and when Russia becomes a member of the League of Nations), Greece, Roumania, and Bulgaria and Turkey (if and when the two latter States become members of the League of Nations). Each Power shall appoint one representative. The representatives of the United States of America, the British Empire, France, Italy, Japan and Russia shall each have two votes. The representatives of Greece, Roumania, and Bulgaria and Turkey shall each have one vote. ...

An outline of proposed terms of the settlement with Turkey had been communicated by the Supreme Allied Council to the United States Government on March 12, 1920. In its reply of March 24th the United States expressed approval of the provision for Russian representation. The note stated:

---

[1] See the statement of Sir Edward Grey, quoted *supra* at p. 160.

[2] The agreement of 1915 had lost its force with the withdrawal of Russia from the war. Article 6 of the Treaty of Friendship which was concluded between Russia and Turkey on March 16, 1921, declared: "Both contracting parties recognise that all treaties concluded heretofore between the two countries do not serve their mutual interests. They therefore agree to consider these treaties as annulled and no longer in force." 1 DEGRAS 237. The other powers also regarded the previous conventions concerning the Straits as terminated by the war. See remarks of Messrs. Politis and Fitzmaurice at the Montreux Conference, ACTES DE LA CONFÉRENCE DE MONTREUX (1936) 117, 254. Cf. Art. 282 of the Treaty of Versailles.

[3] 113 B.F.S.P. 652 (Arts. 37 to 61).

THE REGIME OF THE TURKISH STRAITS

No arrangement that is now made concerning the government and control of Constantinople and the Straits can have any elements of permanency unless the vital interests of Russia in those problems are carefully provided for and protected, and unless it is understood that Russia, when it has a Government recognized by the civilized world, may assert its right to be heard in regard to the decisions now made.

It is noted with pleasure that the questions of passage of war ships and the regime of the Straits in war time are still under advisement as this Government is convinced that no final decision should or can be made without the consent of Russia.[1]

Answering this note, the Supreme Council removed the impression that final decisions on the Straits would await Russian participation, saying: "It has obviously been impossible to defer the drafting of so vital a chapter of the Turkish treaty pending the eventual consultation with Russia." [2]

The Treaty of Sèvres was upset by the nationalist revolution in Turkey. When the powers again sat down with Turkey, at the Conference of Lausanne in 1922–23, the Soviet government claimed the right to be heard. In a note to the British government of September 13, 1922, it stated:

Russia cannot consent to the Straits being opened to the battleships of any country and in particular that Great Britain, with the consent of her allies, should have control of the Straits without the consent and against the wishes of the Powers who have vital interests in the Black Sea and who should have the right of decision as to the fate of the Straits. It is true that all the pre-war conventions regarding the Straits have lost their force. Nevertheless, they were all drawn up with the participation of Russia, and consequently any new regime which is established even *de facto* in the Straits without consultation with Russia cannot be recognized by the Russian Government.[3]

On the following day Russia issued its own proposal for a conference on Near Eastern questions. In this proposal it asserted:

With its allies, the Ukraine and Georgia, Russia is, after Turkey, the country occupying first place among the Powers interested in the freedom of the Straits.

* * *

Russia and Turkey have agreed on the manner in which the freedom of the Straits should be realized, and Russia warns the western Governments against repeating the mistakes which arise from ignoring the vital interests of the States concerned.[4]

---

[1] [1920] 3 FOREIGN REL. U.S. 751.
[2] *Id.* at 755.
[3] 1 DEGRAS 330.
[4] *Id.* at 334, 335.

The reference in the paragraph last quoted was to the Treaty of Friendship between Russia and Turkey of March 16, 1921, which included the following provision:

[Art. 5] In order to secure the opening of the Straits and freedom of passage through the Straits for the commerce of all nations, both contracting parties agree to entrust the final elaboration of an international statute for the Black Sea and the Straits to a special conference of delegates of the littoral countries on condition that any decisions they arrive at shall not involve any derogation of Turkey's complete sovereignty or of the security of Turkey and its capital, Constantinople.[1]

The Turkish Government had thus also taken the position that the question of the Straits could not be settled without the participation of Russia,[2] and an invitation to send a delegation to participate in the examination of the question of the Straits (though not in the other phases of the Lausanne Conference) was in fact extended to Russia on October 27, 1922, by the inviting powers, Great Britain, France and Italy.[3] Bulgaria was also invited for this special purpose only. The preamble to the Final Act of the Lausanne Conference stated that this invitation had been extended to Russia and Bulgaria "as littoral Powers of the Black Sea."[4] Japan, Greece, Rumania, Yugoslavia and the United States were also invited to participate. All except the United States had been at war with Turkey. Germany was still excluded. All of the invited powers accepted the invitation except the United States, which sent only an observer.

The inviting powers circulated in advance an outline of their proposals.[5] Russia presented at the conference draft articles in which she proposed maintenance of the former principle of closure to foreign warships.[6] Departing from her former position that the matter concerned only the countries bordering on the Black Sea, she now suggested a Straits Commission composed of one representative of each of the littoral states (including the Ukraine and Georgia, as well as Russia) and of Germany, the United States, France, Great Britain, Italy and Japan (i.e. all of the great powers). The Russian draft also supported Turkey's

---

[1] *Id.* at 237.
[2] *Lausanne Conference on Near Eastern Affairs 1922–23*, CMD. NO. 1814 at 127 (1923).
[3] 1 DEGRAS 342 ff.
[4] CMD. NO. 1814 at 684 (1923).
[5] *Id.* at 128.
[6] *Id.* at 250.

claim to fortify the Straits, and Chicherin, the leader of the Russian delegation, spoke of demilitarization as a "flagrant violation of the sovereignty and independence of Turkey, which is unacceptable from the point of view of the most elementary requirements of Russia and her allies in respect of safety." [1]

Near the conclusion of the discussion of the Straits question, the inviting powers presented a draft of a Straits convention to which Turkey was ready to agree.[2] This included demilitarization of the zone of the Straits and acceptance of the principle of free passage, while Turkey was at peace, for warships as well as commercial vessels, except that a tonnage limitation was to be placed on naval vessels which outside powers might send into the Black Sea. A Straits Commission, to supervise the new regime, was to be composed of one representative of each of the signatory powers.

At the final session on the Straits, Chicherin objected vigorously to the draft convention, stating that it had resulted from "clandestine negotiations" between the inviting powers and Turkey in which Russia had no part. He asked,

"Do you wish to impose on Russia, the Ukraine and Georgia [3] a treaty which represents the will of other Powers? or are you ready to repair your error and negotiate the draft convention point by point – that is to say, in a sub-commission?"[4]

Turkey, however, had accepted the draft, and Lord Curzon, who was presiding, answered that the discussion would not be reopened. He stated:

"M. Chicherin says: 'Do you want to impose this convention upon us?' Of course not. We are not in a position to impose it upon the Russian delegation. I hope very much that they will sign it. I am largely responsible for their being here, because I have always entertained the conviction that the assent of Russia is both necessary and desirable with a view to a proper, peaceful and permanent solution of the question. I should therefore be very much disappointed if we went away from here with a treaty to which is attached a Straits Convention that is not signed by Russia. But it is not fair to suggest that we are imposing this treaty; for if M. Chicherin is unwilling to sign it, bitterly as we shall regret his action, we shall have to accept it." [5]

[1] *Id.* at 272–273.
[2] *Id.* at 772.
[3] These were treated by the Conference as one delegation representing only one state.
[4] CMD. NO. 1814 at 450–451 (1923).
[5] CMD. NO. 1814 at 435–454 (1923).

When Chicherin failed to influence the conference with his argument that there must be further negotiation over Russia's proposals, he announced that under the circumstances there could be no decision in the Straits question. Russia would not sign and would retain an entirely free hand.[1] Curzon answered:

> ,'If you have a block of nations – eight, nine or ten – on the one hand, and on the other hand a solitary State putting forward views which nobody shares, is it in the spirit of business a practical proposition that the eight, nine or ten Powers should concede the greater part of their case, in which they believe, in order to satisfy the case of a single Power with whom they find themselves in complete disagreement? No man in the world ever conducted business on such a basis.'' [2]

This refusal to allow Russia to exercise a veto over the proceedings was not, strictly speaking, a repudiation of the rule of unanimity in treaty revision, for Russia had conceded that the previous treaties had lost their force. It was rather a refusal to be bound by unanimity as a rule of conference procedure. However, the practical logic of Curzon's remarks would seem as applicable to revision as to other conference decisions. Since the principle of complete freedom of navigation for all but warships was maintained there was no denial of Russia's customary or prescriptive rights.

Although Turkey accepted the draft Convention on the Straits, this first phase of the Conference broke up in disagreement over other matters.[3] Later the disagreements were smoothed over and the Conference reassembled, without Russian participation, to complete the Peace Treaty. The Treaty and the Convention of the Straits were signed on July 24, 1923, by the British Empire, France, Italy, Japan, Bulgaria, Greece, Rumania and Turkey.[4] Just previously the Soviet Government had changed its mind and announced in a note to the Secretary of the Conference:

> While not in agreement with the regime proposed for the Straits, the Soviet Governments, placing the interests of peace and the settlement of international conflicts above all other considerations, consider that they should, by their participation, make the execution of the general agreement possible, in order to realize their own peaceful purposes. ...[5]

---

[1] *Id.* at 456.
[2] *Ibid.*
[3] *Id.* at 837 ff. (1923).
[4] 28 L.N.T.S. 115.
[5] 1 Degras 407.

Russia signed the Convention [1] but later again reversed her policy and never ratified it.

The principle of freedom of passage was declared in Article 23 of the Treaty of Lausanne,[2] as well as in the separate convention on the Straits:

> The High Contracting Parties are agreed to recognise and declare the the principle of freedom of transit and of navigation, by sea and by air, in time of peace as in time of war, in the strait of the Dardanelles, the Sea of Marmora and the Bosphorus, as prescribed in the separate Convention signed this day, regarding the regime of the Straits.

The Convention contained more specific rules for passage through the Straits.[3] It provided that the freedom of navigation for non-military vessels was to be complete, for vessels of all flags, except when Turkey should be at war, In the latter event Turkey might exercise belligerent rights. In regard to warships, the previous principle of closed straits ("the ancient rule of the Ottoman Empire" recognized in the treaties of 1841, 1856, 1871 and 1878) was abandoned. There was to be no limit on the number of warships which a Black Sea power could send into the Mediterranean, but no non-Black Sea power was allowed to send into the Black Sea a force greater than the most powerful fleet of the littoral powers of the Black Sea at the time of passage. Turkey was to have no responsibility in this regard, but the International Straits Commission was given the function of enquiring of each Black Sea power, twice a year, the number of its warships in all classes, and relaying this information to the powers concerned. The Straits Commission was also given the duty "to see that the provisions relating to the passage of warships ... are carried out" and "to prescribe such regulations as may be necessary for the accomplishment of its task." It was to be composed of one representative of each ratifying power. A place was also reserved for the United States and for any independent littoral state of the Black Sea in the event of their acceding to the convention.[4]

[1] This event took place three weeks later at Rome, instead of at Lausanne, because of a diplomatic breach between Russia and Switzerland.

[2] 28 L.N.T.S. 11.

[3] *Id.* at 115.

[4] Article 19 provided: "The High Contracting Powers will use every endeavour to induce non-signatory Powers to accede to the present Convention." This provision was inserted with the United States in mind. The United States, however, maintained its determination not to become a party, and no other state sought to take advantage of the right to accede. It was not renewed in the Montreux Convention of 1936, which provided only for accession by any power signatory of the Treaty of Lausanne.

Article 3 provided that "with a view to maintaining the Straits free from any obstacle to free passage and navigation" (i.e. on the part of Turkey) the zone of the Straits should be demilitarized, and Article 18 compensated Turkey by a guarantee on the part of France, Great Britain, Italy and Japan to meet any threat to the freedom of navigation or the security of the demilitarized zone "by all the means that the Council of the League of Nations may decide for this purpose."

The manner of voting in the new International Straits Commission was not specified in the Lausanne Convention. However, the Commission itself drew up rules of procedure that did not require unanimity in the adoption of decisions.[1] These rules contained the following provisions:

[Article 18] On questions of principle (interpretation of international law, of the Straits Convention, the powers of the Commission, changes in its regulations, etc.) decisions must be taken by a two-thirds majority.

[Article 19] Decisions of the Commission with regard to the despatch of current business and the application of the measures provided in its Rules of Procedure shall be taken by a simple majority, the President [Turkish] being granted a casting vote.

[Article 20] A quorum shall be formed by one-half the number of delegates present in Constantinople plus one.

No very far-reaching decisions were taken, however. The Turkish authorities succeeded in limiting the functions of the Commission largely to the assembling of statistics and the making of recommendations on the improvement of navigation.[2] Its weakness in the face of the territorial sovereign was demonstrated in 1926 when it sought unsuccessfully to require the Turkish government to report to it movement of Turkish war vessels in the Straits. The Turkish government replied that in its opinion the obligation to report passage through the Straits only applied, according to the spirit of the convention, to foreign naval forces. The Commission stated that it "did not consider this reply satisfactory," but there was little it could do about it.[3]

---

[1] *First Report by the Straits Commission for the year 1925*, LEAGUE OF NATIONS OFF. J., 7th year 951, 971 (1926).

[2] They refused to allow the Commission to fly its own flag or its members to exercise diplomatic immunities with respect to Turkish customs and subjected shipping to Turkish health regulations, prohibited the use of wireless in Turkish waters, etc. *Id.* at 957, 966–969.

[3] League of Nations Pub. No. C. 244.M.136.1927. VII. ANNEX. The Soviet government, though not a party to the convention, did comply with a request to furnish

4. THE MONTREUX CONFERENCE OF 1936

In 1936, after Italy's attack on Ethiopia and Germany's remilitarization of the Rhineland, Turkey moved to secure a revision of the regime which would allow her to refortify the Straits. In a note of April 10, 1936,[1] addressed to all the states which had taken part in the negotiation of the Lausanne Convention, Turkey argued that it had been demonstrated in successive political crises that the mechanism of collective guarantee could not be relied on to protect Turkey from a foreign attack. Therefore Turkey requested negotiations for the conclusion of a new agreement "to regulate the regime of the Straits under conditions of security indispensable to the inviolability of Turkish territory."

The resulting conference was convened at Montreux on June 22, 1936. It elaborated a new convention which preserved and reaffirmed the general principle of freedom of transit, but abolished the Straits Commission, the demilitarization provisions and the collective guarantee. A stricter limit was placed on the passage of warships of non-Black Sea powers.[2]

The decision of Turkey to invite all the states which took part in the negotiation of the Lausanne Convention was made so as to include the U.S.S.R. and Yugoslavia, which had not ratified it. The Black Sea powers were the most interested states, and Yugoslavia could by some stretching be considered one of this group because of the Straits-Danube waterway. The decision to invite all signatories of the previous treaty brought in Japan, whose interest was extremely remote, but left out other states with more shipping through the Straits.[3] Japan replied that she accepted the invitation "in view of the fact that the question must be settled by the signatories of the Treaty of Lausanne." [4]

the Commission with a list of its naval forces in the Black Sea. League of Nations Pub. No. C. 596.M.190. 1925. VII.

[1] Text in [1936] 3 FOREIGN REL. U.S. 503–506.
[2] 173 L.N.T.S. 213.
[3] RÉPUBLIQUE TURQUE, MINISTÈRE DES AFFAIRES ETRANGÈRES, [1938] RAPPORT ANNUEL SUR LE MOUVEMENT DES NAVIRES À TRAVERS LES DÉTROITS 75–76.
[4] KEESING'S CONTEMPORARY ARCHIVES 2084 E (1936). A question of state succession arose concerning the British Dominions. They were invited to participate as members of the British delegation (the "British Empire" being a party to the Treaty of Lausanne). Australia accepted the invitation, but the others declined. Each of them informed the Turkish Government that it renounced any right that it might have to object to revision or abrogation of the old convention. It seems likely from the replies that such a renunciation was requested by the Turkish government. None of them expressly asserted a right to be consulted. Canada asserted that

Italy did not attend the conference. Count Ciano informed the Turkish ambassador that this abstention was a result of the campaign against Italy in the Ethiopian affair and that until the sanctions imposed at Geneva had been lifted Italy would "abstain from any form of international collaboration." [1] The Italian government also sent a note to the conference in which it stated that it would not attend because it did not consider the time favorable for the consideration of such grave matters. It added:

> The royal Government, while maintaining this order of ideas, confirms that it is ready to participate in the work of the Conference as soon as the situation in its various aspects is clarified. In the meantime, the royal Government, because of its interest in the matter as a State eminently Mediterranean and in its capacity as a signatory of the Treaty of Lausanne of July 24, 1923, is obliged to formulate the most formal reservations on the discussions which will take place at the approaching meetings, as well as on the entirety of the problems which will there be discussed.[2]

After conveying this message to the assembled conference, the Foreign Minister of Turkey informed the conference that he proposed to reply, stating Turkey's satisfaction

> that Italy promises to be represented here as soon as the hindrances — unconnected with Turkey and with the Conference — which deprive us of the presence of the Italian delegation shall have ceased to exist. I register with satisfaction this part of the letter, even while affirming that the work of the Conference will continue and declaring that Turkey will be happy to see the Italian delegation here at the Conference.[3]

There was no comment from the other delegates, and no hesitation about the continuation of the work of the conference.

There was very little mention of Italy during the discussions, It was noted that she might not sign the new convention, which was intended to abrogate the Convention of Lausanne. This caused no concern to Turkey, which regarded the old convention as lapsed (*caduque*).[4] The British delegate stated that he could she had "no special interest or active obligation" derived from the Lausanne Convention, South Africa made a similar assertion and Ireland stated that revision of the Straits regime was "not a question requiring [its] agreement." Canada reserved, however, "the rights and privileges which are enjoyed in a general manner by the States which are not parties either to the new or to the old Convention." ACTES DE LA CONFÉRENCE DE MONTREUX (1936) 35–36, 42, 119–120.

[1] CIANO'S DIPLOMATIC PAPERS 4 (Muggeridge ed. 1948).
[2] ACTES DE LA CONFÉRENCE DE MONTREUX (1936) 29–30 (Translated).
[3] *Id.* at 30. (Translated).
[4] *Id.* at 276.

not accept this view.¹ However, the more cautions delegates seemed satisfied by the position taken by Mr. Fitzmaurice, of the United Kingdom, who said:

> The signatories accept the new regulation so far as concerns them, without their acceptance binding the other States. It will be up to Turkey to reach an understanding with the latter.²

It was provided in Article 27 of the new convention that it should remain open for the adherence of every power signatory of the Lausanne Treaty.

More discussion was provoked by Turkey's proposal that the new convention should enter into force on signature.³ The U.S.S.R. suggested that it should come into force on the deposit of five or six ratifications (a majority of the signatories), and Turkey accepted this amendment.⁴ The United Kingdom delegate opposed permitting definitive entry into force before all signatories had ratified. He stated:

> ... We have not simply to conclude a new convention, but a convention which abrogates an instrument intended to last indefinitely. Juridically, an instrument of this kind can only be abrogated with the consent of all the parties and this consent is formally attained only when the parties have ratified the new convention⁵.

He acknowledged, however, that this resulted in an impasse "where one feels rather ill at ease," and he suggested that the way out was to adopt a separate protocol permitting provisional entry into force of the convention, or at least freeing Turkey of the demilitarization clauses, in advance of final ratification.⁶ Only Japan, which was least interested, raised further scruples, pointing out that remilitarization would result in an effective modification of the Lausanne Convention without the formal consent of any signatories that did not ratify.⁷

The practical inconvenience of requiring ratification by all signatories before bringing the new convention into force was

---

¹ *Ibid.*
² *Id.* at 254. (Translated). See also *id.* at 115, 117, and the note by "G.F." in 18 B.Y.I.L. 186 at 190 (1937). *Cf.* the removal of the restrictions placed on Italy by the military clauses of the Italian Peace Treaty of 1947. *Supra*, pp. 104–108.
³ ACTES DE LA CONFÉRENCE DE MONTREUX (1936) 285.
⁴ *Id.* at 57–58.
⁵ *Id.* at 116. (Translated).
⁶ *Id.* at 116; *cf.* 57, 253–254.
⁷ *Id.* at 57, 254.

stressed by Messrs. Politis (Greece) and Litvinoff (U.S.S.R.). M. Politis disagreed with the distinction made by the British delegate between the situation facing the Montreux Conference and that of 1923. He stated:

> ... In 1923, the agreement, which was of 1871, was considered fictitiously as non-existent, because it was considered that it had been terminated by the war. In reality it was not a question of legislating in a new situation: one was modifying a state of things which had very ancient precedents going back to the end of the 18th century. The situation does not appear very different today. It is a question of substituting a new convention for the Convention of Lausanne, and the important thing is to produce practical results and not to end in an impasse ... by applying with rigidity the principle of unanimity of ratification.[1]

He added that one must not allow a minority to make the law for the majority. M. Litvinoff stated:

> Governments sign international agreements, then, abruptly, decide not to ratify them. Ratification, in such cases, becomes a sort of plaything. I would be rather inclined, not only so far as concerns this treaty, but also in regard to other international treaties, to be content with the ratification of the majority of the participants.[2]

He thus seemed to concede the validity of the Convention of Lausanne, which the U.S.S.R. had signed but never ratified. These statements reflected the traditional doctrine that treaties become binding only upon ratification. Signature of an instrument authorizing application of the regime in advance of ratification would nevertheless represent consent of all the signatories.

The decisive consideration was that Turkey was determined to remilitarize the Straits, and the other conferees were agreed that a legal way must be found to allow Turkey to do it. The nine participants in the conference all signed the Montreux Convention. It provided that it should enter into force on the deposit of six ratifications, including that of Turkey. There was signed at the same time a separate protocol which allowed Turkey to remilitarize the Straits without waiting for any ratifications and also provided for the provisional application of the provisions

---

[1] *Id.* at 117. (Translated).

[2] *Ibid.* Turkey's delegation presented a theory that the conventional regime of the Straits was of a special kind – an international statute binding on the whole world – and argued that to make a new convention of this kind universally valid, agreement of a majority of the participants in the conference would constitute "a sufficient juridical right." *Id.* at 58, 268–269.

of the convention before its entry into force.[1] Again, there was consent of all the signatories. Neither the protocol not the convention were dependent in any way on Italy's approval.

The Montreux Convention was concluded for a term of twenty years, and thereafter until denounced. The parties agreed, in the event of denunciation, to attend a conference to draw up a new convention.[2] In any event, however, it was declared that the principle of freedom of passage and of seaborne navigation in the Straits (for nonmilitary vessels) should be of permanent validity. The Montreux Convention entered into force on November 9, 1936. The International Straits Commission of the Lausanne Convention had held a last meeting on August 3, 1936, at which, with the single dissenting vote of Italy, it decided to suspend its activities.[3] Italy's aloof attitude began to soften, however, in February, 1937, when at a meeting of the Turkish and Italian Foreign Ministers the latter stated that the reasons for Italy's nonparticipation in the Montreux Convention no longer existed, though she would choose her own time to accede to it.[4] Italy ultimately did accede on May 2, 1938.[5]

The effective revision of the Lausanne Convention without the participation of Italy is a clear-cut departure from the unanimity rule, more noteworthy because the state whose consent was dispensed with was a great power.[6] The British explanation that the new convention was only effective between the parties

---

[1] 173 L.N.T.S. 213 ff.

[2] There was also, in Article 29, a special procedure for a revisory conference in advance of the term for expiration of the convention. It provided that such a conference would only be able to legislate by unanimity, except as to articles 14 and 18 (naval tonnage limits), for which a three-quarters majority would suffice, provided Turkey and three-quarters of the parties which were riparians of the Black Sea were included in the majority.

[3] LEAGUE OF NATIONS OFF. J., 17th year 933 (1936).

[4] CIANO'S DIPLOMATIC PAPERS 93.

[5] [1939[RAPPORT ANNUEL SUR LE MOUVEMENT DES NAVIRES À TRAVERS LES DÉTROITS 7.

[6] C. W. Jenks has suggested that there is a limited exception to the unanimity rule covering instances "when the relations of one member of the international community with that community as a whole have not been normal." He believes that the cases of Russia at the close of World War I and Italy in 1936 fit into this category. Jenks, *The Montreux Conference and the Law of Peaceful Change*, 2 NEW COMMONWEALTH QUARTERLY 242 (1936–37). However, as Sørenson has pointed out, the two cases are not really alike. Russia was left out of the post-war arrangements because the other governments were not in diplomatic relations with it and its participation in the conferences would have involved recognition. This was not the case with Italy. Sørenson, *op. cit. supra* 163–164.

which accepted it is unsatisfactory in view of the clear impossibility of applying two different Straits regimes simultaneously. The text of the Montreux Convention made it clear that it was not limited in any way to *inter se* application. The preamble stated that the parties had "resolved to substitute the present convention for the convention signed at Lausanne," and Article 24 stated without qualification, "The attributions of the International Commission ... are transferred to the Turkish Government." Turkey emphatically stated that she would apply the new regime against all states alike.[1]

It is equally clear that the Turkish argument that the Lausanne Convention had become inoperative because of changed circumstances was not accepted by the other participants in the Montreux Conference. Some writers have maintained that Italy did not register sufficient protests against the substance of the proposed revision, as distinguished from the method of procedure, and thus tacitly renounced the right to object.[2] However, no protest Italy might have made would have prevented the other parties from putting their new convention into effect.

The new convention left intact and even reaffirmed the principle of free transit for commercial vessels, in which other states had customary as well as treaty rights, but it effectively altered the collective system of guarantees and the administrative regime as well as ending the demilitarization restriction.[3]

5. THE NEGOTIATIONS OF 1945–1946

As World War II drew to a close, Russia suggested to Turkey, as a condition for the renewal of their friendship treaty, that the Straits Convention must be revised to provide bases for Russia on the Dardanelles. Turkey's reply made use of the unanimity doc-

---

[1] She even assured nonsignatory states that their rights under the convention were equal to those of the contracting powers. Poland, after receiving this assurance from Turkey, replied that it would "make use of the rights incumbent on it according to the said [Turkish] note." The United States also expressed its "great satisfaction" on receiving this assurance. [1938] RAPPORT ANNUEL SUR LE MOUVEMENT DES NAVIRES À TRAVERS LES DÉTROITS 37–40. The possible acquisition by third states of vested rights in the benefits of the Sraits regime is also discussed by G. F. [itzmaurice] in 18 B.Y.I.L. 189 (1937).

[2] Fernand De Visscher, *La Nouvelle Convention des Détroits*, 17 REV. DE DROIT INTERNATIONAL 669, 703 (1936); DJONKER, LE BOSPHORE ET LES DARDANELLES 138 (1938).

[3] See De Visscher. *op. cit. supra* at 672; 18 B.Y.I.L. 186, 189 (1937).

trine. It stated that the consent of all nine signatory powers would be required.[1]

The matter was next taken up among the Big Three at Potsdam. As part of their agreement there, on August 1, 1945, the United States, United Kingdom and Soviet Union "recognized that the Convention concluded at Montreux should be revised as failing to meet present-day conditions," and it was agreed that "as the next step" (English version), or "as the proper course" (Russian version), there would be direct conversations on the subject between each of the three parties and the Turkish government.[2]

The United States sent a note to Turkey accordingly, on November 2, 1945, suggesting an international conference to revise the convention and indicating a willingness to participate if invited to do so. It suggested that the Straits should be open to warships of Black Sea powers, but closed to those of other countries. It noted that under Article 29 the convention was open to revision every five years and that one such interval would elapse in 1946.[3]

There was no further development until August 7, 1946, when the Soviet Union sent a note to Turkey proposing a new Straits regime in which Turkey and the Soviet Union, "as the powers most interested and capable of guaranteeing freedom to commercial navigation and security in the Straits," would organize to defend them jointly. It also stated that the establishment of a new regime of the Straits "should come under the competence of Turkey and other Black Sea powers."[4] The United States and the United Kingdom both replied that other states besides the Black Sea powers were concerned in the matter.[5] A French note of August 14, 1946, addressed to the three Potsdam

---

[1] KEESING'S CONTEMPORARY ARCHIVES 7737A (1946); Sadak (Turkish Foreign Minister), *Turkey Faces the Soviets*, 27 FOREIGN AFFAIRS 449, 458 (1949).

[2] Both versions were quoted in 16 DEP'T STATE BULL. 144 (1947). It was later specified that the inconsistencies with present conditions which the western powers had in mind were the old definition of warships, the references to the League of Nations and the inclusion of Japan. The Soviet Union meant to exclude all but riparians of the Black Sea. See Howard, *Some Recent Developments in the Problem of the Turkish Straits, 1945–1946*, 16 DEP'T STATE BULL. 143–151 (1947), where the exchanges of notes, 1945–1946, are reviewed in detail.

[3] 13 DEP'T STATE BULL. 766 (1945); 16 *id*. 144 (1947). Turkey replied that it was willing to participate in such a conference. The United Kingdom also stated its willingness to attend. 16 *id*. 144–145 (1947).

[4] 16 *id*. 146 (1947).

[5] *Id.* at 146–147.

powers and Turkey, claimed the right, as signatory and depository of the Montreux Convention, to participate in any revision.[1]

The positions thus taken continued to be maintained in later correspondence, and a deadlock resulted. The Soviet Union, by asking too much, got no revision at all. It continued to maintain that Turkey and the Black Sea powers should elaborate the new regime.[2] The United States, United Kingdom and Turkey maintained that Japan should be excluded from the contemplated revisory conference, but that all the other signatories of Montreux should participate.[3] The determination to exclude Japan, but not Bulgaria, Rumania and Italy, reflected the view that Japanese interest was too remote. The war did not automatically terminate Japan's rights under a multipartite convention of this kind.[4] However, Japan could be, and was, forced to renounce her rights under the Montreux Convention by the Treaty of Peace.[5] Turkey insisted that the method of revision provided in Article 29 of the Montreux Convention must be followed.[6]

Although the United States was not a party to the Montreux Convention, and had in 1945 only indicated its willingness to participate "if invited," in 1946 it seemed to assert that it had a right to participate in the revision, or at least that the Soviet Union was not entitled to object to its participation if invited by other parties. It based this claim on an argument that the Potsdam agreement constituted a recognition by the Big Three that the United States was one of the "interested powers." [7]

6. SUMMARY

From 1840 to 1914 the Straits regime was a matter agreed and guaranteed by all the European great powers, and Turkey, the territorial sovereign. Revision of the regime, if it was to be accomplished without war, required unanimous consent of all

---

[1] Tchirkovitch, *La question de la révision de la Convention de Montreux*, 56 REV. GÉN. DE DROIT INTERNATIONAL PUBLIC 189, 206–207 (1952).
[2] 16 DEP'T STATE BULL. 148 (1947).
[3] *Id.* at 149–151.
[4] RÄNK, "EINWIRKUNG DES KRIEGES AUF DIE NICHTPOLITISCHEN STAATSVERTRÄGE 51–53 (Publications de l'Institut Suédois du Droit International, No. 8, 1949).
[5] See Article 8 (b) of the Japanese Peace Treaty of September 8, 1951. T.I.A.S. No. 2490.
[6] 16 DEP'T STATE BULL. 150 (1947).
[7] 15 *id.* 722 (1946); *cf.* 13 *id.* 766 (1945).

these powers as a practical political matter. There was no revision in this period because the great powers were never able to agree on it. When Prussia, a signatory of the Convention of 1841, was brought into the negotiations at Paris preceding the Treaty of 1856, the point stressed was that it was "of European interest for her to participate" – i.e. the political principle of the Concert of Europe. Russia went about her efforts to secure revision by attempting to get advance commitments from the powers, separately, to favor the modifications she wanted. It seemed that a conference would be called only if support of all the powers for such modifications had been first secured by this procedure.

During World War I, England, France and Russia, without consulting Italy, agreed upon a revision of the Straits regime in Russia's favor, on which they undertook to insist when peace was concluded. While thus denying Italy's right to be consulted in advance, the Allies counted on their ability to secure her consent at the time of final disposition by the peace conference.

In the revisions which took place after World War I the consent of Turkey, the territorial sovereign, was clearly essential. On two occasions, however, (1923 and 1936) a new convention was adopted without the consent of a clearly interested great power. On both occasions they had been invited to participate. The decision to proceed without Russia in 1923 was an abandonment of unanimity as a rule of conference procedure. The parties did not consider that they were revising a convention in force, for the previous conventions had all been terminated by the war, but Russia's interest had been recognized in all such conventions and it was recognized again in the decision to invite Russia to the Montreux Conference in 1936 even though she was not a party to the Convention of Lausanne.

The decision to proceed without Italy in 1936 was a refusal to allow one state, even a great power, to block revision by its refusal to attend a conference when all the other parties to the previous treaty agreed that revision was necessary.

The British delegation asserted as a justification for this action of the Montreux Conference the right of the other parties to renounce individually their right to insist on the old regime, but this interpretation is weakened by the fact that the Montreux Convention was not by its terms limited to the relations between

the signatory powers, and could not be so limited in practice. Also the new convention revised the Convention of Lausanne in other respects besides removing the restriction against militarization. Turkey emphatically rejected any obligation to secure the consent of Italy.

Both the Conference of Lausanne and the Conference of Montreux evoked emphatic statements that no state should be allowed to block action on which the great majority were agreed.

In the negotiations of 1945–1946 Russia ignored the requirement of unanimous consent of previous parties and sought to confine a revisory conference to the Black Sea states, which she regarded as the only ones legitimately interested. The western powers and Turkey upheld the right of all parties to the Montreux Convention, except Japan, to participate in its revision. There was no suggestion, however, that unanimity would have been insisted on at such a conference. The readiness to exclude Japan reflected a belief that her interest had become minimal. It was contemplated that Japan should be compelled to renounce her treaty rights.

CHAPTER VI

INTERNATIONAL REGIMES IN COLONIAL AFRICA

1. THE TREATIES OF MADRID, BERLIN AND BRUSSELS

The scramble for African territory at the end of the nineteenth century was moderated by agreement on international regimes for application to certain areas. The oldest such regime, of customary origin, was the one which developed in the city of Tangier, the port of entry into Morocco and the seat of the diplomatic corps accredited to the Sultan.[1] The representatives of the Christian powers early began to act in common in matters concerning the city. An international Sanitary Council was functioning at least from 1792, and in the course of time the Sultan confirmed its authority over many municipal matters. Each of the consuls of the Christian powers represented in Morocco participated on this body, and when it became necessary to regulate by treaty other matters concerning Morocco this practice of common action by the diplomatic body made it natural that all of the Christian powers represented in Morocco should take part. The first such treaty was the one of 1865, which provided for the maintenance of the important lighthouse at Cape Spartel.[2] It vested control of the lighthouse in the diplomatic corps at Tangier.

In 1880 twelve Christian powers joined with the Sultan in regulating, by the Convention of Madrid, the practice of claiming the privileges of extraterritoriality for Moroccan protégés of the diplomatic missions.[3] The parties to this convention were Germany, Austria-Hungary, Belgium, Denmark, Spain, the United States, France, Great Britain, Italy, the Netherlands, Portugal,

---

[1] The revision of the treaties concerning Tangier has been the subject of a recent case study: Blix, *The Rule of Unanimity in the Revision of Treaties: a Study of the Treaties Governing Tangier*, 5 INTERNATIONAL AND COMPARATIVE LAW QUARTERLY 447–465, 581–596 (1956). See also, STUART (former Adviser to the American Legation at Tangier), THE INTERNATIONAL CITY OF TANGIER (2d ed. 1955).

[2] 1 MALLOY 1217. The parties to the Convention were Austria-Hungary, Belgium, France, Great Britain, Italy, the Netherlands, Portugal, Spain, Sweden and Norway, and the United States. Germany adhered to the Convention in 1878, and Russia in 1899. STUART, *op. cit. supra* at 29.

[3] 1 MALLOY 1220.

Sweden and Norway, and Morocco. Apparently all of the Christian powers represented at Tangier had been invited to the Madrid Conference. Brazil, alone among them, did not attend the Conference, but reserved the right to adhere to the regulations to be established by the other interested powers.[1] The Convention contained no provision for accession, however, and Brazil did not formally accede to it. Russia was permitted to accede to the Madrid Convention by a special protocol in 1881, although she did not establish a legation at Tangier until 1898.[2]

The application of the Madrid Convention was not limited to the signatories. It laid down uniform rules applicable to all diplomatic protection in Tangier. Article 11 recognized that all foreigners possessed the right to hold property in Morocco, though the purchase must take place with the previous consent of the Moroccan government. Article 13 provided that "gate taxes" on the introduction of merchandise into towns should not be increased as applied to foreign nationals, without the consent of the signatory powers. Article 17 provided: "The right to the treatment of the most favored nation is recognized by Morocco as belonging to all the powers represented at the Madrid conference."

In 1885 a conference was held at Berlin on the initiative of the German Government to bring order into the rivalry for control of Central Africa. Germany extended invitations in the first instance to Belgium, France, Great Britain, the Netherlands, Portugal, Spain and the United States, as "the various powers interested in African commerce." Subsequently a second round of invitations was sent, "in order that the resolutions come to by the Conference should receive general consent," to Italy, Russia, Austria-Hungary, Sweden-Norway, Denmark and Turkey.[3] All of the invited States became signatories of the resulting General

---

[1] FRANCE, MINISTÈRE DES AFFAIRES ÉTRANGÈRES, 73 DOCUMENTS DIPLOMATIQUES (Ser. A) 133.

[2] 71 B.F.S.P. 639; cf. STUART, op. cit. supra at 39.

[3] CMD. NO. 4205 at 5–6, 12 (1884). This language may indicate that the acts of this conference like that of the Conference of Madrid were not to be limited to application between the signatories, but were intended to create general international law binding among all the civilized states. Except for Morocco and Turkey the invited powers were the same states as had been parties to the Convention of 1880 on Diplomatic Protection in Morocco. However, a commission of the representatives of the states first named was formed to do the real work of the Berlin Conference. 10 NOUV. REC. GÉN. (2 sér.) 215.

Act of Berlin of February 26, 1885,[1] and all of them ratified it excepting the United States. The purposes of the act were stated to be to set favorable conditions for the development of commerce and civilization in the Congo Basin, to obviate disputes over occupations of territory and to promote the moral and material well-being of the native populations. It contained agreements on freedom of commerce for all nations (the "open door"), on suppression of the slave trade, on freedom of navigation of the Congo and the Niger, and on rules to be observed by the powers in the case of future occupations on the coast of Africa.

The first chapter of the Act provided:

> 2. All flags, without distinction of nationality, shall have freedom of access to the whole coast of the territories named above, to the rivers which flow therefrom into the sea, to all the waters of the Congo and its tributaries. ...
>
> * * *
>
> 5. No Power which exercises or shall exercise rights of sovereignty in the territories named may concede any monopoly or privilege of any kind in commercial matters.

It was planned that an International Commission for the Navigation of the Congo, made up of one delegate of each of the signatory powers, should have the responsibility for overseeing the application of these principles. The International Commission was never appointed, however, and the principles of Chapter I remained without the planned machinery of supervision.[2]

It was later recognized that other states besides the parties to the Act of Berlin derived rights under the general principle, thus established, of free navigation of these rivers. In 1888 the United States, although not a party to the Berlin Act, protested against interference by the Congo authorities with an American ship, and the Congo State, which had adhered to the General Act on February 26, 1885,[3] conceded that the right of free navigation might be insisted on on by all nations.[4]

Article 37 of the Berlin Act provided that other powers besides the original signatories might adhere to it, thus accepting all of

---

[1] 76 B.F.S.P. 4.
[2] 1 OPPENHEIM, INTERNATIONAL LAW 467n. (8th ed. by Lauterpacht, 1955).
[3] 76 B.F.S.P. 1053.
[4] [1888] 1 FOREIGN REL. U.S. 34–38. Further material on rights derived by nonparties is given at p. 174, *supra*, and pp. 234–244, *infra*.

the obligations and receiving all of the benefits of the Act. But by Article 36 adhering powers were to be excluded from participation in revision. This article stated:

> The Signatory Powers of the present General Act reserve to themselves to introduce into it subsequently, and by common accord, such modifications and improvements as experience may show to be expedient.

There was no provision for denunciation.

The report of the Commission of the Conference, which adopted these articles, contains a commentary which explains the drafters' intention.[1] It shows that they were anxious that the system should be capable of effective revision, which they foresaw as a probable necessity, and assumed that unanimity would be required. It was pointed out that the Signatory Powers "indeed constitute the group of States most interested in the questions governed by the General Act," and they should be able to revise it. To admit a right of adhering powers to take part in revision would be "to run the risk of rendering an understanding very difficult." Certain adhering powers whose interests might be directly at stake could always be specially invited to participate. It was particularly foreseen that the future State of the Congo, if it were not constituted in time to be a signatory of the Berlin Act, would be in this category.[2]

In 1890 the signatories of the Berlin Act did revise it by unanimous consent. They did this in the General Act and Declaration of Brussels, which added new and detailed provisions to combat the slave trade and the traffic in firearms and spirituous liquors, and permitted a new tax on imported merchandise to meet the cost of these measures.[3] The Brussels Act contained the same provisions respecting general revision and accessions as had the Act of Berlin.[4] In addition there was a special provision concerning revision of the prescribed import duties on spirituous liquors. On this subject Article 92 provided:

---

[1] 10 NOUV. REC. GÉN. (2 sér.) 401–403.

[2] The Congo Free State was constituted in July, 1885. It was absorbed by Belgium in 1908.

[3] 82 B.F.S.P. 55. The United States ratified these agreements. They were also participated in by the Congo Free State, Persia and Zanzibar.

[4] Arts. 97 and 98 of the Brussels Act. There was again no general provision for denunciation, although certain provisions were terminable after twelve or fifteen years.

The Powers having Possessions or exercising Protectorates in the regions of the zone ... undertake to levy on these spirituous liquors an import duty of 15 fr. per hectolitre up to 50 degrees centigrade for the three years next after the present General Act comes into force. At the expiration of this period the duty may be increased to 25 fr. for a fresh period of three years. At the end of the sixth year it shall be submitted to revision. ...

The Act does not state whether this limited revision was to be undertaken by all the contracting parties or only by "the Powers having Possessions or exercising Protectorates in the zone," nor do the protocols of the conferences shed any light on this point.[1] When Article 92 was revised in 1899, however, Great Britain, Germany, Belgium, Spain, the Congo, France, Italy, the Netherlands, Portugal, Russia, Sweden-Norway and Turkey took part.[2] Not all of these powers had possessions in the zone of Africa in question. Article III of the Convention which they adopted stated:

It is understood that the Powers who signed the General Act of Brussels, or who have acceded to it, and who are not represented at the present Conference, preserve the right of acceding to the present Convention.[3]

The Brussels powers which did not collaborate in drawing up this convention, Austria-Hungary, Denmark, Liberia, Persia and the United States, did accede to it before the deposit of the ratifications of the signatories.[4] The same procedure was followed when this provision was revised again in 1906.[5] The minutes of the conference which made this second revision indicate that the parties to the General Act of Brussels which were not represented had been invited to attend but had chosen not to send delegations. The protocol states that their abstention was "due to the slight interest which the revision of the regime of spirituous liquors in Africa presents for them." [6]

To return to the General Act of 1890, its final clauses provided that it should be ratified within one year and should come into force sixty days following the signature of a protocol of deposit of the ratifications. A year from the date of signature several rati-

[1] *Cf.* ACTES DE LA CONFÉRENCE DE BRUXELLES 393–403 (1890).
[2] 91 B.F.S.P. 6.
[3] *Ibid.*
[4] *Id.* at 8.
[5] 1 NOUV. REC. GÉN. (3e sér.) 722.
[6] *Id.* at 647. It was also stated that Norway and Turkey, parties to the Convention of 1899, had made it known "that they reserved the right to adhere to the decisions to be taken."

fications were still lacking and France had raised specific objections to articles which allowed visit, search and detention of vessels suspected of engaging in the slave trade. The powers therefore drew up a protocol stating their decision, "animated by a sincere desire that an unanimous understanding amongst the Powers should be reached," to extend the delay fixed for the deposit of ratifications. On January 2–3, 1892, representatives of all of the signatories except the United States (all of them except the United States, Portugal and Persia had now ratified) signed a protocol to bring the General Act of Brussels into force.[1]

2. THE ALGECIRAS CONFERENCE

When, in 1905, France sought to impose on the Sultan of Morocco a program of administrative and financial reforms which would have tended to bring that country under French influence, having first by a series of bilateral agreements secured a free hand in the matter from the governments of Italy, England and Spain, Germany objected.[2] In a circular to the signatories of the Convention of 1880 she claimed that decisions to alter the *status quo* could only be taken by a conference of such signatories and that any one of them might veto a change:

> ... The opposition of a single signatory power would suffice to remove all legal justification from any pretention to special rights of any nature which were not compatible with the rights of the most favored nation possessed by the other powers.[3]

The German argument, which was based on the most favored-nation-clause of the Convention of 1880,[4] was disputed by France and it was not stressed in the correspondence which led up to the Algeciras Conference.[5] Seeking the support of the United States and England, Germany emphasized rather the principle of the open door.[6]

[1] 84 B.F.S.P. 53. The United States, which was not a party to the previous General Act (Berlin, 1885), ratified the Act of Brussels one month later, on February 2, 1892. 2 MALLOY 1964.
  [2] STUART, *op. cit. supra* at 41–46.
  [3] 20 GROSSE POLITIK (pt. 2) 413–414.
  [4] *Supra*, p. 180.
  [5] For the opposing French position that Article 17 referred only to matters of diplomatic protection, see TARDIEU, LA CONFÉRENCE D'ALGÉSIRAS 38–41 (1909). The United States later took the same position as Germany. 2 RIGHTS OF NATIONALS OF THE UNITED STATES IN MOROCCO, PLEADINGS, ORAL ARGUMENTS, DOCUMENTS 228 (I.C.J. 1952).
  [6] See 1 BISHOP, THEODORE ROOSEVELT AND HIS TIME 467 ff. (1920).

Germany's political support encouraged the Sultan to resist French pressure and to invite all the governments represented at Tangier to attend a conference to discuss the needed reforms.[1] France was at first opposed to any conference, and the British government also opposed the Sultan's suggestion on the ground that no procedure would be "less likely to bring about the salutary reforms which were so much needed in Morocco than a discussion undertaken by ten or a dozen Powers, some of whom had virtually no concern whatever in the country."[2] Germany proposed that, instead of a discussion by the powers represented at Tangier, the conference should be of the signatories of the Convention of 1880, and it was to all such signatories that the invitations to the Algeciras Conference were finally addressed.[3] Since the subjects to be discussed (organization of the police, suppression of the arms traffic, financial reform, taxes and public services) did not include diplomatic protection or the right of all foreigners to own Moroccan property, it was not clear that any real revision of the Madrid Convention was contemplated. The essence of the German position seems to have been that all powers with commercial treaties with Morocco and commercial intersts in the country had a right to be consulted concerning any changes there wich might affect their interests, and that the category of "interested powers" had received an authoritative definition in the earlier convention.

All of the other parties to the Madrid Convention except Denmark and Norway were represented at the conference that ultimately met at Algeciras, Spain, on January 16, 1906. None of them except Germany had insisted on a right to consideration of the contemplated reforms by a conference. Denmark had accepted the invitation only on condition that all the interested great powers should also accept, but she later decided not to participate.[4] The fact that the Act of Algeciras made no provision for accession by the absent signatories of the Madrid Convention, although Norway had asked that it be given the opportunity to accede,[5] seems to show that participation in the Madrid conven-

[1] [1905] FOREIGN REL. U.S. 668; 3 BRIT. DOCS. 88, 92–93.
[2] 3 BRIT. DOCS. 90.
[3] *Id.* at 114, 146–147.
[4] *Id.* at 101; Blix, *op. cit. supra* at 448n.
[5] Norway, whose union with Sweden was dissolved on Octoger 26, 1905, declined an invitation to attend the conference but asked to be given the opportunity to adhere to the agreement which should result. Blix, *op. cit. supra* at 448–449n.

tion was not thought to give a right to participate in the new act.[1]

The conference at Algeciras followed the unanimity rule of conference procedure.[2] It was evident, however, that Morocco's consent would be compelled, if necessary. On several occasions the European delegates were not content to accept the announced opposition of the Moroccan delegates and required them to consult their government further, in view of "the unanimous assent of the Powers" to the propositions in question.[3]

The Act of Algeciras affirmed the principle of "economic liberty without inequality," i.e. the open door.[4] The right of foreigners to acquire property in Morocco, as stated in the Madrid Convention, was reaffirmed and extended. Chapter VI contained provisions to ensure that concessions for public works should be issued on an equal and competitive basis under the supervision of the Diplomatic Body at Tangier. The Act also affirmed the independence and territorial integrity of Morocco. However, France and Spain were given special authority to train the Moroccan police, and Article 30 recognized French and Spanish zones of authority for the enforcement of regulations concerning the contraband trade in arms. Other provisions were aimed at internationalization. Supervision of the Moroccan police was to be exercised by the Diplomatic Body at Tangier. Switzerland as a neutral country was to provide an Inspector-General for the police force, and appeals in litigation involving the Moroccan State Bank were to go to the Swiss Federal Court of Lausanne. Supervision of the Bank was to rest with "censors" appointed by the German, English, Spanish and French state banks, and all of the powers repre-

---

[1] A theory that parties to the Madrid Convention were under a duty to attend the Algeciras Conference was advanced by Secretary of State Root in his effort to get the Senate to ratify the Act. Root also seemed to consider the Act of Algeciras as a revision of the Convention of 1880. His biographer reports: "[Root's] argument was that we had made treaties with Morocco in 1787 and 1836 and had then become a party to the General Convention of Madrid signed by all the great powers of Europe in 1880. The new Algeciras Treaty 'merely modifies and extends the provisions of the treaty of 1880 in accordance with the requirements of the present day.' The United States, Root said, could not 'with decency' have refused to go into a conference with the other parties to modify the treaty of 1880 and if we declined to ratify this new treaty 'we will be for the first time in one hundred and twenty years, without any treaty relation with Morocco whatever ... we have merely done what our participation in the Madrid Convention of 1880 made it incumbent upon us to do. ... '" 2 JESSUP, ELIHU ROOT 60 (1938).
[2] CONFÉRENCE INTERNATIONAL D'ALGÉCIRAS (1906).
[3] *Id.* at 44, 57–58.
[4] 2 MALLOY 2156.

sented at Algeciras were to have equal rights to subscribe to shares of the Bank's stock.

Chapter IV of the Act, a declaration concerning taxes, also delegated a number of duties to the Diplomatic Body at Tangier. It authorized the imposition of a tax on city buildings and provided that at Tangier a portion of this revenue, to be applied to municipal improvements, was to be turned over to the International Sanitary Council, which should decide as to its use "until the creation of a municipal organization" (Art. 61). The proceeds of a tax of $2^1/_2$ per cent on the entry of foreign merchandise into Morocco were to be devoted to the execution of a program of public works, as "determined jointly by the Shereefian Government and the Diplomatic Body at Tangier" (Art. 66). The Diplomatic Body was also to have a voice in awarding public contracts, in establishing regulations concerning customs storage dues and in determining the amount of opium imported under the government's opium monopoly. By Chapter V the Diplomatic Body at Tangier was also given responsibilities relating to the collection of the Moroccan customs.

Provisions concerning revision of parts of the Act showed an assumption of the requirement of unanimity of the parties as the rule ordinarily governing treaty revision. Article 75 provided that the provisions of the declaration concerning tax matters might be modified by an understanding between the Maghzen (the Moroccan government) and the Diplomatic Body. Article 76 stated that the Diplomatic Body should reach decisions by a majority of votes in some cases, but specifically excluded from that rule decisions under Article 75. Article 104 provided that Chapter V, concerning customs, might be revised by "unanimous decision of the Diplomatic Body at Tangier and in accord with the Maghzen."

3. THE FRENCH PROTECTORATE IN MOROCCO

France, having sent troops into Morocco in 1911, departed from the principle of the independence of the Sultan which had been recognized in the Act of Algeciras by forcing him to accept a French protectorate under the terms of the Treaty of Fez of March 30, 1912.[1] She had obtained Germany's approval of this

[1] 6 NOUV. REC. GÉN. (3 sér.) 332.

action, in return for territorial compensations in Equatorial Africa, in the Franco-German Convention of November 4, 1911.[1] Germany, while "reserving the commercial liberty envisaged by the previous treaties," agreed to offer no hindrance to the establishment of the French protectorate. Article 13 of the convention provided that all clauses of previous agreements which might be contrary to its terms were abrogated. Article 14 provided that the convention should be communicated "to the other signatory Powers of the Act of Algeciras, with regard to whom the two Governments agree to lend mutual support to obtain their adherence."

The British, Russian, Italian and Swedish governments did adhere promptly to the Franco-German agreement.[2] None of the other parties to the Act of Algeciras gave their approval in advance of the establishment of the French protectorate. It was generally recognized that the extension of French (and Spanish) control was not consistent with the Act of Algeciras.[3] However, the Franco-German agreement represented the solution of a European crisis which had carried a serious threat of general war. In these circumstances there were no formal legal objections to the procedure followed. The problem of obtaining the consent of the parties to the Act of Algeciras, or of the effect if they did not consent, was postponed for later consideration.[4] The Franco-German agreement recognized, however, that their agreement should be obtained if possible.

[1] 5 *id.* 643.
[2] The British government did so with the understanding that the agreement did not affect the special character of Tangier. 7 NOUV. REC. GÉN. (3 sér.) 124–125. The adherence of the other powers is referred to in a French note to the United States of December 6, 1911. [1911] FOREIGN REL. U.S. 623. The *quid pro quo* for Italy's adherence was freedom of action in Libya. See 8 NOUV. REC. GÉN. (3 sér.) 144.
[3] The German Chancellor stated his view, before Germany's agreement with France, that subordination of the Sultan to French control would destroy the basis of the Treaty of Algeciras. 7 BRIT. DOCS. 197. Sir Edward Grey wrote on July 20, 1911, "France, Spain, and Germany have all stepped outside the Algeciras Act together." *Id.* at 382. See also, 40 H.C. DEB. (5th ser.) 2007–2008 (1912).
[4] The British Ambassador in Paris had written home on August 3, 1911: "Another difficulty which will arise supposing that the German and French Governments come to terms will be how the acquiescence of the other Powers parties to the Algeciras Act is to be obtained either in a Conference or without one. Germany may be able to answer for Austria-Hungary and perhaps Sweden and possibly but not probably Italy. France can make sure of Russian and British consent, but who is to answer for the United States of America, Belgium, Holland and Portugal. Will they require compensations on the principle and example instituted by Germany and if so who is to provide them." 7 BRIT. DOCS. 431.

The French government has stated that all the powers signatory to the Act of Algeciras except the United States did ultimately adhere to the Franco-German agreement.[1]

The United States, to which the Franco-German agreement was communicated by the French government, replied that to adhere to the provisions relating to commercial rights and the administration of justice "would involve a modification of our existing treaty rights with Morocco, which under our Constitution could only be done by and with the advice and consent of the United States Senate." [2] The Franco-German agreement had stated an intention to take up with the powers signatory to the Convention of Madrid revisions of the provisions concerning diplomatic protection. As to this the United States declared that it would be willing to negotiate at "the proper time." The United States recognized the French protectorate in 1917, but without abandoning its "capitulatory and other rights" under the previous treaties.[3] It continued to protest regularly against any French encroachments on these treaty rights.[4]

Article 141 of the Treaty of Versailles provided:

> Germany renounces all rights, titles and privileges conferred on her by the General Act of Algeciras of April 7, 1906.... All treaties, agreements, arrangements and contracts concluded by her with the Sherifian Empire are regarded as abrogated as from August 3, 1914.

By Article 142 Germany also renounced the regime of capitulations. Similar provisions were contained in the peace treaties with Austria and Hungary. Discussions at the Peace Conference made it clear that there was no intention, by these provisions, to affect the rights of any other powers.[5] France's representative did suggest that she desired "the repeal of the Treaty of Algeciras," but when questioned by the representative of Great Britain

---

[1] 1 RIGHTS OF NATIONALS OF THE UNITED STATES IN MOROCCO, PLEADINGS, ORAL ARGUMENTS, DOCUMENTS 46–47 (I.C.J. 1952).

[2] [1911] FOREIGN REL. U.S. 623.

[3] 1 HACKWORTH, DIGEST OF INTERNATIONAL LAW 89.

[4] 1 RIGHTS OF NATIONALS OF THE UNITED STATES IN MOROCCO, PLEADINGS, ORAL ARGUMENTS, DOCUMENTS 669–733 (I.C.J. 1952). With respect to departures from the provisions of the Act of Algeciras concerning customs, Secretary of State Hull stated on February 9 and on March 16, 1933: "This Government strongly believes that it is obligatory that the parties to the Act of Algeciras should not only be consulted but that each Power should acquiesce before any changes are made in the customs regime in Morocco." *Id.* at 706–707, 805.

[5] Blix, *op. cit. supra* at 453–454n.

he conceded that the Peace Conference could not affect the rights of absent powers.[1] The remarks of Mr. Balfour and M. de Peretti on this subject were reported as follows:

> Mr. Balfour: He would like to enquire whether the Peace Conference had any right without consulting Spain to remove or abrogate a Treaty in which Spanish interests appeared to be very intimately concerned. ... The five Great Powers were there as guardians of the Treaty rights of the world. Therefore he would deeply regret if anything were done which might have the appearance of an attempt to impose conditions on neutrals, apparently depriving them of their rights.
>
> M. de Peretti: There was no question of imposing anything on any country not represented at the Conference. All that France asked was that the Powers represented at the Conference should voluntarily renounce the privileges which they had acquired by the Act of Algeciras.

The language of Article 141 indicates, however, that the renunciation of rights was made by Germany alone.[2]

All of the other parties to the treaties of Madrid and Algeciras, except the United States, eventually agreed to renounce their capitulatory rights in Morocco. The United States alone reserved all its treaty rights.[3] When, in 1952, the International Court of Justice was asked to decide what these rights were, as to the French Zone of Morocco, the parties argued the correct interpretation of the Act of Algeciras, but the validity of its provisions as between them was not disputed by France. The Court took it for granted that all rights derived by the United States from the Act of Algeciras continued to exist, and based its finding that the United States remained entitled to exercise consular jurisdiction in French Morocco in part on that Act.[4] It stated that France, as the protecting power, remained bound "by all treaty obligations to which Morocco had been subject before the Protectorate and which have not since been terminated or suspended by arrangement with the interested States."[5] The Court equally

---

[1] 4 FOREIGN REL. U.S., PARIS PEACE CONFERENCE 1919 at 135, 128–129 (1943).

[2] *Cf.* the language of Arts. 31 and 435 (referring to treaties concerning Belgium and the free zones of Upper Savoy and Gex).

[3] The United States renounced its capitulatory rights in 1956. 35 DEP'T STATE BULL. 844 (1956).

[4] Case concerning Rights of Nationals of the United States of America in Morocco, [1952] I.C.J. Rep. 175.

[5] *Id.* at 188. Four dissenting judges were more explicit on this point: "The Act of Algeciras is a great multilateral convention directly binding upon Morocco and the United States as well as the other signatory Powers. ... The scheme of rights and obligations which it established ... as between Morocco and the United States can not, therefore, be allowed to be impaired by any transactions concluded between

assumed, however, that the other parties were entitled to renounce the benefits of the Act so far as they were concerned.[1]

4. REVISION OF THE ACTS OF BERLIN AND BRUSSELS BY THE PEACE CONFERENCE OF 1919

At the Paris Peace Conference the Council of Foreign Ministers of the Big Five Allied Powers decided on a revision of the General Acts of Berlin and Brussels. Drafts of conventions to replace them were drawn up by the British and French delegations and sent by them to the governments of the United States, Italy, Belgium, Japan and Portugal, and the Council of Foreign Ministers agreed that these seven Allied governments were the "interested Powers" which should participate in a Commission to examine the drafts.[2]

The Commission met and drew up a Convention Revising the General Acts of Berlin and Brussels, which was signed at St Germain on September 10, 1919.[3] Article 13 of the new convention provided:

> Except in so far as the stipulations contained in Article I of the present Convention are concerned, the General Act of Berlin of February 26, 1885, and the General Act of Brussels of July 2, 1890, with the accompany-

any of the other signatories without the concurrence of both Morocco and the United States. This appears to us to be fundamental." *Id.* at 217. They added that the provisions of the Convention of Madrid and the Act of Algeciras were undoubtedly still in force "so far as the United States is concerned." *Id.* at 219, 224.

[1] See especially pp. 188 and 198–199 of the Court's opinion, and *cf.* pp. 232–233. The United States also apparently assumed that the other parties were entitled to renounce the benefits of the Act of Algeciras, but that such action did not affect the rights of the United States. Its agent argued before the Court: "The Government of the French Republic has pointed out that the United States is the only country which was a party to the Act of Algeciras which has not adhered to both the Franco-German Convention of November 4th, 1911, and to the Treaty of Fez. This is true, just as the corollary is true that the United States is the only country whose representative in Morocco retains official diplomatic status and who is accredited to the Sultan. The United States does not agree, however, with the intimation of the French Government that its refusal to agree to these two Conventions places it in an invidious position. Every one of the leading countries interested in Morocco which adhered to the Franco-German Convention and to the Treaty of Fez did so in return for a specific *quid pro quo*. . . . The United States did not ask for any *quid pro quo*. . . . [It] merely asked that it retain the treaty rights which it already had in Morocco." 2 PLEADINGS, ORAL ARGUMENTS, DOCUMENTS 222–223.

[2] 4 FOREIGN REL. U.S., PARIS PEACE CONFERENCE 1919 at 856–857 (1943).

[3] 1 HUDSON, INTERNATIONAL LEGISLATION 343. The new convention freed the colonial powers from certain restrictions of the Berlin Act. In place of the prohibition of any possession of a monopoly or commercial privilege Article 4 now provided: "Each State reserves the right to dispose freely of its property and to grant concessions for the development of the natural resources of the territory, but no regulations on these matters shall admit of any differential treatment between the nationals of the Signatory Powers and of States . . . which may adhere to the present Convention."

ing Declaration of equal date, shall be considered as abrogated, in so far as they are binding between the Powers which are parties to the present Convention.

Besides the exclusion of Russia, which was a common feature of post-war treaty revision procedure, none of the neutral signatories of the Berlin and Brussels Acts (Spain, Norway, Sweden, Denmark and the Netherlands) had participated or been consulted.[1] The new convention provided that these states might adhere to it, and that the Signatory Powers would use their best endeavors to obtain their adherence (Article 14), but in providing for a revisory conference at the end of ten years it was specified that this function was to be performed by the signatory powers, with no mention of those adhering (Article 15).[2]

These was no discussion in the Commission itself concerning the departure from the revision procedure laid down in the Berlin and Brussels General Acts, that matter having been decided for them by the Big Five's Council of Foreign Ministers, and the effect of the new convention on the other signatories of the previous acts was only discussed briefly.[3] The interest of those other signatories was in fact slight. None of them had possessions in the Congo Basin, and the International Commission for the Congo River, on which they would have had representation under the Berlin Act, had never come into existence. The members of the Commission therefore feared that these other signatories would see no advantage to be gained by adhering to the new convention, and would prefer to retain their rights under the Acts of Berlin and Brussels. The President of the Commission (M. Peretti of France), apparently assuming that the Act of Berlin was not intended to be permanent, although it contained no express denunciation clause, suggested that it would be possible to denounce the Berlin Act without qualification and that this would be one way to force the opening of negotiations with the states not participating in the new convention. The delegate of Belgium thought that this

---

[1] In the Peace Treaties Germany, Austria, Hungary and Turkey all undertook to accept the new convention, or renounced their pre-war rights. See Art. 126 of the Treaty with Germany, Arts. 95 and 234 of the Treaty with Austria, Arts. 79 and 217 of the Treaty with Hungary, and Art. 100 (12) of the Treaty of Lausanne (Turkey)

[2] The right to adhere was denied to Russia, at least temporarily, by a clause (directed primarily against Germany) which required that adhering states, if not the possessors of African territories, must be members of the League of Nations.

[3] 2 DROIT COLONIAL INTERNATIONAL, CONFÉRENCE DE LA PAIX DE PARIS 168–169, 179–180 (1931).

was unnecessary, for "sooner or later there will be negotiations with them on other subjects, and these will offer the occasion to impose on them adherence to this Convention as a condition of granting the advantages claimed by them." [1] The first draft of the new convention had provided simply that the Acts of Berlin and Brussels were now abrogated, but this was amended in the course of the deliberations to add the words, "in so far as they are binding between the Powers which are parties to the present Convention." [2] It was agreed that under this wording the parties which refused to adhere to the new convention would continue to possess rights under the Act of Berlin.[3]

The Convention of St. Germain had no denunciation clause. Article 15 provided for future revision as follows:

> The Signatory Powers will reassemble at the expiration of ten years from the coming into force of the present Convention, in order to introduce into it such modifications as experience may have shown to be necessary.

This Article was adopted by the Commission after the Belgian delegate had commented that at such meetings it was usual to seek to act unanimously.[4] There was a difference of opinion as to what would be the effect if at such a meeting there was no agreement. The majority, however, seemed to believe that each power would then be at liberty to withdraw from the Convention.[5] No revisory conference pursuant to this Article was ever held.

None of the other parties to the Berlin Act ever did adhere to the Convention of St. Germain. It was stated in 1934 in the opinion of the Permanent Court of International Justice in the *Oscar Chinn* case that there was no evidence that any of them ever challenged its validity.[6] This lack of interest is perhaps explained by the fact that the provisions of the Act of Berlin which purported to open up the Congo to the free trade of all nations had proved in practice to be illusory.[7]

---

[1] *Id.* at 180. (Translated).
[2] *Id.* at 147, 168.
[3] *Id.* at 168, 179.
[4] "Dans des réunions de ce genre, il est de règle que l'on s'efforce de voter à l'unanimité." *Id.* at 172.
[5] *Id.* at 170–172. The Belgian delegate stated that he could not accept "the idea that one could impose on the African Powers a sort of perpetual contract." *Id.* at 172. (Translated).
[6] P.C.I.J. Ser. A/B, No. 63 at 80 (1934).
[7] Besides the failure to effectuate the International Commission, King Leopold had established monopolies in the Congo contrary to the provisions of the

The validity of the Convention of St. Germain as a revision of the Berlin Act was discussed by the Permanent Court of International Justice in 1934 in the *Oscar Chinn* case.[1] The case concerned a claim by the United Kingdom against Belgium on behalf of a British national who owned a river transport business in the Congo. The claim was for damage resulting from preferential treatment accorded to a rival company, controlled by the Belgian Government. In their arguments before the Court neither the United Kingdom nor Belgium sought to go behind the Convention of St. Germain of September 10, 1919, but based their rights on that convention and on general principles of international law. The majority of the Court, rejecting the British claim, noted that it was not open to the Court to consider the effect of the Acts of Berlin and Brussels where both parties were relying on the Convention of St. Germain as the source of their contractual rights and obligations.[2] Judges van Eysinga and Schücking, who dissented and urged further inquiry into the facts, thought that the Act of Berlin was the only treaty which the Court could apply, since the revision of that act by less than all of its parties must have been devoid of legal effect. Judge van Eysinga reached this conclusion on the basis of general principles, and regarded Article 36 of the Berlin Act, which authorized revision "by common accord" of the signatories, as superfluous.[3] He urged that the constitutional character of the Act should preclude *inter se* modifications.[4] Judge Schücking's position was different. He

Act. SAYRE, EXPERIMENTS IN INTERNATIONAL ADMINISTRATION 83–87 (1919). One author notes that Sweden, Norway, the Netherlands, Denmark and Spain were all among the signatories of a Geneva Slavery Convention of September 25, 1926, which referred in its preamble to the need to give effect to the intentions in regard to the slave trade expressed by the signatories of the "Convention of Saint Germain-en-Laye of 1919 to revise the General [Acts] of Berlin [and Brussels[." From this and other circumstances he concludes that those states acquiesced in the abrogation of the Berlin Act. Muûls, *Le Régime International du Bassin Conventionnel du Congo*, 2 MÉLANGES OFFERTS À ERNEST MAHEIM 226 (1935). However, it could equally well have been concluded, at least with respect to the Act of Brussels, that that Act was recognized to be still effective, since the Slavery Convention of 1926 also stated the parties' desire "to complete and extend the work accomplished under the Brussels Act." All of the parties to the Act of Brussels, except Russia and Turkey, signed the 1926 Convention. 3 HUDSON, INTERNATIONAL LEGISLATION 2010.

[1] P.C.I.J., Ser. A/B, No. 63 (1934).
[2] *Id.* at 80.
[3] *Id.* at 132–136.
[4] "The General Act of Berlin does not create a number of contractual relations between a number of States, relations which may be replaced as regards some of these States by other contractual relations; ... it provides the Congo Basin with a

emphasized Article 36 as a specific expression of the intention of the parties to the Berlin Act, and it was from this Article, rather than from general principle, that he decuded the nullity of the Convention of St. Germain. His opinion states:

> Once it is recognized that the intention was to create a Staute of the Congo which should not be liable to be altered by some only of its authors, the will of the Powers must be interpreted as being that no convention can acquire valid existence that is contracted in disregard of the rule. ... [The Convention of St. Germain] remains null and void, because it transgresses the bounds which the authors of the Berlin Act established for themselves when they subscribed to that Act.[1]

Judge Schücking thought that in these circumstances the Court should be governed by "considerations of international public policy" and should refuse to apply the Convention of St. Germain, regardless of the position taken by the parties to the dispute.[2] It must be emphasized, however, that the majority of the Court did not accept the van Eysinga-Schücking viewpoint.

It may be pertinent to consider here some other decisions of international tribunals bearing on this point. The theory of the dissenting judges that a treaty violative of the preexisting treaty rights of third parties should be considered legally void is not supported by any international judicial decision unless it be the dictum of the Central American Court of Justice in the cases of *Costa Rica* v. *Nicaragua* and *El Salvador* v. *Nicaragua*, decided in 1916–17.[3] The court found in those cases that a treaty between Nicaragua and the United States, conceding to the United States special rights in the San Juan River and in the Gulf of Fonseca, violated rights acquired by the other Central American republics in previous treaties with Nicaragua. Though it found that Nicaragua was without legal power to enter into an

---

regime, a statute, a constitution. This regime, which forms an indivisible whole, may be modified, but for this the agreement of all contracting Powers is required." *Id.* at 133–134.

[1] P.C.I.J., Ser. A/B, No. 63 at 148–149 (1934).

[2] Sir Cecil Hurst, who dissented on other grounds, also noted that the parties to the Act of Berlin might have intended to adopt a special rule excluding *inter se* modifications, but he agreed with the majority that the Court should not go into that matter since "Both the United Kingdom and Belgium are parties to the Convention [of St. Germain] and have in this case treated it as the operative instrument." *Id.* at 122–123.

[3] Reported in 11 A.J.I.L. 181, 674 (1916). See also the dissenting opinion of Judge Schücking in the Case of the S.S. "Wimbledon," P.C.I.J., Ser. A, No. 1, at 47, and the concurring opinion of Judge Anzilotti in the Case of the Austro-German Customs Regime, P.C.I.J., Ser. A/B, No. 41, at 64 (1931).

agreement of this character with the United States, the court found itself without legal competence, since the United States was not before it, to declare the later treaty void. It should be noted that the United States was not a party to the earlier treaty and that no no intent to revise the earlier treaty was involved. The effect on the rights of third parties aside, the view of the majority of the Court in the *Oscar Chinn* Case that the later agreement could not be questioned in a dispute exclusively between the parties to it is supported by the decision of the Permanent Court of International Justice in the Case of the *Jurisdiction of the European Commission of the Danube*[1] as well as by a dictum in the Case of the *Mavrommatis Palestine Concessions*.[2] In the latter case between Great Britain and Greece, Great Britain contended that Protocol XII of the Treaty of Lausanne, to which Great Britain and Greece were parties, withdrew from the Permanent Court the jurisdiction which it would have had under the terms of the British Palestine Mandate, to decide disputes between the Mandatory and any other Member of the League. The Court, although disagreeing that the Protocol was intended to have such effect, stated:

> Although the provisions of the Mandate possess a special character by reason of the fact that they have been drawn up by the Council of the League of Nations, neither of the Parties has attempted to argue that a Member of the League cannot renounce rights which he possesses under the terms of the Mandate.
>
> * * *
>
> The fact that ... the Protocol is more recent in date than the Mandate, does not justify the conclusion that the Protocol would only be applicable in Palestine in so far as it is compatible with the Mandate. On the contrary, in cases of doubt, the Protocol, being a special and more recent agreement, should prevail.[3]

5. THE TANGIER CONVENTION OF 1923

The establishment of the French protectorate in Morocco created a new situation which made it necessary to have some new agreement about the status of Tangier. All of the powers recognized that the Sultan of Morocco was its legitimate sovereign, though his administrative control had, in the words of the Tangier correspondent of the London *Times*, "gradually become

---

[1] *Supra*, pp. 140–142.
[2] Judgment of August 30, 1949, P.C.I.J., Ser. A, No. 2 (1949).
[3] *Id.* at 30–31.

diminished by a sort of superimposed, and often usurped, form of internationalization." [1] With France now controlling the Sultan, England and Spain were determined to restrict the latter's powers in Tangier.[2]

The "special character" of Tangier had been acknowledged in a series of bilateral accords starting in 1904. Article 7 of the British-French agreement of that year stated that no fortifications should be erected on this part of the coast.[3] The Franco-Spanish agreement of the same year stated that Tangier was to keep "the special character which the presence of the diplomatic corps and its municipal and sanitary institutions have given it." [4] The British government stated a similar condition for its adherence to the Franco-German Convention of November 4, 1911,[5] and the treaty which established the French protectorate provided also that the city would retain this "special character." [6] The French-Spanish agreement of 1912 defined the boundaries of the Tangier zone and stated that it would be "endowed with a special regime which shall be determined subsequently." [7]

The drafting of a special regime for the zone of Tangier was started in 1912 by British, French and Spanish experts. Despite the fact that numerous provisions of the Act of Algeciras applied to the government of the zone, none of the other parties to the Act were invited to participate in this work. When Germany reminded France that she had not renounced any of her rights in Tangier, the French government conceded that Germany's consent to the eventual settlement would be required. It also appears to have been contemplated by the British government that the project should be submitted to the signatories of the Act of Algeciras before its final acceptance.[8] The tripartite commission had prepared the text of an international convention to be signed by the powers signatory to the Act of Algeciras,

[1] The Times (London), September 28, 1923.
[2] England's interest was primarily strategic, the denial of control of this port on the Straits of Gibraltar to any single foreign power. Spain considered Tangier as properly within her zone of influence but was willing to accept internationalization as a lesser evil than French control.
[3] 97 B.F.S.P. 39.
[4] 102 *id.* 432.
[5] 7 NOUV. REC. GÉN. (3 sér.) 124–125.
[6] 6 *id.* 332.
[7] *id.* 124–125, 326; STUART, *op. cit. supra* at 59-62.
[8] STUART, *op. cit. supra* at 61.

when the outbreak of World War I interrupted the negotiations.[1]

After the war tripartite negotiations were resumed, with France now claiming a larger share of control than she had been willing to accept in 1912.[2] Agreement of the three governments on a statute for the city was finally reached at a conference held in Paris at the end of 1923. It had been announced that the conference would be limited to representatives of Great Britain, France and Spain.[3] When Italy asked to participate, as a party to the Act of Algeciras and as an important Mediterranean power, her request was refused. It was explained that the conference had already commenced its work and was a continuation of the tripartite discussions of before the war, and the French government reminded Italy of their joint declaration of October, 1912, in which Italy had promised to raise no obstacle to France's plans in Morocco.[4] It appeared that the three powers were having considerable difficulties in reaching agreement among themselves, and it was probable that they felt there was a better chance of reaching agreement if the conference was kept small and private.[5] No report of the discussions was published.

Except for Italy, none of the other parties to the Act of Algeciras claimed a right to participate in the 1923 conference. The position of the United States was unusual. It had signed the Act of Algeciras subject to a reservation which stated that it had no particular interest in Morocco and would assume no obligation or responsibility for the enforcement of the act.[6] In reply to the French invitation to adhere to the Franco-German agreement in 1911 Secretary of State Knox wrote that in conformity with its traditional foreign policy the United States would "refrain from any expression of opinion for or against such part or parts of the Franco-German agreement in relation to Morocco as may be

[1] *Id.* at 62–64.

[2] 169 H.C. DEB. (5th ser.) 134–135 (1924).

[3] [1923] 2 FOREIGN REL. U.S. 579–580. It was pointed out in the House of Commons that the Sultan of Morocco, being under French protection, would be properly represented by France. 156 H.C. DEB (5th ser.) 2097 (1922).

[4] STUART, *op. cit. supra* at 78–80, 96–97; *cf.* 8 NOUV. REC. GÉN. (3 sér.) 144. Italy placed more reliance on her right as a great Mediterranean power to political equality in the adjustment of a "Mediterranean" question than she did on her rights as a party to the Act of Algeciras. STUART, *op. cit. supra* at 97–98.

[5] They later informed the Belgian government that it was impossible to make any changes in their convention because of the difficulty which had been encountered in reaching an agreement. [1924] 2 FOREIGN REL. U.S. 457.

[6] 2 MALLOY 2182–2183.

deemed of a political nature."[1] It therefore seemed very unlikely that the United States would have been willing to participate in the 1923 Conference if it had been invited. The United States nevertheless gave notice that it would insist on its existing treaty rights. After being informed of the approaching conference, Secretary of State Hughes cabled to London, Paris and Madrid:

> This Government takes this occasion to remind the Governments participating in the Conference ... that its fundamental interest in Tangier is to maintain the principle of the Open Door. ... It presumes that at the forthcoming conference nothing will be done to interfere with the maintenance of the principle above mentioned or the rights or interests of the United States.[2]

On October 31, 1923, the British Foreign Office assured the United States Ambassador that no power signatory to the Act of Algeciras would be considered bound by the decisions of the tripartite conference and that they would be given full opportunity to approve or disapprove of the scheme adopted.[3]

The 1923 Convention was based on the principles of permanent neutrality and nonfortification of the Tangier zone and maintenance of the open door.[4] The functions previously performed by the Sanitary Council, or entrusted by the Act of Algeciras to "the Diplomatic Body at Tangier," were now to be the responsibility of new international agencies: a Legislative Assembly, an Administrator, a Mixed Court, a Port Commission and a Committee of Control. The Legislative Assembly was to include representatives of all the Algeciras powers, except for those which had renounced their rights by the peace treaties and Russia, whose Soviet government was still not recognized by the other powers, but France, Spain, England and Italy were to receive weighted representation.[5] The Mixed Court was to be composed only of French, British and Spanish judges. The entire governmental structure was to be supervised by the Committee of Control, composed of the consuls of the powers signatories of the Act of Algeciras. It would take decisions (including the veto of legislation) by majority vote.

[1] [1911] FOREIGN REL. U.S. 623.
[2] [1923] 2 *id.* 580.
[3] *Id.* at 583.
[4] 28 L.N.T.S. 542. Text also printed in STUART, *op. cit. supra* at 201.
[5] Four each for France and Spain, three for England and two for Italy (Art. 34). There were also nine nominees of the Moroccan government, likely to be under French control.

Several of the articles of the Convention referred to the continuing validity of the Act of Algeciras.[1] Other articles, however, made changes in the scheme of the Madrid and Algeciras treaties in terms of general application. Thus, it was provided in Article 13:

> As a result of the establishment at Tangier of the Mixed Court ... the capitulations shall be abrogated in the Zone. This abrogation shall entail the suppression of the system of protection.

And in Article 48 it was stated that the Mixed Court should have general jurisdiction over nationals of foreign powers, replacing the existing consular jurisdictions. Article 42 provided that anchorage dues, which by the Act of Algeciras could be revised only with unanimous consent of the diplomatic corps, were to be replaced by the berthage dues provided for in the port concession described in the Convention. Article 49 provided that with entry into force of the new administration the diplomatic agencies at Tangier would be replaced by consulates. Article 50 provided: "The existing commissions and committees at Tangier shall be abolished."

The signatories of the Act of Algeciras were to be given an opportunity to adhere to the Convention, and the contracting governments agreed to "lend each other mutual support in obtaining the accession of those Powers." However, entry into force of the Convention was not made dependent on such accession, and Article 55 provided: "All clauses of previous treaties, conventions, or agreements which may be contrary to the provisions of the present Statute are abrogated."

Revision of the Convention, if necessary, was to be "by common agreement."

The new Statute was put into operation in the spring of 1925.[2] Of the Algeciras powers to which it had been communicated, Sweden and Belgium acceded at the end of 1924, Belgium having won some minor modifications in her favor, the Netherlands acceded in October, 1925, and Portugal in 1926.[3] The United States, after consulting with the other Algeciras powers, replied to the invitation to accede that it would be willing to consider the possibility of surrendering its extraterritorial rights in the Zone,

---

[1] See Arts. 22, 23, 24, 38.
[2] STUART, *op. cit. supra* at 88.
[3] *Id.* at 82–83; see also [1924] 2 FOREIGN REL. U.S. 457–459.

and acceding to the Convention, if certain conditions were met (added assurances of economic equality, acknowledgement by the signatories of international responsibility for the acts of the administrative authorities of the Zone, the right to designate associate judges in any cases involving American citizens, etc.). It repeated that the United States had no political interest in Tangier and did not want to participate in the administration of the Zone.[1] The three signatories stated their willingness to grant most of these conditions.[2] However, the negotiations were dropped after the United States requested further clarifications and indicated that its accession to the convention would require in any event "an appropriate Convention to that end with the approval of the Senate ... or appropriate legislative sanction of the suspension of extraterritorial rights." [3] The three powers, on putting their Convention into effect, expressed the hope that the United States, having raised no objections "of a fundamental character," would accept the necessity of establishing the new regime without further delay.[4] The United States replied reserving all its rights.[5] Secretary of State Hughes instructed the United States Chargé in Morocco:

> It is not the purpose of the United States to pursue a policy of obstruction in the face of the effort made by the signatory powers of the Tangier Convention to provide the Tangier Zone with a satisfactory form of government, an effort which will of necessity alter in some degree the previously existing administrative machinery.
> A distinction therefore must be made between those acts of the authorities of Tangier which adversely affect substantial American rights and interests and those which merely involve unimportant departures from or nonobservance of practices established under the Act of Algeciras. ...
> Incidents of the latter sort need not be made the subject of formal complaint. ...[6]

Italy, however, was unwilling to co-operate even to this extent. The first clash came over the attempted abolition of the Sanitary Council. Article 61 of the Act of Algeciras had con-

---

[1] [1924] 2 FOREIGN REL. U.S. 459–463. The Under Secretary of State added his assurance "that our spirit in the matter was one of cooperation and that we desired to place no obstacles in the way of the proposed regime so long as our interests were properly safeguarded." *Id.* at 463.
[2] *Id.* at 463 ff.; STUART, *op. cit. supra* at 84–85.
[3] [1924] 2 FOREIGN REL. U.S. 470–472.
[4] [1925] 2 *id.* 591–593.
[5] *Id.* at 599.
[6] *Id.* at 590–591.

ferred municipal functions on this body "until the creation of a municipal organization." [1] The United States representative noted that the disappearance of the Sanitary Council would not, "in practice, have much bearing on the existing rights of the United States, beyond, of course, depriving the American Representative of a voice in the municipal and port regulations and government in Tangier." [2] He suggested that the United States might acquiesce in this alteration.[3] However, when the Sultan purported to rescind the decree of 1879 which had created the Sanitary Council, the Italian Minister, as its president, called a meeting and read a message of his government refusing to recognize the abolition of the Council "so long as an agreement shall not have been reached among the Powers signatory to the Act of Algeciras." He refused to sanction the transfer of the Council's funds and archives to the new administration.[4]

In other respects also the parties to the 1923 Convention were prevented from applying it as against Italy and the United States. The latter continued to pay anchorage dues on the old scale, while vessels of the other powers were liable to higher berthage dues introduced by the new administration. They also continued to maintain legations instead of consulates at Tangier, and to insist upon their capitulatory rights.[5] In *Mackay Radio and Telegraph Co. v. El Khadar* [6] the Court of Appeal of the Tangier International Jurisdiction held in 1954 that the Mixed Court had no jurisdiction over an American corporation because the purported abrogation of the capitulatory regime was binding only on the signatories of the 1923 Convention and not on the United States.[7]

[1] *Supra*, p. 187.
[2] [1925] 2 FOREIGN REL. U.S. 596.
[3] *Id.* at 592.
[4] *Id.* at 594 ff.; see also, Blix, *op. cit. supra* at 457–459. Thereafter, it has been reported, the representatives of Italy and the United States, as the only active members, alternately assumed the presidency and maintained custody of the funds and archives. Even after Italy adhered to the Statute in 1929 the United States Legation continued to exercise certain of its functions and to disburse its funds until they ran out in 1942. STUART, *op. cit. supra* at 26.
[5] Blix, *op. cit. supra* at 460–464.
[6] Digested, 49 A.J.I.L. 413 (1955).
[7] The Court stated that provisions of the 1923 Convention which established jurisdiction of the Mixed Court over "nationals of foreign Powers" must be taken to refer "only to the nationals of countries which have renounced the capitulations and whose consular tribunals have been replaced by the Mixed Court." It added that even the United States' participation in the international organization of Tangier

An attempt to use the terms of the 1923 Convention to alter the control of the Cape Spartel Lighthouse as stipulated in the convention of 1865 also failed of success. Article 53 of the 1923 Convention stated:

> The Contracting Governments recognize that the Shereefian Government retains its property rights in the Cape Spartel Lighthouse, the Convention of March 31st, 1865, remaining provisionally in force.

On the basis of this provision the Moroccan government proposed in 1926 to assume responsibility for modernizing the light and in the future to take over from the International Commission its supervision and operation. Vigorous opposition by the United States representative resulted in insistence by the International Commission on the maintenance of the international character of the lighthouse under the 1865 Convention.[1]

The institutions of government of the Zone were, however, effectively altered as a result of the 1923 Convention.[2]

From the foregoing it appears that, while the United States was determined to preserve all its important rights under the previous treaties, the only strenuous opposition to the regime in its entirety came from Italy.[3] That Italy's opposition was not based on devotion to the unanimity principle was made clear in 1928 when she adhered to the regime at the price of concessions to Italian interests but without prior consent of any of the parties

---

from 1945 onwards in no way presupposed a renunciation of "acquired privileges," as to which "the only normal mode of extinction is *express renunciation*." See [1955] ANNUAIRE FRANÇAIS DE DROIT INTERNATIONAL 325–326.

[1] [1926] 2 FOREIGN REL. U.S. 743–756. Another area in which the 1923 Convention remained ineffective was its prohibition of games of chance (Art. 52). This provision was successfully defied by Italian nationals whose gambling establishments did a thriving business. Blix, *op. cit. supra* at 581.

[2] For example, the United States conceded that an American plaintiff wishing to sue a Belgian defendant should do so in the Mixed Court, and it agreed that testimony of American citizens and protégés, who would not voluntarily testify in the Mixed Court, should be taken in the form of depositions before an American Consular Officer, on the exhibition of an order of the Mixed Court. [1926] 2 FOREIGN REL. U.S. 718–719. The International Court of Justice has also referred to the "former Committee on Customs Valuation," established by Article 96 of the Algeciras Act, as having been "abolished by Article 50 of the Convention [of 1923]." 2 RIGHTS OF NATIONALS OF THE UNITED STATES IN MOROCCO, PLEADINGS, ORAL ARGUMENTS, DOCUMENTS 295 (I.C.J. 1952); see also, Blix, *op. cit. supra* at 464–465.

[3] See, however, the statement of Secretary of State Kellogg to President Coolidge, that the United States had "never recognized the validity of the Statute." [1926] 2 FOREIGN REL. U.S. 736. Stuart, on the other hand, reports that the United States co-operated loyally in trying to make the international government a success. *Op. cit. supra* at 186.

to the the treaties of Algeciras and Madrid beyond the circle of the original signatories of the 1923 Convention.[1]

Professor Hudson has concluded that, as to the United States, Italy and Russia, the Statute was "not so much illegal as inoperative, and the nationals of these Powers remain outside the new régime." [2]

6. THE REVISION OF THE TANGIER STATUTE IN 1928

Besides the obstacles placed in the way of the new regime by Italy and the United States, their nonadherence resulted in a larger share of control by France than Spain had bargained for. In the summer of 1926 the Spanish Government announced that in its view the international regime tried in Tangier had proved inapplicable as a practical matter.[3] On August 23, 1926, it addressed a note to all the signatories of the Act of Algeciras except Germany, Austria, Hungary and Russia, asking that Tangier be incorporated in the Spanish zone.[4] It was Spain's position that the powers to whom this note was adressed included all the Algeciras signatories "who retain interest in Tangier." [5]

The United States replied that it would accept this invitation "provided that all of the major Powers interested in Morocco should be present." [6] The Soviet Government reacted with a note to the British, French, Swedish and Italian governments, in which it asserted that in any conference to review the Act of Algeciras it had the right to participate "on an equal footing with other participants in the Algeciras Conference." [7] The French and British governments insisted, however, that the nego-

---

[1] Italy had continued to press the necessity to consider her interests at Tangier as those "of the most essentially Mediterranean of all Great Powers," and to claim "equality with the other powers concerned," by which she apparently meant only England, France and Spain. STUART, *op. cit. supra* at 98.

[2] Hudson, *The International Mixed Court of Tangier*, 21 A.J.I.L. 231, 233 (1927).

[3] [1926] 2 FOREIGN REL. U.S. 727.

[4] *Id.* at 731.

[5] *Id.* at 741.

[6] *Id.* at 739. The Spanish Government agreed that the conference would not be useful without the participation "of the principal Powers interested in Morocco." *Id.* at 741.

[7] 2 DEGRAS 134.

tiations, in the first instance at least, should be between Great Britain, France and Spain.[1]

A preliminary agreement between France and Spain was reached on March 3, 1928, and four-power conversations including Italy then followed at Paris, which resulted, on July 25, 1928, in the signature by the four powers of an "Agreement revising the Convention of 18th December, 1923." [2] The principal changes were to increase the share in the government of Tangier which was allotted to Italy.

None of the four states which had become parties by accession to the Convention of 1923 had been invited to participate in the conference for its revision, and this despite the provision of the convention (Art. 56) that its revision should be by "common agreement." Nor was entry into force of the new agreement made dependent on their accession. It provided:

> The present agreement shall be communicated by the Government of the French Republic to the Powers which have acceded to the Convention of the 18th December, 1923, relating to the organization of the Tangier Statute, as well as to the Government of the United States of America as a signatory of the Act of Algeciras.

There was not even the reference, contained in the 1923 Convention, to mutual efforts to obtain the accession of the nonsignatory powers. By limiting the right to accede to parties to the Convention of 1923 and the United States, Russia was purposefully excluded.

All of the other four parties to the 1923 Convention did accede to the 1928 revision. Belgium, which had taken the most active part in the international administration, did so on the same day on which the new agreement was signed.[3]

The attitude of the United States was the same as it had taken in 1923. In advance of the four-power conference it notified the participants "that it presumed that nothing would be done

---

[1] [1926] 2 FOREIGN REL. U.S 740–741. The British Foreign Secretary stated that these discussions would be "preliminary to a discussion with the other Powers." 199 H.C. DEB. (5th ser.) 1–2 (1926). The London Times reported that the French government believed other interested powers, "such as the United States, Belgium and, presumably, Italy" should be consulted at a later stage. The Times (London), Aug. 28, 1926.

[2] 87 L.N.T.S. 211; text also in STUART, *op. cit. supra* at 235. An accompanying protocol stated that the four powers had agreed to amend the Convention of 1923 "and to recognize that the Italian Government becomes a contracting party to the said Convention as thus revised."

[3] STUART, *op. cit. supra* at 104.

by the conferring Powers to interfere with the principle of the Open Door or with the rights and interests of the United States" and again made full reservation of all its rights and interests in Morocco and Tangier.[1] The Spanish government replied that it contemplated no interference "with the protection which American citizens and interests enjoyed under the Algeciras Act." [2]

7. TANGIER SINCE 1945

During World War II Spain occupied Tangier in violation of the Statute, and the United States became deeply involved in French Morocco. In 1945 the Soviet Union also claimed the right to participate in postwar arrangements for Tangier. At Potsdam it was agreed to hold discussions on the subject between representatives of the U.S.S.R., the United States, the United Kingdom and France. Spain was excluded because of the refusal of the U.S.S.R. to deal with the Franco government.

At the Conference on Tangier which these four powers held in Paris in August, 1945, they agreed that within six months there should be a conference of "the Powers parties to the Act of Algeciras," including the U.S.S.R. in the this list but omitting Germany, Austria and Hungary, for the purpose of considering "amendments to the Conventions in force." "Conventions in force" was a term evidently thought to include the revised Convention of 1923, even though all the parties to the Act of Algeciras had not accepted it, for the Final Act of the Paris Conference stated that such amendments as any of the Algeciras powers wished to propose should be communicated "to the President of the Committee of Control at Tangier" and that Committee was given the task of drawing up a draft general convention for the use of the future conference. The four powers also approved an agreement of the United Kingdom and France for the re-establishment, as a provisional measure, of the prewar international administration based on the Convention of 1923-28, but with important amendments.[3]

---

[1] [1928] 3 FOREIGN REL. U.S. 371–372.

[2] *Id.* at 372. France invited the United States to send an observer to the four-power conference, but the invitation was not accepted. STUART, *op. cit. supra* at 103. A British government spokesman stated in the House of Commons on November 21, 1928, that the United States was not bound by the provisions of the 1928 revision protocol. 222 H.C. DEB. (5th ser.) 1741 (1928).

[3] Final Act of the Conference Concerning the Reestablishment of the International Regime in Tangier, 13 DEP'T STATE BULL. 613 (1945). The Anglo-French Agreement is also printed in STUART, *op. cit. supra* at 249.

The Final Act also recorded a unilateral declaration by the Soviet delegation that Spanish participation in the administration of the Zone should not be allowed until Franco was replaced by a democratic regime. The other three powers agreed that it would not be desirable that Spain should be invited to the future conference as long as the Franco government continued in power but stated that it was a practical necessity to include Spain, in the meantime, in the provisional administration.

The Anglo-French Agreement for restoration of the international regime altered the 1923 Convention without consulting the other parties – Belgium, Spain, Italy, the Netherlands, Portugal and Sweden.[1] Spain was deprived of all administrative posts and the Administrator was henceforth to be of Belgian, Netherlands, Portuguese or Swedish nationality, as were the officers and advisers of the police force. The composition of the Legislative Assembly was revised to entitle the United States and the U.S.S.R. to three members each, and those powers were given the right to appoint their representatives in Tangier as members of the Committee of Control. A new provision (Article 8) was included, which stated:

> The Committee of Control may at any time while the present Agreement remains in force adopt by unanimous vote any amendments thereto which it considers desirable.

This return to unanimity seems to have been a practical expedient to satisfy the demands of Russia and the United States.

Despite these substantial modifications of the prewar regime (albeit only "provisional") the new agreement was to be put in force immediately, without awaiting accession by the other parties to the convention it revised. The United Kingdom and France did agree to collaborate in inviting the subsequent accession of all of these states except Italy.[2] All of them did accede promptly.

The United States exercised the right given it to appoint a representative to the Committee of Control, making a formal

---

[1] Spain had violated the prewar treaties by her wartime occupation of Tangier. Italy's consent could be compelled.

[2] Article 11 stated that Italy should be invited to accede at a time to be determined later "subject to any relevant provisions of the peace treaty." Italy's representation in the Legislative Assembly was reduced to one member. Italy apparently did later accede to the agreement, for she participated in its revision in 1952. STUART, *op. cit. supra* at 252. See also Art. 41 of the Italian Peace Treaty. 49 U.N.T.S. 142.

reservation at the time, however, that such action did not imply adherence to the 1923 Statute or any modification of the United States' extraterritorial jurisdiction or other customary or treaty rights.[1] The U.S.S.R. did not appoint such a representative.

As instructed by the Final Act of the Paris Conference, the Committee on Control proceeded to draw up the text of a draft general convention to be submitted to the planned Conference of the Algeciras Powers.[2] However, because of the continuance of the Franco regime, the Conference was never held and the provisional regime continued in effect.

In 1952 Spain asked for revision so as to restore her former share in the administration. The Spanish Foreign Minister argued that since the changes made in 1945 had not been made "by common agreement," as stipulated in the 1923 Convention, they were illegal. He intimated that if no action were taken Spain might apply to the International Court of Justice. He was willing, however, to accept revision of the 1945 agreement, as provided in Article 8, by the Committee of Control.[3]

The result of this procedure was that the Soviet Union and Sweden, which had failed to appoint representatives to the Committee of Control, took no part in the revision of the 1945 Agreement in 1952. The amending protocol of November 10, 1952, adopted unanimously by the Committee of Control, restored Spain to her prewar position.[4] On the same day Spain, France, the United Kingdom and Italy signed a separate convention revising the provisions of the 1923 Convention relating to the International Courts of the Zone.[5] They provided, however, that this provision should become effective only when all the powers which had adhered to the 1923 Convention, as well as the United States, should have given it their adherence. All of them did adhere. The United States did so on July 8, 1953, but still with reservations, maintaining its extraterritorial jurisdiction and providing:

[1] Blix, *op. cit. supra* at 591–592. See also [1955] ANNUAIRE FRANÇAIS DE DROIT INTERNATIONAL 328.
[2] STUART, *op. cit. supra* at 153–155.
[3] *Id.* at 162–163.
[4] T.I.A.S. No 2752. The official text shows no reservation in this instance by the United States.
[5] Text in STUART, *op. cit. supra* at 254.

The adherence of the United States does not in any way imply adherence to the Statute of Tangier of December 18, 1923, as modified on July 25, 1928, which the Convention of November 10, 1952 amends.[1]

The final chapter of the international history of the Tangier zone was the reincorporation of the zone in Morocco in 1956 as a consequence of the termination of the French and Spanish protectorates and the restoration of the independence of the Sultan.[2] This was essentially a unilateral declaration of independence from all foreign control and resumption of control over this part of his territory by the Sultan, which the powers represented at a conference held at Tangier in October, 1956, recognized.[3] The language of the "Final Declaration" of the 1956 Tangier Conference supports this interpretation. It states:

> [The signatory Governments] have agreed to recognise the abolition of the international régime of the Tangier Zone and hereby declare abrogated, in so far as they have participated therein, all acts, agreements, and conventions concerning the said régime.[4]

Annexed to this declaration was a protocol settling questions raised by the abrogation of the international regime.[5]

The states which Morocco had invited to participate in this conference, and which signed these acts, were only those which had been represented on the Committee of Control.[6] This left out Sweden (which had not appointed a representative after World War II) and the U.S.S.R.

It has been reported that the Soviet Union protested the failure to invite it to the Tangier Conference.[7] The author has

[1] The text of the United States letter of adherence is printed in STUART, *op. cit. supra* at 264. The United States thus maintained its Consular Court while also having an American Judge on the Bench of the International Courts of Tangier. For criticism of this attitude of "collaboration without adhesion," see [1955] ANNUAIRE FRANÇAIS DE DROIT INTERNATIONAL 328.

[2] The French protectorate was terminated by an agreement of May 28, 1956. In the Spanish Zone transfer of authority was completed on August 1, 1956. KEESING'S CONTEMPORARY ARCHIVES, 14946, 15110 (1956).

[3] See N.Y. Times, October 14, 1956.

[4] 35 DEP'T STATE BULL. 842 (1956).

[5] *Ibid.*

[6] Preliminary negotiations had been between the Foreign Minister of Morocco and the Committee of Control. The Committee informed the Foreign Minister on May 18, 1956, that it was not opposed to integration of the zone with the rest of Morocco and suggested that negotiations should be opened to modify the Tangier Statute. KEESING'S CONTEMPORARY ARCHIVES 14946 (1956). On July 5, 1956, these authorities signed an interim agreement under which the Administrator of the international zone was replaced by a Governor appointed by the Sultan and the police were brought under Moroccan national control. *Id.* at 15110.

[7] N.Y. Times, September 29, 1956.

been informed that the Swedish government also addressed a note to all the states which were invited, calling attention to Sweden's rights under the Act of Algeciras and the 1923 Convention and claiming the right to participate. The reply of the British government referred to Sweden's voluntary lack of participation in the Committee of Control.

8. SUMMARY

The Conference of Algeciras assumed that unanimity would be necessary to revise its own acts, even while it dispensed with the consent of parties to the Madrid Convention which did not take advantage of the opportunity to attend. It applied the principle of unanimity in its own conference procedure. Very soon, however, the parties began the practice of revising the African treaties by action of a few of the most interested parties. (In the case of modification of the Act of Algeciras by the Tangier Statute of 1923 the revising states were not even a majority.) The nonparticipating states were ordinarily given the right to adhere and thus to participate in the revised regime, and there was general recognition that parties to the previous treaties which were unwilling to adhere to the new arrangements, and which refused to acquiesce in the termination of their treaty rights, retained all their rights under the previous treaties. The new arrangements were nonetheless effective so far as concerned the parties thereto.

The method of drafting new arrangements in negotiations limited to the most interested states (those whose participation was as a practical matter vital for the success of the new regime) was followed in respect to Morocco in 1912, 1923, 1928, 1945 and 1952. In each case parties to the preceding regime were invited to give their adherence afterwards. The validity of this method of procedure was not contested by any of the smaller states which were regularly excluded from the negotiations. In the case of modifications of the regime of Tangier they were content to accede and thus retain the privilege of participating in the international administration. It was demonstrated on several occasions that the failure to exercise this privilege of participation might result in the loss of it. Thus, Brazil lost her right to be invited to later conferences by her failure to attend the Con-

ference of 1880. Denmark and Norway similarly lost it in 1906. Russia, whose unrecognized government was excluded in 1923, was not consulted again (though she protested this exclusion) until her political power made her insistence on the right to participate effective in 1945, and the U.S.S.R. and Sweden, as a result of nonparticipation on the Committee of Control were no longer considered "interested powers" when Morocco came to convene the Tangier Conference of 1956.

While Germany in 1905, Italy in 1923 and Spain in 1952, in protesting their exclusion from negotiations to modify a previous regime, argued that it was necessary to observe the rule of unanimity, it was apparent that this was what Scelle has called "a reflex of political defense." [1] Subsequent actions of Germany and Italy showed that they were willing to dispense with the consent of some of the parties to previous treaties provided that they, themselves, were consulted. The deference paid to Italy's claims by Great Britain, France and Spain in 1928 was a recognition that Italy's co-operation must be secured in order for the Tangier regime to function properly. It was a practical rather than a legal necessity.

When the Acts of Berlin and Brussels were revised by the parties to those Acts which were represented at the Paris Peace Conference of 1919, the formula chosen was that of *inter se* agreement, which left to the absent parties the alternative of adhering to the new treaty or preserving their rights under the previous treaties. None of the states which were excluded from the Conference challenged the validity of the Convention of 1919, and the Permanent Court of International Justice held in the *Oscar Chinn* case that it was not open to the Court to question its validity in a suit between two states which were parties to it and relied on it as defining their rights. The legal validity of the Tangier Statute of 1923, an administrative regime which could not be strictly limited to *inter se* application, seemed to be recognized by the Paris Peace Conference of 1945, despite the fact that Russia and the United States, parties to the Act of Algeciras, were not parties to the Statute. The United States had not seriously challenged the validity of the 1923 regime, although it followed Italy's lead in maintaining the fictional existence of the

[1] SCELLE, THÉORIE JURIDIQUE DE LA RÉVISION DES TRAITÉS 6 (1936).

Sanitary Council as a way of securing American rights in pensions and other benefits.

While this practice supports the legal validity of new regimes adopted without unanimous consent, it also supports the principle that other parties to the previous treaties, as to whom the revision is *res inter alios acta*, are entitled to continue to maintain their acquired treaty rights. The continuance of acquired treaty rights of the United States in Morocco was recognized by the parties to the Convention of 1923 and by the International Court of Justice, and affirmed also by the International Court of Appeals of Tangier. Similarly, the Paris Peace Conference of 1919 recognized that it could not abrogate the rights which the absent neutral states derived from the Act of Algeciras.

These two principles – validity of the revision and maintenance of the rights of the nonconsenting states – may appear at first sight to be inconsistent. However, a way of reconciling them is indicated by the position taken by the United States in regard to the 1923 Tangier Convention. While insisting on its acquired rights under previous treaties, it was unwilling, as a result of its "non-entanglement" policy, to take the responsibility of participating actively in the new regime. It never asserted that a rule of unanimity was applicable to Morocco. It reserved its rights while conceding the validity of the new regime (at least after 1945), but still refusing to accede to it. It seemed that the effect of the United States' refusal to participate in the new administration was a decision to withdraw or abstain from this international activity. This would mean that the United States could no longer insist upon the old method of government of the Tangier Zone. The United States' other substantive rights under the old treaties could still be maintained, however, and their continued existence was conceded by the other parties. Such were the United States' right to have its citizens tried only in consular courts, the right of diplomatic protection, the right to be free from certain taxes, the right to do business, etc. These rights could have been maintained even if the United States had acceded to the new regime, by a reservation accepted by the other parties. The United States chose to do so instead by abstaining entirely from participation in the new Convention – reserving its rights while conceding the validity of the new regime but still refusing to accede to it.

The history of the African regimes supports the right of a party to renounce the benefits of a mutlipartite treaty so far as it is concerned. It need not be consulted in a revision thereafter. Germany, Austria and Hungary did so in respect to the Act of Algeciras. Other states individually renounced their rights under the Convention of Madrid.

The exclusion of Spain from the 1945 Paris Conference was clearly a political decision which provides no useful legal precedent. Similarly, the 1945 plan to call a conference of the Algeciras powers was a formula adopted as a political response to the unavoidable demands of Russia and the United States. The formula was abandoned as soon as Russia's cooperation was no longer thought essential, and actual participation in the Committee of Control became the criterion for inclusion in future negotiations.

The international regime introduced in Tangier in 1923 continued in effect, with modifications, until 1956. It was originally made necessary by the new situation of fact brought about by the establishment of protectorates of France and Spain in Morocco, and its termination in 1956 represented the recognition by each of the powers represented at the 1956 Tangier Conference of the resumption of independent Morocco's sovereignty over Tangier.

CHAPTER VII

TREATY REGIMES REINFORCED BY CUSTOM

1. THE AALAND ISLANDS

a) *The Convention of 1856*

The Aaland Islands archipelago lies between Finland and Sweden at the mouth of the Gulf of Bothnia. The islands are Swedish in population. However, Russia forced Sweden to cede them to her in 1809 and incorporated them in Russian Finland. They are recognized to possess great strategic importance in the Baltic area.[1]

Conversion of the archipelago into a demilitarized area was imposed on Russia as a result of the Crimean War. This took the form of a separate Convention of April 27, 1856, concluded between Great Britain, France and Russia, as the three powers which had been active belligerents in the Baltic.[2] It provided:

> His Majesty the Emperor of all the Russias, in order to respond to the desire which has been expressed to him by Their Majesties the Queen of the United Kingdom of Great Britain and Ireland, and the Emperor of the French, declares that the Aland Islands shall not be fortified, and that no Military or Naval Establishment shall be maintained or created there.

The Convention was annexed to the General Treaty of Paris, in which Austria, Prussia, Sardinia and Turkey also participated, with "the same force and validity as if it formed a part thereof."[3] Sweden was not a party to either agreement. She was, however, the Baltic ally of Great Britain and France, which had guaranteed her integrity against Russian encroachment by a treaty of November 21, 1855, and she was clearly intended as a beneficiary. The demand for demilitarization was put before the Congress by the victorious powers as a special condition "in the interest of Europe."[4]

The status of the islands remained unchanged throughout the remainder of the nineteenth century. When, after the turn of the

---

[1] For the history of "The Aaland Islands Question" to 1939, see article with that title by Padelford and Andersson, 33 A.J.I.L. 465 (1939).
[2] 46 B.F.S.P. 23.
[3] Art. 33 of the Treaty of Paris.
[4] 46 B.F.S.P. 67, 71.

century, Russia made attempts to free herself from the restrictions of the 1856 Convention, Sweden, though not a party to the treaty, was the state which raised the strongest objections.

The union of Sweden and Norway had been dissolved in 1905. This raised the question of arrangements to replace the British-French guarantee of 1855. Russia found this treaty distasteful, and she also wished to end the Aaland Islands restriction. Germany also wished to exclude British influence from the Baltic.

Russia's first move appeared designed to feel out the determination of the other powers to maintain the islands' demilitarized status. In 1906 she landed troops in the archipelago, but when this aroused vigorous expressions of alarm in Sweden, echoed in the British Parliament, the troops were withdrawn and Russia explained, reportedly in a note to England and France, that they had been sent only for the purpose of preventing the smuggling of arms into Finland.[1] It was noted in the Swedish press that,

> Such a statement as the above-mentioned, if made by Russia probably as the result of an interchange of views on the subject with the Western Powers, would be of the greatest importance as establishing the maintenance of the measure in question within treaty limits.[2]

There were also warnings of the danger of further encroachments if the treaty obligations were allowed to lapse or to be considered obsolete.[3]

In June of 1907, in the course of Russian-British discussions of a draft treaty for a collective guarantee of Norwegian neutrality, Russia asked abrogation of the old British-French guarantee. At the same time she also argued that the Aaland Islands Convention had lost all practical significance for England and France, while for Russia it constituted a serious obstacle to the restoration of the naval balance in the Baltic which had been upset by the destruction of Russia's fleet in her war with Japan. Therefore Russia wished to terminate the Convention of 1856 "by a special declaration to be signed by the contracting parties of that act, that is France, England and Russia." [4]

England made the consent of Sweden a precondition for abro-

---

[1] The Times (London), Aug. 6, 1906.
[2] *Ibid.* (as reported by the correspondent of The Times). See also *id.*, Aug. 10, 1906.
[3] *Id.*, Aug. 6, 1906.
[4] 8 BRIT. DOCS. 115–116.

gation of the Convention. The British Ambassador reported that he had informed the Russian Foreign Minister on December 16, 1907:

> I presumed that when he had settled matters with Sweden he would address himself to London and Paris: and the Cabinets would decide in what light they would regard the arrangements which might be concluded. [1]

England also gave a specific commitment to Sweden that she would not agree to abrogate the Aaland treaty without prior consultation with Sweden.[2]

Russia also made approaches to Germany. In August, 1907, in course of a meeting between the Tsar and the Kaiser at Swinemuende, there were discussions of a treaty in which the riparians of the Baltic alone should take part, containing a mutual guarantee of the Baltic *status quo*.[3] Russia hoped that such a treaty would clear the way for abrogation of the Aaland Islands Convention. As a first step Russia proposed to Germany the signature of a bilateral secret protocol in which the two governments would declare their intention to maintain the territorial *status quo*. In addition the Russian draft contained an agreement "not to recognize in the future, as interested in the affairs of the Baltic, any other Power except the riparian States, which are: Germany, Russia, Sweden and Denmark." It also spoke of "complete exclusion from the affairs of the Baltic Sea of all foreign political influence." [4]

Germany accepted the secret protocol on October 29, 1907, only after insisting on the elimination of the words quoted above. The German opposition to this language was based, not on reasons of legal principle, but on a policy of avoiding any "unnecessary" provocation of England and fear that the protocol might become known there.[5] Germany recognized, however, in the words of Count von Metternich, that "The legal situation forbids annulment of stipulations of the Treaty of Paris without the consent of all the contracting parties." [6] To appease

---

[1] *Id.* at 153.
[2] *Id.* at 168.
[3] 23 GROSSE POLITIK (pt. 2) 463.
[4] *Id.* at 463–464. (Translated).
[5] *Id.* at 464–465.
[6] *Id.* at 487.

the Russians it was agreed that Germany for her part would not object to eventual abrogation of the 1856 Convention.[1]

To quiet Sweden's fears the Russian government ultimately gave assurances, by way of a newspaper article, that Russia had no present desire to set aside the existing restriction on the Aaland Islands although it should not be sought to "eternalize" it by a new treaty.[2]

Agreement was thus reached on three treaties all of which were signed on April 23, 1908. A Declaration by Great Britain, France and Sweden declared the termination of the treaty of 1855 concerning the integrity of Sweden and Norway.[3] In place of it a Declaration was signed by Germany, Denmark, Russia and Sweden in which each agreed to preserve the territorial *status quo* in the regions bordering on the Baltic, and another Declaration was signed by Great Britain, Denmark, France, Germany, the Netherlands and Sweden performing the same function for the territories bordering on the North Sea.[4] An interpretive memorandum was appended to each Declaration stating that it could "in no case be invoked where the free exercise of the sovereign rights of the High Contracting Parties over their above-mentioned respective possessions is in question." Thus Russia preserved her hopes for future termination of the 1856 Convention. In an exchange of notes Sweden accepted this language but interpreted it as "not implying any prejudice to existing treaties."[5] In England Sir Edward Grey stated in Parliament that the Aaland Islands Convention remained unaffected by the new agreement.[6]

In this diplomatic discussion Russia took the position, ignoring Article 33 of the Treaty of Paris, that "Germany of course was not a party to the Treaty of 1856, but was interested in the Baltic," and in the Aaland question.[7] The British took the same position. Sir Arthur Nicolson told the Russian Foreign Minister, "I did not quite see how the Aaland Islands could be a question

---

[1] *Id.* at 485.
[2] *Id.* at 545. See also The Times (London), March 14, 1908.
[3] 101 B.F.S.P. 188. A new treaty guaranteeing the independence and territorial integrity of Norway had been signed by Great Britain, France, Germany, Norway and Russia on Nov. 2, 1907, 2 A.J.I.L. Supp. 267 (1908).
[4] 2 A.J.I.L. Supp. 270–274 (1908).
[5] 8 BRIT. DOCS. 182–183.
[6] 187 PARL. DEB. (4th ser.) 1395 (1908).
[7] 8 BRIT. DOCS. 147.

of interest to Germany who was not a party to the 1856 Treaty." [1] Also Sir Edward Grey stated in Parliament that if and when it should become necessary to consider modification of the status of the Aaland Islands England would "of course consult with both the other parties to the Treaty, and take into account the feeling of Sweden and every other circumstance which is relevant, before coming to a decision." [2] Only within Germany were there broader views as to what states had treaty rights in the matter. Thus a memorandum written by von Jagow for the German Foreign Office noted that the Aaland Islands Convention, while concluded between Russia, England and France, was by Article 33 of the Treaty of Paris "acknowledged as forming part thereof ... and hence also entered into in a certain measure (*gewissermassen*) by all the Signatories of the latter," [3] and von Metternich, in a despatch from London, wrote:

The legal situation forbids abrogation of provisions of the Treaty of Paris without the consent of all the contracting parties (Article 33 of the Treaty of Paris of March 30, 1856).[4]

However, none of the parties to the negotiations of 1907-08 ever officially suggested that there was any need to consult the non-Baltic parties to the Treaty of Paris, Austria-Hungary, Italy and Turkey, nor has there been found any evidence that any of those states ever requested the right to be heard.

During the First World War Russia, with the consent of England and France, proceeded to fortify the islands. This aroused such concern in Sweden that the Allies feared she might enter the war on the side of Germany, and they hastened to assure her that the defences were temporary and would be removed at the end of the war.[5]

After the Bolshevik Revolution Finland's independence was recognized by the Soviet Government. On December 31, 1917, the inhabitants of the Aaland Islands voted for union with Sweden. In January, 1918, civil warfare broke out in Finland, and Sweden sent troops to the islands, with the consent of the

[1] *Id.* at 153.
[2] 184 PARL. DEB. (4th ser.) 1020–1021 (1908).
[3] 23 GROSSE POLITIK (pt. 2) 464. (Translated).
[4] *Id.* at 487. (Translated).
[5] The Times (London), May 19, 1916; *id.*, May 25, 1916; 32 KRASNYI ARKIV 35–36 (1929).

Soviet government and both contending factions in Finland, to protect the Swedish population.¹ In an exchange of views at this time England and France pointed out to Sweden that a solution of the Aaland question would require their concurrence.² Sweden assured them that her action in sending troops was not the beginning of a permanent occupation.³ Subsequently, at the request of the Finnish government, German troops were also sent.⁴

The treaty of Brest-Litovsk, signed March 3, 1918, between Germany, Austria-Hungary, Bulgaria, Turkey and Russia, provided in Article 6:

> The fortresses built on the Aaland Islands are to be removed as soon as possible. As regards the permanent non-fortification of these islands as well as their treatment in respect to military and technical navigation matters, a special agreement is to be concluded between Germany, Finland, Russia and Sweden; there exists an understanding to the effect that, upon Germany's desire, still other countries bordering upon the Baltic Sea would be consulted in this matter.⁵

The same provision was contained also in Article 30 of the German-Finnish Treaty of Peace of March 7, 1918.⁶ By Article 292 of the Treaty of Versailles, however, Germany recognized the abrogation of these treaties with Russia and Finland.

On December 30, 1918, Finland, Germany and Sweden agreed to detailed arrangements for the demolition, under the supervision of a joint military control commission, of the fortifications which had been erected in the islands during the war.⁷

The Opinion of the League of Nations Commission of Jurists

The question of sovereignty, now hotly disputed between Sweden and Finland, was brought to the attention of the Council of the League of Nations by the British government on June 19, 1920. The Council in turn appointed a Commission of Jurists to advise it on this subject, and also as to "the present state of the

---

¹ [1918] 2 FOREIGN REL. U.S., RUSSIA 754.
² See note of Swedish Delegation to the Peace Conference dated April 22, 1919, LEAGUE OF NATIONS OFF. J., Spec. Supp. No. 1 at 33–34 (1920).
³ [1918] 2 FOREIGN REL. U.S., RUSSIA 754.
⁴ Padelford and Andersson, *op. cit. supra* at 470.
⁵ U.S. DEP'T OF STATE, TEXTS OF THE RUSSIAN "PEACE" 18 (1918).
⁶ 112 B.F.S.P. 1014.
⁷ 113 *id.* 993.

international obligations regarding the demilitarisation of the Aaland Islands." [1]

The League's Commission of Jurists was composed of Professors Larnaude, Struycken and Huber. Their Opinion, dated September 5, 1920, found the demilitarization provisions of the Convention of 1856 to be still in force.[2] They rejected Sweden's theory that the Convention had created a servitude, noting that such a concept was "not generally admitted" in international law and in any event Sweden could not be a *praedium dominans* since it was not a party to the Convention, nor even mentioned in it.[3]

They rejected also the theory that Sweden had contractual rights as a third-party beneficiary, saying on this point:

> Neither can [Sweden] make use of these provisions as a third party in whose favour the contracting parties had created a right under the Treaty, since – though it may, generally speaking, be possible to create a right in favour of a third party in an international convention – it is clear that this possibility is hardly admissible in the case in point, seeing that the Convention of 1856 does not mention Sweden, either as having any direct rights under its provisions, or even as being intended to profit indirectly by the provisions[4].

The Commission of Jurists found, however, that the obligations concerning the islands went beyond the parties to the Convention, for the powers in 1856 had intended to create "true objective law." The significance of the incorporation of the Convention in the Treaty of Paris was that all of the powers recognized this nature of the obligation. On this subject the opinion stated:

> ... If the wording of the Convention of 30th March, 1856, alone be considered, it might be thought that it was merely a question of an undertaking given by Russia to France and Great Britain, and that the last two Powers might release Russia at any moment. An examination, however, of the political conditions under which the agreement was entered into, shows that the Convention has in reality a much wider bearing. Sweden, which, at the time of the negotiations at Fredrikshamn, tried, without success, to obtain an assurance that the Aaland Islands would not be fortified, in 1856 appealed to the great western Powers in order to attain her object through the Peace Congress.

[1] LEAGUE OF NATIONS OFF. J., 1st year 249 (1920).
[2] *Id.*, Spec. Supp. No. 3 at 14–19 (1920).
[3] *Id.* at 16–17. *Cf.* McNair, *So-called State Servitudes*, 6 B.Y.I.L. 111 (1925); 1 OPPENHEIM, INTERNATIONAL LAW 535–543 (8th ed., Lauterpacht 1955).
[4] LEAGUE OF NATIONS OFF. J., 1st year, Spec. Supp. No. 3 at 18 (1920). *Cf.* the opinion of the Permanent Court of International Justice in the case concerning the Free Zones of Upper Savoy and Gex, cited *supra*, pp. 101–102.

It is certain that the provisions agreed upon at Paris between the Powers and Russia went beyond purely Swedish interests. As a matter of fact there was a general European interest arising out of the strategic importance of the Aaland archipelago.

<center> *</center>*

Indeed the Powers have, on many occasions since 1815, and especially at the conclusion of peace treaties, tried to create true objective law, a real political status the effects of which are felt outside the immediate circle of contracting parties.[1]

The opinion went on to cite the history of the Congress of Paris in support of this "European" interest. It also noted that the "permanent international interests" in the maintenance of the situation created in 1856 were evidenced again after the constitution of Finland as an independent state by the agreement of December, 1918, between "those of the Powers most directly interested on account of their geographical position, namely, Sweden, Finland and Germany," to demolish fortifications built during World War I.[2] The jurists felt that this character of the settlement had the effect that it remained binding even on the new state of Finland and gave Sweden a right to insist on compliance with its provisions even though Sweden was not one of the contracting parties.

The opinion gave no clear answer to the question how the status of the islands might be modified. The passage quoted above seemed to suggest that the agreement of Russia, France and Great Britain would not be enough. In another place it stated: "Sweden may, as a Power directly interested, insist upon compliance with the provisions of this Treaty in so far as the contracting parties have not cancelled it." [3] It seemed that the reference here was to the Parties to the Treaty of Paris and that the jurists did feel that all of the great powers would be competent to end this provision of the European law. They also stated:

It becomes obvious that such a settlement cannot be abolished or modified ... by conventions between some few of the Powers which signed the provisions of 1856.[4]

They noted that Russia, though no longer the territorial sov-

[1] *Id.* at 17.
[2] *Ibid.*
[3] *Id.* at 18–19.
[4] *Id.* at 18.

ereign, remained a contracting party and was entitled to rely on the islands' special status, but added:

... The fact that its present Government cannot, owing to its abnormal position, take part in the meeting, cannot prevent the other contracting parties from undertaking this meeting [to consider revision], should it appear necessary.[1]

Later treaties

After receiving this opinion, the Council of the League took jurisdiction of the matter. It ultimately awarded sovereignty to Finland, and directed the Secretary-General to issue invitations to a conference to replace the Convention of 1856 with "a broader agreement, placed under the guarantee of all the Powers concerned, including Sweden." [2]

To determine what states should be invited to this conference, the Secretary-General consulted Finland and Sweden, as parties to the dispute, and Great Britain and France, as signatories of the Convention of 1856. Sweden suggested that invitations be sent to Denmark, Finland, France, Germany, the British Empire, Italy, Poland and Sweden. At the instance of Great Britain Estonia and Latvia were added to the list. [3]

The conference, participated in by these ten governments, was held at Geneva in October, 1921.[4] The new Convention was signed and ratified by all ten participating states.[5] It was far more detailed than the Convention of 1856. It provided that Finland, confirming for her part the declaration made by Russia in 1856, undertook not to fortify the islands. In exceptional circumstances, however, Finland was authorized to send armed forces into the zone temporarily to mintain order. In time of war the islands were to be a neutral zone, and Finland was authorized to lay mines in territorial waters to protect this neutrality. Article 7 provided for referring any violation of the convention to the Council of the League of Nations and obligated the parties to assist in such measures as the Council might decide

---

[1] *Ibid.*
[2] LEAGUE OF NATIONS OFF. J., 2d year, 699–702 (1921).
[3] *Id.* at 1081.
[4] For the minutes of the meetings, see LEAGUE OF NATIONS, SECRETARIAT, CONFÉRENCE RELATIVE À LA NON-FORTIFICATION ET À LA NEUTRALISATION DES ISLES D'ALAND (1921).
[5] 9 L.N.T.S. 211.

upon for this purpose. It added that the vote of the representative of the power accused of having violated the provisions of the Convention should not be necessary to constitute the unanimity required for the Council's action. In the event of a sudden attack Finland was authorized to take measures in the zone to repulse the aggressor until such time as the parties to the convention should be able to intervene to enforce respect for the islands' neutrality. Article 9 seemed to express an intent to make the status of the islands a rule of general international law. It provided:

> The Council of the League of Nations is requested to inform the Members of the League of the text of this Convention, in order that the legal status of the Aaland Islands ... may, in the interests of general peace, be respected by all as part of the actual rules of conduct among Governments.

Russia had protested vigorously against her exclusion from the 1921 Conference,[1] and in the course of it an attempt was made to perpetuate the Convention of 1856 as far as Russia was concerned. Thus a committee of the representatives of Great Britain, France and Italy, which had been set up to reconcile the Swedish and Finnish drafts, added to the preamble a provision stating that the new convention was intended "to supplement, without prejudice thereto, the obligations assumed by Russia in the Convention of March 30th, 1856." This clause was adopted without any discussion reported in the minutes of the Conference. While purporting to perpetuate Russia's "obligations" it gave Russia no right to accede to the new convention. The conferees appeared to regard it as within their discretion to exclude Russia permanently, for they made accession of other states a matter dependent on their unanimous consent.[2] The justification for this provision was the supplemental, rather than revisory, character of the Convention.

There is no evidence that the parties ever did seek Russian adherence. After the new Convention was signed, Russia sent another protest, on November 13, 1921, to the governments of

---

[1] Russian note of July 22, 1921, to Sweden and Finland, 1 DEGRAS 251. See also earlier Russian notes to the Allies and Sweden and Finland claiming the right to be consulted, *id.* at 169–170, 190.

[2] Article 9 provided: "With the unanimous consent of the High Contracting Parties, this Convention may be submitted to any non-signatory Power whose accession may in future appear desirable, with a view to the formal adherence of such Power."

all the participating states, stating that she would not recognize any change in the juridical status of the Aaland Islands made without Russian participation as having any legal effect.[1] The Soviet government protested "in particular against the transfer to the League of Nations, which it does not recognize, of juridical functions concerning the Aaland Island zone." Russia's protests did not directly refer to the Treaty of 1856. Emphasis was placed rather on Russia's special interest owing to the islands' situation at the entrance to the Finnish Gulf.[2]

In spite of Russia's displeasure at being excluded from the 1921 Conference it was evident that the continuance of the demilitarized status of the islands was to Russia's strategic interest now that she was no longer the territorial sovereign, and this became all the clearer when in 1934 she became a member of the League of Nations, with a voice in Council deliberations on effectuation of the guarantee. When in 1939 Finland and Sweden sought to revise the Convention of 1921, so as to permit Finland to fortify the islands, Russia refused her consent.

This Finnish-Swedish proposal was made in a joint note of January, 1939, which referred to the weakening of the security system of the League of Nations and thus of the guarantee system provided in the 1912 Convention, and proposed that Finland should be authorized for a period of ten years to take defense measures in the islands up to a maximum of men and material to be fixed by joint agreement with Sweden.[3] It also asked that Sweden be given the right to assist Finland in applying defensive measures, in the event of imminent danger, pending the application of the guarantee system of the 1921 Convention. Sweden and Finland sent this note to the Soviet Union, as well as to the signatories of the 1921 Convention, asking it, as a member of the Council of the League of Nations, "to lend its assistance in regard to the adoption of the foregoing measures." [4] They also sent copies of the notes to the Council of the League, requesting "the Council's assent to the measures referred to therein, in so far as they come within its competence." [5]

---

[1] 1 DEGRAS 276–277.
[2] Id. at 251, 277.
[3] LEAGUE OF NATIONS OFF. J., 20th year, 284–285 (1939).
[4] Id. at 288–289.
[5] Id. at 284.

All of the signatories of the 1921 Convention gave their consent to the Finnish-Swedish proposals.[1] Approval by the Council of the League was blocked by Russia's refusal to consent.[2] In a speech before the Supreme Soviet on May 31, 1939, Foreign Minister Molotov referred to this incident as follows:

> In 1921 ten countries ... signed a convention prohibiting as formerly the fortification of the Aaland Islands. The Governments of the capitalist countries did this without the participation of Soviet representatives. In 1921, weakened by war and foreign intervention, the Soviet Government could only protest against this act, illegal as far as the Soviet Union was concerned. But even then, we declared clearly and more than once that the Soviet Union cannot be indifferent to this question, that any change in the juridical status of the Aaland Islands is impossible, as a violation of the interests of our country.
>
> * * *
>
> At the instance of the Finnish and Swedish Governments the question of revising the 1921 convention was discussed at the session of the League of Nations Council which has just ended. ... Owing to the objections advanced by the Soviet representative, the Council did not reach unanimity, which is necessary for a decision to be taken. ... It did not sanction the revision of the 1921 convention.[3]

Sweden and Finland maintained that they were under no obligation to await the Council's consent before putting into effect the revision which had been accepted by all the signatories of the 1921 Convention.[4] There was no reference during the brief Council debate to Russia's rights under the Convention of 1856. The Swedish government, however, subsequently withdrew from the Rikskag a bill authorizing the government to co-operate with Finland in the fortification of the islands, giving as the reason that the attitude of the Soviet government necessitated further negotiations.[5] After Russia's attack on her at the end of 1939, Finland built defenses in the islands and notified the Council of the League of Nations of this exercise of her rights according to Articles 6 and 7 of the 1921 Convention.[6]

After the "Winter War" of 1939–40 Finland was forced by Russia to destroy these fortifications. This requirement was contained in a Russian-Finnish agreement of October 11, 1940,

[1] *Id.* at 285–288.
[2] *Id.* at 279–282.
[3] 3 DEGRAS 338.
[4] LEAGUE OF NATIONS OFF. J., 20th year 280–282 (1939).
[5] Padelford and Andersson, *op. cit. supra* at 487 n.
[6] LEAGUE OF NATIONS OFF. J., 20th year 510 (1939).

which provided: "Finland agrees to demilitarise the Aaland Islands, not to fortify them, and not to place them at the disposal of the armed forces of any other Powers." [1] Russia was given the right to oversee the observance of the demilitarization through a consular representative in the islands, and a right to require the Finnish authorities to allow a joint investigation if the Russian representative should observe circumstances which in his opinion ran counter to the agreement.

Needless to say, the agreement of October 11, 1940, was not submitted for approval to the signatories of the 1921 Convention. It was restored in effect, after the second Russian-Finnish war, by the armistice of September 19, 1944.[2] On February 10, 1947, a Treaty of Peace with Finland was signed by the U.S.S.R., the United Kingdom, Australia, Byelorussia, Canada, Czechoslovakia, India, New Zealand, the Ukraine and South Africa.[3] This treaty, without referring to any of the previous treaties by name, provided in Article 5: "The Aaland Islands shall remain demilitarised in accordance with the situation at present existing." An official British commentary states:

> The Aaland Islands were demilitarised under an International Convention concluded in 1921, to which the Soviet Government, however, was not a party. In 1940, the Soviet Government concluded an agreement with Finland which provided equally for the demilitarisation of the Islands. This demilitarisation has now been confirmed in the present Treaty.[4]

There are thus now four treaties each of which can be adduced as the basis of obligations concerning the demilitarized status of the Aaland Islands. These are:

1. The Convention of 1856, which the signatories of the 1921 Convention sought to perpetuate as the source of an obligation binding on Russia, and which Russia apparently relied on before World War II as the source of Russian rights.

2. The Convention of 1921, still in force between the United Kingdom, Denmark, Finland, France, Germany, Sweden, Italy, Poland (assuming the extinction of Esthonia and Latvia).

---

[1] 144 B.F.S.P. 395.
[2] 145 *id*. 513 (Art. 9).
[3] 148 *id*. 339.
[4] CMD. NO. 7026 at 29 (1947). The Treaty of Peace, in Article 12, gave the Allied Powers the right to notify Finland of pre-war treaties which they desired to keep in force. The U.S.S.R. later exercised this right with respect to the Aaland Islands agreement of 1940. 67 U.N.T.S. 139.

3. The 1940 Agreement between the U.S.S.R. and Finland.

4. The Peace Treaty of 1947, in force between Finland, the U.S.S.R., the United Kingdom, Australia, Canada, Czechoslovakia, India, New Zealand, South Africa (and, nominally, the Ukraine and Byelorussia).

Although there are differences in the matter of remedies for infringement, these treaties are all consistent in respect to the principle of demilitarization.

2. THE SUEZ CANAL

a) *The Convention of 1888*

Free navigation of the Suez Canal is secured by the Convention concluded at Constantinople on October 29, 1888, between Great Britain, Austria-Hungary, France, Germany, Italy, the Netherlands, Russia, Spain and Turkey.[1] However, the principle that the Canal should always be open on equal terms to the ships of all nations was recognized even previous to the conclusion of the Convention. The Viceroy of Egypt had "solemnly declared" this principle in his concession of 1856 to the Universal Suez Canal Company.[2] Lord Granville conceded it in his circular despatch to the great powers of January 3, 1883.[3] The differences between Great Britain and France, the powers principally interested, were not over the principle but over France's efforts to have control of the canal entrusted to an international commission. Great Britain, which had effective control, was opposed to anything more than a general agreement not to violate the free navigation of the canal.[4] It was to establish a definitive regime to guarantee the accepted principle of free use of the Canal that the conference which drafted the Convention met in Paris in 1885.

It was originally felt that the matter was one which should be regulated by the great powers. A declaration issued at London on March 17, 1885, by these powers stated that they would appoint commissioners to prepare the definitive regulation, and

---

[1] 79 B.F.S.P. 18; translation in U.S. DEP'T OF STATE PUB. NO. 6392, THE SUEZ CANAL PROBLEM [cited hereafter: THE SUEZ CANAL PROBLEM] 16.
[2] THE SUEZ CANAL PROBLEM 4 (Art. XIV).
[3] 75 B.F.S.P. 676.
[4] HALLBERG, THE SUEZ CANAL 264–291 (1931).

that a delegate of the Khedive of Egypt would also be admitted "with a consultative voice." [1] On March 18th, however, the governments of the Netherlands and Spain asked to participate. The Netherlands called attention to the fact that it was third on the list of nations using the Canal and "next to Great Britain, the principal Colonial Power in Asia." [2] Spain claimed "a direct and important interest" because of possession of the Philippines.[3] Next, Portugal, which had seen the claims of Spain and the Netherlands reported in the newspapers, asked also to be admitted.[4] Similar requests were later received from Greece and Sweden.

The British government favored the admission of all the maritime powers. The other great powers, however, drew the line at the Netherlands and Spain. It was pointed out that "by the most recent statistics of navigation through the Canal, Portugal stood last on the list," and that Greece and Sweden had also been unable to support their requests by showing important interests at stake.[5] Although the Netherlands and Spain were present when the meetings at Paris opened, the other parties at once showed the minor role allowed to them by forming a subcommittee, from which those states were excluded, to do the real work of the Conference.[6]

The differences between England and France concerning the means of securing the protection of the Canal delayed signature of the Convention until 1888. Its signature in that year was only made possible by France's acceptance of a British reservation which postponed its application indefinitely.[7]

The principle of free use was reaffirmed in Article 1:

The Suez Maritime Canal shall always be free and open, in time of war as in time of peace, to every vessel of commerce or war, without distinction of flag.

The Canal shall never be subject to the exercise of the right of blockade.

---

[1] CMD. NO. 4599 at 6–7 (1885). This implied that while the rule of unanimity would be followed as a matter of conference procedure, the vote of the Egyptian delegate would not be counted.

[2] *Id.* at 7.

[3] *Ibid.*

[4] *Id.* at 9.

[5] *Id.* at 17, 29.

[6] *Id.* at 77. The Netherlands' delegate was later admitted to the subcommittee and took part in the discussions. The Spanish delegate took no further part, except to claim a seat for Spain on the supervisory commission to sit at Cairo. *Cf.* the similar procedure at the Berlin Conference of 1885 on Central Africa, *supra*, p. 180.

[7] *Infra*, p. 229.

Articles 7, 8 and 9 outlined a procedure for enforcement of the treaty and protection of the Canal. Article 7 authorized each of "the Powers" to station two warships in the ports of access of Port Said and Suez. Article 8 provided for supervision of the execution of the Convention as follows:

> The Agents in Egypt of the Signatory Powers of the present Treaty shall be charged to see that it is carried out. In any circumstance threatening the security and free passage of the Canal, they shall meet at the summons of three of them and under the presidency of their Doyen, to make the necessary verifications. They shall inform the Khedivial Government of the danger perceived, in order that it may take proper steps to assure the protection and free use of the Canal. In any case, they shall meet once a year to take note of the due execution of the Treaty.
> These latter meetings shall be presided over by a Special Commissioner appointed for that purpose by the Imperial Ottoman Government. A Khedivial Commissioner may also take part in the meeting, and may preside over it in the absence of the Ottoman Commissioner.

Article 9 provided that the Egyptian government should take the necessary measures to enforce the Convention, with the assistance, if need be, of the government of the Ottoman Empire. None of these three articles ever became fully effective.

Article 16 stated that the parties would bring the Convention to the knowledge of those states which had not signed it, inviting them to accede. This article, like the similar article of the Lausanne Convention concerning the Turkish Straits, has never been made use of.

b) *The British reservation*

The British government permitted the Convention of 1888 to go into effect only with a reservation of full freedom of action so long as it remained in occupation of Egypt.[1] The occupation was referred to at the time as a "transitory and exceptional" condition,[2] but it soon became permanent, with the result that the Convention remained completely inoperative for sixteen years.[3]

---

[1] 79 B.F.S.P. 500, 511–512; HALLBERG, THE SUEZ CANAL, 287, 291 (1931).

[2] FRANCE, MINISTÈRE DES AFFAIRES ETRANGÈRES, 106 DOCUMENTS DIPLOMATIQUES (ser. A) 115 (1887).

[3] In 1898 the Under-Secretary of State for Foreign Affairs informed a questioner in the House of Commons that, as a consequence of the British reservation, the Convention had "not been brought into practical operation." 61 PARL. DEB. (4th ser.) 667 (1898). In February, 1904, the Under-Secretary stated in answer to another question: "In view of these reservations the other Signatory Powers have abstained from any steps for the purpose of bringing the Convention into active operation." 130 PARL. DEB. (4th ser.) 981–982 (1904).

In 1904 England succeeded in getting France's acceptance of the permanency of the British occupation, as part of the general settlement of colonial questions between them. In return the British government agreed that the Convention of 1888 should be put into force. This provision of the agreement stated:

> In order to ensure the free passage of the Suez Canal, His Britannic Majesty's Government declare that they adhere to the stipulations of the Treaty of the 29th October 1888, and that they agree to their being put in force. The free passage of the Canal being thus guaranteed, the execution of the last sentence of paragraph 1, as well as of paragraph 2, of Article VIII of that Treaty will remain in abeyance.[1]

The British reservation was therefore narrowed somewhat. It now applied in terms only to the provision for annual meetings of the council of the agents of the signatory powers.[2] However, the result of the occupation was that the British government would guard the Canal instead of the Egyptian, which was a modification of the terms of the Convention. The British government apparently meant that the Convention would be effective only in so far as other governments accepted this change. In effect, therefore, the reservation remained the same as before, but the British government had the added assurance of explicit French acceptance of this situation.

Besides French consent, England also sought acceptance of her occupation of Egypt by the other great powers. On August 8, 1904, the Under-Secretary for Foreign Affairs was able to report to the House of Commons that Germany, Austria-Hungary and Italy had accepted the same terms in return for guarantees of most-favored-nation treatment for their commerce in Egypt.[3] The consent of Spain was obtained indirectly as part of the Franco-Spanish agreement on Morocco of October 3, 1904.[4]

Russia was urged by France to come to terms with England, and she gave her assent to that part of the Anglo-French agreement which concerned the reorganization of Egypt's finances,

---

[1] 97 B.F.S.P. 39.

[2] When the British government first suggested that Article 8 should be eliminated as incompatible with the British occupation, the French government replied that it could be modified only with the concurrence of the other signatories. HALLBERG, THE SUEZ CANAL 306. However, this was a matter of the consent required for treaty reservations rather than for revision of an effective treaty, and in any event the French ultimately abandoned their position on this point.

[3] 139 PARL. DEB. (4th ser.) 1352 (1904); see also CMD. NO. 2409 at 4 (1905).

[4] 98 B.F.S.P. 703.

but the Russian Emperor balked at the other provisions which seemed to affect the liberty of the Suez Canal. He asked for clarification over the proposed suppression of the two sentences of Article 8 of the Canal Convention, and inquired of the French Foreign Minister whether the control to be exercised by the agents of the powers was not essential to the value of the Convention.[1] Faced with these objections, the British dropped their request for Russian adherence.[2] Nor did Turkey consent. On April 22, 1904, she addressed a note to England and France, reserving her rights with respect to the Anglo-French agreement and asking clarification in view of assurances frequently given in the past concerning maintenance and respect for the rights of the Sultan.[3] The British reply argued that the agreement introduced no change in the relations existing between Egypt and the Ottoman Empire and stated that in these circumstances the British government did not consider that there was any reason to refer to Turkey before the conclusion of the agreement.[4] The French government adopted the same reasoning in its reply.[5]

It should be noted that besides its effect on the Convention of 1888 the British occupation of Egypt was a subject that involved the guarantee of the territorial integrity of the Ottoman Empire, under the Treaties of Paris, London and Berlin.[6] In addition, shortly before the British military intervention in Egypt began, the same six powers had signed a protocol agreeing that in any arrangement that might ensue from their efforts to regulate the affairs of Egypt they would seek "no territorial advantage, nor the concession of any exclusive privilege, nor any commercial advantage for their subjects, which those of all other nations might not equally obtain."[7] With these commitments in view, as her occupation took on permanent character, Great Britain spared no effort to clothe it with legality by obtaining the consent of the great power signatories of the earlier treaties. In

---

[1] FRANCE, MINISTÈRE DES AFFAIRES ÉTRANGÈRES, 5 DOCUMENTS DIPLOMATIQUES FRANÇAIS 1871–1914 (2e sér.) 58, 129, 136–137 (1934).
[2] *Id.* at 163–164.
[3] *Id.* at 59.
[4] *Id.* at 162n.
[5] *Ibid.*
[6] *Supra*, pp. 88–91.
[7] 73 B.F.S.P. 1179.

this respect there was never more than accidental or unintended departure from the rule of unanimity.

Another formal change which made very little difference in substance was the conversion of the occupation of Egypt into a British protectorate in 1914, following England's declaration of war on Turkey. By Article 147 of the Treaty of Versailles Germany recognized the protectorate, and by Article 152 she consented to the transfer to the British government of the powers conferred on the Sultan of Turkey by the Convention of 1888. Article 282 (11) provided that the Convention of 1888 should continue in force between Germany and those of the Allied and Associated Powers party thereto. The treaties of peace with Austria and Hungary contained similar provisions. By the Treaty of Lausanne Turkey renounced all right and title over Egypt.[1] The British protectorate had been previously recognized by France, Russia and Italy. Spain and the Netherlands were not consulted in regard to any of these arrangements.[2]

Great Britain later took the position that by these treaties she succeeded to the position of the Ottoman government "as the guardian of the canal in the second degree" under Article 9 of the Constantinople Convention. Her representative to the United Nations Security Council stated in 1947 (in answer to an Egyptian complaint):

> Egypt was, of course, at that time [1888] under the sovereignty of the Ottoman Sultan. Later on, the United Kingdom replaced the Ottoman Sultan as the sovereign of Egypt as a result of the establishment of its protectorate over Egypt, and at the same time, succeeded to the position of the Ottoman Government as the guardian of the Canal in the second degree. Both these two things were recognized by the Powers in the peace treaties which followed the First World War. ...
>
> In other words, [after the termination of the protectorate] Egypt was the guardian of the Canal in the first degree and the United Kingdom the guardian in the second degree. ...[3]

The failure to seek the Netherlands' consent for Great Britain's assumption of the rights of Turkey was not the result of any decrease in her shipping using the Canal. In 1920, as in 1885,

---

[1] 28 L.N.T.S. 11. Article 99 stated that the Convention of 1888 should continue in force.

[2] Spain had, it is true, recognized England's special position in Egypt in 1904. *Supra*, p. 230.

[3] U.N. SECURITY COUNCIL OFF. REC., 2d year, 169th meeting 1890–1891 (1947).

she still stood third on the list in this respect.[1] However, the legal questions raised by these facts concern state succession and the effect of reservations, rather than treaty revision.

In 1922 the British government issued a unilateral "Declaration to Egypt" in which it purported to recognize Egyptian independence but explicitly reserved the right to defend Egypt and the Canal.[2] The notification which communicated this declaration to other powers made it clear that the protectorate was to continue in all but name.[3] In 1936 Great Britain and Egypt signed a Treaty of Alliance.[4] It was only in 1954, however, that British occupation of the Canal Zone was terminated.

The Anglo-Egyptian Treaty of October 19, 1954, provided for the withdrawal of British troops from the Suez Canal Base (although they retained the right to return in the event of an attack on Egypt by any power other than Turkey, Israel or a member of the Arab League).[5] Article 8 provided:

> The two Contracting Governments recognise that the Suez Maritime Canal, which is an integral part of Egypt, is a waterway economically, commercially and strategically of international importance, and express the determination to uphold the Convention guaranteeing the freedom of navigation of the Canal signed at Constantinople on the 29th of October, 1888.

There is no indication that any of the other signatories of the 1888 Convention were consulted with respect to this Treaty. However, it returned the situation closer to that envisaged in 1888 than under the previous arrangement.

In summary, the Convention of 1888, as a consequence of the British reservation, did not become effective between any of the parties until 1904, and for some of the parties, which did not accept the terms on which Great Britain was willing to put it in

---

[1] HALLBERG, THE SUEZ CANAL 380 ff. (1931). After World War I Japan replaced Germany in second place.

[2] *Id.* at 355–356.

[3] CMD. NO. 1617 (1922).

[4] 140 B.F.S.P. 179.

[5] CMD. NO. 9298 (1954). This was the net effect of Article 4 of the Treaty and an Agreed Minute signed the same day. Article 4 provided: "In the event of an armed attack by an outside Power on any country which at the date of the signature of the present Agreement is a party to the Treaty of Joint Defense between Arab League States ... or on Turkey, Egypt shall afford to the United Kingdom such facilities as may be necessary ...." The Agreed Minute provided that the term "outside Power" should mean "any country other than (i) the countries named [in the treaty] and (ii) Israel."

effect, it would seem to have remained ineffective until the end of the British occupation in 1954.[1]

c) *Discussions of revision in 1956*

The nationalization of the Suez Canal Company by the Egyptian government on July 26, 1956, represented for Egypt the culmination of her long struggle for independence, and for Great Britain an attack on the prime symbol of her world position. The repercussions were primarily political, but they resulted in widespread discussion of new conventional arrangements which might supplement or replace the Convention of 1888 and which would provide additional safeguards for free navigation of the Canal. The subject was discussed at the London Conference of August 3–15, at the Cairo Meeting of September 3–10, in the Security Council and in diplomatic negotiations until this chapter of events was ended on October 29, 1956, by the Israeli attack on Egypt. While there was no thought of altering the principle of free navigation of the Canal, and the primary emphasis was upon the need for supplementary arrangements, there were frequent statements that revision of the Convention of 1888 was contemplated.[2]

The United States, which was not a party to the Convention of 1888, joined the United Kingdom and France in the preliminary talks in which the decision was made to hold a conference on the Suez Canal.[3] The invitations were issued to twenty-four states, eight as "Parties to the Convention of 1888" and sixteen as "Other Nations largely concerned in the use of the Canal either through ownership of tonnage or pattern of trade."[4]

While it was conceded that the parties to the Convention of 1888 were entitled to invitations, there was some debate over what states were parties. The Tripartite Statement of August 2, 1956, accepted the U.S.S.R. as a party. It also included Egypt in this category, as well as Turkey. Egypt was not an original signatory, having been treated as a vassal of Turkey in 1888, and

---

[1] In 1954 the Soviet Union asserted its right to be regarded as a party to the Convention. U.N. SECURITY COUNCIL OFF. REC., 9th year, 664th Meeting 10 (1954).
[2] THE SUEZ CANAL PROBLEM 107, 126, 172, 214–217, 329; U.N. Docs. Nos. S/3649, S/3650 (1956).
[3] THE SUEZ CANAL PROBLEM 34.
[4] *Id.* at 36.

TREATY REGIMES REINFORCED BY CUSTOM 235

was evidently called a party by virtue of state succession.[1] However, Austria and Hungary were not invited, although the Austro-Hungarian monarchy had been a party to the Convention of 1888 and the peace treaties of 1919 had specified that the Suez Canal Convention should again be applied as between Austria and Hungary and those of the Allied and Associated Powers party thereto. Austria, which had always supported the position that she was not the same state as prewar Austria-Hungary, announced that she made no claim to participate in the conference.[2] The government of Hungary, however, stated that it should have been invited.[3] The Soviet Union argued that, in addition to Austria and Hungary, Czechoslovakia and Yugoslavia should also have been invited as successors of Austria-Hungary.[4] Prime Minister Nehru of India also stated that Yugoslavia should have been invited, "by virtue of being a succession state in respect of the Convention of 1888 and a maritime power." [5]

The larger group of states was invited to the London Conference as users of the Canal rather than as parties to the Convention of 1888, and throughout the discussions the rights that were emphasized, aside from those of Egypt, were the rights of the user-nations which were economically dependent on the Canal.[6] There were arguments that still other users should have been invited. Panama and Israel protested to the British government against their exclusion.[7] Prime Minister Nehru said that Burma should have been invited.[8] The Egyptian government took the

[1] See statements of Secretary of State Dulles, 35 DEP'T STATE BULL. 335, 611 (1956). Egypt also repeatedly referred to herself as a party to the Convention. See Letter from President Nasser to Prime Minister Menzies, Sept. 9, 1956, THE SUEZ CANAL PROBLEM 317. See also U.N. Docs. Nos. S/3650, (1956) and S/3818 (Letter to the U.N. Secretary-General, 24 April, 1957); U.N. SECURITY COUNCIL OFF. REC., 11th year, 736th Meeting 3 (1956); *cf.* Art. 8 of the Anglo-Egyptian Agreement of October 19, 1954, THE SUEZ CANAL PROBLEM 22.
[2] THE SUEZ CANAL PROBLEM 64.
[3] N.Y. Times, August 12, 1956.
[4] THE SUEZ CANAL PROBLEM 59.
[5] N. Y. Times, Aug. 9, 1956.
[6] It was repeatedly asserted, without contradiction, that all users of the Canal derived rights from the Convention of 1888. THE SUEZ CANAL PROBLEM 37, 54, 73, 147–148, 163–164, 336, 353, 365. The representative of Ethiopia at the London Conference stated: "Under this Treaty Egypt recognised that in a clearly defined part of her territory there is set up the perpetual right of way or easement accepted by Egypt herself in favour of the freedom of commerce of the entire world." *Id.* at 148.
[7] N. Y. Times, Aug. 4 and Aug. 16, 1956.
[8] *Id.*, Aug. 9, 1956.

position that all of the forty-five states which used the Canal in 1955 had the right to participate.[1] The Soviet government argued that all of the Arab states should have been invited because "politically and economically they are profoundly interested in the settlement of the Suez Canal and the uninterrupted functioning of the canal," and Poland, Bulgaria, Rumania, Burma and Finland should have been invited as "maritime states which widely use the Suez Canal." [2] It also asserted that the People's Republic of China should have been invited by virtue of being a great power.[3] It charged that bias had been shown in the invitation of some only among the user-states.[4]

The French Foreign Minister replied to the Soviet charges, saying:

"We took three particular cases: the first, of those powers signatory to the 1888 Convention ...; secondly, the main users, based on tonnage figures, and the third, which was of equal importance, ... those countries which by their economic structure have the greatest possible interest in ensuring the normal functioning of the canal, and I think we chose those whose foreign trade passing through the canal represented more than 50 per cent. of their total foreign trade. These are criteria which might be discussed, but they were objective. ..." [5]

He explained the omission of Austria and Hungary despite their status as parties to the Convention of 1888 accorded them by the Treaties of Trianon and St. Germain by stating that they were not "as directly interested in the question of the canal as others. They have no Mediterranean or Adriatic ports." [6]

Secretary of State Dulles spoke of the users as "beneficiaries" of the Convention of 1888.[7] It seems doubtful that he meant to refer to the doctrine of third-party beneficiaries, previously repudiated by the United States. The Hay-Pauncefote Treaty of 1901 between the United States and Great Britain, like the Suez Convention, had provided that the Panama Canal should be

---

[1] THE SUEZ CANAL PROBLEM 51–52, 317–318.
[2] *Id.* at 59–60.
[3] *Id.* at 59.
[4] *Id.* at 60.
[5] *Id.* at 63.
[6] *Id.* at 64. *Cf.* the statement of Secretary of State Dulles, on October 9, 1956, that there were invited to the London Conference "all seven of the unquestionably surviving signatories of the Suez Canal Treaty of 1888." 35 DEP'T STATE BULL. 611 (1956).
[7] THE SUEZ CANAL PROBLEM 354.

free and open to the vessels of commerce and of war of all nations ... on terms of entire equality, so that there shall be no discrimination against any such nation, or its citizens or subjects, in respect of the conditions or charges of traffic, or otherwise.[1]

Nevertheless, Secretary of State Hughes stated that "other nations ... not being parties to the treaty have no rights under it." [2]

If the principle of third-party contract rights be rejected, however, other states may nevertheless have rights resting on custom and prescription. When the Soviet government protested to the United States in April, 1957, against delays and security precautions to which a Soviet ship had been subjected in the Panama Canal, it based the protest on "the principle of complete equality in the use of canals of international importance to all countries proclaimed in respect to the Panama Canal in the treaty [of 1901] ... and confirmed through usage." [3] Sir Anthony Eden also claimed, in a speech to the House of Commons on September 12, 1956, that the user countries had in the course of time acquired customary rights apart from those derived from the 1888 Convention. He said:

> As the House knows, the rights of the user countries are not derived from the 1888 Convention alone. They have also become established by long and uninterrupted use of the canal. They are not limited to the free right of passage defined in the 1888 Convention. The users are also entitled to insist upon the efficient operation, administration and maintenance of the canal, in the interests of all the countries, without any discrimination. They have also the right to expect that the level of dues shall be reasonable, and it follows from this that the revenues of the canal cannot lawfully be exploited by one country for its own purpose[4]

The Egyptian government declined the invitation to attend the London Conference on the ground that Egypt, the state most directly concerned, should have been consulted beforehand. It made a counter-proposal in which it stated that it would be willing to join with the other signatories of the Convention of

---

[1] 1 MALLOY 782.
[2] 5 HACKWORTH, DIGEST OF INTERNATIONAL LAW 221–222; see also *supra* pp. 101–102, 220, and *infra* p. 242. See also Arechaga, *Treaty Stipulations in Favor of Third States*, 50 A.J.I.L. 338 at 350 (1956).
[3] N. Y. Times, April 10, 1957; *cf.* the United States' insistence on its right in the free navigation of the Congo although it was not a party to the act which established it. *Supra*, p. 181.
[4] N. Y. Times, Sept. 13, 1956.

1888 in sponsoring a conference of all the user-states to reconsider the Convention.[1]

The Soviet Union and Egypt subsequently suggested that a proper procedure would be to form a preparatory commission, "balanced in such a way as to prevent in advance the prevalence of any one point of view," which would draw up a draft of a new Suez Canal convention.[2] The U.S.S.R. proposed that this commission include Egypt, India, the United States, Britain, France and the Soviet Union (leaving out some states which were unquestionably parties to the Convention of 1888 and including two which were not).[3]

The London Conference met from August 16 to 23, 1956.[4] Twenty-two states were represented, including all those invited except Egypt and Greece.[5] It was at once apparent that in the absence of Egypt the Conference would attempt no final decisions.[6] The delegates were all agreed that its nature was preliminary and that it must be followed by negotiations with Egypt. Secretary of State Dulles stated the accepted view when he said:

This is not a conference to take decisions binding on those who do not agree. The effectiveness of our group increases as we manage to find agreement among ourselves, and surely we have a duty to seek that. But no majority, however large, can bind any minority, however small.[7]

The Conference therefore tacitly decided to take no decisions

---

[1] THE SUEZ CANAL PROBLEM 47, 51–52. Egypt later expanded on its reasons for refusing to attend in the debate before the Security Council. Her representative stated that Egypt should have been consulted on the holding of the conference, the place, the time and the countries to be invited. He also argued that the conference was preceded and accompanied by threats of force, and added, "We were not facing a conference, but a trial; we were not invited to a meeting, but assigned to a court." U.N. SECURITY COUNCIL OFF. REC., 11th year, 736th Meeting 9 (1956).

[2] U.N. SECURITY COUNCIL OFF. REC., 11th year, 736th Meeting 26 (1956); U.N. Doc. No. S/3650 (1956); THE SUEZ CANAL PROBLEM 329.

[3] THE SUEZ CANAL PROBLEM 217–218; U.N. SECURITY COUNCIL OFF. REC., 11th year, 736th Meeting 26 (1956).

[4] For record of the proceedings, see THE SUEZ CANAL PROBLEM 55–293.

[5] The Egyptian government sent an observer to London, to be available for behind-the-scenes negotiations. N. Y. Times, August 15, 1956. The delegates of India and Pakistan stopped in Cairo on their way to London to acquaint themselves with Egypt's point of view. *Id.*, August 13, 1956.

[6] See, for example, the statement of the delegate of Indonesia: ". . . Other interested countries are not in the conference, and especially the most important contracting party, that is, Egypt. If we reach here a majority of votes, how could we implement those decisions against the wish of Egypt, if not by force . . . ." THE SUEZ CANAL PROBLEM 62.

[7] *Id.* at 178; see also statements by the United Kingdom and French delegates, *id.* at 67, 266, 65.

at all by voting.¹ When eighteen of the twenty-two states represented had united on a set of proposals they wished to present to the Egyptian government, it was successfully insisted by the other four that these views must be presented by their proponents individually and not put forward as the views of the Conference.² It seemed, however, that the decision not to act as a conference unless unanimity was attained was one made *ad hoc*. Mr. Dulles stated, "If Egypt had accepted the invitation to attend then our conference might have assumed a different aspect."³ It was in any event a matter of conference procedure rather than of the consent necessary in treaty revision.

At the conclusion of the London Conference the eighteen states that were in agreement formed a committee to present their proposals to the Egyptian government.⁴ These proposals were based on operation of the Canal by an international authority.⁵ Egypt rejected the proposals because of her firm opposition to conceding to such an authority any jurisdiction within her territory.⁶

In rejecting the eighteen-power proposals, President Nasser recalled his statement of August 12, 1956, that he was willing to sponsor a conference of all signatories and all user-nations, to review the 1888 Convention.⁷ The eighteen powers announced at London on September 21 that they considered this proposal "too imprecise to afford a useful basis for discussion." ⁸

The next step taken by the eighteen user-states was a new meeting at London at which they considered the formation of a "canal users association." ⁹ Only fifteen of the group decided to

---

[1] *Id.* at 56–72, 251–286.
[2] *Id.* at 251–286.
[3] *Id.* at 178; see also 265.
[4] *Id.* at 267.
[5] *Id.* at 308, 310.
[6] *Id.* at 317–322. Egypt's attitude in this respect was reminiscent of that taken previously by the Netherlands in regard to the Rhine, Rumania in regard to the Danube and Turkey in regard to the Straits. On this indisposition of sovereign states to permit limitations by international bodies acting on their territory, see F. de Visscher, *La Nouvelle Convention des Détroits*, 17 REV. DE DROIT INTERNATIONAL 669, 670 (1936).
[7] THE SUEZ CANAL PROBLEM 329.
[8] *Id.* at 366. The Egyptian government later announced on September 17, 1956, that it had received formal acceptances of this proposal from twenty-one countries. U.N. Doc. No. S/3650 (17 September 1956).
[9] THE SUEZ CANAL PROBLEM 353–367.

become members of such an association.¹ This was not a meeting to consider revision of the 1888 Convention. It was rather an attempt to form a pressure group to defend the users' interests.

In all of these discussions it was apparent that Egypt exercised a real veto power over any revision of the Convention of 1888. It was also apparent that the eighteen-power majority at the London Conference chose to try the method of obtaining Egypt's consent by the exercise of pressure, rather than the method of compromise. At the London Conference India urged the latter method.² The Indian proposals, which included provisions for equitable tolls and proper maintenance of the canal, the "association of international user interests with the 'Egyptian Corporation for the Suez Canal,'" and annual reports to the United Nations, probably represented the maximum concessions that Egypt could have been prevailed upon freely to accept.³

The Conference seemed agreed that the next step should be negotiations by a committee of powers with Egypt. However, the majority chose to negotiate separately on the basis of their own views, without including any representative of the dissenting group. The Soviet Union contended that representatives of the opposing points of view should be included on the negotiating committee, not because this was the right of parties to the Convention of 1888, but because it was the way to reach an agreed solution.⁴

The effort to force Egyptian consent to operation of the Canal by an international authority did not succeed. By attempting too much the eighteen powers, like the Soviet Union in regard to the Turkish Straits ten years before, got no new agreement at all. However, it is important to note that if the eighteen powers had succeeded in getting Egyptian consent to the solution they proposed they would have effectively revised the Convention of 1888 without the participation or prior approval of two parties

---

[1] *Id*. at 369.

[2] *Id*. at 173-178.

[3] Id. at 174-175. The Indian delegate, Mr. Krishna Menon, also offered the alternative suggestion that Article 8 of the Convention of 1888, which had been inoperative, might "be brought to life again," so that "the Egyptian Government in accepting the Convention of 1888 would be bound by this Article as by any other." *Id*. at 171-172. For text of that Article, see p. 229, *supra*.

[4] *Id*. at 217-218, 253-254, 269-270. U.N. SECURITY COUNCIL OFF. REC., 11th year, 736th Meeting 26 (1956). The Egyptian government made the same arguments. THE SUEZ CANAL PROBLEM 329; U.N. Doc. No. S/3650 (17 September 1956).

to the Convention – the Soviet Union and Hungary. The latter might have given their assent but it would not matter very much whether they did or not.[1] It was only Egypt which held a veto power, and that was in her capacity as the territorial sovereign rather than as a party to the prior treaty. The other parties would not have been bound by a new treaty arrived at without their consent, but their only practical alternative to giving their consent would have been withdrawal from participation in active regulation of the Canal.

There was no mention at the London Conference of the Declaration of London or the rule of unanimous consent. There were reaffirmations of the basic principle that the previous convention could not be abrogated by unilateral action of one of the parties.[2] Egypt had declared that the Anglo-Egyptian Treaty of 1954 was terminated by the British attack in November, 1956, but on April 24, 1957 she filed with the Secretary-General of the United Nations a unilateral declaration in which she reaffirmed her intention "to respect the terms and spirit" of the Convention and outlined supplementary obligations which Egypt stated that she would observe.[3] This appears to be a supplement to the 1888 Convention, rather than an attempted revision.

3. SUMMARY

The conventions concerning the Aaland Islands and the Suez Canal differed from the other conventions we have been considering in that their most important effect was the establishment of a principle rather than a detailed regime.[4] The early treaties concerning the Turkish Straits (before the establishment of detailed rules in 1923), whereby the powers recognized the traditional Turkish principle of closure to foreign warships as a rule of European

---

[1] *Cf.* statement by Secretary of State Dulles, September 19, 1956; "The 18 here do represent the countries which in their own right, and in a sense as typical countries interested in the Canal, can, with Egypt, bring about a solution which, if accepted by Egypt and by us, would be, I think we can say, accepted by all of the world." THE SUEZ CANAL PROBLEM 358.

[2] *Id.* at 336. See also statement of the Soviet delegate in the Security Council. U. N. SECURITY COUNCIL OFF. REC., 11th year, 736th Meeting 16 (1956).

[3] Text in 36 DEP'T STATE BULL. 776 (1956).

[4] In the case of the Aaland Islands, the Convention of 1856 stated nothing more than a principle. In the case of the Suez Canal, a similar net effect was produced by the Convention of 1888 and the British reservation which made the more detailed provisions a dead letter.

law, were similar in nature. In each instance there was an intent to establish the principle as an objective rule of international law.

The principle (demilitarized status of the Aaland Islands, freedom of transit of the Suez Canal) in the course of time received the added support of general recognition and reliance by the other states of the world. Their acceptance of its binding force was evidenced by other treaties between other groups of states, by express declarations, and by long-continued user. The original law-giving effect of the treaty between a few states (the great powers of the nineteenth century) may be doubted, but the process of transformation into customary international law gives the principle a wider basis than the original agreement.[1] The latter becomes little more than one piece of evidence supporting the existence of a rule of customary international law.

The effect of such transformation of a conventional principle into customary international law is that other states besides the parties to the treaty come to have a legal right to rely on it, and are bound by it as well. If it is desired to change or abolish it, general consent to the change will be required. This means that all of the states with substantial interests should normally participate if a conference is called to consider changes. Other states whose interests are remote may be expected to accept whatever decision the conference reaches. Under these circumstances participation in the treaty which originally established the principle becomes only one convenient criterion of what states are so "interested" that they ought to be invited.

The alternative theory that the Conventions of 1856 and 1888 created contractual rights for outside states as third-party beneficiaries is not a satisfactory explanation. No third states were specifically named in either convention. The League Commission of Jurists specifically rejected the doctrine in its application to the Aalands Islands, and the United States firmly rejected it in regard to the clause providing that the Panama Canal should be open on equal terms to the ships of all nations. Nor does the explanation of these restrictions as state servitudes seem to accord with the general nature of the reliance on the right.[2]

The practice concerning the Aaland Islands and the Suez

---

[1] McNair, *So-called State Servitudes*, 6 B.Y.I.L. 111, 126 (1925).

[2] *Cf.* McNair, *So-called State Servitudes*, 6 B.Y.I.L. 111 (1925); 1 OPPENHEIM, INTERNATIONAL LAW 535–543 (8th ed. by Lauterpacht, 1955).

TREATY REGIMES REINFORCED BY CUSTOM 243

Canal supports the above-stated view that other states besides the treaty parties had rights under the principles concerned. In the period before World War I England and France made the consent of Sweden a condition of any revision of the Aaland Islands Convention, clearly preferring Swedish consent to that of the signatories of the General Treaty of Paris. Sweden's right to be consulted was also recognized by the three signatories in 1916. Russia's diplomatic initiative of 1907 looked to the consent of Germany and Sweden, the most interested Baltic states, as more essential than that of France and England, though the latter's consent would doubtless have been sought also. Germany, though not a party to the Convention, appeared to recognize the special status of the islands as legally binding on her also. When Sweden sent troops to the islands in 1918 she sought the consent of Russia and Finland before that of England and France. When the latter claimed the right to be consulted they seemed to recognize that there was a binding obligation running between them and Sweden although there was no treaty with Sweden. Sweden, Germany and Finland, though not parties to the 1856 Convention, all recognized the obligation to maintain the islands' demilitarized status in 1918. In 1939, when Finland and Sweden sought to modify this status with the consent of all their co-signatories of the Convention of 1921, they were prevented from doing so by the refusal of the consent of Russia, to whom they were linked by no treaty. They would probably have proceeded with their plans if Russia had been a less powerful state, but Russia's refusal was stated to be based on a vested legal interest in the islands' status.

The 1920 opinion of the League of Nations Commission of Jurists found that all states were entitled to rely on the special status of the islands resulting from the 1856 Convention until those provisions should be replaced, and that it remained binding on the new state of Finland. The opinion did not specify what states' consent would be required for revision.

Sweden's interest and her right to participate in the new arrangements was recognized by the League of Nations in 1921. The list of invitees to the 1921 Conference, composed by Sweden and Great Britain, shows that the states having an interest in the islands' status sufficient to entitle them to participate in its revision were thought to be many more than the signatories of the

Convention of 1856. Those invited included seven Baltic states, and Italy as a great European power.

The Suez Canal Convention of 1888 only reaffirmed the already recognized principle of unrestricted navigation. The same accepted principle has been reaffirmed also in other treaties and declarations. The discussions of 1956 concerning new arrangements to secure this principle demonstrate that important users of the Canal have a right to participate in new arrangements which is at least equal to the right of parties to the Convention of 1888.

Austria and Hungary were omitted from the list of invitees to the London Conference, although they were parties to the Convention of 1888. Austria, by agreeing that her exclusion was proper, appears to have waived her right to be considered as an interested party in the future. Hungary made no such waiver, but was nevertheless excluded because the inviting powers thought her interest insufficient. It appeared that lack of consent by the Soviet Union would not have prevented revision of the Convention if Egypt had consented. There was general acceptance of the right of the majority of the confereees to attempt to reach agreement with Egypt by negotiations outside the Conference on the basis of the majority's proposals.

Egypt was recognized to possess the right to veto new arrangements supplementing the 1888 Convention, but it must be concluded that she possessed this right as territorial sovereign rather than as a party to the Convention of 1888.

CHAPTER VIII

CONCLUSIONS

The striking growth of international organization in the period since the Congress of Vienna has been effected through the legal instrumentality of the treaty. The familiarity of the treaty form for a time hid the fact that in its new multilateral use it was required to perform a quasi-legislative function quite different from the earlier function of recording a simple bilateral bargain.

Among other features of the new development, the use of the multipartite treaty gave rise to an entirely new problem of the degree of consent necessary for revision. Yet it was not at first appreciated that any new problem was involved. The rule that treaties might not legally be terminated or modified without the consent of all the parties was simply assumed. It seemed to be the logical extension on the multilateral plane of the accepted bilateral principle that contracts must be carried out. No serious analysis of the new doctrine, either on a logical or on a teleological basis, was ever undertaken.

Backed by such eminently citable authority as the Declaration of London, the assumed requirement of unanimity has been useful as a weapon in the arsenal of the legal adviser. It has often been invoked when it was desired to cite a legal basis for an essentially political protest against action that a state has been unwilling to accept. However, the seriousness of a government's reliance on the principle must be judged in the light of its total course of conduct rather than on the basis of isolated notes of protest. So judged, there is no government that has been consistent in its support of the principle. Nevertheless, because of the feeling that to abandon the unanimity principle would be to weaken the principle that treaties must be observed, governments have hesitated to question the existence of the principle and have tended, when circumstances made unanimity unattainable, to justify their departures from it in practice on the basis of other limiting principles.

After more than a century of increasing use of the multipartite treaty, it now seems clear that the rule of unanimity requires re-examination. If it were as rigid a principle of international law as it has generally been assumed to be it would have been a serious obstacle to treaty revision. This survey of practice proves that such has not been the case. It also appears to be an unreasonable requirement. No useful purpose is served by granting to a state, regardless of the extent of its interest in a given treaty regime, a purely formal veto power over revision, which may incline it to set an unreasonable price upon its consent to changes desired by the other parties. This may explain the fact that the assumed rule has never been allowed to hamper revision in practice. Where a rule is so little regarded in practice we must doubt its existence as law. It therefore seems evident that the principles governing treaty revision must be found elsewhere than in the concept of unanimity.

In the nineteenth century the authoritative statements of the unanimity principle were issued by the great powers. The concept of the Concert of Europe – the special mandate of the great powers to preserve the peace and to make "European" law – was then in vogue. For the great powers to exercise this "mandate" it was necessary that they speak with one voice. Many of the statements concerning the need for unanimity referred to this concert principle of unity of the great powers. Differences between them were negotiated through diplomatic channels, and political conferences were not convened until it was apparent that unanimity would result. When the great powers did meet in conference unanimity was a rule of voting procedure.[1] It was only where there was unanimity that any conference decision was taken, regardless of whether treaty revision was involved. While adhering to unanimity among themselves, which was necessary if their decisions were to be peacefully effective, the great powers often took decisions affecting the interests of lesser states without the consent of the latter. Because their rule of conference procedure required unanimity, they often consciously excluded the smaller states from their conferences so that the latter might hold no veto over the proceedings.

[1] " ... if an unanimous conclusion was arrived at there was an end of the matter; ... if it were not so, each Power would, with its own opinion, retain full liberty of action." Statement of Drouyn de Lhuys (French Ambassador to England) concerning a proposed great-power conference in 1866. 57 B.F.S.P. 384.

As Lande has pointed out, the unity of the great powers broke down toward the end of the nineteenth century, and the result was a revindication of the legal equality of the smaller states.[1] This development was paralleled by the formation of international unions in nonpolitical matters. In the conferences of such unions the smaller states participated as the legal equals of the great powers. In these conferences practical effectiveness was the controlling consideration, and here the rule of unanimity in conference voting, which had not been distinguished from the rule of unanimity of parties to treaties under revision, began to break down. By 1914 it was common practice for the conferences of the nonpolitical unions to conduct their business by majority voting, while preserving, in the right to withdraw from the union, the principle that no state is to be bound by a conference decision to which it refuses its consent. Every conference now decides for itself the procedure under which it will operate in this regard, unless the matter has been provided for in a constitutional provision of the organization concerned. The principle of unanimity has lingered on, however, in its specific application to treaty revision.

At this point it becomes necessary to note a number of important distinctions. One is the distinction, which has already been mentioned, between conference unanimity and unanimity of parties to previous treaties. A conference may adopt a decision by unanimity of the votes of those present and still not have the consent of a party to a previous treaty which is not represented at the conference. On the other hand, the states whose treaty rights will be affected may unanimously consent in advance to the taking of conference decisions by majority vote. There may thus be conference unanimity without unanimous consent of the parties, or unanimity of the parties without conference unanimity, and there is no necessary connection between the two.

Another distinction is to be made between the rule of unanimity and the rule against unilateral abrogation. It is noteworthy that the Declaration of London and several other authoritative sources of the unanimity doctrine were in fact directed to the latter phenomenon.

[1] Lande, "Revindication of the Principle of Legal Equality of States," 62 POL. SCI. Q 258, 398 (1947).

A third important distinction is between the principle of unanimous revision and the principle that new treaty undertakings will not bind states which do not become parties thereto. This last is the principle of consent. The theoretical basis of the unanimity doctrine is not the principle of consent (state sovereignty) but the principle of effectuating the assumed intent of the parties (*pacta sunt servanda*). It is by no means clear, however, that states concluding treaties generally intend to be limited by a veto over future revision. In fact they usually avoid or postpone consideration of the question.

A fourth distinction is to be made between unanimity which is dictated by the requirement of practical effectiveness (as where the parties are great powers, or states in a position by the exercise of their territorial sovereignty to frustrate any agreement to which they are unwilling to consent), and unanimity which has been dictated by a supposed legal principle where practical effectiveness would not have required it. Instances of the latter type have been practically nonexistent. On the other hand, the smaller states are now more sure of protection of their sovereign rights than they were previously, when there was thought to be a mandate for the great powers to take without their consent binding decisions in matters of the public law of Europe.

A number of methods have been developed to get around the assumed requirement of unanimous consent. The nonpolitical unions have been particularly fruitful in this respect. The terminable character of treaty obligations in this field made departures from unanimity appear less radical than in the field of political treaties. Nevertheless, the parties were generally unwilling to adopt the drastic expedient of terminating an old treaty before concluding a new one, because they wanted if possible to perpetuate the obligations previously undertaken by all the members of their unions. One method of procedure which they often adopted to make new treaty legislation effective was agreement in advance to submit their treaty to periodic revision, coupled with agreement, often tacit or developed by a process of parliamentary evolution, to drop the requirement of voting unanimity and to proceed in their conferences by the majority principle. A similar method of revision is now explicitly provided for in the charters of most international organizations. In both in-

stances revision without unanimity can be explained by consent given in advance.

Another common method which was developed in the revision of nonpolitical conventions was that of adopting new undertakings in the form of an *inter se* agreement, so as to leave the previous agreement still valid except between parties to the new one. Although writers have asserted that no *inter se* agreement should be entered into which would impair the essential purpose of the original treaty, the parties to the new agreement have themselves been the judges of compatibility, and no international tribunal has ever questioned the validity of such an agreement as between the parties thereto.

In respect to multipartite peace settlements occasions for treaty revision were less frequent because of the principle that changes of boundaries, unless they have been protected by an explicit collective guarantee, do not entail the revision of the treaties by which the boundaries were originally established, the latter having exhausted their effect upon completion of the transfers. Other excuses have been found for dispensing with unanimity in the revision of other provisions. One of these was the opinion that such settlements, viewed as a composite of separate agreements of interest to varying groups of parties, are of a specially separable character, constituting an exception to the unanimity principle, so that real interest in the subject matter is the criterion for participation in revision of their clauses. Another concept, which is frequently invoked in the elimination of restrictions imposed by treaty on a defeated state, is that of individual renunciation of the benefit of the restrictions on the part of those of the obligees which are willing to consent to its removal, but without affecting the formal rights of states unwilling to renounce. Such action transforms the question of continuance of the restriction in favor of the states unwilling to renounce into an issue solely between them and the restricted state.

In the field of treaties defining special regimes of a territorial character such devices have often not sufficed. It is usually not possible to limit the effects of the revision of such regimes to the parties to a new agreement. As an administrative matter two concurrent regimes cannot be maintained, and revision therefore

entails the termination of the old regime. It is common practice for the states principally interested in the regime in question to agree to modifications in negotiations among themselves, and then to request the consent or accession of the other parties to the previous treaty. Revision by this method was applied to the Rhine in 1919, and it was planned for the Danube by the great powers in 1948. In regard to the Turkish Straits the method was used in 1936, and Russia contemplated its use in 1945–46. It was frequently applied in the revision of the African regimes, and its validity, as between the parties to the new agreement, has seldom been questioned. We can therefore state with assurance that there is no support in practice for the theory that a treaty which purports to revise an earlier agreement, without the previous consent of all the parties, is void *ab initio*. Though they must be consulted if they are to be *bound* by a new agreement, the parties to a treaty have no general right to take part in all negotiations respecting revision.

The question of what states should be invited to join in discussions of revision is practical rather than legal. It is necessary to bring in all the states whose co-operation will be necessary if the new regime is to work in practice, and all the states whose insistence upon their previously acquired rights would seriously hamper the functioning of the new regime. This means that the degree of interest in the subject matter is the essential criterion for inclusion. Signature of previous treaties is one indication of interest, but the interest of a signatory may later diminish to the point where it may be disregarded, and other states may have important interests based on rights which they have acquired through custom and prescription.

There is, however, one category of states whose consent for changes is indispensable. These are states on whose territory the new treaty provisions must be effectuated. The controlling principle here is not the principle of unanimity but the principle that no state will be bound to a new obligation without its consent. In the case of a river regime limited to the riparian states this requirement will make unanimity necessary for the purely practical reason that the river cannot be united under one regime unless all the riparians do consent.

One must conclude that there is no customary rule of unani-

mity applicable to treaty revision. In place of it the following principles apply:

1) The principle that treaties of permanent character may not be abrogated unilaterally (*pacta sunt servanda*).

2) The principle that no state will be bound by any new obligation to which it refuses its consent (*ex consensu advenit vinculum*).

3) The principle that no treaty among other parties deprives a state of any substantive acquired rights (*res inter alios acta*).[1]

The decisions of international courts bear out these principles. In all cases that have arisen between the parties to a new treaty they have uniformly applied the new treaty, rejecting all contentions that such treaties are to be regarded as void because they modified earlier treaties without the consent of all their parties. It was only in the Central American cases, where states not parties to the new treaty were involved, that an international court held such a treaty ineffective. On the other hand, international courts have always upheld, as still existing, the substantive acquired rights of parties to a previous treaty which did not consent to its revision.

The acquired rights which must be respected include treaty rights and rights founded on custom and prescription. As the result of the transformation of a treaty regime into a customary regime, in such instances as nonfortification of the Aaland Islands and freedom of the Suez Canal, other states besides the parties to previous treaties may have such rights. In both of these instances the rights of outside interested states were recognized when it came to discussions of revision.

No international court has been faced with the more difficult problem concerning rights of a procedural or administrative character, such as the right to be represented on a board with defined powers, which the later treaty reconstitutes or abolishes. However, practice seems to indicate that the principle of respect for acquired rights is here subject to an important qualification, and that the rights which are protected are limited to those which can be divorced from the existence of the old admin-

---

[1] These are the basic principles which were stated by Fitzmaurice in his preliminary Report on the Law of Treaties for the International Law Commission, March 15, 1956. U.N. Doc. No. A/CN.4/101 (1956).

istrative regime. The regime itself may be terminated for all parties by a new agreement between the most interested states.

If it were not for this characteristic – the possibility of termination of a state's right to participate in an international administration – it might be said that the general rule applicable to all revision was that, in the absence of unanimity, revision was legally effective only *inter se*. However, this characteristic indicates that revision of a regime without unanimous consent does have more than *inter se* effect. The result is bound up with the possibility of withdrawal. The state which refuses to participate in changes in an international regime which the majority desires, in effect withdraws from the regime. It is not bound by any new obligations and it reserves its substantive acquired rights, but it may lose the right to participate in the international administration concerned. This conclusion is supported by the fact that the failure to respond to an invitation to participate in a revision conference or to an invitation to accede to the new arrangements has sometimes been regarded as an expression of lack of interest disqualifying the state concerned from the right to participate in future revisions. Except for the possibility of such a waiver, it would seem that all of the parties to the previous regime do have a right to accede to the new regime and so continue their participation if they are willing to accept the revision which the majority has made.

The first principle stated above – the principle against unilateral abrogation – means that some form of collective consent is required for replacement of an existing regime. It seems probable that the minimum consent necessary for such action is that of a majority of the states actively participating in the administration. This is in line with the trend in conference procedure, on abandoning the requirement of unanimity to fall back upon the majority principle. Again, as in other respects, the consent of the largest and most interested states is likely to be necessary also a practical matter. It is clear that the only states having a legal veto, in the absence of specific treaty provisions, are those whose territorial sovereignty will be limited by the new arrangements.

SELECTED BIBLIOGRAPHY

The lists following enumerate the specialized works which have been used in preparing this study. Standard works and series, such as Hackworth's *Digest of International Law*, Oppenheim's *International Law*, the *Survey of International Affairs* and *Documents on International Affairs* issued by the Royal Institute of International Affairs, the *Recueil des Cours* of the Hague Academy, *Foreign Relations of the United States*, *British and Foreign State Papers*, League of Nations and United Nations Official Records and Treaty Series, etc., have been generally omitted; they are cited in footnotes at the appropriate places. Abbreviations used in citing such sources are listed at page XII.

Records of International Conferences

Algeciras. International Conference on Moroccan Affairs, 1906. *Conférence International d'Algéciras*. Madrid, J. Blas y Cia., 1906.
Conférence Danubienne, Béograd, 1948. *Recueil des Documents* . Béograd, Ed. Ministère des Affaires Etrangères de la République Populaire Federative de Yougoslavie, 1949.
Conference for the Codification of International law, Geneva, 1930. *Acts of the Conference*. Vol.I. *Plenary Meetings*. Geneva, 1930 (League of Nations Publication C. 351.M.145. 1930. V).
Conférence Internationale pour l'Etablissement du Statut Définitif du Danube, Paris, 1921. *Protocoles des Séances*. 2 vols. Paris, Imprimerie Nationale, 1921.
Conférence Internationale pour la Protection de la Propriéte Industrielle, Paris, 1883. *Procès-Verbaux* [etc.]. Paris, Imprimerie Nationale, 1883.
Conférence Internationale pour la Protection de la Propriété Industrielle, Brussels, 1897–1900. *Actes de la Conférence*. Berne, Bureau International de l'Union International pour la Protection de la Propriété Industrielle, 1901.
Conférence Internationale pour la Protection de la Propriété Industrielle, Neuchâtel, 1947. *Actes de la Conférence*. Berne, Bureau de l'Union International pour la Protection de la Propriété Industrielle, 1947.
Conférence Internationale pour la Protection des Oeuvres Littéraires et Artistiques, Bern, 1885. *Actes de la Deuxième Conférence Internationale pour la Protection des Oeuvres Littéraires et Artistiques*. Berne, K. J. Wyss, 1885.

Conférence Internationale pour la Protection des Oeuvres Littéraires et Artistiques, Rome, 1928. *Actes de la Conférence.* Berne, Bureau de l'Union International pour la Protection des Oeuvres Littéraires et Artistiques, 1929.

Conférence Internationale sur le Transport des Marchandises par Chemins de fer, Bern, 1952. *Actes de la 5e Conférence de Revision.* 2 vols. Berne, Office Central des Transports Internationaux par Chemins de Fer, 1954.

Conference of States Signatories of the Protocol of Signature of the Statute of the Permanent Court of International Justice, Geneva, 1926. *Minutes of the Conference.* Geneva, 1926. League of Nations Document C.554.1926. VII.

Conference regarding the Revision of the Stature of the Permanent Court of International Justice and the Accession of the United States of America to the Protocol of Signature of that Statute, Geneva, 1929. *Minutes of the Conference.* Geneva, 1929. League of Nations Document C.514.M.173. 1939. V.

Conférence Relative à la Non-fortification et à la Neutralisation des Isles d'Aland, Geneva, 1921. *Actes de la Conférence.* Geneva, 1921. League of Nations Document C.554. 1921. VII.

France. Ministère des Affaires Etrangères. *Conférence Internationale de Bruxelles. 18 Novembre 1889–2 Juillet 1890. Protocoles et Acte Final.* Paris, Imprimerie Nationale, 1891.

———. *Protocoles de la Conférence Sanitaire Internationale. Avril-Août 1859.* Paris, Imprimerie Imperiale, 1859.

Geneva. Conference for Revision of the Geneva Convention of 1864, 1906. *Actes de la Conférence.* Genève, H. Jarrys, 1906.

Hague. International Peace Conference. 2d, 1907. *Deuxième Conférence Internationale de la Paix, La Haye, 15 Juin-18 Octobre 1907. Actes et Documents.* La Haye, Martinus Nijhoff, 1909.

Great Britain. Parliamentary Papers (1923). *Lausanne Conference on Near Eastern Affairs 1922—23.* Cmd. 1814.

International Civil Aviation Conference, Chicago, 1944. *Proceedings.* 2 vols. Washington, Government Printing Office, 1948-49.

International Conference on Private Air Law, The Hague, 1955. *International Conference on Private Air Law, The Hague, September 1955.* 2 vols. Montreal, International Civil Aviation Organization, 1956.

International Radiotelegraph Conference, London, 1912. *Documents de la Conférence Radiotélégraphique Internationale de Londres.* Berne, Bureau International de l'Union Télégraphique, 1913.

International Radiotelegraph Conference, Washington, 1927. *Documents de la Conférence Radiotélégraphique Internationale de Washington.* 2 vols. Berne, Bureau International de l'Union Télégraphique, 1928.

International Telegraph Conference, Paris, 1865. *Documents Diplomatiques de la Conférence Télégraphique Internationale de Paris.* Paris, Imprimerie Impériale, 1865.

International Telegraph Conference, Rome, 1871–1872. *Documents de la Conférence Télégraphique Internationale de Rome.* Berne, Impr. Rieder & Simmen, 1872.

International Telegraph Conference, Brussels, 1928. *Documents de la Conférence Télégraphique Internationale de Bruxelles.* Berne, Bureau International de l'Union Télégraphique, 1928.

International Telegraph Conference, Madrid, 1932. *Documents de la Conférence Télégraphique Internationale de Madrid.* 2 vols. Berne, Bureau Internationale de l'Union Télégraphique, 1933.
Montreux. Conference on the Regime of the Straits, 1936. *Actes de la Conférence de Montreux, 22 Juin-20 Juillet 1936.* Liège, H. Vaillant-Carmanne, 1936.
The Proceedings of the Hague Peace Conferences; Translation of the Official Texts, Prepared in the Division of International Law of the Carnegie Endowment for International Peace under the Supervision of James Brown Scott, Director. 5 vols. New York, Oxford University Press, 1920–21.
Union Postale Universelle. Deuxième Congrès, Paris, 1878. *Documents du Congrès Postal de Paris.* Berne, Impr. Lang & Cie., 1878.
———. Onzième Congrès. Buenos Aires, 1939. *Documents du Congrès de Buenos Aires.* 3 vols. Berne, Bureau International de l'Union Postale Universelle, 1939.
United Nations. Conference on International Organization, San Francisco, 1945. *Documents.* 16 vols. London, and New York, United Nations Information Organizations, 1945–1946.
United States. Department of State. Publication 2868. *Paris Conference to Consider the Draft Treaties of Peace, 1946. Selected Documents.* Washington, Government Printing Office, 1946.

Other Public Documents

Belgium. Ministère des Affaires Etrangères. *Documents Diplomatiques Relatifs à la Revision des Traités de 1839.* Brussels, M. Weissenbruch, 1929.
British Documents on the Origins of the War, 1898–1914. Edited by G. P. Gooch and Harold Temperley. London, H. M. Stationery Office, 1926–1938.
Commission Europeénne du Danube. *Textes du Règlement de la Commission Européenne du Danube et des Accords concernant le Danube Maritime.* Rome, 1954.
Comision Internacional de Jurisconsultos Americanos, *Actas Reunion de 1927.* Vol. 2.
France. Ministère des Affaires Etrangères. *Documents Diplomatiques. Question de la Protection Diplomatique et Consulaire au Maroc.* Paris, Imprimerie Nationale, 1880.
———. *Documents Diplomatiques. Negociations Relatives au Règlement International pour le Libre Usage du Canal de Suez. 1886–1887.* Paris, Imprimerie Nationale, 1887.
———. *Documents Diplomatiques Français (1871–1914).* 2e série. Vol. 5. Paris, Imprimerie Nationale, 1934.
Germany. Auswärtiges Amt. *Die Grosse Politik der Europäischen Kabinette 1871–1914.* 40 vols. Berlin, 1924–27.
Great Britain. Parliamentary Papers (1853). *Correspondence with the Russian Government respecting Obstructions to the Navigation of the Sulina Channel of the Danube.* Cmd. 1669.
———. Parliamentary Papers (1867). *Correspondence Respecting the Grand Duchy of Luxemburg.* Cmd. 3867.

——. Parliamentary Papers. Turkey No. 3 (1878). *Further Correspondence respecting the Affairs of Turkey.* Cmd. 1923.
——. Parliamentary Papers. Egypt No. 34 (1884). *Further Correspondence respecting the Affairs of Egypt.* Cmd. 4205.
——. Parliamentary Papers. Egypt No. 19 (1885). *Correspondence respecting the Suez Canal International Commission, with the Protocols and Proces-Verbaux of the Meetings.* Cmd. 4599.
——. Parliamentary Papers. Danube No. 1 (1883). *Correspondence respecting the Navigation of the Danube.* Cmd. 3525.
——. Parliamentary Papers. Turkey No. 2 (1897). *Correspondence respecting the Introduction of Reforms in the Administration of the Ottoman Empire.* Cmd. 8304.
——. Parliamentary Papers. Egypt No. 1 (1905). *Reports by His Majesty's Agent and Consul-General on the Finances, Administration, and Condition of Egypt and the Soudan in 1904.* Cmd. 2409.
——. Parliamentary Papers. Egypt No. 2 (1922). *Despatch to His Majesty's Representatives Abroad respecting the Status of Egypt.* Cmd. 1617.
——. Parliamentary Papers. Miscellaneous No. 10 (1924). *Correspondence Concerning the Conference to Bring the Dawes Plan into Operation.* Cmd. 2184.
——. Parliamentary Papers. Miscellaneous No. 17 (1924). *Proceedings of the London Reparation Conference July and August 1924.* Cmd. 2270.
——. Parliamentary Papers. Miscellaneous No. 1 (1944). *Protocol on the International Regulation of Whaling.* Cmd. 6510.
——. Parliamentary Papers. Miscellaneous No. 6 (1944). *A Commentary on the Dumbarton Oaks Proposals for the Establishment of a General International Organisation.* Cmd. 6571.
——. Parliamentary Papers. Germany No. 1 (1945). *Unconditional Surrender of Germany.* Cmd. 6648.
——. Parliamentary Papers. Miscellaneous No. 2 (1947). *Commentary on the Treaties of Peace with Italy, Roumania, Bulgaria, Hungary and Finland.* Cmd. 7026.
——. Parliamentary Papers. *Carriage of Goods by Rail, International Convention, 1952.* Cmd. 9065.
——. Parliamentary Papers. Egypt No. 2 (1954). *Agreement between the Government of the United Kingdom and the Egyptian Government regarding the Suez Canal Base.* Cmd. 9298.
League of Nations. Board of Liquidation. *Final Report Presented to States Members of the League of Nations.* Geneva, 1947 (League of Nations Document C.5.M.5. 1947).
Office Central des Transports Internationaux par Chemins de Fer. *Bulletin des Transports Internationaux par Chemins de Fer.* Vols. 58–59. Berne, 1950–51.
United Nations. Interim Commission on Food and Agriculture. *Second Report to the Governments of the United Nations* (1945).
——. Preparatory Commission. *Report of the Preparatory Commission of the United Nations* (1945).
——. Secretariat. *Handbook of Final Clauses.* United Nations Document St/Leg/1 (1951).
——. Secretariat. *Status of Multilateral Conventions of Which the Secretary-General Acts as Depositary.* United Nations Document St/Leg/3 (1955).
United States. Congress. Senate. Committee on Foreign Relations.

The Charter of the United Nations. Hearings before the Committee on Foreign Relations, United States Senate, on the Charter of the United Nations, 79th Congress, First Session (1945).

———. Department of State. Publication 468. *Treaty for the Renunciation of War*. Washington, Government Printing Office, 1933.

———. Department of State. Publication 3177. *Report of the United States Delegation to the International Telecommunication Conference at Atlantic City*. Washington, Government Printing Office, 1947.

———. Department of State. Publication 6392. *The Suez Canal Problem*. Washington, Government Printing Office, 1956.

———. Department of State. *Texts of the Russian "Peace."* Washington, Government Printing Office, 1918.

Books

ADAMOV, E. A. (ed.). *Konstantinopol i Prolivy po Sekretnym Dokumentam B. Ministerstvo Inostrannykh Del*. Vol. 1. Moscow, 1925.

Annuaire Français de Droit International. Vol. 1 (1955).

BISHOP, JOSEPH B. *Theodore Roosevelt and His Time*. 2 vols. New York, Charles Scribner & Sons, 1920.

BYRNES, JAMES F. *Speaking Frankly*. New York, Harper & Bros., 1947.

CHAMBERLAIN, J. P. *The Regime of the International Rivers: Danube and Rhine*. New York, Columbia University Press, 1923.

———, JESSUP, PHILIP C., LANDE, ADOLF, and LISSITZYN, OLIVER J., *International Organization; International Regulation of Economic and Social Questions*. New York, Carnegie Endowment for International Peace, 1955.

CHIESA, PIERRE ALBERT. *Le Régime International du Rhin et la Participation de la Suisse*. Montreux, 1952.

CHODZKO, J. L. *Le Congrès de Vienne*. 4 vols. Paris, 1864.

DEGRAS, JANE (ed.). *Soviet Documents on Foreign Policy*. 3 vols. London, Oxford University Press, 1951–53.

DE VISSCHER, CHARLES. *Theory and Reality in Public International Law*. Translated by P. E. Corbett. Princeton, Princeton University Press, 1957.

DJONKER, M. D. *Le Bosphore et les Dardanelles*. Lausanne, 1938.

Droit Colonial International, Conférence de la Paix de Paris. Paris, Les Editions Internationales, 1931.

DUNN, FREDERICK S. *The Practice and Procedure of International Conferences*. Baltimore, The Johns Hopkins Press, 1929.

DUVERNOY, JEAN. *Le Régime International du Danube*. Paris, 1941.

EYSINGA, JonkheerW. J. M. VAN. *La Commission Centrale pour la Navigation du Rhin*. Leiden, A. W. Sijthoff, 1935.

FANDIKOV, P. G. *Mezhdunarodno-Pravovoi Rezhim Dunaia*. Moscow, 1955.

FAY, SIDNEY B. *Origins of the World War*. 2 vols. New York, Macmillan Co., 1929.

FITZMAURICE, G. G. *Report on the Law of Treaties*. United Nations Document A/CN.4/101 (1956).

———. *Second Report on the Law of Treaties*. United Nations Document A/CN.4/107 (1957).

GAFENCU, G. *Prelude to the Russian Campaign*. London, 1946.

GOODRICH, LELAND M., and HAMBRO, EDVARD. *Charter of the United*

Nations: Commentary and Documents. Revised edition. Boston, World Peace Foundation, 1949.

GUGGENHEIM, PAUL. *Traité de Droit International Public*. 3 vols. Geneva, Georg, 1953–54.

HAJNAL, HENRI. *The Danube*. The Hague, 1920.

———. *Le Droit de Danube International*. The Hague, 1929.

HALLBERG, CHARLES W. *The Suez Canal*. New York, Columbia University Press, 1931.

Harvard Law School. Research in International Law. *Draft Convention on the Law of Treaties*. American Journal of International Law, XXIX (1935), Supplement.

HUDSPN, MANLEY O. *The Permanent Court of International Justice, 1920–42*. New York, Macmillan Co., 1943.

JESSUP, PHILIP C. *Elihu Root*. 2 vols. New York, Dodd, Mead and Co., 1938.

KLIUCHNIKOV, Y. V., I SABANIN, A. V. *Mezhdunarodnaia Politika Noveishogo Vremeni v. Dogovorakh, Notakh i Deklaratziiakh*, Vol. 3. Moscow, 1928.

LADAS, STEPHEN P. *The International Protection of Literary and Artistic Property*. New York, Macmillan Co., 1938.

LANGER, WILLIAM L. *The Diplomacy of Imperialism*. Second edition. New York, Knopf, 1951.

LAUTERPACHT, H. *First Report on the Law of Treaties*. United Nations Document A/CN.4/63 (1953).

———. *Second Report on the Law of Treaties*. United Nations Document A/CN.4/87 (1954).

LISSITZYN, OLIVER J. *International Air Transport and National Policy*. New York, Council on Foreign Relations, 1942.

MANCE, Sir OSBORNE. *International River and Canal Transport*. Oxford, 1945.

McNAIR, Sir ARNOLD. *The Law of Treaties*. New York, Columbia University Press, 1938.

MILLER, DAVID HUNTER. *My Diary at the Paris Peace Conference*. 21 vols. New York, Appeal Printing Co., 1924.

———. *The Drafting of the Covenant*. 2 vols. New York, G. P. Putnam's Sons, 1928.

MUGGERIDGE, MALCOLM (ed.). *Ciano's Diplomatic Papers*. London, Odhams Press Ltd., 1948.

PRIBRAM, A. F. *The Secret Treaties of Austria-Hungary, 1879–1914*. 2 vols. English edition by Archibald C. Coolidge. Cambridge, Harvard University Press, 1920–21.

RÄNK, RICHARD. *Einwirkung des Krieges auf die Nichtpolitischen Staatsverträge*. Publications de l'Institut Suedois du Droit International, No. 8, Uppsala, 1949.

RICHES, CROMWELL A. *Majority Rule in International Organization, a Study of the Trend from Unanimity to Majority Decision*. Baltimore, The Johns Hopkins Press, 1940.

ROSS, ALF. *Textbook of International Law*. New York, Longmans Green & Co., 1947.

Rheinurkunden. 2 vols. Published by the Central Commission for the Navigation of the Rhine. The Hague, Munich and Leipzig, 1918.

Russia. Ministerstvo Inostrannykh Del. *Un Livre Noir, Diplomatie*

d'Avant-Guerre d'Après les Documents des Archives Russes. 3 vols. Paris, Librairie du Travail, 1922–1934.
SAINT CLAIR, ANDRÉ DE. *Le Danube, Etude de Droit International.* Paris, 1899.
SAYRE, FRANCIS B. *Experiments in International Administration.* New York, Harper & Bros., 1919.
SCELLE, GEORGES. *Théorie Juridique de la Revision des Traités.* Geneva, Publications of the Graduate Institute of International Studies, No. 16, 1936.
SCHÜCKING, WALTHER. *The International Union of the Hague Conferences.* Translated by Charles G. Fenwick. New York, H. Milford, 1918.
SHOTWELL, JAMES T. and DEÁK, FRANCIS. *Turkey at the Straits.* New York, Macmillan Co., 1940.
STEPHENS, WALDO E. *Revisions of the Treaty of Versailles.* New York, Columbia University Press, 1939.
STUART, GRAHAM H. *The International City of Tangier.* Second edition. Stanford, Stanford University Press, 1955.
STURDZA, D. *Recueil de Documents Relatifs à la Liberté de Navigation du Danube.* Berlin, 1904.
TARDIEU, ANDRÉ. *La Conférence d'Algésiras.* Paris, Alcan, 1909.
TEMPERLEY, HAROLD. *A History of the Peace Conference of Paris.* 6 vols. London, Henry Froude and Hodder & Stoughton, 1920–1924.
TOBIN, HAROLD J. *The Termination of Multipartite Treaties.* New York, Columbia University Press, 1933.
VEDOVATO, GIUSEPPE. *Il Trattato di Pace con Italia, Documenti e Carta.* Florence, 1947.
VERDROSS, ALFRED VON. *Völkerrecht.* Third edition. Vienna, 1955.
WEGENER, WILHELM. *Die Internationale Donau.* Göttingen, 1951.
WILCOX, FRANCIS O. and MARCY, CARL M. *Proposals for Changes in the United Nations.* Washington, The Brookings Institution, 1955.

Articles

ARECHAGA, JIMENEZ DE. "Treaty Stipulations in Favor of Third States," *American Journal of International Law*, L (1956), 338.
BALLADORE-PALLIERI, G. "La Formation des Traités dans la Pratique International Contemporaine," Académie de Droit International de la Haye, *Recueil des Cours*, LXXIV (1949), 465.
BLIX, HANS. "The Rule of Unanimity in the Revision of Treaties: a Study of the Treaties Governing Tangier," *International and Comparative Law Quarterly*, V (1956), 447, 581.
DE VISSCHER, FERNAND. "La Nouvelle Convention des Détroits," *Revue de Droit International*, XVII (1936), 669.
FITZMAURICE, G. G. "The Juridical Clauses of the Peace Treaties," Académie de Droit International de la Haye, *Recueil des Cours*, LXXIII (1948), 255.
———. "Reservations to Multilateral Conventions," *International and Comparative Law Quarterly*, II (1953), 1.
"G. F." Note, *The British Yearbook of International Law*, XVIII (1937), 186.
HOWARD, HARRY N. "Some Recent Developments in the Problem of the Turkish Straits, 1945–1946." *Department of State Bulletin*, XVI (1947), 143.

HUDSON, MANLEY O. "The First Conference for the Codification of International Law," *American Journal of International Law*, XXIV (1930), 461.
——. "The International Mixed Court of Tangier," *American Journal of International Law*, XXI (1927), 231.
HYDE, CHARLES CHENEY. "The Revision of Treaties and of Settlements Registered in Treaties," *Hungarian Quarterly*, II (1936), 203.
JENKS, C. W. "The Montreux Conference and the Law of Peaceful Change," *New Commonwealth Quarterly*, II (1936–37), 242.
——. "The Relation between Membership of the League of Nations and Membership of the International Labour Organization," *The British Yearbook of International Law*, XVI (1935), 79.
——. "Some Constitutional Problems of International Organizations," *The British Yearbook of International Law*, XXII (1945), 11.
——. "State Succession in Respect of Law-making Treaties," *The British Yearbook of International Law*, XXIX (1952), 105.
LANDE, ADOLF. "Revindication of the Principle of Legal Equality of States," *Political Science Quarterly*, LXII (1947), 258, 398.
MCNAIR, Sir ARNOLD. "Les Effets de la Guerre sur les Traités," Académie de Droit International de la Haye, *Recueil des Cours*, LIX (1937), 523.
——. "The Functions and Differing Legal Character of Treaties," *The British Yearbook of International Law*, XI (1930), 100.
——. "So-called State Servitudes," *The British Yearbook of International Law*, VI (1925), 111.
MARCANTONATOS, L. G. "L'Evolution du Statut International du Danube Maritime de 1938 à 1948," *Revue Hellénique de Droit International*, I (1948), 49, 140.
MUÛLS, F. "Le Régime International du Bassin Conventionnel du Congo," *Mélanges Offerts à Ernest Maheim*, Vol. 2. Paris, 1935.
PADELFORD, NORMAN J. and ANDERSSON, K. GÖSTA A. "The Aaland Islands Question," *American Journal of International Law*, XXXIII (1939), p. 465.
SADAK, N. "Turkey Faces the Soviets," *Foreign Affairs*, XXVII (1949), 449.
SCELLE, GEORGES. "La Revision dans les Conventions Générales," *Annuaire de l'Institut de Droit International*, XLII (1948), 1.
SCHACHTER, OSCAR. "The Development of International Law Through the Legal Opinions of the United Nations Secretariat," *The British Yearbook of International Law*, XXV (1948), 91.
SOFRONIE, G., "Le Statut International du Danube Maritime et la Position de la Roumanie," *Revue Générale de Droit International Public*, XLVIII (1941–1945), 53.
SØRENSON, MAX. "The Modification of Collective Treaties without the Consent of All the Contracting Parties," *Nordisk Tidsskrift For International Ret*, IX (1938), 150.
TCHIRKOVITCH, STEVAN. "La Question de la Revision de la Convention de Montreux," *Revue Générale de Droit International Public*, LVI (1952), 189.
URRUTIA, F. J. "La Codification du Droit International en Amérique," Académie de Droit International de la Haye, *Recueil des Cours*, XXII (1928), 81.
WARNER, EDWARD D. "The International Convention for Air Navigation and the Pan American Convention for Air Navigation: A Comparative and Critical Analysis," *Air Law Review*, III (1932), 225.

INDEX

Aachen, Protocol of, 85
Aaland Islands, treaties concerning, 88, 214–227, 241–244, 251; Geneva Conference (1921), 222–223, 243
Abrogation, unilateral, 6–8, 247, 251–252
Acquired rights, 155, 181, 212, 250–252
Air navigation, conventions on, 39–41
Algeciras, Conference (1905–6), 184–187; Act of, 186–191, 196–213
Anzilotti, Dionisio, 195n
Australia, official statements, 64
Austria, admission to Danube Commission (1957), 152; official statements, 235
Austria-Hungary, official statements, 21, 86–87, 122, 230

Balfour, Arthur J., 190
Barcelona Convention on Freedom of Communications and Transit, 130
Belgium, official statements, 56, 58, 65, 135, 136, 147, 149n, 150, 192–193; and navigation of the Rhine, 128; treaties concerning, 84–85, 97–99, 114
Belgrade, Convention (1948), 149–152, 154
Berlin, Conference (1885), 180–182; Congress of (1878), 89–90, 157; General Act (1885), 180–182, 191–195, 211; Treaty of (1878), 89–92, 124–125, 231
Bilateral form, multipartite treaties in, 107
Bismarck, 89–90, 127n
Bosnia, agreements concerning, 89–92, 159
Boundary provisions, 85–86, 113, 249
Brazil, official statements, 64, 66, 180
Brest-Litovsk, Treaty of, 219
Brussels, General Act (1890), 182–184, 191–195, 211

Canada, official statements, 60, 64
Carol I, King of Rumania, 127

Cecil, Lord Robert, 52
Central American Court of Justice, 195–196, 251
Chicago Convention on International Civil Aviation, 40–41
Chicherin, 165–166
Concert of Europe, 7, 85, 89–92, 114, 122–123, 152–153, 156, 176–177, 227–228, 246–248
Congo Basin, 181–184
Connally, Senator, 63n
Copyright, protection of, 30–31
Costa Rica, 195–196
Cracow, treaties concerning, 86–87
Curzon, 165–166
Customary rights in treaty regimes, 214–244
Czechoslovakia, official statements, 148

Danube river, Conference (1921), 134–138, 154; Conference (1948), 147–151, 154; treaties concerning, 121–127, 133–155, 250
Denmark, official statements, 185

Egypt, concession to Universal Suez Canal Company, 227; nationalization of Suez Canal Company, 234; official statements, 227, 235, 237–241; treaties with Great Britain, 233–241
El Salvador, 195–196
Ethiopia, official statements, 235n
European Rail Transport Union, 26–28
Eysinga, W. J. M. van, 57, 120, 194

France, and navigation of the Rhine, 117–120, 128–129, 133; official statements, 7, 99, 101n, 104–105, 108, 110, 129, 134, 135, 137, 145, 147–151 154, 175–176, 184n, 189–190, 192, 198, 201, 204–208, 218–219, 223, 227–228, 231, 234, 236; protectorate in Morocco, 187–191, 196–197, 209, 213
Finland, official statements, 224–225

262 INDEX

Fitzmaurice, G. G., 5, 61, 107n, 171, 174n, 251n
Food and Agriculture Organization, 42–43
Free Zones of Upper Savoy and the District of Gex, 100–102, 114

Geneva, Conference concerning the Aaland Islands (1921), 222–223; Convention on the Condition of Wounded in Armies in the Field, 31–32
George, Walter F., 63n
German Confederation, 87
Germany, admission to the European Commission of the Danube, 144; agreements concerning (1945), 112; denunciation of provisions of the Treaty of Versailles, 132, 143; official statements, 38, 48, 88, 125, 135, 145–146, 184–185, 188, 189, 197, 216–219, 230; reparations, 94–96, 118
Granville circular, 227
Great Britain, occupation of Egypt, 229–234; official statements, 6, 28–29, 37, 38–39, 61, 63, 65, 83–84, 86, 89–92, 97, 103–105, 107, 108–111, 135–137, 139, 145, 147–151, 154,158, 160, 170–171, 173–175, 188–190, 198, 199, 201, 204–208, 210, 216–219, 223, 227–230, 232–234, 237; reservation respecting the Suez Canal, 229–234
Great Powers, unity of, 7, 85, 89–92, 114, 122–123, 152–153, 156,176–177, 227–228, 246–248
Greece, official statements, 135, 136, 147, 149n, 150, 172; share of Danube traffic, 134n
Grey, Sir Edward, 160–162, 218

Hackworth, Green, 55, 61
Hague, Conference for the Codification of International Law (1930), 46; Peace Conferences, 46–49
Harvard Draft Convention on the Law of Treaties (1935), 1, 3, 9, 50
Havana Convention on Treaties (1928), 8–9, 46
Hay-Pauncefote Treaty, 236–237
Huber, Max, 49, 60n, 80, 220
Hudson, Manley O., 8, 47–48, 57n, 58–60, 67n, 204
Hughes, Charles Evans, 237
Hull, Cordell, 189n
Hurst, Sir Cecil, 195n

India, official statements, 64n, 70, 235, 240
Indonesia, official statements, 238n
Industrial Property, protection of, 28–30
Inter se agreements, 28–39, 47–48, 51, 249, 252
International conferences, procedure, 11–12, 48–51, 53–55, 80–81, 166, 186 246–248, 252
International Copyright Union, 30–31
International Court of Justice, Advisory Opinion on Reservations to the Convention on Genocide, 9–10, 50; International status of South-West Africa, 37, 76–78; Rights of Nationals of the United States of America in Morocco, 190–191, 203n
International Institute of Agriculture, 41–43, 51
International Labor Organization, 58, 66–68
International Telegraph Union, 22–26
Ireland, exclusion from revision of agreements on whaling, 44–45, 51
Israel, official statements, 235
Italian Peace Treaty (1947), 102–114
Italy, official statements, 57, 108, 110, 135, 149n, 150–151, 161, 170, 173, 188n, 198, 201–204, 208, 223, 230; withdrawal from the Central Commission of the Rhine, 133

Japan, official statements, 66, 169, 171
Japanese Peace Treaty (1951), 107
Jencks, C. W., 68, 140

Kellogg, Frank, 203n

Lande, Adolf, 247
Larnaude, Professor, 220
Lausanne, Conference (1922–23), 162–168, 178; convention, 107, 166–168
Lauterpacht, Sir Hersch, 5, 11
Law-making treaties, 46–48, 50
League of Nations, Committee for Communications and Transit, 142–143; Committee of Jurists on the Aaland Islands question, 219–222, 243; Covenant, 52–55; replacement by the United Nations, 32–37, 72–78, 80
Lissitzyn, Oliver J., 41n
Litvinoff, Maxim, 172
London, Conference concerning the Suez Canal (1956),234–244; Declaration of (1871), 6–8, 89, 91–92, 241,

INDEX 263

245, 247; Treaty of, 127, 142, 157, 231
Luxembourg, treaties concerning, 84–85

Madrid, Convention of (1880), 179–180, 210, 213
McNair, Sir Arnold, 77–78, 85n, 98–99, 148
Metternich, 86
Mexico, official statements, 64, 65n
Miller, David Hunter, 54
Molotov, Vyacheslav, 147
Montreux Conference (1936), 169–174, 178
Moore, John Bassett, 141–142
Morocco, restoration of independence of, 209, 213; treaties concerning, 179–180, 184–191, 196–213

Narcotics conventions, 32–36, 50–51
Negulesco, Judge, 125, 136
Netherlands, and international whaling agreements, 44; official statements, 53, 57, 64, 65, 119, 130–132, 228; and regulation of the Rhine, 118–120, 128–133, 153
Nicaragua, 195–196
Nicolson, Sir Arthur, 88, 160n, 217
Niemen river, 138–139n
Nonpolitical conventions, 13, 17–51, 247, 248; denunciation of, 17–20, 39–41, 46–47, 49–50, 248; revision provisions, 20, 28, 30–31, 39–40, 51
Norway, official statements, 57, 68, 71–72, 183n, 185
Nyholm, Judge, 135–136, 142

Palieri, G. Balladore, 82n
Palmerston, 83, 86
Panama Canal, 236–237
Panama, official statements, 235
Pan-American treaties, air navigation 40–41; copyright, 31; patents and trade marks, 31
Paris, Peace Conference (1919), 66–67, 93–102, 189–193, 211, 214, 220–221, 231; Treaty of (1856), 87–92, 121
Pasvolsky, Leo, 63n
Peace settlements, 82–114, 249
Peretti, 190, 192
Permanent Court of International Justice, Austro-German Customs Regime, 195n; Free Zones of Upper Savoy and the District of Gex, 100–102, 114, 220n; Interpretation of Art. 3, para. 2 of the Treaty of Lausanne, 5n; Jurisdiction of the European Commission of the Danube, 125, 135–136, 140–142, 154, 196; Mavrommatis Palestine Concessions, 196; Oscar Chinn case, 194–196, 211; revision of the Statute, 55–62, 79; S. S. Wimbledon, 195n; Territorial Jurisdiction of the International Commission of the River Oder, 79n, 130–131n
Pilotti, Massimo, 57, 59–60, 80
Poland, Treaties concerning (1815), 83–84
Politis, 172
Prescription, rights based on, 234–244, 251
Procedural rights, 251–252
Provisional agreements, 111–112, 114

Read, Judge, 60, 77
Renunciation of benefits of treaty, 107–108, 113–114, 171, 177–178, 213, 249
Reservations, 9–11, 212
Rhine river, treaties concerning, 93, 117–120, 128–133, 250; Central Commission, 118–120, 128–133
Rhineland, occupation of, 93
River regimes, 2–3, 115–155, 250
Root, Elihu, 186n
Ross, Alf, 7–8
Rumania, official statements, 126–127, 135–136, 149; and regulation of the Danube, 124–127, 134–136, 140–150, 152–154
Russia, exclusion from revision of pre-Soviet treaties, 97–99, 109–111, 137–140, 154, 177, 192, 223; official statements, 6, 25n, 63–64, 70–71, 84, 91–92, 105–106, 117, 138–140, 145–151, 158, 163, 165–167, 171, 172, 175–176, 204, 209, 215–219, 223–226, 230–231, 234n, 235–238, 240; and regulation of the river Niemen, 138–139n; withdrawal from WHO, 70–72

Saint Germain, Convention of, 191–195
Salisbury, Marquis of, 90–91, 157
Savoy, neutralization of, 99–100
Scelle, Georges, 4–5, 211
Schachter, Oscar, 69–70n
Schücking, Walther, 48–49, 194–195
Separability, principle of, 82, 85, 87, 93–96, 104, 113, 249
Servitudes, 220
Smuts, Jan Christian, 54
Sørensen, Max, 3–4
Spain, exclusion from revision of trea-

ties after World War II, 33, 35, 62n, 213; offical statements, 198, 201, 204, 208, 228, 232
State succession, 235
Struycken, Professor, 220
Suez Canal, Convention of 1888, 227–244; rights of users, 234–244, 251; treaties and negotiations concerning, 227–244, 251; users' association, 239–240
Sweden, beneficiary of Aaland Islands Convention (1856), 214–222; official statements, 210, 217, 219, 224–225; rights of, in the Aaland Islands, 221
Switzerland, and navigation of the Rhine, 128; official statements, 29n, 53, 56, 71, 100; treaties concerning, 99–102

Tacit consent, 12
Tangier, Courts, 199–204, 208–209, 212; treaties concerning, 179–180, 184–191, 196–213
Temporary agreements, 111–112, 114
Termination of treaties, 6–8, 17–20, 39–41, 46–47, 49–50, 52, 55–58, 62–72, 78, 212, 247–252
Territorial conveyances, 85–86, 113, 249
Third parties, beneficiaries of treaties, 102, 181, 220, 236–237, 242, 251
Tobin, Harold J., 5
Treaty for the Renunciation of War, 47
Trieste, Free Territory of, 108–112
Turkey, guarantee by the great powers, 87–92, 156, 231; official statements, 122, 164, 170–176, 183n, 231
Turkish Straits, treaties concerning, 156–178, 240–241, 250

Union for the Protection of Industrial Property, 28–30

Union of Soviet Socialist Republics, see Russia
United Kingdom, see Great Britain
United Nations, Charter, 62–66, 79–80; International Law Commission, 5–6, 10–11; legal committee of the General Assembly, 33–37; legal opinions of the Secretariat, 34–37, 69
United States, admission to the Central Commission of the Rhine, 133; official statements, 10n, 38, 42, 51, 55–56, 58, 61, 63, 66, 69, 96, 103–105, 107, 108–111, 148, 150, 162–163, 175–176, 189–191, 198–209, 212, 234–239, 241
Universal Postal Union, 22, 24
Universal Suez Canal Company, 227, 234
Urrutia, F. J., 9
Uruguay, official statements, 56, 64

Verdross, Alfred von, 7–8
Versailles, Treaty of, 66–67, 93–102, 107, 114, 128–143, 146, 153–154, 189–190, 219, 232
Vienna, Règlement on the rank of diplomatic agents, 83; Treaty of (1815), 82–87, 117–118, 126, 155
Vyshinsky, Andrei, 139, 149

Warsaw Convention (1955), 37–39, 50–51
Whaling, agreements on, 43–46, 51
Wilson, Woodrow, 51–54
Withdrawal, right of, respecting international organizations, 52, 55–58, 62–72, 78, 212, 252
World Health Organization, 68–72, 78

Yugoslavia, official statements, 106, 109–110, 135, 144, 148–149, 151

ST. CHARLES PARISH LIBRARY
160 W. CAMPUS DRIVE
P.O. BOX 1029
DESTREHAN, LA 70047

A SEAL'S PLEDGE

By Cora Seton

Copyright © 2016 Cora Seton
Print Edition
Published by One Acre Press

All rights reserved. No part of this publication may be reproduced,
distributed or transmitted in any form or by any means, or stored in
a database or retrieval system, without the prior written permission
of the publisher.

Author's Note

A SEAL's Pledge is the third volume in the SEALs of Chance Creek series, set in the fictional town of Chance Creek, Montana. To find out more about Boone, Clay, Jericho and Walker, look for the rest of the books in the series, including:

A SEAL's Oath
A SEAL's Vow
A SEAL's Consent

Also, don't miss Cora Seton's other Chance Creek series, the Cowboys of Chance Creek and the Heroes of Chance Creek

The Cowboys of Chance Creek Series:

The Cowboy Inherits a Bride (Volume 0)
The Cowboy's E-Mail Order Bride (Volume 1)
The Cowboy Wins a Bride (Volume 2)
The Cowboy Imports a Bride (Volume 3)
The Cowgirl Ropes a Billionaire (Volume 4)
The Sheriff Catches a Bride (Volume 5)
The Cowboy Lassos a Bride (Volume 6)
The Cowboy Rescues a Bride (Volume 7)
The Cowboy Earns a Bride (Volume 8)
The Cowboy's Christmas Bride (Volume 9)

The Heroes of Chance Creek Series:

The Navy SEAL's E-Mail Order Bride (Volume 1)
The Soldier's E-Mail Order Bride (Volume 2)
The Marine's E-Mail Order Bride (Volume 3)
The Navy SEAL's Christmas Bride (Volume 4)
The Airman's E-Mail Order Bride (Volume 5)

Visit Cora's website at www.coraseton.com
Find Cora on Facebook at facebook.com/CoraSeton
Sign up for my newsletter HERE.
www.coraseton.com/sign-up-for-my-newsletter

CHAPTER ONE

THE ELEVENTH OF July dawned warm and still, and Harris Wentworth, only two months out of a sixteen-year stint with the Navy SEALs, knew a storm was brewing. He woke early, like he always did, but for once he was the only one up in Base Camp. All the men in the small tent community were ex-SEALs. All of them had served until recently. They were a vigilant, early rising bunch.

Usually.

Today would be an exception, Harris knew. Last night they'd celebrated the marriage of Clay Pickett and Nora Ridgeway—a wedding that could have as easily been a funeral. A stalker had followed Nora from Baltimore, where she used to teach high school, here to Chance Creek, Montana. He'd gotten Nora alone and nearly killed her before Clay managed to track her down. He'd nearly killed Clay's father in his attempt to shoot Clay, too. It had been touch and go there for a while with Nora, so her recovery—and marriage—had given everyone a lot of reasons to make toasts and drink

to the newlyweds last night.

Champagne, wine, beer and mixed drinks had flowed, and as Harris got up and dressed he could hear snoring from several of the tents around his. So far they'd only managed to build two permanent homes in the community—the tiny house Boone Rudman and his wife, Riley, had moved into last month, and the one that Clay and Nora had moved into last night.

There'd be more, though. One of them would be his—just as soon as he was married, too. The wedded couples got first dibs, and it wasn't his turn yet.

He'd have to be patient.

Luckily, Harris was good at that.

He knew most of the men who'd joined the small community had come because of their dedication to sustainability. Because they wanted to get the word out to the wider world there was a different way to live— one that saw humans acting as stewards of the planet's finite resources. Harris believed that, too, and he was proud of the work he was doing here, helping to build the tiny houses.

But that wasn't the reason he'd decided to join up.

He could still remember the ad he'd answered back in April. Boone had posted it on a private online forum for Navy SEALs. It had been succinct:

Six men needed to join planned eco-community. Must be knowledgeable about sustainability, committed to the goals of our organization, comfortable with being filmed for a reality television show documenting our progress— and willing to marry within the year. Wives provided for those lacking them.

Harris would never admit that while he was all for sustainability, it was that last line that had jolted him into action.

Wives provided...

Harris wanted a wife—badly. But while he'd received medals for bravery, commitment and his sharpshooting skills, he would never be commended for his ability to talk to women. He tried—now and then. Truth was, he was a doer, not a talker, and his dates had a depressing tendency to start off okay, but soon slide into a silence that neither side could pierce. Harris had almost given up on the idea of having a family of his own before he saw the ad.

Now he had hope.

The other men who'd joined Base Camp seemed resigned to the idea of marrying. Martin Fulsom, the eccentric billionaire who was funding the whole venture, and whose idea it was to create the reality TV show documenting it, had made it very clear marriage was required. The hooking up aspect was what drew crowds to watch the show, and Fulsom was nothing if not dedicated to creating publicity for the venture. None of the other men seemed to look forward to marriage the way Harris did, though. Maybe they were keeping their feelings to themselves, but Curtis Lloyd, a burly man with a normally cheerful temperament, had been the latest one to draw the short straw that meant he was required to marry next—and he hadn't been cheerful about that at all.

Harris supposed he couldn't blame the man given

the circumstances; it was strange enough being on a television program that required you to marry, but it was even stranger to find out you had to marry someone you'd never met. Clay was the one who'd originally drawn that short straw—on the day after Boone and Riley's wedding just over a month ago—but while Clay wanted to marry Nora right from the start, she'd been reluctant before her stalker attacked her. Back then, when it wasn't at all clear to Clay that he could convince Nora to say yes before the deadline was up, he had agreed to let Boone find him a backup bride to marry, but he'd made Boone agree not to bring her to Base Camp or tell anyone anything about her until his time was up.

After Nora was attacked by her stalker and nearly killed, everyone agreed it wouldn't be fair to push her to marry Clay—or to push Clay to marry someone else, either. Faced with a looming deadline for the television show, the rest of the men had drawn straws again, and Curtis had picked the short one. He'd been furious.

"I thought I was going to get to choose my own girl," he'd kept saying. "I didn't think I'd get Clay's leavings." When Boone had tried to show him Samantha Smith's photograph and bio, he'd waved them away. "What good will it do me to know ahead of time I won't like her?" he'd burst out. "You're forcing me to marry her no matter what!"

That had been a very uncomfortable forty-eight hours at Base Camp. They'd managed to keep the tension hidden from Clay and Nora, thank goodness, so

it was a surprise to everyone when Nora rallied at the last minute—the very day before the deadline. She and Clay had married in a matter of hours, and Curtis, realizing he'd been given a forty-day reprieve, had partied harder than anyone else last night.

"You saved my ass, man," he kept saying to Clay whenever he bumped into him. "I was due at the altar to marry some loser Boone caught trolling the Internet. But you beat the deadline. I've got forty more days. And I'm going to put them to good use. Starting tonight."

From what Harris could tell, Curtis had hit on every female guest at the wedding. He wasn't sure if he'd had any luck, but Harris was certain the man would be nursing a hangover the size of Montana today.

So would everyone else.

Which meant no one had thought about the backup bride.

Harris exited his tent, zipped the flap shut behind him and made his way to the bunkhouse, where he got a pot of coffee going. Pouring a mug and heading back outside to the fire pit where they ate many of their meals, he sat down on a log and pondered the situation.

Boone had mentioned the woman's plane was due in early this morning. Before Clay and Nora's wedding, the plan had been to hold a small ceremony just before noon today and host a lunch to welcome the backup bride to the community. With Nora struggling to get over the attack, Clay so worried about her and Curtis so unhappy about stepping into his shoes, no one had wanted to make a fuss about the wedding.

Now there didn't need to be a hasty wedding. Harris had overheard Boone explain the situation to Reverend Halpern last night, so there was no danger of him turning up again. Harris wondered what would happen next. Maybe Curtis would fall for this Samantha Smith after all once they'd spent some time together.

But what if he didn't? What would happen if Curtis refused to marry her? Would Boone find a backup bride for the backup bride?

What would happen to Samantha?

Harris skimmed an eye over the quiet campground, and the empty pastures beyond. He thought about waking Boone to remind him it was time to go fetch the woman, but Boone deserved the chance to sleep in with his wife. He'd taken a lot on his shoulders when he'd helped found Base Camp. A natural leader, the others looked to him for direction, which left him in charge of the bulk of the responsibilities.

Harris was fine with that. He'd had his time of being in charge—of being the man everyone else depended on. He was happy to be one of the followers now.

"Harris Wentworth. Just the man I've been looking for."

Harris nearly dumped his coffee in his lap, and bit back a groan as he realized who had spoken. Renata Ludlow, the show's director. A sharply dressed, thirtysomething Hollywood type whose mannish, tailored clothing contrasted with her scarlet lipstick, heavy mascara, and the lacy bra that peeked out from the vee of her buttoned shirt, she was notorious for her skewer-

sharp questions. She was followed by three camera crew members who looked like they'd drunk as much last night as some of the wedding guests. What the hell were they all doing up this early?

"You've been avoiding me." The director shook a finger in his face. "Time for an interview."

"Not now."

"Yes—now." Her tone brooked no disagreement and Harris knew he was well and truly trapped. This was part of his job—to talk about what he did. He didn't think he'd ever get used to it. Spending your days being followed by people wanting to film your every word and move was as hellish as it sounded.

"Fine. Shoot." He drained his coffee and stared straight into the camera. He knew they all hated that.

"Harris. Harris!" Renata snapped when he didn't avert his gaze. "Oh, for fuck's sake. Have it your way. Look like an ignorant prick on the show."

That made him look at her. As much as he didn't want to admit it, he didn't want to look like an ignorant prick.

"So, Harris... Curtis Lloyd says you've given up on finding a wife in the normal way, and are looking forward to having one assigned to you. Why is that?" She made a show of scanning him top to bottom. "You're a handsome devil. I bet you have a way with the ladies."

Damn Curtis for throwing him under the bus. Harris tamped down his rising anger and simply shrugged. Aside from staring at the camera, it was the best way to

rile up Renata and her crew.

"Use your words, sailor."

No, Harris thought. He wasn't going to use his words. He wasn't in the Navy anymore, and Renata couldn't give him an order. He shrugged again.

She narrowed her eyes. After a long moment, she said in a silky tone, "Tell me, Harris, do you think disaster follows you?"

Harris blinked, then cursed himself for letting her get to him. "Can't say I've ever thought about it like that."

"You were ten when Hurricane Andrew hit Florida." She cocked her head. "You were already the man of the family, weren't you? Where did your father go?"

Harris shrugged again. Who knew? He certainly didn't.

"You saved your mother and sisters."

He shifted. That old story. "I didn't save anyone." They'd done what any sane person would do—spent the duration of the storm in the trailer park's cinder block recreation building with the rest of the tenants who couldn't—or wouldn't—evacuate before the storm hit. It had easily withstood the driving winds and rain.

Nothing else had.

Harris had rescued his family, but not in the way Renata meant. He'd never forget walking out of the building into the wasteland the storm had left behind, or the way his mother, Audrianna, had collapsed into a sobbing heap not twenty paces from the door. He'd left his younger sisters clinging to her and raced ahead to

examine what was left of their home. Trouble was, he couldn't find it. It was completely gone, along with every possession they'd owned, including the beater Subaru his mother drove to work at the laundromat, and the three hundred and fifty dollars she'd squirreled away behind one of the trailer's paneled walls for a rainy day.

It had taken weeks before they could make their way to family in New Orleans, and during that time Harris had been the one to find food and water, the one to get them to the emergency shelters and sign up for aid. He'd been the one to wrangle a phone call to his aunt and uncle and persuade them to wire money for bus tickets, and he'd kept his grieving mother and terrified sisters safe until they pulled into the Greyhound station in New Orleans and were met by their kin.

Normalcy had returned, although it took years for his mother to get over that storm. The four of them had settled into one room at his aunt and uncle's house. His mother and sisters shared the double bed. He slept on a foam mat they tucked away underneath it each morning. When she wasn't working at the corner store where Aunt Olivia had helped her find a job, Audrianna spent hours on the little house's front porch, staring into the distance.

Seeing nothing.

Harris was the one to make sure his sisters made it to school. He was the one to remind her to buy them clothes, go in and talk to the teachers, make them get their homework done. Aunt Olivia did her best, but she

had four kids of her own to raise, along with a full time job.

"You were twenty-three when Katrina hit," Renata said, breaking into his thoughts.

As if he'd ever forget. Five years into his service, he'd come home on leave to see his family and make sure his sisters were walking a path that would get them out of the kind of poverty and desperation they'd grown up in. So far it had been working. Della was already at LSU with a full scholarship. Belinda was starting eleventh grade with straight A's and a slew of after-school activities. He was so proud of them—and of his mother, who despite her fears and struggles always held down a job and did her best to keep her girls on the straight and narrow path.

They should have gotten out. He'd wanted them to evacuate. But by then Uncle Manny was in a wheelchair with a crushed hip, and the nine members of the combined two families still at home depended on one Chevrolet Cavalier to get around. No way they could pile into it for a drive that might take days, let alone carry the food and clothing they'd need for the trip. No way Uncle Manny could bear that much time in a car, anyway. His aunt refused to leave Manny behind, and Audrianna refused to leave her sister, no matter how many times Harris urged her to take Belinda on one of the city buses and get out of town.

"The dikes will hold," Uncle Manny kept saying.

Of course, they hadn't.

"Tell us what happened," Renata encouraged in a

low voice. She must have seen the traces of his memories on his face.

"I got them to the roof. Kept them safe until help came."

"Which took days," Renata prompted.

Days. Nights. A nightmare passage of time that still haunted his dreams. The water had risen so fast he'd nearly lost his uncle before he'd gotten the rest of them to the roof. He'd had to dive under the rising water in the narrow stairwell to rescue Manny from the bottom of the stairs where he'd been waiting his turn in his wheelchair, and drag him up into the attic, out a window and onto the roof, his sisters, cousins and aunt screaming and straining to get him up over the eaves trough. He'd spotted his nephew's inflatable beach boat on the way out, grabbed it and used it to rescue neighbors, strangers—even a couple of cats and dogs.

"I did what I could."

"You saved twenty-seven people that day, counting your family—and in the days following you kept them fed and alive. You're the kind of hero this country needed during that disaster. What kept you going through that nightmare?"

The memory of the four awful days before help finally arrived hit Harris like a punch to the gut. The water. The heat. The smell. The bodies. During the long, hot days he'd foraged for food and water as best he could. At nights, he'd perched on one end of the roof and kept watch, crouching there, straining to see and hear as screams and shots rang out in the distance

from time to time. Someone had thought to grab the bugout bag his uncle—ex-soldier that he was—always kept stocked. Manny had handed him the revolver and ammunition it contained that first day. "There was a time I'd be the one keeping watch and saving lives. Now it's on you," he'd said.

Harris had kept that revolver near to hand until rescue finally came.

On the fourth morning, he must have been sleeping just as dawn broke, because it was as if he had stepped out of his body and watched himself watching the hushed, watery world that surrounded him. In that instant, he'd known this was his fate—not just for those few days, but forever. To be the watcher. The man on the edge of the roof, the man who saw danger before anyone else.

The man who took care of it.

In his dream or vision, or whatever it was, he'd seen himself on one end of the roof, everyone else on the other end, and he'd known that was the price of his family's safety. His country's safety.

He would be alone.

"Do you think those early experiences led you to become a sniper?" Renata asked, as if reading his thoughts.

He met her gaze. Nodded. Of course it had.

"Not much need for a sniper around here." Renata gestured to the bunkhouse and the little, sustainable community taking shape on the hillside a stone's throw away. "This is Chance Creek, Montana. Pretty safe

country here."

Harris swallowed. Renata knew damn well that wasn't true. "Tell that to Nora." Guilt flooded him, the way it did every time he thought about the stalker tracking Nora down, playing with her, leaving clues they'd all been too stupid to acknowledge, and then snatching her out from under their noses.

The truth was that when Harris arrived at Base Camp he'd told himself his vigil on the rooftop was over, and he'd behaved like it was. He'd looked forward to being found a wife, marrying her and starting his family. Finally getting to be one of the crowd at the other end of the roof.

And three people had nearly died.

Harris wouldn't make that mistake again. Trouble was, he didn't know what to do. Keeping vigilant meant keeping apart from other people—and in order for Base Camp to succeed, he would have to marry when he drew a short straw.

The way this game went, ten male inhabitants of the sustainable community had to marry within the year. Three of the wives needed to be pregnant before next June. If he left the community, they'd be up shit's creek. If he stayed, he'd be going against the future fate had obviously picked for him. As soon as things calmed down around here he meant to take his conundrum to Boone and sort it out.

Renata sighed. "You don't want to talk about Katrina? Let's talk about your nickname. Hawk, isn't it? So, Hawk—tell me. What kind of woman are you hoping to

marry?"

Harris stood up, unable to take any more questions. He'd always hated that nickname, and he'd left it behind when he'd left the Navy. "I'll marry who I'm assigned to marry," he said tightly. "Now I've got to go."

Renata's face lit up. She obviously sensed an interesting development. "Where?"

Hell, he couldn't tell her. She'd drag her film crew along to the airport and the last thing Harris wanted was to break the news on camera to the backup bride she wasn't getting married today. Renata would love it, though. She'd make sure to get a close-up of Samantha Smith's disappointment. She'd pray for tears.

Harris wouldn't be any part of that.

"Nature's calling," he said bluntly. "Want to film that?"

Renata rolled her eyes and made a chopping motion with her hand. The crew stood down and Harris headed for the bunkhouse, which held the only flushing toilet in Base Camp. He bypassed the restroom, though, walked straight through the kitchen and out the side door. Five minutes later, he'd managed to take a circuitous route to the main road, where he called a cab on his cell phone.

He walked along the country highway toward Chance Creek, knowing sooner or later he'd meet up with the cab coming to fetch him, and mulled over the irony of the situation. He'd wanted to stop looking out for everyone and here he was taking charge again. Solving another problem. Keeping an eye on things as if he was the shepherd of this operation rather than just

one of the sheep on the comfortable end of the roof.

He didn't know why he fought against fate. He was meant for vigilance.

Meant for being alone.

WHEN HER PLANE landed at the Chance Creek Regional Airport in Montana, Samantha Smith found she couldn't make herself leave her window seat. She let the other passengers file by until the plane was empty and the flight attendant made her way over to her.

"Everything all right?" A blond woman about ten years older than Sam, the flight attendant's expression was kind, but tired, and Sam felt bad for holding things up.

"I think so. I'm making a big change," she confessed. "I guess I'm nervous."

"What kind of change?" The woman helped her gather her things as Sam finally stood up and made her way into the aisle.

"I'm getting married. Today." Sam still couldn't believe it. She'd always been the steady one in the family, now here she was taking a flying leap into matrimony with a man she'd never met.

"Congratulations! I hope you two will be very happy!"

"Thank you." Reluctantly, Sam moved up the aisle toward the exit. So far things hadn't exactly gone smoothly. She'd made the decision to join the sustainable community at Base Camp without telling any of her family, and she had to admit she was more than a little

concerned with the fact the first man she'd been matched with—Clay Pickett—had turned out to be in love with someone else. She'd gotten a phone call from Boone Rudman, the SEAL who seemed to head the community—who'd matched her with Clay to begin with. He'd apologized profusely and explained the whole story of Clay's rocky relationship with his new wife, Nora, but told her another man was ready to take Clay's place.

She still felt strange she'd been matched to a second man in such a short period of time, but since all she had to judge the men by was their photographs and bios on the show's website, and what she'd seen of them when she'd watched them on TV, she'd decided the friendly, stocky Curtis Lloyd seemed just as likely a partner as the slimmer, more serious Clay Pickett.

But the switch had dampened any flight of fancy she might have had that her marriage was ordained by fate, and she was having trouble maintaining her original excitement for this mad adventure.

"Have a wonderful wedding day," the flight attendant said when they reached the top of the stairs. "Watch your step going down and kiss your husband for me!"

Sam nodded, her nerves twisting tight in her belly. She gripped the railing, shifted her purse and carry-on bag into her other hand and began to descend to the tarmac.

It had all started with her mother's craving for hummus. They'd been halfway across Kansas in the big,

twelve-sleeper bus they'd long-since dubbed the Evermobile—an amalgamation of her parents' band's name and the fact they never seemed to leave it for very long. Sam had been driving, as usual, when her mother rushed up the aisle waving an empty container in her hand.

"Sam? Sam, we're out of hummus again! I told you at our last stop we needed more!"

Sam pressed on the accelerator and tried to block out the sound of her mother's voice. It wasn't hard to do since the noise level in the 1998 sleeper coach had just hit a high mark. She'd been driver, tour manager, advisor and den mother to *Deader Than Ever*, a popular 60s hippie-esque cover band, for the last seven years, and she'd grown up on this bus—and its predecessors—since she was a baby in her mother's arms. She would have been born on one, but they'd made it to the hospital on time.

For someone who'd been surrounded by music since she was conceived, the irony was she hadn't been gifted with a drop of musical talent. Her parents, Rachel Flick and Henry Smith, had passed her instrument after instrument, sung her song after song, allowed their friends to try various methods of imparting musical knowledge, and finally had given up, much to Sam's relief. Her sister, Melissa, had talent enough for both of them, and the same stadium-sized ego their parents had. That was enough of both for one family, Sam always thought.

Besides, someone had to have their head on straight in this zoo.

"Sam? Did you hear me?" Rachel reached the front of the bus and waved a plastic container in Sam's face. "There isn't enough in here to spread on a rice cracker. We need to stop."

"We're in the middle of Kansas, Mom." Sam pointed out the window at the fields of knee-high cornstalks spreading in every direction around them. "When there's a place to stop, I'll stop."

Rachel huffed out a breath and turned back toward the kitchenette.

Sam kept driving, pressing down against the discontent that sizzled inside her all the time these days. She was sick of the bus. Sick of being on the road. Sick of the temporary gigs and housing they parked themselves in between tours. She didn't understand how the rest of her family could ride along, day after day, their enthusiasm for the life and the road unflagging. Her parents had toured for years before she'd even been born.

"It's the best life," Rachel always said when she asked.

"It's the only life," Henry always added.

"Everyone's equal on the road. There's no patriarchy out here," Rachel liked to insist. "Just a whole lot of freedom. What more could you want?"

Freedom.

Sam didn't define the word the way her family did. Her parents seemed to think it meant a lack of commitments of any kind. A lack of responsibility, too. Never married, and never exclusive to each other, either, as far as Sam could tell, they'd met when the

band formed and Rachel had signed up as a backup singer, while Henry played guitar. They'd loved each other, brought two daughters into the world in two years and raised them together while each pursued a number of dalliances and relationships that left Sam bewildered, Melissa wild and both of them cynical far beyond their years.

Sam had never been able to play those games, and her dating life could only be summed up as a disaster. She spent her days in the company of musicians, roadies and fans, but none of them were interested in long term or stable, the only things she wanted from a relationship.

Now she was twenty-seven. Single.

Fed up.

"Don't suppose anyone's going to deliver us a pizza out here."

Sam glanced over her shoulder and saw that Chris Castle, the lead singer, had taken the nearest seat.

"I don't think so."

"I'll whip something up in back. That should help keep the grumbling down."

She nodded. Chris always read a brewing situation right, whether in the bus or in a stadium, and always worked to diffuse it. He was the opposite of a diva, she thought. There should be a word for that.

"Everything all right, Sam?"

She knew he expected her to say yes, like usual, but she couldn't. Not anymore. Things weren't all right. This was never the life she'd wanted for herself and she

didn't know how she'd gotten here. Time was slipping by like the cornfields outside her window.

"Sam?" He reached out and put a hand on her shoulder.

She shook her head. "No. It's not. I'm going to leave pretty soon." She didn't know when, or where she'd go or what she'd do. She'd never had any life except on this bus.

"I know, honey. I've been wondering for a while what you're waiting for."

"I need a plan. I don't know what to do first, or where to go." She tried to keep her eyes on the road. She couldn't take chances driving a rig this big. Chris squeezed her shoulder and stood up.

"Stop overthinking it. You don't need a plan. You need to throw yourself into the mix and let the universe sort it out for you." He patted her shoulder a couple of times. "I'll bring you dinner in a few."

Let the universe sort it out for you, Sam thought when he was gone. Far easier to say than to do. At least for her.

But she was willing to try it if it got her off this bus.

Two hours later, after the night driver took over, Sam was sitting on a bench seat with her laptop perched on her lap, sending follow up texts and e-mails to all the upcoming venues on this leg of the tour when everyone else piled into the bus's media area. She was only halfway through her list when Rachel turned on the big-screen television and turned up the sound.

Sam tried to concentrate, but as music blared into the small space, she lost her place and had to re-read

what she'd written so far before she could finish the sentence she was trying to type.

A narrator's rich tones overlaid the quasi-patriotic song ringing out from the television. "Welcome to Base Camp, where ten men must pit themselves against time and technology to build a model sustainable community. They must build ten houses that consume a tenth of the power of a normal North American home. They must create a renewable power grid from which to run all their appliances, lights and machines. They must grow all the food they'll need to last through the winter. They must each marry before the year is up, with three babies on the way, or risk losing everything."

By the time the announcer finished the ridiculous list of goals, Sam was watching the screen with as much concentration as everyone else. "What is this?" she asked her father.

"It's *Base Camp*." There was no mistaking his contempt. "Apparently the US Military is going to solve global warming, if you can imagine that. Ten Navy SEALs getting together to form a sustainable society."

"This show is the Patriarchy's wet dream," her mother called over from her seat. "Just watch the way these men give each other orders. And see what they're making the women wear! It's straight out of the dark ages."

"Out of the 1800s, you mean—and they're wearing those clothes because they want to. Now shh!" her sister told them. "This is the best part!"

"Meet the men of Base Camp," the announcer in-

toned. One by one, men flashed up on the screen, their images subtly enhanced to make them look like comic book super-heroes. "Look at them," Melissa said. "No one's that buff. The military probably got them all hopped up on steroids."

Sam ignored her sarcastic tone. Those men were something, she had to admit. Each more handsome than the next, although it was the fifth man they showed—one named Harris Wentworth, of all things— who made her breath catch. It wasn't his bulging muscles, she told herself. It was something about his eyes, the way they seemed to scan the distance for trouble. That's what she always had to do, whether it was scanning the road ahead for actual danger, or thinking about the future to avoid potential pitfalls on tour.

When the announcer had tolled through all the men, he said, "Meet the women of Westfield!" The background, which had showed a cluster of tents and a building or two on a Montana ranch, now changed to show a beautiful old stone house perched on a rise of ground.

"Wow," Sam said. That was some house. She could only imagine what it would be like to live in a place like that. Everyone would get their own room—a room with a lock. They could shut the door, turn the key and be blessedly alone for hours.

Her mother turned on her. "Can you imagine how wasteful it is to live like that? Just a handful of women in that great, big pile of stone? Can you say *white privi-*

lege?"

"I can say *privacy*, white or otherwise," Sam told her.

"You might as well dig up all the coal and oil in the world and set it on fire if you're going to live like that," Rachel said.

"Wait a minute. You got mad at the Army guys living in tents and tiny houses a minute ago. You can't be mad at the women for living in that house, too."

"Navy guys," the drummer put in. "They're Navy SEALs, not soldiers."

"Whatever. You can't have it both ways, Mom."

"I'll have it anyway I want to. They all should be ashamed of themselves."

"Shh!" Melissa said again. "Watch."

"Wait—why are they dressed like that?" Sam asked, leaning forward to get a better look at the women appearing on screen one by one. Each of them wore clothing like a character in one of the Regency period dramas she loved to watch, but never got to because everyone else on the bus hated them.

"They came to the ranch to lead a Jane Austen life," Melissa said as the announcer said the same thing in the background. "Their clothing represents their commitment to pursuing their creative passions. You'd know that if you'd watched episode one with us last week."

Sam made a face at her. Last week she'd been fighting with a venue operator who'd wanted to cancel their concert at the last minute.

"Now the women of Westfield must divide their time," the announcer intoned. "They spend mornings at

chores in the manor, then help the men with their projects in Base Camp, before returning to the manor for an afternoon of reading, writing, painting and music, much like characters in a Jane Austen novel."

"They host paying guests at the manor—and Regency weddings, too," Melissa told her.

"Trussed up like Vienna sausages in the corsets they wear under those gowns for the enjoyment of the men," Rachel put in.

"It *is* rather enjoyable." Henry waggled his eyebrows suggestively.

Rachel smacked him.

"Oh, come on. I saw you eyeing those hot young SEALs. Made you feel all patriotic for a second. Admit it."

"That's as bad as saying I'd ogle the CEO of a financial institution on Wall Street."

Sam tuned her parents out. Despite her resolve to finish her work, the reality television show was as fascinating as it was crazy.

"Clay has to marry next," Melissa informed her as the cameras focused on him. She moved to sit next to Sam. "He wants Nora, but Nora wants to take things slow, and he's only got a couple of weeks until he has to marry someone. I don't think he's going to convince her to go through with it."

"Yes, he will," Chris said. "Come on, the dude's in love with her. How can she resist that?"

"Marriage is an outdated institution," Rachel put in.

"Not everyone's as cynical as you, Rachel," Chris

said.

Melissa caught Sam's eye and pretended to gag. They'd been hearing this argument their whole lives, and had known since they were teenagers Chris had an unrequited crush on their mother.

Sam watched the men of Base Camp working at their various tasks as the others argued around her, and realized that underneath the silly goals there was something far more serious going on. Ten men had pledged their lives to try to build a model community. They were willing to give up their homes, their military careers—and even the chance to pick whom and when to marry—in order to meet their goals. When the cameras panned in on the one completed tiny house and the second one under construction, Sam was enchanted, even though she knew what living in a small space could entail. The beautifully constructed houses on the television screen were everything this old sleeper coach wasn't. The materials were organic, the setup brilliant, and instead of sitting around drinking beer and yelling at the TV, the participants were working hard to build a something special.

"Sustainable means that something can keep working forever without degrading its environment," one of the characters on-screen explained in an interview.

Sam let out an uneven breath. That was her problem in a nutshell; her situation was unsustainable. She couldn't live like this for another minute, let alone the rest of her life. She needed a way out. She needed something like Base Camp—a community to join in

which she would be allowed to do something real.

As she watched, an ache grew in her chest. If only she belonged on that ranch...

When the show ended, she was nearly in tears because all that faced her now was typing out emails, answering questions, cleaning up beer bottles and dirty dishes after everyone else hit the hay in their sleeper bunks—and then getting up tomorrow to do it all over again.

"Oh, my God. Look at that," Melissa said just as Sam turned her attention back to her e-mail.

Sam looked up. "What?"

Melissa pointed to the screen where a photo of Clay had been posted under the headline, "Backup Bride Needed."

"Are you female, single, between twenty-five and thirty-five years of age? Looking for a husband? Think you've got what it takes to join Base Camp?" the announcer said. "Follow the link below to apply now."

"Oh, my God; they don't think Clay can marry Nora in time. They're finding someone else for him just in case," Melissa squealed.

"Who the hell would volunteer for that?" Rachel asked.

"No one in their right mind," Henry said.

Melissa laughed and socked Sam on the arm. "Three hundred and fifty-eight."

"Ouch." Sam rubbed her arm, but didn't retaliate. She knew exactly why Melissa had punched her: their parents agreed so seldom, they'd begun counting the

times they did when Sam was thirteen and Melissa was twelve. Melissa kept a tally on the wall of her sleeper bunk.

Sam snapped down the cover of her laptop before Melissa could see what she'd just typed: the URL to apply to be Clay Pickett's backup bride.

At the time, she hadn't planned to go through with it, of course.

But it had proven too tempting.

Now, just three weeks later, here she was crossing the tarmac to the small terminal, her heart pledged to Curtis Lloyd and Base Camp, the sustainable community she'd watched with such interest back in the bus. Her heart beat triple time as she crossed the short distance to the entrance. Was Curtis Lloyd watching her with equal trepidation from inside the terminal? Did he like what he saw?

Or was he regretting this as much as she currently was?

No. No regrets, she told herself. She was boldly stepping into the next phase of her life. The phase in which she got to stay in one place and dedicate herself to a cause she believed in with all her heart.

The phase in which she married a man.

A stranger.

Sam stumbled. Caught herself.

Kept going.

CHAPTER TWO

HARRIS DIDN'T KNOW what to do.

He'd made it to the airport without Renata following him. He'd placed himself by the door and watched every passenger exit the small plane when it landed, searching the crowd for single females. There'd been several, but each time he'd moved forward to greet them, they'd rushed into the arms of a husband or family member and marched happily off toward the baggage carousel along with the other passengers.

The stream of people getting off the plane had slowed to a trickle and then stopped altogether.

Samantha Smith hadn't come, after all.

Problem solved.

Still, Harris lingered. He didn't like to leave a job uncompleted. Loose ends were messy. They formed an entryway for trouble. Had Samantha gotten in touch with Boone to let him know she wouldn't arrive? Or had she gotten held up along the way? Should he call Boone and risk waking him the one time the man got to sleep in? Should he question someone from the airline?

Harris was just turning to scan the small terminal again, in case Samantha had somehow passed him by in the earlier crush of passengers, when a movement at the top of the metal stairs to the airplane caught his attention, and he swiveled around.

Two women emerged: a stewardess and a passenger. The stewardess said something and waved. The passenger began to descend the stairs.

Samantha Smith. It had to be her.

Harris stepped closer to the window and stared.

She was nervous. He could tell from here because she kept shifting her purse and carry-on bag from hand to hand even as she climbed down the stairs. Once on the ground, she took a moment to smooth her skirt, a straight, navy blue number that stopped just above her knees. She wore a white blouse and navy pumps she didn't seem altogether comfortable walking in. She'd dressed up to meet her husband-to-be, Harris realized with a jolt.

A husband-to-be who hadn't come to meet her.

As she raised a hand to pat her hair into place, she moved closer, and her vulnerability stabbed him like a knife to the heart. Her hair was a shiny chestnut, and had been corralled into a sleek twist that showed off a slim neck and fine features. This woman had courage, but she was worried, as well she might be, Harris thought. She was walking into a situation with very little information. A kind of human sacrifice to the television gods who demanded sex and tension from a show that was supposed to be about sustainable living.

In a few moments, he was going to have to tell her Curtis didn't want her, after all.

He knew without a shadow of a doubt the news would crush this woman's heart. And he knew—somehow he knew—she'd soldier on despite it. He read it in the proud angle of her jaw, the tight grip on her carry-on and the firm steps she was taking.

Harris nodded to himself. She'd get hurt, but she'd recover. She'd do okay. He moved closer to the door to greet her when she walked in—

And Samantha stumbled on the tarmac.

She caught herself and kept walking. *She's fine*, Harris told himself firmly.

But it was too late. In that moment—in that one, unguarded moment in which he'd read the fear, panic and desperation in her face as she nearly fell—Harris's heart squeezed hard, and he knew his fate was irrevocably tied to hers.

Samantha Smith had come here to marry. She wanted a husband. Needed one badly enough to risk everything on a stranger. She couldn't know Curtis was reluctant to marry her. She had to believe she was wanted—because Curtis *would* want her as soon as he saw her. She was beautiful. Determined. Oh, so feminine.

Ready to fall in love.

Harris would be the shepherd one last time. He'd make sure Samantha and Curtis made it to the altar—today—and then he'd go have that conversation with Boone, the one in which he explained he'd been

wrong—that it wasn't in the cards for him to marry.

He'd thought Boone might have an idea for how he could stay on in some ancillary capacity. He'd hoped they'd be able to find a man to replace him on the show. Now he knew he'd have to leave Base Camp altogether.

Because the one thing he knew for sure:

He couldn't watch Samantha Smith fall in love with another man.

WHAT IF CURTIS wasn't there to meet her? What if he'd already left? Or hadn't come at all? What if this was all a huge joke and she was about to be humiliated on camera? Would there be cameras? Or would they wait? What would her wedding be like?

What would happen if she threw up right now?

Cameras. Film crew. People watching, she told herself and lifted her chin as the door into the terminal opened automatically. She needed to make a good first impression both on her husband-to-be and the viewing public. After all, her family would only learn of what she'd done when they watched the next episode of *Base Camp*. She'd fled the bus in the middle of the night, leaving a note that said she was all right and needed to make a life for herself. She'd neglected to say how—or where. She knew in order to make this break from them, she had to operate without their input. She was far too used to doing what they wanted her to do. This time she needed to trust her own gut.

The terminal had emptied out by the time she walked in, and at first she thought there was no one to

greet her. Her heart plunged into her stomach and she fought the urge to be sick again.

Until she spotted a man standing off to one side, and realized she'd seen him before.

Harris, she thought. *Harris Wentworth, the sniper.*

The one who'd caught her attention the first time she'd watched the show. Since that day she'd watched it online a dozen times, and had gone back to catch the first episode, too. She'd focused on Clay, of course, and then Curtis when Boone called her and told her the news about the attack on Nora. Both men were good, decent men who were dedicated to their cause and ripe for marriage.

Still, whenever the sniper was on-screen—a rare enough occurrence—Samantha found her eyes drawn to him. He rarely spoke, but he was still compelling. A strong, silent, vigilant man who seemed constantly on the lookout for trouble. Samantha couldn't help sympathize with the urge to look for danger and do what you could to prevent it. She'd spent her whole life doing that for her family and the band.

She hesitated just inside the door, unsure what to do next. Why was Harris here instead of Curtis?

Had Curtis found another woman to love—like Clay had?

As Harris stepped toward her, Samantha realized that had to be the answer, otherwise Curtis would be the one reaching for her bag, not this silent man whose eyes searched hers. He was dressed in jeans, boots, a plaid shirt unbuttoned over a black T-shirt that

stretched across a muscled chest. But all Samantha could focus on was Curtis's absence.

"He's not coming, is he?" Her voice was so high and thin, she barely recognized it. "He doesn't want me."

"He's—"

Sam cut Harris off. "He's taken one look at my photograph and decided he can do better." That had to be it. She'd never photographed well, and besides, she wasn't a woman who could compete like that. Her sister was the one to get all the men. Hell, her mother did better than her in that department, with a string of beaus half her age parading in and out of the bus. Sam was nowhere near as beautiful as either of them. She was too... practical. Too plain.

"He hasn't looked at your photograph."

Sam blinked. "Hasn't looked at it?" That meant he'd been against this marriage from the start. "What am I doing here?" She hated the desperation in her voice. What must this man think of her?

Harris shifted uncomfortably and Sam choked back a wild laugh. Where were the television cameras? Surely they'd want to capture this moment of humiliation for the whole world to see.

When she thought of how hard she'd worked to secretly prepare for this moment, she wanted to die. When the band had made a stop in Phoenix, she'd slipped away to buy a wedding dress. She'd packed it carefully in the luggage she'd purchased and hidden in the bus's undercarriage storage until it was time to leave.

She had makeup, jewelry—she'd even bought a pair of etched wineglasses in a fit of romantic impulse, in order to toast her new husband on their wedding night.

She was such a fool.

"What am I doing here?" she repeated, tears stinging her eyes. Where would she go? Could she crawl back to her family after this? Get her job back driving the bus?

She was shaking. She didn't know what to do with her hands. She hadn't realized how badly she'd wanted this to work until it had become clear it wouldn't. She'd been so stupid to think there could be one quick answer to all her problems. Her cheeks burned as she remembered her daydreams about marrying into Base Camp, pulling on one of those beautiful Regency gowns, becoming close friends with the other women and helping run the Jane Austen Bed & Breakfast, and maybe being one of the first three women to become pregnant to help secure Base Camp for good.

What an idiot. No man wanted her like that.

"Why am I here…?" she breathed, unable to stop herself, although it was clear Harris didn't want to answer her questions.

It was a good thing he reached out to steady her before he spoke, because his words when they came nearly swept her feet out from under her.

"Because you're going to marry me."

WHAT WAS HE doing?

Harris moved like an automaton, carrying the heavy

suitcase Sam had pointed out to him on the carousel. The plain black bag was easy to spot as it traveled slowly around the apparatus, the only luggage still unclaimed. He led the way through the small airport and out into the parking lot where the taxi he'd rode here in still waited for them, just as he'd asked.

"Back to Westfield?" the cabby asked when they were settled inside.

Harris nodded, then quickly changed his mind. They couldn't go to Westfield. Not until he'd sorted out this mess.

"No—to Silver Falls," he blurted, naming the closest town over from Chance Creek. He needed to go where no one knew him so they could talk this through. He had to admit the truth—that Sam was still supposed to marry Curtis, whether Curtis was willing or no, but that she'd have to wait until another forty days were up. That was the way the show went: one wedding every forty days. By then, Curtis would have fallen as hard for Sam as Harris had.

How the hell did he make that clear to her, though?

Her gratitude when he made his declaration had nearly undone Harris. As soon as he'd blurted out the words, he'd expected her to laugh at him. Women didn't want to date him, let alone marry him. Instead, she'd clung to him like he was a lifeline.

She'd... smiled.

And in that moment, she'd set hooks into his heart he knew he'd never shake off. He wanted what she was offering so badly.

A wife.

A family of his own.

His sisters were grown now, both of them married. His mother had remarried, too, after he'd convinced her to enter counseling and she'd been treated for the reversals of fortune that had nearly undone her. Everyone had a home and a partner—except him.

All Harris knew was that the minute they reached Base Camp, Renata would swoop down on them with her cameras. Boone would take over and organize things. Curtis would claim Samantha for his bride.

He should tell the cabdriver to drive to Westfield, but somehow the words wouldn't come.

As long as they kept going, Samantha was his.

WHY WASN'T HARRIS saying anything?

Sam kept taking surreptitious glances at the man seated next to her in the cab, but she couldn't read anything in his expression. He took up far more room than she did on the narrow seat, his legs wide, his hands resting on his jeans-encased thighs. He was rugged, with strong features and eyes that seemed to see everything, although he didn't move a muscle for the first five minutes they rode in the cab.

"Why are we going to Silver Falls?" she finally managed to ask. "I thought Base Camp was in Chance Creek." She'd done her research. Base Camp was the name the men had given their tiny community, which sat on part of a large ranch named Westfield. Westfield had been owned by the Eaton family for over a hundred

years. Riley Eaton—now Riley Rudman—had expected to inherit it from her uncle, but her uncle had sold it to a billionaire named Martin Fulsom instead. Fulsom was the one backing Base Camp and the television show named after it.

"We're going to Silver Falls..." He trailed off as if he didn't know the answer. Sam turned toward him. She'd known from the start something had gone wrong, and now all her fears were back.

"For the wedding?" she pressed him.

After a short pause, he nodded. "For the wedding. There's...a chapel there." A muscle in his jaw tightened and Sam wished she knew what he was thinking. Was he here of his own free will, or had he drawn the short straw in yet another round of *who's going to marry next* on the show?

"A chapel," she prompted. "But... what about the marriage license?"

That muscle in his jaw flexed again. "We'll have to stop to get it at the courthouse."

"Okay." But she had more questions. "Won't we... be filmed?"

"Is that why you came?" The look he fixed on her drew her up short.

"I'm not some publicity whore," she retorted, then closed her eyes and got a hold of her temper. "That's not why I'm here," she assured him, and faltered when he suddenly smiled.

Sam's heart skidded to a stop and then thump, thump, thumped to catch up again. She'd never seen

Harris smile on-screen, and she wanted to reach out and smooth a thumb over the curve of his mouth. The sense of humor it betrayed warmed her to the core. This wasn't a hard-hearted man she'd pledged to marry; Harris had depths she'd only begun to suspect.

"Publicity whore," he said, trying out the phrase. "That sums it up pretty good."

"I've known my fair share." She felt a twinge of guilt. That was a rough expression to use to describe her family and the other members of the band, but sometimes, when they were out at a bar after a show, everyone competing to out-drink, out-laugh and outdo the others in their wild, attention-getting antics, Sam couldn't help feel like the whole lot of them ran on publicity rather than food and water. They could never just stop and relax, and act like normal people. Whenever she hinted they should try, her mother, father and sister shouted her down for even suggesting it.

"I don't like it. Being on-screen," Harris said.

"I don't think I'll like it either," she admitted.

"So why'd you volunteer?"

"I guess for the same reason you did. I want my life to be meaningful." As Harris waited for her to go on, Sam realized she didn't want there to be any secrets between them. "I've traveled for most of my life," she admitted, "which hasn't made it easy to meet a man. I want to settle down and raise a family." Was she blushing? She was pretty sure she was blushing. "I just... couldn't wait any longer."

Harris didn't respond. The way he was looking at

her, he must think she was crazy. Sam dropped her gaze to where her hands sat entwined in her lap. She'd said far too much. Maybe he didn't want kids.

Maybe this marriage wasn't supposed to be real.

"I... want that, too." Harris's deep voice wrapped around her like a caress.

"Really?"

He nodded. "It's why I came."

"So... we're going to a chapel?" She needed to make sense of all of it. Needed to know the sequence of events so she could stop feeling so close to shattering.

"Right after we stop at City Hall in Silver Falls."

"WHEN IS THE wedding?" the middle-aged woman sitting behind the desk at City Hall asked. They'd already made it through the line once, picked up the correct paperwork and retired to a bench to fill it in. If the situation had been awkward before, it had become more so as it sunk in how little they knew about each other. Luckily, the paperwork was straightforward, and they had enough identification on hand to prove who they were. Harris noticed Sam's hands were still shaking, however, and he wondered if she was having second thoughts.

Sam looked to him to answer. "In about an hour," he said.

"You folks are in a hurry," the woman commented, with a fairly obvious glance at Sam's flat belly. Sam hugged her arms over her chest.

"Can't wait." Harris meant for it to sound romantic,

but it fell flat and came off as indifferent, instead. The woman looked them over again.

"Any reason for the rush?"

"Is that one of the questions you're supposed to ask?" He was losing his temper. All he needed was for this busybody to slow them down and give Sam enough time to change her mind. Lord knew he should change his—he wasn't meant for marriage. Fate had shown him that time and again. He was supposed to stay aloof.

He felt anything but aloof right now.

"Just making sure both parties know what they're getting into. Marriage is forever, you know. It's not just a lark."

She finished looking over the forms while Harris looked anywhere but at Sam. When neither of them answered, the woman sighed and gathered everything up. "I need to make copies of your IDs."

She stood up and shuffled away, leaving them waiting again. The minutes ticked by so slowly Harris wondered if time had stopped altogether.

"You don't have to, you know," Sam said suddenly when the silence between them had gone far too long. Harris was reminded of every date he'd ever been on.

"Have to what?" He didn't mean to growl like that, but where was the damned woman with their IDs? He had the feeling his one chance at happiness was slipping away. If he let Sam—or himself—think about this much longer, it would disintegrate in his hands.

"Have to marry me. I understand if you don't want to."

She had no idea how much he wanted to. Harris didn't think he'd ever wanted anything this much. "We're going to get married—just as soon as we get some service around here," he growled.

The office fell silent as everyone turned their way. Sam looked like she wanted to melt into the floorboards. The woman who'd served them ambled back their way. "Someone's looking forward to his wedding night," she said loudly.

Hell.

If Sam had been flushed before, now her cheeks were scarlet.

"Wait a minute," a woman in the next line over said. "Aren't you that man from the show? From *Base Camp*?"

This was getting worse and worse.

"It *is* him," a teenage girl cried out. "It's Harris Wentworth. The sniper."

The woman in the next line craned her neck. "You're getting a marriage license? Is this your bride? Is your wedding going to be on the next show?"

"I thought Curtis was marrying next," the teenager said, coming closer. She was a willowy wisp of a thing, but Harris swore her voice was like a foghorn. "Mom! Mom—it's the guy from the show. The one Aunt Carol likes. The sniper—he's getting married."

"How much do I owe you?" Harris growled at the woman who still held their forms in her hand.

"Hold your horses."

"I'm not holding my horses. My horses are about to

42 | CORA SETON

stampede, got it? How much?"

She must have seen something in his eyes, because suddenly the woman began to move double time. In a flash she'd returned their paperwork and IDs, handed over the license and took Harris's debit card. As soon as the transaction was complete, Harris grabbed Sam's elbow and hustled her out of the building. "Where's that goddamn taxi?"

"There!"

Fifteen minutes later, when the taxi pulled off the highway into a gravel parking lot, Harris couldn't blame Sam for staring at the small white building and the large, blinking sign perched on a metal scaffolding on top of it.

"Heaven's Gate?" she read aloud. "This is where we're getting married?"

"That's right." Harris leaned forward to speak to the driver. "You'll wait, right?"

"You're racking up a bill, man. You gonna pay for all this?"

"Damn straight I will."

"Then I'll wait."

Harris got out of the taxi, went around to the other door and opened it for Sam. As he helped her out, he took in her wide-eyed expression and realized how strange this all had to seem to her.

"Where are the cameras?"

He frowned. "Cameras?"

"The camera crews? Won't this be on the show?"

Hell, she had him there. Now he'd have to confess

everything.

"Or do we marry first and then re-enact it for the show?" Sam said. "I could see how that would be best, because then the bride and groom wouldn't care if they had to stop for all the different shots and makeup touch-ups and things."

Harris let her talk. She was nervous. She talked when she was nervous. He liked knowing that about the woman who was going to be he wife.

"Is that it?" she concluded, and it took a second for him to catch up to her.

"Something like that," he managed to say. It was nothing like that, but he was too far in now to call a halt to what he was doing. He'd marry Sam first and sort out the rest later. "Come on."

"What kind of a chapel is this?"

Heaven's Gate was Montana's answer to Vegas. Harris only knew of it because he'd seen a story about it in the local paper once, and had driven past it several times. It was open twenty-four hours a day and the columnist had complained its owner shouldn't be allowed to make a profit on the drunken exploits of Montana's casino crowd. If there was a way to get it shut down, the good citizens of Montana would have done so, but apparently the chapel wasn't breaking any rules.

"It's non-denominational," he managed to say.

"Seems like Elvis should be here to greet us," Sam said.

She was right; it was as campy as a Vegas one-stop

chapel, and there were only two other vehicles in the parking lot.

"It'll get the job done," Harris said brusquely.

"I need my bag."

"The whole thing?"

She nodded, not meeting his eye.

With a glance over his shoulder down the highway, Harris leaned down to talk to the taxi driver through the window. "Open the trunk."

The man did so. Harris pulled out Sam's bag. "I'll carry it up," he told her and set off toward the chapel's front door.

Inside, they found themselves in a small vestibule that led into a waiting room with plastic seats. Facing them sat a worn desk with a laptop, printer and stacks of paperwork on it. The walls, carpet and furniture were all white, and Harris briefly wondered how the owner managed to keep it that way. Lord knew what he was dragging in here on his boots.

A silver-haired woman came out of a door from a side room, and blinked when she saw them. Her clothing was as white as the rest of the chapel; a sensible skirt, shoes and blouse with a bow on it that made Harris think of libraries and church dinners. She wore a silver name tag with the word *Honey* on it.

"Oh, I'm sorry; I didn't know anyone was here. Can I help you?"

"We're here to get hitched," Harris told her. "Right now."

"Well, the reverend is just—"

"Now."

Honey raised an eyebrow, but nodded. "All right then, I'll let him know you're in a rush." She hurried off, and Harris glanced back at the entry to the chapel. He hoped like hell none of the people at City Hall had managed to snap photos of him and Samantha, or had posted online about spotting them. All he needed was Boone tracking him down before he'd pulled off the wedding.

"I need to change," Samantha said. "There's a ladies' room over there. I'll be right back."

"Hurry up." Harris caught himself. "Those people at City Hall," he explained. "Fans of the show—"

"Believe me, I understand," Samantha told him. "We don't want them spoiling our moment."

Harris watched her hurry away and bump the swinging door to the ladies' room open with her hip. Samantha was amazing. Curtis would have wanted her the moment he laid eyes on her. Harris was fucking with fate—fucking with the television show.

If he had one shred of decency in him, he'd put a stop to this, drive Samantha back to Base Camp and give Curtis his chance with her.

But Harris had learned a long time ago that decency got you nowhere. Only vigilance did.

He'd been the one who remembered she was coming today.

He'd been the one sober enough this morning to go to the airport.

He'd been the one to assure Samantha she was

wanted at Base Camp.

For once being the man on the lonely side of the roof had paid off.

CHAPTER THREE

SAM SMOOTHED HER shaking fingers over the satin folds of her wedding dress. She'd meant to buy something simple—something befitting the situation. A plain, white sheath, with just a hint of embroidery or beadwork to mark the occasion. A wedding dress that made sense.

Unfortunately, when she'd slipped away to go shopping, she'd stumbled into an empty showroom and found herself face to face with four bored salespeople who'd lit up at their first customer of the day. She hadn't wanted to disappoint them, so when they began pulling dresses off racks to show her, she agreed to try them on. In the end she must have climbed in and out of nearly thirty gowns, but it was number seventeen she fell in love with. When she'd put it on, stepped out of the changing room and stepped up onto the pedestal in the viewing area surrounded by mirrors, she felt like a princess in a fairy tale who'd just had her life transformed.

The dress represented everything she wanted—her

happily ever after of a settled life, a meaningful life.

A life in which she had a partner as dedicated to her as she wanted to be to him.

Its strapless bodice fit close, plumping up her breasts over its sweetheart neckline. A band of satin ringed its natural waistline and delicate needlework gave interest to its panels, but while above the waist, the dress was elegant and even understated, below the satin band, it spread to the floor in a spill of organza puffs like a froth of foam. The skirt was so wide and so fluffy, Sam had laughed out loud, even as she'd fallen head over heels for it.

"You can pull this off," a saleswoman had told her enviously. "Most women can't, but you can. You look beautiful."

She did look beautiful, Sam thought as she quickly arranged her hair in a bun at the nape of her neck and fastened the comb of her veil just above it. The swoop of white netting crowned the outfit and for one moment Sam wished her family could see her now. Then she shook the thought away. If she'd held a traditional wedding with her family in attendance, her mother would spend the whole ceremony lecturing her on the patriarchal symbolism of white wedding attire, Melissa would show up in something see-through or plastic just to grab her share of attention, and her father would scan the congregation looking for his next conquest.

Despite the twist of nerves in her belly and the hollow ache of going alone to her wedding, Sam preferred it this way. She would meet Harris at the altar free of all

encumbrances. She would make the decision she'd come here to make without interference from her well-meaning but exasperating family.

She'd marry Harris.

Her way.

She was so lucky, she told herself as she reapplied her makeup. Harris was so handsome, he took her breath away. Not model pretty—a man's man through and through—his broad shoulders and muscled arms made her melt inside. But it was his eyes... and that smile—

If she could make him smile again today she thought her life would be complete. Never in a million years did she think she'd have a husband like him.

This was a fairy tale come true.

With a final look in the full-length mirror thoughtfully provided in the ladies' room, Sam headed for the door, took a deep breath as she pushed it open and stepped outside.

Harris, who'd evidently been pacing the waiting room, turned and stopped. Hands jammed in his pockets, brow furrowed, he was a man who'd obviously been questioning what he was doing in this chapel, but as she watched, his forehead smoothed, his back straightened and he smiled again—that quirk of his mouth that sent a ripple of emotion through her she couldn't quite name.

Happiness?

Longing?

His gaze drank her in and the interest in his eyes

was all too clear. Not the casual interest of a man looking at a women in a pretty dress: the intense, personal interest of a man who knows he's about to win the right to take that dress off and possess what's underneath it.

Sam's breath hitched. Of course she'd thought about sex—first with Clay, then with Curtis. She felt slightly sick to remember that now, but in an instant it didn't matter, because it was Harris she'd stand next to in front of the altar, and if she was truthful, it had been Harris who'd caught her eye every time she watched *Base Camp*. Fate had led her to the man she'd truly hungered for.

Was he thinking about what would come later? Sam thought he might be, and she wondered what that would be like. When would they be together? Would they be compatible? The butterflies in her stomach swooped and dove until she wasn't sure if she could stay standing.

"There's the beautiful bride," Honey called out as she entered the room again, breaking the spell between them. "Give me your extra things; I'll stow them behind my desk." She took Sam's suitcase and purse and squirreled them away out of sight. "Now, come on, both of you. Let's get ready for the ceremony."

Before she knew what was happening, Honey had taken her arm and clamped a hand around Harris's bicep, too, and marched them toward the white double doors behind the reception area.

Sam expected to see rows of benches and an altar

when they passed through the doors. Instead, they entered another ante-room. It was as white as the waiting room had been, but it was lined with display cases and white metal shelves, like a heavenly gift shop.

"Many of our couples come a tiny bit unprepared," Honey said, "so we've stocked some things you might be wishing you had."

Sam wasn't sure whether to laugh or be horrified by this new development.

"You have a veil already," Honey went on, leading them past a spinning rack of them. "But I notice you don't have flowers. It's traditional to carry a bouquet when you walk down the aisle." She pointed at several shelves. Most of the bouquets were dried arrangements, but there were several that were surprisingly fresh. A small bouquet of wildflowers caught her eye and Sam bit her lip. Honey, following her gaze, scooped up the flowers and presented them to her. "Lovely!" she proclaimed. "Just nineteen ninety-five. A bargain."

"But—"

Sam didn't get another word out before Honey had them standing in front of a large display of cups, wineglasses, champagne flutes, cake cutters and more. She began to pick items up and present them one after another to Sam.

"I already have champagne flutes," Sam managed to say. Honey's mouth straightened into a thin line. She returned the items one by one. Harris guided Sam between the shelves, but somehow Honey nipped forward and got ahead of them again.

"These are pretty special: we take your photo and transfer it to a pillow or throw blanket. Perfect for your bed to remind you of your wedded bliss! Only fifty-nine ninety-five." She held up a tasseled, tan pillow with a grainy depiction of an unfortunate couple in their wedding attire.

"Definitely not," Harris told her.

"Music?" Honey chirped, darting forward again. "A commemorative CD of popular tunes from the current year?"

"No," Harris said.

Undeterred, she hurried on. "Candles! Every wedding night needs candles. These are citrus scented—"

"No." Harris kept walking.

Honey squeaked as he elbowed past, but she darted around, ducked past Sam and got ahead of them again.

"Luggage?" She indicated a set of turquoise bags. "For your honeymoon! We've got sunscreen, too, if you're headed for warmer climes—"

"No." Harris pulled Sam forward as they reached the far side of the displays. Sam thought he was about to make a run for the double doors that hopefully led into the chapel's sanctuary, when Honey looped around them one more time.

"How about—"

"We're not buying anything else!"

Honey quailed and Sam didn't blame her. The woman had pushed Harris to the edge of his patience, and he was formidable when he was angry.

"Not even rings?" Honey managed, holding up a

tray of them.

Harris stopped in his tracks. Sam held her breath.

Rings. She hadn't even thought of them.

"Hell," Harris said. He turned her. "I didn't—"

"That's okay," she said hurriedly.

Honey drew herself up. "It absolutely is *not* okay. This is your bride. This is the woman pledging her heart to yours for the rest of her life. This is a *holy* occasion."

For a moment Sam thought Harris would point out the irony of that statement, standing where they were, but to his credit he didn't. Instead he nodded.

"We need rings."

"Come over to the display. We have lots of lovely ones to choose from," Honey said.

As Sam and Harris followed her slowly, Sam wondered again if she was doing the right thing. Back in the ladies' room she'd thought she was. Every time Harris looked her way, she was sure she was, but standing next to him in this tacky salesroom at this ridiculous chapel, she had to wonder if she'd lost her mind.

"Take a look," Honey said, lining up several trays of rings. Some of them belonged in the bottom of a cereal box, but Sam was surprised to see Honey was right; they did have some lovely ones. "You're a traditional girl," Honey told her. "You need a traditional ring that will stand by you through the years. I always think it's sad how people today turn their back on the tried and true. There's a reason for traditions, don't you think? They worked for those who came before us, and they'll work for us, too."

She pulled a ring out of its slot in the tray and held it out. "Try this on."

Sam did and a tremor ran through her when it fit perfectly. It was a single diamond in a beautiful silver setting.

"That's an engagement ring, of course," Honey said. "Here's the band that goes with it. It'll fit," she assured them. "You'll want to wait for the ceremony to put it on. Now for you," she said to Harris and considered the rings, "Here's one." She held out a thick, silver masculine band that Sam thought would suit him to a T.

"We'll take them."

Sam slid the engagement ring off and handed it to Honey. Honey took the flowers and led the way to a cash register tucked discreetly to one side. She rang up the purchases. "Plus the fee for the ceremony." She tapped in a few more numbers and named a total that made Sam wince. She reached for a purse that wasn't there.

Harris pulled out his wallet without comment, presented a credit card and paid the bill.

"Come this way," Honey said graciously when the transaction was done. She opened the double doors, and Sam, flustered at the thought of being thrust suddenly into the sanctuary when she was unprepared, sighed in relief to see yet another ante-chamber. This one was furnished only with a bench and a beautiful stained-glass window on one side. "I'll give you two lovebirds a moment alone." Honey kept the flowers and wedding bands, but presented Harris with the engagement ring in

a small velvet box. "Perhaps you'd like to propose," she said to him in a penetrating whisper. With a lift of her eyebrows toward Sam, she slipped through another set of double doors and disappeared.

Sam closed her eyes at absurdity of it all, but when she opened them again, Harris stood before her, studying her again. Without a word, he led her to the white upholstered bench and she sat down. He sat beside her.

"She's right. We should take a minute. This is a big step. It deserves some thought."

"I've thought it through," she assured him. If he changed his mind now, she didn't know what she'd do.

"Have you?" He scanned her face. "It isn't an easy life I'm offering. Most women want more. A big house, fancy cars, lots of furniture. Do you think you'll be able to live like we do?"

Sam laughed. "Harris, I've lived in a bus almost my entire life. A bus I shared with eleven other people, most of whom weren't related to me. There's nothing Base Camp can throw at me I haven't seen before."

When she took in his quizzical expression, Sam figured he was wondering about the circumstances of her upbringing, but before she could explain, he shook his head with a small chuckle.

"What?" she asked.

"It's good to hear you call me that," he explained. "In the Navy it was always Hawk this, Hawk that."

"Hawk? Is that your nickname?"

"It's a stupid name. I don't like it, and I've put it to

56 | CORA SETON

rest." He examined his hands where they rested on his knees. He'd set the small velvet box aside on the seat.

"Is it because... you're a sniper?"

"*Was* a sniper. That's not who I am anymore." His expression darkened and he looked away. "Can't say I know for sure who I am these days."

She understood that. "Maybe we can create something new together." She reached out tentatively and touched one of his hands. She was so curious about him, but as soon as her fingertips slid over his skin, she pulled back, embarrassed. "Sorry."

Harris caught her hand in his, a lightning-quick move she wouldn't have believed if not for the pressure of his fingers around hers. "Don't ever be sorry for touching me. Don't ever be sorry for anything you do."

"I'm not sure what's allowed," she confessed to him. "We're getting married, but we don't know anything about each other. I want... I want to love you, but I'm not sure what you want."

Harris didn't answer for a long time. Then he reached for the little box, drew the ring out of it and pushed off the bench to kneel before her.

"I don't know you, but I know what this represents to me." He held up the ring. "It represents the commitment I'm making to you. I will love you and only you for the rest of my life. I will stay with you no matter what happens until my dying day. I will protect you from anything that wants to harm you for all time. When I put this ring on your finger, I'm giving you a promise. And I don't ever walk away from a promise."

He took her hand and raised it, hesitating. "This ring means forever. Is that what you want?"

Sam's heart expanded until she didn't think her rib cage could contain it. "Yes," she said. "That's exactly what I want."

As HARRIS SLID the ring onto Sam's slender finger, his heart was banging away in his chest like the rattle of a snare drum announcing a military charge on some old-fashioned battleground. Fate was handing him the gift of everything he'd ever wanted and all he could think was this had to be some mistake. Surely he wasn't allowed to be this happy.

Sam's green eyes watched his every move as he stood and lifted her along with him. She tilted her chin for a better view, and he spotted the dark curve of a single eyelash resting on the apple of her cheek. He automatically leaned closer and brushed it away.

Her delicate fragrance, the tendrils of her hair coming loose from her updo, the smoothness of her skin under his fingertips fired up a longing in him he'd always managed to keep in check until now. Sam took a ragged breath and he fought the urge to crush her against him and taste the promised sweetness of her mouth.

Not yet.

Fire throbbed through his veins as she pulled back, watching him again, raising a hand to the spot where he'd just touched her.

"An eyelash," he explained, his voice unexpectedly

gruff.

Honey opened the door and leaned around it. "Ready, you two?"

"Yes," Harris forced himself to say. He was ready. To hell with the consequences; there was no way he'd back out now.

This time when they went through the double doors, they finally entered the sanctuary of the chapel. Harris bit back a chuckle at the décor: as white as the rest of the building. Whoever owned this place had a heaven-complex. White carpet flowed over the floor. White wooden benches stood in straight lines facing front, where a white raised dais stood lined with white vases full of white chrysanthemums. A white lectern stood waiting for the officiant, who was nowhere to be seen, and for one moment Harris wondered if Honey played that role, too, until a door opened and a man walked out.

"That's Reverend Gabriel," Honey whispered loudly. "The Reverend of Love."

Harris's fingers twitched. He caught Sam's eye and found her biting her lip, obviously fighting against laughter. So his future wife had a sense of humor.

Good. She was going to need it back at Base Camp.

"Harris, you go down front there and stand before the reverend. Samantha, you stand back here. When the music starts, you walk down that aisle—slowly, like a real lady."

Samantha made a choking sound and coughed to hide it. Harris touched her hand as he passed with what

he hoped she'd read as an encouraging squeeze. As Honey fussed around her and Samantha composed herself, he moved to the head of the chapel, where Reverend Gabriel nodded benignly at him. He wore a white outfit that was a cross between a tuxedo and ministerial garb with a stiff collar and a large, white crucifix hanging around his neck. He held a white calfskin Bible between manicured fingers. Harris shuddered to think how the ceremony might go.

But then his attention was taken by Honey hurrying up the aisle. She presented him with the ring box that held their wedding bands. "Don't lose it," she admonished him, and clucked over him as she straightened his plaid shirt.

"How the hell am I going to lose it? I'm standing right here at the altar," Harris blurted before thinking better of it.

Honey huffed. "Respect! You're in the presence of God!" She pushed past him, climbed onto the dais and sat herself at a white baby grand piano in the corner. She fanned herself for a moment with a set of sheet music before arranging it and preparing to play.

Harris was still looking around for the Deity when the first chords of the bridal march crashed over him. Honey was an exuberant musician, and casting aside all thought about the irregularities of the Heaven's Gate Chapel, Harris focused instead on the woman walking down the aisle toward him.

The woman he was about to marry.

Samantha looked like a queen as she floated down

the aisle toward him, an angel descended from the heavens to escort him into certain bliss. It didn't matter to him that Honey's music was more loud than accurate, or that the officiant was puffing out his chest as if he meant to belt out an opera rather than speak the words that would bind them together.

It didn't even matter that he'd told himself he wasn't meant for marriage.

He was here, and so was Samantha. That was all that counted.

When Samantha reached his side, he took her hand as if they'd known each other for years, not hours. Her fingers curved around his and held on as if he was her lifeline. Harris swore to himself that was exactly what he'd be to her—a pillar of strength in an uncertain world. A lookout for danger. A sword at the ready.

But when she turned to him, lifted her gaze to his and smiled as Honey's music came to a crashing close, Harris realized his methods of dealing with life's problems weren't going to work anymore. He wasn't a lone shepherd guarding his flock from the wolves. He wasn't the sniper on a roof pinpointing a target and eliminating it.

He was a man holding a woman's hand, and that woman would expect to share his world, his life and his thoughts. He couldn't hold her at arm's length while he protected her. She'd want to enter the circle of silence he'd always surrounded himself with, that space that allowed him to be more vigilant than everyone else. Harris's throat thickened with an unfamiliar feeling that

made him want to step away a few paces. To re-establish that buffer zone between him and the rest of the world.

But he couldn't. Not anymore.

"Dearly Beloved," Reverend Gabriel announced suddenly in a baritone that belonged on Broadway. "We are gathered here today to join this man and this woman for all eternity in holy matrimony."

Harris swallowed. Samantha was as fine as a china statue. Her beautiful eyes, pale cheeks and curved mouth made up the stuff of fantasies for a man like him. Despite what she'd said about growing up in a bus, he could tell from the openness of her expression she'd lived a privileged life of safety. She didn't know poverty or desperation or disaster. She had no idea the dangers the world contained. How could he care for her and keep her close, all at the same time?

"Let us consider the nature of marriage," the reverend went on, oblivious to Harris's internal struggle. "A wedding isn't a party." He fixed Harris with a stern look. "It's an occasion to take stock."

Harris tuned him out. He was taking stock, damn it. Taking stock and finding that the shelves were empty and he'd set his storehouse on fire. He couldn't do this. He couldn't put everyone around him in danger by pursuing this selfish path. Look what had happened to Nora when he relaxed his vigilance. He was the watcher.

Not the lover.

Harris looked down at Samantha again. Found her looking up at him, a tiny crease forming between her

eyebrows. He knew she was sensing the turmoil inside him. If he left now—

Samantha squeezed his hand again encouragingly, sending Harris whirling into a memory from the distant past, before either of the hurricanes had torn apart his life. He was up on top of a slide at some playground. His elementary school, maybe. He had the impression of a small, blonde girl, someone in his kindergarten class. Laurie... Lanie? Lanie Sudeker. He couldn't believe he could still pull that name out of his memory.

His legs were splayed before him. He was looking down the sweep of the slide, an enormous distance off the ground, although Harris was sure it wasn't nearly as high as it had felt back then. Lanie, standing behind him on the ladder waiting her turn, took another step up, plopped herself on the platform, scooted up behind him, her legs to either side of his, and put her arms around his waist. "I'm scared, too," she announced. "We'll do it together."

They'd pushed off, slid down and spent the rest of that recess racing up the ladder and sliding down again.

Harris, reeling from the unexpected memory, realized for the first time how much he'd lost of his early years. Hurricane Andrew had wiped the slate clean with the force of the catastrophe his family had lived through. Those first hungry weeks, the constant worry and tears of the people all around him, the never-ending bus ride to New Orleans and the herculean task of starting over in a brand-new city had all conspired to erase his time in Florida. But there had been good times

back then. Memories of a different life he could draw on. A time when a hug and an offer of friendship could solve any problem.

Harris squeezed Samantha's hand back. This beautiful woman standing next to him was offering him more than friendship. She was offering her heart. Shouldn't he at least try to be worthy of it?

As Reverend Gabriel wound down his sermon on the wedded state and slid into the familiar wording of the vows, Harris stood tall. Damn straight he'd try to be worthy of it. He'd give it his all. Maybe he'd fail, but it wouldn't be for lack of trying.

He was going to make a life with the woman standing by his side.

HE WAS WAVERING. Harris was wavering, she was sure of it, and Sam couldn't blame him one bit. They were rushing this wedding, the venue was ridiculous, the officiant obviously loved the sound of his own voice and things like this didn't—couldn't—turn out well.

What had she been thinking running away from her family and joining up with a group of strangers who for all she knew were some sort of cult that had gotten television sponsorship? What was she doing marrying this... sniper? Why was she in this fairy-tale dress, in this merengue of a chapel, like Cinderella—doomed to a hard return to earth when the clock struck twelve and exposed this whole venture as the farce it was?

Harris kept swallowing as if fighting to find the words to stop the proceedings. His hand in hers had

grown lax and cold. He was having second thoughts. He wanted out. And so did—

No.

Sam got a hold of herself and slowed her breathing, which had grown shallow and fast. No, she didn't want out and from what he'd said back on the bench outside the sanctuary, Harris didn't, either. She tried to come up with a rational explanation for his behavior. Her own concerns were that she wouldn't live up to Harris's expectations—that she'd disappoint him somehow and he'd feel tethered to a woman who didn't suit him for the rest of his life.

Could Harris be thinking something similar? Was he worried he wasn't good enough for her?

When she glanced up, he was glancing down again and the worry in his gaze made her think maybe she was right. She squeezed his hand to encourage him. Of course he was good enough for her.

Too good.

If anyone was to disappoint, it would be her.

What did she know of marriage, after all? It wasn't like she had any examples to base her actions on. Henry and Rachel hadn't managed to stay faithful more than a year and a half, and even that was debatable, Sam had often thought. Their devotion to *Deader Than Ever* was the only constant thing in their lives.

Would her body hold interest for Harris? She wasn't the flamboyantly sexual being her sister was. Nor was she the free spirit her mother had always been. Maybe she was too uptight for Harris's tastes.

Maybe she'd disappoint him the first time they made love.

It was her turn to let her hand go slack in Harris's, but just as she'd encouraged him, now he gripped hers firmly, tugged a little until she looked up at him. He caught her gaze and held it, and all Sam's doubts fled before the intensity of his deep blue eyes staring back at her.

She'd do whatever it took to keep this man happy, she decided. She'd love him with everything she had. More, even.

She'd do her best, and hope like hell that was enough.

SPEAKING HIS VOWS, Harris barely heard the reverend's prompts. Somehow he knew what to say. Somehow the traditional words echoed everything he was feeling in his heart. When Sam repeated the words and pledged herself to him, he could hardly breathe. This was happening. She was becoming his wife. She would be his in a matter of moments.

Her hands trembled as he slid the wedding band on her finger, but then a tremor ran through his, too, as she slid the larger band on his ring finger. They were taking this leap together. God knew where they'd land, but as soon as they touched down, Harris would throw himself into building a life for Sam—a life where she'd be safe and cherished. A life they could live together.

"I now pronounce you husband and wife. You may kiss the bride."

As the officiant's words passed over him, Harris knew the next thirty seconds would change his life forever. They were already bound together in marriage, but this kiss would tell him what to expect from the future. Casting away his worries, Harris cupped Samantha's pretty face with both hands and bent to cover her mouth with his.

She was sweet. So sweet. So pliable and soft under his lips. He drank her in like he'd been waiting for her all his life, and in a way he had. Samantha was the answer to all his unspoken prayers. She was the hope he'd been waiting for—a reason to walk a new path in life. As he kissed her, he let go of thought and worry and plans and for one moment—one wonderful moment—allowed the present to be everything.

His wife—his beautiful wife—slid her arms up around his neck and kissed him back, the swell of her breasts pressing against his chest in a tantalizing way. Harris knew he'd have to earn the right to touch her, and he swore to himself he'd do just that.

When Reverend Gabriel cleared his throat, Harris reluctantly broke the kiss and pulled away. Sam was flushed, her eyes shining, and when she smiled at him, he bent down and took her in his arms again. This time he deepened the kiss and she kissed him back, answering his need with her own. But they were still in the chapel. This would have to wait.

"Ahem." The reverend was growing impatient. "There are forms to sign."

"Of course." Harris kept a tight hold on Samantha

even as he turned to take the pen the reverend handed to him.

WHEN HARRIS LED her out of the chapel, Sam felt as if she was at the top of a roller coaster looking down at the parking lot, the taxicab and the road leading to the rest of her life. Her heart was pounding, her breath short and a strange combination of light-headedness and exhilaration made her head swim.

"Are we going to Base Camp now?" she asked Harris.

"No."

Startled at his vehemence, Sam stopped halfway down the steps. "Why not?"

"Because... I'm not ready to share you yet." He tugged her hand as he continued down toward the taxicab. "I've got somewhere I want to show you first."

"Should I change?" She lifted the skirts of her princess-style wedding gown doubtfully.

Harris stopped and looked her over. Sam's skin tingled at the smile that curved his mouth. "You probably should change, but I wish you wouldn't."

She smiled back at him, her concern forgotten. "Why?"

"I like you in that getup."

She liked the way he was looking at her. "I'll keep it on, then."

He held her gaze. "I'll carry you over the rough parts."

Sam's heart throbbed in response to his words. She

looked forward to that. Harris looked strong enough to carry her all day. She wondered what it would feel like to be in his arms.

"We'll have to make a few stops, but it'll be worth it in the end."

"It already is," she assured him.

Harris, who'd turned to move on, stopped again. "Why's that?"

"Because I'm with you," she said simply. She'd never in her wildest dreams thought the day could go this well, or that she'd feel such an instant connection to the man she'd married at first sight. As they made their way to the waiting cab, she felt like she was floating, and that sensation continued through several stops—the first for a rental pickup truck they could keep for the next twenty-four hours, the next for picnic supplies, food and drinks before they drove back along the highway and finally turned onto a rutted dirt road.

Sam had to bite back a laugh as she wondered what her family would think if they could see her now. Embracing the patriarchy: married. To a former Navy SEAL. A sniper.

Rachel would have a lot to say.

Melissa would ask about their sex life, or lack thereof. She'd have snarky comments about what might happen next.

Suddenly, Sam's hands were clammy and she searched for a handkerchief in her purse so as not to have to wipe them on her dress.

When would she and Harris become intimate? They

hadn't talked about that. They hadn't really talked about anything. She swallowed in a mouth that had become very dry. Was that why he was taking her to a secluded place? Did he think they were going to have sex—right now?

Of course, she knew intimacy would be part of their marriage, but Sam hadn't figured on jumping into the sack with a stranger right off. She'd pictured some kind of Hollywood honeymoon, actually. She'd packed a swimsuit and pretty outfits for a trip. Now she realized she'd been silly. She'd watched the other episodes. Boone and Riley had honeymooned for all of two days in a tent on the far side of the ranch. She had no idea what Clay and Nora were doing.

"Harris, are we—?" Sam bit off the rest of the question. Asking him if they were going on a honeymoon trip was ridiculous when he was driving her into the wilderness. Maybe this picnic was her honeymoon.

Maybe he'd done all this simply to get laid.

What kind of a man went on a show and let someone else pick out his wife?

What the hell was she doing here?

"What's wrong?" Harris turned her way. Sam couldn't find any words to explain her panic. What would she say? That she'd just realized she was driving into the backcountry with a man trained to kill? That she was afraid she'd be dead in a matter of minutes? That she wanted out?

"Samantha?" Concern laced his voice.

"I don't... I don't think... I want—look out!" Sam

pointed and screamed as Harris jerked the wheel, accelerated, went right off the road, barely avoided a tree before swerving back into the rutted lane. Her seat belt snapped her back against the seat when he slammed on the brakes and she struggled to recover her breath as Harris opened his door and raced back the way they'd come.

Sam pressed a hand to her beating heart, composed herself and climbed out of the truck, her legs wobbling beneath her before she got her wits about her again. She lifted her skirts and walked slowly back to where Harris was kneeling in the road, dreading what she would see. The dog had leaped out from nowhere. One minute the track had been empty; the next the animal's pleading eyes had filled her vision before Harris jerked the truck out of the way. They must have hit him. There was no way—

"Not a scratch," Harris said, his voice thick. "Jesus, I almost ran her over. Why didn't she move?"

Sam reached them and bit back a sob of relief when she saw the way the skinny yellow dog was seated in the track, calmly allowing Harris to run his hands all over her frame, looking for injuries.

"I can't believe I didn't hit her," Harris said again. The dog shifted a little and licked his face.

"She's taken a shine to you." Sam cleared her throat, got her emotions under control and knelt down carefully to stroke its fur. "Look at you. You're a beauty. What are you doing way out here?" The dog whined a little, and she took in its gauntness. "She's hungry."

"Someone must have left her out here. Or else she wandered off and got really lost." Harris checked for a collar, but Sam had already seen there wasn't one. "I guess we'll have to take her to the pound when we go back."

"Why?" Sam demanded. She took a breath and tried again. "Why?" she asked again in a softer voice. "If she doesn't belong to anyone, we could take her in."

The dog turned her way and licked her chin, as if in thanks.

"Are you sure about that? We're going to be living in a space the size of a small bedroom, and this girl here isn't exactly a lapdog."

No, she wasn't, Sam agreed. She wasn't any breed Sam could distinguish, but she had long fur, a husky build, and sweet, brown eyes. "I have a pretty big lap," she told the dog. "You're welcome to sit in it any time." As she leaned forward to hug the animal, an age-old pain shifted a little in her heart. She'd wanted a pet for as long as she could remember, but of course that was impossible, given the life they'd led. She'd learned young never to fall for a stray because there wasn't even a hint of a chance that they'd take one aboard the bus, and after several heartbreaks, Sam couldn't stand that pain anymore. She shouldn't let her heart go out to this animal, either. Harris was right; they were going to live in a house even tinier than the sleeper bus had been and she had no idea what Base Camp's policy on pets was. Still, she found herself saying, "I'd like to keep her. What do you think?"

His silence spoke volumes, and Sam began to steel her heart against yet one more disappointment when he touched her shoulder. She looked up to find him closer than she expected. When his mouth brushed her cheek, she let out a little gasp of surprise. "What was that for?"

"I'd like to keep her, too. I haven't had a pet since... well, since ever."

"You weren't allowed one as a child?"

"There wasn't room for one."

She waited for him to say more, but he didn't.

"But you'd be okay with one now?" She had to be sure she'd heard him right.

"Definitely. We'd better make sure she doesn't belong to someone else, but I have a feeling she's ours if we want her."

"We'd better go get her some food."

He nodded. "I'd still like that picnic, though."

She smiled, her heart full. "Me, too."

CHAPTER FOUR

B Y THE TIME they'd made the short run to Silver
Falls, picked up some dog food, a couple of bowls,
a jug of water, a collar and a lead, then made it back
down the long dirt road where they'd started, over an
hour had passed and Harris's stomach was rumbling. He
judged it was past twelve. The clouds were still heavy,
the temperature warm, and the sight of Sam in the
passenger seat, tendrils of her lovely hair coming free of
her updo, her veil slightly askew, still made his heart
throb every time he looked at her. He knew there'd be
trouble when they returned to Base Camp, but he didn't
care. It would be worth it.

She was worth it.

Daisy, as Sam had named the dog, lay across Sam's
feet patiently.

"Why would anyone let her go?" she asked again
when he pulled into a turnout near the head of a path,
and shut the engine off.

"We might never know." They'd left word at the
feed store that they'd found her, but Harris was confi-

dent no one would come looking for the dog. She had an air of neglect about her that said it had been a while since she'd had a home.

They'd given her food and water back at the feed store, so now it was picnic time. Harris got out, gathered up their things and came around the truck to where Sam and Daisy stood. "Ready?"

Sam nodded, although she eyed the track they were going to take uneasily. "Let me grab those champagne flutes I bought first."

"It's not too long a walk, and the view is worth it when you get there," he promised her, leading her to the back of the truck, where he moved her suitcase within reach.

"It looks like it's going to rain."

"It'll hold off for a few more hours," Harris assured her.

"Okay."

Harris waited patiently for her to rummage through her things until she pulled out the two delicate glasses. He found himself grinning as he walked, despite the load of groceries and supplies he was lugging along. He couldn't have picked a better companion if he'd searched for one for months. Sam seemed up for anything. She wasn't complaining about the rugged circumstances she found herself in. She'd been patient through the trip back for food for Daisy—especially considering the looks she'd gotten in the feed store in that wedding dress.

She liked dogs. That had to be a sign.

A SEAL'S PLEDGE | 75

As they walked in silence, however, Harris wondered if all that was enough to base a relationship on. Shouldn't he be talking to her right now, for instance?

He wasn't sure what to say.

These woods reminded him of the hills of Afghanistan, but he was smart enough to know you didn't talk about battles on your honeymoon. Maybe he should talk about the honeymoon.

The fact that there wouldn't be one.

With a sigh, Harris decided he needed a positive topic. Like Daisy.

Except they'd covered that ground in the truck on the way to and from the feed store.

A trickle of sweat snaked down between his shoulder blades, its tickling track hard to ignore. Not much longer to go, he told himself, but it wasn't that the load he carried was heavy; it was the knowledge that Samantha was walking behind him in her beautiful dress, expecting him to have some sort of plan about what came next. She'd done her part: she'd shown up and married him.

He needed to figure out how to make this marriage real.

Harris was relieved when Daisy barked once and trotted ahead, stopping every now and then to look back to make sure they were following.

"Good dog. Go check it out for us," he encouraged her. Looking back over his shoulder, he asked, "You doing okay back there?"

"I'm great."

The cheerful tone of her voice relieved him. Just a few steps more.

There.

Harris came to a stop when he stepped out of the woods onto the edge of a hillside where the land fell away and the view was panoramic.

"Oh, it's beautiful," Samantha breathed. "It's the perfect place for a picnic."

Daisy barked as if in agreement and Harris grinned again. When had he ever smiled so damn much in one day?

SAM MADE SANDWICHES while Harris got the cork out of the bottle of champagne they'd bought. He poured a generous amount into Sam's two champagne flutes and handed her one. In exchange, she passed him a paper plate of food. Daisy flopped down in the shade a half-dozen feet away and settled in for a contented snooze. Sam imagined it had been a while since she'd had a full belly and hoped her doggy dreams were happy ones.

She and Harris both sat down on the rough wool blanket Harris had found in the back of the rental truck. Sam's full skirts billowed around her and she sighed in satisfaction. Was there anything as romantic as wearing your wedding gown to a picnic?

"I hope we don't spoil that dress," Harris said.

"I hope we do." Sam bit her lip. She hadn't meant to say that out loud. The truth was her stomach was full of butterflies and her heart still tripped with anticipation. Maybe she wasn't ready to be fully intimate with

this man, but she hoped he would kiss her again.

A lot.

She was sure the color was high in her cheeks and when she chanced a glance his way, the interest in his eyes was equally elevated.

He raised his champagne flute. "To us."

"To us. To a future together."

They clinked the glasses together and both drank.

The champagne's bubbles tickled her throat and Sam immediately felt a buzz. She hadn't eaten since lunch the previous day. She'd been far too anxious last night as she'd slipped away from the tour bus in Austin, picked up a rental car and driven five hours to an airport where her family wouldn't think to look, and waited overnight to catch her flight. She'd been even more anxious this morning before boarding. She'd had almost no sleep and should be exhausted right now, but instead she was exhilarated.

"I want to know all about you," she said.

"That'll take time."

"I know, but we've got to start somewhere. Tell me something I don't know."

Harris sat with his legs in front of him, leaning back against one braced hand. His dark hair was military-short. Thick, dark eyebrows framed his eyes, which tended to look off into the distance, searching for something. Watching. A strong jaw made him serious, and his shoulders filled out his plaid shirt nicely. He was athletic, but in a capable way, rather than a record-breaking way, she mused. He was a man built to work

hard and long at a physical job. "You're a carpenter," she prompted.

"Not really. I can frame up a house, but I'm not like Clay." He stopped short and frowned. "Guess you expected to marry him."

She shook her head. "At first, but then Boone called and told me about Clay and Nora's wedding, so I was already prepared to marry Curtis."

He nodded. "Maybe I should apologize for stepping in."

"I'm not sorry—but I guess I'd like to know why Curtis didn't come."

He seemed to think this over, swirling the remains of the champagne in his glass. "Maybe you're not sorry yet, but you might change your mind."

"You didn't answer my question."

"Curtis was... indisposed."

"What does that mean?" she asked sharply. "Like, he was sick?"

"Drunk, more like it. Had a little too much fun last night."

She thought about that. "He must not have been in too much of a hurry to meet me."

"I think he was nervous. Like I said, maybe I should apologize for stepping in."

"You mean, he didn't actually ask you to?"

Harris shook his head. "No."

A wave of vertigo crashed over her. Harris had stepped in on his own accord? But... what about Curtis?

"He never saw your photo. None of us did. He wasn't eager to marry someone he didn't know—he wanted Boone to give him an array of women to choose from. It didn't work out that way, so when Nora married Clay last night, and he got a forty-day reprieve, he... got a little carried away. Celebrating." Harris shrugged. "I just came to take you back to the ranch to meet him. But when I saw you..." He trailed off.

"When you saw me...?" she prompted, hardly able to comprehend what she was hearing. She'd assumed Curtis had begged Harris to take his place.

"I decided I wanted you for myself."

"So you just..." She didn't even know how to sum up the situation.

"Stole you." He looked away, but he was smiling a little.

She should have been outraged.

Instead, she was incredibly... turned on.

Harris wanted her. Badly enough to break all the rules.

"What will Curtis say about that?" she made herself ask. She was proud of how steady her voice sounded, given the circumstances.

"He'll be pissed." He glanced up. "But I'm not sorry. Hope you're not, either."

What could she say to that?

The truth, she decided. "I'm not. Besides, it's too late. We're married now, and that's forever."

Harris stilled. "You really believe that?"

"Don't you?"

"Lots of people don't these days."

Sam sighed and withdrew her touch. "Some people don't even get married in the first place." When he raised a questioning eyebrow, she went on. "My parents didn't. They barely stayed together long enough for me and my sister to be born. They weren't exactly role models for the settled life."

"Did you divide your time between them?"

Sam laughed. "I didn't have to. We all lived together for the most part on a tour bus, with eight other people, sometimes more, sometimes less. My parents are both in a band. So is my sister now. I drove the bus."

Harris grinned. "You drove the bus?"

"I did. I'm not musical to save my life, unfortunately."

"I'm glad. If you were, you wouldn't be here now. Would you?"

"Probably not. I wouldn't be searching to figure out where I belong." She cut off, afraid she'd said too much.

"Base Camp is a good place to belong." But he seemed to run out of words, too, and gazed out at the landscape in front of them as if he'd like to retract that last sentence.

"Tell me about Base Camp. Why did you join up?"

Harris thought a moment, his gaze still distant. "I wanted a wife," he said bluntly.

Sam, who'd just lifted her glass to take a sip, nearly choked. "You joined Base Camp to get a wife?"

"I suck at this. All of it. Meeting women, talking to them. Getting anywhere with it."

"You suck at this?" Sam didn't know what to say next. If he sucked at it, she must be a colossal failure. "I'd have thought you'd be thronged with women wanting to date you."

Harris snorted. "Yeah. Thronged."

"Come on. A man like you?"

"Like what?" He took a swig of his champagne. "What's a man like me?"

She nearly joshed him about fishing for compliments, but she had a feeling Harris was serious; that he didn't know what an intriguing, intimidating man he was.

"A man who isn't afraid of commitment. A man who relishes hard work. A man who's faced danger and lived to tell about it. A very handsome man."

He made another noise. "I think that's about all I can stand to hear right now."

"You realize if you put yourself down, you're putting me down, too. I chose to marry you, after all." She finished her champagne and held out her glass for more. Harris put his down and refilled hers, then poured more for himself.

"Never thought about it like that," he admitted.

"You were raised not to brag."

"I was raised—I mostly raised myself," he finished. "Not sure how I turned out."

"Seems to me you turned out pretty good."

HARRIS DREW OUT the meal, knowing that soon enough he'd have to face the music back at Base Camp. He felt

an ease out on this hillside with Samantha and Daisy he hadn't felt in far too long, and he didn't look forward to reality bursting the fragile bubble of peace this day had brought him.

"How about you? You must have left some man behind," he made himself say. She was right; he didn't want to drag her down by thinking the worst of himself, but what he'd said was true; dating had never been his strong suit and he hated to think he might mess up.

She shook her head. "Not a one. I always had a hard time competing."

"With who?"

"My mom. My sister. All the groupies."

"Your mom?"

Samantha sighed and pulled her cell phone out of her bag. She turned it on, punched in her code and chuckled. "Oh, they're pissed. Listen to this text my mom sent: 'Who's going to drive the bus?' Really? Her daughter goes missing and that's what concerns her?" Another sigh as she scanned a few more. A moment later she handed him the phone. "That's my family."

Harris took the phone and examined the image. A man in his late fifties, bald with a crescent of gray hair, stood between two beautiful women. The one on the left was also in her fifties, the fine lines on her face only making her beauty more interesting. She had long hair and a knowing expression, and wore a deep purple tunic over black, flowing pants. The one on the right was in her twenties. She, too, had long dark hair, but her face was unlined, her cheekbones like a model's. Still, she

had the same knowing look, like she'd seen a bit too much for her years.

"See what I mean?" Samantha asked.

"You have a nice looking family." They were familiar, too, although Harris couldn't say why.

"Nice. That's an understatement. No one looks at me when Mom and Melissa are around."

"Sure they do."

She looked surprised, and Harris went on.

"They look at you and realize you're a keeper. You're a woman a man has to work for. You come with expectations, the kind of woman a man settles down with, not the kind of woman a man screws for the hell of it."

Her lips parted, and Harris pressed on. He'd probably offended her, but he was only speaking the truth. "Those men—the ones who see your mom and sister but not you. Are they the settling down kind?"

She shrugged. "My mom's had proposals. So has my sister."

"From men they just met."

She nodded.

"Those aren't proposals. Those are propositions. There's a difference."

"We just met and we got married."

Hell, she had him there. "But both of us are the settling down kind. We make promises we mean. Don't feel bad about those men passing over you for someone easier. And I don't mean to sound harsh toward your mom or sister, either. I'm sure they make the choices

84 | CORA SETON

that are right for them." Was he putting his foot in it? He had a feeling he needed to backtrack.

But before he could, Samantha said, "You're right. I don't want to judge how they are, but it's not for me, and the men who come around—they're not for me, either."

"Good, because you're taken." He meant it, too—even if he did sound like a Neanderthal.

Samantha smiled. "I'm glad."

Time to kiss her again. Harris might not have a way with words, but he didn't need to explain what he wanted. He just needed to touch her. He set his drink aside and began to pack away the food and trash. Samantha joined in, and when they were done, and the blanket between them was clear, Harris moved closer, lifted her into his lap and pressed his mouth to hers.

Samantha eagerly kissed him back. Her skirt spilled over their legs and when she leaned into him, her bodice barely contained her breasts. Harris had been looking at those breasts all morning, wondering what they'd feel like in his hands, but the time wasn't right for that yet.

First they needed to get to know each other. He brushed his mouth over hers, tasting her sweetness and the tang of champagne. He wasn't satisfied with such chaste kisses, though, so he slid his hand up her back to cup her neck, pulled her closer and deepened the encounter. She braced her hands on his shoulders and met his ardor with her own, wordlessly encouraging him when she tightened her fingers over his muscles and pressed her breasts against his chest.

When he'd drunk his fill of her mouth, he moved to kiss her neck, down under her ear to her shoulder and then slid lower across her collarbone and dipped down into the soft valley between her breasts.

Samantha sighed and leaned closer. Did she want more?

He did.

He replaced his mouth with one hand and slid his knuckles up and along the edge of her bodice, dipping his fingers gently underneath it to brush her breast. Her intake of breath brought her nipple within reach and he allowed a finger to trail across its tight bud.

Samantha arched back and Harris understood what she wanted. He wanted it, too, but they needed to go slow. Today was only the beginning of their time together and while his body was ready for anything, he knew that moving too fast could backfire.

He gently laid her down on the blanket, slid a hand underneath her bodice and lifted her breast free. As he bent down to take her nipple into his mouth, Samantha moaned, and the sound stirred the desire that was already threatening to overwhelm him.

It was hard to remember they needed to take it slowly when she arched back farther to press her breast into his mouth. Harris decided to follow his instincts and he soon lost himself in the texture of her tight nipple and soft breast. When he'd lavished enough attention on one, he switched to the other side. With every moan and movement, Samantha was turning him on even more. He ached to be able to feel every part of

her, but he knew he had to get himself under control.

Samantha opened her eyes as if she'd heard the debate he was having in his head. She reached up to trail a finger over his jaw. Harris had grown lax about shaving over the last few weeks and he wondered if she minded. Not if her expression was anything to go by. She looked as if she wanted to touch him as much as he wanted to touch her. Harris had to shift to make himself more comfortable.

"I…" Samantha trailed off.

"What?" He ducked down and kissed her pert nipple. He couldn't help himself.

"I want you. Is that bad? It's crazy, right?"

"No, it's not bad. Or crazy." Harris lifted her hands over her head and linked his fingers with hers, the wool blanket rough against them. "I want you, too. But I don't want to blow this, so let's take it one step at a time."

"I suppose you're right," she said, but the way she shifted underneath him told him she wanted more.

He did, too. That didn't change their circumstances, though.

"We'll get there. Soon. But you have to be sure of me first. Maybe you're swept up in the romance of what we just did."

"Harris, look at me."

He already was. He liked the way she used his given name instead of Hawk. Hawk felt too contrived. Too obvious, given he was a sniper. Harris was who he was when he wasn't playing hero.

"I married you," Samantha said. "I'm not going to change my mind."

With a groan, Harris bent to kiss her, all his desire flooding through him like a warm wave. He wanted to make love to her so badly he ached with it, but like he'd said, he didn't want to ruin what they had. His body tried to overrule his mind, but Harris hadn't spent a lifetime watching the horizon, anticipating trouble, narrowing in on a target not to see all the potential pitfalls in making love to Samantha right now.

"There's nothing I want more than to bury myself deep inside you," he told her. "If I didn't think you'd regret it later, I would."

"I won't regret it."

"Samantha." He brushed a strand of her hair from her eyes. "You've known me only for a morning." When her expression fell, he swooped down and stole another kiss. "I swear, the next time you ask me I'll say yes, no matter what. When you're ready—really ready— I'll be there." He chuckled. "Any time."

That got a small smile from her. "Okay."

"Meanwhile, there are other things we can do."

Her eyebrows lifted. "Like…?"

He eased backward and began to fold her skirt up, exposing her legs. Silky white stockings were held up by garters and Harris nearly lost his resolve to take things slow. When he exposed the slip of fabric that formed her panties, he decided he'd played it safe enough for both of them. Time to show her how much he wanted her.

88 | CORA SETON

He snapped the thin satin bands of her panties in two, drew them off her and tossed them aside. He pushed her legs apart and bent to kiss one smooth, sexy thigh.

Samantha gasped, and twisted her hands into the fabric of his shirt as he slid his mouth over her skin to her hot, wet core. She was slick with need and as he teased and tasted her, her restless movements and small sounds let him know how much she liked what he was doing.

He slid his hands under her thighs and lifted her for better access. He knew it wasn't the same as making love, but he couldn't think of a more intimate experience to share. She opened to him willingly and her trust in him only bound his heart more tightly to hers. He'd been given a gift he'd never looked for—something he'd wanted for as long as he could remember, but always seemed out of reach. He'd do anything for Samantha, he decided. He'd wait as long as she wanted—or he'd take her now, today, if that's what she asked of him. He'd do more than that. He'd get to know her every wish and desire and build a life with her that fulfilled them.

When Samantha came, she lifted her hips, dug her hands into his shoulders and cried out. Harris rode the wave with her, hanging on to his self-control... barely. He told himself he'd jump into Pittance Creek when they got home if that's what it took to calm his libido.

But when Samantha had shuddered to a stop, and caught her breath, she tugged on his shoulders to bring

him closer to her. Pressing him down beside her, she turned to fumble with his belt. "My turn."

"Sam—"

"Listen, Mr. Navy SEAL, you don't get to call all the shots in this marriage."

Surprised, he let her push him over on his back. "I don't?"

"No." She knelt above him and got to work on his belt buckle again. When it came free, she slipped her fingers under his waistband and undid the button of his jeans. When she undid his zipper, he let her tug down his jeans and boxer briefs, all the while wondering if this was right.

It felt right.

"Samantha—"

She gave a sigh of exasperation, slid him free, bent down and took him in her mouth.

Harris made a strangled noise and gave up. Her mouth was so warm and wet, her tongue sliding over his skin made every nerve in his body jump with want and need. He clutched the blanket and twisted it in his hands, needing every bit of his self-restraint to hold back.

It was a lost cause.

Cradling him in her hands, caressing him with her tongue and lips, Samantha soon brought him to the edge of a precipice he couldn't make it back from.

He tried to warn her. Tried to shift away, unsure how far she wanted to take this, but Samantha took him deep in her mouth and there was no way he could stop

himself from letting go.

He'd never experienced anything as erotic as giving in to her. Trusting her to make up her mind for herself what she did and didn't want to do. In that moment, he wondered if he'd kept them from something special by not making love to her when she asked him to. Should he have taken her at her word instead?

This was no time for deep thoughts, though. When he came, shudders wracked his body until he collapsed back and stared at the deep blue sky far above him. "Samantha," was all he could say. She released him after a final caress or two, lay down beside him and snuggled up under his arm. Harris held her, still staring up at that unknowable sky. How could he feel so comfortable with a woman he'd just met? How could his life have changed so inexorably in so few hours?

Is this where I'm supposed to be? He wasn't sure who his question was aimed at—or who could answer it.

Still, the answer came loud and clear in his mind.

Yes.

He turned to Samantha. She was smiling at him, examining him with as much interest as he'd been examining the sky moments before.

"I like you," she said.

Something eased a little in his heart. Something that had been tight and hard for far too long.

"I like you, too."

"HOW DO I look?" Sam asked an hour later when Harris turned the truck onto the rutted dirt lane leading into

the ranch. With her gown smoothed back into place and a new pair of panties fetched from her bags—she'd stashed the ones he'd ripped deep in her suitcase—she felt more or less presentable, although she was sure anyone who looked closely could tell from her flushed face what she and Harris had been doing. She'd been reluctant to leave their peaceful sanctuary, and had a feeling she'd count those first few hours alone with Harris as some of the happiest of her life, but it was time for them to return to Base Camp and face the music—and the cameras.

Harris had told her a little about what life was like being filmed twenty-four/seven. She wasn't looking forward to it, but she felt she could handle the attention, although she dreaded to think what her family would say when they first saw her on-screen.

She was far more concerned with how she'd fit in with the other members of Base Camp. As she'd said to Harris, it was like meeting a bunch of movie stars— movie stars with a shared past she hadn't been part of. She wasn't sure she'd fit in.

And then there was Curtis. She told herself the man hadn't bothered to get up and fetch her from the airport. He probably wouldn't care that she'd married Harris—and if he did, it was his own fault.

But as they drove, Harris's silence unnerved her and she had a feeling he was thinking of the other man. Samantha hoped he was blowing this out of proportion. After all, Curtis had been relieved not to have to marry right away. Now he had time to find his own wife.

By the time they arrived, however, Sam was as nervous as she'd been when she got off the plane. The clouds were even darker now, but Harris had been right; so far it hadn't rained. A cluster of men and women were gathered near an empty fire pit chatting. The men wore work clothes, but the women were dressed in the same kind of Regency finery that Sam had seen them wearing on television. A sense of unreality washed over her. It was as if she had stepped into a movie, not just driven up to a ranch. Harris climbed out of the truck first. Daisy followed, barking excitedly. Sam meant to follow them, but she couldn't seem to get her limbs to move. Harris came around the truck to open her door and Sam climbed out gingerly, arranging the skirts of her wedding gown. Already, people were beginning to turn their way, gesture toward them, point at Sam's dress and the dog, and come to meet them. Cameramen followed in a throng, and Sam froze, intimidated by the idea that everything she did from now on would be filmed.

"Where have you been?" a man Sam recognized as Boone Rudman asked.

"I went to the airport," Harris said.

Boone nodded at Sam. "The backup bride."

"That's right," Harris said.

"I went to get her, too, but she was already gone. I thought maybe she'd changed her mind."

"Nope."

Sam wasn't sure what to make of the confrontation between the two men. Neither seemed angry, but there

was definitely tension between them. Boone looked beyond Harris at her. When he moved to greet her, Harris stepped in his way.

Boone hesitated, as if waiting for Harris to say more. When he didn't, he asked, "You must've picked her up hours ago. What have you been doing ever since?"

"Marrying her."

Boone stiffened. "Marrying her? What do you mean marrying her? She's Curtis's bride."

"Not anymore," Harris said.

The gathered crowd went quiet. Sam clutched her hands before her, her palms damp. She looked for a friendly face among them, but only saw confusion and concern. They were all just like they had been on-screen, the men weathered warriors, the women beautiful in their Regency gowns. Except instead of welcoming her with open arms, they were staring at her like she'd dropped in uninvited to a party.

Harris stepped back to take her arm and lead her forward. "Everyone, meet my wife, Samantha Smith… Samantha Wentworth now."

Samantha tried to smile, but she was afraid it wasn't convincing. The silence that had settled over the crowd deepened and just as she became afraid it would never end, a woman stepped forward, her bonnet framing her sweet face, her bodice encasing a beautiful figure. She wore a green gown that set off her fair features. Savannah Edwards, if Sam wasn't mistaken.

"Welcome to Base Camp," she said. "We're glad to have you."

Sam relaxed just a bit. Maybe everything would be all right after all.

But even as she thought this, another woman pushed forward. Unlike the beauty in the green gown, she was dressed all in black in modern clothes, and Sam wondered how she could negotiate the rough ground in her high heels. She recognized this woman, too. Renata Ludlow. She was the one who always conducted the interviews on the show, and her piercing questions often reduced the men and women of Base Camp to stuttering answers.

"Say that again," Renata demanded of Harris.

"This is my wife, Samantha Wentworth." Harris stared her down, but Renata didn't even blink.

"You are mistaken; this is not your wife. For one thing, you haven't married her. For another thing, Boone's right, Samantha is Curtis's bride. Curtis will romance her for the next forty days, and then he will marry her in front of the cameras, so our viewing audience can see every minute of the ceremony, just as they've been promised. Whatever foolishness you two have concocted between you is over right now."

"There's no mistake about it." Harris stepped closer to Renata, looming over her. "And you'll stay away from her if you know what's good for you."

"You'll stay away from her, if you know what's good for you," Renata parroted in a squeaky voice. "You might think this is all a big game, but it's not, and I have the contracts to prove it. You don't get to marry until you draw the short straw, which you haven't. You definitely

don't get to marry the bride who's been promised to another man. Curtis drew the short straw, he's going to marry next. And he's going to marry *her*."

"Over my dead body."

Renata was as formidable in person as she was on-screen. Sam was glad she was addressing Harris and not her. Just when Sam thought it couldn't get any worse, a man pushed his way through the crowd to stand before them. Curtis Lloyd. She recognized him from the show. She remembered how Boone told her it wasn't fair to demand Clay and Nora decide their future while Nora was recovering from the attack. It wasn't fair to demand that Clay marry somebody else and live a life of regret because he couldn't wait for the woman he loved to heal. Curtis, who had drawn the short straw, had manfully agreed.

But he must have changed his mind about going through with it if he'd gotten so drunk last night he couldn't be bothered to come and pick her up this morning. She didn't blame him for wanting to choose his own bride. Still, it was strange to see him in real life and know if he hadn't slept in, she'd have married him today.

"What's all this?"

"Just introducing everybody to my bride," Harris said. "Curtis, meet Samantha Wentworth."

"Samantha?" Curtis looked her over, took in her wedding dress, and understanding dawned. "Samantha?" he said again. "Wait...you married my bride?"

"I married *my* bride. You said you weren't interested.

You hit on every woman you saw at the wedding last night. You couldn't be bothered to get up and go to the airport to meet her this morning. You made it perfectly clear that you didn't want to marry Sam. So I stepped in and married her for you."

Curtis sputtered. "But... but... I just wanted a chance to meet her first. To—" He broke off, color rising in his handsome face. "Damn it, Harris!"

"You didn't want her," Harris said again.

"I didn't know she'd look like that!"

Samantha took a step back. If all Curtis cared about was her face and figure, she was glad he hadn't come to marry her this morning. The connection she shared with Harris went far deeper. At least, she thought it did.

"What's done is done." Harris's tone said it was his final word on the matter.

Renata and Curtis erupted simultaneously.

"You agreed to be filmed every moment for one year."

"I never even got to meet her!"

"You can't marry until I say you can marry," Renata said, stepping forward to waggle a finger in Harris's face.

"You can't run off and steal my bride before I even have a say," Curtis added.

Sam took another step back. She didn't like this one bit. In her fantasies about this moment, she'd arrived at Base Camp to a welcome of open arms and instant camaraderie.

"Enough. Enough!" Boone stuck two fingers in his

mouth and whistled. The shrill noise pierced through the commotion, and everyone fell silent. "Harris, Samantha, Curtis, Renata, in the bunkhouse, now. Let's sort this out."

Harris took her hand and led the way, not waiting to see if the others followed. Sam followed reluctantly, feeling like she'd stepped into a hornet's nest. She wasn't sure how to behave. Should she speak up and assert her right to be with Harris? Or keep quiet and let Harris stand up for both of them? He knew the others, after all. She didn't.

Looking back, she saw Daisy trot over to inspect Curtis and lick his hand. Sam stifled the urge to go and get the dog. Didn't Daisy know she was consorting with the enemy? This was the man who'd hit on every woman he met last night because he was so relieved he didn't have to marry her. The man who couldn't be bothered to get out of bed this morning and tell her himself he'd changed his mind. Daisy obviously didn't care about that. She licked Curtis's hand again and stuck close to him.

Inside the building, Sam took in the rough surroundings, just like she'd seen on-screen. The large room had a battered wooden floor, and metal folding chairs were scattered around. A wooden desk sat in one corner, piled with paperwork and a laptop. Other than that the room was empty.

Harris grabbed two chairs and moved them close together. He waved Samantha into one of them and she sat down carefully, although her dress had already taken

a beating. Curtis paced the room before finally taking a seat at Boone's command, but Renata refused. She stood there, toe tapping, arms folded over her chest, as several crew members followed them in and set up to record the scene.

"Well, this is a cluster fuck," she said. "Fulsom isn't going to be pleased."

"We can figure this out," Boone said reasonably.

"There's nothing to figure out," Harris said. "Sam and I are married, end of story."

"Like hell you are," Curtis said. "That's my wife,"

"She's *my* wife," Harris asserted. "Nothing you can say or do is going to change that."

"Don't be so sure about that," Renata said. "You haven't shown us any paperwork. How did you manage to get married anyway?"

Samantha shifted in her seat, uncomfortable with the way that they were all talking about her as if she wasn't there. She wanted to speak up, but she was all too aware of the cameras filming everything. This was as bad as band meetings back on the bus, but at least there she hadn't been filmed. Here, every word she spoke would be captured for posterity.

"We went to the Heaven's Gate Chapel," Harris said.

"How the hell do you even know about that place?" Boone asked him.

"Seen it driving to Bozeman," Harris said. "They did a real fine job of the wedding."

"Which we have no way of corroborating, since

none of us were there to film it," Renata exploded. "I'll remind you again, your contract says that we have the right to film you whenever you are awake and outside your tent. This is in direct violation of that contract, which means that anything you did during the period in which you left Base Camp is null and void."

"That's not the way it works," Harris said, keeping his cool. Samantha wondered how he was doing it. She was beginning to lose her temper.

"That's right," Curtis said. "Your marriage isn't valid. It's like it never happened."

"It happened," Harris asserted, before Sam could do it herself. "Nothing you can do will change that now." He pulled out his wallet, fished out a copy of the paperwork they'd been given back at the chapel and handed it over.

Renata snatched it from his fingers, pulled out a slim, black cell phone, tapped at it and lifted it to her ear. "Get me Fulsom," she said, unfolding the paperwork. She surveyed Harris and Samantha. "Fulsom has the resources to change anything he wants to. Your marriage will be annulled within the day. Then we'll start over and do this right."

Harris stood up. "You can't annul anything. What's done is done. We're married."

Renata looked at him coolly. "Are you telling me you two have consummated this marriage?"

Harris swallowed. Samantha lowered her head, unable to look at anybody, sure her cheeks were red with heat. They hadn't consummated the marriage, but they'd

come incredibly close. Did that count? Should she speak up?

"Not... not exactly," Harris admitted.

"Not *exactly*?" Curtis sputtered, leaping to his feet. "What the hell does that mean? If you put your hands on my bride, you're going to pay."

"I'm not your bride!"

Everyone stared at Sam as if Daisy was the one who'd spoken. "I'm not. I'm his." She pointed to Harris.

"Just how far did you two go?" Renata demanded of them, still pressing the phone to her ear.

Clutching at the folds of her dress, not sure when she'd ever felt so humiliated, Sam found herself at a loss for words.

"Far enough." Harris glared at Curtis.

Curtis glared back. "That's it. You get this marriage annulled," he demanded of Renata. "You get this joker out of here. That's my bride, and he doesn't get to touch her."

"I get to touch her anytime I want," Harris said. "She's my wife."

"She's not your wife until I say she's your wife," Renata said.

"She's not ever going to be your wife," Curtis roared.

Harris shoved him. Curtis shoved him back. Boone stepped between the two men, just as it seemed they were about to come to blows. "Settle down."

"Fulsom? It's Renata." She turned her back on the

rest of them as if the scuffle didn't concern her in the least. Harris and Curtis backed away from each other. "We've got a problem. Harris went off half-cocked and married Curtis's backup bride." She listened for a moment. "That's right. Um-hm. Yes. Yes, you read my mind. Of course. I like that idea. I'll take care of it." She ended the call and put the phone in her pocket. "Okay, that's that. Harris, I understand you feel you have a prior claim. So does Curtis. Luckily, we have forty days until the next wedding is scheduled to occur. You and Curtis can both try to woo Samantha. Samantha will choose her groom—but not until a month from now. August tenth is when she'll announce her engagement. That's when she'll name her husband-to-be. And not before then." She turned to Samantha. "You got that?"

"No." Samantha finally found her voice again. "No, I don't understand it at all. I married this man today. I pledged my life to him. I intend to keep my promise. I don't want to be courted. I don't want to pretend that I'm not already married to Harris. I want to be his wife."

Curtis strode off a few paces, spun around and came back again. "This is bullshit. I don't know what you did to her out there, but whatever it is, it sucks. You had no right to pick up my bride. You had no right to marry her. I think you should have to leave the show."

"No one's leaving the show," Boone said. He turned to Renata. "If these two *have* fallen for each other, and gotten married, then what's really the harm of it? We can re-create the wedding. We can move on to the next

couple."

Renata was already shaking her head. "Absolutely not. We promised the viewers ten romances and ten marriages. It's bad enough that they didn't get to see you woo your wife. We're not going to stiff them on any of the other romances. We will annul the marriage. Harris and Samantha will start over. Curtis will get his shot, too—I'll make sure of that. It's only fair to him, and it's only fair to the viewers."

"Fuck that," Harris ground out. "I'm not going to stand around and watch Curtis go after my girl."

"You don't have a choice," Renata said.

"Like hell I don't," Harris said. "I'll take her and leave."

Sam's breath hitched. She wanted to be with Harris—but she didn't want to leave. She had done all this to be part of a community—not to run away from one.

Renata glared at him. "You'll take her and leave?" she repeated, putting her hands on her hips. "Fine. Go right ahead. We'll just shut this whole thing down right now. You'll all lose, and you know the consequences of that. The developer Fulsom has on standby will win. I've got Montague on speed-dial. Give me an hour and I'll have him here with his machinery. He'll tear down the bunkhouse and the manor, flatten the tiny houses you've built so far and start the prep-work for the 325 houses he wants to build on this property. I'll film all of it for the final episode of *Base Camp*. Remember the contract you signed at the beginning of the show? If the ten of you and your wives don't meet the conditions,

the game is over, and this ranch becomes a housing tract."

Harris stared at her, wet his lips, opened his mouth to speak and shut it again.

"You're not serious," Boone said.

"Try me," Renata said. "We're going to begin filming in five minutes. We'll either re-film Samantha's arrival at Base Camp, Curtis's reaction to meeting his bride and Harris realizing she's the woman he's always dreamed of—or we'll film the scene in which you all decide your free will is more important than your commitments, more important than the television show and more important than this community. We'll show the American viewing public all the reasons they can't band together to create a better life. Which do you want it to be? I'll be waiting outside for your answer."

She strode out of the building, the tapping of her high heels loud on the wooden floorboards.

Boone scrubbed a hand over his jaw. "Sit down," he told Curtis and Harris.

To Sam's surprise, they did.

"It's like Renata said," Boone told Harris. "We don't have a choice. We're in this thing together, and we have to see it through. Curtis, you made it clear to everyone last night you weren't interested in marrying a woman you hadn't known and chosen for yourself. You can't blame Harris for stepping in and taking the opportunity you turned down. You might regret your decision, but that doesn't mean you get to ruin what Harris and Samantha have found between them. On the other

hand, Harris, you and Samantha broke the rules. You knew when you took her to the chapel to get married that you were violating your contract and the spirit in which our community is formed. Your rush to the altar shows that you knew damn well you weren't doing the right thing."

"The hell with that," Harris said.

Boone interrupted him. "We don't have time for a debate. We're going to do what Renata said. We really don't have a choice. Samantha will get a tent and bunk down with the other women. She'll spend her days working on the B&B. She'll also help out with the carpentry, and during that time she'll get the chance to know both you and Curtis better. You both will get the opportunity to date her—but neither one of you will lay a hand on her until she's had the chance to make up her mind. You heard Renata; on August tenth, Samantha will tell us who she's chosen. The wedding will take place on August twentieth, as scheduled. Until then, there will be no physical contact among any of you."

"That's ridiculous," Harris said. "She's my wife."

"Are you willing to take all of us down with you?" Boone asked. "Because that's what it means if you balk at this. Base Camp will be history. All of our plans will be for nothing. My wife will lose the home she loves, the home she fought for. We'll all lose everything we fought for." Boone rubbed his jaw again. "Harris, if you and Samantha are meant to be together, you'll be together. You'll wed again on August twentieth with all of our blessings. You owe Samantha a chance to get to

know the man she was intended for. You owe it to Curtis to give him the chance to prove to her that he's the man for her. Time will tell how this really should sort out. Meanwhile, you need to abide by your contract to Renata and Fulsom—and all of us. That's what being a part of this group means."

"What about me?" Samantha asked when he finally took a breath. "Doesn't anybody care what I want?"

"Of course we do." Boone softened. "You've got to understand; being part of Base Camp isn't like regular life. It's more like serving in the military, where you've given over part of your independence in order to belong to a group that has a higher purpose. Harris and Curtis both knew that when they signed up. I explained it to you, too, when you expressed your interest in being the backup bride. You said you understood that. Here's your chance to show me you do."

Samantha bit back the words that she'd intended to say, because what Boone said was right. She had told him she understood what being part of Base Camp would be like. She'd been wrong, but that wasn't Boone's fault. Belonging to a tight-knit group like the one here, and being part of a grander vision, was what had attracted her in the first place. She turned to Harris. "What do you want to do?"

Harris hesitated a long time, and she could almost see the thoughts churning inside his mind. "Like all the other men here, I made a promise to help make this a better world for everyone. I believe in what we're trying to do here. Not all this—" he gestured to the film crew

"—but what's outside. The tiny houses, the green energy we're tapping. Sharing our resources. Living small on the land. But then I made a promise to you, too—that we'd be together forever. I married you in good faith, and I meant everything I said." His gaze bore into hers, and Samantha knew what he was asking, knew what he wanted her to understand. He wanted to be with her, she didn't doubt that for a moment, but he also wanted to carry through on the promises he'd made to these men. He wanted to keep his word, even if the promises he'd made were turning out to contradict each other. She wouldn't respect him if he was any other way.

That didn't make this any easier.

"I guess… I guess I can abide by what Boone has said," she began uncertainly. "But I need to be clear." She turned to Curtis. "My heart is engaged. I said my wedding vows and I meant them. I'll do what I have to, because I understand how much Base Camp means to you, and I want it to mean that much to me. I'll gladly work on the houses and on running the bed-and-breakfast. I'll take the time to get to know you, but it would be unfair to pretend that Harris doesn't already have my heart."

Curtis took a step closer to her. "Harris picked you up at the airport, he swept you off your feet, he took you to a chapel and married you. That doesn't mean either one of you knows the first thing about each other. As far as I'm concerned, he and I are starting off on even ground. If you're asking me to take your wedding into consideration, I'm not going to do that, because

that would be losing before I even began to fight. And I'm going to fight for you, Samantha. You were supposed to be my bride, and I deserve a chance."

Uneasiness filled her at his words. He was right; she didn't know much about Harris, but every instinct told her he was the one for her. She had ached for him to make love to her earlier. If he had been willing, she would have been, too. She didn't think she could backtrack from that enough to give Curtis a fair shake, but she would abide by the rules of this game, even if she didn't like them.

"I've agreed to do what you're asking," she said. "I'll do my best to be fair. That's all I can say."

Harris reached for her, but Curtis lunged forward and knocked his hand away. "You don't get to touch her. Those are the rules. You heard Renata."

"For God's sake, I just married her."

"Curtis, back off," Boone said. "All right, you two. One last kiss. Then everything starts over."

Samantha swallowed hard and licked her lips. Without wasting another second, Harris tugged her close and kissed her, hard, a kiss that went on and on until Boone cleared his throat.

"That'll do," he said.

Samantha pulled away from Harris reluctantly. She wanted him more than ever, and the thought of living at Base Camp and not being with him filled her with impatience. Curtis's face looked like thunder, and Boone stepped in again.

"For all intents and purposes the two of you have

just met," he said to Sam and Harris. "I know it's difficult, but it's what you have to do. Let's go out there and show Renata we're not even remotely ready to shut this all down. Harris, you first."

And that was that. Her marriage was over just as quickly as it had begun. Samantha felt numb as she filed out with the rest of them and faced Renata. She looked for Daisy, but the dog kept close by Curtis's side.

"Samantha, Harris," Renata said. "Get back in the truck, and pretend you've just driven up. Harris, you've picked up Samantha from the airport, because Curtis was too hung over to get up and do it himself. There are sparks of interest between you and Samantha. That's obvious to anybody who's looking at you. But Samantha is here to marry Curtis in forty days. You know you have to step back and let this happen, but you don't want to. You're in turmoil. Curtis, you are here to greet your bride, you're sheepish that you slept in and you are unsure you even want to marry her. But now that you've seen her, you know that she's the girl for you. We'll roll cameras and see what happens. You both know the rules."

Samantha swallowed hard, and turned back to the truck.

"Wait. Hold on," Renata said suddenly. "For crying out loud, she can't be wearing that wedding gown. She has to change."

The whole crowd waited for Samantha as she fumbled with her suitcase in the back of the rental truck, pulled out an outfit, headed back into the bunkhouse

bathroom and changed, her hands shaking all the while. She didn't want to do this. She wanted her fairy tale to continue. Why did Renata—and Curtis—need to ruin it all?

She told herself this was only temporary. It was acting, as if she was in a play. She could stand forty days of anything—hadn't she stood twenty-seven years on a bus?

But she'd been so close to what she wanted. It hurt so bad to have it ripped away again. When she was back in her plain navy skirt and white shirt, she looked as blank and plain as she felt. The fairy tale was over. She was Samantha Smith again—not Samantha Wentworth.

When she returned, Harris silently held the truck's door open for her. "Come on, Daisy," he called, but Daisy, standing next to Curtis, didn't move.

Curtis reached down absently to pat her head. She licked his hand and sat down.

"Daisy," Harris tried again.

"Think she wants to stay with me."

Sam, hearing the challenge in Curtis's voice, shut her eyes. "Daisy," she called.

The dog didn't move.

"Forget the dog," Renata said. "Move it; we don't have all day."

Harris closed Sam's door, went around the truck, got in on his side and shut his door, too.

"Here. I guess you'd better hold on to these for safe keeping." Sam reluctantly slid off the two rings he'd put on her finger only hours before. She knew she was

losing far more than a couple of pieces of jewelry, and she blinked against the tears stinging her eyes.

"I'm sorry. I'm more sorry than I can say." He took the rings she held out to him, slid his own wedding ring off his finger and put all of them into his shirt pocket before taking her hand and squeezing it. "No matter what they say, no matter what they do, no matter what *we* have to do over the next forty days, we're married. I believe that. Nothing can change it."

"I'll spend the next forty days learning everything that I can about you and about Base Camp," Samantha promised. "I'll become the best wife I can be for you, because this is where we're going to spend our future, and I need to know everything about it. It's going to be hard," she added. "Hard not to touch you."

He squeezed her hand again. "I know. Real hard. Let's get started, so we can get to the end of it."

She nodded. "I'm ready." She wasn't, though. She wasn't ready for any of this. She'd wanted to be by Harris's side. She'd pictured the two of them living in a tent together until their tiny house was ready for them. Pictured them moving in and creating a life.

Sleeping with Harris tonight.

Now all of that would have to wait. Could she last for forty days?

She was about to find out.

CHAPTER FIVE

A S HARRIS CLIMBED out of the truck again a minute later, opened Sam's door and helped her out, he knew everything had changed. As much as he and Samantha assured each other they could get through the next forty days, he knew that would be more difficult than Samantha realized. For one thing, she would have to get used to all the different personalities of the people already at Base Camp. She would become part of the tensions and conflicts that could crop up at any time when you had a number of adults living in the same place. For another, Curtis would do his best to showcase each and every one of Harris's faults. And God knew Harris had plenty of those. He had a tendency to hold back and stay separate in group situations, while Curtis's jovial, larger-than-life personality made him welcome wherever he went.

Harris told himself he would have to change. He would have to put himself out there so Samantha knew he really wanted her. He would have to take part in group activities, linger around the campfires at night and

volunteer to help out when the women had guests at their B&B.

As they stepped in front of the cameras, he saw a grin playing around Renata's mouth, and realized that far from being angry, she was enjoying all of this. And why not? Controversy was what made the show interesting to its viewers. Two men vying over one woman would make for great television. Didn't Renata know that they were all human beings, and they all had feelings that would suffer in the process? If so, she didn't seem to care.

As for the viewers, they were another loose cannon in the situation. Renata and her people loved the concept of interactive television. They constantly updated the website with information, quizzes and games. She would definitely exploit this competition between him and Curtis. In fact, she would play that for all it was worth. He needed to warn Samantha that the director would make this even more difficult than it needed to be. She would probably set up situations that threw them together in awkward pairings. She would do whatever it took to shake up the bad blood between him and Curtis, and to give Samantha all the opportunity she needed to change her mind and fall for the other man.

With the cameras rolling, Boone strode forward again, and Harris was struck at how comfortable they'd all become with being filmed. Boone was as confident as any television show actor when he raised a hand and called out, "Welcome, Samantha."

A SEAL'S PLEDGE | 113

Samantha moved to greet him as if she were in a dream, and they shook hands. "Hello," she said awkwardly. "Thanks for having me."

"Not at all, thank you for joining us. We're always looking for a few good men and women to build our community. We hope you'll soon feel like you're one of us."

Samantha looked as if she didn't believe that were likely, but Boone was already turning to Harris. "Thanks for picking Samantha up, Harris. I appreciate you running out to the airport early, when the rest of us were still sleeping."

"My pleasure," Harris said. When Renata smiled and nodded in approval, he cursed himself for not finding a way out of this.

"Curtis? Curtis," Boone called heartily. "Come look who's here. It's your bride."

Out of the corner of his eye, Harris saw Samantha frown. It was all too clear to him, and anyone else watching, she wasn't happy to see her supposed intended. Renata was certainly getting what she wanted here. Curtis strode up, Daisy trotting by his side, but he didn't just greet Samantha, he pulled her into a bear hug, one arm around her waist, one hand cradling the nape of her neck, as if he meant to kiss her.

Harris couldn't help himself; he surged forward, pushed between them and shoved Curtis away. "You're not allowed to touch her," he said. "The next time you do, my fist is going to have a talk with your face." He turned to Renata. "That's right, isn't it? Those are the

rules you laid out."

"Cut, cut! For God's sake, you can't talk to me like I'm on screen," Renata said. "I can't be the one to explain why the two of you aren't going to touch her. So we're going to use what we filmed right up until the moment you started talking, Harris. We'll cut the rest of it out, and you two are going to confront each other. Harris, you're going to admit that you've fallen for Samantha, and you want her for your own. Curtis, you're going to be upset, but you're not going to fight him. The two of you are going to talk it out until you come to an understanding. Boone, maybe you'll step in and help sort it out. Maybe some of the rest of you will step in and help, too. The end result is that both of you men will agree to the rules. And you, too, Samantha."

Harris fumed as Renata moved around putting all of them in their places again. Then she made a motion to the cameramen, who had kept filming. "Okay, we're all set up. Keep going."

There was an awkward pause during which Samantha stood to one side, and the two men faced off as if Harris had just pushed Curtis. Harris contemplated decking Curtis, but then they'd have to do another take.

"What the fuck?" Curtis said.

"I don't want you to touch her," Harris said. He didn't think he'd ever felt more wooden while being filmed.

"Why the fuck not?" Curtis demanded. "She's my bride."

"Because I want to marry her. You didn't even

bother to get up and go to the airport to pick her up. Samantha and I spent the morning together. We got to know each other. I'm the man for her." He wouldn't be taking home an Oscar for his performance anytime soon, Harris thought.

"To hell with that," Curtis said. "If you spent time with her, you took advantage of a situation, and that's not right. Samantha came here to marry me, and I intend to see it through."

Boone stepped in, just as Renata had suggested. "Neither one of you knows Samantha, and Samantha hasn't had the time to get to know either one of you, either. There's an obvious solution for this."

Both men faced him. "Yeah?" Curtis asked. "What's that?"

"We give Samantha time enough to get to know both of you. During that time, neither one of you gets to put the moves on her. No kissing, no touching, no nothing."

"For how long?" Harris found himself asking, as if he didn't already know, as if he wasn't playing a game. It disturbed him how easily he could fall in with this, even though the whole thing made him furious. Still, what were his options? If he didn't follow the rules, he could ruin things not just for himself, but for everyone.

"Someone has to marry in forty days, so we'll give it one month. Thirty days from now, Samantha will announce on the show who she's going to marry. Until then, nobody touches, nobody kisses. Your courtship will have to take place with words and actions, not

physical displays of affection. It's a civilized way to figure this out, and I expect all of you to abide by it. Do you understand me?" He included Samantha in his question.

Samantha nodded. Harris waited for Curtis to react, but the other man only said, "I still say she's supposed to be *my* wife. I don't see why I should have to agree to this."

"Samantha and I already have a connection," Harris countered. "I think you should find a different bride."

"I've already told you both how it's going to be," Boone said. "Do we have an understanding or not? Shake on it."

The last thing Harris wanted to do was shake Curtis's hand, but he was all too aware of the cameras filming everything. Reluctantly, he reached out. Curtis grasped his palm, and shook, trying to crush Harris's hand in his. But Harris was strong enough to withstand that kind of attack. He gripped Curtis's hand with equal pressure and shook back.

"Enough." Boone sighed. "Samantha, I'm glad you're here. You're a brave woman for coming and agreeing to marry somebody so quickly, so the least we can do is to give you the time to get to know both Curtis and Harris and see which man suits you best before you make up your mind. For now, I'll hand you over to the other women. They can show you around and get you settled in your tent. Riley, you and the others can give her a tour of the manor, too, and make sure she has everything she needs. We'll all meet again at

dinnertime. Until then, you two men should get back to work. We've got houses to build, including the tiny house that Samantha will live in when she's chosen her man and married him."

The women closed ranks around Samantha, and the last Harris saw of her they were heading toward the women's side of the camp. He knew he would see her in a matter of hours, but Harris couldn't help feel he was already beginning to lose her. He knew Curtis could be a very stubborn man. Plus, the others in the community liked him. He was fun to be around. A joiner. Samantha was such a sunny, happy person. Wasn't it likely in the end she would be drawn to a man more like her?

Maybe. But Harris wasn't ready to call it quits.

He'd fallen in love with his wife in the few short hours they'd spent together.

It didn't matter if it made sense, it didn't matter if there hadn't been enough time for him to get to know her, it didn't matter that it was the most unreasonable thing he had ever done in his life. It was true. And nothing was going to change that.

He watched her go, then turned toward the building site where he worked each day with Curtis—and Clay, when the man wasn't on his honeymoon. Behind him, he heard Boone say, "Time to get to work. And I expect you to behave like a grown-up. No fighting."

"Harris is the one who should behave like a grown-up," Curtis said. "He's the one in the wrong here."

"I don't want to hear any more about it." Boone was getting angry. That was something. Harris had

begun to feel the whole situation was stacked against him. "If you wanted her so bad, you could've gotten your ass out of bed this morning and got to the airport to get her yourself. You know you told everybody you didn't want to marry her last night, so cut the crap and stop playing the victim. If anyone's the victim here, it's Samantha. She's the one who's going to have to deal with the two of you. Get to work."

"I've got to get this rental truck back," Harris told him when the other man approached.

"Jericho and I will handle it; I was about to head into town anyway. He'll give me a ride back," Boone said.

So much for putting some distance between him and Curtis. It took all Harris's strength of will to walk toward the building site instead of running after Sam, tossing her in the rental truck and getting the hell out of here. Just this morning, he'd been proud of being part of Base Camp. Now, he was finding its constraints hard to swallow.

He knew if he turned he'd find a camera crew following them, and he could only imagine what the rest of the afternoon would be like.

He heard a sharp bark and glanced over his shoulder. Daisy was trotting next to Curtis. That was one ungrateful dog, he thought, and couldn't help wonder if Daisy's disloyalty was a harbinger of things to come. The dog had taken one look at Curtis and decided he was a better master than Harris. Would Sam switch sides, too, when she got to know the man?

Harris stalked on, his mood growing worse and worse. Clay was the one who had designed the tiny homes, and was in charge of building them, but would be long gone on his honeymoon by now, and Harris knew what he had to do. At least Clay and Nora would be having a good day. They hadn't gone far; just to the Cruz ranch, where they'd stay at the guesthouse run by Autumn and Ethan Cruz. After all she'd been through, Nora had needed something familiar, easy and safe, and the Cruz guesthouse would offer them plenty of privacy—and wonderful food. Autumn was reputed to be a fantastic cook.

Ordinarily Harris didn't mind his days working on the houses, but while he was good at framing them up, it wasn't really his calling. He wasn't entirely sure what his calling was, but where Clay was drawn to think about elevations and angles, and the way people lived in their homes, Harris was drawn to the outdoors, to the wild—and to animals. He felt most at home when he was surrounded by nature. He wasn't sure how to turn that into a useful skill for the community, but he hadn't given up hope yet that his inclinations might not lead him to a job that made sense for all of them. Today he longed for nothing more than to grab a rifle and head out into the woods.

Instead, Harris surveyed the work they had done on the third tiny house. Like the others, it was built into the side of the hill, enclosed on the back and the sides by the grassy slope. It would eventually have a green roof that would give it even more protection from the

elements. The front walls would be made mostly of glass to let in the sun and warmth. The roof was pitched in such a way to let in any sun that a winter's day might offer, but block the too harsh rays of the summer afternoon. Harris admired the way that Clay had designed the homes, both for the way they used minimal energy, and for the way they suited people, even though their interior space was small.

The community was set up in such a way that most of the cooking was done for the group in the bunkhouse kitchen, rather than in their individual houses. The bunkhouse also offered space for large projects and group get-togethers. Homes were reserved for times when people needed a little space, or privacy. Thus, none of them needed to be too large.

When they began this house, it was with the intention it would soon be Curtis's. Now Harris found himself thinking of it as his. That was jumping the gun, though. Who knew how things would turn out? Still, Harris imagined maneuvering around the small space with Samantha. He imagined preparing a breakfast with her on a morning they wished to be alone. Relaxing in the afternoon on the small couch it would contain. Going to bed together in the loft bed at night. He touched a 2x4 that was framing in the front wall. Could this be his home?

"Don't even think about it." Curtis walked up behind him, and Daisy circled both of them. "That's my house, just like that's my wife back there. None of this is going to belong to you. In fact, when Samantha

chooses me, I think you should leave the community. None of us needs a sneak like you."

"We've got thirty days ahead of us like this," Harris said. "If we're fighting all the time, nothing's going to get done, and we've got a house to build. In fact, we've got eight houses to build. You can sit there jawing all you want, but I'm ready to work. Ready to build this community, because it's where I intend to stay."

"We'll see about that."

Harris ignored him, grateful the two of them tended to do different jobs. He worked on the framing, Curtis worked on the finish work. So while Harris got to the work at hand, Curtis gathered up some supplies and headed off toward one of the barns, where he would work on interior elements that would go into the house later.

Kai Green, passing by, stopped to ask Harris, "How are the two of you going to make it through the next thirty days without coming to blows?"

"Who says we are?"

HERE SHE WAS in Base Camp, Samantha thought, as she walked with the rest of the women toward the cluster of tents near one side of the bunkhouse. There was Riley, Boone's wife. And Savannah, who had been the one to greet her first. According to Sam's sister, sooner or later she would marry Jericho, a blond Navy SEAL who Samantha thought should've been an actor, not a warrior. Nora Ridgeway—Nora Pickett now—was gone on her honeymoon, of course. Avery Lightfoot rounded

out the original group of women who had come to Base Camp in order to get away from their modern lives. She had auburn hair and a lively expression, and Samantha had liked her the best when she had been watching the show.

Win Lisle had arrived in Base Camp a little later than the other women. She had attended the first Regency wedding that the women had thrown at their bed-and-breakfast, and had decided that she didn't want to leave. On the show, she was often seen flirting with Angus, a burly man with a Scottish accent. Samantha wasn't sure why they hadn't already married, except she supposed Angus hadn't drawn the short straw, so he wasn't allowed to yet. There wasn't any mystery about them, though. They were definitely an item. They were just biding their time.

"Here's where the women sleep, Samantha," Riley said. "And here comes Jericho with a tent. We'll help you set it up."

"Thanks."

Jericho placed the tent roll on the ground, and added to it a blowup mattress. "Do you want some help?" he asked, but he directed the question at Savannah, rather than Sam.

"That won't be necessary," Savannah said shortly.

Samantha wondered about the currents that were running through this conversation. She knew from watching the show that Jericho and Savannah had clicked at first, but then something had seemed to come between them. Maybe there had been a misunderstand-

ing, or maybe they had grown to learn they weren't as compatible as they first thought.

Samantha didn't want to think about that possibility.

"We'll take it from here," Riley said. "Then we'll need to find Samantha a dress. I had meant to set up a fitting for her, but in all the last minute fuss over Clay and Nora's wedding, I completely forgot about it. Who has the phone today? We should call over to Two Willows, and see if Alice has anything suitable for Samantha, at least to get her started."

When Jericho had gone again—reluctantly, Samantha thought—Avery leaned close and murmured, "Did you really marry Harris?"

Samantha nodded. "I really did. And I meant it, too." She was about to say she didn't appreciate having to play act for the next thirty days, when she glanced up and realized the cameras had followed them and they were being filmed even now. She supposed this was what it was going to be like for the next year. Always on film. Always having to watch what she said.

She began to have more of an appreciation for what these women had gone through already. But when she caught sight of Avery's pursed lips, she felt a surge of worry. What did the women think about her?

"I didn't think Curtis had any interest in marrying me," she explained in an undertone. "From what I understood, Harris had stepped in to fill his boots."

"I think that's because he liked what he saw," Avery murmured back. "Like Renata said, he saw his chance and he took it."

"Do you blame me for what I did?"

"No, it's just…" She fumbled to a stop and glanced at the cameras and the other women. Riley and Win were debating where to put Sam's tent, and the cameras seemed focused on them for now. "The thing is you originally signed on to the show to marry Clay, right?"

"That's right," Sam said slowly.

"Nora liked Clay right from the beginning, you know," Avery explained. "But she was so torn about leaving her students in the lurch, and she'd really been affected by that man who stalked her—even before he tried to kill her. Here she was, trying to heal—and you were ready to come and marry the man she loved. I mean, I don't blame you for being attracted to Clay—"

Sam knew she had to put an end to this fast. "I wasn't particularly attracted to him," she rushed to say. "But I understand why what I did seems callous to you. I guess—I didn't even think about Nora when I answered the ad," she admitted shamefacedly. "I thought about Base Camp—about how much I wanted to be a part of it. Doing something meaningful with my life— gaining a husband, a family—and friends," she added, although she saw that was in jeopardy now. "That's what I was after."

"I guess I can understand that," Avery said. "I think all of us were hoping that coming here would change our lives for the better."

Sam was grateful she seemed to understand.

"But Nora might not see it that way. She might see you as a threat."

"I'm not a threat. Not at all. Harris is the only man I'm interested in," Sam told her. "I wish I could be with him right now."

"You really fell for him that fast?"

"I think I'm as surprised as anyone," Sam said. "I mean, I thought I would have to work at relating to the man I married here. I thought it would be hard. Instead, I saw him at the airport waiting for me, and I just… I…" She didn't know how to explain it. "God, he's so… amazing."

Avery grinned. "You've got it bad for him, don't you?"

Sam nodded. "Will you help me? With Nora? I don't want her to feel weird around me."

"I'll try—but, you get it, right? Why it's a little uncomfortable? I mean, you flipped from Clay to Curtis to Harris really fast. You don't know Walker yet, for example—the man I'd like to marry. You don't know any of the other single men. What if you change your mind again?"

"I won't," Samantha insisted. She'd never been accused of being fickle before. Just the opposite. If she hadn't cared so much what the women thought of her, she'd have been hurt at the implication. As it was, she was terrified. These were supposed to be her new friends. If Avery didn't trust her, none of them would, and she'd be alone here.

She couldn't blame them if they thought she was a flake, given the situation. To an outsider, it must look like she'd bounced from man to man as if marriage

meant nothing more than a walk in the park.

It meant far more than that to her, though. How long would it take to prove that to everyone that was the case?

A month?

More?

What if she never belonged here at Base Camp?

When tears stung her eyes, Samantha decided she'd had enough. "I'm going to set up my tent, and then I'll come up to the manor," she told Avery.

She bent down, gingerly picked up the bag that held the tent, fumbled with the drawstring and worked to pull the tent free. As she spread it out, tears blurred her vision, and she wasn't sure she would be able to make out how to set it up by herself. But she wasn't going to ask for help, either. Not if all the women felt like Avery did.

Win said brightly, "I'll help Samantha. The rest of you head up to the manor, and call Alice about those clothes for Sam. We'll come up as soon as we're done with the tent."

"Sam—"

Samantha looked up when Avery said her name.

"I didn't..." She looked at the cameras and shrugged. "I just... Well, I'll see you later."

She left with the other women and Sam wondered if she'd already lost the chance to be friends with them. Win got to work helping Samantha set up the tent with little talk between them. When it was done, they fetched Samantha's bags together and put them inside.

"I'll blow up the air mattress later," Sam said. "I don't want to keep you from your work."

"I don't do too much up at the manor," Win said. "I spend most of my time in Base Camp, working in the gardens." She cocked her head. "Is everything all right?"

"It's just something Avery said. That Nora might not trust me right away since I signed up originally to marry Clay."

Win nodded. "Give the others some time to get used to you. They nearly lost their best friend recently. Even after Clay saved Nora, she was really...she was slipping away. It was like she couldn't come back from wherever that man had taken her. We were all terrified she might...well...give up—if not worse. Anyway, don't take it personally. Those three will do whatever it takes to make sure Nora doesn't get upset again. It might take time before they trust you all the way."

"What about you? Do you trust me?"

"Let's just say I know what it's like to find that the man you're engaged to isn't the man for you," Win said with a rueful grin. "They don't entirely trust me, either. I was engaged—and a real bitch—when I first came to Westfield. This place turned me around."

"On TV, Base Camp looks magical."

"Wait until you've spend a few weeks living in a tent. It's not quite so magical then." Win made a face.

"I've pretty much spent my entire life in a sleeper bus," Samantha told her. "I don't think it will be hard for me to adapt. Unless I get kicked off the island," she added, with a glance at the figures of the other women

climbing the hill to the manor.

"Give them time," Win said again. "They have to get to know you. And once Nora realizes you aren't after Clay, and Avery realizes that you don't want Walker, everything will be okay. I promise."

"As long as I can get through the next forty days."

Win looked at her curiously. "Harris really has you hooked, huh?"

Samantha nodded. "I'm afraid so."

Up at the manor fifteen minutes later, they found the others gathered in the kitchen, a room Sam recognized from the show. It was large with a high ceiling, and a long table in the middle of it, where the women had gathered. Savannah looked up when they walked in, and said, "Alice says to come over at three. She has several dresses you can try on, and then she'll do the alterations. I called Maude and James, as well, and James is coming at two-thirty in their barouche to pick us up."

Despite everything that had happened in the past hour, Samantha smiled. How many times had she seen the women riding with Maude or James in the barouche, pulled by a pair of horses? How many times had she seen similar scenes in Jane Austen movies? Now she would get her chance to experience it for herself.

CHAPTER SIX

THE AFTERNOON DIDN'T go smoothly. While Harris did his best to concentrate on his work, he couldn't stop thinking about Samantha and what she might be doing. Were the women being friendly to her? Would she feel comfortable with them? Was she rethinking the whole thing and wishing she could go home?

He'd known there would be trouble when they got back to Base Camp, but he'd hoped against hope things wouldn't be so awkward. In truth, Curtis's reaction didn't surprise him. As much as he'd said he wanted to pick his own bride, he couldn't have found a better candidate than Samantha. Maybe he could have found his own match online, or in town, but if that was the case, wouldn't he have done so already? Letting Boone pick a woman for you was a heck of a crapshoot to take on the rest of your life. So when Sam appeared, dazzling in that beautiful white dress of hers, with an open, sweet expression and a warmth of character that was all too clear, Curtis must have done the math in his head and realized he'd be hard pressed to find a better wife.

Working on the house was tolerable while Curtis had been in the barn, but now he was back, things weren't going so well, and a camera crew was making sure to document every moment of it.

Curtis was taking measurements for cabinets for the interior of the kitchen space. For the last ten minutes he'd kept up a constant string of curses Harris knew would eventually blow up into something more.

He was right.

"You call these walls square?" Curtis shouted suddenly. "Do you even know how to measure?"

Harris ignored him. The man was trying to get a rise out of him, and he wasn't going to cooperate.

"I'm talking to you," Curtis called belligerently. "I'm telling you your measurements are off. You better get your ass in here and fix this."

Harris refused to let him get under his skin. He made his way into the shell of the tiny house, joined Curtis in the kitchen and pulled out a measuring tape. With each span he measured, he called off the reading. "Sixteen inches. Sixteen inches. Sixteen inches. He let the measuring tape slide back into its container and pocketed it. "It's square."

"The only reason you're working on this house is because we're short of labor," Curtis said. "I heard Clay say that to Boone. Any guy off the street could do what you do. Even a teenager. You don't have any real skills to offer this community. Not like me."

Harris went back to his job, and kept on ignoring him. But Curtis had found a weak spot, and he knew it.

As the afternoon wore on, he kept probing at it, returning to his theme again and again, until Harris found it difficult to concentrate on his task. Only Daisy's antics as she explored her surroundings offered him any relief. As long as the two men stayed near each other, she gave them equal attention. God knew what He was doing when he made dogs, Harris mused. What the heck he was thinking when he got to men like Curtis was anyone's guess.

Still, it was hard to ignore the man's incessant talk. The problem was, Curtis was right. The framing work wasn't difficult. He knew he was doing a good job—possibly a better job than most teenagers would, he assured himself with a private smile—but most men could handle the work. He wasn't a finish carpenter like Curtis was.

But while that was galling, it wasn't the worst thing. Curtis was also right he didn't really have a place here in this community. He'd come here determined not to end up the watchman again. Then, when he'd finally relaxed, trouble had reared its head and Nora had nearly died. Now he didn't know what to do. Nora's attack was an isolated incident, and the man who'd perpetrated it was dead, but still there was nothing to say there wouldn't be more trouble ahead. He'd promised himself he'd take up a watch again, but that was before he'd met and married Sam. How was he supposed to keep framing these houses and mount some kind of one-man guard of Base Camp—and woo Sam all at the same time?

Harris had no idea, and that bothered him. He was a

man who needed to know where he fit in. He needed to feel needed. Curtis was undermining that with every complaint and comment.

Now Curtis was muttering again, and Harris braced himself for another attack. He didn't have to wait long. Suddenly Curtis erupted, "For God's sake, how am I supposed to fit anything in here when the job you've done is this shoddy?"

Harris reached the end of his patience. "The only one doing shoddy work is you. Why don't you shut your mouth and get to it?"

Curtis was on him in a second, darting out of the half-finished house and shoving Harris hard. "Say that to my face, asshole."

"Gladly. Shut your mouth and get to work."

Harris was ready for the punch Curtis threw at him. He struck back, and landed a blow on Curtis's jaw. The bigger man came at him again, but while Harris's job in the Navy rarely called for it, he'd always excelled at hand-to-hand combat. Curtis was so angry it was hindering his ability to fight. Harris could predict his moves and dodge his blows. The ones he returned hit their mark. Daisy barked and jumped around them but kept her distance. She didn't like what was going on, but she was too timid to get involved.

He had no idea how long the fight would have gone on, or what the result would have been, because Walker arrived before things got too out of hand. One of the founding members of Base Camp, Walker was a Native American who, like the others, had served as a Navy

SEAL for years before coming home to Montana.

"Break it up. Break it up!" He pushed his body between them and suffered a blow or two before they each got a hold of themselves and backed off. "What is this?"

"This is fucked," Curtis said. "Harris couldn't frame up a square house if his life depended on it."

Walker eyed him. "This really about framing a house?"

"This is about Samantha." Harris was done playing games.

"Come with me. Just you." Walker pointed to Harris. "You get back to work," he said to Curtis.

Harris put away his tools, and followed Walker gladly. Daisy whined, but in the end she stayed with Curtis.

Figured.

Harris wished he could punch Curtis a few more times for stealing his dog, but the two of them needed to find a way to coexist. He wasn't sure if that was possible, but he refused to be the one to prove it wasn't.

"Where are we going?"

Walker strode toward the barn and outbuildings. "Horse threw a shoe. Going to need some help."

"You know how to shoe a horse?"

"Farrier's on his way."

Harris followed him with interest. He hadn't grown up with horses like many of the other men at Base Camp. He had begun to learn to ride, but he had a long way to go to catch up. Meanwhile, he was curious to see the farrier at work.

The farrier arrived in a battered old silver truck and began unloading his tools. He was a man in his seventies, with a hitch in his gait, but a youthful, cheerful face. He whistled while he worked, and although Harris suspected he had already visited several other ranches that day, he seemed eager to get on with the business at hand, and meet his patient.

Walker brought him to the stables, where a black gelding named Spirit shifted restlessly in his stall. Walker motioned Harris back, and the two men watched the farrier approach the horse.

"Roy Egan is a wizard with them," Walker said. "Just watch."

As far as Harris could tell, Walker was right. Egan spoke softly to the horse the entire time, as he unlatched the stall door and entered it. He let the horse out gently, and soothed him until the horse settled, then asked, "What happened?"

"He was scrambling up a rocky incline," Walker said.

The farrier nodded. As he got to work, Harris watched with growing curiosity. He had expected the horseshoes the man used to be prefabricated, but somehow he got the sense that Egan had made them himself. They looked like works of art rather than pieces of metal that had been stamped and shaped by machines. As Egan got to work on the horse's hoof, filing and shaping it correctly for the shoe, Harris found himself edging closer for a better look.

"You'd better stop there," Egan said in a soft voice,

keeping the same tone he'd been using to speak to the horse the entire time. "I'll show you everything you want to see later. Nothing I like better than talking over the trade with an interested man. Right now, though, this fellow is mighty anxious, and I don't want harm to come to either him or me."

A little embarrassed, Harris edged back. He didn't bother to apologize, though. He knew the man understood his curiosity, and had only spoken up to keep everybody safe. After a while, Harris realized there really wasn't anything for him or Walker to do, and he wondered why they were there. Maybe Walker had just made up the errand to get him away from Curtis for a while. It didn't take a genius to see that things were going from bad to worse back there.

A half-hour later, Spirit was shod again, and back in his stall munching his feed. Walker had gone off to speak to Boone, and Harris followed Egan to his truck, where instead of loading his tools, the man laid them out on the tailgate. He began to explain each one, the rasps and files he used on the horses' hooves, the hammer and clinchers he used to pound the nails into the horseshoes and bend over the ends, and so on. But Harris was most interested in the way he manufactured the horseshoes.

"These look homemade," he said, lifting one.

"That's right. Not many of us do that anymore, but it was the way I was trained, and it's the way I like to do things. It allows me more control over the way the horseshoe fits the hoof. I'm old-fashioned that way."

136 | CORA SETON

"You must have a forge."

"I do." Egan beamed. "Don't suppose you'd want to see it?"

"I'd like that. If you have the time."

"I definitely keep busy, but I have time to show a man who takes an interest. There's not many who find blacksmith work compelling these days."

"Don't know that I'd be any good at it, but I am interested." Harris leaned against the truck. "Seems a solid kind of work to me."

"Don't want to put the cart before the horse, so to speak." Egan began to pack his tools away. "But I'll have to retire someday, and when I do this town's going to need another farrier. I don't have any backups. Next one is 50 miles away, and some days I can't keep up with the work. If you're interested, you can take a course to cover the basics, but I'd be happy to teach you, too. If it's the blacksmithing part that interests you most, you'd better come around to my forge, and take a look. There's plenty I can show you there, too."

"I'd appreciate that."

"Any time." Egan handed him a card that was a little bent and worse for wear for being in his pants pocket. "Give me a call, we'll set something up."

"I'll do that."

"I DON'T KNOW how this is going to look without stays. The dresses are made to be worn with them," Riley told Samantha. They'd gone up to Riley's room to find Sam a spare dress to wear until they got to Alice's.

"If it doesn't work I can wear my normal clothes until I get one of my own," Samantha assured her, surveying the pretty room they stood in with something close to avarice. She'd always wanted to live in a house like this, and had spent many hours reading Jane Austen novels on the bus in between gigs. The idea of having so much space to herself nearly overwhelmed her. In between tours, the band spent a lot of time in temporary housing, where they doubled up in order to save money. The band had always done well, but there were many people to split the money among, and in truth, the members partied hard and weren't exactly pillars of the community as far as savings were concerned.

"It must've been hard for you to move down to a tent after living here," Samantha told Riley.

"It was," Riley admitted, "but I love my tiny house. What it lacks in space, it makes up in character by far. Besides, I get to come up here to work every day, so it's not like I've left the manor behind for good. When we have guests, we'll sleep in our rooms in order to be close to them. I guess you could say I have the best of both worlds. Here," she said, "try this on."

She held up a plain blue gown and a large white apron. Sam thought the dress looked beautiful. "I can't believe you work in these."

"I know." Riley smiled. "That's how I felt in the beginning, but they're made of a very washable fabric. Our dressy ones are much harder to keep clean." Riley handed Samantha some undergarments. "I loved your wedding gown, by the way. I'm sorry the day didn't go

as planned."

"Do you really think Renata can annul my wedding?" Samantha stepped into the petticoat and slid the chemise over her head. Riley helped her into the blue gown. As she did up the fastenings in the back, Samantha surveyed herself in the mirror. Riley was right, the gown didn't quite fit as well as the other women's did. She wasn't sure if that was because it had been made for Riley, or because she wasn't wearing stays, which acted like a corset to shape the body.

"It's not Renata you have to worry about, it's Fulsom. Billionaires have a way of getting what they want." She stepped back and looked at Samantha critically. "That's much better than I thought it would be. You have a beautiful figure."

"Thanks," Samantha said. She allowed Riley to help her on with the voluminous apron. Now she looked like a character straight out of a Jane Austen period drama. "I can see why she'd make us act like we'd just met, in order to make the show better, but I don't see why she'd actually annul our wedding."

"Because she hopes you'll act differently because of it," Riley explained. "She's trying to drive a wedge between you and Harris. She wants there to be controversy in the show, so people keep watching." She tied the apron strings behind Samantha's back. "What did your family think about you coming here?"

Samantha made a face. "They don't know I'm here. And they're not going to like it when they find out."

"When are you going to tell them?"

"I'm not. But they watch *Base Camp* every week, so they'll find out pretty soon."

Riley laughed. "What will they object to? Our emphasis on sustainability? Or the fact that you married a stranger?"

"Well, they won't know about the marrying the stranger part, since I have to pretend that didn't happen. Basically, they'll object to all of it. They consider themselves to be environmentalists. But they don't think about their actions too deeply. They really don't like the idea that a bunch of men who have been in the military could be the ones leading the way on this. It offends their sensibilities."

"I'm sorry you don't have their support. Family is important." Riley stepped back. "You know, when we chose to wear these clothes, it was because we wanted an outward symbol for the choice we were making to pursue our dreams. What about you? What does joining us mean? Why bother to dress in Regency clothes?"

Sam didn't have to think about her answer. "I'm finally choosing the life I want to lead. One that means something special to me. I believe in what you all are doing here and I want to be a part of it. I want to decide for myself what's important and pursue that. I'm not just along for the ride on someone else's trip anymore."

Riley nodded. "I like that. You're taking control of your destiny."

But was she? Sam wondered if that was true. Right now it seemed like Renata was the one calling the shots.

"What about children?" Riley asked, interrupting her

thoughts. "Have you and Harris talked about children?"

"Not really," Samantha said, grateful for the change in topic. "I definitely want them. I think Harris does, too, but I guess we'll have to put that off for a while. How about you and Boone?"

"We definitely want them," Riley said. "Whether or not we can have them, we'll have to wait and see."

Samantha wasn't sure how to answer that. "You can't have been trying for too long," she ventured. "I'm sure it'll happen in time."

"But what if it doesn't?" Riley asked with a sigh. She smoothed the folds of the comforter on her bed. "Three of us need to be pregnant by the end of the year. I wanted to be one of those people. We've been trying ever since the wedding, but I've got my period again. I just want this so bad."

Samantha hadn't had much experience talking to women about pregnancy. The women in the band and those she met on the road were generally trying to keep from getting pregnant, not anticipating it. "Sometimes it takes a while," she said awkwardly. "Just have faith. I'm sure it will happen."

Riley nodded. "Let's go downstairs and join the others."

Downstairs, they found the rest of the women still gathered around the kitchen table. All eyes were on her as she entered the room, and Samantha smoothed her skirts self-consciously. She knew the dress she wore didn't look quite right because she wasn't wearing her stays. She hoped the others realized that, too, and as she

took in the cameras filming them, she was grateful they hadn't followed her and Riley upstairs while she changed. She doubted she would have had such an intimate conversation with Riley if they did, and she would've hated being exposed like that on television. She sat down, and there was a general shifting around as Avery handed her and Riley cups of tea.

"We're discussing the itinerary for when our guests come," she said. "They'll arrive a week from Friday, and stay until Sunday night. It's a short visit, so we'll have to make the best of it. We want them to have a great experience, and talk about it online, to get the word out."

"We're going to do a lot of the same things we did when we held the wedding here," Savannah said. "We'll start on Friday with a tour of the manor and the property, fittings for the Regency clothes that the guests have ordered and a short dancing lesson after dinner."

"On Saturday," Avery said, "we'll start with a carriage ride. Maude and James have already said they'll help out with that. They would like to host a lunch at their cottage, followed by a tour of their gardens. We'll return to the manor for another dance lesson, and then everybody will get dressed for dinner and a small party Saturday night. We expect that to be a late night, so Sunday we'll start with brunch."

"It will be a picnic brunch with the men of Base Camp," Savannah picked up. "And then we'll do a tour of the sustainable community. We'll finish with tea and snacks mid-afternoon, and they'll leave before dinner."

"That all sounds perfect," Riley said.

"How can I help?" Samantha asked.

The others looked at each other, and when the silence went on a little too long, Riley spoke up. "There will be plenty for you to do when the guests actually arrive, but for now we've got it all taken care of," she said. "You know, we're going to have even more women before all is said and done. We should think of ways to make use of all that manpower."

"*Women* power," Avery corrected her.

"Let's wait until Nora's back from her honeymoon to assign jobs for the weekend," Savannah said.

Samantha wondered how that would go. How would Nora react to her? After what Avery had said back at the tent site, she was paranoid that Nora would hate her.

Sam tried to imagine how she'd feel if she knew someone had come to Base Camp to marry Harris.

She'd be pretty pissed.

It would take time and consistency on her part to convince Nora she wasn't a threat, Samantha decided. She'd be patient and vigilant. That was all she could do.

"Would it be easier if I stayed away from the B&B?" she asked.

"Let us talk it over with Nora," Savannah said again. "She might need time to get used to you," she added apologetically.

"In the meantime, I'll go talk to Boone and find out what I should do," Sam told them, trying—but failing—not to be disappointed.

A SEAL'S PLEDGE | 143

"Boone's already told me you'll be working on the houses with Harris and Curtis," Riley told her. "But that's only for two hours a day. "There's plenty of time for your own projects. What do you like to do?"

Put on the spot, Sam froze. "Um…" What did she like to do? She wasn't sure. She'd had far too many responsibilities back on the bus to have hobbies.

"Are you an artist?" Avery asked curiously.

"Or is music your thing?" Savannah suggested.

"No, music is definitely not my thing," Sam said with a laugh. "I don't really have a thing."

The others exchanged a look. "Well, I'm sure you'll figure it out in time," Avery said. "We try to spend most of our afternoons on personal projects."

Sam knew this from the show. Nora was a writer, and had begun to work on a school curriculum; Riley was a painter, Savannah a gifted pianist and Avery was writing a screenplay. Sam didn't really do anything like that.

Which was pathetic, she realized.

"I'll…think about it," she told them.

When the meeting broke up, the women dispersed, including Riley, who said she needed to head back down to Base Camp. "Savannah will take you to Alice's," she told Sam.

As Sam helped carry the teacups to the sink for washing, Savannah commented, "We didn't even think about what to do with extra help for the B&B. I hope it isn't boring for you when our guests are here."

"I'm the newbie here. I'll take whatever leftover jobs

you have, if Nora's all right with that, and work my way up from there."

"You're stubborn, I'll give you that," Savannah said.

"I'm worried," Sam corrected her. "Worried my being here is going to upset Nora, and I know she's been through so much already. I wish I'd thought about that before I'd come."

"It might take time," Savannah said, "but I'm sure she'll come around. Maybe don't fawn all over Clay for now," she added with a grin.

"I'll put off any fawning for the time being," Sam assured her. "So, now what?"

Savannah smiled. "Now we wait for the barouche. James will be here soon. We'll go to Alice's house and find a dress for you that fits."

"That sounds great."

Ten minutes later, Sam bounced on the balls of her feet like a little girl when the carriage came rolling down the driveway and pulled up in front of the house. Savannah, standing beside her, was still grinning.

"I'd forgotten how exciting this was at first," she said. "It's fun to relive it through you."

Samantha waited until the driver came to a stop and climbed down from the carriage. "It's James, isn't it? I recognize you from watching the show."

"At your service." James lifted her hand and kissed it gallantly. In his sixties, dressed in impeccable Regency clothes, he was just as endearing in person as he'd been on the episodes Sam had watched.

"Oh, that's so strange," Savannah said. "I never

even thought about the fact you've watched us on TV."

"It's strange from my end, too," Samantha confessed. "I feel as if I know you far better than I should, but you don't know me at all. It's nice to meet you in person," she said to James.

"I never thought I'd be a TV star," James said. "It's nice to meet you, too. Let me help you up."

Samantha climbed up into the barouche, and Savannah took a seat next to her. Several camera crew members climbed in and sat across from them, ruining the moment just a little. Samantha decided not to pay any attention to them. That was both easier and harder than she'd expected. Easier, because everything was so exciting. Harder, because they tended to stay closer than she'd expected. They were constantly shifting around, adjusting their cameras and the boom microphone.

James climbed up to the driver's seat and clucked to the horses. As they lurched to a start, Sam clung to the side of the carriage to keep in her seat. This was better than she'd even dreamed. It was as if she had travelled back in time to a world far different than her own. "It's wonderful," she said to Savannah.

All too soon, they'd made the journey to Two Willows and pulled up in front of the large, old, white farmhouse where Alice Reed and her sisters lived. Alice was standing on the porch to greet them, and she led them first inside for a cup of tea in the kitchen, and then out the back door to a carriage house several hundred feet away, where her studio was.

"Come on in. Watch your step on the stairs." Alice

led the way into an old-fashioned garage, through a door to an enclosed stairwell and up to the second floor, where they entered a large open space like a loft.

Samantha gasped as she stepped inside. Large arched windows let light stream into the open room. Several large work tables were positioned in the center, surrounded by racks and racks of clothing and costumes Alice must have made. At one end of the room, in a corner, was a makeshift change room. At the other end was a studio kitchen. Alice had everything she could possibly need.

"If you go to the change room," Alice said, "you'll find several dresses to try on. Put on the one you like best, and come on out to show me. We'll get it fitted to you in a jiffy."

As Sam made her way across the room, she heard Alice and Savannah talking together in low voices behind her. She paused before entering the small cubicle, one hand poised to draw the curtain for privacy, and looked back. Alice was examining the gown that Savannah wore. "It's the bodice," Savannah said, loudly enough for Sam to hear. "It's too tight."

"Again?" Alice laughed. "That was fast."

"It's not funny," Savannah said.

Alice sobered. "You're right, it isn't. I'm sorry. Does Jericho—" Alice looked up, spotted Sam, turned her back and continued in a lower voice. Sam could no longer hear the discussion, and as she entered the change room and drew the curtain over the door, she wondered about what she had heard. She remembered

that in one of the episodes she'd watched, Savannah had said that she had a doctor's appointment. And now her dress needed alteration because it was too tight. There was a logical explanation, but nothing had been said on any of the episodes about Savannah being pregnant.

Sam figured she'd better stay out of it. The last thing Savannah would want was for a newcomer to poke her nose into her business. She would wait until Savannah brought up the topic herself. Meanwhile she would keep her mouth shut.

Inside the change room, she pulled off her apron and work dress, switched into the new chemise and petticoat Alice had laid out for her and surveyed the stays with interest. Putting her arms through the arm-holes, she tried to look over her shoulder and figure out how to lace them up behind her.

"Samantha? Can I help you with those stays?" Alice said from outside the change room.

"Yes, I have no idea how I would do this myself." Samantha opened the curtain again. She turned her back, and Alice began to lace the ties up.

"There's really no way you can," Alice said. She made quick work of them, then tugged until the stays cinched her waist a little. "Because only the bodice fits tightly in a Regency gown, and the skirts hang straight, we don't have to pull these as tight as we would with a Civil War–era gown."

"Thank God," Samantha said. "I like breathing." She noticed the crew had trained their cameras on her, and sucked in her stomach.

"Most of us do."

When Sam's stays were done, Alice helped her on with a deep blue Regency gown made from a fine material that felt light and airy over her underthings. Alice led her out of the change room and over to a three-way mirror. "That looks fantastic on you."

Samantha turned one way and then the other in order to get a better look. Alice was right; the color suited her, and she loved the gown.

"I've got some shoes for you, and a reticule, an apron and a jacket." She showed all of them to Samantha and Sam was amazed that everything fit so well.

"It's as if you knew I was coming," she told Alice.

Alice smiled. "Well, I did. Riley called me earlier."

She was teasing, and Samantha said, "Did she tell you my shoe size, too?"

"I made an educated guess."

"Don't let her fool you," Savannah said, coming over. "Alice has a sixth sense about these things. About a lot of things."

The other two women exchanged a glance, and again Sam wondered what Savannah's secret was. There was no way to see if she was in the early stages of pregnancy while she was wearing a Regency gown.

"Let me take a couple of measurements," Alice said. "Your dress fits well, but it's not perfect, so I'll make a couple of quick adjustments. Meanwhile, try on those other gowns, and I'll bring you a couple of work gowns, as well."

Samantha did as she was told, and an hour later she

left with two complete outfits, one for work, which Alice had packed in tissue paper, and one for leisure, which she was currently wearing. Alice assured her she would deliver the rest of the clothes the following day, and she whispered something in Savannah's ear that sounded like a promise to deliver another gown for her, too.

Samantha enjoyed the carriage ride home even more than the earlier one, decked out in an outfit that was tailor-made for her. They travelled through beautiful countryside, past ranch after ranch, until they pulled into Westfield again. When the barouche travelled up the winding driveway, and the manor came into sight, Samantha's heart swelled. Despite her rocky beginning here, it felt like coming home. She couldn't wait for the guests to arrive, and to actually sleep in the manor. If Nora was okay with that.

When they pulled to a stop, the camera crew got out first and established the shot as Samantha and Savannah exited the barouche. James helped them down, but then said he was needed back at his own house and couldn't come in for tea. As he drove away, it occurred to Sam she didn't know what came next.

Before she could ask Savannah, the other woman said, "We'll head down to dinner in half an hour. What would you like to do until then?"

"Would you give me a full tour of the manor?"

"Of course."

Savannah led the way, and they made a circuit of the first floor. To the left of the front door was a parlor,

with a couch and easy chairs, a grand piano and a desk. "This is where we spend our time when we're working on our own creative pursuits," Savannah said.

"I know." Sam bit her lip, realizing she didn't really need a tour of the manor house; she'd seen it all on TV. The parlor was already familiar, as was the kitchen, and to a lesser extent the great room that formed the other side of the house. Upstairs it was the same. Samantha showed her the guest rooms on the second floor, each one more beautiful than the last. On the third floor were the rooms the women had held back for themselves. Only then, Samantha realized she'd made another assumption that wasn't true.

"I guess there really isn't a place for me to stay when the guests are here," she said slowly, trying to hide her disappointment. "I thought we'd all stay in the house, but that doesn't make sense. I'd be taking a room that's meant for guests."

It was obvious Savannah hadn't thought about that either. "Sometimes there will be fewer guests than there are rooms. But pretty soon there'll be other women at the ranch..." She trailed off.

"Right. We'd end up filling up the whole house." So much for having a beautiful room to herself.

"As soon as you marry Harris or Curtis, you'll have your own tiny house," Savannah said by way of encouragement.

Samantha knew she was only trying to help, but she didn't feel cheered up. She'd always had to share the bus or a hotel room, and even the rooms they'd had in

rental houses and apartments. She'd never had a space of her own, and now it looked like she never would. "I need to freshen up," she told Savannah. "We still have a few minutes before we have to go to dinner, right?"

Savannah nodded. "That's right. I bet you could use some privacy before you meet everyone again. Why don't you use my room, and you can join us downstairs when it's time to leave."

"Thanks." Samantha held it together until Savannah had gone, and the camera crew that had trailed them went with her, and then she sank down on Savannah's bed in defeat. What had she done? She'd gone straight from a bus to a stupid tent. She wasn't really wanted here. Renata had erased her wedding as if it had never happened.

This was all a huge mistake.

Samantha allowed herself five minutes of self-pity, and then she wiped her eyes and stood up again. Base Camp wasn't the same as the tour bus; it was whatever she made it. She had come here to make a difference, not to live in a beautiful room. She would get to enjoy the manor whenever there were guests here, and whenever it was time for the women to pursue their creative pursuits. She didn't have to sleep in a room in order to enjoy it. Besides, she did have a space of her own—for now.

Her tent.

She would make the best of that, too. It was more than she'd ever had before, she told herself ruefully.

The most important thing was she had Harris. And

no matter what Renata had said, she was sure the connection they'd shared this morning was real. She had to trust any hardship she endured in the next month would all be worth it when she married him again.

Ten minutes later, she hoped she'd erased all traces of her tears. She held her head high and descended the stairs lifting the skirts of her gown. As the women walked the quarter mile down the dirt track that led to the encampment, Samantha hung back, but she listened intently to the others' conversations. Riley was quiet, and when Avery asked if she was feeling well, she nodded.

"Too well," she said acerbically. "I'm definitely not pregnant."

"Next month," Avery assured her, putting a hand on her back.

Riley just nodded.

Savannah didn't say anything, but Sam noticed her briefly rest her hand on her belly.

Sam bit her lip. If Savannah was pregnant, how would Riley react? And why hadn't Savannah told Jericho? Or had she, but Jericho didn't want to marry her? That didn't make sense; Jericho was always mooning around after Savannah.

It was hard to keep her questions to herself, but Samantha managed it. The last thing she wanted to do was start a controversy between the other women. Besides, the cameras were following them like always. She would have to be on her toes while she was here.

When they arrived in Base Camp, Win was there to

greet them. "It's taco night tonight. My favorite. One thing I love about Base Camp is I do enough physical work here I can eat all I want and not gain weight."

"Wish I could say that," Savannah said, and then blushed. "I mean, I'm not doing as much physical work as you are."

"That's because you're supposed to be a concert pianist," Win said. "I'm just a lowly gardener."

"A lowly gardener who used to be a highly paid executive," Savannah reminded her. "There's nothing lowly about you. Or if there is, it's because you've chosen it."

"I've chosen a better life."

"Why are you so comfortable giving up everything you used to have?" Savannah asked her. "I mean, the rest of us had things we wanted to leave behind, but you were sitting pretty. How did you walk away from it all so easily?"

Sam wondered if she was the only one surprised by the conversation. Win had been a friend of Savannah's cousin Andrea, and had come to Westfield to attend Andrea's wedding here. As far as she knew from the episodes she'd watched, Savannah and Win had grown to like each other over the past few months. Why was Savannah confronting her now?

"I'm not the only one here with rich parents," Win reminded her tartly.

"I was supporting myself before I came here," Savannah retorted. "And I hated my job."

"Maybe I hated my job, too."

"Andrea told me your parents were subsidizing that rock-star lifestyle of yours."

"Savannah," Riley warned her.

"I'm not throwing stones," Savannah said. "I'm genuinely curious. Win has gone from living in a palace to living in a tent—and she's thriving. I want to know why."

"It wasn't a palace," Win told her. "I'm here because I believe in Base Camp. Money isn't everything."

"Here, here," Riley cheered.

Sam noticed Win's answer didn't reveal anything about her past. The show had highlighted her wealthy family during one episode, but had never explained much about the fiancé she'd left behind. Why *had* a woman who could live in a palace chosen to come here and live in a tent? Unfortunately, they'd already reached camp. The women split up. Harris spotted her and came to meet her. Samantha forgot everything else.

When he drew near, Harris reached for her, but quickly pulled back his hand. "How was your day? Are you settling in?"

She lifted the skirts of her new gown a little to show him. "Yes, I am. Do you like my dress?"

"It's almost as beautiful as your wedding gown."

"Cut, cut!" Renata, nearby, stepped forward through the crowd. "Remember, as far as our viewers are concerned, you have not seen her wedding gown. You just met her, and this is the first time you're going to get to ask her out. Focus. Do it again."

She made a rolling motion with her hand. Harris

rolled his eyes and Sam could tell he was biting back a cutting retort. He got himself under control and turned back to Samantha. "Uh, yes, I do like that dress."

They stared at each other for a moment, and once more Samantha took in those broad shoulders she'd grasped earlier, his handsome features and the mouth she couldn't resist when he smiled. She wished he was smiling now. She searched for what to say next. "Alice is bringing several more for me tomorrow."

Harris nodded. "I met a farrier today."

Samantha wasn't sure what that was, so she just nodded. God, was it always going to be this stilted in front of the cameras?

"A farrier puts horseshoes on horses," Harris explained. "I'm going to check out his forge sometime." He looked away. Was he embarrassed? Why? Did he think she'd find that boring?

Far from it; Samantha was intrigued. "I'd like to see a forge," she said.

"You would?"

She nodded. "Can I come along?"

"I don't see why not. I was planning to go tomorrow. You can come with me." There was that smile.

Sam melted inside. If only she could kiss him. "It's a date."

His smile grew. "Huh. I was thinking for our first date I'd take you out to dinner, but I guess a forge will do. How about we go tomorrow afternoon?"

"That sounds lovely." Samantha's heart swelled. This wouldn't be so hard after all. And even if they

couldn't touch, they could communicate how they felt. She read Harris's inclinations in the way he stayed close to her, the way his gaze caught hers and held it. The way his smile reached his eyes.

"The day after that, you can go on a date with me," Curtis interrupted loudly. Samantha had been so caught up in talking to Harris, she hadn't even noticed him arrive. Curtis didn't look happy, probably because Harris had gotten to her first.

Well, that was too bad for him, Samantha thought. She wondered what Curtis was really after. He didn't know her at all, and from all accounts he hadn't been eager to be married anyway, so why was he pushing this so hard? She found it hard to believe he'd taken one look at her and decided she was the one. She was worried this was more about competition between the two men than anything to do with her. Which didn't make any of them look good.

She swallowed, and nodded again, reaching down to stroke Daisy's head. Had the dog spent the whole day with Curtis? Didn't she have any loyalty for the people who'd saved her? Daisy licked her hand almost apologetically. "Okay," Sam said slowly. She looked to Harris, worried about how he might react. Harris didn't betray any emotion, but his expression was hard.

"I've got somewhere special to take you," Curtis went on. "Just the two of us. It'll give us an opportunity to get to know each other better."

"Just the two of you and a camera crew," Harris corrected. "It's not like you'll be alone." It sounded like

a warning, and Sam was pretty sure it was.

"I've gotten pretty good at ignoring the camera crew," Curtis said, "and I'm sure Sam can, too. Isn't that right, Samantha?"

"I'm pretty hungry," Samantha said, hoping to deflect the tension. "Harris, would you show me where to get some food?"

"I'll show you." Curtis moved toward her.

Before Harris could intercept him and escalate things, Samantha spoke up. "I asked Harris this time." Daisy whined a little, standing in the middle of the three of them. But Sam didn't back down. So far, Curtis struck her as a bully. And she didn't like bullies.

She braced herself for an angry reply, but to her surprise Curtis fell back. He looked more chagrined than anything. "A-all right, I'll catch up to you later."

He walked away. "Smart move," Harris said under his breath. When he caught Samantha looking at him, however, he added, "I'm sure Renata will make sure he gets his chance."

Daisy gave her one last look, and trotted along after Curtis.

"I don't like the way you two argue over me," Samantha told Harris, watching Daisy go. Why did she have such a strong preference for Curtis? It was galling—and also made Sam wonder what she was missing. Weren't dogs supposed to have some kind of sixth sense about people? Was Daisy trying to tell her Curtis was the man she should choose?

Sam dashed the silly thought from her mind.

"I don't like it, either," Harris said, "but I'm not going to stand back and let him make a move on you. I don't like what he was hinting at."

"But like you said, there will always be a camera crew with us, we'll never be alone, so you don't have to worry about that."

He looked at her fondly, and touched her cheek. "Honey, what you don't seem to realize is that every man in this camp, except the ones holding cameras, are Navy SEALs. If Curtis wants to get you alone, he'll get you alone."

Samantha mulled over that a few minutes later as she stood in line with Harris to be served their food. A tall, blond man with a laid-back California surfer smile served the meal. Harris introduced him as Kai Green.

"Nice to meet you," Kai said. "Hope you enjoy your dinner."

"I'm sure I will," Samantha said. She followed Harris back outside to the campfire ring. It was a warm day, and there was no fire burning, but it was a good place for the members of Base Camp to gather together and share their meals. They sat down on a log together, and Samantha took a bite of her taco. She hadn't realized how hungry she was until now. "Oh, that's good."

"Kai is a wizard in the kitchen," Harris said. "He does as much of the cooking as possible using solar ovens. He's got it all down to a science. We'll soon have the kitchen hooked up to solar power. That's Jericho's department."

"I guess tomorrow I'll start working with you," Sa-

mantha said.

Harris nodded, but his expression was grim.

"What's wrong?"

"You'll be working with me *and* Curtis," he reminded her. "Could be ugly."

"At some point the houses will be done," she said. "What will happen then? Will there be other building projects?" There was nothing either of them could do about the fact that they would be working with Curtis. All she could hope was that the man kept his temper under control.

Maybe she could talk to him when they had their date. Maybe away from Harris, Curtis would see the light and accept this relationship wasn't going anywhere. She would make sure to point out all the ways in which they were incompatible. She would remind him that Boone would find another woman—a better one—for him.

"I'm sure there'll always be building projects," Harris said. "But I don't think I'll be working on them. The farrier this afternoon asked me if I'd be interested in learning his trade—both shoeing horses and blacksmithing. Don't know if I'll be any good at it, but I'd like to try. Could be useful around here."

The surge of envy she felt surprised Samantha. But then she'd always wanted to have a calling, like her parents and her sister. A job that was more than a job. Something that set her on fire the way music set ablaze the rest of the members of her family. Harris was obviously more interested than he was letting on in the

idea of becoming a blacksmith. She didn't blame him; it was an unusual job that struck her as requiring both mental and physical skill. It was a job that would engage a man in the doing of it.

What could she do that would be a help to this community and establish her place here?

Samantha wasn't sure. She'd hoped her organizational skills would be useful at the B&B, but she was beginning to think that was a dead-end. She would do her best to help out during the upcoming visit, but Nora wasn't due back until the end of the week, which left little time before the guests arrived for the two of them to sort things out. If Nora made it clear she wanted Sam to back off, she would.

"What does Base Camp need that it doesn't have already?" she asked Harris. "Something I can do. Something like blacksmithing."

Harris grinned. "You want to be a blacksmith, too?"

She shoved him with her shoulder. "You know what I mean."

Harris thought about it. "I'm not sure, but I'll let you know if I come up with anything."

"Thanks."

"The other women are artistic. Riley paints, Nora writes, that kind of thing. What about you?"

"Nope. No talents here."

"I doubt that," Harris said. "You said you drove the bus."

"Driving the bus isn't a talent."

"I think it is. It means you can handle large equip-

ment. You could probably drive a backhoe, things like that. That might come in handy."

Samantha rolled her eyes. "I'm not sure large equipment is my future," she said.

"Well, you're starting over here. You can do anything you want. Maybe you should take a few days to think about all the possibilities before you decide on one."

"I guess so," she told him. "Starting with blacksmithing."

She loved to see his smile. He leaned in, and for a second she thought he would kiss her, but he must've realized his mistake. He straightened again, frowned and took another bite of his food. "This sucks," he said when he'd swallowed.

"The food? I think it's terrific."

"Not getting to be with you." He met her gaze. Lowered his voice. "I made a hell of a mistake this afternoon, didn't I?"

Her heart plummeted. Made a mistake? Did he mean when they fooled around? Did he regret that now?

Harris leaned even closer. "Not making love to you."

Samantha sucked in her breath, and desire pulsed through her. "Yeah," she said. "I think that was a mistake, too."

The look he gave her promised that soon they would be together, but she knew they would have to wait at least thirty days. As if she'd spoken aloud, he

shook his head and leaned close again. "There are ways to get alone—if we really want to."

They were being filmed. It seemed as if they were always being filmed. Harris was taking a chance talking like this. But he had his mouth close to her ear, and he was whispering, so she didn't think that anybody could hear.

"How?" she whispered back.

"I'll let you know as soon as I come up with a plan."

HARRIS WAS JUST congratulating himself for solidifying his relationship with Samantha, when Curtis approached and sat down on the other side of her on the log. Daisy settled down at Curtis's feet.

"Seems like the two of you are having an interesting conversation," he said. "Thought I'd come and see what it was about."

Samantha's cheeks were stained with color, and Harris knew it was up to him to rescue the situation. "Blacksmithing."

"Bullshit," Curtis said conversationally. "Seems to me the two of you are figuring out how to sneak off together. Which wouldn't be fair given the situation. In fact, I don't think I'm prepared to wait until you've spent another afternoon together before I get my chance. So after dinner, Samantha, I'm taking you out on the town."

"I don't think—" Samantha said.

"It's only fair." Curtis took an enthusiastic bite of his taco, and wiped his mouth with a napkin. He

chewed and swallowed, and then added, "I'll pick you up at seven-thirty."

"Wait a minute—"

Curtis put his plate down on his lap and faced Harris. "Here's the thing, buddy. You and I, and Samantha, here, all know the two of you are already stuck on each other. She was supposed to be my bride, and I don't have a chance with her. So the least you can do after stealing her away from me is give me one evening to prove the two of you are making a mistake. If Samantha can honestly say at the end of one night she's not interested, I will back off and play-act through the rest of this month. We'll give Renata what she wants, but that's it. You'll have won. Deal?"

"No way," Harris said quickly. This was a trick, and Curtis was a fool if he thought Harris would fall for it. He wanted to tell Sam point-blank he and Curtis both been trained to manipulate situations—to flip people over to their side. Whatever happened, he couldn't let Curtis be alone with her until he and Sam had spent more time together. Their relationship was too new—too fragile. She had no idea how underhanded a SEAL could be.

"Harris—"

"No," Harris said again. "Bad enough he gets a shot at you tomorrow. He doesn't get tonight, too."

"It's not going to change anything—"

"I said no."

Her mouth dropped open and Harris would have given anything to rewind ten seconds and change his

tone, but it was too late. The damage was done.

Samantha pulled back. Turned to Curtis. "I'd be happy to spend some time with you tonight."

"Sam—"

"You don't get to boss me around," she snapped.

Curtis grinned. Harris clenched his fists, but instead of going off half-cocked, he stood up. "Daisy, come," he said. If Curtis wanted to steal Sam back, he couldn't have his dog, too.

"Where are you going?" Sam asked. Daisy didn't budge.

"I'm done here." He could shoot like nobody's business, but talking—that was a whole other matter. He'd already stuck his foot in it, and he didn't know how to fix that. Best to leave before he'd made it even worse. "Daisy, come."

"I'm only going with Curtis because it's the right thing to do," Samantha told him heatedly, standing up, too, her plate clutched in her hands. "The sooner he realizes he and I aren't compatible, the sooner you and I can move on. Once you learn not to order me around."

She was offering an olive branch of sorts and he needed to grab hold of it. If he didn't, Curtis would succeed in driving a wedge between them.

"That's right, Harris." Curtis stood, too. "Why *are* you so concerned about Samantha spending a single evening with me? Just what do you think I could do to change her mind?" He stood too close to Sam for comfort, but it was the triumphant look on his face that made Harris's good intentions dissolve in a puff of

smoke. Curtis was a smooth talker, the life of the party. He knew how to make people laugh, and Harris had a feeling that would count a lot to Sam. The life she'd described had left her on the outskirts far too much. She wanted to belong.

Curtis could give her that. Harris wasn't sure he could.

He would lose her.

"Don't go with him," he said to Sam. He'd meant it as a plea—and he'd stretched far beyond his comfort zone to ask it of her. His words came out too harsh—too commanding.

Another order, not a request.

Samantha's spine stiffened and her chin lifted. Harris knew he'd screwed up again. He'd given her an ultimatum—in front of Curtis—and one thing Samantha possessed in spades was pride.

He knew what she would do before she did it, and as he watched her turn to Curtis, his heart plummeted in his chest. Damn it, he was going to lose her over a pissing contest with another man. He had to say something. Do something.

Instead he stood frozen in place as Samantha touched Curtis's arm. "I'm going to go freshen up. Where should I meet you?"

"I'll come fetch you up at the manor," Curtis said. "Like a real date. Looking forward to it."

Anger, hot and sharp, flooded Harris. He wanted to swing at the other man. He wanted to sweep Samantha into his arms and kiss her until she remembered what

they'd experienced together on the ridge. He wanted to let the whole world know that she belonged to him, and only him.

But he'd blown it.

So now the only thing he could do was stand right where he was while Curtis and Samantha took their dishes back to the bunkhouse kitchen and then parted ways, Daisy trotting at Curtis's heels like she'd known him all her life.

He was still standing there when Boone took his plate from his hand. "Go sleep it off, or work it off, or whatever you have to do not to turn this camp upside down."

Harris shoved past him and strode down the path that led to Pittance Creek as the first fat drops of rain began to fall from the leaden sky, and all the other people around the campfire scrambled to get inside. He should have read the signs in the landscape and known this day—and his marriage to Samantha—was doomed before it even started. The storm would be a whopper.

Who knew what its aftermath would bring?

"POOR HARRIS," AVERY said, as the women trudged up the hill toward the manor. The clouds that had threatened all day were becoming downright ominous, Sam thought, glancing up at them with concern.

"What about Curtis? He thought he was getting a bride today," Savannah said.

"I just know what it's like to think about the person you love being with someone else. I can only imagine

what Harris is feeling tonight."

"He should have handled it differently," Riley said.

"That's for sure," Samantha said. The walk was giving her time to calm down, though, and when she replayed Harris's words she wondered if he'd meant to give her an order, or something else altogether.

It had felt too much like being on the bus though—being at everyone's beck and call, never getting to make her own decisions.

She'd married him, for heaven's sake. They'd spent one of the best mornings of her life together. Maybe they'd only known each other for a few hours, but they'd connected—with their words and their bodies. Being intimate with Harris meant something to her.

Didn't he understand that?

She looked up again as a drop of rain hit her cheek. The last thing she wanted to do was spend an evening with Curtis. She would've preferred to go to bed, pull the covers up over her head and fall into a blissful sleep in which she didn't remember anything except being alone with Harris. She looked down at her gown and smoothed out the wrinkles that had appeared as she sat at the campfire.

"Do you think there's any way I can get out of this date?"

"I don't think so," Riley said. "Besides, what you said back there was right; the sooner you and Curtis see if you are meant to be together, the sooner all of this can be straightened out."

"That's not what I said at all. I said the sooner Cur-

tis realizes he doesn't like me, the sooner we can sort this out. I know I'm meant to be with Harris. At least... I thought I was." She didn't want to be with a man who didn't trust her.

"But that's the thing," Savannah said. "You don't actually know Harris, and he doesn't actually know you. Until you give Curtis a chance, how do you really know how you'll feel? I think it's a good thing that you're going out with him tonight—and that you're going to take the time to get to know both of them. I think if the three of you can keep your tempers, you'll be able to figure this out."

"Come on upstairs," Riley said as they reached the manor, just as the spattering of raindrops turned into a deluge. The women hurried in the back door and the ever-present camera crew pushed in behind them. "Let's freshen up your hairstyle; that will make you feel better."

Samantha thought it would take far more than a new hairstyle to improve the day, but when they'd all reached Riley's bedroom, she allowed Riley to unpin her hair, comb it out and begin to style it. Aware of the cameras capturing this moment, she fiddled with her dress.

Avery glanced out the window. "Where do you think Curtis will take you?"

"I have no idea," Samantha said. "What do you know about him?"

"He's nice. Usually. I'm not sure I've ever seen him angry before today," Avery said.

"His carpentry is amazing," Savannah added. "You

should see the interior of Riley's house—and Nora's."

"He does amazing things with his hands," Avery said impishly. "He might be a wonderful lover."

Samantha rolled her eyes. "I thought you were sweet on Walker."

Avery blushed. "I am."

"I don't know much about Curtis's past," Riley mused. "He was a Navy SEAL, of course. I'm not sure what made him come here."

"An overwhelming urge to save the world," Savannah said with a sigh. "Just like all the other men."

Avery laughed. "That's right; it's like even though they left the military, they can't stop wanting to make the world a better place. They're kind of cocky that way."

"That's what I admire about all of them," Samantha said. "When I first watched the show, I thought it was going to be ridiculous. But then I saw how seriously the men were taking it. They really believe in what they're doing. I think it's admirable."

The others exchanged a glance. "I think it's admirable, too," Riley said. "I just wish their solutions had a few less composting toilets and solar showers, and a few more hot tubs and shopping trips." She chuckled. "I didn't know what a heathen I was about these things until I came here."

"There are advantages to their system though," Savannah said. "I love the evenings here. I love it that we all eat together, and spend time together outside, especially when we linger until the sun goes down and

the stars come out. I haven't spent so much time outside since I was a kid. It's really wonderful. I like how we do all the chores together. I even like helping Jericho with the solar stuff. I thought I'd hate that, but it's pretty interesting."

"I think because it's so important to all of us that our community succeeds, we have this camaraderie." Riley finished styling Samantha's hair and turned her to face the mirror to see the effect. She had pulled it up into a high loose bun, and left tendrils to soften the line of her face. Samantha liked it.

"I agree," Savannah said.

If that was true, Sam wondered why Savannah was keeping secrets. But it wasn't her place to judge.

Avery nodded to the clock on the bureau. "We better go downstairs. Curtis should be here soon."

Samantha suddenly realized that if they went into town, she'd still be dressed like a Regency character. She lifted her skirts. "I can't go on a date like this," she said. "Everyone's going to stare at me if he takes me to Chance Creek."

"They'll be staring at the cameras," Avery told her. "Everybody in town has seen us now. They're used to the way we dress. But they're still fascinated by the filming process."

"For God's sake," one of the crew interrupted loudly. "Stop talking about us. You know we can't use that footage."

"Fascinated, and annoyed," Savannah went on, ignoring him. "You should see us when we go shopping.

A SEAL'S PLEDGE | 171

We troop around the grocery store followed by our entourage, and we take up a whole aisle at a time. People get a little testy sometimes."

"You want your funding, you have to deal with us," the cameraman said. "Now quit it. Back to getting ready for Sam's date."

Sam didn't like her life being a plot point, but it was what she'd signed up for. "Let's head down," she told the others.

She had just reached the bottom of the stairs when a knock on the door announced Curtis's arrival. The crew made sure to film her answering the door. When she opened it, Curtis stood on the stoop, and his own entourage of cameras stood behind him in the rain. Samantha bit back a grin.

"Would you like to come in?" she asked him.

"How about we hit the road instead," Curtis said. "Let's go into town and have a drink."

"Okay."

Avery rushed up carrying the little fitted jacket Alice had given her earlier. "You'd better wear your spenser," she said. "It's not waterproof, but it'll help keep the rain off you. And don't forget your bonnet."

"I've got an umbrella," Curtis said.

Samantha allowed Avery to help her on with the garments, moving as quickly as possible so that the men outside wouldn't get soaked through. When she was ready, the others said good-bye, and shut the door behind her, as Samantha and Curtis dashed to the truck under the protection of Curtis's umbrella. Several

cameramen stuck close to them and climbed into the backseat.

She was damp, but luckily the evening was warm, so it wasn't too unpleasant. The sunlight had faded early under the onslaught of the storm, and Samantha was glad Curtis was doing the driving. She had spent far too many nights driving hour after hour struggling to keep the tour bus on the road under difficult conditions. She'd had enough of that, and hoped never to do it again. Thinking about the tour bus made her think of her family, though, and Samantha drooped a little. Were they worried about her? Were they angry that she'd left them in the lurch? Both her parents were just as capable of driving the tour bus as she was, so it wasn't like she'd left them stranded, but they'd still be upset. Everyone in the band depended on her to make so many of the little decisions, and the big ones, too. If it wasn't for the controversy between Curtis and Harris, she was sure that right now she would be filled with a vast sense of relief. She'd left her phone with her things in her tent, wanting to be as much like the other women as possible—and wanting to get away from her family's angry messages.

"Where's Daisy?"

"Back at the bunkhouse with Boone. She's sure taken a shine to me."

"Um-hmm." Sam wasn't going to say more than that. His implication had been easy to read: Daisy had picked Curtis. So should she.

The drive to town was quiet, while Curtis gave the

road his full attention. Samantha appreciated he was giving the weather its due. So many men liked to pretend that they could handle anything, as if it was somehow less masculine to take care in a difficult situation.

When they pulled into the parking lot of the Dancing Boot, she could feel the beat of a bass drum even inside the truck.

"I think they've got live music tonight," Curtis said. "I hope you like dancing."

Samantha loved dancing. That was the best thing about traveling with a band, one of the few perks of a situation that hadn't suited her in a long time. She sometimes grew tired of dancing to the same songs that *Deader Than Ever* played, but in between gigs the band often went out to hear new music. In any given week, she got to see several live shows and dance her heart out. It allowed her to blow off steam, get some exercise and socialize with people outside the band, all at once. Kind of like a yoga class—with alcohol and a beat.

Curtis got out of the truck and came around to open her door. They dashed through the rain again and hurried inside the club where the music was much louder, and the dance floor was full.

Samantha hadn't listened much to country music. Usually her family and the rest of the band opted for funk, bluegrass or folk. Besides, Harris wasn't here with her—and their parting had been anything but amicable. She wished she could go back and soothe his fears that Curtis might change her mind.

The band was quite good, though, and despite her worries, she wondered if an hour on the dance floor would ease the tension that pulled her neck and shoulder muscles tight. She followed Curtis to the bar, feeling guilty. It would be far too disloyal to Harris to do that.

But if Harris hadn't kicked up such a fuss, she could have had a simple evening with Curtis, then told him to back off. They would have finished out the month acting their parts, but there wouldn't have been any more hassle between them.

Harris was the one who'd decided it all had to be difficult. This was her wedding night, and instead of spending it with the man she'd married, she was at a bar with a stranger.

Which meant it was his fault she was here about to dance with Curtis.

Curtis seemed to like the music as much as she did. He quickly got them each a beer at the bar, gave her just enough time to take a couple of swigs, set them aside on a table out of the way and led her to the dance floor.

Dancing in a Regency gown was a little tricky at first, but only because she was self-conscious about it. As soon as she decided that she didn't care—and no one else did, either—Samantha gave herself up to the beat. Curtis turned out to be a terrific dancer. This day had been bizarre from start to finish, and Sam decided it might as well end as strangely as it had begun.

The songs were fast-paced, and soon she had worked up a sweat. She was glad Curtis didn't try to hold hands and dance with her. She didn't want that

from him and he seemed to understand her need to have her own space. Instead he allowed her to move exactly like she wanted to, and followed along with her. She decided to let go of her worries for the time being and tried to relax.

They spent an hour like that, dancing, going back to the table for a drink now and then, enjoying the music and the night. Unfortunately, when a particularly good song ended, the lead singer leaned into the microphone and said, "Let's slow this down, shall we? This song is called *Loving You*."

The band launched into a ballad and before Samantha had time to move away, Curtis placed one hand lightly at her waist and twined the fingers of his other hand through hers. She had the feeling if she tried to pull back, he'd hold on tight and she'd end up making a scene. Sam gave in, but as they began to sway to the music, the evening was spoiled for her. Now she was aware of Curtis as a man, not an acquaintance who was sharing a fun night out. Curtis was a couple of inches taller than Harris. He was heavier set, too. But whereas when she got close to Harris, she tingled all over with anticipation, with Curtis it was different. She didn't feel that tug way down deep inside. She didn't want to, either. All she felt was annoyed.

Still, when Curtis gently pulled her a little closer, she didn't fight him. Instead, she rested her head against his chest and allowed him to put his arms around her. She would give him his chance so he couldn't say she hadn't, even though she already knew the outcome. At the end

of the night, she would have to let Curtis down. She hoped that would be the end of it.

Still, she was aware she was being filmed, which made an uncomfortable situation downright awkward. Had she looked foolish dancing in her Regency gown?

What did she look like now?

"I came to Base Camp because I needed something in my life to believe in," Curtis said softly into her ear. "When I left the Navy, I thought I wanted to be a free man. Turned out I was wrong. Turned out I needed something to guide my days. It's always like this. Before I make a commitment to something, it scares the crap out of me to think that I won't be able to change my mind later on. You should've seen me before I enlisted. Agonized over it for months. Then the minute I signed the paperwork, I knew it was going to be the best thing I ever did, and I never looked back. Same thing when I applied to come and live at Base Camp. Went back and forth, back and forth. Nearly drove my friends nuts. But the day I arrived, I knew this was the place for me. It's like that with marriage, too. Fucking terrifies me." He chuckled grimly. "I was serious about a woman once. Took me ages to get up the nerve to propose—" He cut off.

"What happened?" Sam looked up.

"Didn't work out in the end."

A pang of sympathy squeezed her heart. So Curtis was capable of love—and of being hurt. And she was about to hurt him again.

"You'd think I'd have learned my lesson by now,"

he continued. "Yesterday, when I found out that the pressure was off, and I didn't need to get married, I was so relieved I got stinking drunk. Hit on everybody I could see. But today, when you walked into camp, I got that same feeling I always get. I'm supposed to marry you, Samantha. We're supposed to spend our lives together. I know it's not fair of me to say so, since you already married Harris. I know I'm an asshole. But what I feel is real, and if we don't end up together, I don't know what I'm going to do. I'm supposed to be here in Base Camp. You're supposed to be my wife. That's just the way it is."

He tightened his arms around her as if he didn't mean to let go, and Samantha didn't know what to do. Those were heady words he'd said to her, and they spoke to her of the kind of belonging and finality she'd always hoped for. She had a feeling if her marriage to Harris actually was annulled, and she wed Curtis today, he would stick with her for the long haul. They might not have the instant, passionate connection she had with Harris, but that didn't mean that they couldn't build a life together, or that she couldn't fall in love with him someday.

But even as she thought it, she knew it wasn't true. Maybe they would find contentment together, and maybe love would grow between them, but Curtis deserved to find a woman who felt about him the way she felt about Harris. That glow of instant recognition—and the hunger he inspired in her—were something really special. If she gave that up, she would

always long for it. Curtis needed to find that with someone else.

She tried to extricate herself from his embrace, but Curtis wasn't willing to let her go. "Let's just dance," he said. "I'm not asking you for anything more tonight."

Maybe she owed him that much. It was already late, and soon enough the band would finish playing and they would go home. She'd tell Curtis she had made up her mind. Tomorrow at breakfast she'd let Harris know she'd done so. She was sure he would've calmed down overnight and regretted how he'd behaved.

"He's a hell of a man," Curtis said, as if reading her mind. "I'll never say it to his face, but I respect the hell out of Hawk. He has quite a record, you know."

"What you mean?" She tilted her head to look up at him, noting that Curtis had used the nickname Harris hated.

"Of kills. He's a sniper, and a really good one. The Navy was sorry to see him go. More successful shots than anyone else. When he gets you in his target, you're dead, whether you're fifty feet away from him or a mile. I couldn't do it. Don't get me wrong; I've done plenty of things in the heat of action. But lining up a shot like that, watching your target, spending all that time planning for it before you pull the trigger; that's something else. That takes a kind of detachment I just don't have."

He kept swaying gently to the music, and Samantha kept swaying with him, but the visions of violence Curtis had conjured shocked her. She couldn't picture

Harris as a cold-blooded killer. But then again, he was a SEAL. Of course he'd seen military action; all the men at Base Camp had. But Curtis was right—there was something about a sniper. Something—removed. Controlled.

Calculating.

She hadn't seen any of that in the time she'd spent with him, but they'd only been alone together for a few hours. What did she really know about the man?

Once again, she was all too aware of the cameras that had followed them everywhere tonight. She needed time alone to think this through—to decide if she knew Harris well enough to declare for him tonight when they got home.

Now she wasn't entirely sure. Curtis's words had driven a wedge of doubt in her mind. Was Harris cold and calculating? Was that the kind of man she wanted?

But was Curtis any different? He wasn't an innocent here either. He was targeting her, as sure as Harris had targeted his victims. Saying exactly the right thing to make her doubt her choice.

"I'm getting tired," she said. "I think I need to go home. I had a very early flight this morning, and it's been a long day."

Curtis nodded and led her from the dance floor.

"So what's the verdict?" he asked when they reached their table. He drained his current drink, and Samantha drained hers, too, buying more time. She'd been so sure she would choose Harris when the night was up, but now she was second guessing herself. What

did she really know about him? About either of them?

Would it be so bad to take a month to find out more before she chose?

"I'm going to take those thirty days to make my decision." It hurt to say it out loud—to admit her doubts—but it was the smart thing to do, she told herself.

To Curtis's credit he didn't gloat. "Thank you for giving me a chance" was all he said as he helped her on with her spenser. He took her hand as he led her from the bar, and Samantha swallowed hard, wondering what she'd done.

Outside, the storm had blown over, leaving the air cooler but still humid, lacking the freshness that usually came after a strong rain. It was as if there was another storm coming.

There probably was, she decided.

CHAPTER SEVEN

HARRIS WAS UP early the following morning, despite staying awake most of the night. He'd heard Curtis and Sam come home and go to their respective tents just before midnight, heard Sam talking to the other women as they'd all prepared to settle in for the night. He was pleased Curtis hadn't managed to keep her out later, but they'd been gone long enough for plenty to have happened. All night long he replayed the conversation he'd had with Sam before she returned to the manor. He heard himself order her away from Curtis. Heard how cold he sounded—how domineering. That was no way to win Samantha's heart.

Unable to sleep any longer, he got up well before six, dressed, left his tent and headed out toward Pittance Creek. He'd stalked its banks last night for hours, pacing up and down before finally giving up and heading to bed. This time he took the long way around, feeling the need to walk the perimeter of their encampment. The most threatening thing he saw was a hawk circling high above him. All was quiet in their neck of the woods, so

eventually he found his way down to the creek banks, and stood, hands shoved into his pockets, watching the water run past.

Last night's rain hadn't dispelled that hushed, close, *storm is coming* feeling, and clouds hung low and threatening in the sky. He stared into the creek's depths for a long time, thinking about what he wanted to say to Samantha when they met at breakfast, and became so deeply engaged in the exercise he didn't hear footsteps approaching. Jolted out of his thoughts at the sound of a twig breaking, he spun, prepared for anything, but stopped short when he saw Samantha.

"I'm glad I found you," she said. She was dressed in a plain gown today, in a soft shade of violet that set off her lovely skin. She wore a bonnet, as all the women did when they were outside, and—as always—he had to smother a flicker of irritation about the way the bonnets' brims blocked the wearer's vision. He wanted to warn the women they were making themselves vulnerable by hampering their peripheral vision, but so far he'd managed to stop himself before he said such a ridiculous thing to any of them.

"I'm glad you did, too." He hesitated. For all the thought he had put into it, he still didn't know what to say now she was here. How could he let her know how sorry he was? How much he wished he could take back what he'd said yesterday?

"Harris, I—" She stopped, as if she didn't know what to say, either. Harris couldn't interpret the way she was looking at him. It was different than the way she'd

looked at him yesterday. Almost as if she'd grown shy—or nervous—around him. Was it because she'd spent time with Curtis last night?

Had she done something she felt badly about?

Harris couldn't ask her. He'd only upset her again. He figured there was one way he could make sure of where he stood with Samantha, though. They were alone—no camera crew nearby to film them. He stepped forward to close the gap between them, pulled her into his arms and kissed her. As soon as their mouths met, he had his answer. She melted against him, and the way she responded to his touch told him she wanted him as much as he wanted her. Whatever it was that sparked between them hadn't been put out by last night's storm.

As long as he was holding her, things would be all right.

If only he never had to let her go.

"I want to be with you," Samantha whispered against his neck.

"I want to be with you, too," Harris said. "I didn't mean what I said last night."

"I know. You were angry. I was angry, too."

"That doesn't make what I did right. It's just—" Harris didn't know how to put it into words. He worried he couldn't be enough for her. He felt he never quite belonged. He was beginning to be afraid that even if Samantha joined him, they would both end up on the far side of the roof, instead of becoming part of the community together. He didn't want to do that to her.

He didn't want to be alone, either.

"This is a difficult situation," she said, pulling back. "We're hardly ever going to be alone together like this. I'm going to be forced to go on dates with Curtis. You're going to be forced to watch us. It's all unnatural. But we have to take the time to get to know each other. It'll be worth it in the end."

Harris stilled. So Curtis had gotten to her.

"You didn't tell him to back off." It wasn't a question. He could read the answer in her face.

"No, I didn't. Not because I've changed my mind about you, but because neither of us knows the other well enough to make a decision that will affect the rest of our lives."

She hadn't felt that way yesterday when she'd married him. Curtis had changed her mind.

"You'll pick him." He hadn't meant to say that out loud, but it was true. What woman wouldn't pick an outgoing, fun-loving man over him?

"What happened to make you think no one could love you?"

Harris stepped back. He had a sudden, uncomfortable memory of being seven, standing at the cheap metal screen door of his family's trailer, both hands pressed against its frame, waiting for his father. His dad had left one day and simply hadn't returned. Harris hadn't been able to understand how someone so important could disappear like that.

"Don't bother," his mother had said tiredly as she passed him for the fourth time doing chores around the

trailer. "I told you; he's not coming back."

His mother had been right. He'd never seen his father again. When he'd asked her later what had happened, she waved his question away with that same tired, glazed look he remembered from their first days alone. *He doesn't love us, Harris. Sometimes you just don't win.*

Harris swallowed against a lump that had risen in his throat. He'd overcome all that. He'd made something of himself, kept his family together through thick and thin, made it possible for his sisters to attend college. If his father was stupid enough to throw away the love of an entire family, they didn't need him.

Samantha was waiting for his answer, though. "I know who I am," he said. "All I'm saying is Curtis might suit you better. You don't know yet."

"You're right; I don't," she said quietly. "I'm going to give it thirty days. That will give us all a chance to make the right decision."

He'd lost. No matter what she was saying to soften it, he'd lost.

"We better be getting back." Harris couldn't talk about this. He didn't have the words. He wanted to kiss her again, but after everything she'd said, he couldn't make himself reach out to her.

"I know." She nodded, but didn't move. "Listen, we might not get any more chances to speak like this before the thirty days are up. So whatever happens, whatever this television show makes us do, you need to know that I care about you."

It was Harris's turn to nod, but caring wasn't

enough. She had to love him to make this work, and that's what this conversation was really about. She was telling him she didn't love him. Not yet.

Maybe not ever.

A month of dates with Curtis could change everything.

"I need to know if you feel the same way," she added when he didn't say anything.

Harris nodded. Of course he did. He'd made his pledge to her; she was his life now. She was the wild card here. Didn't Sam know that?

She didn't seem entirely satisfied, but even as she opened her mouth to speak again, voices carried on the wind toward them—Jericho and Boone. Harris knew if they were found alone together like this, the men would assume they'd broken Renata's rules.

"See you back at the camp."

She nodded quickly, and tilted up her chin as if she expected a kiss. Harris wanted to kiss her, wanted that more than anything else, but if he started, he wasn't sure he would be able to stop. It was hard enough, knowing what was to come. So instead, he touched her cheek and strode away.

THE MORNING SEEMED endless to Samantha. She'd greeted Boone and Jericho, exchanged some small talk with them about the weather and hurried back to her tent. When she heard the other women talking as they got ready for the day, she joined them. Avery, who'd also been up early, had lent her the fresh work gown

until Alice brought the rest of the clothes over, and helped her with her stays earlier, but Sam took advantage of the time in her tent to smooth her hair again and re-tie her bonnet.

Ten minutes later, Harris walked up the dirt path from Pittance Creek, whistling. His hair was wet and slicked back, and it looked as if he taken an early morning swim. Renata met him at the edge of the camp, and appeared to be scolding him for not telling one of the camera crews where he was going.

"We'll re-create that scene later today," she said. "A wet, bare-chested Navy SEAL will do wonders for our ratings."

Samantha wondered what Renata would say if she knew the two of them had been together. She would probably want to re-create that, too, although Samantha had a feeling Renata would prefer an R-rated version to the conversation they'd actually had.

It still hurt to think about Harris's expression when she'd let him know she hadn't told Curtis to keep his distance. It had gone hard, as if he was filing this loss with all the others he'd suffered in his life, and Sam had wanted to assure him it wasn't like that.

But it kind of was.

After eating breakfast near the other women, she joined Harris and Curtis at the building site. Clay and Nora were still on their honeymoon, which left the three of them alone. Curtis and Harris each had a job to do, and each of them tried to co-opt her as his assistant. She did her best to take turns, but the two men had her

running back and forth, and soon she grew irritated.

She was bracing a 2x4 for Harris when Curtis called from the makeshift workbench he'd set up on two sawhorses nearby, "Sam? I need an extra pair of hands here."

"I'll be there in a minute," she called back.

"I need you now."

"You'll have to wait."

A second later, Curtis stormed over to see you what the delay was, just as Harris finished his task.

"You managed to do all of this without her before," he told Harris.

"So did you," Harris said.

"Clay was here working with me, or did you forget him?"

"I haven't forgotten anything." Harris straightened, the drill in his hand, and his watchful, steady stance called forth an image in Samantha's mind—one that Curtis had put there only the night before. Harris in uniform, a gun in his hand, his eagle gaze locked on the target. Samantha inadvertently took a step back, realizing too late that left her closer to Curtis. A flicker of Harris's gaze let her know he noticed. His expression tightened. "Go on. Help him now," he said, then turned around without another word and got back to work.

Samantha, kicking herself for what she'd done, followed Curtis to the sawhorses.

"This piece needs to be sanded down until its smooth all over," Curtis told her. It was an interestingly curved piece of wood that he told her he was planning

to use over the mantle of one of the doors. It had once been a tree branch, but he had cut away all the excess wood, leaving just the stubs of branches. "It will take some time, so go easy. You don't have to push hard on the wood; let the sandpaper do the work for you."

He demonstrated what he wanted, and left her to it, moving to sort through a stack of logs like the one she was working on.

Samantha expected Harris to call her back at any moment, but as seconds stretched out into minutes, and a half hour passed, and then an hour, she realized he wasn't going to play the game anymore. It hurt her feelings more than she'd expected. Maybe he was taking the higher road, refusing to treat her like a ping-pong ball in a match between him and Curtis, but it felt to her like he had given up already. She wanted him to fight for her.

As the time went past, Curtis set up another pair of sawhorses and got to work on another piece of wood. He asked her questions about her childhood, her family and her aspirations. She did her best to answer him, although she considered her words carefully. Curtis was capable of playing dirty if it meant he got what he wanted. Still, now that Harris was keeping to himself, he proved an affable, easy companion. Despite her intentions to stay disengaged, she found herself relaxing as the morning went on, and asked him questions, too. He was a man she could've been friends with if not for the circumstances. Maybe someday they would laugh about this, all of them together.

At the moment, that seemed unlikely.

After an hour and a half, Boone came by to check on them. He examined the piece of work that Samantha was just finishing up. "That looks great."

"Thanks." Samantha was feeling proud of what she'd done. When she'd stopped bouncing back and forth between the two men, she'd had enough time to accomplish something.

"I'm going to steal Samantha from you, if you don't mind," Boone said loudly enough for both men to hear. "It's time she had a tour of the whole operation here. She needs to be able to understand the big picture."

Samantha put down her sandpaper gratefully and rubbed her shoulder. She wasn't used to this kind of work, and her arm was sore. She waved to Harris as they passed, and he nodded, but got right back to work without comment. Frustrated, Samantha decided to make the most of the tour and find out everything she could about Base Camp. She wasn't going to let the tension between Harris and Curtis get her down.

"Everything going smoothly this morning?" Boone asked, when they were far enough from the building site so that the men wouldn't overhear.

"Smoothly enough," she said. "They make everything into a competition, don't they?"

Boone chuckled. "Yeah, I guess you could say that."

As he took her around to various points of interest, Samantha began to get a better idea of how things ran at Base Camp. Of course, she'd seen most of it on television, so there weren't any real surprises, except that the

A SEAL'S PLEDGE | 191

people seemed as cheerful and hardworking in real life as they came across on TV. She viewed everything with interest, and listened to all that Boone had to say, but it wasn't until they reached their last stop, the gardens, that her heart quickened and she really wanted to know more.

As they walked through the rows of vegetables, and in and out of the greenhouses, Samantha knew she had to become a part of this, especially when Boone began to demonstrate the ways in which they were working to make their whole system self-sustaining. Win was there, cheerfully harvesting snap peas. She smiled and waved as they walked past.

At one point, as Boone was showing her how they controlled the temperature in the greenhouses, he stopped and smiled. "You're glowing," he said.

"I find it all fascinating," she told him. "Do you have any books I could read to learn more about closed-system gardening?"

"Sure," Boone said. "Most of them are in my house, but I can move them into the bunkhouse and get Clay to build a bookshelf. We should have a library of resources that anyone can access. Let's go find one or two to get you started."

CHAPTER EIGHT

ROY EGAN WAS hard at work when Harris and Sam—and a camera crew—arrived at his property later that afternoon, but he set down his hammer, wiped his hands on his apron and came to greet them.

"Welcome. Glad you could come." He immediately began to give them a tour of the forge, pointing out tools and half-finished projects. The entire space was neat and tidy, every tool clean and in its place, and Harris recognized the trappings of a real expert. It had been a little awkward when he and Sam had met up again at lunch and she'd reiterated her desire to meet Egan and see his forge. Harris had thought she might have changed her mind after how surly he'd been this morning. He'd hated himself the whole time for acting that way, but didn't know what else to do. Should he have kept calling her back to help him? Should he have flattened Curtis with his fists?

Something told him he needed to give Sam time— but he also knew he had to pull it together and show her who he really was.

A SEAL'S PLEDGE | 193

Maybe this was his chance.

Egan worked on everything from horseshoes to latches and hinges to fancy metalwork gates. "Pretty much, if you can draw me a picture of what you want, I can make it," he said at one point.

Harris's fingers itched to pick up the tools and get to work. He'd had a metalwork class or two back in high school, and had always excelled at it. While the other kids had created clumsy ashtrays and candlesticks, he had made each of his sisters an intricate metal bracelet. His teacher had insisted that the bracelets be displayed in the yearly art show, much to his embarrassment.

Egan must've seen his interest, because he took up a horseshoe-shaped piece of metal and a pair of tongs, held it over his forge to heat, put it on the anvil and gave a whack or two with his hammer, before turning to Harris and saying, "Now it's your turn to give it a go. You can't hurt this horseshoe, and it'll give you a feel for the work."

Harris donned the protective gear Egan gave him, took the hammer and tongs, heated the metal again and gave it a try. He ignored the cameramen zooming in on his hands. He was confident he could learn the trade, and if he didn't do it right from the first, that was okay.

The movement was as reflexive as if he was coming home to a job he'd always done, and Harris knew he'd found something he hadn't even known he was looking for. He worked at the horseshoe, shaping it until he instinctively knew it was ready for use. When he looked up, Egan was nodding. "You've got the feel for it," he

said. "I had a hunch you would."

"I'd like to watch you work for a bit," Harris told him. "I'd like to see how you do that fancy work."

Egan took over again without comment, set the horseshoe aside and picked up a long piece of metal. For the next hour, Harris and Sam watched in awe as Egan over and over again turned raw pieces of metal into art. Harris wasn't sure when he'd seen the camera crews so intent; they were getting great footage for the next episode.

Sam leaned close to him. "That's what you want to do, isn't it?" she asked in a low voice.

Harris nodded. He wanted it more than anything else. "I've got responsibilities at Base Camp, though." He made sure Egan overheard his words. "I'd like to study blacksmithing, but I need to do my part."

"Seems to me there will be plenty of uses for a blacksmith in that community of yours," Egan said. "Plus, like I said, I've been looking for somebody to take over when I retire. As long as there's horses, there will be a need. It will be a way to bring in a little extra cash for your operation."

"I'll talk it over with Boone and the others. See what they have to say. But if you'll have me, I'd like to spend a couple hours a day here."

"Any time."

When Egan was done with his demonstration, he showed the two of them over the rest of his property, and ended by ushering them into his small home, where his wife, Bertie, served them coffee, handing cups to the

crew, as well.

"What will you do when you retire?" Samantha asked, accepting a cup and placing it on the table in front of her.

Bertie, a jolly woman several years younger than Egan, answered for him. "We got ourselves a travel trailer a few years back, and we plan to see the country. We've been too busy up until now."

Samantha's smile looked a little strained, and Harris remembered what she told him about her upbringing. Touring the country in a small vehicle probably didn't hold the charms for her that it held for Bertie. Samantha held her tongue, however.

The forge had distracted Harris, but as they walked back toward the truck a half hour later, alone except for the cameras, he couldn't help focusing on Samantha again. As if they'd planned it, they stopped by the truck, Samantha leaning against it, and Harris standing in front of her. Despite the presence of the crew, he took both of her hands. "I miss you. Thought about you all last night." There, that was better than he'd managed lately.

"I thought about you, too."

Harris wanted to believe that, but she'd spent hours in Curtis's company. He knew he should leave that alone, but he found himself asking, "How did it go? Last night?"

Samantha looked away. "It went fine. But Curtis isn't you."

Harris wanted to kiss her. Needed to kiss her. But with the cameras right there, he wouldn't be able to get

away with that. Instead, he tried to tell her with his fingers, squeezing hers, and with his gaze. Finally he said, "I need you."

"I know," she said softly. "We have to be patient."

"I'm not sure I know how to do that." He wasn't being fair, but he wanted her to know that if it was possible, he'd be willing. "Remember before? Where we met this morning?" he whispered, and noticed the cameramen leaning in, pressing closer to record every word.

She nodded, almost imperceptibly.

"Any time." That was all he could get away with now, but he hoped she understood. If she gave him a sign—any sign—he'd meet her by the creek.

Aching to touch her, but gratified he'd managed to smooth things between them a little, he swallowed down his desire and opened the door to the passenger side for her. He helped her in, touching her more than was necessary, and then reluctantly shut the door. As he climbed in on his own side, the crew got in behind them. They wouldn't even have privacy during the ride back to Base Camp. Harris had never been tortured like this over a woman. All he could do was count the days, and pray he somehow won Samantha forever.

THEY GOT HOME in time for dinner, but Samantha was far too distracted to think about eating. She filled her plate with the lettuce wraps Kai had made, and picked up a glass of water, following Harris out to sit on one of the logs around the empty fire pit, but once there, she

only played with her food. When Harris had taken the hammer and tongs Egan had offered him and tried them out, his body had been as much a work of art as Egan's metal gates. His biceps were sculpted, his shoulders bunching and releasing under his cotton T-shirt. She'd had to swallow hard against the ache in her throat, and another one deep inside her.

Every blow of his hammer had made his muscles ripple in a way that reminded her of being alone with him—touching him. She wanted to touch him again. All of him.

Sam thought about what he had said back at Roy Egan's. That any time she wanted, he would meet her at the creek again. It was too big of a risk; she couldn't jeopardize everything for a few minutes alone with him, but she wanted to. Badly. Surely that would wash away any trouble between them, along with her fears of who he might really be.

Instead, she'd keep busy—and keep getting to know him. She needed to keep her head, for both their sakes. Still, her mouth was dry, her fingers ached to touch him and she had no idea how she would last twenty-nine days until she could announce her choice.

When Curtis came to sit beside her on the log, Samantha let out a low sound of displeasure, then bit her lip as he scowled. "Did you have fun on your *field trip*?" he asked derisively.

"I did. It was fascinating, especially watching Harris swing the hammer."

Curtis's eyes narrowed, and Sam knew she was play-

ing with fire making her preference so clear. But at the moment, she didn't think she could continue this game. She wanted Harris, and she didn't care who knew it. Why on earth hadn't she put an end to this contest last night? She could kick herself for letting Curtis make her second-guess herself.

"You spent the afternoon with Harris, so it's my turn tonight," he said.

"Hell, no," Harris spoke up. "We already said it's my turn tonight. Stop trying to horn in on things."

"I don't see how that's fair. You get too much time alone with her, you'll trick her into thinking that you're the one she wants."

"I *am* the one she wants."

"That remains to be seen until the time's up." Both men were leaning forward, talking over her as if she wasn't there. Samantha lost her temper.

"I'm going out with Harris tonight," she said. "That's what we agreed to, and that's what I'm going to do. Your turn comes tomorrow."

Curtis turned toward the nearest cameraman. "You all had better keep watching them every minute," he said. "I don't trust this guy farther than I could throw him, and while I could throw him pretty far, that's still saying something."

"You couldn't lift me off the ground," Harris told him, setting his plate aside and dusting off his hands.

"Like hell I couldn't," Curtis said, doing the same.

Samantha had had enough. She stood up, her plate and glass in her hand, and went to sit near the other

single women. She hated that she'd turned her back on Harris as well as Curtis, but she wasn't going to participate in their game. For one thing, it would alienate both of them from the rest of the members of Base Camp, and that was the last thing she wanted.

"Can I join you? I'm sorry for the commotion," she said to the gathered women. She settled in next to Win on another log and set her plate in her lap.

"Must be nice, having two men fight over you," Avery said, a little sourly, Samantha thought.

"I don't find it fun. I know who I like, and I wish I could just be with him." Again, she wished she'd made her preference clear the night before. What had she been afraid of? That Harris had been a sniper? Every one of the men here had a long career in the military. None of them were saints.

Still, it was reasonable to spend a month getting to know a man before committing to him forever, she reminded herself.

"Join the club," Avery said.

"What's the deal with Walker?" Samantha asked her, ready to change the subject.

"Yeah, what *is* the deal with Walker?" Win echoed.

"I don't know," Avery said. "He doesn't tell me anything. I thought after his grandmother began working with Nora on the curriculum they're writing together, she'd change her mind about me. Nora told me at the wedding she thought Sue wasn't as opposed to me as she used to be, but maybe Walker doesn't know that. He hovers around like he's interested, but he never asks

me out. He never touches me. With Nora and Clay still on their honeymoon, Sue hasn't come near the place. When she does, I'm going to confront her. I need to know once and for all if she'll ever give Walker her blessing to care for me." She shrugged. "But then I wonder if I'm making a fool of myself. Maybe Walker doesn't care for me at all, and Sue is giving him an easy way out."

"He cares for you," Savannah said. "That's evident to anyone who looks at him. If something's holding him back, it's for an honorable reason."

"What about you and Jericho?" Avery asked her. "Are you two ever going to act on the passion that's always smoldering between you? Inquiring minds want to know."

"I have no idea," Savannah said, sounding so discouraged that Samantha wanted to pat her on the back and tell her it would all be okay. But she didn't know Savannah, and she had no idea if it would be okay. None of them needed to be lied to.

"Oh!" Win cried out, half standing, as Curtis took a swing at Harris across the way. Boone and Jericho had already sprung up to push them apart.

"That's it," Curtis said. "I don't want him anywhere near me. I don't want him anywhere near my houses. You find him another job."

"They're as much my houses as they are yours," Harris answered him. "I'll work there if Boone needs me there. But if he doesn't, I'll be happy to move on." He turned to Boone. "I want to build a forge. I'll be

studying with Egan, and it won't be long before I can handle the horseshoes and any other metalwork we might need around here. When Egan retires, I'll take over the jobs he's got going. It'll be an income stream for the community."

After a moment, Boone nodded. "That makes sense. You go ahead studying with Egan. The framing on the current house is done, right?"

"Near enough," Harris said.

"If Curtis and Clay need an extra pair of hands, Sam will be there to help, anyway."

Samantha saw Harris's face darken. She quickly stood up. "I'm not going to work on the houses either," she said loudly, hardly believing she was being so bold when she was so new in the community. "I want to work in the gardens. That's where my interests lie." She lifted her chin and met Boone's gaze. "Besides, you need to keep my time fair between Curtis and Harris. I can't work with one and not the other."

Boone only hesitated for a moment. "You're right, that wouldn't be fair. I'd be glad to have you join us in the gardens."

Samantha let her shoulders relax. She met Harris's gaze from across the fire pit and smiled. His expression relaxed, and the corners of his mouth turned up. He nodded.

That was a step in the right direction.

CHAPTER NINE

THE NEXT FEW days passed more rapidly than Harris could've imagined, but the nights seemed endlessly long. During the daytime, he spent most of his time over at the Egans' place, learning his new skill. The work was hard, and sometimes his fingers felt so clumsy he thought he'd never get the hang of what Egan was showing him, but with each day his touch grew surer, and his repertoire of metalworking skills grew broader. Along with working at the forge, Egan was also teaching him more about horses. Each day, Egan gave him a quick riding lesson on the tracks around the property, during which he taught Harris about horse anatomy and what factors affected the fit of a horseshoe.

On the trail, Egan would point out different conditions of the ground, and how they might affect a horse's gait and its ability to hold on to a shoe. He pointed out what to look for on a horse's hoof, and the shoe itself, when one got thrown. Along the way, he threw in every bit of information that crossed his mind, saying that if Harris was going to settle in Chance Creek, he needed

to know about the landscape as well as horses.

That was a lesson Harris had learned many times over during his time with the SEALs. The landscape was everything. The animals and people that inhabited it were shaped by it in all aspects. Most people never realized that, but once you did, you were far more able to predict people's movements, and that anticipation could mean the difference between life and death.

He was a quick learner, and he knew that made Egan feel proud. "Always wanted a son to take over for me," he said once, "but the Lord didn't see fit to give me one. Now here you are."

Harris didn't like to admit, even to himself, the comment had thickened his throat. He'd had to clear it a time or two before he'd been able to speak. "I'm glad to be here," was all he managed to say. It'd been enough. Egan's nod had told him that.

He enjoyed Bertie's company, too. She was such a cheerful woman, and she was always happy to have someone to talk to. Harris told her all the latest gossip from Base Camp, and she admitted she watched the show every week on television.

"Glad to hear it, ma'am," he told her. "That's the reason we're doing the show. So that people can learn from us."

"I think what I'm learning is that it's dangerous to have so many single men in one place," she said with a big laugh.

"You think Base Camp is bad," Harris said. "Try being in the military."

Tonight it was his turn to take Samantha out again, for which he was grateful. The nights she went out with Curtis were even longer than the rest of them. And they were all long. He lay in his tent wound up tighter than a bowstring, with no relief. He kept waiting for that sign, but Samantha never gave it to him. When he pressed her, she whispered it wasn't safe. She couldn't put everybody in jeopardy over her desire to be with him. He told himself to be grateful she wanted to be with him at all, but it was hard to keep his frustration in check. Until she'd made her announcement at the end of thirty days, he'd be wound up no matter what happened.

Deciding to focus on one day at a time, he had made reservations at a restaurant in town, so at least they would be away from the others. Delmonaco's was a busy restaurant that served a killer steak, and was always hopping on a Friday night. Surrounded by the camera crew, it was hard to see the rest of the patrons, and when he did glance their way, it was to find most of the other diners staring back at him. Harris tried to focus on Samantha, instead.

When they had ordered, he took Samantha's hand across the table. "How goes the gardening?"

"I love everything about it. I'm learning so much; Boone is a whiz at this."

"From what I've heard, his parents kept a big garden. He grew up with it, but all the sustainable stuff he's learned on his own. He's been on fire for it for years."

The waitress appeared with their salads. "Enjoy."

"Tell me more about your family," Harris said. Renata had given him a nudge earlier in the day to ask the question, and while normally he hated to do anything she said, he figured it was harmless. They'd already gone over some of that ground the first day they'd met. In truth, he was interested in the family that he hoped to stay married into. He vaguely knew the band her parents and sister played for, but it had never been one of his favorites. He was more aware of the controversy they sometimes kicked up when they joined environmental protests.

Samantha sighed. "My parents both joined *Deader Than Ever* before I was born," she said, and he realized she was talking to the cameras and must have understood it was time for her to explain more about her past. "They've always been passionate about music, and about protesting. The band champions all kinds of causes. Everything from racial equality to environmentalism."

"How do you think they'll feel about your joining Base Camp?" he asked. Another line he'd been fed by Renata.

"They'll hate it." She smiled and shrugged at him.

"I don't understand. If they're environmentalists, won't they support what we're doing here?"

Samantha shook her head. "It's not about what we're doing here; it's about who's doing it. My parents hate everything about the military. They hate war, and they feel like having a large military causes more problems than it solves."

"Is that the way you feel?" They were trespassing on dangerous ground. Harris hoped they weren't stumbling into a fight.

"Honestly? I don't know the answer to that question. I mean, I don't know if having a big military leads to more problems, or vice versa. What I've learned since I've been here is that all of you had the best of intentions when you joined the military. None of you did so to cause problems; you did it because you thought you would be able to solve them. And that's the same reason you joined Base Camp. I admire that. I'm here for the same reason."

"Do you think your parents will understand that?" He squeezed her hand, willing her to understand that no matter what the differences in their backgrounds, he wanted to be with her. In fact, he was ready to be done with the conversation and cut to some serious fooling around. That wasn't on the table tonight, though.

"No, I don't. All they'll see is the ways in which Base Camp resembles a military outfit. Face it, Base Camp has a definite hierarchy. Boone's on top, running everything. We women are on the bottom, taking orders. My parents will hate that."

Harris leaned forward. "What about you? Do you hate that?"

"I'm okay with it, for now. I'm assuming that someday this dictatorship will transform into a democracy, but I don't hear you guys talk about it much."

Harris took a bite of his salad to give himself a moment to form an answer. "The thing is, a dictatorship

makes it easy to get stuff done quickly. We all understand that, having spent years in the military. I know it's not that palatable for civilians, but it works."

Samantha leaned forward, too. "But it can't last. There has to be a way that Base Camp can grow and mature into a democracy."

Harris nodded. "Of course." He stabbed another forkful of lettuce. "Do you think your parents' way is better?" It wouldn't surprise him if she did. Families had a strong influence.

Samantha sat back, and in doing so slid her hand from his. Harris missed its soft warmth. "No, I don't think their way is better. All they do is sing. And protest. They never get their hands dirty, they never do anything real. What's changed in their lifetime? They're still singing. People are still polluting, still consuming far too much, still filling their landfills with crap." As if suddenly realizing her words were being recorded, Samantha shut her mouth with a snap and bit her lip. "The salad is wonderful," she said suddenly. "What do you think is going to happen with Savannah and Jericho?"

Knowing she was hoping to provide the camera crew—and Renata—with something more interesting to focus on than her family, Harris took the bait. They analyzed the situation between Savannah and Jericho for a number of minutes, coming up with more and more outlandish reasons for why the couple kept apart when it was so obvious to everyone they were interested in each other.

"Maybe Savannah secretly pledged herself to celiba-

cy when she was young," Sam was saying when the waitress appeared again to clear away their salad plates and serve the main course. "Maybe she's afraid to go back on a deal she made with God."

"Maybe Jericho is already married, and is frantically getting a divorce as we speak," Harris said. "Or maybe he has a gay lover stashed somewhere." He would probably pay for that later, but he was willing to feed Jericho to the wolves, if it kept Samantha's unkind words about her parents off the air.

"I wish I could kiss you," Sam said suddenly.

Harris swallowed, and shifted in his seat. Throughout everything, his desire for her had raged unabated. Now it surged all over again. "I wish I could kiss you, too," he said. "Hell, I wish I could take you to bed right now."

She smiled, and Harris realized that she was playing it up for the cameras. She must be really desperate to keep what she'd said off the show. He'd go with it, but not because he cared about her parents' feelings. He simply enjoyed the verbal foreplay. "If I had you alone, I'd get that gown off of you, and anything else you're wearing underneath it, and I would lay you out on my bed and take a good long look at you, before I got down to the matter at hand."

She licked her lips again. "And if I got you alone, I'd get you naked as fast as humanly possible, and welcome you to do whatever you liked."

Harris nearly growled, his need for her was so bad. "I'd make the most of it."

"That's what I'd be counting on."

Harris wasn't sure how much longer he could do this without making a spectacle of himself. Samantha must've understood. She took a mouthful of her manicotti and moaned with pleasure.

"That's not helping," he said.

"Maybe I don't want to help," she said. "Maybe I want to drive you wild."

"Honey, if you're trying to drive me wild, you succeeded days ago."

"WIN, COULD YOU help me with my gown?" Samantha asked the following afternoon when she had finished up her work in the gardens. Her muscles ached, she was exhausted, and she couldn't remember ever being happier. All day, as she'd transplanted seedlings from the greenhouse into the dirt outside and helped to start set up their hydroponics system, she'd replayed her date with Harris in her mind, especially the last parts, in which he'd made it all too clear how much he wanted her. This was so much more satisfying than driving the bus, and so much more meaningful, too. She wished she could show her parents around the gardens, and show them what she was doing. She wanted to explain to them she didn't mean to hurt them by leaving them behind.

She tried to picture who had taken over her job. Had her mother or sister done so? Or had the band brought in somebody from the outside? She hoped there hadn't been too much disruption in their schedule

while they made the transition.

"Sure thing," Win said.

They'd had many chances to chat during the day and Sam had enjoyed Win's sharp sense of humor. She gathered up everything she needed and led the way to the bunkhouse bathroom. Win helped her change, waiting while Sam washed up and then lacing up her new gown.

"Who's the lucky man tonight?"

"It's Curtis tonight." Sam sighed. She wasn't looking forward to another round of sparring with the man. With each date, he was working harder to impress her, and the worst of it was she was pretty sure they could've been friends if he wasn't trying to make her his wife. Curtis was nice enough when he wasn't being pushy, but there wasn't a single spark between them. She wasn't sure if Curtis was blind to that, or if his pride refused to allow him to back down. She'd tried hinting she'd changed her mind about giving it thirty days and wanted him to stop pursuing her. He'd only shaken his head. "That was a one-time offer. You chose to give me a month. I expect you to keep your word. Besides, it's what Renata wants."

Sam couldn't argue that.

More than once, she'd wondered about that other woman Curtis had mentioned; the one he'd proposed to, but hadn't ended up marrying. Was she the reason he wouldn't take no for an answer?

Whatever made him so stubborn, Sam was getting tired of it.

A SEAL'S PLEDGE | 211

"Where is he taking you?"

"I don't know. But I'm going to miss dinner here." That annoyed her. She didn't mind going out when it meant she and Harris could be together, but if she kept missing all of the group dinners at Base Camp, it would keep her separate from the others. It was as if she was still on trial here, rather than a full member of the community. As long as Curtis and Harris were fighting over her, it would stay that way.

"Want me to do your hair?" Win gathered Samantha's long hair into her hands, took the brush Sam offered her and got to work. Sam stood in front of the mirror and watched her progress. This was something that she hadn't known in her former life. It had always been as if her mother and sister were in competition with her, and she'd never felt like pushing hard enough to win. She'd always held back, and that had kept a certain distance between them.

Here, the women helped each other because they had to. Their old fashioned clothing was designed for an era far different than the current one. You couldn't lace up your own stays. It was difficult to do up the fastenings of your gown by yourself. Their daily interactions made them closer.

"There," Win said.

Samantha looked at her reflection. Win had rolled the bulk of her hair into a neat chignon. "Thank you."

When she came out of the bunkhouse, Harris was waiting for her. "Don't fall for him," he said, with a lazy smile that told her he wasn't too worried about it

anymore.

"I won't," she said. "I think I know which man I want."

Harris stepped closer. "Maybe I'd better think about buying a ring," he said loudly for the cameras present, winking to remind her he had their wedding rings for safe-keeping. She nodded back, aching to cross the distance between them and press a kiss to his mouth.

"Samantha, you ready to go for a ride?" Curtis drawled the words in a lazy twang that gave them a meaning they shouldn't have. When she turned, startled, his knowing smile implied a far closer relationship than the one they had.

"Watch it," Harris said.

"Relax," Curtis said. "Samantha will be in good hands tonight. I know exactly how to treat her."

Every sentence made it worse, and Samantha backed away, afraid the men would come to blows again. Instead, Curtis took her elbow. "Come on, sweetheart, we don't want to be late for our date. I've been looking forward to this all day. Couldn't get you out of my mind."

With a final warning look at Harris she hoped would keep him from rising to Curtis's bait, Sam accompanied him to the truck and climbed in. Curtis waited until she'd arranged her skirts around her legs, and shut the door. He said something to Harris she didn't quite catch, and a minute later he was in the truck, too, and had started the engine.

A half-hour later, she was holding a paper bag of

take-out food in her lap as Curtis drove. They were going on a picnic, although Curtis had yet to tell her where. The ride had been quiet, the inevitable cameramen in the backseat shifting in the silence, as if begging them to give them something to film. Samantha didn't mind the lack of conversation, however. She wasn't sure how much more she had to say to Curtis, and she had a feeling things were coming to a head between them.

It wasn't until Curtis pulled off from the highway onto a rutted road that Samantha began to recognize her surroundings. He was taking her down the same track Harris had the day she'd met him. The day she'd married him.

"No," she said. "Not here."

"Yes, here. Trust me, it's one of the prettiest spots around, and it's where we're going to have our dinner."

Samantha couldn't say more in front of the cameras, but heading up this road felt like trespassing. She had no idea if Curtis had somehow figured out where she and Harris had gone that first morning, or if this was purely a coincidence. When Curtis pulled over and climbed out, she refused to move. "Anywhere but here," she said when Curtis opened her door.

Curtis leaned in across her, undid her seat belt and lifted her down from the truck. He held her like that a moment, a hand on each hip, and leaned in close. She was afraid he would try to kiss her, but instead he whispered in her ear, "Look, I don't know another picnic spot, and the sun's going down. If we have to stop now and retrace our steps, it's going to screw

everything up, and we'll have to do it again tomorrow night. Is that what you want?"

Someone swiped the paper bag from her hand; one of the cameramen.

Curtis's hands remained on her hips, and she covered them with hers, trying to peel his away. "No." Curtis was right; she didn't want that. Tomorrow night she wanted to be with Harris, which meant she would have to get through this the best she could.

"So you're okay with this?"

She definitely wasn't okay with it, but she nodded. "Let's go."

Curtis finally stepped back, took her hand and led the way to the small track that curved into the woods. When he turned back, flashed a grin at the cameramen and gave them a thumbs up, Samantha wanted to smack him, but she kept her cool and walked as quickly as she could, wanting to get this over with. Curtis kept a hand on her arm and slowed her down. Sam was fuming by the time they reached the overlook.

"Where's the food?" she snapped, then realized one of the crewmembers must have darted ahead of them, and set up the scene as if Curtis had done it himself earlier. A beautiful blanket was laid out on the ground. A picnic basket was artfully arranged, its lid open, displaying silverware and tempting food, including the take-out fare, which now was presented in covered containers.

"Have a seat," Curtis said.

Against her will, Samantha did so, a growing sense

of unease in her gut. All of this was too well thought out. The camera crew seemed to be in on it. She didn't know what that meant, but she had a feeling it wasn't good.

"What's going on?" She decided on a direct approach.

"What's going on is our time is running out," Curtis said. "We only have a few weeks to get to know each other before you make your decision. I want you to really know what kind of man I am."

"What kind of a man are you?" Sam wondered if she'd just stepped into a trap.

"The kind of man who wants you. The kind of man who would do just about anything to get you." As he spoke, he leaned forward again, and once more, Samantha braced herself for a kiss. It never came, which almost disappointed her; because if it did, she could cry foul and Curtis would lose.

Of course he knew that, too. Instead of kissing her, he touched her cheek, slid his hand along her jaw and around to the nape of her neck. He leaned even closer. It was as intimate a gesture as possible without taking anything too far. "We could be happy together," he told her. "I would worship the ground you walked on. I would do everything I could to make you happy—work hard, stay by your side, be a man you could depend on." He searched her face with his gaze. "Think about it, Samantha. I'm more a part of this community than Harris could ever be. I don't just hang on the sidelines of things, I get involved. The people here are connected

to me. Can't you see how suspicious Harris is? How he holds himself apart from everybody else? It's like he doesn't trust any of us, and he never will. As his wife, you'll always be an outsider, too."

Curtis's words hit home. She had observed what he said; Harris did tend to keep himself apart from the others. She was afraid that as his wife, his distance from the group would extend to her, too. Sometimes, she worried what their relationship would be like over time. Would a distance grow between them, too? She didn't think she could stand that. And what if they had children? How would he behave toward them?

"I'm a family man," Curtis said, as if he'd read her mind. "I want a big family. I already belong to one, and I've always enjoyed it. When the time is right, my relatives will come and visit, and you'll see how it is. No one's ever lonely around us."

The picture he was painting touched desires Sam had hardly admitted to herself she had. It must've shown in her face, because he leaned in closer. "Imagine us, living at Base Camp, our children running around with all the other kids in the community. Sharing meals with them, visiting back and forth in the evenings. You hanging out with the other women, knowing that everything is right between me and the other men. We'd be the ones to organize social events. Our kids would be friends with everyone else. Right in the center of the community, that's where we'd be. Now imagine it with Harris. You know he'll keep to himself rather than joining in. If you have children—*if*—he'll train them to

be the same way. You'll always be on the outside of things. Is that what you want?"

Samantha shook her head before she even knew what she was doing, and a tear slid down her cheek because he was naming all of her own fears. Before she could wipe it away, Curtis beat her to it, his thumb smearing the wetness across her cheek.

"Don't cry." He spoke so loudly she jumped and pulled back. "It's going to be all right," he continued in that clear, distinct voice. "I'm here. You don't have to marry Harris."

"What? That's not what I—" Before Samantha could set him straight, Curtis turned toward the picnic basket and began to fix her a plate of food. She sat there, fuming, knowing everything that he'd said and done had been for the cameras. When he handed her the plate, she took it ungraciously, picked up a piece of fried chicken and stared at it, trying to figure out how to fix what he'd done. What could she do to make him back off and stop providing the cameras with fodder for the show?

But Curtis seemed to have lost interest in doing so. He spent the rest of the evening chatting with her so politely she began to doubt her sanity. She remained aloof, but as the meal went on, with Curtis doing his best to lighten the mood, she couldn't keep up her sullen responses. She finally gave up. It was hard to remain curt when he was being so sociable. With the cameras filming, she realized she was only helping his case. Curtis was coming across as a cultured, respectable

man. She looked like a sulky idiot. There was nothing for it but to answer his questions and make conversation, which wasn't all that difficult with a man as knowledgeable and witty as Curtis could be. Once again, she found herself feeling that if it wasn't for the show they could've been friends. But not when he kept playing dirty.

When the meal was finished, he poured her a glass of wine and one for himself, and leaned back on one hand to gaze up at the stars. He began pointing out the constellations he knew, and after a time she joined in. They discussed stars and galaxies, the age of the universe and how it got there in the first place. When she finished her glass, he refilled it again. He hadn't said or done anything objectionable in over an hour and she finally relaxed. How long had it been since she'd had a night to merely gaze up at the sky and contemplate the universe? She couldn't remember the last time she'd done so. Curtis turned out to be a wealth of information about heavenly objects, and in the end, they had a lively debate about the cause of the Big Bang.

Samantha had lost track of how much time had passed, and how many glasses of wine she had drunk, when Curtis finally said, "It's probably time to get back. More work tomorrow."

"That's right," she said with satisfaction. She couldn't wait to get up in the morning and get her hands back into the dirt again. She stood and began to help Curtis pack up, surprised to find herself swaying a little on her feet. More than once Curtis had to steady her,

but he made a joke of it and put her at ease.

They stumbled back down the little track toward the truck by the light of Curtis's phone. He had taken her hand at the beginning, but soon she needed to lean on him in order to navigate the bumps and curves in the dark. By the time they reached the truck, Curtis's arm was around her, supporting her over the uneven ground. He opened the passenger side door for her and helped her in. Leaning across to fasten her seat belt around her, he took advantage of his position to snatch a kiss the cameras couldn't see.

Samantha sucked in a surprised breath. "Don't," she hissed, as quietly as she could; she didn't want the cameramen to even suspect something had happened.

Curtis tucked her skirt around her legs and shut the door on her, without acknowledging her words. When he climbed in the driver's side, she asked loudly, "Are you even safe to drive?"

"I'm not the one who's been drinking," he answered just as loudly, and started the truck. A moment later the truck was bumping down the rutted road back toward the highway.

Stunned, Samantha kept quiet. Hadn't he been drinking, too?

Maybe not. She couldn't actually recall him refilling his own glass, although she remembered him lifting it to his mouth many times. Had he deliberately gotten her tipsy? How had all of that looked for the cameras?

All the way home, Samantha replayed that kiss. How had she let it happen? What would Harris think if he

knew? She wanted to tell herself she had been repelled by it, but in truth it wasn't repellent—and it hadn't moved her, either. The problem with Curtis was he couldn't see she didn't want to be with him. He could be a good conversationalist, he was funny, and he was right; he could give her a place in the center of the community if she married him. It was flattering in an uncomfortable way how badly he wanted to win her. But she didn't like the underhanded way he tried to achieve his means—the way he didn't care about her feelings when he played his tricks.

She only realized how late it was when they pulled into the parking area near Base Camp, and everything was dark, except the lone light that stayed lit in the bunkhouse overnight.

"We'd better be quiet," she said, and bit back a groan when she realized she had a problem; she had no one to help her out of her dress and stays. It looked like all the other women had already gone to sleep.

She got out of the truck and shut the door behind her, the click sounding like a thunderclap in the quiet of the camp. Heading into the bunkhouse, she didn't look to see if Curtis was following her. Of course he was. She hesitated near the door to the washroom. She had two choices; she could sleep in her clothing tonight, or she could ask Curtis to help her undo the things she couldn't do herself.

Under any other circumstances, she would've slept in her clothes. But like the women of Jane Austen's time, she only had a few gowns. Avery had instructed

her how to care for them when she arrived, and she was overly conscious of how expensive they were and how it was her duty to make sure they weren't ruined.

She took a breath and turned to Curtis. "I'm going to need your help. I can't get out of these clothes by myself. Can you help me without taking advantage? Because this isn't an invitation."

"I'll be a gentleman," Curtis promised her.

He followed her into the bathroom, and so did the cameras. She wanted to protest, but she knew it was better for them to keep filming, to document that nothing happened between them. She turned her back to Curtis, and he began to undo the ties that held her dress together. When he had them undone, he took a step back. "There."

Samantha realize the next problem. He couldn't reach her stays while she still had her dress on. She would have to take it off. After a long hesitation, she did so, and presented her back to Curtis again.

"Jesus, my hands are shaking," Curtis said a moment later. "Don't know when the last time was that happened."

Samantha didn't want to answer, but it seemed worse to let such a provocative statement hang between them like that. "Why are they shaking?" she asked reluctantly.

"Because you're so beautiful."

His fingers brushed her skin at the top of her stays as he began to undo the ties that held them tight. Samantha shivered involuntarily and told herself he had

tickled her, that she wasn't reacting to his touch.

But she couldn't deny how erotic it was to have a man undo her stays. In any other circumstances, this would be the prelude to something far more intimate. He stood so close, she could feel the brush of his breath on her neck. Curtis took his time, as if savoring the situation. Bit by bit, he undid the cords that bound the garment. As her stays loosened, so did her chemise, and its neckline lowered to display more of her cleavage. Looking in the bathroom mirror, she caught Curtis's eye in the reflection. He was much taller than her. Standing so close behind her, he must have a terrific view of all her curves.

When he had undone her stays, he peeled them off her in a gesture that was far too intimate for the circumstances. Samantha turned around to face him, and then realized her mistake. Her chemise was made of thin, delicate linen. She wasn't wearing a bra underneath it, because Regency women didn't wear bras. Her nipples were hard from the coolness of the evening, and she was afraid they were all too obvious beneath the thin fabric.

"You're so beautiful," Curtis said again, and lifted his hands to undo the strings of her bonnet. Samantha knew she had to stop him, but somehow she couldn't. This was all wrong, but the words she meant to say were strangled in her throat when he lifted the bonnet off her head, and in a quick movement she hadn't anticipated, undid her chignon, sending her hair swinging down over her shoulders.

"Beautiful." Curtis leaned close.

He wouldn't kiss her. He couldn't—

Samantha held her breath as his mouth came within a fraction of an inch of hers. "Wait for me," he breathed. "Don't make up your mind until you know me. That's all I'm asking, Samantha." His lips almost brushed her ear. "We could be so good together."

Then he was gone from the room, leaving Samantha breathless, leaning against the sink for support. What was wrong with her? She wanted Harris, not Curtis. How had Curtis gotten under her skin?

She looked up, noticed the cameramen still filming her and kicked the bathroom door closed in their faces.

CHAPTER TEN

THE SHAFT OF the ax felt good in his hands, but even better was the burn of the muscles in his arms and shoulders. There was nothing as efficient for releasing anger as chopping wood. Harris stood in a clearing not too far from Base Camp, and set another chunk of wood on the stump he was using as a base. He swung his ax and cleaved the wood in two, tossing both parts into the pile that was growing a few feet away. It was early, but he had already been at work for two hours. He hadn't slept a wink last night.

Samantha and Curtis had come home late. Very late. He'd been exiting the door of his tent, having waited for them, when they climbed out of the truck, and both of them headed into the bunkhouse. They were in there a long, long time. Harris had held back, aware of the camera crew filming the proceedings. He knew if he burst into the building there would be a confrontation, and they would document it.

When the bunkhouse door finally opened again, Curtis had come out alone, whistling. His hands had

been jammed in his pockets, and there was no mistaking the bounce in his step.

It was several more minutes before Samantha emerged, much more slowly. Even in the dim light, Harris could tell that her clothing was awry. The back of her dress was undone, and her silhouette was bulky, as if her stays were off. Had she let Curtis do the honors? Had the man gotten a good look at her curves?

He told himself the cameras had been there with them the whole time. It's not as if they could have done much of anything—let alone made love. But if Samantha was allowing Curtis to touch her, things had changed. Undressing was undressing, no matter how you sliced it.

The thought of Curtis's hands on her burned him, and Harris grabbed a new chunk of wood and swung the ax again. As hard as he worked, he couldn't get the wayward thoughts out of his mind, though. He had to talk to her. He had to see if Curtis had changed her mind about him. Once again, he wondered how he could ever compete with the other man.

The sun rose in the sky, and he knew it had to be breakfast time. Time to face the music. When he got back to camp, he would look at the way Samantha and Curtis positioned themselves, and he would know how things stood between them. As he approached the fire pit, he breathed a sigh of relief when he noticed Curtis chatting with some of the other men, and Samantha sitting and eating with the women. Nothing too momentous could've happened the night before, he told

himself.

But then Samantha looked up, caught Curtis's eye and blushed.

The rise of color in her cheeks stopped Harris in his tracks. He stood just beyond the circle of logs that surround the fire pit. Curtis must have felt his presence, because he turned and gave Harris an ironic salute. The burning bands of anger that had squeezed his chest earlier tightened again.

Harris wasn't sure how he got through the rest of the day. As usual, he made his way over to the Egans' right after breakfast. But even Egan noticed his distraction, and gave him a good dressing down after lunch when he broke a piece of metal that he was working on by hammering too long after it had cooled down.

At the end of a long, long day, he returned to Base Camp. Every instinct made him want to grab a plate of food and take it somewhere he could be by himself, but that was how Curtis would win. For once, he couldn't use distance to avoid an uncomfortable situation. If he wanted Samantha—and he did want her—he needed to try something different. He took a seat next to Samantha on a log, but he was still struggling to figure out what to say when she spoke up.

"Are we—? Are we going out tonight?"

"Do you want to?" Harris growled. Damn it—he needed to keep his cool, but he kept picturing the way Curtis had left the bunkhouse whistling last night—and the way Sam had slunk out a few minutes later with her clothes all awry.

"Of course I want to. If you do." There was a question in her voice, and Harris hated that he got some satisfaction from it. Despite whatever gains Curtis had made last night, she still wanted to know if he cared about her. He still had a chance, but he needed to make the most of it.

Harris thought fast. What would really make an impression on Sam?

She liked it when they connected. When they spoke about things that meant something.

When he was real with her.

Had Curtis ever been real with her? Or had he dished out a constant stream of engaging—but ultimately meaningless—conversation?

Harris had definitely connected with her that first morning they were together. First with their words and then with their bodies. Something told him that despite what had happened last night, Curtis and Samantha hadn't done either of those things.

"Where do you want to go?" he asked her to buy time.

"I—I don't know."

"How about… ice cream?"

"Ice cream?"

"Why not?" It didn't matter where they went. Only what they said—and did.

Sam nodded. "Ice cream it is."

They didn't speak much on the way to town, but that was all right with Harris. Curtis was the big talker. When he reached over and took Sam's hand, her fingers

curled around his willingly, and the smile she sent his way made him relax.

This was better. He had to stop reading so much into everything Curtis said and did. Sam kept telling him he was the one she wanted to be with.

He couldn't seem to make himself believe her.

At the ice cream shop, they each ordered a cone, then sat on the hood of the truck to eat it. Just being with Sam was good enough for him, but he'd begun to worry again it might not be enough for her when she said, "I wish we could be alone." She nodded at the cameras.

"You sure about that?"

Samantha turned toward him and licked her cone from bottom to top in a big swirl. "I'm absolutely sure about that."

Harris's spirits soared, and more of his tension drained away, but he needed to be clear. "What would you do if we were alone?"

Samantha gave her ice cream another long, sensuous lick, swallowed, opened wide, took most of the ice cream into her mouth and pulled the cone away, letting her lips slide over the creamy mound. "Get the picture?" she murmured.

"Yes." Harris took a moment to tamp down his rising libido. "I was beginning to wonder if you'd changed your mind about Curtis," he admitted.

"I haven't changed my mind. I'm not going to."

She couldn't be any clearer than that. Samantha held her cone in her right hand and her left braced against

the hood of the truck. Harris switched his cone from his right to his left, and tangled the fingers of his free hand in hers. He hoped his touch conveyed everything he wanted her to know. How much he wanted to be with her. How much he hated having to wait.

"Remember what you said?" she asked softly. "Any time?"

Harris's pulse jumped. "Yeah," he said just as softly, not quite believing his ears.

"Tonight. Please."

"You got it." At this point, Harris was willing to risk everything. If she'd let him be with her tonight, he didn't care what happened tomorrow. "Later," he said. "First, we have to have a date."

They walked along Chance Creek's main street, such as it was, window shopping in the few stores that made up the downtown, checking out restaurants they hadn't tried yet, and commenting on the other people they saw. Harris touched her whenever he could get away with it—and she touched him, too, understanding the game without him having to explain it. He accidentally brushed her breast on the way to smoothing aside a tendril of her hair. She accidentally pressed up against him when stepping aside to let others pass on the sidewalk. They stopped in at the Dancing Boot for a beer and slow danced to a couple of fast numbers. Not too many, though; Harris knew much more of that and he would give himself away.

He made sure it was past eleven o'clock before they headed back to Base Camp. They made a show of

saying their good nights, and Harris made sure Win was around to help Samantha pretend to get ready for bed. He'd been half-hard all night and he ached to be with her. The next couple of hours would be long, but worth it.

"One-thirty," he whispered in her ear when he got the chance. "Keep to the shadows on the way to the creek. I'll take a roundabout way and meet you there."

Then he went back to his tent and began the long, long wait.

SAMANTHA'S HEART WAS pounding as she slowly undid the zipper of her tent and climbed outside. Win had helped her prepare for sleep, and while she'd pulled her gown back on, she'd left her stays, chemise and petticoats behind. She felt almost naked, despite the fact the gown fell to her ankles. It swirled around her feet as she tiptoed through the camp and down the track toward the creek. The distance between the camp and the water felt endless, but Sam nearly danced her way there. She couldn't wait to feel Harris's hands on her body. The touches they'd stolen all night had her dizzy with longing, and when she reached the flowing water and there was no one there to meet her, Sam bit back a frustrated groan.

She pace the creek's banks, and nearly screamed when Harris seemed to materialize from nowhere and took her arm. He didn't speak, just drew her close and kissed her. Samantha lost herself in that kiss and all her worries faded away.

Hungry for him, she returned his kisses with an intensity that surprised her. In the past she'd been a much more passive participant in these kinds of games. Now she was the one leading the way. Harris must have wanted her just as badly. He devoured her mouth with a passion that left her breathless—and aching for much more.

"I want you inside me," she gasped into his ear when he bent to slide a series of kisses down her throat. "Now, Harris; I want you in me now."

"Come on." He led her a hundred yards or so into the woods, gathered up the skirts of her dress and tugged the whole garment up and over her head. It slid off easily and Samantha laughed to feel the brush of the cool night air on her skin as Harris tossed it aside.

He held her at arm's length with a grin and she knew he appreciated the fact she hadn't been wearing anything under it. "Hell, you look good" was all he said. He pulled a blanket out of the rucksack he was carrying, spread it on the ground, got to work shucking off his clothes, and a moment later, Harris was as naked as she was. When they came together again, his desire for her was obvious and Sam twined her arms around his neck, wishing he was inside her already. But she could wait. Every touch of his hands on her skin sent tremors through her. She wasn't sure when she'd ever felt so alive, and when they lay down and he gathered her in his arms, she knew she was right where she belonged.

She didn't need a big house or a room with a lock; she needed Harris. He would be her home, and she

would be his. He began a thorough exploration of her body with his mouth that had all her senses reeling and her need for him setting her nerves alight. Sam surrendered to the experience, watching the stars play with the branches of the trees far overhead. Everywhere Harris touched her warmed under his attention, and anticipation swirled through her veins until she was clinging to him, begging him with her body for more. When neither of them could wait a moment longer, he reached to search through his jeans pocket, pulled out a condom and soon had it on. Covering her, he bent down for a thorough kiss, nudged open her thighs with his knees and positioned himself between them. Samantha let out a shaky breath that was almost a whimper. "Are you sure?" he asked. "You're ready?"

She nodded, digging her fingers into his shoulders, wanting him so badly she was trying to pull him in even as he moved into place.

"Good." He shifted above her and pushed inside, filling her with a slow, long stroke that drew an animal-like moan of pleasure from her throat.

Nothing had ever felt so good. Sam realized she'd been ravenous for Harris, needing him to possess her.

She moved her hips, and Harris took pity on her, beginning a rhythm of strokes that soon had her crooning with need. Her arms wrapped around his neck, her sensitive breasts pressed against his hard chest, Samantha wanted more. She urged him on until he was plunging into her with strong, hard thrusts. Even then it wasn't enough.

Samantha ran her teeth over his shoulder, eliciting a groan from him. She liked the feeling of power that gave her and she did it again. Harris redoubled his efforts, one hand cradling her head, the other cupped under her bottom, increasing her pleasure every time he stroked into her.

When he bent down and took one nipple into his mouth, Sam lost the battle; she came with a crash of heat and ecstasy that went on and on, finally leaving her stunned and breathless, panting for air as he continued until he came with a series of thrusts that pushed her over the top a second time. Harris cradled her while she cried out this second release and when she shuddered to a stop in his arms, all she could do was hold on, breathing hard, her mouth pressed against his neck. She wanted to stay like that forever. Wanted to be in his arms for all eternity; joined to him, nothing between them. Two hearts made one.

After a long time, he carefully pulled out of her, but she didn't let him go far, and he wrapped his arms around her, holding her close.

She didn't realize she was crying until Harris wiped her eyes. "What's wrong?"

"Nothing. I just want to be with you. That's all I want."

"It's what I want, too, but we need to make sure no one figures out we were together. We can't stay here long."

"I don't care. You're my husband. You *are* my husband... aren't you?"

"Of course I am." He crushed her against him again. "All that bullshit Renata said about annulling our marriage? They wouldn't go through the effort. We're married. They can't take that away."

She clung to him even more tightly. "Make love to me again. Make love to me all night. I need to know I'm yours. Please, Harris."

"Just for a little while." He rolled over, pulled her on top of him, and she straddled his hips, anticipation building again for what would come next. Harris would fill her, move inside her—make love to her.

And she would love every minute of it.

CHAPTER ELEVEN

IT TOOK ALL Harris's strength the following day not to allow his actions to betray what had happened between him and Samantha the previous night. At breakfast, he took his plate of eggs, bacon and hash browns to one side and sat by himself. Each time he stole a glance at Samantha, he met her gaze, and she quickly looked away, her cheeks reddening. It was a good thing he'd be spending his morning at the Egans', Harris thought. Or they'd never get away with this.

It helped that Clay and Nora had returned from their extended honeymoon, and everyone's attention was on them. Nora looked far healthier than she had when she'd left, and Clay was beaming with happiness. Still, the other women bustled around Nora solicitously and decided she would spend her day up at the manor, taking it easy but helping finalize the plans for the guests who were to arrive on the weekend.

"Listen up, folks," Renata called. "Let's meet in the bunkhouse in ten minutes to watch the next episode."

A good-natured groan rose up from the crowd, but

people began to finish their meals, return their plates to the bunkhouse kitchen and get ready for the showing.

"Just wait, you'll see," he heard Avery say to Samantha as he followed the rest to the door. "You won't even recognize yourself on the show. It's incredible what they do with the footage they have. It looks totally different than real life."

Sam turned back to him, worry creasing her brow. She waited for him to catch up. "Harris—about the show…"

"Don't worry about it. It's always awful, but we get over it."

"But that's the thing. Curtis—"

"Move it, people!" Renata broke in before Sam could finish what she was saying. She pushed between them and herded everyone inside.

Harris ended up on the far side of the room from Sam, which was probably for the best if they wanted to keep last night's exploits to themselves. He wanted to touch her—badly. He was losing patience with having to wait so long. Today she looked sweet in her Regency gown, with her hair tucked up under her bonnet. But he couldn't help remembering how she looked last night. Flushed, wanton—fully satisfied. He couldn't wait to be with her again, and he had to forcefully wrench his thoughts away before he became too uncomfortable.

"Everybody ready?" Renata said a few minutes later. She nodded to Boone, who clicked the button on his laptop, and the show began to play on the large screen behind them. Everyone settled in and there was an

uncomfortable lull as the opening credits started in the semi-patriotic music played behind them.

This week's episode began with a recap of the events that preceded Nora and Clay's wedding. Watching Samantha, Harris saw her wince along with everyone else at the footage of Nora's lifeless body being wheeled out of the old schoolhouse on a gurney and lifted into an ambulance. Clay looked pale as he watched himself on-screen at the hospital pacing, waiting for news. Harris doubted that there was a dry eye in the room when the surgeon came out to announce that Nora had made it. They covered Nora's convalescence, and the plans that had been previously made behind the scenes to find a backup bride for Clay. They showed Boone and the other men making the decision to allow Clay to wait for Nora's recovery, and the drawing of straws to see who would marry a stranger in his place.

When on-screen, Renata narrated that Curtis was the one who drew the short straw and would marry Samantha Smith when she arrived, Curtis said audibly, "You got that right."

Harris forced himself to unclench his fists. Last night had proved he and Samantha belonged together. He didn't have to worry about Curtis. Soon enough Sam would announce her choice, and he would marry her all over again.

As the show continued, he found himself sinking lower in his seat, however. Somehow Renata had managed to piece together footage that showed him slinking off from Base Camp as if had deliberately

planned to steal Curtis's bride away from him. He couldn't believe how much Renata had fabricated.

The footage of his return to Base Camp with Samantha, however, was all too real, as was the scuffle between him and Curtis afterward. The show played up the tension between the two men, but instead of focusing on Samantha's desire to be with Harris, Renata and her crew had managed to make it look like Samantha was torn between them.

Then there was the scene at Delmonaco's. None of their tricks had worked. All their flirting had been cut out, but the show made much of Sam's description of her parents as singing about environmentalism but accomplishing nothing. A helpful graphic popped up detailing the environmental costs of *Deader Than Ever*'s constant touring to drive the point home.

When Harris glanced at Samantha again, she was biting her lip, her hands clutched together in her lap. Curtis, on the other hand, looked far from beaten. He was sitting back in his seat, his legs wide and his arms crossed over his chest. The smirk on his face seemed to say he knew something Harris didn't.

Harris soon found out what it was. The footage on the screen jumped to Samantha's date with Curtis just two nights ago. The scene began with Curtis solicitously helping Samantha into his truck, and getting in himself. They took a long drive down a winding highway to an area Harris recognized with a sinking heart. When Curtis turned off in the very place Harris had taken Samantha on their wedding day, he leaned forward,

dread and anger knotting together in his stomach. He'd forgotten he'd pointed out the track to Curtis once on a trip to Bozeman. He couldn't believe the man would take Sam there.

The cameras caught Curtis lifting Samantha down from the truck, speaking together in low tones, Curtis's hands resting on her hips. They were obviously talking about something important, but the cameras didn't pick up their words. At the end it was clear that Curtis had asked her a question. Samantha nodded, allowed him to take her arm and lead her into the woods. Just as they disappeared around a bend in the path, Curtis turned around and gave the cameras a big thumbs up.

What the hell? Harris was on his feet, but Jericho grabbed his arm and yanked him back down again.

"Renata is fucking with you," he said. "Don't make an ass of yourself."

Harris's heart raced as the scene unfolded in front of him. Curtis and Samantha sat having an intimate picnic on the very same ledge where she'd been with him that first time. The two of them talked and laughed as the sun went down. Curtis moved closer. Samantha allowed him to. The cameras faded away just as Curtis bent toward her, obviously moving in for a kiss.

But that wasn't the worst of it. Harris couldn't believe his eyes when the scene jumped again to show the two of them arriving back at Base Camp, getting out of the truck and heading together into the bunkhouse. He'd seen that with his own eyes, but knowing what had come before made it even worse. Curtis and Samantha

240 | CORA SETON

had to know the cameras were catching their every move, so he expected some kind of slow good-bye. Perhaps a peck on the cheek. Maybe Curtis would linger too long holding her hand.

Instead, Samantha gestured for Curtis to join her in the bathroom. Harris's jaw dropped open. The cameras followed them even then, and he was forced to watch his rival unlace his wife's dress, help her pull it over her head and get to work on her stays as she leaned forward over the sink to give him access. Curtis took his time, and Samantha didn't rush him, even when he slid a hand over her exposed skin.

When Curtis peeled off her stays, Samantha turned to face him, and Harris tensed again. Jericho's grip was tight on his arm, but Harris didn't think that would stop him if Curtis kissed Samantha on-screen.

He didn't, but he might just as well have. It was clear Samantha wanted him to, clear that she was dying for him to do more. When Curtis left her, flushed, almost panting, Samantha kicked the bathroom door closed in the camera's face. The episode ended.

No one said a word.

"IT WASN'T LIKE that at all," Samantha said loudly when she finally caught her breath. People were already standing, hurrying toward the door as if they were desperate to escape. She didn't blame them; they all knew she was married to Harris. "None of it happened like that; they manipulated everything to make it look worse than it was."

No one was listening to her. A few of the men had gathered around Harris, muttering consolations. Riley confronted Curtis and was shaking her head at him. Most of the women were already slipping out the door, the glances they threw back at her making it all too clear they weren't sure what to think.

Samantha stood up, panic clawing at her throat. They had to believe her. This couldn't be happening. With one episode, Renata had managed to turn everyone against her. "Harris?" She took a step back when he turned her way, cold, hard anger tightening his features.

She tried again. "Harris, I swear—"

"Don't want to hear it." He was out the door in two long strides.

Tears stung Samantha's eyes. She moved to follow him, but Win blocked her way. "Give him time to cool off," she said. "He knows as well as anyone else how much Renata manipulates the footage. That doesn't make it any easier to watch another man undress you."

"I just needed help with my stays. No one else was around," Sam protested.

"Except an entire camera crew," Win pointed out.

"We're not supposed to talk to them. What was I supposed to do? Wear my stays to bed?"

"Maybe this once it would have been the wiser choice."

"WE ALL KNOW Renata is completely capable of twisting things to suit her needs," Boone said when he caught up with Harris in the barn. The other men filed

in after him. Camera crew members followed, too—a whole horde of them. Harris wondered if there were any left to film the women.

"Fuck it. If she likes him that much, let him have her." His chest pulsed with white-hot anger, and he flexed and clenched his fists, wishing there was someone to fight. He didn't know where Curtis had gone; probably after Samantha. They were probably together right now, laughing at him.

"I can't believe how much happened in the few days Nora and I were gone," Clay said. "But Boone's right, I don't think all that footage went together the way they showed it."

"Don't try to look for ways to explain it," Harris said. "It's clear to me."

"You're going to let Curtis win?" Boone asked. "You said yourself you brought Samantha here to marry him."

"I brought Samantha here to marry Clay, but that's changed several times, hasn't it?"

Harris didn't care. If Samantha hadn't slept with Curtis, she might as well have. He didn't know what kind of game she was playing. Maybe she got off on pitting them against each other. Maybe she was the kind to sleep around. Maybe she wanted the notoriety of being the bad girl on a television show.

Whatever had happened, he was over it. He might be slow, but he wasn't stupid. The message from the universe was clear: he still wasn't the marrying kind.

"Tell them they have my blessing," he said, and

moved to leave the barn, but Walker took a step in front of him and blocked the way. "Move it."

Walker shook his head. "One day." He held Harris's gaze.

"One day what? What the fuck are you saying?" Harris tried to push past him, but Walker wouldn't budge.

"Wait one day. Say nothing. Do nothing." He looked for Harris's acquiescence.

Harris shook his head. "Fuck that. I'm done with this. Maybe I'm done with all of this."

Walker crossed his arms over his chest. "You can stand one day."

"Listen to the man," Clay said. "He won't steer you wrong."

"What good will it do?"

"What good will it do to throw away your wife before you even know for sure what happened?" Clay challenged him.

Before Harris could answer, Boone stepped in. "Aren't you due at the Egans'? Get in the truck and head over there. Do your work. Take the opportunity that man's giving you. Cool off. We'll talk about this again tomorrow."

"Fine," Harris growled. He was out the door before anyone else could say another word.

"COME WITH ME," Savannah said quietly when Sam finally left the bunkhouse. "James will meet us with the carriage out on the street. We're going to sneak off to

Alice's house for the afternoon."

"Okay," Samantha said a little shakily. Anything to get away from Base Camp for a while. She was devastated by how she'd been portrayed on-screen, and the way Harris had reacted. He still was so quick to believe she'd let him down. Sam was beginning to think nothing would make him trust her. She'd given herself to him. Didn't that mean anything?

Only a small camera crew followed the women when they headed up the hill. Most of them had traipsed off after the men when they'd trooped out of the bunkhouse. The rest were deep in conversation with Renata. Once at the manor, Avery picked a loud fight with Riley over whose turn it was next with the cell phone they shared. With the camera crew engaged, Sam and Savannah slipped out the front door and met James. Half an hour later, he dropped them off at the Reeds' big white house, and Alice came out on the front porch to meet them. "I'm glad you could come," she said, holding out a hand to Savannah. "Especially you. I've got a dress I want you to try on. Sam, why don't you go find my sister in the herb garden behind the house. I know she wants to show it off to you."

Alice led Savannah inside, and Samantha took a path that wound around the outside of the house to the backyard. This time, instead of heading straight to the carriage house, where Alice had her studio, she ventured into the gardens, where a young woman was bent over the plants.

The woman looked up as Sam approached, stood

and dusted her hands on her jeans. "Hello. You must be Samantha."

"That's right." Sam shook hands with her, taking in her practical clothing, warm expression and kind eyes.

"I'm Sadie. Sadie Reed. It's nice to meet you. Some of the other women from Westfield have been over to the house, but you just arrived, right?"

"A week ago," Sam told her. "You have a beautiful garden. Do you do all of this yourself?"

"Yes; it's a full time job. Sometimes I get help when I'm completely overwhelmed, but mostly I try to do it on my own. It's important for me to stay connected to what I grow."

"I get that." It was a good way of articulating what Sam felt when she was working in the gardens at Base Camp. No one else seemed to talk that way about it, though.

Sadie was looking at her curiously. "Skullcap, I think. Blackberry leaf. And a little rosemary."

"I beg your pardon?"

"I see sadness. False accusation. A need for clarity. Is that right?"

It was as if the ground shifted beneath Sam's feet. "That's right." To her surprise her voice was thick with tears and her throat ached with them. She hadn't looked for such understanding from a stranger.

"Sometimes I get a sense of what people need to feel better." Sadie shrugged. "It's Two Willows; this place is special. You know—because of the stone." She moved among her plants and harvested a leaf here and a

root there.

"You've lost me." Sam had no idea what she was talking about.

"I'll show you later. I think Alice and Savannah need some privacy." She nodded toward the tall green hedge that bordered the large garden. Alice and Savannah were walking quickly along its base, and as Sam watched, they turned a corner and were hidden from view.

"What is that?"

"The hedge maze. Later," she said again. "Come to my greenhouse. I'll mix this up for you."

Samantha followed behind her, but her gaze kept trailing back to the tall hedge that blocked everything behind it from view. She was curious about the maze Sadie had mentioned. She'd seen them in photographs, but never in real life.

Inside the greenhouse it was warm and humid, and Samantha soon longed for fresh air, but she waited as patiently as she could for Sadie to clean and chop up the herbs and roots, then add them to a pot of water she had boiling on a hot plate. They chatted while the mixture cooked, and Samantha learned Sadie and her sisters had lived here all their lives, each of them helping to keep the ranch running in their own way. "Cass runs the house," Sadie explained. "Lena runs the cattle operation. Alice does her costumes and brings in some extra money. I care for the gardens, make herbal tinctures and sell produce at a roadside stand. Jo takes care of the animals—all kinds. She's really good with them."

After some minutes had passed, Sadie strained out the herbs and poured the liquid into a tall mug. She handed it to Sam. "Here. Drink this."

Grateful it didn't taste too bad, Sam did so as Sadie showed her more of the greenhouse and then led her back outside into the gardens. There they wandered until they met Alice and Savannah leaving the maze and heading toward the carriage house. Savannah was pale, and Alice walked close beside her. Sam sensed they didn't want to be interrupted, so she nodded at them as they passed, but didn't say anything.

"I'll show you the maze now if you like," Sadie said.

"I'd like that."

When they entered it on a grassy path, Sam was surprised at the way the sounds of the outside world fell away behind its green walls. Someone had been mowing in the distance, but now it was hardly a buzz. Sadie led the way to the first crossroads, where she hesitated. "Some people like to pick their own path. Others like us to show them the way."

"I'll pick my path." Sam thought Sadie approved of that. She made her choices at random until Sadie laughed.

"We're doubling back."

"Sorry. Maybe you should lead."

"At least you gave it a try," Sadie said. "Some people are chicken. If you want you can come sometime and spend an afternoon at it. You'll eventually find your way through. My sisters think everyone should be led to the center, but I think it's fun to try to find your own way."

"I agree," Sam said as she followed Sadie's lead. "How did it get here?"

"My mother planted it when she was a teenager. I feel close to her here. I think we all do. She died when I was young."

"I'm sorry to hear that." Sam suddenly wondered if she was taking her own family for granted. Maybe she should call them and warn them about what they'd see on television when the episode aired. Sure, they were annoying sometimes, but she must have worried them when she left, and they were sure to feel offended when they saw the show. Guilt piercing through her, Sam vowed she would make the call when she got home.

"Here we are," Sadie said, breaking into her thoughts.

Sam stopped short and stared at the monolithic stone standing in front of her. At least twelve feet high, it rose from the ground like a lost monument from Stonehenge. She realized this clearing must form the center of the maze.

"What's it doing here?" she asked when she found her voice again.

"No one knows. It was here before the first of my ancestors cleared this ground and started ranching."

"Are you sure?" That seemed improbable.

Sadie nodded. "Someone put it here. We just don't know who."

She took up a position before it, and Sam joined her, craning her neck to see the top. She reached out tentatively and touched its rough surface. It was warm

from the sun, almost alive.

But that was silly.

"You can ask it a question," Sadie said suddenly. "It'll answer."

"Like—it talks?" Sam laughed, grateful from the distraction from her awful day. Even if everything fell apart, this brief visit to Two Willows would give her a story to tell.

"Not with a voice." Sadie smiled, too. "It has a way of letting you know, though."

"That's the… strangest… thing I've ever heard."

"Give it a try. You'll be surprised," Sadie said. "And sometimes getting an answer helps."

After a moment's hesitation, Sam said, "Sure. Why not? How do I do it?" she added.

"Just be sure you're respectful. The stone has a bit of a temper," Sadie warned her.

"Respectful. Okay." Sam took a deep breath. She had so many questions, it was hard to choose one. She shied away from asking about Harris and Curtis. That was far too personal to talk about in front of Sadie. Instead she asked, "Stone, if you know anything you'd like to share, please tell me… Do I belong at Base Camp?"

She waited. So did Sadie. After a moment, though, Sadie took her arm. "The stone will answer when it's ready."

Sam felt a rush of disappointment. It was just a game, after all. Why had she thought it might be real? She knew better than that.

She composed herself as she followed Sadie through the twists and turns of the maze, wondering if it was a trick the young woman liked to play on other people. She felt foolish about asking such a question in front of a stranger.

A breath of wind picked up, lifted the tendrils of her hair where it had escaped her bonnet and ruffled the evergreen boughs of the maze.

"Sam? Sam!" It was Savannah calling from outside of the maze. As Sadie and Sam exited the narrow path into the gardens again, she hurried forward, her pastel dress wrapping around her legs as she came their way. "Look at this!" She held out a magazine. "That's you." Gone was Savannah's worry. She looked far happier now than when she'd come, and Sam hoped that Alice had imparted some piece of wisdom or support that had made the difference.

Sam glanced at the magazine's cover and blinked. Savannah was right; it *was* her.

"*Deader Than Ever* Daughter a Fabulous Fit on Base Camp!" the headline screamed. Sam's heart sank. She'd thought she'd have more time before her parents learned her whereabouts.

"How do they even know I'm on the show?" she asked. "The episode hasn't aired yet!"

"You're forgetting the website and social media. Renata's been posting stuff about you all week," Savannah told her. "You haven't taken a turn with the cell phone yet. I guess we should have offered it to you."

"I was happy not to have one around for a change."

She could have looked at her own in her tent—once she'd charged it up a bit in the bunkhouse or manor. Although she knew the women limited their screen time, they hadn't formally asked her to follow their rules. It had been a mistake not to tell them she wanted to, she realized.

But that was the least of her worries now. If Renata had been posting about her and the press had picked it up, her parents would find out where she was any minute now. Which meant her cell phone was probably blowing up with messages. Maybe she'd let it stay in her tent a little bit longer.

"They love you," Savannah said. "Read it!"

Reluctantly, Sam read on.

"Stars' daughter finds the home of her heart on reality television's biggest series," the sub-headline read. There was a whole article about her, and it continued in the same vein. "Samantha Smith, daughter of *Deader Than Ever* favorites Rachel Flick and Henry Smith, is the latest addition to the sizzling hot new reality television series *Base Camp*, and she brings some drama to a show that's already knocked our socks off. We've seen an advance screening of tonight's episode, and Samantha arrives with a bang, stirring up the romantic desires of two of the show's eligible bachelors, but despite the sparks that fly on her debut episode, what's clear is that Samantha has found the place where she belongs. We can only imagine what it's like to don Regency garb, be assigned a new job, sleep in a tent and have two bachelors fighting over you, but Samantha handles it all with a

grace and charm we could only hope to share under the circumstances. Only a woman who's found her true calling—and home—could exhibit such grace under pressure."

Samantha didn't know what to say. She handed the article to Sadie and waited while she read it.

Sadie laughed. "Sounds like you've got the answer to your question."

"But—"

Savannah turned to her. "You asked the stone a question?"

Sam could only nod. "Did you?"

"Yes." But Savannah didn't say what her question was, and Sam didn't volunteer any information, either. Savannah pulled out the cell phone the women took turns carrying.

"James will be here in a minute to pick us up. Thank you, Alice—for everything."

"Of course." Alice gave her a hug. "Come any time."

"That goes for you, too," Sadie said to Sam. "I enjoyed meeting you."

"Me, too," Sam said, but she was still having trouble wrapping her mind around what had just happened. It was a coincidence, of course.

But it didn't feel like one.

CHAPTER TWELVE

BY THE TIME Harris got back to Base Camp, he'd gotten his temper under control—just. He'd decided he'd keep his mouth shut and avoid the others until the following morning, at which time he'd have another pow-wow with Boone and announce his intention to back off and let Curtis win.

He'd eaten in town and killed time walking the streets until the memories of doing the same with Sam a few days ago had become too much. Back at the ranch, he tried to retire to his tent, but the night was warm and the small structure was stuffy. He was almost grateful when footsteps heralded someone's approach.

A throat cleared. Harris couldn't say how he knew it was Walker, but when he unzipped the tent's flap and climbed out, there he was.

"Bunkhouse."

The big man led the way and Harris followed, keeping his gaze on Walker's back. In the bunkhouse, he parked himself in the chair the man indicated.

"Check this out." The man plopped a laptop in his

lap and Harris grabbed it to keep it from falling on the floor. Walker leaned over, hit a key and a movie began to play on the screen.

"I already watched this," Harris said, moving to rise when familiar footage appeared, but Walker put a hand on his shoulder and shoved him back down.

"Watch."

Harris did so, his jaw tight, but as the images played out in front of him, he relaxed a little bit. Some of the footage was the same he'd seen earlier on the TV episode Renata had played for them, but much of it was new. This was an unedited version, before it had been spliced together in the most provocative way. Boone had been right; Renata's crew had manipulated it carefully to make Samantha's actions worse than they really were. They'd arranged it all carefully to make the audience believe Sam wanted to sleep with Curtis. They'd cut out the parts where Sam had snapped at him and become angry.

But it didn't exonerate her completely. She'd still walked into that bathroom with Curtis and let him touch her. There was no mistaking the moment between them when she'd turned around and Curtis had taken down her hair.

Harris scrubbed a hand across his face. "Must have been hard to get this footage. Why bother?" He couldn't get the image of that intimate scene between Curtis and Samantha out of his mind. Had they met in the woods later? Had she given herself to Curtis with as much abandon as she'd given herself to him?

"Didn't like what was happening." Walker took the laptop back again. "It's hard enough, two people finding each other in the right place, at the right time. Figured I should help if I can." He studied Harris. "But maybe I didn't help enough."

"I appreciate what you tried to do." But he was right; it wasn't enough to contradict the growing certainty in Harris he'd never been meant to have a wife.

Walker sighed. "A blind man doesn't see what's in front of his face."

"That's for sure. But one thing I've never been accused of is being blind." Harris stood to go. "I served as a sniper for over a decade. I see things others miss."

"And sometimes you see things that aren't really there. You're making a mistake."

"I'm making sure I *don't* make one."

Harris headed for the door. Outside, he allowed his gaze to climb to the manor on top of the hill. That's where Samantha would be at this time of day.

He'd keep his distance from here on in.

BACK AT THE ranch, Samantha took a deep breath before she entered the manor. Savannah was still chatting with James outside. Sam wanted to get this over with before she came in. She found the women sitting at the kitchen table, pads of paper in front of them on which they were making lists. They were preparing for the guests who would arrive in about a week.

"Hi," she said awkwardly. "I need to say something. First, thank you for helping me and Savannah escape for

a few hours. I needed that."

"I don't think the camera crew even realized you were gone. We told them you were taking a soak in one of the tubs upstairs," Avery said. "They finally got bored and left."

"Well, thank you, anyway. It helped to clear my head." She wasn't sure how to word this next bit, so she plunged ahead. "I care what you think of me, so I want you to know I didn't fool around with Curtis. We came home late and I needed help getting out of my dress and stays. Curtis was the one who took liberties. Curtis was the one who kept trying to make it look like there was more going on than really happened. He's the one who should be blamed, not me. I'm not that kind of—"

"We get it," Riley interrupted her. "Believe me, we do. I think we were all a little shocked by what we saw, but once we talked about it we realized how much Renata had probably played with the footage."

"Really?"

One by one, the other women nodded.

"Does it make me a bad person that I'm jealous, though?" Avery said suddenly.

"Jealous?" Samantha couldn't fathom that. "Of being made to look... cheap?"

"Of having two men want you. Why is everyone here so damn pretty?"

Savannah let out an aggravated groan. "For God's sake, would you get over yourself, Avery? You are beautiful, and kind, and fun, and sexy. And Walker worships everything about you."

"But he never says or does anything to indicate that," Avery burst out. "I want to go on dates. I want to get kissed. I want someone to help me out of my stays. Is that so hard to understand?"

"No," Savannah said sadly. "Not at all."

"You have to be patient," Riley told her.

"For how long?"

No one could answer that.

After a long pause, Sam tried to bring the conversation to safer ground. "I was wondering—is there anything I can do to help you all next weekend?" She noticed that Nora hadn't said a word. If anyone resented her presence, it would be her. "Nora? I guess I need to hear from you what role I can play. I understand if this is uncomfortable for you—"

"Because you came here to marry my husband? It is a little weird," Nora admitted pertly. "But I just spent my honeymoon with him and I'm pretty sure we're solid," she went on with a smile. "I'm sure we can find you something to do when our guests get here."

"Thank you." Sam was touched by her generosity of spirit. "I wish I knew what to do about Curtis. When he's not being a total ass, he's actually a good guy. But then the things he does... even if it wasn't for Harris, or the fact I'm not attracted to him, I could never marry him, because in the end he doesn't care about me; he only cares about winning!"

"I think both of them need a time out," Avery said. "They're acting like children, so treat them like children."

"A time out," Sam mused. "That's a really good idea."

"A TIME OUT?" Harris repeated the following morning. "She doesn't need to give me a time out; I'm through with her."

Boone scratched the back of his neck. "Well, through or not, Samantha has demanded a break from dating both of you. Curtis isn't too happy about it."

"Fuck him." Harris turned to leave. It was time for him to get to the Egans'. He'd skipped breakfast, and couldn't get away from Base Camp fast enough.

He'd barely slept the night before. Tossing and turning, he'd struggled with his determination to turn his back on Sam. After an hour or two, doubts began to worm their way into his thoughts. Was he overreacting to what he'd seen? Was his pride getting in the way of the best thing that had ever happened to him?

He wanted to believe Sam wasn't interested in Curtis, but when Curtis had leaned close and undone her hair in the bunkhouse bathroom, she'd been affected.

And that was the sticking point.

If she wanted to be with Curtis, he wasn't going to get in her way. He knew the deal; when people left, you didn't get them back.

"Renata isn't happy either." Boone followed him to the truck.

"Can't say I care too much."

"Look, you're not seeing the bigger picture here. Someone's got to marry in about a month. Do I need to

start looking for more backup brides?"

"More of them?" Harris was aghast. "Hell, that's all we need."

As HER WEEK of freedom dragged by, Samantha put her heart and soul into the gardens, heading there early in the morning and working long past when everyone called it a day. She'd made an ally of Kai in the kitchen. Each day he packed her a hamper of food and a bottle of water so she didn't have to return to the bunkhouse for meals.

"I think you're making a mistake," he told her once. "I don't think keeping to yourself is the answer."

"I can't stand having them argue about me," she said. She didn't have to specify Harris and Curtis; he knew exactly who she meant.

She appreciated the food hampers more than he could have known. The other women had the B&B preparations sewn up. She'd take part during the weekend itself, acting as an extra pair of hands wherever she was needed. Meanwhile, she helped make sure the gardens were weeded, seedlings transplanted and beds prepared for the late summer and fall crops. At night she read the books Boone had loaned her. The work was hard, but it was cleansing, too. Things were simple in the garden; not like in the rest of her life.

Curtis still used every opportunity he could to try to engage her in conversation. Sam had taken to turning and walking in the other direction whenever she saw him, which was hard because Daisy always accompanied

260 | CORA SETON

him wherever he went. The dog's loyalty to Curtis was maddening, and Sam had despaired of ever winning her back. Maybe she wasn't meant to have a pet.

Or the man she loved.

Sam thought Harris was avoiding her, because she rarely saw him, and then only at a distance.

She missed him. Especially that smile of his, which she hadn't seen for far too long. When she did get a glimpse of him, he looked far too serious. She hated to think how badly she must have hurt him—no matter how inadvertently.

"What are you going to do tomorrow?" Kai asked on Friday morning when she came to fetch her food.

"The guests are arriving this afternoon, so I'll be up at the manor mostly over the weekend. I guess I'll see where I stand with Harris and Curtis on Monday morning. Maybe they'll both be as sick of this as I am."

"I doubt either one is going to give up."

Sam wasn't so sure of that, and as she picked up the picnic basket Kai had filled for her, she wondered if Curtis would be the only man standing on Monday morning. Harris was making it far too clear how he felt about what she'd done. She'd hoped time would give him more perspective, but that didn't seem to be happening.

Keep working, she told herself, exiting the bunkhouse and striding determinedly toward the gardens. Work was the answer to everything. She'd have to trust the rest would turn out for the best.

That afternoon, she made her way back to her tent

and changed to a clean work dress. Since she was already wearing her stays, this was possible to do alone, although difficult. She combed out her hair and twisted it up into a bun on top of her head. She tied on her bonnet and climbed back out of her tent to make her way up to the manor, a little nervous about how the guests' arrival would go. Once there, she let herself into the kitchen, where she found a woman she didn't know. A small camera crew, looking rather bored, sprang to life and began filming when Sam entered.

The unfamiliar woman wore Regency clothing, too—a kind of uniform the household help might have worn. She put out her hand, and Samantha shook it.

"I'm Mary—the cook. Maud sends me to help when guests come to the B&B. Who are you?"

"My name's Samantha Smith," Sam said. "I just came here recently, and I don't really have a job to do while the guests are here. Could I help you out in the kitchen?"

"Avery helps with the cooking when she can," Mary said. "But I wouldn't say no to adding on a scullery maid, if that was the part you were willing to play."

"Scullery maid suits me fine," Sam said. Her heart lifted. "Put me to work anywhere. Give me all the hardest jobs." She wanted to prove to the others they needed her.

"I'm going to like you," Mary said. When Avery bustled in a moment later, she added, "Hope you don't mind, Avery, but I've found us some new help. This is our new scullery maid, Samantha Smith."

262 | CORA SETON

Samantha dropped a perfect Regency curtsy. "It's a pleasure, ma'am," she said to Avery. "I'm a hard worker. And you don't even need to pay me."

The corner of Avery's mouth lifted. "Scullery maid, huh?"

"At your service, ma'am," Samantha said in her best impression of a Cockney accent.

Avery grinned. "Let's get started then."

The rest of the afternoon passed swiftly as Samantha worked in the kitchen—and in every room in the house—to get it ready for the guests. The other women had already given the manor a thorough cleaning, so she just hit all the high notes, polishing doorknobs, straightening towels, brushing the wrinkles from the beds in between washing sinks full of dishes and scrubbing tables and counters in the kitchen as necessary. The camera crew kept getting in the way, but Samantha dodged and darted around them, and didn't worry about whether or not they were keeping up.

When a taxi finally pulled into the driveway just past four o'clock, Samantha was standing in the line with the other women, her stomach filled with butterflies. It was crucial their guests love every minute of their stay here. The bed-and-breakfast business was still very new, and wouldn't support itself for some time. Samantha wanted to be a part of it, almost as badly as she wanted to work in the gardens. There was something about sharing this beautiful ranch, the Regency dream and the work they were doing at Base Camp with other people that energized her.

Riley and the others had negotiated with Renata to keep the cameras away from the guests over the weekend. Renata wasn't happy with the decision, but as Savannah had pointed out, the guests were paying money for a vacation—not to be part of a television show. To their relief, Fulsom had agreed with the ban on filming at the manor over the weekend, and there wasn't a camera in sight.

Five young women exited the taxi, oohing and ahhing over the beautiful manor house, and the women in their old-fashioned gowns lined up in front of it.

"I can't wait to have a gown of my own," one of the women gushed. "This is amazing."

Riley and the others went to meet them, and soon multiple conversations had sprung up around Sam, but she held back from participating. She was satisfied to be part of the scenery.

As Riley began to herd the women toward the front door, the appearance of another vehicle grabbed Samantha's attention. It was moving fast—far too fast on the winding driveway.

"Who's that?" Savannah held a hand up to shield her eyes. "I don't recognize that car."

"You wouldn't believe who was at the airport, on our flight," one of the guests said. "Some of the members of *Deader Than Ever*. They were seated only a few rows away!"

"I got their autographs," another of the guests said.

But Samantha wasn't listening anymore. She knew without a shadow of a doubt who was in that car

careening up the driveway toward her. She had to stop them, but she didn't know how.

Even as she started forward to block it, the black rental sedan skidded to a stop just feet away from the guests, who jumped back in alarm. Three of the car's doors flung open and her family climbed out. Her mother, father and sister had all arrived.

And they were furious.

Rachel was the first to spot her. Samantha's mother strode across the ground between them and slapped her across the face, hard. A collective gasp behind her told Samantha everyone present had seen. She held a hand to her cheek, too shocked to do anything else.

"I have never been so ashamed of one of my children," Rachel said. "If you deliberately tried to hurt me, you couldn't have done a better job. You've thrown everything your father and I believe in back in our faces. All we do is sing—and that doesn't change anything? How could you say that about our life's work? I hope you're proud of yourself. Because no one else is going to be."

Samantha, her cheek aching, stumbled to find her words. Before she could, her sister was upon them.

"All those years you lectured me about my behavior, and this is what you do? Sign up to marry a complete stranger? A Navy SEAL? Have you lost your mind?"

"Samantha Smith, you get in that car right now. We're leaving. I don't want to hear another word. These people have brainwashed you," her father said. She'd never seen Henry so furious—in fact, she hadn't known

he was capable of it—and she stepped back, wondering if he would slap her, too. Her parents had never believed in corporal punishment. They'd never lifted a hand to her before.

"No," she said, finally finding her voice. "I'm not going anywhere. This is my home now."

"I've heard just about enough," Henry said. "How could you do this to us? Your mother and I—and your sister—have built our careers on standing against everything these people represent!"

"You've built your career on standing against environmentalism? Against being frugal and using only what you need? Against working together to achieve a common goal? Funny, because that's exactly what I thought you stood for!" Her anger loosened her tongue. This was why she'd left; because on the bus there was too much talk and far too little action.

"Don't play word games with me, Sam," Henry said. "Every one of the men in this community has served in the military. Aren't you too old to rebel like this?"

"Every one of these men has risked their life for our country," Sam retorted. "I respect them for that, even if I don't always agree with what our government does."

"Don't split hairs," Rachel said. "Not with issues this big."

"Maybe the issues are more complicated than you make them out to be," Samantha told her furiously. "Maybe people have more sides to them than you want to believe. I'm not going anywhere. I've committed myself to staying here and helping. To marrying the man

266 | CORA SETON

I love. If he'll have me."

"You think any man would have you after the way you acted? That episode was disgusting," Melissa said. "I can't believe you screwed around like that on TV."

Samantha laughed. She couldn't help herself. She'd seen her sister play men off each other more times than she could count. "You've always told me I was too uptight, too repressed. Now I fall in love and you have something to say?"

"You think you're a big shot now, don't you? Starring in a show. Just you wait until the season is over. No one will remember you," Melissa said. "People will remember *Deader Than Ever* forever."

Was that what this was all about? Samantha couldn't believe it.

Or maybe she could.

She'd stepped out of her role in her family, hadn't she? And now everyone else was upset. She was the one who was supposed to remain in the background. She was supposed to drive the bus. Instead, she'd taken center stage on a nationwide television show. Was her family really so shallow they resented that?

"I'm telling you again, young lady," Henry said. "Get in the car. Now."

"Or what? You're going to ground me for the first time in my life?" Samantha laughed at the absurdity of it.

"Or... Or... We'll picket the show. Then you'll see," he finally said. "We'll show the world just what we think of it."

That shut Samantha up. With anyone else's parents, it would've been an empty threat, but the members of *Deader Than Ever* were old hands at protesting, and they tended to garner a lot of publicity.

"Don't you have gigs to play? You don't want to disappoint your fans," she said, putting her hands on her hips. "Nothing you do is going to stop me, so you might as well keep right on going. Maybe someday you'll realize what I'm doing here has merit."

"What you're doing here is allowing the establishment to take over environmentalism," Rachel broke in. "Which means they're going to put an end to it. Greenwashing, that's what they call it. Are you really so stupid you can't see it?"

"You're the ones who are blind," Samantha retorted. "You haven't even looked around to see what we're doing here before you make up your minds about it. Do whatever the hell you want. I don't care." She turned her back on them, but came to an abrupt stop faced with the crowd near the front door.

Riley, Avery, Nora and Savannah quickly sprang into action and escorted their guests inside. Sam turned back to her parents and sister. "You have five minutes to get off this ranch before I sic all those Navy SEALs on you. They know how to get rid of people who aren't wanted."

"Just try it. I don't think you'll like the results," her mother said. But she returned to the car, and Henry and Melissa followed. When they drove off, Samantha breathed a sigh of relief, but she knew that wouldn't be

the end of it and she wasn't sure what to do now. For all she'd love to follow the others inside, get back to cleaning and pretend none of this had happened, that wouldn't solve anything.

She'd probably better walk down to Base Camp and give Boone a head's up. She wished she could talk to Harris. He'd know what to do.

She wondered if he'd ever want to talk to her again.

CHAPTER THIRTEEN

WHEN HARRIS ARRIVED back at the bunkhouse late that afternoon, he realized he'd stumbled into a private meeting of the founders.

"Gotta do something to head this off," Boone was saying when he walked in. Harris stopped in his tracks, and began to back out again. Boone called after him, "Might as well join us. Everyone's going to know about this pretty quick."

"What's going on?"

"We've got a problem," Jericho said. "Samantha's family tracked her down today and they're pissed. They threatened to picket the show unless she agrees to come home with them. Given that they're mighty famous, that's not an empty threat."

"We just heard from the sheriff, too," Clay added. "*Deader Than Ever* fans have already begun to arrive in Chance Creek, along with some press. The vultures are circling, sensing trouble. This could get out of hand.

"We need a plan," Boone agreed.

"What is Samantha's family upset about? The fact

that she's marrying one of us?" He'd meant to say Curtis, but somehow the words hadn't come out that way. He told himself he was done thinking there was anything left between him and Samantha, but his body still hadn't seemed to realize that. Night after night it taunted him with memories of everything they'd done together. He still wanted her—bad. No matter how unrealistic that had become.

"They hate everything about the military," Jericho said. "The idea that their daughter is going to marry someone who served is really steaming them."

"*If* she marries anyone," Boone said.

"I doubt this will scare Curtis off," Harris said and shoved his fists in his pockets. Just saying the man's name made his blood boil.

"This isn't about Curtis. This is about Samantha," Boone told him. "She's made it clear all along she's married to you, and that she's going to stay married to you."

"But that didn't stop her from fooling around with Curtis," he pointed out and immediately wished he hadn't. Boone and the others stared at him like he'd lost his mind.

"She never fooled around with anyone—except you, from what I gather," Jericho told him. "Kai let me know the other day he saw you and Sam sneaking around the campsite late one night. Don't tell me nothing happened out there in the woods. Which put the whole damn community in jeopardy, by the way."

Harris stiffened. Kai had seen them?

Shit, he was losing his touch.

"Look," Boone told him. "I've been with Riley long enough to know how difficult it is for her to get in and out of those clothes. I have to help her every time. What other choice did Samantha have that night with Curtis but to ask him to help in that situation? And how calm and collected would you be in her shoes, a young, beautiful woman being filmed in a bathroom while a strange man helps you off with your dress?"

More doubts crowded into his brain, but Harris didn't want to act the fool. "I'm not going to fight another man for Samantha."

"Why the hell not?" Clay demanded. "If you love someone, you fight for them, no matter what the circumstances. Are you so afraid of being hurt you won't even try?"

Harris bit back a sharp retort. What could he say to a man who'd been willing to take a bullet for the woman he loved? "Here's the thing," he managed when he'd gotten himself under control again. "She doesn't love me."

"Says who?" Jericho asked. "How do you know that?"

"I know it because—" Harris didn't know what to say. Because he wasn't meant for love? Because his role in life was to always be on the outside? It sure seemed that way. "Because that's just how it is."

He left the building, too frustrated to keep on talking. It was too late to return to town, but he couldn't stay here. Couldn't stand to go to bed and toss and turn

all night, either. He'd walk the perimeter of their community, instead. Time to get back to basics. He was at his best when he was alert, focused, the eyes and ears for the others. It was his job to protect the community—not to belong to it.

He'd learned that a long time ago.

LATER THAT EVENING, Samantha's parents were back with a caravan of vehicles, including the tour bus, and with them were the other members of the band and about thirty followers, some of whom Sam recognized. There was nothing her parents and their fans liked better than a cause. And they'd found one.

She walked out to meet them self-consciously, burning with embarrassment that her mother and father would turn a family spat into a full-on crisis. Renata's crews followed Sam closely, but they weren't the only press on hand. And this was nothing. Sam knew if she didn't put an end to this soon it would turn into a media circus.

"You're making yourselves look bad, you know," she called when she neared the tour bus. Her mother and father were talking with Chris Castle and a man she didn't recognize.

"You're the one who looks like a fool in that getup," her mother said.

Sam remembered how she'd felt when she first put on a Regency gown; like she'd finally stepped into the life she wanted to live. No wonder her mother saw her clothing as such a threat. "Chris, you're in on this, too?

You're the one who said I should let the universe guide me."

"I don't think it's the universe that's guiding you. I have to say it hurt, hearing you put us down like you did. We let you be part of our family. We do a hell of a lot more than sing, you know that. And if you don't, I guess you're going to find out." He shrugged and made his way over to where the rest of the band was pulling out tents and luggage from the bus's storage compartments.

Sam hated knowing Chris thought badly of her, but she couldn't let this continue. She turned to her parents. "I mean it; you need to leave before this gets out of hand."

"We're not leaving until we've proven our point." The man she didn't recognize folded his arms over his chest. "You're on the wrong side, Sam. Better switch before it's too late."

"Who the hell is he?" she asked her father.

"Kenny Strike." The man stuck his hand out. Sam didn't shake it. With a sneer, he withdrew it. "You don't know what you're stepping into here."

"I've seen demonstrations before." But she didn't like the way he was trying to intimidate her. Who did he think he was? And why were her parents putting up with his interference?

Melissa clattered down the steps of the tour bus and rushed to join them. "Sam—have you met Kenny?" She took his arm, leaned her head on his shoulder, and Sam understood in a rush. This was another of Melissa's

conquests. Her parents never set boundaries with Melissa.

"Mom, Dad—I'm serious. You have to stop this."

"There's no stopping it now. It's taken on a life of its own." Kenny waved toward the cars and vans that even now were pulling to the side of the road. Sam had seen this before. Once organizers of a demonstration put out the word, social media allowed the message to spread quickly. *Deader Than Ever* were so well known their calls to action reached millions of fans.

"Fine. You had your chance. Just remember when it's all over, and you look like idiots, you chose him over me." She pointed at Kenny and strode off to report back to Boone, telling him as clearly as she could what he needed to expect would happen in the next few days.

Boone called the sheriff, who arrived quickly and told the interlopers in no uncertain terms they couldn't trespass on private property. Sam's parents' reaction was to block traffic on the street, instead.

Cab Johnson called an emergency meeting with the principals of Base Camp in the bunkhouse. Since it was her family causing the issue, Sam joined in.

"You're not using the land closest to the highway," Cab told them. "It's close enough to both the manor and Base Camp you can keep an eye on the protestors if they're there. Bring in porta-potties, make sure they have access to running water. Things like this can get messy fast if they're not handled correctly."

"If we give them facilities and water, that's like an open invitation for them to stay," Boone protested.

"If you don't, those hippies will be using the great outdoors to take care of their needs," the sheriff said. "And those camera crews hovering around will beam the results to the whole world. I don't think that's the image you want to project."

"Those *hippies* are my family," Samantha put in.

"I use the term in the best sense of the word, ma'am," the sheriff said with a smile. "I'm a fan of *Deader Than Ever*. Believe me, I want everything to stay friendly here."

Samantha relaxed a little bit, but later she watched the growing crowd of protesters set up tents in the pasture where Boone and Cab had directed them, and her uneasiness grew. She'd seen this before, and knew how tenacious her parents and their followers could be. She had no doubt they would get a lot of press.

By the time she got up the following morning, the crowd had swelled to several hundred, with more people arriving by the minute. She would've been surprised at how quickly it was all happening, if she hadn't participated in similar protests before. *Deader Than Ever*'s fans were willing to drop anything and pay whatever it took to get to a concert. For the privilege of camping out and protesting with them, they would mortgage their homes and sell their cars. Judging from past events, there'd be several thousand protestors by sundown, and more by tomorrow. She'd hoped people wouldn't be interested in a private argument between her and her parents, but she quickly realized that didn't matter. They weren't here to protest Base Camp so

much as they were here to hang out with the band.

"It's beginning to look like Woodstock out there," Avery said mid-morning when she came to check in with Sam. "We're about to take our guests to Maud and James's house for lunch and a walk in their gardens. If you're coming, you'd better change."

It broke Sam's heart to turn down the invitation, but she couldn't leave the ranch now.

"I'd better stay here," she said. "Have fun."

"I'm sorry this is happening." Avery gave her a quick hug. "I know how frustrating families can be."

"Thanks."

When Sam joined the line at the bunkhouse to get her lunch, she wasn't sure if she'd be able to eat any of it. Outside again, she looked for a place to sit, and finally chose a log that was a little way off from the others.

"I don't know why we don't just run them off," Angus said, his thick Scottish accent making the idea sound almost jolly.

"That would only make matters worse," Clay said.

"I don't understand why they think we're on opposite sides," Boone said. "So what if we were in the military? *Deader Than Ever* is supposed to be supportive of sustainability."

"They are," Samantha said. As angry as she was at her family, it was hard to hear people put them down. "They're very supportive of sustainability, and environmentalism in general. They don't like war."

"No one likes war," Jericho said.

"They think that if the country keeps a standing military it'll find reasons to use it," Samantha told them. She knew it was futile; discussions like this never got anywhere. And besides, she understood both sides. She didn't like war either, and the idea of Harris out there in danger, being shot at, shooting at other people—it was hard to imagine. She didn't *want* to imagine it.

But she wasn't so naïve she thought doing away with the military would end war. Didn't every country in the world have a military of some sort? She didn't think that would change anytime soon.

She straightened when she saw Renata coming their way, wondering if her objective was to chew her out for allowing her parents to disrupt things. Instead, Renata was fairly glowing, and there was a bounce in her step.

"Isn't this fantastic?" she exclaimed. "Think of the publicity. Our ratings are going to go through the roof. Our servers are already getting overloaded by hits on the website. Samantha, you're a genius."

Did Renata think she'd planned this? Samantha glanced around. Did they all think she'd planned this?

"This is all my parents' doing, not mine," she said angrily. "I think my work here shows just how dedicated I am to our cause."

"Damn straight," Boone came to her defense. "You get more done in those gardens than anyone else. No one's questioning that. Renata, don't forget that if Base Camp fails, so does your TV show. With all this publicity, you could do yourself right out of a job."

"There's always another job," she told him, but she

left soon after.

Sam decided she needed a cup of tea. Leaving the men to strategize, she slipped inside to the kitchen and found Kai already cleaning up the meal.

"Aren't you going to eat?" she asked him.

"No appetite. I'm having flashbacks," he told her. "I come from Venice Beach, California, which isn't exactly a hotbed of military support. When I decided to join up, some of my friends picketed my house. It was a joke—kind of. It kind of wasn't, too."

"It's hard to go against family and friends, isn't it?"

"It is. Was," he said sheepishly. "They're proud of me now that I've joined Base Camp. Sometimes they act like I finally came to my senses. Kind of bugs me, you know?"

She nodded. "We live in a complicated world. I wish people would acknowledge that."

"Complicated doesn't make for good soundbites," he said, lifting a stack of dishes into the soapy water in the sink.

"Seems unfair that they make you do all the cooking *and* all the cleaning, too," she said.

"I wouldn't refuse a hand," he said with a quick grin.

"Be glad to." She needed something to keep her mind off the evening she was missing. And the fact that her family was picketing just a few hundred yards away.

Curtis barged into the kitchen, stopped when he saw her, exchanged a look with Kai she couldn't interpret and left again with only a nod.

Complicated, indeed.

CHAPTER FOURTEEN

CLOSE TO MIDNIGHT, Harris lay in the grass, binoculars pressed to his eyes, and once again scanned the encampment of protesters. Their numbers had ballooned up faster than any of them had thought possible, and he estimated about four thousand people were milling around in their field. Tents had sprung up all over, along with campfires and charcoal grills. Harris knew the whole thing was giving Cab nightmares. He didn't like it one bit, either.

It'd taken him half an hour to wriggle his way close, but he had a feeling he could've been far less careful and he still wouldn't have been noticed. Bottles of wine were being passed around from protester to protester, and the air was fragrant with weed. Someone strummed a guitar, and a few people were singing, but the biggest cohort were huddled around listening to Henry.

Who would've thought the mild-mannered guitarist would have so much to say about capitalism, patriotism and the military industrial complex? Henry had obviously put a lot of thought into it over the years, and had

come up with some interesting hypotheses about the way the country was run. Harris had heard them all before, of course. If you wanted conspiracy theories, just hang around a military compound.

Backing him up was another, younger man. Kenny Strike. Where Henry was focused on his theories, Kenny was all fire and brimstone. He wasn't interested in debate—he wanted action.

"We need to shut down this show—by any means necessary," he kept saying, even when Henry tried to calm him down.

Harris didn't like the sound of that.

What he wanted to hear was the tactics the group planned to use to disrupt the show. But maybe that was expecting too much from this crowd. For all their talk, neither man outlined a plan. Still, acting as recon for Base Camp was far more satisfying than hanging around moping over Samantha.

He was pretty sure the protesters wanted maximum press coverage, and were waiting to make their stand until television crews could arrive from around the country. He'd already seen several, and he was sure there would be more tomorrow. He began to think about ways to keep the chaos under control. Keeping the crowds contained was the main thing. If the protesters got too close to the manor, or to Base Camp, things could get ugly.

Harris stayed in position for hours, long past when the revelers finally all retired to their tents, and snoring, fueled by alcohol, filled the air. When another hour

passed, and no one stirred, he finally eased away again, got to his feet and went back to catch a quick round of shut-eye himself.

He was up again well before dawn, watching every move the protesters made as they ate their breakfast, stretched and scratched, and began to form up their picket lines again.

Supporters began to stream in as soon as dawn arrived. And with them the press he knew Henry and Rachel craved. Renata strode around issuing orders to the cameramen. "This is fabulous," he heard her say more than once. Her happiness galled Harris more than he could say.

Riley, when she came down to Base Camp from the manor to confront Boone, was far less pleased. "We're trying to give our guests a Regency experience, and these protestors are ruining it," she exclaimed. "Can you imagine what kind of reviews we're going to get? We might as well shut down the bed-and-breakfast right now."

Samantha picked at her breakfast miserably. Harris knew she'd wanted to spend the weekend with the other women and their guests, but he supposed she couldn't do that when her own family was threatening to shut Base Camp down. It was too bad she was missing out. Curtis, standing some distance away, but watching Sam, seemed just as miserable. Harris hadn't seen the two of them interact once during the week that had crawled past. Boone and the others kept telling him Sam had made it clear she didn't want to.

He was beginning to lose his resolve as far as keeping his distance was concerned. Should he talk to Samantha?

Maybe.

Hell, probably. But he'd have to wait until this current crisis was over. He couldn't let Sam—or anyone—distract him when trouble was brewing.

"Nonsense," Renata told Riley. "This publicity is good for all of us. Just you wait, you'll have customers knocking down your doors."

The look Boone and Riley exchanged said neither of them believed it. "I'm sorry," Boone said to his wife. "If I could run them off I would, but you know that would just make it worse."

"Samantha, isn't there something you can do?" Riley asked her.

"I've tried, but I'm the last person they'll listen to," Samantha said. "They hate that I'm getting any attention at all. They want it all for themselves. And—" she sighed "—they've always been against the military. I'm sorry. I thought maybe if I laid low, they'd go away, but that doesn't seem to be working."

"I guess we'll have to give our guests free vouchers for another vacation," Riley said. "I don't know if they'll come back again after the experience that they've had so far, though."

"Maybe I could talk to your guests," Samantha told her. "I can apologize to them on my parents' behalf. I can explain what's going on, make a joke out of it. Maybe they'll see the humor?"

"I'm not sure that will help," Riley said. "We're going to take them back to Maud and James's house in a half-hour or so for lunch, instead of eating down here like we'd planned. We'll skip the tour of Base Camp, too. At least at Maud and James's they'll get away from the noise and crowds for a while."

"I'm sorry," Samantha said again. "I wish I could fix this." She got up to bring her dishes back to the bunkhouse, and Harris's heart squeezed at the way her head was bowed and her shoulders slumped. A minute later she was back outside, heading toward the gardens. He knew she spent most of her time there, and he'd overheard Boone talking about what a green thumb she had. She was finding a place for herself here, or she would be if her parents hadn't interfered.

He'd talk to her, he decided. As soon as the protestors were gone. He'd find out the truth once and for all about her and Curtis, and if she said there was nothing between them, he'd believe her.

A weight slipped off his shoulders as he made his decision, and he realized with chagrin he'd almost chosen the lonely end of the roof again—for no good reason, except his own pride.

He went to talk to Boone about finding a way to get rid of the protestors once and for all. He had a wife to remarry.

If she'd still have him.

"TRAITOR!"

"Sell out!"

Sam ignored the names the protestors called at her, and the cameras filming her progress, as she searched for her parents later that morning in a crowd that had ballooned up to far more than the pasture could bear. The show had arranged for two-dozen blue porta-potties to be delivered to the edge of the field, but there were lines in front of each of them and she'd heard Boone asking Renata to order more.

"...we'll have ten thousand people out there by the time the day's over," she'd heard Renata saying.

This had to stop. And she was the only one who could stop it. She should have realized that earlier.

When she finally spotted her mother, Rachel was in a heated discussion with Kenny Strike.

"...I'm saying is that you're being too soft on them," he was saying. "They've got your daughter, I get that, but that's no reason to hold back."

"There's a right way to do things and a wrong way," Rachel told him. "We're here to show the strength of peaceful protest—" She cut off when she saw Sam. "We'll talk more later," she told the man. Sam thought he would argue, but he left with a disdainful shrug.

"Having fun yet?" Sam asked her sarcastically.

"He's a bit of a hothead," Rachel admitted. There were lines on her mother's face Sam didn't remember, and she wondered if Rachel was regretting what she'd started.

"Why'd you invite him then?"

"I didn't. I can't control who joins in—you know that. Besides, he's Melissa's friend."

"And we all know how good she is at choosing friends."

Rachel rolled her eyes. "Did you come here to pick on your sister?"

"No, I came here to see if you'd come to your senses. We aren't doing anything wrong, Mom."

"That remains to be seen." Rachel led the way a little apart from the others. "You could still join us, you know."

Sam could imagine how her mother would love that. The press would be all over it, resulting in more publicity for the band.

"What's this really about?" Sam asked. "Because I'm beginning to think you're throwing a huge hissy fit because you lost your damn driver."

"You really left us in the lurch, you know that?" Rachel said. "We nearly missed a show because of you."

"You nearly missed a show?" Sam was speechless. "Mom, I nearly missed my life because of *you*. How long were you going to keep me in that bus? Forever?"

"Well, how's that for ingratitude?" Rachel was as furious as she was. "You got to tour with one of the most popular bands of our time—for your whole childhood! You grew up around the best musicians, listening to the best music, seeing our whole country— and other parts of the world. And I'm supposed to feel bad?"

"No, Mom." That wasn't what she wanted at all. "You're supposed to feel good about what I became because of all of that. Not ruin it!"

"Oh, stop being so dramatic." Her mother put her hands on her hips, nodding toward the milling crowds. "I heard your own director say it; we're giving you great publicity, too. It's a win-win situation."

"No, it's not." Sam realized her mother would never understand what Base Camp meant to her.

But Sam knew how important it was. What the men and women who lived here were trying to do transcended any feud she had with her family.

And in order to save it, she had to step away.

Defeat thickened her throat and she closed her eyes, fighting to maintain her composure. She would hate to leave Base Camp. To lose her new friends, her new calling.

To lose Harris.

But it was the only way to stop to what was happening. These crowds were out of control. And while protests could start peacefully, they rarely stayed that way when they ran too long. There was nothing for them to do here on Westfield's lawn. The sun was hot. She'd seen too much alcohol being passed around. Soon they'd get bored. Restless.

Disaster could only follow.

"You know what?" She opened her eyes again. Faced her mother. "Go call off the ravening hordes."

"Why would I do that?"

"Because you won. I'm leaving the show." It hurt to say it, but it was the only way. She'd get over her disappointment somehow. She'd go somewhere else. Somewhere she could garden. Create some kind of life

for herself.

Although how she could possibly do that without Harris she didn't know.

"You're coming back?" Her mother's face lit up and for one second—one very short second—Sam wondered if this was about Rachel missing her.

Sam's heart squeezed. She'd missed her mother, too. All of her family—and the band.

But she couldn't turn back time and be a child again.

"No, Mom, I'm not coming back," she said sadly. "And I'm not going to stay here, either. Not if that gives you an excuse to shut Base Camp down. I'm just leaving. For good."

She turned to go. Rachel rushed after her. "You can't walk out of my life again. I won't let you."

"Watch me."

"Samantha Smith, don't you turn your back on me."

The closest protestors turned to see what was going on. Samantha kept going.

"It won't work. We won't leave," Rachel called out. "We'll shut it down anyway."

"That's right," a male voice chimed in. Kenny Strike. Sam steeled herself not to listen. When she was gone, it would all be over, no matter what her mother said. Rachel would lose steam when she found she couldn't force Sam's hand. She'd move on to the next gig.

It was time to pack her things and call a taxi. But not yet. Not for a few more minutes. She had to say good-bye to Harris.

But first Sam couldn't resist one last look at the only place she'd ever really felt at home.

"AT LEAST THE women's guests are leaving tonight," Jericho said to Harris when they met up near the bunkhouse. "That's one wild card out of the picture. Savannah said they're going to go ahead with giving them vouchers for another stay in the future. That's going to hurt their bottom line, but there isn't much else they can do. Have you seen Samantha lately? I thought I saw her talking to her parents. I wonder how that turned out."

"I just saw her head toward the gardens." Sam had stalked past him without even seeing him, her head down and her arms crossed over her chest. Harris couldn't wait for the protest to end so they could hash things out. He hated to see her so unhappy.

"I'm not sure they could get any worse. This might have sunk the B&B. That makes Savannah and Avery less likely to stay."

"I hope not."

"I can't believe how many people have turned out to protest us. This is out of hand. Curtis just took that dog of his up to the manor for the duration. The people freaked her out."

Harris could understand that and he was glad Curtis had the foresight to get Daisy out of the way. Cab had called in reinforcements. The field near the road was full to bursting. And the protestors were getting sick of their cramped situation and the lack of amenities.

In fact—

Harris held up a hand. Was it his imagination or had the volume of the protest risen in the last few minutes? "Hold up," he told Jericho. "You hear that?"

"They're chanting," Jericho said. "What are they saying?"

At first Harris couldn't make it out. When he did, his blood ran cold.

"Tear it down! Tear it down!"

"Shit, they're going to riot." Jericho turned toward the bunkhouse. "Boone! Clay!"

A roar from the protestors drowned out his words as they broke through the split rail fence and streamed toward the camp, their chant speeding up.

"Tear it down! Tear it down!"

"Stop! Stop!" Harris raced toward them as if he could hold them back single-handedly. He held his arms wide, trying to catch the men and women streaming past, but it was like trying to stop an ocean with a sieve. He heard Boone and Clay yelling. Saw Angus and Walker join the fray.

"Tear it down! Tear it down!" That was Kenny Strike, and Harris had no doubt he was behind all this. Harris lurched for him, but the crowd was so thick he couldn't reach the troublemaker. The protestors ran rampant through the camp, shouting, pulling up tents and trampling them, swarming into the bunkhouse, where Harris heard Kai yelling, followed by a din of pots and pans and breaking glass.

Pushed back by the constant stream of people, Har-

ris fought to keep his feet. Men were shouting all around him as his fellow Navy SEALs tried to stop the chaos, and the protestors kept coming. There were thousands of them—all heading through the camp as if with a common goal.

Harris didn't understand where they were going, but they didn't stop at the edge of the camp. The only thing that way was—

The gardens and greenhouses.

Sam, Harris thought wildly.

He let the tide of humanity carry him toward the gardens, bellowing in rage when he caught sight of what they were doing.

Swarms of protesters had slashed their way through the rows of crops and were flailing against the plastic sheeting of the closest greenhouse. Several of them had torn through the walls and were holding back the plastic to let the others in. A woman's scream pierced the din. Sam?

She was inside, Harris realized. Inside, and trapped by all the protestors. Were they hurting her? He tried to struggle closer, but the whole crowd had dead-ended around the greenhouses and were milling in circles rather than moving forward.

Those who'd made it inside began hurling out the trays and pots of seedlings, dumping their contents on the ground, even as more people tried to force their way in. Dozens of yards away, Harris couldn't move forward or back. Sooner or later someone would be trampled in this crowd.

"Burn it down!" a man yelled. Harris spun around to see who it was, but there was no way to tell where the shout had come from.

"Burn it down!" "Burn it down!" The crowd picked up the refrain.

"There are people inside," Harris yelled, fighting and struggling to break through the press of bodies. "God damn it—there are people in there!"

"Harris!" Curtis appeared a half dozen yards away, caught in the crowd, too. He pointed at the greenhouse, just as Harris smelled smoke, and realized someone had actually started a fire. Panic erupted as the crowd realized what was happening. Screams filled the air. Those still inside began to burst out of the torn walls, but there was nowhere for them to go.

The crowd surged, wavered and heaved him toward Curtis, who caught his arm and held on.

"It's wood," Curtis was yelling. "The whole thing's framed with wood; it's going to go up in a matter of seconds. We've got to get everyone out!"

"Sam's in there!"

Curtis's eyes widened. He linked arms with Harris. They both bent forward and charged against the crowd, which had now turned and was trying to race away from the fire. Curtis lost his footing. Harris yanked him back up. Flames were already licking up the walls of the greenhouse. Heart pounding, Harris yelled, "Where is she? Why isn't she coming out?" They shoved the oncoming protestors aside, and finally gained some ground—

Only to lose it again with another surge of the crowd.

"Damn it!" Harris pressed forward again, Curtis behind him, lending his strength. Flames shot up from a hole in the roof. The crowd was finally thinning as people helped each other race away, but he was still too far away to reach it quickly enough. "Samantha!" Where was she? The structure was nearly engulfed.

"That way!" Curtis pointed and Harris understood what he meant. He fought his way through the press of bodies to a pile of packing crates left behind from some of Jericho's solar equipment. Quickly climbing to a higher vantage point, he scanned the area as Curtis scrambled up beside him.

"There!" Curtis pointed and Harris's heart surged. There she was, pushing through the tattered plastic on the close side of the building.

"Sam!"

She made it almost all the way through before something tugged her back and she nearly fell. As Harris watched, she twisted around, grabbed hold of her skirts and pulled, but nothing happened. She couldn't break free.

"She's stuck! Her skirt's caught," Curtis yelled.

Harris scanned the distance between them. Could he make it to her before the flames reached her? He had to try. Curtis yanked him back just as Harris braced to leap down from the crate. He reached under his jacket, yanked a pistol from his shoulder holster and slapped it in Harris's hand.

"There's no time! Shoot!"

Curtis was right; he couldn't reach Sam in time. The greenhouse would be gone—and so would Sam—in a matter of seconds. He needed to try to sever that twist of fabric. How ironic he hadn't thought to arm himself and Curtis had.

But there were people everywhere. Civilians.

"Can you get a clear shot?" Curtis yelled in his ear.

The crowd was thinning, but the fire was raging higher than before. Time was running out.

"Yeah. I think so." Sam still struggled to get free of the building. The hem of her skirt had wrapped tight around something inside. The angle was right as long as she kept tugging and didn't move back inside.

Curtis must have thought the same thing. "I'll call her name." He leapt off the packing crate and ran crosswise through the crowd.

Harris braced himself and raised the pistol. It wasn't his usual weapon of choice, but it would do. The crowd was finally streaming away. The only one left near the greenhouse was Sam.

He took a breath. Ran through the patterns and habits that made him such a successful sniper. He let everything go except the target; the twist of fabric holding Sam prisoner.

Sound, sights, smell disappeared.

There was only him and the place the bullet needed to go.

"Samantha! Sam!"

Samantha wheeled around at Curtis's shout, saw him

and took a step toward him. The long skirts of her dress stretched out taut.

Harris aimed for that twist of fabric. *Breathe in. Breathe out.*

He pulled the trigger.

Sam pitched forward so suddenly that for one awful second Harris thought he'd missed and killed her. Then she scrambled to her knees and raced toward Curtis. Harris jumped down and ran just as fast to reach her.

"Sam!"

He scooped her into his arms as the greenhouse, completely engulfed in flames, teetered and crashed to the earth in a shower of sparks.

"Harris!"

She clung to him, sobbing into his neck, her arms so tight around him he didn't think she'd ever let him go as he rushed away from the greenhouse's burning remains.

"You're okay. You're safe." He looked around to find Curtis and thank him.

But Curtis was gone.

SAMANTHA WAS STILL shaking when Harris reached the bunkhouse.

She'd nearly died.

And Harris had rescued her.

She should have been terrified when she realized it was Harris's shot that had torn her skirts and freed her. But that's why she loved Harris; because she could trust him utterly. Because he would always do the right thing.

Almost always, she amended. He still had to learn to

trust her. She hoped he would.

Because she couldn't live without him. Wouldn't live without him. She'd been wrong to ever consider going back on her vows. Harris was the man she loved. He was her life. He was her everything.

That was worth fighting for.

The damage the mob had left behind was devastating, though. She'd never forget the sound of the chanting mob as it had raced through Base Camp. She'd never forget the rush of bodies against the plastic greenhouse walls. The way the crowd had pushed and ripped at them until they'd burst inside all around her, pouring in like they'd never stop. To see them toss around the seedlings, dump them on the floor and stomp on them was like watching someone beat her own children. So many people had spilled into the greenhouse she couldn't get out.

She was battered and bruised, and her dress was shredded beyond repair, but that was the extent of her injuries. Now the protestors were streaming toward their vehicles, leaving the ranch as fast as they could. Harris carried her inside the bunkhouse. "Stay here until I come get you." He set her down gently, but kept his arms around her. He buried his face in her hair. "I thought I was going to lose you."

"I know."

"I couldn't bear that." He stepped away as if he couldn't say anymore.

"Where are you going?" She didn't want to be apart from him, even for a moment, but Harris was already

heading for the door.

"To help round up anyone who's decided to linger and get them the hell off our property."

"Be careful," she cried as he shut the door, leaving her alone inside. She paced the small confines of the building, breaking off from time to time to try to see what was happening out the windows. Suddenly, the door flung open again and her family rushed in.

"Sam! You're safe!" her mother cried and rushed to sweep her into her arms. "Oh, my God, baby—I was so scared. I didn't know if you were hurt—"

As her father and sister surrounded her, Sam shoved her mother away. "You were scared? You sicced your fans on us. They nearly killed me! They burnt down my greenhouse. Destroyed everything they could. Did you see it out there? The one place I felt safe—the one place that felt like home—is gone!"

"Sam—" Her mother reached for her again, but Sam lifted her hands to ward her off.

"I nearly died!" She grabbed her dress and held up its hem for them to see. "I would have died if your fans had their way. They set a building on fire with people in it—with me in it! I couldn't get out!" She shook her hem at them, the scorch marks that blackened it giving testament to how close the fire had come. "I was caught. Harris's shot set me free. I'm here right now because of a sniper, do you understand that?"

Her family's stricken expressions told her they understood it all too well.

"We didn't mean for any of that to happen. You

have to know that's not how we operate," her father said. "The crowd got out of control. Most of the trouble-makers weren't even our fans. I don't know where they came from."

"I do! You put out a call on social media for protestors and they came! You said what we were doing here was wrong. You whipped up a bunch of hatred and these are the consequences!" Samantha wasn't letting any of them off the hook. "All because you couldn't stand that I was getting a little bit of attention. Right? Because I dared to get off the damn bus!"

She spun away from them, sick to her stomach. From a window she could see the flat ground where the tent camp had been. Now there was nothing but shredded fabric and people's possessions scattered in the dirt. Tears pricked her eyes and no matter how hard she tried, she couldn't hold them back.

"What if I'd died?" She pointed out the window to where smoke still rose from the ruins of the greenhouse. "What if someone else had?"

"Sweetheart, we're sorry," Rachel said, moving to touch her arm.

Samantha shrugged her off, refusing to turn around. "If you're sorry, then fix it. Make it all go back to what it was! I was growing lettuce, Mom. That's my crime. I was growing fucking lettuce. Harris and Curtis were building tiny houses. Jericho and his crew were setting up windmills." She spun around. "We were trying to make the world a better place—just like you taught me was the most important thing to do!"

She shouldered past all of them, strode to the bathroom, slammed the door behind her and turned the lock. She couldn't look at them anymore and she didn't want to see what was happening outside. Samantha splashed cold water on her face, then reluctantly looked in the mirror. She was a mess, her dress torn and stained, her hair in tangles around her shoulders, her bonnet gone—who knew where.

The truth crashed over her like a tidal wave.

She might love Harris—and Base Camp—but this was all her fault. It was all ruined because of her. The encampment gone. The greenhouses gone. The crops they were depending on for the winter gone. She should have known what would happen when her parents found her. She should have predicted the protests—and the results.

If she'd left with her family when they'd first come, none of this would have happened.

She didn't deserve to stay at Base Camp.

She didn't deserve Harris's love.

She had to leave.

Even if it was too little, too late.

HARRIS STOOD WITH the rest of the men of Base Camp watching a die-hard group of protestors and Samantha's parents and sister finish negotiating with Cab and Boone. The camera crews, who'd broken and run when the riot touched off, had begun to reconvene, but still weren't back to filming.

Renata was having a full-on meltdown. "What do

you mean you didn't get the fire on film?" she was screaming. "Where the hell were you cowards?"

Boone broke off from the meeting and made his way over.

"It's the damnedest thing," he said, scrubbing a hand over his short-cropped hair. "They want to stay and help rebuild."

"Fuck that," Jericho said. "They're just looking for a way to ruin things even more."

"I don't think so," Boone said. "I think the ones who stayed are real fans of *Deader Than Ever,* unlike some of the other people who came to join the fun. They're pretty broken up over what happened. Samantha's family, too. They've apologized for protesting in the first place, and admit they lost control over the crowd."

"You think?" Jericho wasn't having it. Harris knew one of the expensive turbines he was installing had been damaged by the crowd. He understood how his friend felt. Right now he was struggling to contain his anger. Those people had endangered his wife's life. Didn't they know what that made him want to do?

"Look, they're right; we need them. Not just to fix up the place, but to show the nation we've found common ground. Those people aren't the only ones who want to dismiss us because we were in the military. We've all experienced that kind of prejudice. Well, here's a chance to address it." Boone looked around the group. The others nodded. So did Harris.

If he wanted Base Camp to get back to normal, he

needed to be willing to forgive and move on. He'd learned that lesson all too well recently. His inability to do so had cost him a lot of time with Sam. Time he wished he had back. He wasn't going to waste any more pursuing grudges.

The door to the bunkhouse opened and Samantha walked out. Harris forgot everything else and went to her. He tried to take her into his arms, but she eluded him, marching straight over to Boone and the others.

"I have something to say." Her voice was thin, but she was determined. "I'm leaving Base Camp. Today. Right now. I caused all of this. I made a mistake coming here. All I've done is mess everything up right from the start. You'll be better off without me."

"No." Harris's raised voice got everyone's attention. Even the members of *Deader Than Ever*, Renata and the ragtag remnant of the protestors turned to look at him. Harris fought to express what he needed to say, even though he hated being the center of attention like this.

"You can't go. Not now. And not because of me, either," he hastened to add. "You need to stay at Base Camp because you love it here—because this is your home. And you deserve to have what you love." He wasn't being clear enough, and he wished he had Curtis's gift with words, but all he could do was his best. "When I married you just over two weeks ago, I meant every vow I spoke." He heard gasps from some of the onlookers who hadn't known about their wedding, and noticed the camera crews were filming again, but he ignored them. He wasn't playing for an audience. All he

cared about was Sam. "I promised to be with you in good times and bad. In sickness and in health. Until I die. And I'm not dead. Thank God, you aren't either."

Rachel sobbed and buried her face in Henry's shoulder. Henry put an arm around her.

"That means I'm going to keep my promises. I'm going to stand by you. Right here at Base Camp. Where both of us belong. Maybe we lost this battle, but we haven't lost the war—not by a long shot. I made a commitment to the other men here. I have to stay. I'm asking you to stay, too. With me. What do you say?"

A tear slid down her cheek. "I want that more than anything. But this is all my fault—"

"No, it's not. It's mine," Melissa said, stepping forward. She was pale, her expression so careworn Harris thought she looked a decade older than the spoiled girl from the photo Sam had shown him on her phone just weeks ago. "I'm the one who brought Kenny along, and I'm the one who should have stopped him, but I didn't. I thought it was all a game. That's what life has always seemed like to me. It's been like this big candy bowl and I've always gotten to choose exactly what I wanted." She turned to Sam. "I guess I got used to you being the one to fill the bowl and take care of everything else. I thought somehow I deserved the life I had, and you deserved the one you had. When you left, everything changed. I didn't like that, and I wanted it to go back to normal. I wanted you back on the bus. That was pretty selfish of me."

"You weren't the only one who was selfish," Henry

said. "We all owe you an apology for that, Sam," her father said. "We were so wrapped up in our own careers we never thought that there was something else you might've rather been doing."

"I should've spoken up sooner about what I wanted," Sam told him. "I guess I didn't really know, either, until the first time Boone showed me the gardens. Then I knew exactly what I wanted to do."

"I think we all needed to be shaken up to see what was real," Rachel said. "We're all the better for it."

"I know I am." Curtis elbowed forward through the crowd to face them, Daisy at his heels. Harris was glad to see the dog unharmed. "I feel like this is my fault, too. And I have to say—hell, I don't think I've ever been as ashamed of myself as I am now. I was so determined not to be made a fool of again, that I made a fool of myself." He scanned the crowd and suddenly shouted, "These two have been married since the day Samantha appeared on the show. They belong together. Everything else you've seen on television was fake. Just made up to entertain you. I've never met two people more in love and I won't be part of keeping them apart anymore. Samantha, Harris, you have my blessing. Be happy together." He turned to stride away, but in a flash Renata was after him. Her hair loose was from its normal updo, her clothes were smeared with dirt and her shirttail was undone from her trademark pencil skirt, but her disheveled appearance didn't slow her down.

"Wait! Stop right there. *When* were you made a fool of before?" she shouted, chasing him as best she could

in her high heels.

Curtis stopped and his shoulders slumped. He turned. "Really? You want to exploit me, too? Now? After all this?" He waved a hand to encompass the devastation around them.

"Of course I do, and you knew that when you signed up, so stop playing coy. When were you made a fool of before?"

"Two years ago," Curtis said finally, and Harris felt more sorry for the man than he'd ever thought possible. Curtis was throwing himself under the bus to take the heat off him and Samantha. The viewers wouldn't like it when they learned he and Sam were already married—and the show had covered it up. Curtis was giving Renata something new to use to distract the audience. "I was left at the altar by the love of my life. In front of all my friends, and the men I served with. In front of my family. Everyone in my hometown knows about it. Guess your team of spies isn't as good as you think it is, Renata."

"Oh, God," Samantha whispered to Harris. "No wonder he was furious I married you instead of him."

Harris took her hand. "He was the one who didn't want to marry a stranger," he reminded her. "He's playing it up for Renata's sake. For our sake. But he knew what he was doing when he got drunk and played the field the night of Clay and Nora's wedding. He deliberately didn't come to get you at the airport the next day. He's only got himself to blame for what happened."

Samantha nodded. "It still sucks. I hope he finds the woman who's meant for him."

"Yeah. Me, too." He turned her to face him. "But you didn't give me your answer. Will you stay?"

Tears shining in her eyes, she nodded again. "Of course. If the others want me."

"Of course they want you. Come on, let's get you up to the manor. We need to update the women. Looks like things are under control here." He tugged on Sam's hand and, after scanning the crowd, who now circled around Curtis and Renata, she followed him. Her parents and sister were talking earnestly to Boone. Harris hoped they were discussing ways to make amends for the damage they'd done. He'd talk to them later and let them know exactly what he expected from them as his future in-laws. They weren't going to push Samantha around anymore. They'd have him to answer to from here on in.

HARRIS SEEMED SO sure the others would agree that she could stay, but Sam wasn't sure at all. She'd unleashed this disaster on Base Camp; she could hardly blame anyone who wanted her to leave. By the time they reached the top of the hill, she was as anxious as she'd been when Harris had left her in the bunkhouse, but before they reached the manor, Clay overtook them.

"I need to see Nora and let her know we're all okay. Thank God the women stayed up here. I was afraid they'd come running down and get caught up in the mob, but Curtis told me they barricaded the doors when

they saw the riot start. He already let them know the coast was clear when he came to get Daisy back."

Clay hurried ahead, racing up the back steps to the manor and pounding on the door. "Nora? Nora—it's me."

The back door swung open and Nora dashed outside, followed by the rest of the women and their guests. In their Regency gowns they made a colorful crowd, but their faces were somber.

"We heard a gunshot," Nora cried. "Is everyone really all right?"

Samantha hadn't even considered how that must have affected Nora. The woman had been shot herself only weeks ago. Now violence had come to Base Camp a second time—and it was Sam's fault.

Harris didn't let her shrink away. "Everyone's fine," he said loudly. "Only Samantha, here, had a close call. She was in the greenhouse when the protestors set it on fire. She nearly didn't make it out."

All eyes turned to her and Sam cringed, wishing Harris hadn't said anything. "My dress got caught. I couldn't pull free—"

Nora reached her before she could finish, and pulled her into a rough embrace. The others surrounded her. Their questions all came at once.

"Are you hurt?" "Have you seen a doctor?" "Who set the fire?" "How did you get away?"

"I'm okay. Just bruised," she said when Nora let her go. "I don't know who set the fire, but Harris saved me. That was the shot you heard; he tore the fabric with a

bullet." She lifted the ragged hem of her dress to show them. "It's my fault. You all know that, don't you? All of this is my fault. I shouldn't have come—"

"Nonsense," Riley said sternly, just as she had earlier. "You weren't one of the protestors; you've been busting your ass in that greenhouse day in and day out. It's all Boone talks about. He was saying he thought he could expand with your help since you do so much."

"But it's my parents—"

"Uh-oh—are we supposed to be responsible for what our parents do now? Because if we are, I'm in trouble," Avery said. She smiled to show she was joking. "Samantha, that crowd was so big no one could have stopped it."

"She's right," Harris said. "Some of those people came to make trouble and they made it. That won't stop us from cleaning it up again. Samantha's family and some of their fans have volunteered to stay and put things back to right."

Samantha braced herself for a wave of scorn from the other women. Instead, Avery nodded. "That will make things a lot better. They'll get all kinds of publicity and *Base Camp* will get more viewers. More people will learn about sustainability."

"Why aren't you all mad at me?" Samantha burst out. "Look at everything's that happened since I've been here."

"Well," Savannah said after a pause. "You're not boring."

The others nodded in agreement.

"We'd better get back to our guests," Riley said. "Will you come, too, Samantha, and tell them all first-hand what happened? That may go some way to smoothing over their bumpy stay here."

"Yes, of course. And—if any of them wants one after what happened, I'll make sure they get auto-graphed photos from the band," Samantha said.

"They'll get one better than that," Jericho said, arriving out of breath. "*Deader Than Ever* are going to do a benefit concert for Base Camp. Your guests will get backstage passes if they can stay an extra couple of days."

"We'll give them free lodging, too, if they decide to stay. See, it's all going to turn out just fine," Win said. "Besides, Harris loves you, and you love him. That's what Base Camp is really all about—learning what's real. Finding true happiness. You two epitomize that."

"Do you... really want me to stay?"

"Yes!" Savannah said.

"Absolutely," Riley chimed in.

"You're one of us now, no getting away from that," Nora told her.

"It's decided. You'll stay—and marry Harris all over again. I want to be a bridesmaid!" Avery chimed in.

Sam turned to Harris. "Do you really want to marry me again?" She could hardly believe she was getting a second chance.

"Are you sure you want to marry me? You know what you're signing on for now."

"Of course I do."

"Then it's settled."

CHAPTER FIFTEEN

THE FOLLOWING DAY, Harris approached the
building site immediately after breakfast. He hadn't
worked on the tiny house in days, not since he and
Curtis had fought. In the clear morning light, Base
Camp didn't look as bad as it had the night before. The
danger and violence was over, and it was time to
rebuild. Everyone seemed eager to get to work.

After a long discussion with Renata and Boone the
previous evening, Harris knew it was time to finish the
tiny house, too. Renata had agreed to air a modified
version of the events of the previous day, which showed
the building tension, the riot and its aftermath, but not
Curtis's shouted explanation that Harris and Sam were
already wed.

Instead, the next episode would include the part in
which Curtis said Harris and Samantha were meant to
be together, and would also make much of Curtis's
admission he had been left at the altar once before as an
explanation for his behavior. Harris figured *Deader Than
Ever*'s benefit concert footage would probably eat up

most of the episode, anyway. The women's guests had put off their flight home, with the B&B covering the cost of changing their plane tickets. Maud and James were hosting an impromptu ball in the meantime, with all the men of Base Camp slated to dress up and join in. Once it was clear the danger was over, the women's guests had relaxed and even volunteered to help with the cleanup effort.

With his wedding set for August twentieth, they had several weeks to get Base Camp back in order, and it had occurred to Harris this next tiny house would be his. That being the case, he needed to help build it.

He hoped Curtis understood.

He was only beginning to understand how wrong he'd been when he'd thought protecting those he loved meant he had to stay aloof. If Curtis hadn't helped him get close enough to the greenhouse and hadn't handed him that pistol, Sam would be dead right now. On his own, he was only one man, and he couldn't be everywhere at once. Luckily for him, at Base Camp he didn't have to. Every man here was a Navy SEAL—they'd all had experience on the lonely end of the roof.

And now they'd each chosen the other end. They were a true community. They would work together, protect each other, fight off hordes of protestors if need be.

Together.

He couldn't say how much that meant to him. Which meant he needed to put things right between him and Curtis before he could do anything else.

When he arrived, he found Curtis hard at work on finishing touches inside. He was amazed how far he and Clay had gotten in the last few days. Daisy perked up and came to see him, sniffed his hand, gave a doggy sigh and returned to Curtis's side.

"Morning," Harris said, leaning against the door frame.

"Morning," Curtis answered. "Something I can do for you?" He was wary but not belligerent, and Harris relaxed a little.

"More like I'm here to see if there's something I can do for you. I think... this house will be mine and Samantha's." He braced himself for an explosion. He couldn't blame Curtis if that was the way he reacted.

Curtis looked down, and his shoulders sagged. He nodded. "Guess so. Guess you want to help finish it, then."

"Yeah, I'd like that."

"You know what? I'd like that, too." Curtis held out a hand, and after a moment Harris shook it. "We used to do good work together—before I started acting like an ass. I'd like to know I helped build the house you and Samantha will make a life in. I'm rooting for you guys. Really."

"That's good to hear. Thank you for your help during the riot. I don't think I'd have made it in time to save Sam without you."

"Of course." Curtis rubbed his chin with the back of his hand. "That riot made a lot of things crystal clear to me in a very short period of time. Like how I wasn't

going to change Sam's mind, and how I didn't even know if I wanted to. After all that talking we did, I didn't know her very well at the end of it. Guess I was too busy trying to convince her to like me to listen to what she had to say."

"You're not pissed at me anymore, then?"

"Nah," Curtis said. "But when it's finally my turn, and my bride arrives at Base Camp, I'd appreciate it if you kept as far away from her as possible."

Harris laughed. "You got a deal."

"Good. Now let's get to work."

Harris cocked his head and studied Daisy, who was keeping mighty close to Curtis's feet. "How do you do that?" he asked.

"Do what?"

"Keep that dog so loyal? Daisy was supposed to be Sam's. I gotta admit, when she stopped giving me the time of day and wouldn't leave your side, I was worried it was an omen." He inspected the work that had been done since he was last in the house, but when Curtis didn't answer, he looked over to find the husky man looking sheepish.

"That's exactly how I wanted you to feel," Curtis admitted. "So I've been feeding Daisy steak from my secret stash. Kai's a terrific cook, don't get me wrong— but I love steak—and bacon. Kai doesn't serve it enough for my taste." He scratched the back of his neck. "Lucky for me, he's been willing to keep my secret in exchange for me doing some of his dishes. That first day Sam arrived and you brought Daisy, she sniffed my

hand and smelled the bacon I'd cooked on the sly. That's why she kept licking me. After that, I made sure she got a lot of extra treats as long as she kept close."

"You are one sneaky bastard," Harris told him.

"You got the girl. Don't I at least deserve the dog?"

"I guess so." Harris reached down to scratch Daisy's ears. He'd have to find another canine friend for Sam one of these days.

"I HAD NO idea you had such a green thumb," Rachel said when Samantha gave her family a tour of the reconstructed greenhouse several days later. They'd all kept busy getting the community back up and running. Luckily, none of the permanent structures had been damaged. After hearing the news about the riot, the lumber company that had provided the scrap wood for the original greenhouse sent over a new load, and everyone had pitched in to frame it up.

"I never had the chance to try before," Samantha told her. She had spent several hours this morning repotting a bunch of seedlings donated by one of the local nurseries, and this afternoon a whole crew of them would replant the gardens with the more mature vegetable plants they'd been given. A sporting goods company had donated new tents and sleeping bags. Help had been flowing in from all directions since the first news stories went out about what had happened here, and she was overwhelmed at how quickly they'd been able to rebuild.

Her mother hugged her. "I've really missed you, you

know," she said. "The bus isn't the same without you."

"Who did you get to take over my job?" Samantha asked her.

"Me," Melissa said. "Scary, I know. I had no idea how much you did, until I took it on."

"Don't tell me—" Samantha said. "You took on the job in order to prove how easy it was, and what a wimp I was to always whine about it." She laughed when Melissa's mouth dropped open. "Come on, admit it."

Melissa was actually blushing. "I guess that sums it up."

"Well, I'm just glad that everyone's okay, and that things are going so well for all of us," Henry said. "We're all going to miss you, peanut, but we're glad you found Harris and are making a life for yourself."

"Even if he's a Navy SEAL?"

"After that riot? Especially since he's a Navy SEAL."

"HEARD THERE WAS a bit of a scuffle at the ranch," Egan said when Harris finally made it back to his forge several days later.

"You could say that."

"The wife and I snuck in for the concert."

Harris chuckled. "You didn't need to sneak; everyone was welcome."

"That little lady of yours all right?"

"Yes, she is." And he'd spent every spare moment he could with her these past few days. Free from having to hide their relationship, they'd struggled to keep their

hands off each other. Harris never found it difficult to think of something to say now he wasn't worried she'd leave him. They'd decided to wait until their wedding night to make love again, and the anticipation was killing him. "About Sam," he went on. "My wedding is coming up—second wedding," he amended. "I want to make something for her. A gift."

Egan was already nodding. "What do you have in mind?"

"Something for the house. Something to make it ours."

Egan thought a moment. "A door knocker. Something like this." Egan pulled a scrap piece of paper and a stubby pencil out of his pocket. He braced it on the anvil and began to sketch. A few minutes later he held it out for Harris's inspection.

"I like it." Harris admired the man's skill. "Not sure I can pull it off, though."

"We'll do it together, one step at a time." Egan patted him on the shoulder. "I'm proud of you."

"Oh, yeah? What for?"

"For being the kind of man who doesn't quit. You'll be a good husband for Sam."

"I'm damn well going to try."

"IT'S ALL YOURS," Avery said to Sam, throwing open the door to the best guestroom the manor had to offer. All the women had decided to spend the night before her wedding up at the house together—a kind of sleepover bachelorette party, as Avery had put it when she'd come

up with the idea.

"All mine?" Sam's heart squeezed with excitement. A whole room. Just for her.

"Don't forget the en suite." Avery threw open that door, too. "You'd better spend an hour or more luxuriating in that tub. Who knows when you'll next get a chance?"

"Probably never," Sam agreed. "It's solar showers from now on."

Avery laughed. "Solar showers with your husband. That's not so bad, is it?"

"We'll see." But secretly Sam thought she was right. Any time spent with Harris was wonderful—especially now that nothing stood between them.

"We'll meet up at seven for dinner. Until then, take all the time you need. Really—enjoy it," Avery told her. "You deserve every minute of happiness."

"Even if two men fought over me?" Sam poked her in the side.

Avery batted her hand away. "Even if two men fought over you," she agreed with a sigh.

After Avery helped her to undress and went off to prepare for the evening, Sam took her time exploring the room while her tub filled. It was heavenly to have so much space to herself. She could spend a lifetime here—

No, she decided. Not a lifetime. A week or two, maybe, but then Base Camp would call to her again, with all its bustle and busyness. She loved being part of that community, and even Harris had lightened up since

the day of the riot. That smile of his came far more quickly and he wasn't so eager to go off alone.

She missed him already, although she'd been with him only a half-hour ago. She wouldn't see him again until she walked down the aisle. Just the thought of her wedding sent tremors running through her. She wasn't sure why; they'd done this before, after all.

But this time they'd be filmed, and their families would be present. She would meet his mother and sisters for the first time tomorrow. She prayed they approved of her.

Most of all, this time she knew that forever lay on the other side of the ceremony. Renata couldn't keep them apart anymore. Tomorrow night they'd enter their tiny home together—

And start their married life for real.

Her bath stretched on for more than an hour. She couldn't help draining out the cool water and adding more hot. Just this once she would indulge. Then she'd adhere to Base Camp's environmentally sound practices for the rest of her life. As soon as Jericho got his turbines and solar arrays up, things would get more comfortable, anyway. Meanwhile, she'd focus on her husband. On her gardens.

On starting a family.

Sam couldn't wait.

CHAPTER SIXTEEN

THE DAY OF the wedding dawned clear and bright. Harris was grateful to see the sunshine, since they hoped to hold the ceremony and reception outside. They had been prepared to move it to the great room at the manor, but with all the guests they expected, it would've been crowded. Besides, Samantha had said more than once that getting to spend her time outdoors was one of the best parts about moving to Base Camp.

Their tiny house was done, although he had forbidden Samantha to come near it until he was able to carry her over the threshold after the wedding. He couldn't wait to show it to her—including the hand-wrought door knocker he'd installed this morning on the door. He wished he'd had the talent to do all of the fine wood finishing work, but he was proud to be able to say that Curtis had done it to his specifications. Once he'd finished the door knocker, he'd had enough time to forge many of the iron handles and drawer pulls for the cabinets, too, under Roy Egan's tutelage. He had a feeling Samantha would appreciate those touches.

They would spend their first night in their tiny house, and then head up to a cabin in the nearby mountains donated for the occasion by the Mathesons—a nearby ranching family Boone and the other founders had known since they were kids. It was brand-new, rebuilt after a snowstorm had damaged the previous one. Harris had seen pictures, and it seemed the perfect getaway for him and Samantha to spend time alone together.

He and Sam had discussed the future over and over again, and had decided to start their family as soon as possible. Three pregnancies were still required to meet Fulsom's conditions for them to keep the ranch, and Harris looked forward to trying to provide the group with one of them.

Samantha seemed just as intrigued with the idea of becoming a mother as he was with the idea of becoming a father. Now that he knew he belonged here at Base Camp, he couldn't wait to get started. Unlike his own father, he would stay with his family through thick and thin. He was positive the love he shared with Samantha would last forever.

In the days after the riot, he'd had plenty of time to think about cause and effect, and whether or not he could've prevented what had happened. The answer he'd come up with was *possibly*. But no matter what had happened, they'd all come together to restore their community afterward. That was the beauty of life at Base Camp. He didn't need to work alone. He was one man among equals, all of them sharing a common goal.

No longer would he stand on the far side of the roof. From here on in, he would sink or swim with the others.

As had become the custom here at Base Camp, the men were donning Revolutionary War–era uniforms for the wedding—Alice's answer to the kind of uniforms Regency men would have been wearing. But this time, to the men's surprise, Alice brought over blue uniforms instead of the red ones she'd lent them previously. She gathered them all in the bunkhouse for a final fitting that morning.

"It's just too unpatriotic to keep forcing you to dress up as British redcoats instead of American patriots," she said as she worked on fitting Harris's uniform. "I figured with the number of weddings you'll need to have, I'd better come up with the right clothes."

"We could wear normal suits. Or better yet, our good jeans," Harris told her.

"Hush, or I'll stab you with a pin," Alice said. "You have to match the women."

"Of course." Harris didn't mind nearly as much as he made out. Alice was right; at least now their old-fashioned uniforms were from the right continent. Those old red coat uniforms had done in a pinch, but Base Camp was here to stay, and there'd be plenty more Regency weddings down the road.

As if reading his mind, Boone said, "Since we're all gathered anyway, might as well draw straws for the next victim."

There was an uncomfortable shuffling as the as yet-

to-be married men contemplated their future. The cameras, following closely as usual, honed in on the straws Boone had produced in his hand.

"Walker, Jericho, Curtis, Kai, Angus, Greg and Anders, come on down. Let's see who's up next." Boone wasn't going to let anyone off the hook. Harris grinned, glad his marriage was already sewn up.

As the others gathered around Boone, Alice finished her inspection of Harris's uniform. "I'm just going to keep pretending that there is a tear in this seam," she whispered to him. "I've got to see how this ends."

Angus drew first, but his straw was long. He frowned, and Harris wondered if he was anxious to get on with marrying Win. Kai and Greg drew next. Theirs were long, too. Curtis drew a long straw, and exhaled visibly. Anders drew another long one.

"It's down to Walker and Jericho," Boone said. "And rightly so. One of the founders should marry next."

"Don't know about that," Jericho said. "Seems we're all in this together."

"And everyone drew their straw, fair and square," Boone said. He thrust his fist in front of Walker's face. "Don't think keeping quiet is going to make me forget you," he said. "Isn't it time to put Avery out of her misery?"

Harris was glad none of the women of Westfield were present, and he hoped Alice knew well enough to keep her mouth shut. Avery's relationship with Walker was a sore point, and since Walker never talked about

anything, no one knew which way the wind was blowing.

Walker shot Boone a long, brooding look, but reached out and grasped one of the straws. He hesitated, and Harris was sure everyone in the room was holding his breath. When he finally tugged it out of Boone's grasp, he held it up so everyone could see it was long.

"Well, hell," Jericho said. "Guess it was bound to happen sooner or later. Would've liked it to be later, though." He disappeared out of the bunkhouse before anyone could stop him.

"It's for the best," Boone said to no one in particular. "If Savannah doesn't want him, she should tell him once and for all, so Jericho can get on with things."

"It's not always that easy," Clay said. Harris knew he was thinking of Nora.

"So far things have turned out," Harris said, speaking up for the first time. "Maybe it'll turn out for them, too."

"Let's hope so," Boone said.

Alice smoothed down the arms of Harris's jacket one last time. "There. You're all set. All of you look very handsome. I'll see everyone at the wedding." She slipped out of the bunkhouse, too.

"The ceremony starts in less than an hour," Boone said. "You ready, Harris?"

"Never been readier."

As SAMANTHA PACED down the grassy aisle between the rows of white folding chairs the men had set up that

morning on the lawn in front of the manor, she didn't think her wedding day could be more perfect. Savannah had made sure her beautiful wedding gown was cleaned and pressed, and Alice had repaired any damage it had sustained. It wasn't a traditional Regency gown, but she'd worn it for her first wedding to Harris and nothing else would do for her second walk down the aisle to marry him. She leaned on her father's arm, feeling closer to him than she'd felt in years. Her mother sat in the first row, and had twisted around to watch her progress. Her sister took her place next to the three other bridesmaids Samantha had chosen: Win, Savannah and Avery. And her dress was a respectable peach Regency affair, the same as the other women wore.

All her new friends sat waiting for the ceremony to begin. Members of the band, and the core group of fans who had stayed behind to rebuild Base Camp, sat in many of the chairs on her side of the aisle. Alice and several of her sisters sat there, too, along with other people from the community she'd met over the weeks that she'd been here.

On the other side of the aisle were the Egans, Harris's mother and sisters, who'd come up from Louisiana with their husbands and children, his aunt, uncle and cousins, and more members of the community whom he'd met along the way. Samantha realized they were already well on their way to belonging in Chance Creek.

She allowed her gaze to stray to Harris and the men standing beside him as she neared the altar. He'd chosen Curtis, Kai, Jericho and Walker as his groomsman.

She'd heard Jericho was due to marry next, and even in the middle of her own wedding, she couldn't help but be curious as to the state of things between Savannah and him.

Her father dropped a kiss on her head before moving to sit next to her mother in the first row. Harris came to stand beside her, and for the second time in six weeks she faced an officiant and waited for her wedding to begin. Maybe two weddings wasn't such a bad idea after all, she thought several minutes later as she realized this time around she was relaxed enough to hear every word Reverend Halpern said.

When Harris repeated the vows he'd sworn to her only weeks before, this time they rang even truer. She knew now he'd meant everything he'd said back then, and she was glad she'd get to speak her vows again, too. Today she truly knew the man she was standing beside, and that knowledge had grown her regard for him into a love strong and deep.

"I now pronounce you man and wife. You may kiss the bride," Reverend Halpern said, and Harris lifted her delicate veil over her head. He leaned forward, and Samantha met him halfway, eager to feel his touch again.

The wait had been worth it. Every nerve in her body came to attention as Harris cupped her chin in his hands and kissed her. This was her husband.

This was the man with whom she'd spend the rest of her life.

When he finally pulled away, amid thunderous clap-

ping and cheers, Samantha leaned forward again and whispered in his ear, "I can't wait to be alone with you tonight."

"I can't wait, either."

They had to wait, though—through dinner, and dancing to an intimate set played by *Deader Than Ever*. Neither her parents nor her sister seemed upset to share the limelight with her on this special day, and Samantha was brimming over with love for everyone present by the time the evening wound down.

She once caught sight of Jericho and Savannah in a heated discussion by the front door of the manor, but didn't think of them again until late that night as Harris led her toward the brand-new tiny house they'd both helped to build. She wished them well in her heart and hoped that one day they would be as happy as she and Harris were.

"Hold on," Harris said when they got close. He scooped her into his arms and carried her easily up and over the threshold, although he had to turn sideways to get them both safely inside. When he set her down again and pointed to the door knocker, Samantha covered her mouth with her hands.

"It's... beautiful." The door knocker was shaped like a hawk, its head protruding from the door toward her. In its beak it held a carefully crafted iron ring made to look like several different herbs and flowers twisted together. She knew instinctively they were meant to represent her love of gardening. Just like the hawk represented Harris's desire to keep her—and everyone

else in Base Camp—safe. "You and me," she said.

"That's right. You and me together. Like we should be." He shut the door and led her farther inside. Sam was nearly overcome by what she saw. The whole interior seemed crafted just for her. She recognized the other iron work Harris had done right away; handles for the cabinet doors wrought into familiar species of plants she was cultivating in the greenhouse, the stems and leaves works of art. Like the other tiny houses, this one had been built with organic curves so that it felt like it had grown out of the earth, rather than being man-made. Set into the hillside, its large front glass windows let in lots of light. "I love it. Harris, I adore it." She threw her arms around his neck and realized with a renewed surge of joy she was allowed to hug him like this now. No one stood in their way as man and wife, and judging by the look in Harris's eyes, he was as pleased as she was by the thought.

"Come here." He led her toward the little bedroom and showed her how he'd built the bed as a loft over a closet, storage space and built-in chest of drawers. He helped her up and she saw at once how the high bed felt like an escape from the rest of the world.

"I feel like a kid in a treehouse," she told him.

"What I've got in mind is for grownups." He kissed her and Samantha's heart felt full to bursting. How had she managed to come so far in such a short period of time? From being frustrated and thwarted back in her family's bus to feeling like every dream she'd ever had was coming true.

326 | CORA SETON

"I love you," she said.

"I love you, too. But I want to get you out of that dress."

There was nothing she wanted more. She felt a pang at putting aside the beautiful gown, but it had served its purpose, making her feel like a queen on her wedding day—not once, but twice. Now she wanted nothing to come between her and Harris.

"We'd better do this on the ground," he said a moment later. Helping her down again, he got to work on the complicated fastenings and had the beautiful gown off her in no time at all. Samantha hung it carefully in the closet, and noticed other items of her clothing there. She smiled, knowing her friends had transferred her things to her new house while she'd been busy at the reception. She didn't wear stays under this modern gown, but Harris took his time undoing her strapless bra, kissing each new inch of skin laid bare by his skillful fingers. Samantha buzzed all over with the delicious knowledge that soon those hands would caress her everywhere. As if reading her mind, he set aside her bra, ran his hands up to cup her breasts and softly squeezed.

His touch made Samantha weak in the knees, and she sagged back blissfully against Harris's muscled chest and let him explore her body. As she stepped out of her modern panties, he turned her around and bent to press his mouth to one nipple. Sam moaned, almost overcome again.

Waiting to be with Harris had been such sweet torture, and now she wasn't sure she could hold back, but

Harris moved slowly, teasing and touching her until her skin burned and she ached to feel him between her legs.

Harris urged her up the ladder after he'd undressed, too, taking liberties all the way up that left her even hungrier for him to fill her. Up on the bed, she lay back and stretched her arms over her head. "Would you take me already?"

"We have all night," he said, lying beside her and running one hand over her body.

Samantha turned and pounced on him. "I'm not waiting all night for the good stuff. I've been patient long enough." He chuckled good-naturedly and let her climb up to straddle his waist. Feeling the hard length of him against her was enough to draw another sigh from her throat. "Harris, I'm not kidding. I need you."

"I'm right here." He lifted her hips and held her over him so that he was just pressing against her. Samantha wriggled, wanting him to push in deeper. "I'll always be here for you. Every night from now on."

"Promise," she begged him. "Because I never want to be apart from you again."

"I promise." Harris pushed into her, gently at first until she wanted to scream with impatience, and then with more authority until he filled her. Without a condom between them, the sensation was heavenly, and when he began to move inside her, Samantha closed her eyes and rocked with him, her breasts hanging heavy, almost within reach of his mouth.

She swallowed, trying not to be overcome by the feel of him inside her. Harris pushed up to take her

nipple into his mouth, and ran his teeth over her sensitive skin. She gasped and leaned forward for more, each stroke of him inside her bringing her closer to the brink.

"Harris." She couldn't think of anything else. That said it all; she loved him, felt loved by him and was satisfied to think that this could be her whole world from here on in. The way he held her, the way he moved inside her showed his intimate knowledge of who she was and what she wanted. That was Harris through and through; a man who cared enough to take the time to learn her preferences and to put her desires in front of his.

She couldn't wait to share her life with him—all of it.

And this was the start.

When she crashed over the edge a moment later, Samantha gave herself up to loving him, loving her life and loving whatever might come next. Harris came with her, his groans echoing her cries, until both of them collapsed, panting and gasping, against the bed. Samantha lay on Harris's chest, breathing hard, and found herself blinking back tears.

"Hey, you all right?"

"More than all right. Perfect. How can you be mine?" she asked him.

"The same way you can be mine. Because we were meant for each other. Because Fate wanted us to be together—and we wanted it, too," he told her.

"Once isn't nearly enough," she warned him a few

minutes later, when her heart had slowed down and her breathing was normal again.

He chuckled. "No?"

"No. Not by a long shot. I want to be pregnant by the time the night's over. Is that all right with you?"

"Hell, yeah." Harris flipped her on her back and began to make love to her all over again.

To find out more about Harris, Samantha, Boone, Riley, Clay, Jericho, Walker and the other inhabitants of Westfield, look for *A SEAL's Consent*, Volume 4 in the *SEALs of Chance Creek* series.

Be the first to know about Cora Seton's new releases! Sign up for her newsletter here! www.coraseton.com/sign-up-for-my-newsletter

Other books in the SEALs of Chance Creek Series:

A SEAL's Oath
A SEAL's Vow
A SEAL's Consent

Read on for an excerpt of Volume 1 of
The SEALs of Chance Creek series – *A SEAL's Oath*.

NAVY SEAL BOONE Rudman should have been concentrating on the pile of paperwork in front of him. Instead he was brooding over a woman he hadn't seen in thirteen years. If he'd been alone, he would have pulled up Riley Eaton's photograph on his laptop, but three other men ringed the table in the small office he occupied at the Naval Amphibious Base at Little Creek, Virginia, so instead he mentally ran over the information he'd found out about her on the Internet. Riley lived in Boston, where she'd gone to school. She'd graduated with a fine arts degree, something which confused

Boone; she'd never talked about wanting to study art when they were young. She worked at a vitamin manufacturer, which made no sense at all. And why was she living in a city, when Riley had only ever come alive when she'd visited Chance Creek, Montana, every summer as a child?

Too many questions. Questions he should know the answer to, since Riley had once been such an integral part of his life. If only he hadn't been such a fool, Boone knew she still would be. Still a friend at least, or maybe much, much more. Pride had kept him from finding out.

He was done with pride.

He reached for his laptop, ready to pull up her photograph, whether he was alone or not, but stopped when it chimed to announce a video call. For one crazy second, Boone wondered if his thoughts had conjured Riley up, but he quickly shook away that ridiculous notion.

Probably his parents wondering once again why he wasn't coming home when he left the Navy. He'd explained time and again the plans he'd made, but they couldn't comprehend why he wouldn't take the job his father had found him at a local ranch.

"Working with horses," his dad had said the last time they talked. "What more do you want?"

It was tempting. Boone had always loved horses. But he had something else in mind. Something his parents found difficult to comprehend. The laptop chimed again.

"You going to get that?" Jericho Cook said, looking up from his work. Blond, blue-eyed, and six-foot-one inches of muscle, he looked out of place hunched over his paperwork. He and the other two men sitting at the table were three of Boone's most trusted buddies and members of his strike team. Like him, they were far more at home jumping out of airplanes, infiltrating terrorist organizations and negotiating their way through disaster areas than sitting on their asses filling out forms. But paperwork caught up to everyone at some point.

He wouldn't have to do it much longer, though. Boone was due to separate from the Navy in less than a month. The others were due to leave soon after. They'd joined up together—egging each other on when they turned eighteen over their parents' objections. They'd survived the brutal process of becoming Navy SEALs together, too, adamant that they'd never leave each other behind. They'd served together whenever they could. Now, thirteen years later, they'd transition back to civilian life together as well.

The computer chimed a third time and his mind finally registered the name on the screen. Boone slapped a hand on the table to get the others' attention.

"It's him!"

"Him, who?" Jericho asked.

"Martin Fulsom, from the Fulsom Foundation. He's calling me!"

"Are you sure?" Clay Pickett shifted his chair over to where he could see. He was an inch or two shorter than Jericho, with dark hair and a wiry build that

concealed a perpetual source of energy. Even now Clay's foot was tapping as he worked.

Boone understood his confusion. Why would Martin Fulsom, who must have a legion of secretaries and assistants at his command, call him personally?

"It says Martin Fulsom."

"Holy shit. Answer it," Jericho said. He shifted his chair over, too. Walker Norton, the final member of their little group, stood up silently and moved behind the others. Walker had dark hair and dark eyes that hinted at his Native American ancestry. Unlike the others, he'd taken the time to get his schooling and become an officer. As Lieutenant, he was the highest ranked. He was also the tallest of the group, with a heavy muscular frame that could move faster than most gave him credit for. He was quiet, though. So quiet that those who didn't know him tended to write him off. They did so at their own peril.

Boone stifled an oath at the tremor that ran through him as he reached out to accept the call, but it wasn't every day you got to meet your hero face to face. Martin Fulsom wasn't a Navy SEAL. He wasn't in the military at all. He'd once been an oil man, and had amassed a fortune in the industry before he'd learned about global warming and had a change of heart. For the last decade he'd spearheaded a movement to prevent carbon dioxide particulates from exceeding the disastrous level of 450 ppm. He'd backed his foundation with his entire fortune, invested it in green technology and used his earnings to fund projects around the world aimed at

helping him reach his goal. Fulsom was a force of nature, with an oversized personality to match his incredible wealth. Boone liked his can-do attitude and his refusal to mince words when the situation called for plain speaking.

Boone clicked *Accept* and his screen resolved into an image of a man seated at a large wooden desk. He was gray-haired but virile, with large hands and an impressively large watch. Beside him stood a middle aged woman in a severely tailored black suit, who handed him pieces of paper one at a time, waited for him to sign them and took them back, placing them in various folders she cradled in her arm.

"Boone!" The man's hearty voice was almost too much for the laptop's speakers. "Good to finally meet you. This is an impressive proposal you have here."

Boone swallowed. It was true. Martin Fulsom—one of the greatest innovators of their time—had actually called *him*. "It's good to meet you, too, Mr. Fulsom," he managed to say.

"Call me Martin," Fulsom boomed. "Everybody does. Like I said, it's a hell of a proposal. To build a fully operational sustainable community in less than six months? That take guts. Can you deliver?"

"Yes, sir." Boone was confident he could. He'd studied this stuff for years. Dreamed about it, debated it, played with the numbers and particulars until he could speak with confidence about every aspect of the community he wanted to build. He and his friends had gained a greater working knowledge of the fallout from

climate change than any of them had gone looking for when they joined the Navy SEALs. They'd realized most of the conflicts that spawned the missions they took on were caused in one way or the other by struggles over resources, usually exacerbated by climate conditions. When rains didn't come and crops failed, unrest was sure to follow. Next came partisan politics, rebellions, coups and more. It didn't take a genius to see that climate change and scarcity of resources would be two prongs spearheading trouble around the world for decades to come.

"And you'll start with four families, building up to ten within that time frame?"

Boone blinked. Families? "Actually, sir…" He'd said nothing about families. Four *men*, building up to ten. That's what he had written in his proposal.

"This is brilliant. Too brilliant." Fulsom's direct gaze caught his own. "You see, we were going to launch a community of our own, but when I saw your proposal, I said, 'This man has already done the hard work; why reinvent the wheel? I can't think of anyone better to lead such a project than someone like Boone Rudman.'"

Boone stifled a grin. This was going better than he could have dreamed. "Thank you, sir."

Fulsom leaned forward. "The thing is, Boone, you have to do it right."

"Of course, sir, but about—"

"It has to be airtight. You have to prove you're sustainable. You have to prove your food systems are self-perpetuating, that you have a strategy to deal with waste,

that you have contingency plans. What you've written here?" He held up Boone's proposal package. "It's genius. Genius. But the real question is—who's going to give a shit about it?"

"Well, hell—" Fulsom's abrupt change of tone startled Boone into defensiveness. He knew about the man's legendary high-octane personality, but he hadn't been prepared for this kind of bait and switch. "You yourself just said—"

Fulsom waved the application at him. "I love this stuff. It makes me hard. But the American public? That's a totally different matter. They don't find this shit sexy. It's not enough to jerk me off, Boone. We're trying to turn on the whole world."

"O-okay." Shit. Fulsom was going to turn him down after all. Boone gripped the arms of his chair, waiting for the axe to fall.

"So the question is, how do we make the world care about your community? And not just care about it—be so damn obsessed with it they can't think about anything else?" He didn't wait for an answer. "I'll tell you how. We're going to give you your own reality television show. Think of it. The whole world watching you go from ground zero to full-on sustainable community. Rooting for you. Cheering when you triumph. Crying when you fail. A worldwide audience fully engaged with you and your followers."

"That's an interesting idea," Boone said slowly. It was an insane idea. There was no way anyone would spend their time watching him dig garden beds and

install photovoltaic panels. He couldn't think of anything less exciting to watch on television. And he didn't have followers. He had three like-minded friends who'd signed on to work with him. Friends who even now were bristling at this characterization of their roles. "Like I said, Mr. Fulsom, each of the *equal* participants in the community have pledged to document our progress. We'll take lots of photos and post them with our entries on a daily blog."

"Blogs are for losers." Fulsom leaned forward. "Come on, Boone. Don't you want to change the world?"

"Yes, I do." Anger curled within him. He was serious about these issues. Deadly serious. Why was Fulsom making a mockery of him? You couldn't win any kind of war with reality television, and Boone approached his sustainable community as if he was waging a war—a war on waste, a war on the future pain and suffering of the entire planet.

"I get it. You think I'm nuts," Fulsom said. "You think I've finally blown my lid. Well, I haven't. I'm a free-thinker, Boone, not a crazy man. I know how to get the message across to the masses. Always have. And I've always been criticized for it, too. Who cares? You know what I care about? This world. The people on it. The plants and animals and atmosphere. The whole grand, beautiful spectacle that we're currently dragging down into the muck of overconsumption. That's what I care about. What about you?"

"I care about it, too, but I don't want—"

"You don't want to be made a fool of. Fair enough. You're afraid of exposing yourself to scrutiny. You're afraid you'll fuck up on television. Well guess what? You're right; you will fuck up. But the audience is going to love you so much by that time, that if you cry, they'll cry with you. And when you triumph—and you *will* triumph—they'll feel as ecstatic as if they'd done it all themselves. Along the way they'll learn more about solar power, wind power, sustainable agriculture and all the rest of it than we could ever force-feed them through documentaries or classes. You watch, Boone. We're going to do something magical."

Boone stared at him. Fulsom was persuasive, he'd give him that. "About the families, sir."

"Families are non-negotiable." Fulsom set the application down and gazed at Boone, then each of his friends in turn. "You men are pioneers, but pioneers are a yawn-fest until they bring their wives to the frontier. Throw in women, and goddamn, that's interesting! Women talk. They complain. They'll take your plans for sustainability and kick them to the curb unless you make them easy to use and satisfying. What's more, women are a hell of lot more interesting than men. Sex, Boone. Sex sells cars and we're going to use it to sell sustainability, too. Are you with me?"

"I…" Boone didn't know what to say. Use sex to sell sustainability? "I don't think—"

"Of course you're with me. A handsome Navy SEAL like you has to have a girl. You do, don't you? Have a girl?"

"A girl?" Had he been reduced to parroting everything Fulsom said? Boone tried to pull himself together. He definitely did not have a *girl*. He dated when he had time, but he kept things light. He'd never felt it was fair to enter a more serious relationship as long as he was throwing himself into danger on a daily basis. He'd always figured he'd settle down when he left the service and he was looking forward to finally having the time to meet a potential mate. God knew his parents were all too ready for grandkids. They talked about it all the time.

"A woman, a fiancée. Maybe you already have a wife?" Fulsom looked hopeful and his secretary nodded at Boone, as if telling him to say yes.

"Wel...."

He was about to say no, but the secretary shook her head rapidly and made a slicing motion across her neck. Since she hadn't engaged in the conversation at all previously, Boone decided he'd better take her signals seriously. He'd gotten some of his best intel in the field just this way. A subtle nod from a veiled woman, or a pointed finger just protruding from a burka had saved his neck more than once. Women were crafty when it counted.

"I'm almost married," he blurted. His grip on the arms of his chair tightened. None of this was going like he'd planned. Jericho and Clay turned to stare at him like he'd lost his mind. Behind him Walker chuckled. "I mean—"

"Excellent! Can't wait to meet your better half.

What about the rest of you?" Fulsom waved them off before anyone else could speak. "Never mind. Julie here will get all that information from you later. As long as you've got a girl, Boone, everything's going to be all right. The fearless leader has to have a woman by his side. It gives him that sense of humanity our viewers crave." Julie nodded like she'd heard this many times before.

Boone's heart sunk even further. Fearless leader? Fulsom didn't understand his relationship with the others at all. Walker was his superior officer, for God's sake. Still, Fulsom was waiting for his answer, with a shrewd look in his eyes that told Boone he wasn't fooled at all by his hasty words. Their funding would slip away unless he convinced Fulsom that he was dedicated to the project—as Fulsom wanted it to be done.

"I understand completely," Boone said, although he didn't understand at all. His project was about sustainability. It wasn't some human-interest story. "I'm with you one hundred percent."

"Then I've got a shitload of cash to send your way. Don't let me down."

"I won't." He felt rather than heard the others shifting, biting back their protests.

Fulsom leaned so close his head nearly filled the screen. "We'll start filming June first and I look forward to meeting your fiancée when I arrive. Understand? Not a girlfriend, not a weekend fling—a fiancée. I want weddings, Boone." He looked over the four of them

again. "Four weddings. Yours will kick off the series. I can see it now; an empty stretch of land. Two modern pioneers in love. A country parson performing the ceremony. The bride holding a bouquet of wildflowers the groom picked just minutes before. Their first night together in a lonely tent. Magic, Boone. That's prime time magic. *Surviving on the Land* meets *The First Six Months.*"

Boone nodded, swallowing hard. He'd seen those television shows. The first tracked modern-day mountain men as they pitted themselves against crazy weather conditions in extreme locations. The second followed two newlyweds for six months, and documented their every move, embrace, and lovers' quarrel as they settled into married life. He didn't relish the idea of starring in any show remotely like those.

Besides, June first was barely two months away. He'd only get out of the Navy at the end of April. They hadn't even found a property to build on yet.

"There'll be four of you men to start," Fulsom went on. "That means we need four women for episode one; your fiancée and three other hopeful single ladies. Let the viewers do the math, am I right? They'll start pairing you off even before we do. We'll add other community members as we go. Six more men and six more women ought to do it, don't you think?"

"Yes, sir." This was getting worse by the minute.

"Now, I've given you a hell of a shock today. I get that. So let me throw you a bone. I've just closed on the perfect piece of property for your community. Fifteen

hundred acres of usable land with creeks, forest, pasture and several buildings. I'm going to give it to you free and clear to use for the duration of the series. If—and only if—you meet your goals, I'll sign it over to you lock, stock and barrel at the end of the last show."

Boone sat up. That was a hell of a bone. "Where is it?"

"Little town called Chance Creek, Montana. I believe you've heard of it?" Fulsom laughed at his reaction. Even Walker was startled. Chance Creek? They'd grown up there. Their families still lived there.

They were going home.

Chills marched up and down his spine and Boone wondered if his friends felt the same way. He'd hardly even let himself dream about that possibility. None of them came from wealthy families and none of them would inherit land. He'd figured they'd go where it was cheapest, and ranches around Chance Creek didn't come cheap. Not these days. Like everywhere else, the town had seen a slump during the last recession, but now prices were up again and he'd heard from his folks that developers were circling, talking about expanding the town. Boone couldn't picture that.

"Let me see here. I believe it's called... Westfield," Fulsom said. Julie nodded, confirming his words. "Hasn't been inhabited for over a decade. A local caretaker has been keeping an eye on it, but there hasn't been cattle on it for at least that long. The heir to the property lives in Europe now. Must have finally decided he wasn't ever going to take up ranching. When he put

it on the market, I snapped it up real quick."

Westfield.

Boone sat back even as his friends shifted behind him again. Westfield was a hell of a property—owned by the Eaton family for as long as anyone could remember. He couldn't believe it wasn't a working ranch anymore. But if the old folks were gone, he guessed that made sense. They must have passed away not long after he had left Chance Creek. They wouldn't have broken up the property, so Russ Eaton would have inherited and Russ wasn't much for ranching. Neither was his younger brother, Michael. As far as Boone knew, Russ hadn't married, which left Michael's daughter the only possible candidate to run the place.

Riley Eaton.

Was it a coincidence that had brought her to mind just moments before Fulsom's call, or something more?

Coincidence, Boone decided, even as the more impulsive side of him declared it Fate.

A grin tugged at his mouth as he remembered Riley as she used to be, the tomboy who tagged along after him every summer when they were kids. Riley lived for vacations on her grandparents' ranch. Her mother would send her off each year dressed up for the journey, and the minute Riley reached Chance Creek she'd wad up those fancy clothes and spend the rest of the summer in jeans, boots and an old Stetson passed down from her grandma. Boone and his friends hired on at Westfield most summers to earn some spending money. Riley stuck to them like glue, learning as much as she

could about riding and ranching from them. When she was little, she used to cry when August ended and she had to go back home. As she grew older, she hid her feelings better, but Boone knew she'd always adored the ranch. It wasn't surprising, given her home life. Even when he was young, he'd heard the gossip and knew things were rough back in Chicago.

As much as he and the others had complained about being saddled with a follower like Riley, she'd earned their grudging respect as the years went on. Riley never complained, never wavered in her loyalty to them, and as many times as they left her behind, she was always ready to try again to convince them to let her join them in their exploits.

"It's a crime," he'd once heard his mother say to a friend on the phone. "Neither mother nor father has any time for her at all. No wonder she'll put up with anything those boys dish out. I worry for her."

Boone understood now what his mother was afraid of, but at the time he'd shrugged it off and over the years Riley had become a good friend. Sometimes when they were alone fishing, or riding, or just hanging out on her grandparents' porch, Boone would find himself telling her things he'd never told anyone else. As far as he knew, she'd never betrayed a confidence.

Riley was the one who dubbed Boone, Clay, Jericho and Walker the Four Horsemen of the Apocalypse, a nickname that had stuck all these years. When they'd become obsessed with the idea of being Navy SEALs, Riley had even tried to keep up with the same training

regimen they'd adopted.

Boone wished he could say they'd always treated Riley as well as she treated them, but that wasn't the truth of it. One of his most shameful memories centered around the slim girl with the long brown braids. Things had become complicated once he and his friends began to date. They had far less time for Riley, who was two years younger and still a kid in their eyes, and she'd withdrawn when she realized their girlfriends didn't want her around. She still hung out when they worked at Westfield, though, and was old enough to be a real help with the work. Some of Boone's best memories were of early mornings mucking out stables with Riley. They didn't talk much, just worked side by side until the job was done. From time to time they walked out to a spot on the ranch where the land fell away and they could see the mountains in the distance. Boone had never quantified how he felt during those times. Now he realized what a fool he'd been.

He hadn't given a thought to how his girlfriends affected her or what it would be like for Riley when they left for the Navy. He'd been too young. Too utterly self-absorbed.

That same year he'd had his first serious relationship, with a girl named Melissa Resnick. Curvy, flirty and oh-so-feminine, she'd slipped into his heart by slipping into his bed on Valentine's Day. By the time Riley came to town again that last summer, he and Melissa were seldom apart. Of all the girls the Horsemen had dated, Melissa was the least tolerant of Riley's

presence, and one day when they'd all gone to a local swimming hole, she'd huffed in exasperation when the younger girl came along.

"It's like you've got a sidekick," she told Boone in everyone's hearing. "Good ol' Tagalong Riley."

Clay, Jericho, and Walker, who'd always treated Riley like a little sister, thought it was funny. They had their own girlfriends to impress, and the name had stuck. Boone knew he should put a stop to it, but the lure of Melissa's body was still too strong and he knew if he took Riley's side he'd lose his access to it.

Riley had held her head up high that day and she'd stayed at the swimming hole, a move that Boone knew must have cost her, but each repetition of the nickname that summer seemed to heap pain onto her shoulders, until she caved in on herself and walked with her head down.

The worst was the night before he and the Horsemen left to join the Navy. He hadn't seen Riley for several days, whereas he couldn't seem to shake Melissa for a minute. He should have felt flattered, but instead it had irritated him. More and more often, he had found himself wishing for Riley's calm company, but she'd stopped coming to help him.

Because everyone else seemed to expect it, he'd attended the hoe-down in town sponsored by the rodeo that last night. Melissa clung to him like a burr. Riley was nowhere to be found. Boone accepted every drink he was offered and was well on his way to being three sheets to the wind when Melissa excused herself to the

ladies' room at about ten. Boone remained with the other Horsemen and their dates, and he could only stare when Riley appeared in front of him. For once she'd left her Stetson at home, her hair was loose from its braids, and she wore makeup and a mini skirt that left miles of leg between its hem and her dress cowboy boots.

Every nerve in his body had come to full alert and Boone had understood in that moment what he'd failed to realize all that summer. Riley had grown up. At sixteen, she was a woman. A beautiful woman who understood him far better than Melissa could hope to. He'd had a fleeting sense of lost time and missed opportunities before Clay had whistled. "Hell, Tagalong, you've gone and gotten yourself a pair of breasts."

"You better watch out dressed up like that; some guy will think you want more than you bargained for," Jericho said.

Walker's normally grave expression had grown even more grim.

Riley had ignored them all. She'd squared her shoulders, looked Boone in the eye and said, "Will you dance with me?"

Shame flooded Boone every time he thought back to that moment.

Riley had paid him a thousand kindnesses over the years, listened to some of his most intimate thoughts and fears, never judged him, made fun of him or cut him down the way his other friends sometimes did. She'd always been there for him, and all she'd asked for was one dance.

He should have said yes.

It wasn't the shake of Walker's head, or Clay and Jericho's laughter that stopped him. It was Melissa, who had returned in time to hear Riley's question, and answered for him.

"No one wants to dance with a Tagalong. Go on home."

Riley had waited one more moment—then fled.

Boone rarely thought about Melissa after he'd left Chance Creek and when he did it was to wonder what he'd ever found compelling in her. He thought about Riley far too often. He tried to remember the good times—teaching her to ride, shoot, trap and fish. The conversations and lazy days in the sun when they were kids. The intimacy that had grown up between them without him ever realizing it.

Instead, he thought of that moment—that awful, shameful moment when she'd begged him with her eyes to say yes, to throw her pride that single bone.

And he'd kept silent.

"Have you heard of the place?" Fulsom broke into his thoughts and Boone blinked. He'd been so far away it took a moment to come back. Finally, he nodded.

"I have." He cleared his throat to get the huskiness out of it. "Mighty fine ranch." He couldn't fathom why it hadn't passed down to Riley. Losing it must have broken her heart.

Again.

"So my people tell me. Heck of a fight to get it, too. Had a competitor, a rabid developer named Montague."

Fulsom shook his head. "But that gave me a perfect setup."

"What do you mean?" Boone's thoughts were still with the girl he'd once known. The woman who'd haunted him all these years. He forced himself to pay attention to Fulsom instead.

Fulsom clicked his keyboard and an image sprung up onscreen. "Take a look."

Letting his memories go, Boone tried to make sense of what he was seeing. Some kind of map—an architect's rendering of a planned development.

"What is that?" Clay demanded.

"Wait—that's Westfield." Jericho leaned over Boone's shoulder to get a better look.

"Almost right." Fulsom nodded. "Those are the plans for Westfield Commons, a community of seventy luxury homes."

Blood ran cold in Boone's veins as Walker elbowed his way between them and peered at the screen. "Luxury homes? On Westfield? You can't do that!"

"I don't want to. But Montague does. He's frothing at the mouth to bulldoze that ranch and sell it piece by piece. The big, bad developer versus the environmentalists. This show is going to write itself." He fixed his gaze on Boone. "And if you fail, the last episode will show his bulldozers closing in."

"But it's our land; you just said so," Boone protested.

"As long as you meet your goals by December first. Ten committed couples—every couple married by the

time the show ends. Ten homes whose energy requirements are one-tenth the normal usage for an American home. Six months' worth of food produced on site stockpiled to last the inhabitants through the winter. And three children."

"Children? Where do we get those?" Boone couldn't keep up. He hadn't promised anything like that. All he'd said in his proposal was that they'd build a community.

"The old-fashioned way. You make them. No cheating; children conceived before the show starts don't count."

"Jesus." Fulsom had lost his mind. He was taking the stakes and raising them to outrageous heights... which was exactly the way to create a prime-time hit, Boone realized.

"It takes nine months to have a child," Jericho pointed out dryly.

"I didn't say they needed to be born. Pregnant bellies are better than squalling babies. Like I said, sex sells, boys. Let's give our viewers proof you and your wives are getting it on."

Boone had had enough. "That's ridiculous, Fulsom. You're—"

"You know what's ridiculous?" Fulsom leaned forward again, suddenly grim. "Famine. Poverty. Violence. War. And yet it never stops, does it? You said you wanted to do something about it. Here's your chance. You're leaving the Navy, for God's sake. Don't tell me you didn't plan to meet a woman, settle down and raise some kids. So I've put a rush on the matter. Sue me."

He had a point. But still—

"I could sell the land to Montague today," Fulsom said. "Pocket the money and get back to sorting out hydrogen fuel cells." He waited a beat. When Boone shook his head, Fulsom smiled in triumph. "Gotta go, boys. Julie, here, will get you all sorted out. Good luck to you on this fabulous venture. Remember—we're going to change the world together."

"Wait—"

Fulsom stood up and walked off screen.

Boone stared as Julie sat down in his place. By the time she had walked them through the particulars of the funding process, and when and how to take possession of the land, Boone's temples were throbbing. He cut the call after Julie promised to send a packet of information, reluctantly pushed his chair back from the table and faced the three men who were to be his partners in this venture.

"Married?" Clay demanded. "No one said anything about getting married!"

"I know."

"And kids? Three out of ten of us men will have to get their wives pregnant. That means all of us will have to be trying just to beat the odds," Jericho said.

"I know."

Walker just looked at him and shook his head.

"I get it! None of us planned for anything like this." Boone stood up. "But none of us thought we had a shot of moving back to Chance Creek, either—or getting our message out to the whole country." When no one

answered, he went on. "Are you saying you're out?"

"Hell, I don't know," Jericho said, pacing around the room. "I could stomach anything except that marriage part. I've never seen myself as a family man."

"I don't mind getting hitched," Clay said. "And I want kids. But I want to choose where and when to do it. And Fulsom's setting us up to fail in front of a national audience. If that Montague guy gets the ranch and builds a subdivision on it, everyone in town is going to hate us—and our families."

"So what do we do?" Boone challenged him.

"Not much choice," Walker said. "If we don't sign on, Fulsom will sell to Montague anyway."

"Exactly. The only shot we have of saving that ranch is to agree to his demands," Boone said. He shoved his hands in his pockets, unsure what to do. He couldn't see himself married in two months, let alone trying to have a child with a woman he hadn't even met yet, but giving up—Boone hated to think about it. After all, it wouldn't be the first time they'd done unexpected things to accomplish a mission.

Jericho paced back. "But his demands are—"

"Insane. I know that." Boone knew he was losing them. "He's right, though; a sustainable community made only of men doesn't mean shit. A community that's actually going to sustain itself—to carry on into the future, generation after generation—has to include women and eventually kids. Otherwise we're just playing."

"Fulsom's the one who's playing. Playing with our

lives. He can't demand we marry someone for the sake of his ratings," Jericho said.

"Actually, he can," Clay said. "He's the one with the cash."

"We'll find cash somewhere else—"

"It's more than cash," Boone reminded Jericho. "It's publicity. If we build a community and no one knows about it, what good is it? We went to Fulsom because we wanted him to do just what he's done—find a way to make everyone talk about sustainability."

"By marrying us off one by one?" Jericho stared at each of them in turn. "Are you serious? We just spent the last thirteen years of our lives fighting for our country—"

"And now we're going to fight for it in a whole new way. By getting married. On television. And knocking up our wives—while the whole damn world watches," Boone said.

No one spoke for a minute.

"I sure as hell hope they won't film that part, Chief," Clay said with a quick grin, using the moniker Boone had gained in the SEALs as second in command of his platoon.

"They wouldn't want to film your hairy ass, anyway," Jericho said.

Clay shoved him. Jericho elbowed him away.

"Enough." Walker's single word settled all of them down. They were used to listening to their lieutenant. Walker turned to Boone. "You think this will actually do any good?"

Boone shrugged. "Remember Yemen. Remember what's coming. We swore we'd do what it takes to make a difference." It was a low blow bringing up that disaster, but it was what had gotten them started down this path and he wanted to remind them of it.

"I remember Yemen every day," Jericho said, all trace of clowning around gone.

"So do I." Clay sighed. "Hell, I'm ready for a family anyway. I'm in. I don't know how I'll find a wife, though. Ain't had any luck so far."

"I'll find you one," Boone told him.

"Thanks, Chief." Clay gave him an ironic salute.

Jericho walked away. Came back again. "Damn it. I'm in, too. Under protest, though. Something this serious shouldn't be a game. You find me a wife, too, Chief, but I'll divorce her when the six months are up if I don't like her."

"Wait until Fulsom's given us the deed to the ranch, then do what you like," Boone said. "But if I'm picking your bride, give her a chance."

"Sure, Chief."

Boone didn't trust that answer, but Jericho had agreed to Fulsom's terms and that's all that mattered for now. He looked to Walker. It was crucial that the man get on board. Walker stared back at him, his gaze unfathomable. Boone knew there was trouble in his past. Lots of trouble. The man avoided women whenever he could.

Finally Walker gave him a curt nod. "Find me one, too. Don't screw it up."

Boone let out the breath he was holding. Despite the events of the past hour, a surge of anticipation warmed him from within.

They were going to do it.

And he was going to get hitched.

Was Riley the marrying kind?

RILEY EATON TOOK a sip of her green tea and summoned a smile for the friends who'd gathered on the tiny balcony of her apartment in Boston. Her thoughts were far away, though, tangled in a memory of a hot Montana afternoon when she was only ten. She'd crouched on the bank of Pittance Creek watching Boone Rudman wade through the knee-deep waters, fishing for minnows with a net. Riley had followed Boone everywhere back then, but she knew to stay out of the water and not scare his bait away.

"Mom said marriage is a trap set by men for unsuspecting women," she'd told him, quoting what she'd heard her mother say to a friend over the phone.

"You'd better watch out then," he'd said, poised to scoop up a handful of little fish.

"I won't get caught. Someone's got to want to catch you before that happens."

Boone had straightened, his net trailing in the water. She'd never forgotten the way he'd looked at her—all earnest concern.

"Maybe I'll catch you."

"Why?" She'd been genuinely curious. Getting overlooked was something she'd already grown used to.

"For my wife. If I ever want one. You'll never see me coming." He'd lifted his chin as if she'd argue the point. But Riley had thought it over and knew he was right.

She'd nodded. "You are pretty sneaky."

Riley had never forgotten that conversation, but Boone had and like everyone else he'd overlooked her when the time counted.

Story of her life.

Riley shook off the maudlin thoughts. She couldn't be a good hostess if she was wrapped up in her troubles. Time enough for them when her friends had gone.

She took another sip of her tea and hoped they wouldn't notice the tremor in her hands. She couldn't believe seven years had passed since she'd graduated from Boston College with the women who relaxed on the cheap folding chairs around her. Back then she'd thought she'd always have these women by her side, but now these yearly reunions were the only time she saw them. They were all firmly ensconced in careers that consumed their time and energy. It was hard enough to stay afloat these days, let alone get ahead in the world—or have time to take a break.

Gone were the carefree years when they thought nothing of losing whole weekends to trying out a new art medium, or picking up a new instrument. Once she'd been fearless, throwing paint on the canvas, guided only by her moods. She'd experimented day after day, laughed at the disasters and gloried in the triumphs that took shape under her brushes from time to time. Now

she rarely even sketched, and what she produced seemed inane. If she wanted to express the truth of her situation through her art, she'd paint pigeons and gum stuck to the sidewalk. But she wasn't honest anymore.

For much of the past five years she'd been married to her job as a commercial artist at a vitamin distributor, joined to it twenty-four seven through her cell phone and Internet connection. Those years studying art seemed like a dream now; the one time in her life she'd felt like she'd truly belonged somewhere. She had no idea how she'd thought she'd earn a living with a fine arts degree, though. She supposed she'd hadn't thought much about the future back then. Now she felt trapped by it.

Especially after the week she'd had.

She set her cup down and twisted her hands together, trying to stop the shaking. It had started on Wednesday when she'd been called into her boss's office and handed a pink slip and a box in which to pack up her things.

"Downsizing. It's nothing personal," he'd told her.

She didn't know how she'd kept her feet as she'd made her way out of the building. She wasn't the only one riding the elevator down to street level with her belongings in her hands, but that was cold comfort. It had been hard enough to find this job. She had no idea where to start looking for another.

She'd held in her shock and panic that night and all the next day until Nadia from the adoption agency knocked on her door for their scheduled home visit at

precisely two pm. She'd managed to answer Nadia's questions calmly and carefully, until the woman put down her pen.

"Tell me about your job, Riley. How will you as a single mother balance work and home life with a child?"

Riley had opened her mouth to speak, but no answer had come out. She'd reached for her cup of tea, but only managed to spill it on the cream colored skirt she'd chosen carefully for the occasion. As Nadia rushed to help her mop up, the truth had spilled from Riley's lips.

"I've just been downsized. I'm sorry; I'll get a new job right away. This doesn't have to change anything, does it?"

Nadia had been sympathetic but firm. "This is why we hesitate to place children with single parents, Riley. Children require stability. We can continue the interview and I'll weigh all the information in our judgement, but until you can prove you have a stable job, I'm afraid you won't qualify for a child."

"That will take years," Riley had almost cried, but she'd bitten back the words. What good would it do to say them aloud? As a girl, she'd dreamed she'd have children with Boone someday. When she'd grown up, she'd thought she'd find someone else. Hadn't she waited long enough to start her family?

"Riley? Are you all right?" Savannah Edwards asked, bringing her back to the present.

"Of course." She had to be. There was no other option but to soldier on. She needed to get a new job. A

better job. She needed to excel at it and put the time in to make herself indispensable. Then, in a few years, she could try again to adopt.

"Are you sure?" A tall blonde with hazel eyes, Savannah had been Riley's best friend back in school, and Riley had always had a hard time fooling her. Savannah had been a music major and Riley could have listened to her play forever. She was the first person Riley had met since her grandparents passed away who seemed to care about her wholeheartedly. Riley's parents had been too busy arguing with each other all through her childhood to have much time left over to think about her. They split up within weeks after she left for college. Each remarried before the year was out and both started new families soon after. Riley felt like the odd man out when she visited them on holidays. More than eighteen years older than her half-siblings, she didn't seem to belong anywhere now.

"I'm great now that you three are here." She wouldn't confess the setback that had just befallen her. It was still too raw to process and she didn't want to bring the others down when they'd only just arrived. She wasn't the only one who had it tough. Savannah should have been a concert pianist, but when she broke her wrist in a car accident several years after graduation, she had to give up her aspirations. Instead, she had gone to work as an assistant at a prominent tech company in Silicon Valley and was still there.

"What's on tap for the weekend?" Nora Ridgeway asked as she scooped her long, wavy, light brown hair

into a messy updo and secured it with a clip. She'd flown in from Baltimore where she taught English in an inner-city high school. Riley had been shocked to see the dark smudges under her eyes. Nora looked thin. Too thin. Riley wondered what secrets she was hiding behind her upbeat tone.

"I hope it's a whole lot of nothing," Avery Lightfoot said, her auburn curls glinting in the sun. Avery lived in Nashville and worked in the marketing department of one of the largest food distribution companies in North America. She'd studied acting in school, but she'd never been discovered the way she'd once hoped to be. For a brief time she'd created an original video series that she'd posted online, but the advertising revenue she'd generated hadn't added up to much and soon her money had run out. Now she created short videos to market low-carb products to yoga moms. Riley's heart ached for her friend. She sounded as tired as Nora looked.

In fact, everyone looked like they needed a pick-me-up after dealing with flights and taxis, and Riley headed inside to get refreshments. She wished she'd been able to drive to the airport and pick them up. Who could afford a car, though? Even when she'd had a job, Riley found it hard to keep up with her rent, medical insurance and monthly bills, and budget enough for the childcare she'd need when she adopted. Thank God it had been her turn to host their gathering this year. She couldn't have gotten on a plane after the news she'd just received.

When she thought back to her college days she realized her belief in a golden future had really been a pipe dream. Some of her classmates were doing fine. But most of them were struggling to keep their heads above water, just like her. A few had given up and moved back in with their parents.

When she got back to the balcony with a tray of snacks, she saw Savannah pluck a dog-eared copy of *Pride and Prejudice* out of a small basket that sat next to the door. Riley had been reading it in the mornings before work this week as she drank her coffee—until she'd been let go. A little escapism helped start her day off on the right foot.

"Am I the only one who'd trade my life for one of Austen's characters' in a heartbeat?" Savannah asked, flipping through the pages.

"You want to live in Regency England? And be some man's property?" Nora asked sharply.

"Of course not. I don't want the class conflict or the snobbery or the outdated rules. But I want the beauty of their lives. I want the music and the literature. I want afternoon visits and balls that last all night. Why don't we do those things anymore?"

"Who has time for that?" Riley certainly hadn't when she was working. Now she'd have to spend every waking moment finding a new job.

"I haven't played the piano in ages," Savannah went on. "I mean, it's not like I'm all that good anymore—"

"Are you kidding? You've always been fantastic," Nora said.

"What about romance? I'd kill for a real romance. One that means something," Avery said.

"What about Dan?" Savannah asked.

"I broke up with him three weeks ago. He told me he wasn't ready for a serious relationship. The man's thirty-one. If he's not ready now, when will he be?"

"That's tough." Riley understood what Avery meant. She hadn't had a date in a year; not since Marc Hepstein had told her he didn't consider her marriage material. She should have dumped him long before.

It wasn't like she hadn't been warned. His older sister had taken her aside once and spelled it out for her:

"Every boy needs to sow his wild oats. You're his shiksa fling. You'll see; you won't get a wedding ring from him. Marc will marry a nice Jewish girl in the end."

Riley wished she'd paid attention to the warning, but of course she hadn't. She had a history of dangling after men who were unavailable.

Shiksa fling.

Just a step up from Tagalong Riley.

Riley pushed down the old insecurities that threatened to take hold of her and tried not to give in to her pain over her lost chance to adopt. When Marc had broken up with her, it had been a wake-up call. She'd realized if she waited for a man to love her, she might never experience the joy of raising a child. She'd also realized she hadn't loved Marc enough to spend a life with him. She'd been settling, and she was better than that.

She'd started the adoption process.

Now she'd have to start all over again.

"It wasn't as hard to leave him as you might think." Avery took a sip of her tea. "It's not just Dan. I feel like breaking up with my life. I had a heart once. I know I did. I used to feel—alive."

"Me, too," Nora said softly.

"I thought I'd be married by now," Savannah said, "but I haven't had a boyfriend in months. And I hate my job. I mean, I really hate it!" Riley couldn't remember ever seeing calm, poised Savannah like this.

"So do I," Avery said, her words gushing forth as if a dam had broken. "Especially since I have two of them now. I got back in debt when my car broke down and I needed to buy a new one. Now I can't seem to get ahead."

"I don't have any job at all," Riley confessed. "I've been downsized." She closed her eyes. She hadn't meant to say that.

"Oh my goodness, Riley," Avery said. "What are you going to do?"

"I don't know. Paint?" She laughed dully. She couldn't tell them the worst of it. She was afraid if she talked about her failed attempt to adopt she'd lose control of her emotions altogether. "Can you imagine a life in which we could actually pursue our dreams?"

"No," Avery said flatly. "After what happened last time, I'm so afraid if I try to act again, I'll just make a fool of myself."

Savannah nodded vigorously, tears glinting in her eyes. "I'm afraid to play," she confessed. "I sit down at

my piano and then I get up again without touching the keys. What if my talent was all a dream? What if I was fooling myself and I was never anything special at all? My wrist healed years ago, but I can't make myself go for it like I once did. I'm too scared."

"What about you, Nora? Do you ever write these days?" Riley asked gently when Nora remained quiet. When they were younger, Nora talked all the time about wanting to write a novel, but she hadn't mentioned it in ages. Riley had assumed it was because she loved teaching, but she looked as burnt out as the rest of them. Riley knew she worked in an area of Baltimore that resembled a war zone.

Her friend didn't answer, but a tear traced down her cheek.

"Nora, what is it?" Savannah dropped the book and came to crouch by her chair.

"It's one of my students." Nora kept her voice steady even as another tear followed the tracks of the first. "At least I think it is."

"What do you mean?" Riley realized they'd all pulled closer to each other, leaning forward in mutual support and feeling. Dread crept into her throat at Nora's words. She'd known instinctively something was wrong in her friend's life for quite some time, but despite her questions, Nora's e-mails and texts never revealed a thing.

"I've been getting threats. On my phone," Nora said, plucking at a piece of lint on her skirt.

"Someone's texting threats?" Savannah sounded aghast.

"And calling. He has my home number, too."

"What did he say?" Avery asked.

"Did he threaten to hurt you?" Riley demanded. After a moment, Nora nodded.

"To kill you?" Avery whispered.

Nora nodded again. "And more."

Savannah's expression hardened. "More?"

Nora looked up. "He threatened to rape me. He said I'd like it. He got... really graphic."

The four of them stared at each other in shocked silence.

"You can't go back," Savannah said. "Nora, you can't go back there. I don't care how important your work is, that's too much."

"What did the police say?" Riley's hands were shaking again. Rage and shock battled inside of her, but anger won out. Who would dare threaten her friend?

"What did the school's administration say?" Avery demanded.

"That threats happen all the time. That I should change my phone numbers. That the people who make the threats usually don't act on them."

"Usually?" Riley was horrified.

"What are you going to do?" Savannah said.

"What am I supposed to do? I can't quit." Nora seemed to sink into herself. "I changed my number, but it's happening again. I've got nothing saved. I managed to pay off my student loans, but then my mom got sick... I'm broke."

No one answered. They knew Nora's family hadn't

had much money, and she'd taken on debt to get her degree. Riley figured she'd probably used every penny she might have saved to pay it off again. Then her mother had contracted cancer and had gone through several expensive procedures before she passed away.

"Is this really what it's come to?" Avery asked finally. "Our work consumes us, or it overwhelms us, or it threatens us with bodily harm and we just keep going?"

"And what happened to love? True love?" Savannah's voice was raw. "Look at us! We're intelligent, caring, attractive women. And we're all single! None of us even dating. What about kids? I thought I'd be a mother."

"So did I," Riley whispered.

"Who can afford children?" Nora said fiercely. "I thought teaching would be enough. I thought my students would care—" She broke off and Riley's heart squeezed at Nora's misery.

"I've got some savings, but I'll eat through them fast if I don't get another job," Riley said slowly. "I want to leave Boston so badly. I want fresh air and a big, blue sky. But there aren't any jobs in the country." Memories of just such a sky flooded her mind. What she'd give for a vacation at her uncle's ranch in Chance Creek, Montana. In fact, she'd love to go there and never come back. It had been so long since she'd managed to stop by and spend a weekend at Westfield, it made her ache to think of the carefree weeks she spent there every summer as a child. The smell of hay and horses and sunshine on old buildings, the way her grandparents

used to let her loose on the ranch to run and play and ride as hard as she wanted to. Their unconditional love. There were few rules at Westfield and those existed purely for the sake of practicality and safety. *Don't spook the horses. Clean and put away tools after you use them. Be home at mealtimes and help with the dishes.*

Away from her parents' arguing, Riley had blossomed, and the skills she'd learned from the other kids in town—especially the Four Horsemen of the Apocalypse—had taught her pride and self-confidence. They were rough and tumble boys and they rarely slowed down to her speed, but as long as she kept up to them, they included her in their fun.

Clay Pickett, Jericho Cook, Walker Norton—they'd treated her like a sister. For an only child, it was a dream come true. But it was Boone who'd become a true friend, and her first crush.

And then had broken her heart.

"I keep wondering if it will always be like this," Avery said, interrupting her thoughts. "If I'll always have to struggle to get by. If I'll never have a house of my own—or a husband or family."

"You'll have a family," Riley assured her, then bit her lip. Who was she to reassure Avery? She could never seem to shake her bad luck—with men, with work, with anything. But out of all the things that had happened to her, nothing left her cringing with humiliation like the memory of the time she'd asked Boone to dance.

She'd been such a child. No one like Boone would have looked twice at her, no matter how friendly he'd

been over the years. She could still hear Melissa's sneering words—*No one wants to dance with a Tagalong. Go on home*—and the laughter that followed her when she fled the dance.

She'd returned to Chicago that last summer thinking her heart would never mend, and time had just begun to heal it when her grandparents passed away one after the other in quick succession that winter. Riley had been devastated; doubly so when she left for college the following year and her parents split. It was as if a tidal wave had washed away her childhood in one blow. After that, her parents sold their home and caretakers watched over the ranch. Uncle Russ, who'd inherited it, had found he made a better financier than a cowboy. With his career taking off, he'd moved to Europe soon after.

At his farewell dinner, one of the few occasions she'd seen her parents in the same room since they'd divorced, he'd stood up and raised a glass. "To Riley. You're the only one who loves Westfield now, and I want you to think of it as yours. One day in the future it will be, you know. While I'm away, I hope you'll treat it as your own home. Visit as long as you like. Bring your friends. Enjoy the ranch. My parents would have wanted that." He'd taken her aside later and presented her with a key. His trust in her and his promises had warmed her heart. If she'd own Westfield one day she could stand anything, she'd told herself that night. It was the one thing that had sustained her through life's repeated blows.

"I wish I could run away from my life, even for a little while. Six months would do it," Savannah said, breaking into her thoughts. "If I could clear my mind of everything that has happened in the past few years I know I could make a fresh start."

Riley knew just what she meant. She'd often wished the same thing, but she didn't only want to run away from her life; she wanted to run straight back into her past to a time when her grandparents were still alive. Things had been so simple then.

Until she'd fallen for Boone.

She hadn't seen Uncle Russ since he'd moved away, although she wrote to him a couple of times a year, and received polite, if remote, answers in turn. She had the feeling Russ had found the home of his heart in Munich. She wondered if he'd ever come back to Montana.

In the intervening years she'd visited Westfield whenever she could, more frequently as the sting of Boone's betrayal faded, although in reality that meant a long weekend every three or four months, rather than the expansive summer vacations she'd imagined when she'd received the key. It wasn't quite the same without her grandparents and her old friends, without Boone and the Horsemen, but she still loved the country, and Westfield Manor was the stuff of dreams. Even the name evoked happy memories and she blessed the ancestor whose flight of fancy had bestowed such a distinguished title on a Montana ranch house. She'd always wondered if she'd stumble across Boone someday, home for leave, but their visits had never coincided.

Still, whenever she drove into Chance Creek, her heart rate kicked up a notch and she couldn't help scanning the streets for his familiar face.

"I wish I could run away from my dirty dishes and laundry," Avery said. Riley knew she was attempting to lighten the mood. "I spend my weekends taking care of all my possessions. I bet Jane Austen didn't do laundry."

"In those days servants did it," Nora said, swiping her arm over her cheek to wipe away the traces of her tears. "Maybe we should get servants, too, while we're dreaming."

"Maybe we should, if it means we could concentrate on the things we love," Savannah said.

"Like that's possible. Look at us—we're stuck, all of us. There's no way out." The waver in Nora's voice betrayed her fierceness.

"There has to be," Avery exclaimed.

"How?"

Riley wished she had the answer. She hated seeing the pain and disillusionment on her friends' faces. And she was terrified of having to start over herself.

"What if... what if we lived together?" Savannah said slowly. "I mean, wouldn't that be better than how things are now? If we pooled our resources and figured out how to make them stretch? None of us would have to work so hard."

"I thought you had a good job," Nora said, a little bitterly.

"On paper. The cost of living in Silicon Valley is outrageous, though. You'd be surprised how little is left

over when I pay my bills. And inside, I feel... like I'm dying."

A silence stretched out between them. Riley knew just what Savannah meant. At first grown-up life had seemed exciting. Now it felt like she was slipping into a pool of quicksand that she'd never be able to escape. Maybe it would be different if they joined forces. If they pooled their money, they could do all kinds of things.

For the first time in months she felt a hint of possibility.

"We could move where the cost of living is cheaper and get a house together." Savannah warmed to her theme. "With a garden, maybe. We could work part time and share the bills."

"For six months? What good would that do? We'd run through what little money we have and be harder to employ afterward," Nora said.

"How much longer are you willing to wait before you try for the life you actually want, rather than the life that keeps you afloat one more day?" Savannah asked her. "I have to try to be a real pianist. Life isn't worth living if I don't give it a shot. That means practicing for hours every day. I can't do that and work a regular job, too."

"I've had an idea for a screenplay," Avery confessed. "I think it's really good. Six months would be plenty of time for me to write it. Then I could go back to work while I shop it around."

"If I had six months I would paint all day until I had enough canvasses to put on a show. Maybe that would

be the start and end of my career as an artist, but at least I'd have done it once," Riley said.

"A house costs money," Nora said.

"Not always," Riley said slowly as an idea took hold in her head. "What about Westfield?" After all, it hadn't been inhabited in years. "Uncle Russ always said I should bring my friends and stay there."

"Long term?" Avery asked.

"Six months would be fine. Russ hasn't set foot in it in over a decade."

"You want us to move to Montana and freeload for six months?" Nora asked.

"I want us to move to Montana and take six months to jumpstart our lives. We'll practice following our passions. We'll brainstorm ideas together for how to make money from them. Who knows? Maybe together we'll come up with a plan that will work."

"Sounds good to me," Avery said.

"I don't know," Nora said. "Do you really think it's work that's kept you from writing or playing or painting? Because if you can't do it now, chances are you won't be able to do it at Westfield either. You'll busy up your days with errands and visits and sightseeing and all that. Wait and see."

"Not if we swore an oath to work on our projects every day," Savannah said.

"Like the oaths you used to swear to do your homework on time? Or not to drink on Saturday night? Or to stop crank-calling the guy who dumped you junior year?"

Savannah flushed. "I was a child back then—"

"I just feel that if we take six months off, we'll end up worse off than when we started."

Savannah leaned forward. "Come on. Six whole months to write. Aren't you dying to try it?" When Nora hesitated, Savannah pounced on her. "I knew it! You want to as badly as we do."

"Of course I want to," Nora said. "But it won't work. None of you will stay at home and hone your craft."

A smile tugged at Savannah's lips. "What if we couldn't leave?"

"Are you going to chain us to the house?"

"No. I'm going to take away your clothes. Your modern clothes," she clarified when the others stared at her. "You're right; we could easily be tempted to treat the time like a vacation, especially with us all together. But if we only have Regency clothes to wear, we'll be stuck because we'll be too embarrassed to go into town. We'll take a six-month long Jane Austen vacation from our lives." She sat back and folded her arms over her chest.

"I love it," Riley said. "Keep talking."

"We'll create a Regency life, as if we'd stepped into one of her novels. A beautiful life, with time for music and literature and poetry and walks. Westfield is rural, right? No one will be there to see us. If we pattern our days after the way Jane's characters spent theirs, we'd have plenty of time for creative pursuits."

Nora rolled her eyes. "What about the neighbors?

What about groceries and dental appointments?"

"Westfield is set back from the road." Riley thought it through. "Savannah's right; we could go for long stretches without seeing anyone. We could have things delivered, probably."

"I'm in," Avery said. "I'll swear to live a Regency life for six months. I'll swear it on penalty of… death."

"The penalty is embarrassment," Savannah said. "If we leave early, we have to travel home in our Regency clothes. I know I'm in. I'd gladly live a Jane Austen life for six months."

"If I get to wear Regency dresses and bonnets, I'm in too," Riley said. What was the alternative? Stay here and mourn the child she'd never have?

"Are you serious?" Nora asked. "Where do we even get those things?"

"We have a seamstress make them, or we sew them ourselves," Avery said. "Come on, Nora. Don't pretend you haven't always wanted to."

The others nodded. After all, it was their mutual love of Jane Austen movies that had brought them together in the first place. Two days into their freshman year at Boston College, Savannah had marched through the halls of their dorm announcing a Jane Austen film festival in her room that night. Riley, Nora and Avery had shown up for it, and the rest was history.

"It'll force us to carry out our plan the way we intend to," Savannah told her. "If we can't leave the ranch, there will be no distractions. Every morning when we put on our clothes we'll be recommitting to

our vow to devote six months to our creative pursuits. Think about it, Nora. Six whole months to write."

"Besides, we were so good together back in college," Riley said. "We inspired each other. Why couldn't we do that again?"

"But what will we live on?"

"We'll each liquidate our possessions," Savannah said. "Think about how little most people had in Jane Austen's time. It'll be like when Eleanor and Marianne have to move to a cottage in *Sense and Sensibility* with their mother and little sister. We'll make a shoestring budget and stick to it for food and supplies. If we don't go anywhere, we won't spend any money, right?"

"That's right," Avery said. "Remember what Mrs. John Dashwood said in that novel. 'What on earth can four women want for more than that?—They will live so cheap! Their housekeeping will be nothing at all. They will have no carriage, no horses, and hardly any servants; they will keep no company, and can have no expenses of any kind! Only conceive how comfortable they will be!'"

"We certainly won't have any horses or carriages." Savannah laughed.

"But we will be comfortable, and during the time we're together we can brainstorm what to do next," Riley said. "No one leaves Westfield until we all have a working plan."

"With four of us to split the chores of running the house, it'll be easy," Avery said. "We'll have hours and hours to devote to our craft every day."

Nora hesitated. "You know this is crazy, right?"

"But it's exactly the right kind of crazy," Riley said. "You have to join us, Nora."

Nora shook her head, but just when Riley thought she'd refuse, she shrugged. "Oh, okay. What the hell? I'll do it." Riley's heart soared. "But when our six months are up, I'll be broke," Nora went on. "I'll be homeless, too. I don't see how anything will have improved."

"Everything will have improved," Savannah told her. "I promise. Together we can do anything."

Riley smiled at their old rallying-cry from college. "So, we're going to do it? You'll all come to Westfield with me? And wear funny dresses?"

"And bonnets," Avery said. "Don't forget the bonnets."

"I'm in," Savannah said, sticking out her hand.

"I'm in," Avery said, putting hers down on top of it.

"I guess I'm in," Nora said, and added hers to the pile.

"Well, I'm definitely in." Riley slapped hers down on top of the rest.

Westfield. She was going back to Westfield.

Things were looking up.

End of Excerpt

The Cowboys of Chance Creek Series:

The Cowboy Inherits a Bride (Volume 0)
The Cowboy's E-Mail Order Bride (Volume 1)
The Cowboy Wins a Bride (Volume 2)
The Cowboy Imports a Bride (Volume 3)
The Cowgirl Ropes a Billionaire (Volume 4)
The Sheriff Catches a Bride (Volume 5)
The Cowboy Lassos a Bride (Volume 6)
The Cowboy Rescues a Bride (Volume 7)
The Cowboy Earns a Bride (Volume 8)
The Cowboy's Christmas Bride (Volume 9)

The Heroes of Chance Creek Series:

The Navy SEAL's E-Mail Order Bride (Volume 1)
The Soldier's E-Mail Order Bride (Volume 2)
The Marine's E-Mail Order Bride (Volume 3)
The Navy SEAL's Christmas Bride (Volume 4)
The Airman's E-Mail Order Bride (Volume 5)

The SEALs of Chance Creek Series:

A SEAL's Oath
A SEAL's Vow
A SEAL's Pledge
A SEAL's Consent

About the Author

NYT and USA Today bestselling author Cora Seton loves cowboys, hiking, gardening, bike-riding, and lazing around with a good book. Mother of four, wife to a computer programmer/backyard farmer, she recently moved to Victoria and looks forward to a brand new chapter in her life. Like the characters in her Chance Creek series, Cora enjoys old-fashioned pursuits and modern technology, spending mornings in her garden, and afternoons writing the latest Chance Creek romance novel. Visit **www.coraseton.com** to read about new releases, contests and other cool events!

Blog:
www.coraseton.com

Facebook:
www.facebook.com/coraseton

Twitter:
www.twitter.com/coraseton

Newsletter:
www.coraseton.com/sign-up-for-my-newsletter

Made in the USA
Lexington, KY
17 July 2017